HANDBOOKS IN INFORMATION SYSTEMS
VOLUME 4

Handbooks in Information Systems

Advisory Editors

Ba, Sulin
University of Connecticut

Duan, Wenjing
The George Washington University

Geng, Xianjun
University of Washington

Gupta, Alok
University of Minnesota

Hendershott, Terry
University of California at Berkeley

Rao, H.R.
SUNY at Buffalo

Santanam, Raghu T.
Arizona State University

Zhang, Han
Georgia Institute of Technology

Editor

Andrew B. Whinston

Volume 4

United Kingdom ● North America ● Japan
India ● Malaysia ● China

Emerald

Information Assurance, Security and Privacy Services

Edited by

H. Raghav Rao
State University of New York at Buffalo

Shambhu Upadhyaya
State University of New York at Buffalo

Emerald

United Kingdom • North America • Japan
India • Malaysia • China

Emerald Group Publishing Limited

Howard House, Wagon Lane, Bingley BD16 1WA, UK

First edition 2009

British Library Cataloguing in Publication Data
A catalogue record for this book is available from the British Library

ISBN: 978-1-84855-194-7
ISSN: 1574-0145

Awarded in recognition of
Emerald's production
department's adherence to
quality systems and processes
when preparing scholarly
journals for print

INVESTOR IN PEOPLE

Contents

Part II: Incentive Mechanisms and Web Security

CHAPTER 4
Incentive Mechanisms for Internet Security
Manoj Parameswaran and Andrew B. Whinston

Part III: Human-Centric Aspects of Security

CHAPTER 7
Social Engineering in Phishing
Markus Jakobsson and Christopher Soghoian

CHAPTER 8
Human-Centered Security
Vidyaraman Sankaranarayanan, Shambhu Upadhyaya and
Kevin Kwiat

CHAPTER 9
An Exploration of the Design Features of Phishing Attacks
Jingguo Wang, Rui Chen, Tejaswini Herath and
H. Raghav Rao

Part IV: Security, Privacy and Access Control Theory

CHAPTER 10
Identification and Access Management and Data Privacy
Sateesh S. Kannegala

CHAPTER 11
Children's Online Privacy: Issues with Parental Awareness and Control
France Bélanger, Robert Crossler, Janine Hiller, Michael Hsiao and Jung-Min Park

CHAPTER 12
Usable Mandatory Access Control for Operating Systems
Ninghui Li, Ziqing Mao and Hong Chen   335

CHAPTER 23
Incentive-Based Methods for Inferring Attacker Intent and Strategies and Measuring Attack Resilience
Wanyu Zang, Meng Yu and Peng Liu

PREFACE

"Information Assurance, Security and Privacy Services" is the state-of-the-art handbook in the area.

This volume with 23 chapters provides a detailed resource in the emerging areas of cyber security. The aim of this edited volume is to provide an up-to-date examination of the current trends in information assurance, security and privacy services, recent advances and future projections. The specific topics covered are: data security and authentication, incentive mechanisms and web security, human-centric aspects of security, security, privacy, and access control theory and applications, economics aspects of security, and threat modeling, intrusion, and response.

There are three major aspects of any system—technology, process, and users. The book brings out some of the significant advancements in security technology by considering issues and advances in authentication and biometrics, web technology, mobile *ad hoc* networks, and sensor networks. It also presents advancements in access control and trust management process. Yet, cyber security is still an unresolved problem unless one talks about the users. Why are we not able to address security in day-to-day applications despite significant research and innovation? Is it the human, who is the system user being the weakest link? The book provides the various human-centric aspects of security by going into enforceable security policies, user cooperation and the human factors of phishing.

The volume covers both technical and business aspects with a focus on new concepts, techniques and practices that would help bring security to users' desktops and make security proximate. Chapters include a survey of current state-of-the-art in chosen topics along with an in-depth look into emerging concepts. A unique feature of the book is that many of the chapters are based on multidisciplinary research by authors from multiple disciplines such as information systems and computer science and engineering. In addition, the handbook reflects a truly international flavor with contributions from researchers at universities in the United States, Norway, Canada, Switzerland, Germany, and Portugal, as well as industries such as Microsoft, Nokia, and IBM, and government research labs.

It would be remiss if we did not thank all the referees for their dedicated efforts in reviewing the chapters. We thank Professor Andrew B. Whinston, editor-in-chief of the book series for his encouragement with regard to this endeavor, and Insu Park, who has spent hours and hours in keeping track of all the submissions, reviews, and helping us in coordinating the book project. We would like to acknowledge the support provided by the National Science Foundation through grant no. DUE0723763 and the Department of Defense through grant no. H98230-07-1-0243 to conduct our research on information assurance and computer security. The usual disclaimer applies. Finally, we would like to thank Diane Heath and Emma Smith of Emerald publishers, without whom this project would not have ended!

H. Raghav Rao and Shambhu Upadhyaya

Part I
Data Security and Authentication

Rao & Upadhyaya, Eds., *Handbooks in Information Systems, Vol. 4*

Chapter 1

Distributed Proof Systems for Cross-Domain Authorization

Kazuhiro Minami

Department of Computer Science, University of Illinois at Urbana-Champaign,
201 N. Goodwin Avenue, Urbana, IL 61801, USA

David Kotz

Department of Computer Science, ISTS, Dartmouth College, 6211 Sudikoff Laboratory,
Hanover, NH 03755-3510, USA

Abstract

The ability to access information resources across organizational boundaries is vital for today's corporate, military, and educational organizations, which must be able to quickly pool their resources to respond to opportunities and threats. Since each organization protects its resources with its local authorization policies, we need mechanisms for cross-domain authorization to achieve information sharing among multiple organizations. Unfortunately, traditional identity-based authorization approaches are impractical, because the identity of a requester is not a useful clue for authorization in a decentralized environment. Many distributed authorization schemes, therefore, consider a requester's properties (e.g., employer and physical location) to make an authorization decision and use a logic-based approach to specify authorization policies in a flexible way. Such a distributed proof system makes an authorization decision by constructing a proof with information provided by different entities in a distributed environment. In this chapter, we provide an overview of distributed proof systems for cross-domain authorization. We first cover major language constructs and proof-constructing algorithms of existing distributed proof systems and then introduce an emerging issue of protecting confidential policies and credentials (facts) in a distributed proof system involving multiple security domains. We finally describe our distributed proof system for cross-domain authorization in detail and show how our cryptographic protocol allows mutually untrusted principals to construct a proof in a decentralized way while preserving each principal's security policies.

1 Introduction

As our society becomes increasingly dependent on rapid information flow, shared resources, and Internet-based interactions, it has become common for multiple organizations to work as a single virtual organization. An emergency response team (National incident management system, 2004) for disastrous incidents (e.g., fires, earthquakes, and terrorism) is one example. First responders in such a team belong to different local, state, and federal agencies. An electric power infrastructure that consists of many utilities is another example. Such a virtual organization needs an information infrastructure that enables information sharing across organizations. For example, first responders in an emergency response team need to access situational information (e.g., the locations of casualties) and information about available resources (e.g., medical facilities) to respond to the disaster in a timely manner. However, the information about the incident is distributed across the systems managed by different organizations, and each system protects its information with local security policies.

Therefore, an information infrastructure for a virtual organization must support mechanisms for cross-domain authorization to achieve resource sharing among multiple organizations. Identity-based authorization based on a Public Key Infrastructure (PKI) does not scale to a large number of users because it requires systems in each organization to register users in other organizations in advance. Also, an administrator in one system cannot trust unknown users in other organizations, solely based on their identities. Therefore, rather than basing authorization decisions in a decentralized environment on a requester's identity, we need to consider the attributes (properties) of the requester (e.g., her employer or her role in an organization).

To support flexible policies that consider statements from remote principals, many systems (Appel and Felten, 1999; Bauer et al., 2005; Becker and Sewell, 2004; DeTreville, 2002; Gunter and Jim, 1997; Jim, 2001; Jim and Suciu, 2001; Li et al., 1999, 2002) take a logic-based approach to express authorization policies; that is, an authorization policy consists of a set of rules that refer to the properties of entities and resources across different administrative domains. An authorization decision is therefore made by constructing a distributed proof of a certain statement that derives a granting decision.

Authorization in such systems will depend on collecting information from multiple independent hosts. However, in many realistic authorization policies for virtual organizations, sources of information considered by those authorization policies are inherently distributed among many administrative domains that define different security policies. For example, an emergency response system could have an authorization policy that depends on role membership maintained by a police department and location information maintained by a wireless network operator.

Earlier rule-based authorization systems have a universally trusted central server that collects all the information necessary to make authorization decisions. However, this approach does not work when each host maintains its own security policies. To achieve such information sharing among hosts in a decentralized environment, we must address two trust issues. First, each administrative domain (organization) defines integrity policies that specify whether to trust information from other domains in terms of the integrity (correctness) of that information. We assume that these trust relationships are defined by principals, each of which represents a specific user or organization, and that each host is associated with one principal (e.g., the owner of a PDA, or the manager of a server). Second, each administrative domain defines confidentiality policies to protect information in that domain. Confidentiality of facts might be used to protect organizational attributes in virtual business coalitions, or the sensitive context information (e.g., location) in pervasive environments. In both cases, principals will not want to reveal such information to other administrative domains indiscriminately, and thus it is important to model confidentiality policies. Therefore, a requester must satisfy the confidentiality policies of an information provider to access the requested information.

Existing systems allow each principal to specify integrity policies, but the question of *confidentiality* is largely unaddressed. To the best of our knowledge, only PeerAccess (Winslett et al., 2005) explicitly supports mechanisms for protecting confidential policies and facts in each host of the system. However, the discretionary access-control (DAC) model, which is adopted by PeerAccess, fails to construct a proof if a requester principal in the system does not satisfy the confidentiality policies of the principal handling that query.

In this chapter, we present our secure distributed authorization system (Minami and Kotz, 2005a,b) that enables mutually untrusted principals, which have partial knowledge about authorization rules and facts about entities, to evaluate a logical query without a universally trusted principal or a centralized knowledge base. The core of the approach is to decompose a proof for making an authorization decision into a set of subproofs produced on multiple different hosts, while preserving the confidentiality and integrity policies of the principals operating those hosts. Thus, rather than depending on a central trusted server (Fig. 1a), we decompose a proof into subproofs produced by multiple hosts (Fig. 1(b)). This collaboration is only possible if the querier can trust the integrity of other hosts (to provide correct facts and to properly evaluate rules) and if the other hosts can trust the querier with confidential facts. Our contributions are as follows:

1. A new security model for distributed proof systems that defines trust relations among principals in terms of confidentiality and integrity of information they maintain.

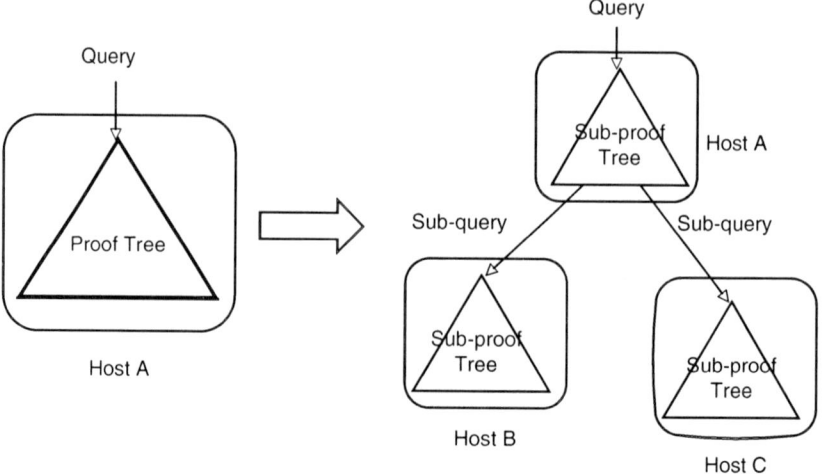

(a) Centralized authorization server   (b) Decentralized multiple authorization servers

Fig. 1. Decentralized evaluation of an authorization query. The proof of a query is decomposed into subproofs and produced on distributed multiple hosts. On the left, Host A generates a whole proof on a centralized server. On the right, Hosts A, B, and C produce only a subtree of the proof.

2. A scalable, distributed algorithm that constructs a proof as a set of subproofs produced by different principals, according to the integrity requirements of those principals.
3. A confidentiality-preserving, cryptographic protocol capable of constructing a proof even when systems that enforce DAC policies by controlling a reply to the querier fail.

The rest of the chapter is organized as follows. We give background on distributed authorization systems in Section 2 and introduce our security model for distributed proof systems in Section 3. Section 4 describes our secure distributed proof system for the simpler case, where policies apply only to facts. We describe the architecture of our system and the enforcement mechanism for confidentiality policies. We also describe algorithms for handling queries in a distributed way. Section 5 describes the general case that supports policies on rules as well, following the structure of the preceding section. We describe the representation of a proof and additional features for supporting the general case. Section 6 covers some design issues and security properties in our system, and Section 7 concludes.

2 Background

In this section, we provide a brief survey of existing distributed authorization schemes based on logic. We first introduce logic-based authorization system with a central server and describe how authorization policies are expressed as a set of logical rules. Next, we cover distributed authorization systems that have multiple information sources; that is, those systems collect information necessary to make an authorization decision from multiple servers. We discuss additional functionalities that those distributed authorization systems need to support. Finally, we explain recent authorization systems where peers in those systems construct a proof that derives a granting decision in a peer-to-peer way. Our distributed proof system, which is presented in the following sections, is such a peer-to-peer authorization system whose main focus is to protect each peer's confidential policies and facts.

2.1   Centralized authorization systems based on logic

We first introduce important concepts of logic-based authorization with a central model. Such a centralized system has a trusted central server that maintains all the authorization policies, which are represented as a set of rules and facts in its knowledge base. Figure 2 shows the structure of the system where a central authorization server consists of a knowledge base and an inference engine. When the inference engine receives an authorization query from a remote server managing a resource, it tries to derive the fact in that query by constructing a proof with rules and facts in the knowledge base. If the engine succeeds in constructing a proof, it returns a Boolean value *TRUE*; otherwise, it returns *FALSE*.

In pervasive computing (Satyanarayanan, 2001), many authorization systems take this centralized approach, and the major difference among those centralized systems is a choice of an authorization language they support. For example, generalized role-based access control (GRBAC) (Covington et al., 2001), open architecture for secure interworking services (OASIS) (Bacon et al., 2002), and Tripathi's resource discovery system (Tripathi et al., 2004) apply a propositional logic, whereas Cerberus

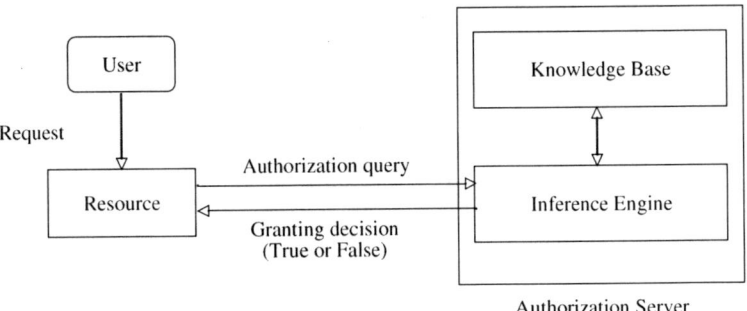

Fig. 2.   Structure of an authorization server.

(Al-Muhtadi et al., 2003) adopts a general first-order logic. Some systems do not support a logic-based language directly, but provide a language that expresses logical expressions. For example, Myles (Myles et al., 2003) adopts Extensible Markup Language (XML) to express rules in the propositional logic, and the KNOW system (Kapadia et al., 2004) represents a Boolean formula as a decision tree.

Datalog as an authorization language: Many recent logic-based authorization systems have adopted variants of Datalog (Ullman, 1989), which is a subset of Prolog, and, as we see in Section 3, our distributed proof system also adopts Datalog as an authorization language. Therefore, we here describe the notion of a proof tree based on Datalog. Datalog represents rules and facts as Horn clauses. The syntax of a Horn clause is $b \leftarrow a_1 \wedge a_2 \ldots \wedge a_n$, which says that simple statements called atoms a_1 through a_n, if all true, imply b. The atom b is called the head of the clause, and the atoms $a_1, \ldots, a_n$, the body of the clause. An atom is usually used to state a fact. An atom is formed from a predicate symbol followed by a parenthesized list of variables and constants.

An authorization decision is made by constructing a proof of a certain predicate that indicates that access should be granted. We assume that an atom *grant(P)* represents the fact that a principal P is granted access to some resource. For example, a medical database may define an authorization policy that requires a requester P to hold a role membership "doctor" and to be physically located at the "hospital" as follows:

$$grant(P) \leftarrow role\ (P, doctor), location\ (P, hospital)$$

The atoms *role(P, doctor)* and *location(P, hospital)* on the right side of the clause are the conditions that must be satisfied to derive the granting decision *grant(P)* on the left. If a user Bob issues a request to read a medical database, the proof tree in Fig. 3 could be constructed based on the earlier rule. The root node in the tree represents the rule and the two leaf nodes represent the facts, respectively. Note that variable P in the rule is replaced with a constant Bob. In general, a proof tree consists of nodes that represent rules (or facts) and edges that represent the unification of the atom in the body of the rule in a parent node with the head of the rule in a child node. Every leaf node contains a fact that has no atom in its body.

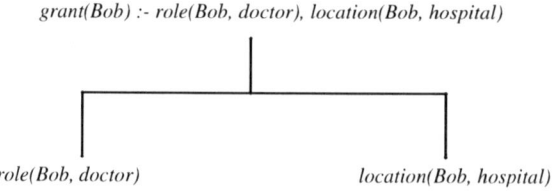

Fig. 3.   Sample proof tree.

2.2 *Distributed authorization with multiple information sources*

We next cover distributed authorization systems in which an authorization server fetches information from remote servers while making an authorization decision. Those systems are distributed in the sense that a policy maker can define policies that refer to facts in remote servers. However, the evaluation process of authorization (i.e., the construction of a proof) is still centralized; a central authorization server that collects all the necessary information from remote servers makes the authorization decision. We consider trust-management systems, such as PolicyMaker (Blaze et al., 1996) and KeyNote (Blaze et al., 1999), as variants of distributed authorization systems since those trust-management systems provide a compliance checker that decides an authorization decision by considering credentials received from remote principals. However, those systems do not provide mechanisms for fetching those credentials, assuming the existence of such fetching mechanisms.

Figure 4 shows an architectural overview of a distributed authorization system. Each information server maintains facts in its knowledge base, and the credential-fetching module in the authorization server fetches facts from those information servers. In many distributed authorization systems, the credential-fetching module fetches credentials from other principals, checks their digital signatures, and converts them into logical statements in the local knowledge base.

Since the authorization server considers rules and facts in multiple knowledge bases in a distributed environment to make authorization

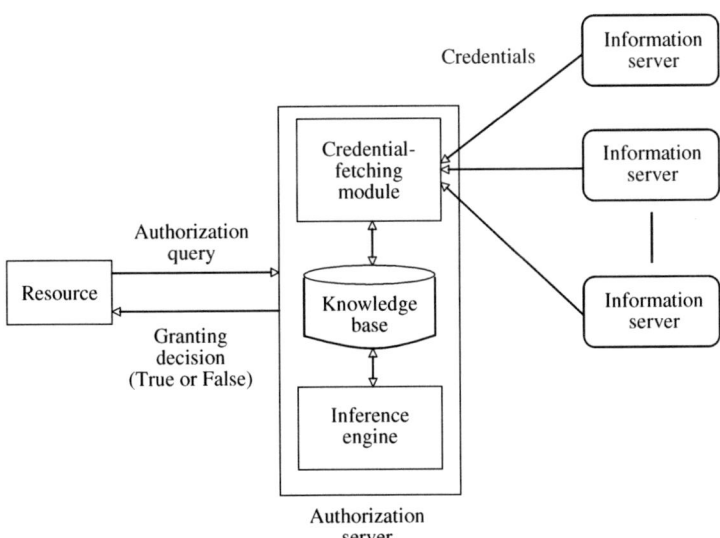

Fig. 4.   Distributed authorization with multiple information servers.

decisions, we need language constructs for associating each fact with the publisher of that fact. Many distributed authorization systems support quoted facts in their logical languages; that is, when a principal receives a signed fact f from principal p_i, that principal maintains the received fact as the quoted fact "p_i *says* f" in its local knowledge base. To make an authorization decision using quoted facts, we need a rule that derives a local fact from quoted facts. For example, an authorization system grants access to a principal P when receiving from Bob the fact that P holds role *doctor* if the system maintains the rule below in its local knowledge base.

$$grant(P) \leftarrow Bob \; says \; role \; (P, doctor)$$

In general, a rule can contain multiple quoted facts associated with different principals in the body of the rule. A rule containing quoted facts expresses trust in the principals in those quoted facts to provide correct information. For example, the principal that defines the earlier authorization policy trusts Bob to make a correct statement about principal P's doctor role membership. Note that it is useless to collect facts from remote principals if the imported quoted facts are not mentioned in any of the local rules. Therefore, each principal fetches facts from remote principals only when it has a rule containing a quoted fact involving those remote principals.

In summary, there are two additional features that are necessary to achieve a distributed authorization system that collects facts from remote principals. First, an authorization language must provide a policy maker with a way to specify the location of remote facts to derive local facts from the imported quoted facts. Second, a system provides mechanisms for fetching signed credentials from remote servers, verifying their signatures, and converting them into quoted facts in the knowledge base. Next, we introduce several examples of such distributed authorization systems. Note that not all of the following systems support the second feature.

Secure dynamically distributed datalog (SD3) (Jim, 2001) is a distributed authorization system that uses an extension of Datalog as an authorization language. SD3 extends Datalog with simple distributed security infrastructure (SDSI)-linked local names (Rivest and Lampson), which are local names paired with public keys. The expression $K\$f$ refers to a fact f maintained by a principal holding key K. The inference engine of SD3 constructs a proof by retrieving certificates that correspond to remote facts of the form $K\$f$ from the remote hosts automatically, and the whole proof tree is constructed by the inference engine on a central server.

Proof-carrying authorization (PCA) (Appel and Felten, 1999) applies higher-order logic to define authorization policies with application-specific modal logics. The goal of PCA is to prove application-specific rules, which appear in Abadi's logic and simple public key infrastructure (SPKI), as lemmas proved from a single set of inference rules. Since higher order logic is undecidable, PCA puts the burden of constructing a proof on a client sending a request. Bauer et al. (2002) later developed a web-based authorization system based on PCA. In Bauer's system, a client constructs a proof by responding to a challenge issued from the server. However, PCA does not provide a client with a mechanism for fetching credentials automatically.

The International Telecommunication Union-Telecommunication Standardization Sector (ITU-T) X.812 (Security frameworks for open systems, 1995) defines a general framework for distributed authorization systems, whose components correspond to those in Fig. 4. X.812 does not specify particular mechanisms for implementing the framework. The framework is designed to support control of access according to context information (e.g., time of attempted access and the location of a requester) in a decentralized environment where multiple security domains are involved. An access-control system in the architecture consists of an access control decision function (ADF) and an access control enforcement function (AEF). An ADF function makes access-control decisions by applying access-control policies, and an AEF function enforces the decisions made by the ADF. We consider that ADF and AEF correspond to the inference engine in the authorization server and the enforcement mechanism in the client managing a resource, respectively, in Fig. 4. To make an authorization decision, ADF collects from other system entities, called access control information (ACI), attributes of a requester and a resource. In the X.812 framework, it is possible that an ADF or an AEF consists of multiple entities in different security domains. However, the X.812 framework does not define a trust model that enables information sharing between those entities.

The OASIS eXtensible access control markup language (XACML) 2.0 (OASIS, 2004) is an authorization language based on the XML. XACML enables a policy maker to define an attribute-based authorization policy: a request from a user contains attributes of the requester and the requested resource, and only the policies whose attributes match the attributes in the request are evaluated to make an authorization decision. In XACML, it is possible to define additional constraints as Boolean conditions combined with disjunction and conjunction operators; a policy in XACML is equivalent to a statement in propositional logic. A policy can refer to subpolicies defined by other servers, and, therefore, the policy can contain nested subpolicies of an arbitrary depth. Since multiple policies for a given request might derive different authorization decisions, XACML provides a mechanism for resolving such a conflict using a policy-combining algorithm.

XACML also defines a distributed architecture that involves four types of system entities: a policy enforcement point (PEP), a policy decision point (PDP), a policy information point (PIP), and a policy administration point (PAP). When a PEP receives a request from a user, it enforces an authorization decision made by a PDP. When it receives a request from a PEP, a PDP makes an authorization decision by evaluating applicable policies and returns a response that contains a granting decision. The PDP obtains authorization policies and attribute values from PAPs and PIPs, respectively. XACML defines the formats of request and response messages between a PEP and a PDP. However, it does not specify a protocol for transporting messages between the two parties. Furthermore, how a PDP collects policies and attributes from PIPs and PAPs is outside the scope of the XACML 2.0 specification.

Trust-management systems: Trust-management systems are distributed authorization systems whose authorization policies express trust relations among principals. PolicyMaker (Blaze et al., 1996) first introduced the notion of a trust-management system that determines whether a set of credentials satisfy authorization policies for the given request. The definition of trust-management systems is similar to that of distributed authorization systems that collect information from information servers. However, PolicyMaker puts more focus on supporting delegation of authority in its policy language. The core of the PolicyMaker trust-management system is a function that takes as inputs a request, a set of local policies, and a set of credentials and that returns a Boolean decision (yes or no), depending on whether the credentials constitute a proof that the request complies with the policies. This functionality is called compliance checking. Note that a proof in PolicyMaker is a chain of delegation from the local authority to a requester principal, and thus different from that in logic-based authorization systems in Section 2.1.

PolicyMaker expresses both policies and credentials as an assertion that consists of a set of predicates, and one or more public keys. Predicates check the attributes of a request and its environment (including information about the current context). If a source principal that issues an assertion holds authority for the compliance checking of a request, that assertion is applied to the request to obtain a list of principals to which the authority is delegated; that is, if the predicates in the assertion are evaluated to be true, the authority for compliance checking is delegated to the set of principals in the assertion. Initially, a local principal that handles a request has the authority for compliance checking and, therefore, a local policy is applied to the request first. Once the authority is delegated to other principals, credentials signed by those principals can be applied to the request in the same way. This process is iterated until the principal that issued the request gains the authority for the request or until the function exhausts all applicable assertions. Thus, the problem of compliance checking is to find a sequence of assertions that derive a requesting principal as the authority for claiming the statement in the request. The collection and verification of credentials is outside the scope of Policy-Maker; that is, an application that issues a query to PolicyMaker is responsible for collecting credentials and checking cryptographic digital signatures.

KeyNote (Blaze et al., 1999) is a descendant of PolicyMaker. In addition to the original goals of PolicyMaker, KeyNote aims to standardize a language syntax for policies and credentials and to ease the integration of the trust-management engine into applications. KeyNote requires that policies and credentials are written in a specific language so that they can be handled smoothly with KeyNote's compliance checker. KeyNote is responsible for checking cryptographic digital signatures. However, it does not automatically fetch credentials from remote hosts.

Delegation-based authorization systems: Delegation-based authorization systems provide language constructs for expressing delegation of authority in their authorization languages based on logic. Abadi's logic of authentication (Abadi et al., 1993) introduces the speaks for operator that allows us to define principal *A*'s belief based on principal *B*'s belief. The statement *A* speaks for *B* means that if principal *A* believes that a statement *s* is true, then principal *B* also believes *s* to be true; that is, this statement allows principal *B* to delegate its authority to principal *A*. A request is granted if the system generates a proof that a requesting principal *p* speaks for one of the principals in the access-control list on the requested resource.

The SPKI (Ellison et al., 1999) defines a standard for authorization certificates. An SPKI certificate binds either a name or a key to authorization. SPKI defines an internal representation of certificates as well as its own certificate format to handle PGP certificates (OpenPGP Message Format) and X.509 certificates (Internet, 1999). SPKI's internal representation encodes the delegation of authorization rights as a 5-tuple that consists of an issuer, a subject, a Boolean flag, authorization, and validity dates. Snowflake (Howell and Kotz, 2000) is a delegation-based authorization system based on SPKI. In Snowflake, a client who makes a request is responsible for constructing a proof. When the client issues the request, a server returns a principal that the client must speak for. The client's prover object constructs a proof that derives a statement that a client speaks for the given principal by traversing search space from that principal.

Delegation logic (DL) (Li et al., 2003) is an extension of Datalog that supports explicit constructs for expressing delegations with integer depths and complex principal structures, such as a *k*-out-of-*n* threshold that requires agreement among *k* out of *n* principals. DL supports quoted facts with the says operator to express a rule or a fact stated by a remote principal. DL uses the construct delegates to express the delegation of authority, for example,

Bob delegates access(docZ)$^\wedge$1 to David

The earlier rule states that Bob delegates the authority to access docZ to David, and the depth of the delegation is 1, which means that Bob does not trust people whom Dave trusts.

Li et al. (2003) show that there exists a function that converts a DL program into the equivalent Datalog program by introducing the predicates holds and delegates. An authorization engine that supports DL needs to collect all the credentials that are necessary to make an authorization decision and translate those credentials into rules in DL. However, DL itself does not provide a mechanism for retrieving credentials from remote servers. Li et al. (2002) later developed the Role-based Trust-management language (RT) that supports role-based access control (RBAC) (Sandhu et al., 1996) policies. RT provides a language syntax that allows each principal to define a local role and to delegate authority to another principal by including the remote principal's role in the local role. The semantics of RT is defined with a transformation function from RT to Datalog. Li et al. (2003) also developed a goal-directed bidirectional search algorithm for credential chain discovery in RT in a distributed environment and introduced a storage-type system for credentials in RT to ensure traversability of credential chains.

2.3 Peer-to-peer authorization systems

Peer-to-peer authorization systems consist of multiple peers, each with an inference engine and a knowledge base. Those peers could have different rules and facts in their knowledge bases. Peer-to-peer authorization systems not only distribute information necessary to make an authorization decision, but also distribute the responsibility for constructing a proof among multiple peers in the system. Binder (DeTreville, 2002) is a logic-based authorization language that extends Datalog with a modal operator says. In Binder, inference engines on different servers can exchange statements (facts or rules) as signed certificates. When a statement is imported into an inference engine, that statement is automatically quoted with the says operator to differentiate it from local statements. In Binder, a proof for an authorization decision can be decomposed into subproofs produced by different peers. However, Binder provides no mechanism for protecting confidential rules and facts.

Bauer et al. (2005) developed a distributed proving system that constructs a proof that grants access to a resource; a principal that constructs a proof could delegate a task of building a subproof to another principal rather than collecting all the certificates that are necessary to construct a whole proof. The principal receiving the query returns the subproof that contains multiple certificates and thus a whole proof for the initial query is eventually constructed by the principal issuing the initial query. Bauer's authorization language is based on the logic of authentication (Abadi et al., 1993), and provides the modal operators such as says and speaks for. Like Binder, Bauer's system does not address the issue of protecting confidential information in certificates, which are used to construct a proof.

PeerAccess (Winslett et al., 2005) is a framework for reasoning about authorization in a distributed environment. PeerAccess consists of a set of peers maintaining a local knowledge base. Each peer can construct a proof by collecting rules and facts maintained by other peers. Like Bauer's system, a peer that makes an authorization decision needs to collect subproofs from other peers. Each peer's knowledge base also contains release policies that protect its local rules and facts. Release policies in PeerAccess are sticky in the sense that those policies are permanently attached to the information they protect; that is, PeerAccess assumes that all peers that exchange their rules and facts with each other enforce the original publishers' release policies correctly.

An automated trust negotiation (ATN) system (Winsborough and Li, 2002; Yu and Winslett, 2003; Yu et al., 2003) enables two parties to establish mutual trust through bilateral disclosure of credentials. An ATN system protects confidential policies of two parties by treating them as resources to be protected with other policies. However, since an ATN system only supports collaboration between two parties, we do not consider them as a peer-to-peer distributed authorization system involving multiple principals in this chapter.

Although there are many distributed authorization systems, there is little research on confidentiality in those systems except for PeerAccess. A system like PeerAccess that simply applies DAC model fails to construct a proof if a requester principal in the system does not satisfy the confidentiality policies of the principal handling that query. Therefore, we developed a crypto-graphic protocol for distributed authorization systems. Our scheme enables mutually untrusted principals to construct a proof even when systems based on the DAC model fail. Deriving a granting decision while protecting each peer's confidential information is considered as a special problem of secure function evaluation (SFE) (Goldreich et al., 1987; Yao, 1986) where each peer's private input contains the information in its knowledge base and that of its security policies. However, our protocol does not need multiple rounds of messages to be exchanged among principals, and thus is much more efficient than that of the general solution. Many protocols for special problems (e.g., finding association rules) of SFE have been developed in the context of privacy preserving data mining (Vaidya et al., 2006), but those are different special problems than that in this chapter. In Section 3, we present the design and implementation of our secure distributed proof system.

3 Security policies

Our distributed proof system belongs to the category of peer-to-peer authorization systems in Section 2.3, and it consists of multiple hosts managed by different principals. Like many existing distributed authorization systems (Bauer et al., 2005; DeTreville, 2002; Jim, 2001; Li et al., 1999), our distributed proof system uses Datalog, which is described in Section 2.1, as an authorization language; that is, each principal of the system maintains rules and facts in Datalog in its knowledge base. In addition to the Datalog authorization language, our system supports two types of security policies, which we introduce in this section. Confidentiality policies allow each principal to specify which other principals are granted access to rules and facts in its knowledge base. Integrity policies allow each principal to specify whether it believes that facts or rules received from other principals are correct.

3.1   Rule patterns

We first introduce the notion of rule patterns, which are mechanisms for expressing these security policies in our security model. A rule pattern is just a regular Horn clause to be unified with a rule or a fact in the knowledge base. A rule pattern is used to define a policy for any rules or facts that match it through unification, a pattern-matching process that makes a rule pattern and an actual rule in the knowledge base identical by instantiating variables in the rule pattern. For example, the rule pattern *location(bob, X)* matches the fact *location(bob, hanover)* in the knowledge base, because the variable X can be instantiated to *hanover*. However, it does not match the fact *location(alice, hanover)*. The rule pattern *role(X, Y) ← occupation(X, Y), location(X, hospital)* can match the rule *role(P, physician) ← occupation(P, physician), location(P, hospital)* by instantiating X to P and Y to physician. A principal may define as many security policies as it chooses. Each security policy *(rp, t)* is represented as a rule pattern *rp* and a set of trusted principals *t*.

3.2   Integrity policies

Integrity policies express trust in the correctness of rules and facts. When a principal p_i defines the integrity policy *ip(rp, t)* it means that p_i trusts those principals in *t*, which we often denote $trust_i(rp)$, to be correct in whatever rules or facts that match pattern *rp*. We use subscript *i* in the integrity policy to denote which principal defines the policy. As we have described in Section 2, many authorization systems express integrity policies using rules with quoted facts. For example, if principal p_j belongs to $trust_i(grant(P))$, then p_i can express an equivalent policy with rule *grant(P) ← p_j says grant(P)*. However, when there are multiple principals that satisfy the integrity policy on a given rule pattern, we need to define a rule with a quoted fact for each principal. For brevity, we choose to express integrity policies as a list of principals. Note that our integrity policy does not support attribute-based delegation, which is supported by some delegation-based authorization systems (Li et al., 2002, 2003).

The integrity of a fact means that the truth value of a fact is correct. For example, if principal p_0 includes principal p_1 in its $trust_0(loc(P, X))$, then principal p_0 believes that p_1's evaluation (true or false) of a location query of the form $?loc(P, X)$ (e.g., $?loc(bob, hanover)$) is correct. However, the integrity of a rule means that the rule itself is able to correctly derive a new fact. For example, if principal p_0 includes principal p_1 in its integrity policy, $trust_0(loc(P, X)) \leftarrow WiFi(P, Y), in(Y, X))$, then p_0 believes that p_1's rule $loc(bob, X) \leftarrow WiFi(bob, Y), in(Y, X)$ is a correct rule to resolve the query of the form $?loc(bob, hanover)$. In other words, principal p_0 believes that the query $loc(bob, hanover)$ is replaced with two subqueries $?WiFi(bob, Y)$ and $?in(Y, hanover)$. Principal p_0 can verify that principal p_1 applied the rule correctly to derive the conclusion by checking the proof tree. We will later show an example where we want to trust the integrity of a rule rather than a fact in Section 5.6.

Note that trust on a fact is a stronger notion than trust on a rule. Trust on a fact implicitly trusts the rules used to derive that fact. For example, the trust on the rule pattern $loc(X, Y)$ implicitly indicates trust of any rule whose head can be unified with $loc(X, Y)$.

3.3 Confidentiality policies

Confidentiality policies protect facts and rules in a principal's knowledge base. A fact must be protected if it contains confidential information. A rule must be protected if confidential information may be inferred from reading the rule. For example, the rule $grant(P) \leftarrow loc(bob, sudikoff)$ says that any principal P is granted access when bob is located at the sudikoff building. If a request is granted, the requester may infer that bob is at Sudikoff, which might not be public knowledge. When a principal p_i defines the confidentiality policy $cp(rp, t)$, it means that p_i trusts those principals in t, which we often refer to as the access-control list $acl_i(rp)$, with facts or rules matching rule pattern rp. Principal p_0 only responds to a query q from principal p_1 if there exists a rule pattern rp that can be unified with the query q and principal p_1 belongs to $acl_0(rp)$. For example, suppose that principal p_0 defines the policy $acl_0(location(bob, L)) = \{p_1, p_2\}$; principal p_0 responds to a query $?location(bob, hanover)$ from principal p_1, because rule pattern $location(bob, L)$ matches $location(bob, hanover)$. Similarly, principal p_0 discloses rule $grant(P) \leftarrow loc(bob, sudikoff)$ only to principal p_1 if p_0 defines confidentiality policy $acl_0(grant(P) \leftarrow loc(bob, sudikoff)) = \{p_1\}$.

3.4 Assumptions

We make a few assumptions to maintain our focus on the confidentiality and integrity issues in a distributed authorization system. First, integrity policies of every principal are public knowledge. Second, each principal can gain knowledge about whether it has a privilege of accessing information on a given fact from other principals. It is possible for a principal to infer that knowledge by issuing a query about that fact to those principals. If the requesting principal receives a query result, that principal possesses the privilege. If the request is denied, it means that the principal does not possess the privilege. However, the denial of a query request does not reveal any information on whether the principal receiving that query actually maintains the queried fact in its knowledge base. Third, we assume that each principal's confidentiality policies on rules are not public knowledge because a confidentiality policy on a rule discloses the fact that the principal possesses a rule that matches the rule pattern of that confidentiality policy. Fourth, a PKI is available and every principal can obtain the public key of other participants, so that they can establish secure channels with a session key and verify the authenticity of messages with digital signatures.

4   Authorization on the basic security model

In this section, we describe our authorization system for the simpler case, where policies apply only to facts. We first describe the architecture of the system and introduce the notion of proof decomposition in a distributed environment. We then cover a mechanism for enforcing confidentiality policies and give a distributed algorithm for evaluating a logical query in a peer-to-peer way.

4.1   Architecture

With no central server to make authorization decisions, we use multiple hosts that are administered by different principals. Without loss of generality, we assume that each host i is administered by a different principal p_i, although in many realistic environments there may be principals that own or manage many hosts. Each host stores a local copy of its principal's integrity and confidentiality policies. Each host provides an interface for handling queries from remote hosts, and may ask other hosts to resolve any subqueries necessary. In Fig. 5, a user sends a request to the server that maintains some resource, and the server issues an authorization query to a host it chooses to make a granting decision.

The structure of a host is shown in Fig. 6. The query handler handles queries from other hosts and enforces the local confidentiality policies. The inference engine constructs a proof for a given query based on the rules and facts in the local knowledge base. If some query cannot be evaluated locally, the inference engine issues a remote query to another host through the query issuer. The query issuer refers to its local integrity policies to choose a principal that is trusted to return a correct query result; the integrity policies

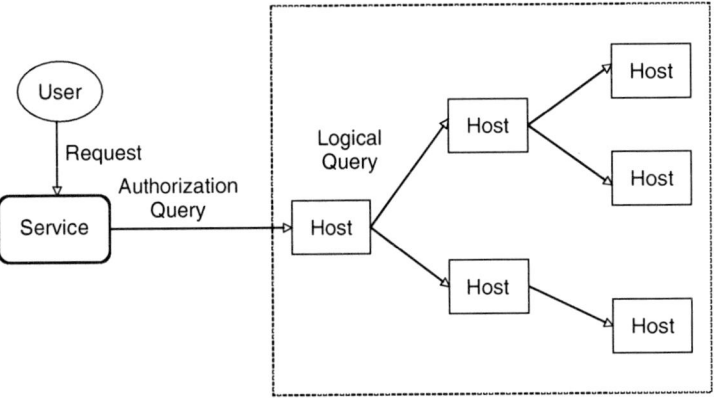

Fig. 5.   Architectural overview. The hosts enclosed in the dotted lines make an authorization decision in a collaborative way.

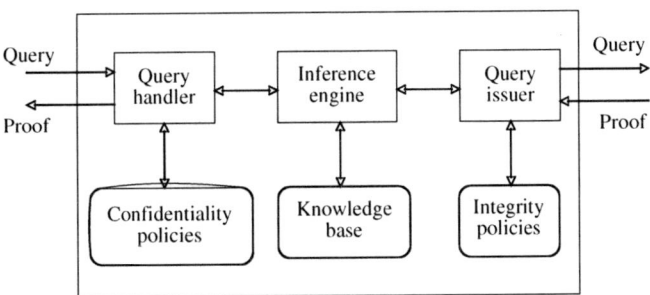

Fig. 6.   Structure of a host.

serve as a directory service to choose a principal to which it sends a query. The query issuer receives a proof for the query and checks its integrity based on the integrity policies.

4.2   *Proof decomposition in distributed query processing*

Multiple servers in different administrative domains handle an authorization query in a peer-to-peer way, since there need not be any single server that maintains all the rules and facts; a server must issue a remote query to another server when it does not have necessary information in its local knowledge base. However, the principals running those servers must preserve their confidentiality and integrity policies. The key idea for this goal is that when a principal who issues a query trusts a principal who handles a query in terms of the integrity of the query result, the handler principal does not disclose all the information in the proof. It might be sufficient to return a proof that simply states the fact in the query is true, and a proof thus is decomposed into multiple subproofs produced by different hosts.

Figure 7 describes such collaboration between a querier and a handler hosts. Suppose that host A run by principal Alice, who owns a projector, receives an authorization query *?grant(Dave, projector)* that asks whether Dave is granted access to that projector. Since Alice's authorization policy in her knowledge base refers to a requester's location (i.e., *location(P, room112)*), Alice issues a query *?location(Dave, room112)* to host B run by Bob. Alice chooses Bob, because Bob satisfies Alice's integrity policies for queries of the type *location(P, L)* (expressed by the statement *trust(location(P, L)) = {Bob}*). Alice decides to which principal a query should be sent by looking up her integrity policies. Bob processes the query from Alice, because Alice satisfies Bob's confidentiality policies for queries of the type *location(P, L)* as defined in Bob's policy *acl(location(P, L)) = {Alice}*. Bob derives that Dave is in room112 from the location of his device using the facts *location(pda15, room112)* and *owner(Dave, pda15)*. However, he only needs to return a proof that contains a single root node that states that *location(Dave, room112)* is true, because Alice believes Bob's statement about people's location (i.e., *location(P, L)*) according to her integrity policies. The proof of the query is thus decomposed into two subproofs maintained by Alice and Bob. In general, Bob may derive a proof tree that contains multiple nodes. If Alice only trusts Bob's rule that derives Bob's location instead of Bob's fact, he would need to submit a larger proof tree to satisfy Alice's integrity policies. We cover this general case in Section 5.

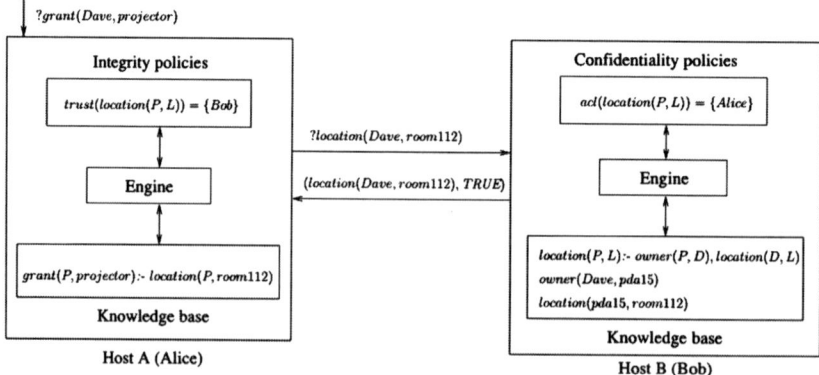

Fig. 7.   Remote query between two principals. Alice is a principal who owns a projector, and Bob is a principal who runs a location server.

4.3 *Enforcement of confidentiality policies*

Each principal who participates in constructing a proof enforces his confidentiality policies by encrypting a query result with a receiver principal's public key. A principal who returns a query result is allowed to choose a receiver principal from a list of upstream principals in a proof tree; a query is appended with a list of upstream principals that could receive the query result. Therefore, it is possible to obtain an answer for a query even when a querier principal does not satisfy the handler principal's confidentiality policies. Figure 8 shows the collaboration among five principals: p_0, p_1, p_2, p_3, and p_4. When principal p_0 issues an authorization query f_0 to principal p_1, p_1 issues a subsequent query f_1, which causes principal p_2's queries f_2 and f_3. Since a receiver principal of a proof might not be a principal who issues a query, a reply for a query is a proof $(p_i, n, (pt)_{Ki})$ where p_i is an identity of a receiver principal, n a nonce that prevents reply attacks, and $(pt)_{Ki}$ an encrypted proof tree with the receiver p_i's public key. (We name the third element pt of a proof a proof tree because, in the general case in Section 5, it contains a proof tree that shows how the queried fact is derived.) We omit the field of a nonce n in a proof for brevity in the following discussion. We assume that, in this example, each principal who issues a query trusts the integrity of the principal who receives that query in terms of the correctness of whether the fact in the query is true or not. For example, p_0 defines an integrity policy $trust_0(f) = \{p_1\}$.

Suppose that query f_1's result (i.e., true or false) depends on the results of queries f_2 and f_3, which are handled by principals p_3 and p_4, respectively, and that p_3 and p_4 choose principal p_0 and p_1 as a receiver, respectively, since p_2 does not satisfy their confidentiality policies. Each principal receiving a query chooses a receiver from a list of upstream principals associated with the query. Because principal p_2 cannot decrypt the results from principals p_3 and p_4, p_2 encrypts those results with the public key of principal p_1, which p_2 chooses as a receiver; that is, the proof for query f_1 is

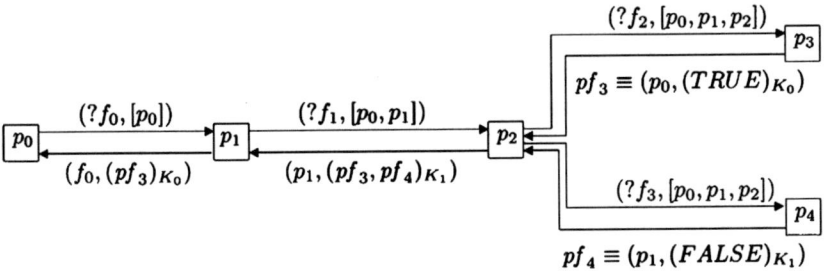

Fig. 8. Enforcement of confidentiality policies. Each query is associated with a list of upstream principals. The first item in a proof tuple is a receiver principal, and the second item is a proof tree encrypted with the receiver's public key.

the conjunction of two encrypted proofs published by principals p_3 and p_4 because the query result of f_1 is the conjunction of the Boolean values in those encrypted proofs. In general, a proof could be the conjunction of subproofs in which multiple Boolean values are encrypted in a nested way.

Principal p_1 decrypts the encrypted result from p_2 and obtains the encrypted results originally produced by principals p_3 and p_4. Since p_1 is a receiver of the proof from p_4, p_1 decrypts the proof that contains TRUE. Since a query result for f_0 depends on the encrypted proof from p_3, principal p_1 forwards it in the same way. The principal p_0 finally decrypts it and obtains an answer for query f_0.

In general, each proof must be signed with a sender principal's public key so that a principal who receives a proof that contains subproofs produced by multiple principals can check its integrity. (These signatures are not shown in Fig. 8.) In this example, since each querier principal trusts the integrity of the principal handling the query, intermediate principals p_1 and p_2 do not have to forward the digital signature of the received proof to its upstream principal. Thus, principal p_0 is not aware of the fact that the query result is originally produced by principal p_3.

Nested encryption: When a principal constructs a proof that contains encrypted proofs received from downstream principals, that proof must be encrypted recursively with the public key of a principal that receives that proof, as we see in the example in Fig. 8. The grammar for a proof is given as follows:

> $PROOF ::= \; '('\; RECEIVER\; ','\; PTREE\; ')'$
> $PTREE ::= \; VALUE \mid PROOF^+$
> $VALUE ::= \; TRUE \mid FALSE$

A proof (PROOF) is a pair of a receiver principal (RECEIVER) and a proof tree (PTREE), which is encrypted with the receiver's public key. (This encryption is not shown in the grammar earlier for brevity.) The receiver's identity is thus necessary in the proof so that a principal that receives the proof can decide whether it should attempt to decrypt the proof tree. A proof tree (PTREE) could contain a single Boolean value (VALUE), which is either TRUE or FALSE, or contain multiple subproofs (i.e., $PROOF^+$) in a nested way.

This nested encryption is necessary to prevent an attack by colluding upstream principals that modify a list of upstream principals attached with a query. We describe such an attack with an example in Fig. 9. Suppose that principals p_1 and p_2 are malicious colluding principals. When p_1 issues a query f_1, p_1 attaches the list $[p_1, p_0]$ after swapping the position of the two principals in the correct list. Another malicious principal p_2 issues a query f_2 with the list of upstream principals $[p_1, p_0, p_2]$; principal p_2 just appends itself at the end of the list received from p_1. Principal p_1 needs p_2's cooperation because, if p_2 is not a colluding principal, p_2 detects p_1's modification on the list because p_1 is not at the end of the list. When principal p_2 sends a query to

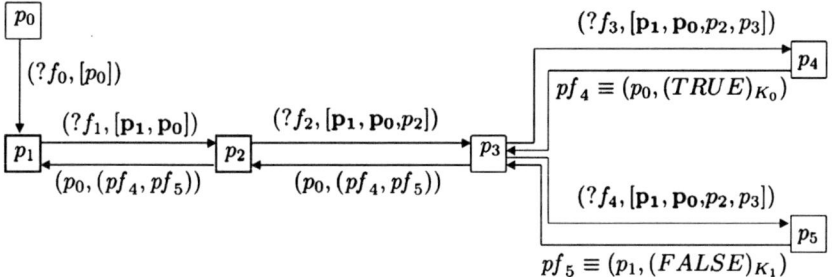

Fig. 9.   Principals p_1 and p_2 are malicious colluding principals. Principal p_1 swaps the position of principals p_0 and p_1 in the list of upstream principals for query $?f_1$.

p_3, p_3 cannot detect the modification of the list by p_1 because principal p_2 is at the end of the list of upstream principals.

Suppose that principal p_3 chooses p_0 as the receiver of p_3's proof, which contains proofs obtained from principals p_4 and p_5 and that principals p_4 and p_5 choose principals p_0 and p_1 as the receivers of their proofs, respectively. If principal p_3 does not encrypt the proofs from p_4 and p_5 with p_0's public key recursively, principal p_1, who receives those proofs before p_0 does, decrypts the proof from principal p_5. Principal p_1 knows the query result for f_2 without a legitimate privilege if p_5's proof contains FALSE, because the result of f_2 is the conjunction of the Boolean values contained in the encrypted proofs pf_4 and pf_5. Though, if p_5's proof contains TRUE, p_1 is still not sure about the query result for f_2.

Constraint on a choice of a receiver principal: When a principal returns a query result that contains an encrypted result received from a downstream principal, the principal needs to make sure that the encryption that principal performs on the query result will be decrypted before it arrives at the principal that is able to decrypt the inner encrypted result from the downstream principal. For example, in Fig. 8, principal p_2 cannot choose p_0 as a receiver principal even if p_0 satisfies p_2's confidentiality policy on fact f_1. Principal p_1 cannot decrypt proof pf_4 produced by principal p_4 because it is further encrypted with principal p_0's public key. In general, a proof could contain multiple encrypted results from different downstream principals, and a principal returning such a proof needs to make sure that the aforementioned constraint is satisfied for each encrypted result in the returning proof. In our algorithm in Section 4.4, each principal actually trims the list of upstream principals when it issues subsequent queries to satisfy this constraint.

4.4   Algorithms for the base case

Each host (run by some principal) provides an interface *HandleRemote Query* for handling a query from a remote host. It takes as parameters a query string q and a list of upstream principals receivers. The function *HandleRemoteQuery* calls the function *GenerateProof* to obtain a proof.

Figure 10 shows the algorithm for the function *GenerateProof*, run on principal p_h's host to build a reply tuple $(p_r, (pf)_{K_r})$ for query q while enforcing p_h's confidentiality policies. The function takes several parameters: principal p_q that issues a query, principal p_h that handles a query, a query string q, a list of upstream principals receivers, p_h's integrity policies *i_policies$_h$*, p_h's confidentiality policies *c_policies$_h$*, and p_h's knowledge base KB_h.

Lines 2 and 3 check whether there is any principal in the list receivers that satisfies principal p_h's confidentiality policies. The principals that belong to the intersection of receivers and the union of the access-control lists in p_h's confidentiality policies for query q are eligible to receive a proof from p_h. We treat the ordered list receivers as a set in line 2, and denote by *acl* the result set. If there is no such principal (i.e., the set *acl* is empty), line 4 returns a tuple with a REJECT value to querier principal p_q.

GENERATEPROOF($p_q, p_h, q, receivers, i\_policies_h, c\_policies_h, KB_h$)

1   ▷ Check if some principal in $receivers$ satisfies p_h's confidentiality policies.
2    $acl \leftarrow receivers \cap (\bigcup_i t_i)$ for all policies $(rp_i, t_i) \in c\_policies_h$ where rp_i matches q
3   **if** $acl = \emptyset$
4   **then return** $(p_q, (REJECT)_{K_q})$
5    $p_r \leftarrow minIndex(acl, receivers)$
6   **if** $\exists$ fact $f \in KB_h : f$ matches q
7   **then return** $(p_r, (TRUE)_{K_r})$
8   **elseif** $\exists$ rule $R \equiv A \leftarrow B_1, \ldots, B_k \in KB_h : A$ matches q
9   **then** unify q and $A \leftarrow B_1, \ldots, B_k$, resulting in $A' \leftarrow B'_1, \ldots, B'_k$
10   **for** $i \leftarrow 1$ **to** k
11   **do** $pf_i \leftarrow$ GENERATEPROOF($p_h, p_h, B'_i, receivers, i\_policies_h, c\_policies_h, KB_h$)
          where $pf_i = (p_{r(i)}, (v_i)_{K_{r(i)}})$, and $r(i)$ is the receiver principal of pf_i
12       $pfs \leftarrow \wedge_1^k pf_i$
13       $pf \leftarrow$ DECRYPTPROOF(p_h, pfs)
14   **if** $pf = TRUE$
15   **then return** $(p_r, (TRUE)_{K_r})$
16   **elseif** $pf = FALSE$
17   **then** ▷ do nothing.
18   **else return** $(p_r, (pf)_{K_r})$
19   ▷ If p_h fails to construct a proof with its local knowledge base, p_h attempts to obtain a proof from a remote principal.
20    $contacted \leftarrow \emptyset$
21    $rcvrs \leftarrow concat(sublist(receivers, 0, index(receivers, p_r)), p_h)$
22   **while** $\exists$ principal $p_l \notin contacted, \exists$ policy $p = (rp, t) \in i\_policies_h : rp$ matches $q \wedge p_l \in t$
23   **do** $(p_{r'}, (pfs)_{K_{r'}}) \leftarrow$ ISSUEREMOTEQUERY($p_l, q, rcvrs$)
24       $pf \leftarrow$ DECRYPTPROOF($p_h, (p_{r'}, (pfs)_{K_{r'}})$)
25   **if** $pf = TRUE$
26   **then return** $(p_r, (TRUE)_{K_r})$
27   **elseif** $pf = FALSE$
28   **then** ▷ do nothing.
29   **else return** $(p_r, (pf)_{K_r})$
30       $contacted \leftarrow contacted \cup \{p_l\}$
31   **return** $(p_r, (FALSE)_{K_r})$

Fig. 10.   Algorithm for generating a proof.

Line 5 chooses a principal that receives a proof from p_h. The receiver principal must belong to list *acl* and have the minimum index in the ordered list *receivers*. The function *minIndex(acl, receivers)* in line 5 returns such a receiver principal. Line 6 checks whether query q matches fact f in p_h's knowledge base KB_h. If so, line 7 returns a proof with a TRUE value to principal p_r.

Lines 8–18 cover the case that query q matches the head of rule R in p_1's knowledge base. Line 9 unifies query q and rule $R \equiv A \leftarrow B_1, \ldots, B_k$, resulting in the instantiated rule $A \leftarrow B'_1, \ldots, B'_k$. Lines 10 and 11 obtain subproofs for the subqueries $B'_1, \ldots, B'_k$ iteratively. Line 12 sets the conjunction of all the subproofs into a variable *pfs*, and line 13 decrypts subproofs that can be decrypted by principal p_h by calling the function *DecryptProof* in Fig. 11. If function *DecryptProof* returns TRUE, it returns a tuple $(p_r, TRUE)$ in line 15. If the function returns FALSE, we do not return a proof that contains FALSE immediately, because we may be able to find a proof from a remote principal in lines 19–28. If the function returns an undecrypted proof *pf*, line 18 returns a tuple $(p_r, (pf)_{Kr})$. Note that principal p_h recursively encrypts the proof *pf* with the receiver principal p_r's public key.

If lines 6–18 fail to construct a proof that derives query q, our algorithm does not return a proof that contains FALSE immediately. Instead, it tries to obtain a proof from a remote principal in lines 20–28. Line 20 creates an empty set contacted that will contain a set of remote principals. In line 21, we modify the *receivers* list to constrain the choice of a receiver principal as described in Section 4.3. The function *sublist* returns a sublist of receivers'

DECRYPTPROOF$(p_h, (p_r, (pfs)_{K_r}))$

```
 1  if p_h ≠ p_r
 2     then return (pfs)_{K_r}
 3  pfs ← DECRYPT(p_h, (pfs)_{K_r})  ▷ Decryption with p_h's private key
 4  if pfs = TRUE
 5     then return TRUE
 6  elseif pfs = FALSE
 7     then return FALSE
 8  elseif pfs = ∧₁ⁿ pf_i
 9     then for i ← 1 to n
10          do pf'_i ← DECRYPTPROOF(p_h, pf_i)
11             if pf'_i = FALSE ∨ pf'_i = REJECT
12                then return FALSE
13          if ∀i :  pf'_i = TRUE
14             then return TRUE
15          elseif
16             then return ∧ pf'_i where pf'_i = (p_{r_i}, (pf''_i)_{K_{r_i}}) and p_{r_i} ≠ p_h
```

Fig. 11. Algorithm for decrypting a proof.

list from index 0 to that of principal p_r, and the function *concat* appends p_h at the end of that sublist. We maintain the produced list in another ordered list *rcvrs*. This ordered list *rcvrs* is used as one of the parameters for remote queries later.

Lines 22–30 obtain a proof for query q from a remote principal. Line 22 checks whether there is any principal p_l that satisfies p_h's integrity policies for query q and does not belong to the set contacted yet. The set contacted maintains a list of principals to which the remote query has been already issued. Line 23 calls the function *IssueRemoteQuery* with the remote principal p_l, the query q, and the ordered list *rcvrs* as parameters, and that function returns a tuple of the form $(p_r, (pfs)_{Kr})$ from principal p_l. In line 24, the function *DecryptProof* decrypts the returned proof with p_h's private key and return a decrypted proof pf. If a proof pf contains TRUE, line 26 returns a tuple $(p_r, (TRUE)_{Kr})$ after p_h encrypts the TRUE value with the receiver p_r's public key. If a proof pf contains FALSE, we do not return a proof with FALSE immediately because we may be able to find a proof from another remote principal. If the function returns an undecrypted proof pf, line 29 returns a tuple $(p_r, (pf)_{Kr})$ after the proof pf is recursively encrypted with principal p_r's public key. Line 30 adds the remote principal p_l into the set contacted. This process is iterated until the while loop in lines 22–30 obtains a proof or finishes trying all the remote principals. Finally, line 33 returns a tuple $(p_r, (FALSE)_{Kr})$ since there is no other way to construct a proof for query q.

Algorithm for decrypting a proof: Figure 11 shows an algorithm for decrypting a proof. The function *DecryptProof* takes as parameters a principal p_h whose private key is used to decrypt a proof and a tuple $(p_r, (pfs)_{Kr})$ where the proof pfs is encrypted with a principal p_r's public key. Line 1 checks whether principal p_h can decrypt the proof, and, if not, line 2 returns the proof given as a parameter. Line 3 decrypts the proof with principal p_h's private key. If the proof contains TRUE, line 5 returns TRUE. Similarly, if the proof contains FALSE, line 7 returns FALSE. Lines 8–16 cover the case where the proof pfs in the parameter contains subproofs $pf_1, \ldots, pf_n$. Line 10 decrypts each subproof pf_i by calling the function *DecryptProof* recursively. If any subproof pf_i contains either FALSE or REJECT, line 12 returns FALSE regardless of the truth of other subproofs. If all the subproofs contains TRUE, line 14 returns TRUE. If there are subproofs that cannot be decrypted by principal p_h, line 16 returns the conjunction of those undecrypted subproofs.

4.5   Example application

The teams responding to a large-scale disaster are coordinated by experts drawn from multiple disciplines (fire, police, medical) and often multiple jurisdictions (city, state, federal). Increasingly, incident commanders use software to assist with incident management and situational awareness. The National Incident Management System (2004) defines clear roles for the many participants in a large-scale response, so RBAC (Sandhu et al., 1996) is a natural basis for protecting resources in an incident management system (IMS). Such an IMS needs to dynamically link people, resources, and information from multiple domains, providing information to those who need it in a time of crisis.

Suppose that an incident occurs at an airport. There is a surveillance camera image server managed by the airport, and the chief of operations (bob) wishes to use the camera images to improve his awareness of the situation. Figure 12 shows a set of rules that define the airport's policy to grant access to the camera resource, which allows the local police chief access to the images whenever he is in the airport, as determined by either his Wi-Fi network connection or by the global positioning system (GPS) tracking device in his radio. Rule 1 says that principal P must hold the role operation chief to be granted, and rule 2 defines the two conditions to hold that role. The first condition specifies the prerequisite role police chief in a police department, and the second requires principal P to be in the airport. Rules 3–5 specify how we derive the location of principal P from the raw location information of a device. Given the facts listed in Fig. 12, a centralized system would produce the proof tree shown in Fig. 13 by unifying the query with the rules 1–4 and facts 6–9, substituting variables as needed.

We next consider the scenario where the same proof is constructed in a distributed way. Figure 14 shows how user bob (principal p_0) requests images from the surveillance camera image server managed by the airport (principal p_1). Bob's request is handled by multiple principals $p_1, p_2, \ldots, p_7$. In Fig. 14, every principal issues queries to the principals that satisfy its integrity policies, and every querier except for principal p_2 satisfies the confidentiality policies of the principals to which it sends the queries. Principal

Rules:

$$grant(P) \;\leftarrow\; role(P, operation\_chief) \tag{1}$$
$$role(P, operation\_chief) \;\leftarrow\; roleIn(P, police\_chief, police\_dept) \wedge location(P, airport) \tag{2}$$
$$location(P, L) \;\leftarrow\; owner(P, D) \wedge location(D, L) \tag{3}$$
$$location(D, L) \;\leftarrow\; wifi(D, A) \wedge in(A, L) \tag{4}$$
$$location(D, L) \;\leftarrow\; gps(D, X, Y) \wedge closeTo(X, Y, L) \tag{5}$$

Facts:

$roleIn(bob, police\_chief, police\_dept).$	Bob is chief of the local police department.	(6)
$owner(bob, pda15)$	Bob owns device pda15	(7)
$wifi(pda15, ap39).$	pda15 is associated with access point ap39.	(8)
$in(ap39, airport).$	Access point ap39 is at the airport.	(9)

Fig. 12. Sample set of rules. We use uppercase for variables and lowercase for constants and names.

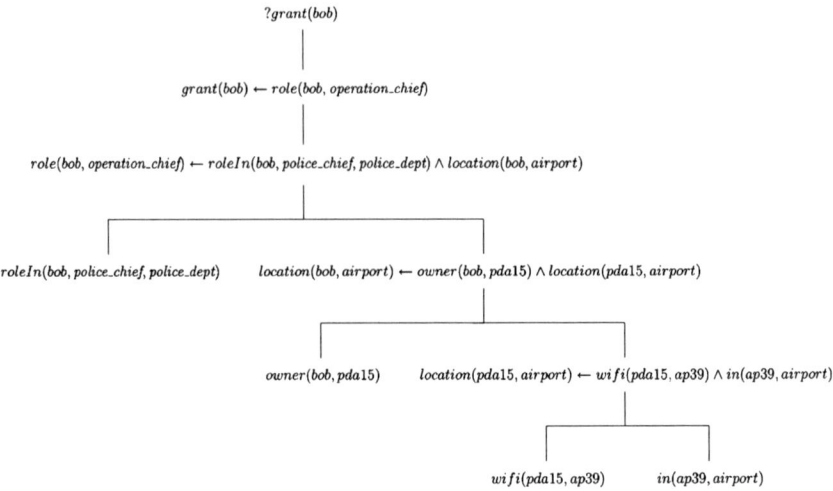

Fig. 13.   Example proof tree based on the rules in Fig. 12.

p_2 does not satisfy p_4's confidentiality policies for query *?location(bob, airport)*, because p_2 is temporarily assigned to manage the role server for the incident, and we assume that principal p_4 has not established a long-term trust relationship with principal p_2. Fortunately, p_1 that runs the surveillance camera image server satisfies p_4's confidentiality policies, principal p_4 encrypts the query result with p_1's public key, and principal p_2 embeds p_4's proof into its own proof, and returns it to p_1. Principal p_1 decrypts the query result in the proof from p_2, but it is not aware of the fact that the query result was created by principal p_4.

5 Authorization for the general case

In this section, we extend our authorization scheme so that it supports security policies on rules as well as on facts. A proof contains a proof tree that describes the derivation of the query's result if the evaluation of a query is true, instead of simply the result TRUE, to satisfy a querier principal's integrity policies. This situation occurs when the querier principal does not trust the integrity of the query result from the handler principal, but trusts handler's rule that is used to decompose the query into subqueries. We describe how our authorization system for the base case in Section 4 should be extended to support security policies on rules.

5.1 Representation of a proof

In the general case, principals in the system exchange proofs that consist of intermediate nodes that represent rules and leaf nodes that represent facts.

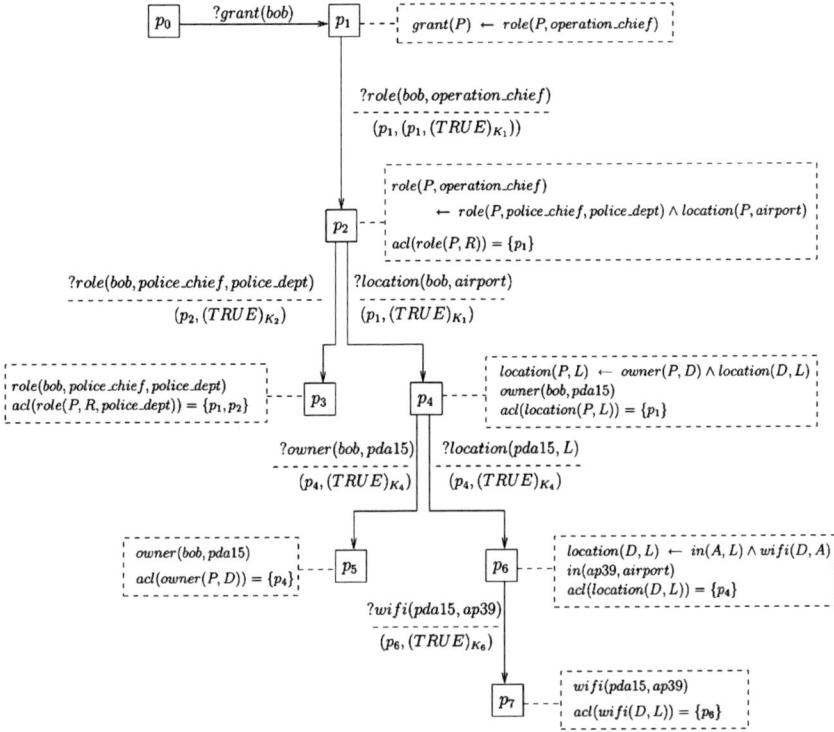

Fig. 14. Example of an emergency response system. Principal p_0 is a first responder whose role is "operation chief." Principal p_1 represents a surveillance camera image server. Principal p_2 is the role membership server of an incident management system (IMS). Principal p_3 is the role membership server of a police department. Principal p_4 represents a location-tracking service. The arrows represent the flow of queries among the principals. Each arrow is labeled with a query and a returned proof. The query is shown above the dashed line and the proof is shown below the line. Each principal's rules, facts, and confidentiality policies are shown in a dashed rectangle.

We therefore need to extend the representation of a proof in Section 4. A proof could have a hierarchical structure when the proof contains a node that represents a rule. Also, since each node of a proof is published by a different principal, we need to associate it with the identity of its publisher principal. A principal that receives a proof checks the authenticity of each node by verifying the digital signature signed by the publisher principal. We represent a proof as a tuple with four fields as follows:

$$
\begin{aligned}
PROOF &::= \ \text{'(' } SENDER \text{ ',' } RECEIVER \text{ ',' } QUERY \text{ ',' } PTREE \text{ ')'} \\
PTREE &::= \ VALUE \mid PROOF^+ \mid \text{'('} RULE \text{ ',' } PROOF^+ \text{ ')'} \\
VALUE &::= \ TRUE \mid FALSE
\end{aligned}
$$

$$RULE ::= HEAD \text{ '} \leftarrow \text{' } BODY$$
$$HEAD ::= ATOM$$
$$BODY ::= ATOM \text{ (',' } ATOM \text{)}*$$

We denote by *SENDER* and *RECEIVER* the sender and receiver principals of a proof, respectively, and by *QUERY* a query string. A proof tree *PTREE* represents the derivation of the queried fact *QUERY*. If the root node of a proof tree is a rule (*RULE*), we represent that proof tree as a tuple *(RULE, PROOF$^+$)* where subproofs *PROOF$^+$* represent the proofs of the subgoals of the rule in the first field of the tuple. If the root node is a fact as we assume in Section 4, a proof tree is either a Boolean value *VALUE* or the nested conjunction of subproofs that contain a Boolean value in their proof trees. The sender principal of a proof digitally signs the proof and attaches the signature with the proof so that a receiver principal can check its authenticity. Also, the sender principal encrypts the proof tree in a proof with the receiver principal's public key; the proof tree is published in an encrypted form. Similarly, if a proof contains other proofs in its proof tree in a nested way, those proofs are attached with the digital signatures of their publishers, and all the proof trees in those proofs are encrypted with the public keys of the receivers of those proofs. The receiver's identity is necessary in the proof for a receiver principal to decrypt the proof tree. We do not show encryption on a proof tree and a digital signature on a proof in the preceding grammar for brevity.

Example. We revisit the example in Fig. 3. Suppose that principal p_1 that maintains the rule *grant(Bob)* ← *role(Bob, doctor), location(Bob, hospital)* obtains facts *role(Bob, doctor)* and *location(Bob, hospital)* from principals p_2 and p_3, respectively. If principal p_1 receives query *?grant(Bob)* from principal p_0, p_1 might return a proof as follows:

> *(p_1, p_0, grant(Bob), grant(Bob)* ← *role(Bob, doctor),*
> *(p_2, p_0, role(Bob, doctor), TRUE)(p_3, p_1, location(Bob, hospital),*
> *TRUE))*

Principal p_1 signs the whole proof, and principals p_2 and p_3 sign the two subproofs *(p_2, p_0, role(Bob, doctor), TRUE)* and *(p_3, p_1, location(Bob, hospital), TRUE)*, respectively. Also, principal p_1 encrypts the whole proof tree with principal p_0's public key, and principal p_2 and p_3 encrypt the Boolean values TRUE in their subproofs with the public keys of principal p_0 and p_1, respectively. For clarity, we do not represent the encryption or the signatures in our notation.

5.2 Integrity of a proof

A principal trusts the integrity of a proof (e.g., believes its result) for a query if each node of the proof satisfies its integrity policies. We formally define the integrity of a proof tree from the viewpoint of a querier principal p_0 inductively as follows. Suppose that principal p_0 issues a query q to principal p_1.

Base case (single-node tree): If a proof from principal p_1 contains a Boolean value or the conjunction of Boolean values, and principal p_0 has an integrity policy $ip(rp, t)$ such that rule pattern rp matches query q and p_1 belongs to the set of principals t, then p_0 trusts the integrity of the proof. Principal p_0 needs to verify the authenticity of a proof by checking a digital signature with the proof.

Induction step: If the proof from p_1 contains a proof tree whose root node represents a ruler, the head of rule r matches query q, p_0 has an integrity policy $ip(rp,t)$ such that rule pattern rp matches r and p_1 belongs to the set of principals t, and p_0 trusts the integrity of the subproof trees under the root node representing r, then p_0 trusts the integrity of the proof.

Example. Again consider the example of Fig. 3, but suppose that principal p_0 has different integrity policies, and, as a result, principal p_1 returns a proof that contains a proof tree. Principal p_0 does not trust the integrity of p_1 to evaluate the query $?grant(bob)$, but does trust the integrity of $rule_1$. Principal p_1 constructs a proof that consists of the rule $rule_1$ as a root node and the subproofs $proof_2$ and $proof_3$ as leaf nodes and returns it to principal p_0. The proof tree constructed by principal p_1 is trusted by principal p_0 because principal p_0 trusts $rule_1$ in principal p_1 and the facts $role(bob,doctor)$ and $location(bob,hospital)$ in principals p_2 and p_3, respectively, according to its integrity policies (Fig. 15).

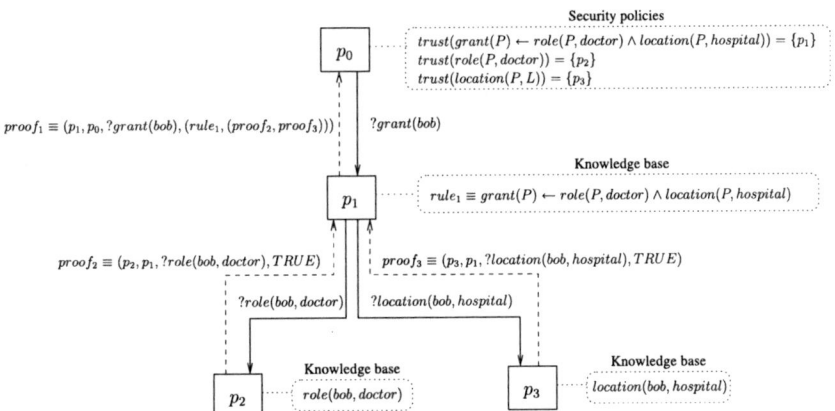

Fig. 15. Construction of a proof tree. The solid arrows are labeled with queries and the dashed arrows are labeled with returned proof trees. The rounded rectangles with dotted lines represent the knowledge bases or security policies of those principals, respectively.

5.3 Decomposition of proof tree

In the general case, a response to a query is a proof that contains a proof tree that satisfies the integrity policies of a querier. When a principal issues a query, it attaches integrity policies to the query so that downstream principals can construct a proof that satisfies those integrity policies. If a principal is an initial querier, it attaches its integrity policies. If a principal issues a subsequent query q to construct a proof for the query q from the upstream principal, there are two cases. If the intermediate principal satisfies integrity policies attached to the query q, it attaches its integrity policies to the subsequent query q. Otherwise, it attaches the integrity policies for the query q to the subsequent query q.

If the integrity of the principal that handles a query is trusted by the querier, it only returns a single-node proof tree that contains the truth of the fact in the query. If there are several principals participating in handling a query, the whole proof tree is decomposed into several subtrees and is evaluated by multiple principals in a distributed way. The facts and rules in those subtrees do not have to be disclosed to a querier principal. In Fig. 16, principals $p_0, p_1, \ldots, p_{10}$ are the participants in handling a query, and each arrow shows how a proof tree flows from one principal to another. We show only the fields for a sender and a receiver principals for brevity,

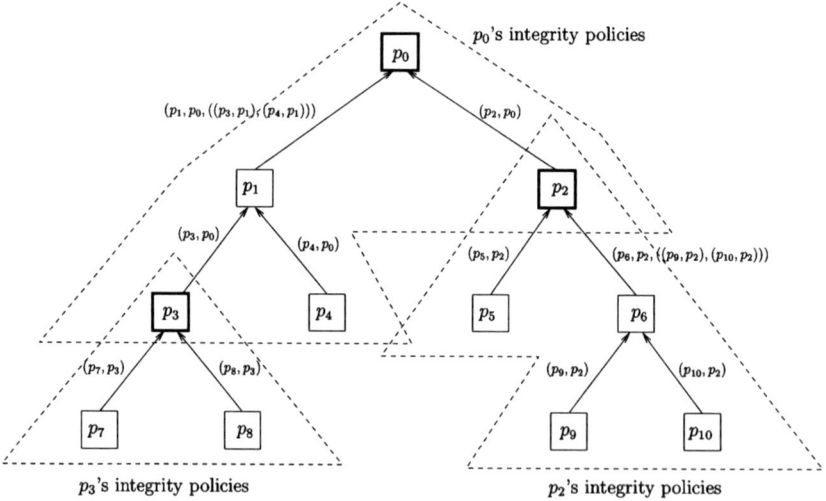

Fig. 16.   Example of subproofs. Principals $p_0, \ldots, p_{10}$ are the participants in evaluating a query. Each arrow shows how a proof tree flows from one principal to another. Each arrow is labeled with the pair of a sender and a receiver principals in a proof, omitting the other fields of the proof for brevity. The dashed lines show which principal's integrity policies are applied to the principals enclosed in the lines. The principals $p_0, p_2,$ and p_3 that represent the root node of the nested subtrees are enclosed in the thick rectangles.

omitting other fields. The dashed lines show which principal's integrity policies are applied to the principals enclosed in the lines.

Because principal p_0 trusts principal p_2 and p_3 in terms of the integrity of the given queries, it is possible to evaluate the query at p_0, p_2, and p_3 rather than collecting all the rules and facts at p_0. Principals p_2 and p_3 construct a proof tree locally based on their own integrity policies, and return only a single-node proof tree that contains a query result. Therefore, principal p_0 does not know how the query results from p_2 and p_3 are derived.

5.4   Enforcement of confidentiality policies

We apply the same mechanism for enforcing confidentiality policies in Section 4.3. The only difference is that a receiver principal must be an upstream principal that evaluates a proof subtree. For example, principal p_7 in Fig. 16 can choose a receiver principal only from two principals p_0 and p_3. We, therefore, define a set of principals $receivers(p_i)$ whose members are eligible to receive principal p_i's proof as follows:

Suppose that in a proof tree there is a sequence of nodes $n_0, n_1, \ldots, n_k$ on the path from the root n_0 to node n_k in the proof tree, and principal p_i is a publisher of a fact or a rule in node n_i for $i = 1$ to k. We assume that principal p_i handles query $q_i - 1$ from $p_i - 1$ for $i = 1$ to k while constructing the proof tree. Principal p_i where $i < k$ belongs to the set $receivers(p_k)$ if it satisfies either of the following two conditions.

- Principal p_i is p_0.
- Principal p_l belongs to $receivers(p_k)$, p_l has an integrity policy $ip(rp, t)$ such that rule pattern rp matches query $q_i - 1$ and p_i belongs to the set of principals t, and there is no other principal p_j (where $l < j < i$) that satisfies this condition.

Note that our new definition covers the definition of upstream principals in Section 4.3, because every principal issues a query to a principal that it trusts in terms of the integrity of evaluating the query. That is, if a querier principal $p_i - 1$ in $receivers(p)$ issues query $q_i - 1$ to p_i, p_i belongs to $receivers(p)$ as well because p_i satisfies the second condition earlier. In other words, all the upstream principals of p belong to the set $receivers(p)$.

5.5   Algorithms for the general case

We summarize the major differences from the algorithm for the base case in Section 4.4. We refer interested readers to our journal paper (Minami and Kotz, 2005b) for more details.

- Each query is associated with the receivers list defined in Section 5.4 rather than a list of upstream principals in Section 4.3.

- A principal insuring a query attaches integrity policies with the query as we describe in Section 5.4, so that a principal handling the query can return a proof that satisfies the attached integrity policies.
- A principal that receives a query could return a proof that contains a proof tree whose root node represents a rule as we describe in Section 5.1.
- Each node of a proof tree is associated with the identity of a publisher principal. Also, the subproof tree under that node is associated with the digital signature signed by the publisher principal of the root node.
- A principal that receives a proof verifies its integrity by checking that every node in the proof tree satisfies the integrity policies sent with the query.

5.6 Example application

We revisit the example of an IMS; in Fig. 14, every querier principal trusts the integrity of the principal that handles its query in terms of the correctness of the query's result. This time, we have some principals that define security policies on rules as well as facts.

Figure 17 shows how user bob (principal p_0) requests images from the surveillance camera image server managed by the airport (principal p_1). Principal p_1 agrees with the policy for role operation chief, that is, *role(P, operation_chief)* ← *role(P, police_chief, police_dept)* з *in(P, airport)* is correct, and principal p_2 that runs the role-membership server of IMS uses that rule to evaluate a query *role(bob, operation_chief)*. However, principal p_1 does not trust the answer from principal p_2, since p_2 is temporarily assigned to manage the role server for the incident, and we assume principal p_1 has not established a long-term trust relationship with principal p_2. Fortunately, principal p_2 trusts the role-membership server of the police department and the location tracking service run by principals p_3 and p_4, respectively, because those are long-running existing services. Principal p_2 is thus able to return a proof tree that contains the proofs from principal p_3 and p_4, and principal p_1 trusts that proof. The proof tree also satisfies the confidentiality policies of principals p_2, p_3, and p_4. Principal p_4 only returns the evaluation result of the query *?location(bob, airport)* because it belongs to *trust(location(P, L))* = *{p_4}* defined by principal p_1.

6 Discussion

In this section, we discuss several design issues, limitations, and security properties of our system.

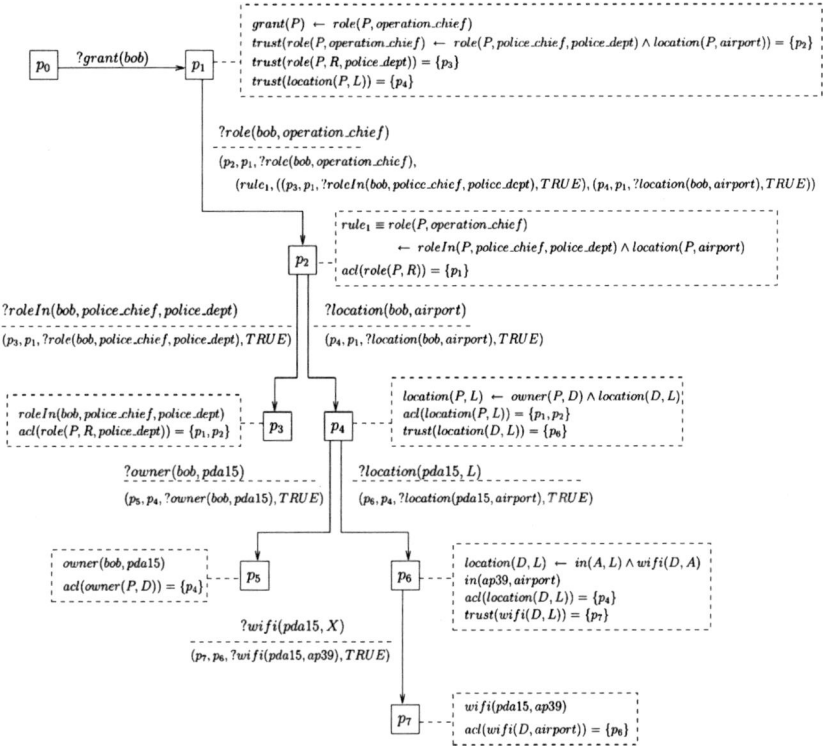

Fig. 17.   Example of an emergency response system. Principal p_0 is a first responder whose role is "operation chief." Principal p_1 represents a surveillance camera image server. Principal p_2 is the role membership server of an incident management system (IMS). Principal p_3 is the role membership server of a police department. Principal p_4 represents a location-tracking service. The arrows represent the flow of queries among the principals. Each arrow is labeled with a query and a returned proof tree. The query is shown above the dashed line and the proof is shown below the line. Each principal's rules, facts, and policies are shown in a dashed rectangle.

6.1   Completeness of our algorithm

The algorithm for the function *GenerateProof* in Fig. 10 is not complete. That is, it is not guaranteed to find a proof that derives a granting decision even if one exists. This situation could happen when a principal who handles a query is able to produce multiple alternative proofs. Suppose that the proof that the principal produces first contains an encrypted subproof obtained from another principal and that encrypted subproof contains a FALSE value. When the principal returns the proof, a principal who receives the proof finds that proof invalid after decrypting its embedded subproof. However, since the principal that returned the proof finished handling the query, that principal is not able to find another alternative proof.

There are two possible ways to make our algorithm complete. One is to add a mechanism that enables a principal that finishes handling a query to resume processing the same query from the previous point of the search space; an inference engine continues to maintain various data structures, such as a proof tree, for a query after a proof for that query is returned, and those data structures must be associated with a unique identifier of the query to resume the query-handling process. This approach does not waste computing and network resources since a proof is constructed on demand. However, it could consume a lot of memory to maintain these data structures. Furthermore, this approach makes it possible for a principal that handles a query to infer the query result in an encrypted subproof produced by another principal; that is, if a querier principal issues the same query again, the handler principal can infer that the encrypted subproof embedded in the previous proof contains a FALSE value. Considering this security issue, we cannot choose the first approach.

The other is to modify an interface for handling a query so that a principal that handles a query can return multiple alternative proofs together. A querier principal specifies the number of proofs he needs as a parameter in a query, and the querier and handler principals maintain a network session until all the proofs are transmitted. This approach does not have the security risk of the first approach. However, we need to extend the representation of a proof in Section 5.1 to evaluate a set of alternative subproofs as the disjunction of the query results in those subproofs. This situation happens when a principal that handles a query issues a subsequent query and obtains multiple alternative proofs together. If the principal cannot decrypt those proofs, the principal must embed the disjunction of those proofs into a proof that the principal returns. Although we believe this approach is feasible, it requires a lot of changes in our current implementation, such as the algorithm for checking the integrity of a proof, the data structure of a proof object, and so on. Therefore, we plan to make our algorithm complete in our future work.

6.2 Performance of our implementation

Our implementation of the system has approximately 12,000 lines of Java code, extending a Prolog engine XProlog (Vaucher, 2003). We used the Java Cryptographic Extension (JCE) framework to implement RSA and Triple-DES (TDES) cryptographic operations. Our experimental results with a 27-node cluster show that the performance overhead of public-key operations involved in the process of a remote query were large. However, we reduced the amortized latency for handling a query significantly by applying caching mechanism to the system. We refer interested readers to our conference paper (Minami and Kotz, 2006) that includes the details of our design and implementation of the system and its performance results.

6.3 Security assurance

Our authorization scheme ensures that each principal's confidentiality policies are preserved while participating in the evaluation of an authorization query. A malicious principal that represents an internal node of a proof subtree cannot inappropriately obtain a rule or a fact from other principals by modifying the receivers list in a subquery it issues, because each principal discloses its rules or facts to other principals only if they satisfy its confidentiality policies. We provide a soundness proof of our algorithms in our journal paper (Minami and Kotz, 2005b).

We use a nonce to prevent a reply attack by a malicious party that is capable of intercepting and modifying a message. All the participating principals that evaluate an authorization query use the same nonce, generated by the original querying principal, because the receiver of a proof might be different from a querier principal. The nonce in a proof must match the nonce in the query, for the proof to be valid.

6.4 User feedback

It would be useful, in the case of a FALSE proof, to provide some feedback for the user about why the proof failed and what policies prevent them from obtaining the desired access. Although to return an incomplete proof is a plausible solution, there are two issues to be addressed. First, due to confidentiality policies the user may not be allowed to receive the incomplete proof, and, as a result, the user is not able to know which subproof failed. Second, because there could be multiple incomplete proofs for a given query, we need some mechanism that chooses a useful proof for the user from them. The KNOW system (Kapadia et al., 2004), which is a centralized rule-based authorization system, uses a cost function to rank proofs for a query based on the likeliness that the user is able to satisfy the conditions in the proofs. It is, however, difficult to define a reasonable cost function in a decentralized system like ours because there is no single administrator who knows all the rules and security policies that are involved in authorization decisions. We leave this complex problem for future work.

6.5 Information leak through inference

We assume that rules maintained by each principal are confidential information. However, colluding principals can gain partial information on a confidential rule as follows. Suppose that a principal p_0 issues a query *?grant(bob, document)* to a principal p_1 that maintains a confidential rule *grant(P, document)* ← *employee(P, IBM)* and that p_1 issues a subsequent query *?employee(bob, IBM)* to principal p_2. If principals p_0 and p_2 collude, they can learn that p_1's granting policy depends on the requester's employment with IBM if p_0 issues the same query multiple times and p_2 returns the different answers for the queries from p_1. Therefore, we plan to formalize confidentiality on rules in a distributed proof system and study new algorithms that protect the confidentiality of rules.

7 Summary

In this chapter, we provide an overview of distributed proof systems for cross-domain authorization. When we make an authorization decision with rules and facts maintained by different administrative domains, a distributed proof system must protect each principal's confidential information while constructing a proof for the granting decision. We introduce a new security model based on integrity and confidentiality policies and present our secure distributed authorization system that adopts a cryptographic protocol among principals. Our distributed algorithm enables multiple principals to construct a proof in a peer-to-peer way while preserving each principal's confidentiality policies. Future work includes the development of a new algorithm that finds all the valid proofs for a given query while preserving the soundness requirement. We also plan to study the issue of user feedback to make our system more usable to end-users.

References

Abadi, M., M. Burrows, B. Lampson, G. Plotkin (1993). A calculus for access control in distributed systems. *ACM Transactions on Programming Languages and Systems (TOPLAS)* 15(4), 706–734.

Al-Muhtadi, J., A. Ranganathan, R. Campbell, D. Mickunas (2003). Cerberus: a context-aware security scheme for smart spaces, in: *Proceedings of the 1st IEEE International Conference on Pervasive Computing and Communications*. IEEE Computer Society, Dallas-Fort Worth, TX, USA, pp. 489–496.

Appel, A.W., E.W. Felten (1999). Proof-carrying authentication, in: *Proceedings of the 6th ACM Conference on Computer and Communications Security*. ACM Press, Singapore, pp. 52–62.

Bacon, J., K. Moody, W. Yao (2002). A model of OASIS role-based access control and its support for active security, in: *Proceedings of the Sixth ACM Symposium on Access Control Models and Technologies*, Vol. 5, Issue 4, Monterey, California, USA, pp. 492–540.

Bauer, L., S. Garriss, M.K. Reiter (2005). Distributed proving in access-control systems, in: *Proceedings of the 2005 IEEE Symposium on Security and Privacy*. IEEE Computer Society, Washington, DC, USA, pp. 81–95.

Bauer, L., M.A. Schneider, E.W. Felten (2002). A general and flexible access-control system for the web, in: *Proceedings of the 11th USENIX Security Symposium*, San Francisco, CA, USA.

Becker, M.Y., P. Sewell (2004). Cassandra: distributed access control policies with tunable expressiveness, in: *Proceedings of the 5th IEEE International Workshop on Policies for Distributed Systems and Networks*, Yorktown Heights, NY, USA, pp. 159–168.

Blaze, M., J. Feigenbaum, A.D. Keromytis (1999). Keynote: trust management for public-key infrastructures (position paper), in: *Proceedings of the 6th International Workshop on Security Protocols*. Springer, London, UK, pp. 59–63.

Blaze, M., J. Feigenbaum, J. Lacy (1996). Decentralized trust management, in: *Proceedings of the 1996 IEEE Symposium on Security and Privacy*. IEEE Computer Society Press, Oakland, CA, USA, pp. 164–173.

Covington, M.J., W. Long, S. Srinivasan, A.K. Dey, M. Ahamad, G.D. Abowd (2001). Securing context-aware applications using environment roles, in: *Proceedings of the 6th ACM Symposium on Access Control Models and Technologies*. ACM Press, Chantilly, VA, USA, pp. 10–20.

DeTreville, J. (2002). Binder, a logic-based security language, in: *Proceedings of the 2002 IEEE Symposium on Security and Privacy*. IEEE Computer Society, Washington, DC, USA, p. 105.

Ellison, C.M., B. Frantz, B. Lampson, R. Rivest, B.M. Thomas, T. Ylonen (1999). SPKI certificate theory. Internet RFC 2693, October, http://www.ietf.org/rfc/rfc2693.txt

Goldreich, O., S. Micali, A. Wigderson (1987). How to play any mental game, in: *Proceedings of the 19th Annual ACM Conference on Theory of Computing*. ACM Press, New York, NY, USA, pp. 218–229.

Gunter, C.A., T. Jim (1997). Design of an application-level security infrastructure, in: *Proceedings of the DIMACS Workshop on Design and Formal Verification of Security Protocols*, Piscataway, NJ, USA, September.

Howell, J., D. Kotz (2000). End-to-end authorization, in: *Proceedings of the 2000 Symposium on Operating Systems Design and Implementation*. USENIX Association, San Diego, CA, USA, pp. 151–164.

Internet X.509 Public Key Infrastructure Certificates and CRL Profile, January 1999, http://www.ietf.org/rfc/rfc2459.txt

Jim, T. (2001). SD3: a trust management system with certified evaluation, in: *Proceedings of the 2001 IEEE Symposium on Security and Privacy*. IEEE Computer Society, Oakland, CA, USA, pp. 106–115.

Jim, T., D. Suciu (2001). Dynamically distributed query evaluation, in: *Proceedings of the 20th ACM SIGMOD-SIGACT-SIGART Symposium on Principles of Database Systems*. ACM Press, New York, NY, USA, pp. 28–39.

Kapadia, A., G. Sampemane, R.H. Campbell (2004). KNOW why your access was denied: regulating feedback for usable security, in: *Proceedings of the 11th ACM conference on Computer and Communications Security*. ACM Press, Washington, DC, USA, pp. 52–61.

Li, N., J. Feigenbaum, B.N. Grosof (1999). A logic-based knowledge representation for authorization with delegation, in: *Proceedings of the 1999 IEEE Computer Security Foundations Workshop*. IEEE Computer Society, Washington, DC, USA, p. 162.

Li, N., B.N. Grosof, J. Feigenbaum (2003). Delegation logic: a logic-based approach to distributed authorization. *ACM Transactions on Information and System Security* 6(1), 128–171.

Li, N., J.C. Mitchell, W.H. Winsborough (2002). Design of a role-based trust-management framework, in: *Proceedings of the 2002 IEEE Symposium on Security and Privacy*. IEEE Computer Society, Washington, DC, USA, p. 114.

Li, N., W.H. Winsborough, J.C. Mitchell (2003). Distributed credential chain discovery in trust management. *Journal of Computer Security* 11(1), 35–86.

Minami, K., D. Kotz (2005a). Secure context-sensitive authorization, in: *Proceedings of the 3rd IEEE International Conference on Pervasive Computing and Communications (PerCom)*, Kauai, Hawaii, pp. 257–268.

Minami, K., D. Kotz (2005b). Secure context-sensitive authorization. *Journal of Pervasive and Mobile Computing* 1(1), 123–156.

Minami, K., D. Kotz (2006). Scalability in a secure distributed proof system, in: *Proceedings of the 4th International Conference on Pervasive Computing (Pervasive)*, Dublin, Ireland.

Myles, G., A. Friday, N. Davies (2003). Preserving privacy in environments with location-based applications. *IEEE Pervasive Computing* 2(1), 56–64.

National incident management system (2004). March, http://www.fema.gov/pdf/nims/nims_doc_full.pdf

OASIS eXtensible Access Control Markup Language (XACML) Version 2.0, September 2004, http://docs.oasis-open.org/xacml/2.0/access control-xacml-2.0-core-spec-os.pdf

OpenPGP Message Format. http://www.ietf.org/internet-drafts/draft-ietf-openpgp-rfc2440bis-15.txt

Rivest, R., B. Lampson. SDSI: a simple distributed security architecture, http://theory.lcs.mit.edu/
    <cis/sdsi.html

Sandhu, R.S., E.J. Coyne, H.L. Feinstein, C.E. Youman (1996). Role-based access control models.
    IEEE Computer 29(2), 38–47.

Satyanarayanan, M. (2001). Pervasive computing: vision and challenges. *IEEE Personal Communica-
    tions* 8(4), 10–17.

Security frameworks for open systems: Access control framework. ITU-T Recommendation X.812,
    1995, http://www.itu.int/rec/recommendation.asp?type=folders&lang=e&parent=T-RECX.812

Tripathi, A., T. Ahmed, D. Kulkarni, R. Kumar, K. Kashiramka (2004). Context-based secure resource
    access in pervasive computing environments, in: *Proceedings of the 2nd IEEE Annual Conference on
    Pervasive Computing and Communications Workshops*. IEEE Computer Society, Orlando, FL, USA,
    pp. 159–163.

Ullman, J.D. (1989). *Database and Knowledge-Base Systems*. Vol. 2. W.H. Freeman & Company,
    New York, NY, USA.

Vaidya, J., C.W. Clifton, Y.M. Zhu (2006). *Privacy Preserving Data Mining*. Springer, New York,
    NY, USA.

Vaucher, J. (2003). XProlog.java: the successor to Winikoff 's WProlog, February, http://www.iro.
    umontreal.ca/<vaucher/XProlog/AA README

Winsborough, W.H., N. Li (2002). Towards practical automated trust negotiation, in: *Proceedings of
    the 3rd International Workshop on Policies for Distributed Systems and Networks (POLICY'02)*.
    IEEE Computer Society, Washington, DC, p. 92.

Winslett, M., C.C. Zhang, P.A. Bonatti (2005). PeerAccess: a logic for distributed authorization,
    in: *Proceedings of the 12th ACM Conference on Computer and Communications Security*. ACM Press,
    New York, NY, USA, pp. 168–179.

Yao, A.C.-C. (1986). How to generate and exchange secrets, in: *Proceedings of the 27th Annual
    Symposium on Foundations of Computer Science*. IEEE Computer Society Press, Toronto, Ontario,
    Canada, pp. 162–167.

Yu, T., M. Winslett (2003). A unified scheme for resource protection in automated trust negotiation,
    in: *Proceedings of the 2003 IEEE Symposium on Security and Privacy*. IEEE Computer Society,
    Oakland, CA, USA, pp. 110–122.

Yu, T., M. Winslett, K.E. Seamons (2003). Supporting structured credentials and sensitive policies
    through inter- operable strategies for automated trust negotiation. *ACM Transactions on Information
    and System Security* 6(1), 1–42.

Rao & Upadhyaya, Eds., *Handbooks in Information Systems, Vol. 4*

Chapter 2

Issues and Advances in Biometrics

Sergey Tulyakov and Venu Govindaraju

Center for Unified Biometrics and Sensors, University at Buffalo, 520 Lee Entrance, Suite 202, Amherst, NY 14228, USA

Abstract

Biometrics is the automated recognition of the persons based on the structure of their body or their behavior. The expansion of the technology resulted in the availability of cheap and high performance biometric sensors, and made the functioning biometric systems a reality. In this chapter, we briefly describe the main advances of biometrics research field. In particular, we discuss the most widely used biometric modalities, fingerprint and face, and present the main concepts of the measuring biometric system performance and combining biometric matchers. We also devote our attention to some research directions further enhancing biometric systems: cancelable biometrics, liveness detection, indexing and individuality. The discussions are illustrated by the examples providing additional insight into this field.

1 Introduction

1.1 History of biometrics

General descriptions of a particular person, including the height, color of the skin, hair and eyes, particular traits in appearance and behavior, have been possibly used since ancient times. Though such general descriptions might not be sufficient for person identification with complete confidence, they can be successfully used in constrained situations or for the confirmation of other, more discriminative, biometric features. These features are still widely used (e.g., on driver licenses) and might be called as *soft biometrics*. The fingerprints and face can be considered as the earliest traditional biometrics in use by people. Fingerprints have been known to be used by ancient potters to identify the produced goods (Berry and Stoney, 2001). Face portraits and sculptures might have been used for both

41

identifying the important persons and marking goods. For example, coins bearing king head might serve both to confirm validity of the coin, as well as, help to recognize the king.

The biometric measurement began to play more increasing role with the increased amount of travel and bigger scale of industrial production in recent time. The modern use of biometrics probably began with the development of Henry fingerprint classification system at the end of 19th century. In this system, each fingerprint of the person was checked on whether it had a whorl ridge structure. The total number of possible combinations of whorls for 10 fingers is $2^{10} = 1024$; therefore, each person belongs to one of 1024 possible Henry fingerprint classification classes. The system was first employed in India to avoid the duplicate payments to factory workers. Later, it was adopted by Scotland Yard to track criminals; after arresting a person, the Henry classification system was used to check whether this person already had a criminal record. At the same time, the techniques of lifting latent fingerprints at the crime scenes have been developed and increasingly used in forensics (Berry and Stoney, 2001).

The wide use of face photographs and signatures in passports and other documents can be viewed as further expansion of biometric use in modern society. Until recently the process of biometric matching, for example, between passport photo and person's face or between bank check signature and previously enrolled signature at the bank, relied on human experts. With the proliferation of computers, we expect that computers would perform most biometric-matching tasks. Also, with the development of new sensor technologies, it becomes possible to employ a significant number of new biometric traits.

1.2   Modern use of biometrics

The purpose of biometrics is to provide a confident authentication of a person participating in some activity. Since the biometrics field is still young and the price of biometric systems is high, most of current biometric systems are deployed in high importance applications. Following is a sample list of some current biometric technology applications, clearly incomplete:

- *Access control*: This is probably the most widely used application of biometrics. We can differentiate (1) large-scale applications, such as access to the country; (2) middle-scale applications, such as access to work place, prison inmate control, hospital patient tracking; and (3) small-scale applications, such as controlling access to computer or to the car.
- *Distribution of benefits*: Just as in case of first use of Henry fingerprint classification system to avoid the duplicate payments to workers, biometrics is increasingly deployed for the purpose of controlling the

distribution of social benefits. In contrast with access control applications, the biometric system has to ensure that each person is not enrolled twice and, therefore, the benefits are not distributed twice to the same person. Pensions, salaries, and medical insurance payments can benefit from biometrics use.

- *Financial transactions*: If person's credit card is lost or stolen, a stranger would be able to use. Integrating biometrics with credit, debit, and other types of payment cards can significantly reduce their misuse. It is not even necessary to have a card; a person might use a biometrics alone to identify himself to the financial system and authorize payments.

- *Forensics*: Fingerprints had a long history of usage in forensics due to the property of human skin to leave them on touched surfaces. The development of FBI's Automatic Fingerprint Identification System (AFIS) showed the ability to automate the matching process and to perform a match of latent fingerprints to the database consisting of millions known fingerprints. DNA matching is another recently developed technique used for the purpose of identifying criminals. The proliferation of biometric sensors, for example, surveillance video cameras, will result in the collection of biometric data capturing suspects and in the possibility of such biometrics to be used in forensics.

With the further development of biometric technologies and the falling prices of biometric sensors and solutions, we expect the biometric field to expand widely into modern life. Following are some possible future applications of biometric technologies:

- *Smart environments*: The idea of smart environments is the increased interaction between the person and the surrounding environment enhanced with sensors and computing power. The biometrics might play an essential part in this interaction by recognizing who the person is and providing person-specific actions. For example, by recognizing who entered the room, the smart room might adjust the lighting and temperature according to that person's preferences. Or, the smart car might recognize the person sitting in the driver's seat and adjust rear-view mirrors accordingly.

- *Internet transactions*: Current user-computer authentication is based on remembering passwords; many websites require registration and entering authenticating passwords. Password authentication might be replaced by biometrics; instead of entering password a user might swipe a finger at fingerprint sensor and be authenticated. As another example, the smart video system might stream and show a rated movie only if built-in biometrics sensor recognizes that all people watching it are adults.

- *Total surveillance*: The eventual development of sensor and biometrics technology might lead to the systems identifying and tracking all people at all times. It is hard to predict the consequences of such development, but it is clear that it will have a significant impact on the society; one of the benefits frequently advertised is the elimination of crime. The deployment of citywide surveillance system in London showed that significant progress in biometrics is still required for the system to work as expected.

1.3   The structure of biometric system

The typical biometric system consists of the following elements: biometric scanners located at the points where the person has to be authenticated, biometric matchers, and the biometric database that stores the person's information and biometric templates. Depending on application, the matchers and database can be located either at the dedicated server, at the location of the scanner, or be contained in the smart card belonging to the user. In all cases, biometric system integrators have to ensure that no tampering has occurred to any of the system's elements or communication lines between them.

The workflow of biometric system has two operational stages— enrollment and authentication.

- *Enrollment*: The task of enrollment stage is to create a record about the person in the database together with biometric templates. Since the access to biometric database should be secure, the enrollment stage usually requires the presence of human operator. The operator should verify the identity of the user by alternative means and insert the enrollment record into biometric database. The successfully enrolled user is called enrollee. The protocol for enrollment might include the quality control of biometric templates and the check that this person is not already enrolled in the system or that there is no other enrollee with similar biometric templates (which will be the cause of errors during authentication stage). If some confusion exists, the user might be asked to re-scan the biometrics or to use additional biometric modalities. The biometric system might also update its indexing structure during enrollment.
- *Authentication*: The user is required to present the biometrics to the scanner, and biometric system matches input biometrics with the biometric templates stored in the database. The user might also be required to provide additional authentication information, for example, some identification number, so that the biometric system would perform matching using only selected enrolled templates. The authentication stage might not need the presence of human operator; upon successful authentication, the system might automatically authorize requested action.

1.4   Biometrics and pattern recognition

The research in biometrics uses many techniques of pattern recognition and thus can be considered as a part of this more general field. The processing of biometric input usually has all the traditional steps of generic pattern-matching algorithm—preprocessing and enhancement, feature extraction and matching. Pattern recognition deals with classes and the number of the classes is rather small; some learning of the classes is frequently performed from training samples and the number of the training samples for each class can be large, hundreds or thousands. However, biometrics usually has only one enrolled sample template for each person (class), and class-specific learning is rarely performed. The matching in biometric system can be viewed as simple nearest neighbor matching in traditional pattern recognition field; the input is classified as belonging to person with nearest enrolled template. From this point of view, the biometrics deals with rather simple subset of problems of pattern recognition.

However, the variation in the appearance of samples of the same class in biometrics can be significant, and sometimes bigger than the variation between samples belonging to different classes (see the examples of face images in Section 2.2). Therefore, traditional pattern recognition methods oriented to the learning of class separation functions might not deal adequately with biometric problems. It becomes important in many biometric problems to learn a representational model—all possible ways in how a person's biometric might appear on the scanner. The biometric matching in this case is transformed to matching models, rather than doing classification in the feature space.

2   Biometric modalities

The structure of human body and person's behavior is rather uniquely determined by genetic and environmental factors. Some biometric characteristics, for example, sex, skin, and hair color, are determined by genetic makeup; some biometrics, such as fingerprint and iris, are formed during the fetus development; and other biometrics, such as voice and gait, are the product of the later life of the individual. Even if the face appearance of the person is mostly determined by the genes, the examples with monozygotic twins show that the environment can play a role in the face appearance in the later life.

It is not surprising, therefore, that practically any part of the human body or appearance can serve for the purpose of identifying individuals. The *biometric modality* is the choice of a particular body part or a particular person's behavioral characteristic for the purposes of biometric person authentication. Different biometric modalities usually require different sensors and matching algorithms. The adoption of a particular biometric modality is due to several factors: cost of the sensors, performance of the matching algorithm, convenience and acceptance by the users, and universality of biometrics.

In the rest of this section, we consider in detail most widely used biometric modalities: fingerprint, face and hand geometry. We also discuss in brief the use of other modalities as well.

2.1 Fingerprint

The use of fingerprints for biometric purpose, especially in forensics, has a long history, and older databases were created using ink and paper. Recently, most fingerprint databases are collected using digital scanners directly, and older databases are digitized. The digitization of fingerprint scanning allowed using automatic algorithms for template extraction and matching. But, digital fingerprint templates produced by different types of scanners vary significantly in their appearance. Figure 1 presents sample fingerprint images from three fingerprint scanners taken from FVC 2002 database (Maltoni et al., 2003).

Most fingerprint-matching algorithms rely on the extraction and matching special points of the fingerprint ridge structures—*minutia*. Usually minutia points designate ridge endings and ridge bifurcations, and have a representation (x,y,θ), where x and y are coordinates of the minutia in the image and θ is the direction of minutia coinciding with the orientation of ridges at these coordinates. To extract minutia, the following steps can be followed:

- Find the orientation and strength of ridges in each point (or small blocks) of the image. This can be achieved by different methods, for example, by using wavelet or Fourier coefficients, or by directly analyzing image gradients. The important properties utilized here is the

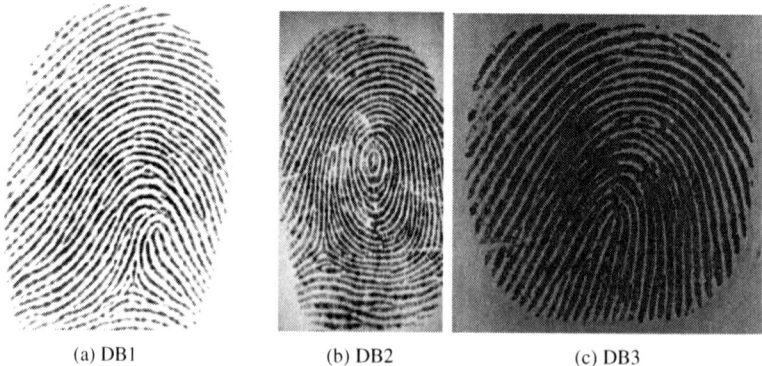

(a) DB1   (b) DB2   (c) DB3

Fig. 1. Samples of fingerprint images from fingerprint verification competition (FVC), 2002. Included images from databases DB1, DB2, and DB3 were obtained using different fingerprint sensors.

wavy nature of fingerprint ridges; the ridge directions change gradually, the image gradients (directions of fastest change in image intensity) are perpendicular to ridge directions, and wave structure makes the use of wavelets or Fourier coefficients natural. Thus, even if different sensors produce quite different fingerprint appearances, the orientation and general ridge structure can be relatively easy to find.

- Enhance and binarize image. Using the found direction and frequency of the ridges in each point of the fingerprint, a filter, for example, in wavelet or Fourier domain, can be applied emphasizing the ridge direction and frequency and removing other directions and frequencies as noise. Consequently, a simple threshold can be used to binarize the image.

- Segment the fingerprint area from the background. This might be considered as the most difficult part of fingerprint image processing. Although some thresholding techniques might be successful on fingerprints with white background (DB1 image in Fig. 1), they will not be sufficient for sensors producing complex background. Additional problem is the frequent presence of residual fingerprints—the latent fingerprints formed on the surface of the scanner by the previous users. Usually, some heuristics, for example, involving the strength of ridges, the confidence in the extracted ridge directions and frequencies, can be used for segmentation.

- Extract minutia positions. Different techniques can be used here—thin the binary image to obtain 1 pixel wide skeleton and find its endpoints and bifurcations, find the contour of the binary image and extract minutia points as the points of large change in direction of the contour, or follow the ridges with perpendicular cuts and find where these cuts end or merge.

Note that presented steps are not necessary and many other techniques have been investigated (Maltoni et al., 2003), for example, it is possible to extract minutia positions directly from the gray-scale image. We present an example of binarized fingerprint image and the candidate locations of minutia positions in Fig. 2; the image was enhanced and binarized using filtering of Fourier coefficients in 16×16 pixel blocks of the image, and the candidate minutia positions were found by following contours of binary image (Chikkerur et al., 2007).

The set of extracted minutia usually represents a fingerprint template stored in the database, but the template might also contain other elements useful for fingerprint matching, for example, ridge orientation map, counts of ridges between minutiae, original gray-scale fingerprint image. The type of the fingerprint, for example, whorl as in Henry's system, can also be automatically extracted and used for matching or indexing.

The task of minutia-matching algorithm is to find correspondences between two sets of minutia. It is usually assumed that the map responsible

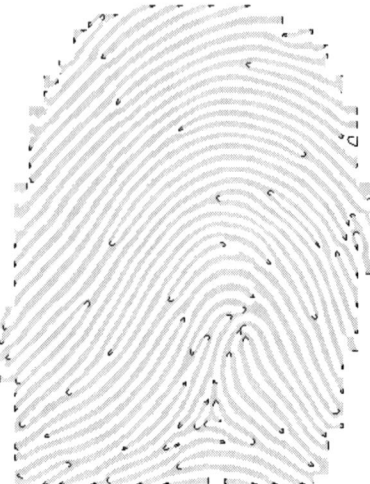

Fig. 2.   Binarized fingerprint with candidate minutia positions.

for minutia correspondences is affine (composed of rotation and translation). The brute force approach to minutia matching will look at all pairs of
minutia in two fingerprints and assume that these minutia correspond to
each other (pivot minutia); this assumption automatically determines the
translation from minutia coordinates and rotation from minutia directions,
and all other minutia are checked for correspondence with found
transformation parameters. The brute force algorithm is somewhat slow,
and many improvements can be made to it. For example, we might want to
consider pivot minutia only if these minutia have similar neighborhood
structure determined by the minutia and its two nearest neighboring
minutia. The features extracted from minutia triplets are called *secondary
features* by Jea and Govindaraju (2005) and can be used instead of original
minutia for more precise and faster matching. The set of matching minutia
in two fingerprints obtained by the method of matching secondary features
is shown in Fig. 3. The final matching score is usually some heuristic
function including number of matched minutia, numbers of minutia in two
considered fingerprints and other parameters.

2.2   Face

The face biometrics can be considered as most convenient and universally
acceptable biometric modality. The number of digital cameras, including
webcams and cellular phone cameras, is significantly more than the number
of fingerprint (or any other biometric) scanners. Therefore, there is a big
incentive to utilize this multitude of cameras for biometric purposes.
    The earliest works on face recognition relied on specialized algorithms
to extract the positions of *landmark points*, such as eyes, eyebrows, nose,

(a)1_1.tif   (b) 1_2.tif

Fig. 3.   Two matched fingerprints with marked matched minutia positions.

mouth, and on measuring the distances between these points. The explicit extraction of landmark points follows traditional pattern recognition approaches of feature extractions, and performing classifications using feature vectors. Though such matching methods have good sense, it turns out that, due to large variations in the appearance of landmark points, it is rather difficult to confidently extract their positions. Subsequently, the implicit extraction of feature vectors by projection methods proved to have better performance and became the most popular face-matching approach.

The work of Turk and Pentland (1991) introduced a technique called *principal component analysis* (PCA) which had a major influence on the development of the face recognition research. Face images can be represented as points in $W \times H$-dimensional space (W and H are the widths and heights of the image in pixels). Points corresponding to faces cannot occupy the whole space since there are images representing other objects. The PCA technique attempts to approximate the region with faces by the linear subspace. Using the criteria that the sum of squared distances from the subspace to sample face images should be minimized, the optimal subspace is the subspace spanned by the first K eigenvectors of covariance matrix constructed using sample face images (K is the desired dimension of subspace; usually it is taken as the one that gives best recognition results). *PCA projection* is the orthogonal projection of original face images onto *PCA subspace*, which is spanned by *principal components*—first K eigenvectors or *eigenfaces* found from training samples. The example of PCA technique is shown in Fig. 4. Each face-like image is a principal component projected back into image space (eigenface); a real face of person can be approximated by the linear sum of these principal components.

The PCA technique can be used for two different purposes. First, by calculating the distance from the test image to the PCA subspace, we can judge whether the test image represents a person's face or some other object. Many *face detection* techniques successfully use PCA. Second, two PCA projections of two different face images are K-dimensional vectors of *PCA coefficients*, and the distance between these two vectors can serve as matching measure between two face images. The PCA and similarly constructed linear (some nonlinear methods are also been investigated) projection algorithms (Delac et al., 2005) make the largest share of face-matching methods.

Though projection techniques are able to get satisfactory matching results on some databases containing frontal and uniformly illuminated face images, their performance decreases significantly when any of the typical face variations appear: change in illumination, head rotation, occlusions, facial expressions, and speaking dynamics. Figure 5 shows the examples of face images from CMU PIE (pose, illumination, and expression) database (Sim et al., 2003). It is clear, that by using eigenfaces of Fig. 4, it will not be possible to properly represent these faces and have a matching algorithm.

We can view the PCA algorithm from two sides: on one side it is a projection of original image onto lower-dimensional feature space, and on

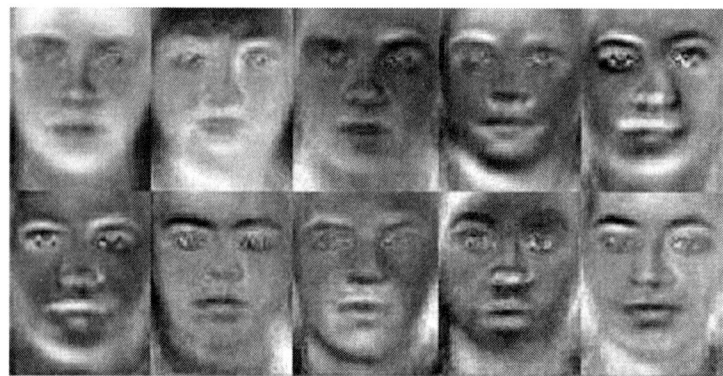

Fig. 4. Sample eigenfaces of PCA model (images provided by R. Rodriguez).

Fig. 5. Samples of face images from CMU PIE (Sim et al., 2003) database. The great variation in the face position and illumination makes most projection-based matching methods and algorithms relying on feature extraction from landmark points ineffective.

the other side it is a representation or the model of the face by K latent variables (same as feature vector). The PCA model of the face is quite simple—the face is a linear combination of eigenfaces and the coefficients in this combination are the latent variables. It is possible to construct more complex face models that more adequately represent the face and face variations.

Active appearance model (AAM) (Cootes et al., 2001) was successfully utilized for face modeling. In this model, instead of using projections of whole face, the principal component projections for small patches around face landmark points are constructed (*texture PCA*). The set of distances between landmark points is also represented by the PCA projection (*shape PCA*). The model is matched to the face image by searching the best position of landmark points. For a particular choice of landmark points, the match confidence is a sum of matching confidences from texture and shape PCAs. AAMs show good performance and are increasingly utilized in many tasks: face detection, face recognition, and facial expression analysis. But AAMs might still not work well with changes in illumination and head rotation, and special adjustments to the algorithm are needed (Ashraf et al., 2008).

Three-dimensional (3-D) morphable model (Blanz and Vetter, 2003) gives an example of even more complex face model. Instead of a set of landmark points in two-dimensional (2-D) plane for AAM, the surface in 3-D space is used to represent the shape of the face. The shape model is learned from a set of separately obtained 3-D face scans by constructing PCA model. In addition to shape model, a texture model is constructed from the appearance of each pixel of the shape model—pixel color values. Again, the PCA model is used to represent textures.

Note that though the 3-D morphable model algorithm represents a face as surface in a 3-D space, it is used to match 2-D images only. The important part of the algorithm is to construct a model from a given face image. During this construction the rotation of the head and the position of illumination source, as well as, shape and texture parameters of the model are estimated. Thus, this algorithm is inherently designed to deal with head rotations and changes in illumination, and it shows superior performance on the images from CMU PIE database of Fig. 5.

2.3 Hand geometry

Different biometric modalities exhibit different levels of variation; as a consequence, the matching algorithms have different complexities. We might think that face matching requires rather complex algorithms (if we want to deal with head rotations and illumination changes) and fingerprint matching has rather medium complexity. Here, we consider an easier biometric modality—hand geometry.

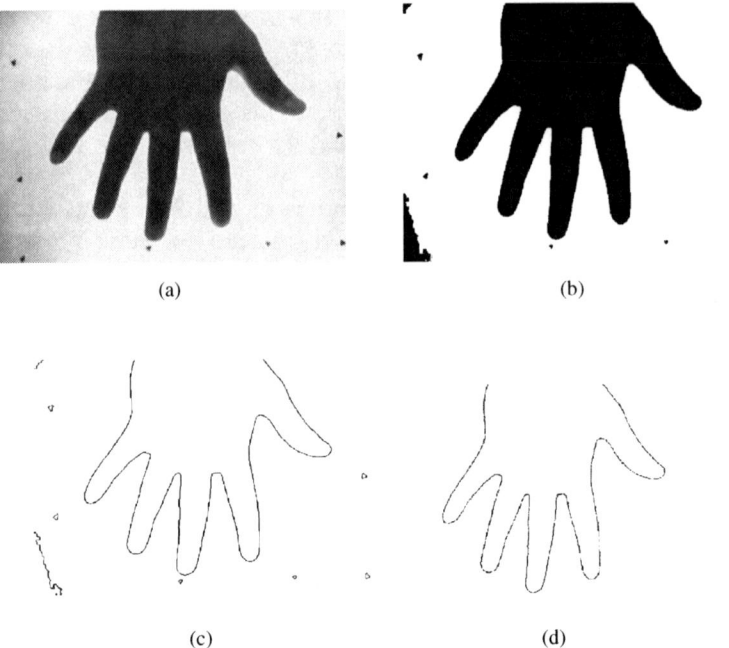

Fig. 6.   Different stages of processing hand image.

We describe an algorithm for hand geometry matching used by Mhatre et al. (2005). Though there are specialized hand geometry scanners (e.g., including pegs for precise positioning of the hand and using laser for scanning), the hand images can be easily obtained with regular digital camera (Fig. 6(a)). Simple binarization is applied in Fig. 6(b) and the boundary contours are extracted in Fig. 6(c). Using some heuristics, all the contours except one corresponding to the hand are discarded in Fig. 6(d).

The set of predefined features is extracted by searching the particular points of the hand contour—extrema where either the direction or the convexity of contour changes (Fig. 7). The features are usually the distances between these points, or some functions of distances (e.g., ratio of distances). The Euclidean distance between feature vectors serves as (inverse) confidence of biometric match.

2.4   Other modalities

It would be impossible to describe all investigated biometric modalities in this short chapter. In this section, we only mention the most popular ones.

The *iris* is colorful ring-like structure around the pupil of human's eye. The iris turned out to provide good properties for person identification: diversity, small intrapersonal and large interpersonal variations, protection

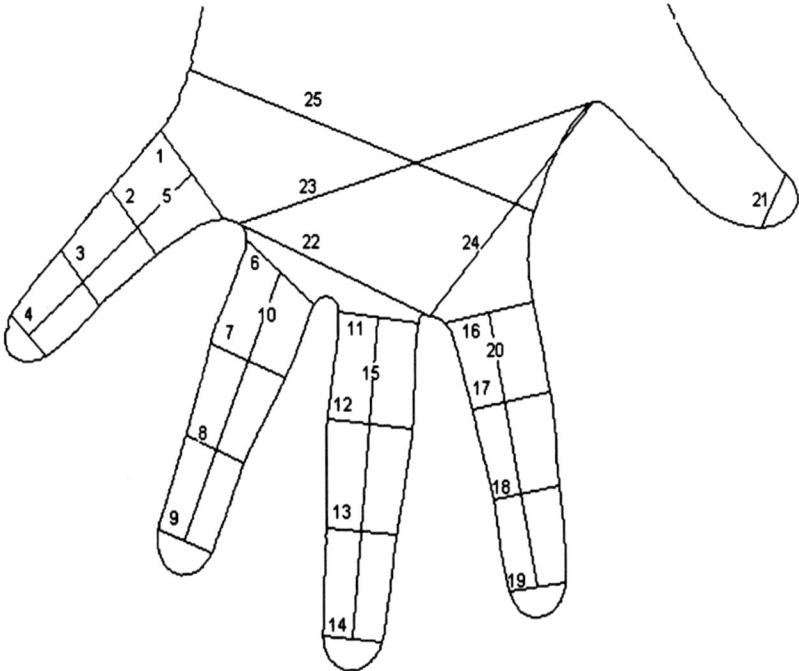

Fig. 7.   The features utilized for hand geometry matching.

from the outer environment, and little change with the passage of time. The binary vector of length 2,048 is extracted by quantizing the responses of Gabor wavelets at the circular grid locations throughout the iris by Daugman (1993). The match distance between two irises is calculated as the Hamming distance between two binary feature vectors. Owing to small variation in the irises of the same person and the relative ease of locating irises in images, we might consider iris biometrics as simple to implement. The most difficulty might be due to making good scans of irises, especially at larger distances.

Speaker identification was one of the first automatic biometric applications investigated. The main advantage of speech modality is the abundance and cheapness of sensors—microphones. But, despite a significant research effort, speaker identification systems have shown only average performance. The performance of speaker identification systems is degraded in the presence of noise, and thus they are not suitable for many applications. Additional drawbacks of speaker biometrics are the inconvenience to the users (the necessity to actively speak) and high nonuniversality. But, so far, it is the only biometrics allowing remote authentication by means of phones, and this is how it is mostly used.

Handwritten signature has been used for a long time to identify the documents belonging to particular persons, and similarly it can be used for the identification of person. Some research into automatic matching of handwritten signatures has been performed, but the reported performance is not very strong. The *online handwritten signature*, providing time of writing in addition to position, has substantially better performance than *offline handwritten signature*. Though it can be used for the current widespread application of signature verification during credit card transaction, it is not clear if it would be more cost effective than replacement of signature by other, more convenient, biometrics, such as fingerprint or face.

Some newly developed biometric modalities rely on specific biometric sensors. *3-D face* (or rather head) uses special sensor (e.g., laser) to obtain a 3-D structure of person's head. *Blood vessel* biometrics might need a camera operating in infrared, and not in traditional visible light, spectrum. *Retina* biometrics uses blood vessels located inside person's eyes; though it has good properties of performance and the preservation of features, many users might object to the intrusiveness of the retina scans. *Gait* biometrics might be useful in surveillance applications, where the distance to the subject is typically large and most of the other biometrics fail to acquire usable templates.

3 Evaluating performance of biometric systems

The important question facing biometric system designers is the evaluation of performance. We are able to say that one biometric matcher will perform better than the other, and, in general, that using a biometrics system is beneficial for the current application. It turns out that the evaluation depends on a particular application—one biometric matcher might have better performance than the other in one application, but worse performance in another application. In this section, we present some ways to evaluate the performance of biometric matchers.

3.1 Operating modes of biometric systems

The biometric system in a particular application is usually utilized in one of the following modes of operation:

- *Verification*: To be authenticated, the user first claims his/her identity, for example, by presenting an ID card or by simply entering his/her name or identification number on the keypad. Then the user's biometric is scanned and matched against a single template corresponding to the claimed enrolled identity. The decision to accept the identity claim or reject it is usually made by comparing a single matching score to the threshold.

- *Identification*: No claim of identity is made by the user, and the user's biometric is matched against all enrolled persons. Closed set identification systems assume that the user is always enrolled in the system; the identification is successful if the score corresponding to the true user's identity is better than all other matching scores. Open set identification systems assume that user might not be enrolled in the database and in such cases the correct decision of the identification system will be to reject identification attempt. Thus, in such systems, not only a best matching score is found, but it is also compared to some threshold.
- *Watch list or screening*: Watch list is the biometric application reverse of open set identification system. The input biometrics is matched against all persons in the database and the decision is made on whether the person is enrolled or not. In contrast with open set identification, we might not need to know which enrollee matches current user.

All modes of operation deal with two types of scores—*genuine matching scores* are the result of matching biometric templates of the same person, and *impostor matching scores* are the result of matching biometric templates of the different persons. The task of verification system is to determine whether a particular score is genuine or impostor, the task of identification system is to make sure that genuine score is higher than any impostor score, and the task of watch list is to make sure that all scores produced during matching are impostors. Different tasks assume that the cost of errors made by a biometric system is calculated differently. Therefore, some biometric systems might be suited for one operating mode, and some might be better suited for other. The example in Section 3.3 shows that changing costs for system errors in verification system might change the choice of biometric matcher.

3.2 Performance of verification systems

The biometric system operating in verification mode makes a decision on whether the score is genuine and has two possible types of errors: *false accepts* (FA), where an impostor score was accepted, and *false rejects* (FR), where a genuine score was rejected. False accept rate (FAR) is the proportion of accepted impostors among all impostors, and false reject rate (FRR) is the proportion of rejected genuines among all genuines. The decision usually consists in comparing the score to the threshold, θ, and both error rates are functions of θ—FAR(θ) and FRR(θ).

Suppose we know what the densities of the scores are: $p_{gen}(s)$, the density of the genuine scores, and $p_{imp}(s)$, the density of the impostor scores. Then, the FAR(θ) and FRR(θ) can be expressed as (assuming accept decision if score is bigger than θ):

$$FAR(\theta) = \int_{s \geq \theta} p_{imp}(s)ds, \quad FRR(\theta) \int_{s < \theta} p_{gen}(s)ds \qquad (1)$$

If we obtain a sample of genuine and a sample of the impostors scores of a biometric matcher, we can approximate $p_{gen}(s)$ and $p_{imp}(s)$, for example, by using mixture of Gaussians or Parzen window method. Though it might be possible to calculate FAR(θ) and FRR(θ) using approximated densities and Eq. (1), it would be easier to simply count the proportion of sample impostors above threshold and the proportion of sample genuines below threshold. Figure 8 shows the densities of genuine and impostor scores of face matcher "C" from NIST biometric score set BSSR1 approximated by Parzen window method. The integrals of Eq. (1) are represented as the areas under corresponding densities; threshold $\theta = 0.4$ was used for acceptance decision.

The graphs of score densities of Fig. 8 might be helpful to visualize the distributions of scores in a biometric system, but they are of little use for making comparisons of biometric systems. Since both FAR and FRR depend on the single parameter, it is possible to construct a graph {FAR(θ), FRR(θ)} representing a trade-off between two types of error depending on threshold parameter θ. Such curve is called *ROC* (receiver operating characteristic) *curve*. Note that this curve might also be called DET (detection-error trade-off) curve, and FRR axis can be changed to GAR (genuine acceptance rate) axis.

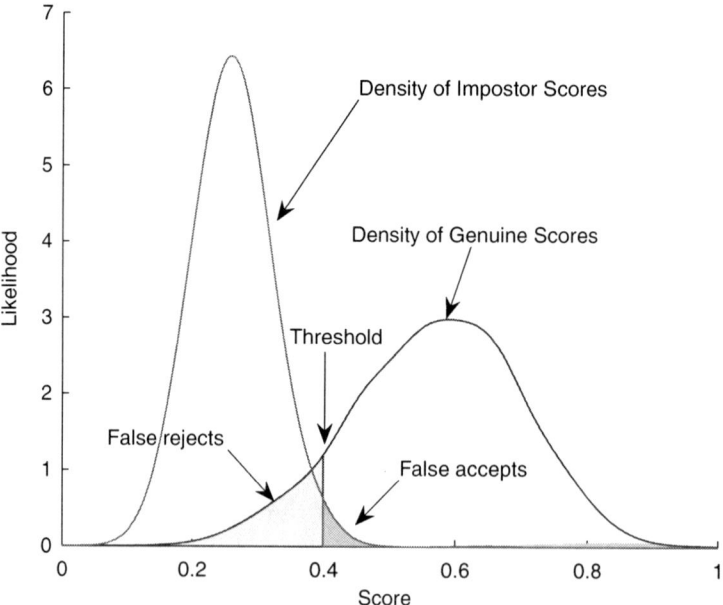

Fig. 8.   The densities of genuine and impostor scores of face matcher "C" (linearly normalized to [0,1]). The areas corresponding to the rates of false accept and false reject errors for threshold 0.4 are shown.

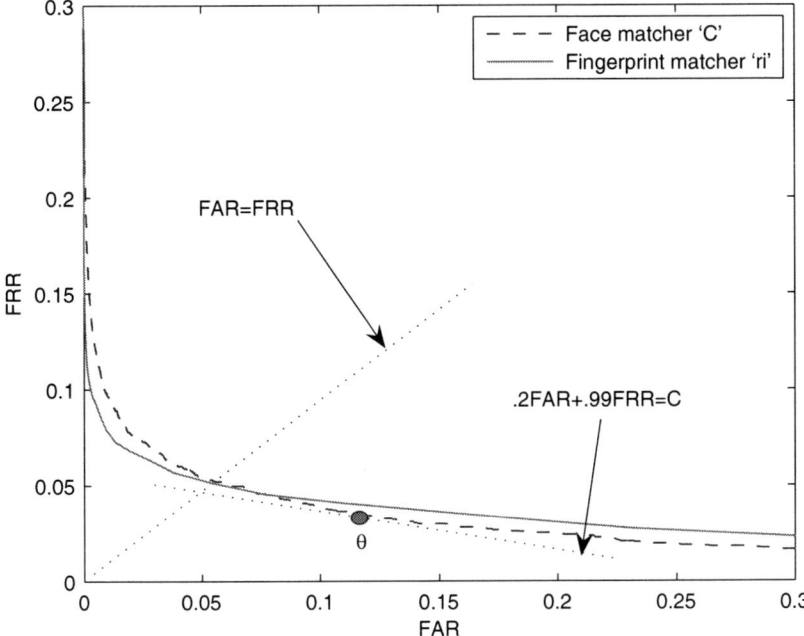

Fig. 9.   ROC curves for face matcher "C" and fingerprint matcher "ri." "C" has better performance for low FRR values, and "ri" has better performance for low FAR values.

The ROC curves for face matcher "C" and fingerprint matcher "ri" (to be precise, "ri" stands for "right index" match scores of fingerprint matcher "V") from NIST BSSR1 database are shown in Fig. 9. The closer the ROC curve to the axes, the less errors biometric matcher has, and consequently, has better performance. As ROC curves for both matchers show, there might not be a short "yes/no" answer that one matcher is always better than another matcher. If our preference is to have lower FAR, for example, in a high-security application requiring fewer false accepts, then we need to use matcher "ri." If we need more convenience to the users and smaller number of false rejects, we need to use matcher "C." Sometimes, the *equal error rate* (EER) is used for comparison, which is defined as the point in ROC curve, where FAR = FRR (as shown in the Fig. 9); in this case EER = FAR = FRR. In the next section, we present a practical example on how the biometric systems can be evaluated with respect to a particular application.

3.3   Example

Consider the application of biometrics to control the access to an amusement park. The user enrolls into the system during the first visit to the park, when her biometrics is scanned and stored in the database. On subsequent visits, the scanned biometric input is matched against the stored template (retrieved with the help of entrance ticket identification number). If match decision is made by the biometric system, the user is let in, and if no match is declared, the user is asked to re-scan biometrics or human supervisor is called to verify the identity of the user by alternative means (e.g., driver's license).

To optimally choose the biometric system for this application, we might want to consider the following cost function:

$$\text{Cost} = C_{\text{FA}}P_{\text{imp}}\text{FAR}(\theta) + C_{\text{FR}}P_{\text{gen}}\text{FRR}(\theta) \tag{2}$$

where C_{FA} is the cost associated with making erroneous accept decision, C_{FR} is the cost of making erroneous rejection, P_{imp} and P_{gen} are the prior probabilities of impostor and genuine matches (impostor or genuine user attempting to get access), and $\text{FAR}(\theta)$ and $\text{FRR}(\theta)$ are error rates of considered biometric system. The costs of making decision errors and prior probabilities should be estimated by the park administration. For example, the cost of making erroneous accept decision, C_{FA}, is the cost of servicing user in a park, say \$20; the cost of erroneous reject (time spent by servicing personnel, dissatisfaction of the user and reduced possibility of making repeated ticket sale to this user, dissatisfaction of other users waiting in line) might be estimated as \$1; the probability of impostors (users with stolen, borrowed or fake ticket trying to get unauthorized access to the park) might be estimated as 1% and the probability of genuines is correspondingly 99%. In this case, the total cost of making biometric decision error is

$$\begin{aligned}\text{Cost} &= 20*.01*\text{FAR}(\theta) + 1*.99*\text{FRR}(\theta) \\ &= .20\text{FAR}(\theta) + .99*\text{FRR}(\theta)\end{aligned} \tag{3}$$

Suppose, as in Fig. 9, we are evaluating two matchers with regard to this cost equation. The lowest overall cost will be achieved by finding the intersection of line $.2\text{FAR} + .99\text{FRR} = C$ with any of the ROC curves. Such intersection is denoted in Fig. 9 as θ and face matcher "C" achieves lowest cost. Note that if we had different estimates on costs of errors or prior probabilities of each type of users, we might have gotten different biometrics preference. For example, if we had $P_{\text{imp}} = 10\%$ of impostors trying to gain unauthorized access to the park, our cost would have been $\text{Cost} = 2\text{FAR} + .9\text{FRR}$ and fingerprint matcher "ri" would have achieved lower cost.

To decide whether the deployment of biometric system would be beneficial, we need to account for more factors. The total cost would be the sum of cost given by Eq. (2), the cost of purchasing and maintaining biometric system, and the implicit cost of inconvenience to the visitors of the park. The additional revenue will be due to reduced number of unauthorized users getting access to the park, consequent increased number of ticket sales, and less dissatisfaction of legitimate users from sharing the park facilities with unauthorized users.

4   Multimodal biometrics

Multimodal biometric system uses more than one biometric modality for the authentication of the user. There are two major advantages for using such systems:

(1) Properly constructed combined system will have better performance than the system using only a single biometric modality.
(2) It is more difficult for an intruder to bypass the security of multimodal system since more modalities need to be faked.

The possible drawback of multimodal systems is the need for additional biometric scanners and more time needed for the user to be authenticated. The drawback might be reduced if scanners of different modalities can be combined in one device. For example, it is possible to have a combined scanner for face and iris utilizing one or two digital cameras with different resolutions in one unit. Or, fingerprint scanner can be combined with finger blood vessel scanner; in this approach, the blood vessel scanner can use similarly positioned camera that is more sensitive to infrared spectrum of light than the camera for the fingerprint ridges.

4.1   Combination in verification systems

Without loss of generality, assume that we have two scanners for different modalities or two matching algorithms using the input of one scanner (instead of arbitrary many scanners or matchers). Both matchers deliver two matching scores, s_1 and s_2, and our task is somehow to combine them in a single matching score, $S = f(s_1, s_2)$, so that the performance of combined matching system is optimal. The problem of finding the combination function f is quite simple for the biometric systems operating in verification mode.

Let score pairs (s_1, s_2) be the points in the 2-D space in Fig. 10(a). This space can be regarded as the feature space for a classification algorithm trying to separate two types of points—points corresponding to either genuine or impostor score pairs (s_1, s_2). The performance criteria of verification systems, minimizing the trade-off between two types of errors, false accepts and false rejects, directly corresponds to the criteria of minimizing misclassification cost of our two-class classification problem. The solution to such problem is well-known in pattern classification field: the optimal decision function f can be taken as the likelihood ratio of two classes:

$$f(s_1, s_2) = \frac{p_{\text{gen}}(s_1, s_2)}{p_{\text{imp}}(s_1, s_2)} \tag{4}$$

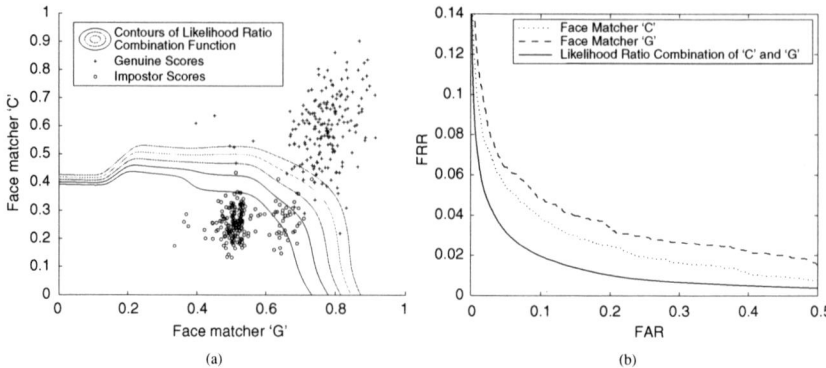

(a)   (b)

Fig. 10.   Likelihood ratio combination of face matchers "C" and "G" from NIST BSSR1
biometric score set: (a) Few samples of genuine and impostor score pairs from both matchers
and the contours of likelihood ratio combination function (scores in both matchers are
linearly normalized to interval [0,1]). (b) ROC curves of standalone matchers and their
combination by likelihood ratio function.

The densities of score pairs $p_{gen}(s_1, s_2)$ and $p_{imp}(s_1, s_2)$ can be approximated
by different methods using a *training set* of sample score pairs.
Alternatively, a classification can be performed by many developed
methods of pattern classification field without explicit approximation of
score densities. Generally, many pattern classification algorithms can
deliver better approximation of decision boundaries than the explicit use
of approximated densities in likelihood ratio method, but the difference is
not significant. Since the dimension of feature vectors in classification
problem coincides with the number of matchers and this number is usually
small, the densities approximation methods will have adequate performance. Figure 10(a) shows the decision boundaries (contours $f(s_1, s_2) = \theta$)
of likelihood ratio combination method for combining face matchers "C"
and "G" of NIST BSSR1 dataset, as well as few samples of genuine and
impostor score pairs. The 2-D densities were approximated using Parzen
window method. Figure 10(b) contains ROC curves of single matchers and
of their combination using likelihood ratio.

4.2   Combination rules

One of the research directions in classifier combination field investigates
the use of the so-called combination rules (Kittler et al., 1998). The
combination rules specify that the matching scores should be combined
in some predetermined fashion, for example, sum rule adds scores
$f(s_1, s_2) = s_1 + s_2$ and product rules multiplies them $f(s_1, s_2) = s_1 \times s_2$.
Usually, some assumptions are made on the nature of scores, and one or the
other rule is justified.

If the matching scores were truly satisfying some required assumptions, the use of particular combination rule might have made sense. In practice, the matching scores are the result of elaborate calculation of distances between two biometric templates, and there is no reason to expect that some assumptions on these scores, for example, scores are approximations of posterior class probabilities, hold. We might try to convert the matching scores to satisfy required condition, but such conversion would require some learning algorithm using a training set of scores. In this case, the task will be somewhat equivalent to learning combination function. Learning combination function directly seems to be an easier approach to combination.

One of the reasons used to justify combination rules is the existence of independence between scores produced by matchers of different modalities. The independence knowledge might be easily exploited for likelihood ratio combination method: instead of approximating 2-D score densities $p_{gen}(s_1, s_2)$ and $p_{imp}(s_1, s_2)$, we can decompose them in one dimensional components

$$p_{gen}(s_1, s_2) = p_{1,gen}(s_1)p_{2,gen}(s_2), \quad p_{imp}(s_1, s_2) = p_{1,imp}(s_1)p_{2,imp}(s_2) \quad (5)$$

and approximate one-dimensional (1-D) components. As our research shows (Tulyakov and Govindaraju, 2006), such decomposition and approximation of 1-D components indeed improve the performance of combination algorithm, but the gains are very small.

4.3 Combination in identification systems

There is almost no research investigating the combination of biometric matchers in identification systems. Usually, it is implied that the same combination function f, which was constructed for verification system, can be similarly used for combinations in identification systems. The likelihood ratio combination function of Eq. (4) seems to be a good candidate for the combinations in identification systems.

As we investigated (Tulyakov et al., 2007b), the likelihood ratio combination function might not deliver the optimal performance for identification systems. It is actually possible, that the combination in identification system using likelihood ratio function will have worse performance than a single matcher used in combination. The optimal combination function for identification systems might not have convenient analytic representation as likelihood ratio function, and finding it is an open research question. We have proposed some combination methods (Tulyakov et al., 2007c) that work better than likelihood ratio in identification systems, but the optimality of these methods is uncertain.

4.4   Increase in performance

Is performance of combined system always better than the performance of any single matchers used in combination? It is clear that in worst case, we can always have a combination function to simply output a score of single matcher, for example, $f(s_1, s_2) = s_1$, and therefore the performance of optimal combination algorithm cannot be worse than the performance of a single matcher. But, the increase in performance is not guaranteed when the number of matchers is increased. If, for example, two matchers operate on the same modality, they might have very similar matching results, and combining them will have little effect. It is usually hypothesized that the increase in performance is largest when combined matchers produce statistically independent matching scores, but no published evidence for such hypothesis seems to exist.

5   Additional topics in biometrics

5.1   Cancelable biometrics

If a traditional security system utilizing passwords is compromised, and the intruder gains access to the passwords, the old passwords can be easily revoked and new passwords issued. If we want to utilize biometrics in the analogous system, we need to ensure that enrolled biometric templates could be revoked and new biometric templates are issued; the intruder possessing compromised biometric templates should not be able to use them. The biometrics implementing this capability is called *cancelable biometrics*.

There are two obstacles for constructing cancelable biometric templates. The first obstacle is the permanent nature of biometrics—it is not possible for the users to change their biometrics as they could do with the passwords. To overcome this obstacle any cancelable biometric system should combine the permanent biometric features with some replaceable key to create cancelable templates. The second obstacle is the variation of biometric measurements and the necessity to match close but nonidentical scanned biometrics. If we are dealing with traditional passwords, one-way hash function (such as MD5) can be applied, and only password hashes could be stored; the password match would succeed only if identical password is entered and its hash exactly coincides with the stored hash. Since the biometric measurements of the same person are not identical, this method cannot be applied directly to the biometric templates.

One idea to deal with the variability of biometric templates is to utilize error-correcting codes. Error-correcting codes are mostly used in the transmission of digital data. If the part of the data is corrupted, the error correction algorithm might be able to recover the original data. Suppose,

b is the binary representation of the biometric template and let c the error correction bits, such that the concatenation $b||c$ represents a valid codeword of the used error correction system. If b' is another sample of the same person's biometric and the difference between b and b' is sufficiently small for chosen error correction system, then $b'||c$ can be corrected to $b||c$. Such application of error correcting codes allows us to eliminate storing biometric template b in the biometric database: instead of b, we store error correcting bits c and some hash of the string b: $h(b)$. During authentication, user presents biometrics b' and using stored c the original b is calculated; the hash of restored template is compared to stored hash $h(b)$ and, if they are identical, the match is declared. Note that if intruder obtains stored values of c and $h(b)$, he would not be able to restore b.

The preceding algorithm for hiding biometric data has been presented by Davida et al. (1998). The biometric b can be combined with replaceable key k, b_k, before calculating c and $h(b_k)$ to make the biometric cancelable, but it is not clear if this enhancement is really needed. Indeed, if we assume that intruder is smart enough to reverse (generally nonreversible) hash function and obtain b_k from the $h(b_k)$, then it is probable that he would be able to obtain k and reverse b_k to get b as well.

Although described algorithm can be applied to many biometric modalities whose templates are represented by a slightly varying binary string b, there are biometric modalities that do not have such representation. For example, the fingerprint templates usually contain a set of minutia, whose quantity, order, and values can change significantly. Most of the recent research in cancelable biometrics deals specifically with fingerprint templates represented as a set of minutia. Juels and Sudan (2002) proposed a construction of *fuzzy vault*, which allows comparison of two nonordered sets of features, and Clancy et al. (2003) applied fuzzy vaults for storing fingerprint templates. Most of the subsequent research into fingerprint fuzzy vaults deals with their two major weaknesses—the corresponding minutia positions of two compared fingerprints should be exactly the same, so the fingerprints should be prealigned before fuzzy vault construction, and the requirement of using unprotected fingerprint during matching to fingerprint stored in fuzzy vault (intruder can simply intercept these unprotected fingerprints instead of trying to break the fuzzy vault). The more detailed analysis of the security weaknesses of fingerprint fuzzy vaults and other cancelable biometrics is presented by Scheirer and Boult (2007).

There are also proposals of hiding fingerprint templates not involving the error correcting codes. For example, in Farooq et al. (2007) and Tulyakov et al. (2007a) authors construct hashes of fingerprint minutia sets so that the matching of two fingerprints is performed by using only their hashes. No fingerprint prealignment is needed, and hashes can be constructed securely at the scanner location so that original templates are never transmitted or stored. Though such approaches are sometimes criticized for the degradation of matching performance, such degradation should be expected.

As we explain in Section 5.5, the combined use of biometrics and user-specific keys can result in apparent perfect performance of biometric systems, but such results are misleading. Therefore, the algorithms constructing cancelable biometrics and claiming performance superior to the original noncancelable biometrics should be considered with caution.

5.2 Liveness

Even if an intruder gets access to unprotected templates stored in the biometric database, these templates might be of no use if the biometric system implements some kind of liveness test during biometrics acquisition. For example, by presenting a face photo to a camera, the intruder might trick the face biometric system to perform a match of the photo instead of live face. If the stored biometric templates use some features and not original images of faces, it is usually easy to construct an artificial face image having same features as a particular biometric template and use such image for breaking the system. By implementing additional liveness test, the biometric system can avoid such break-ins.

The particular technique for liveness detection would greatly depend on biometric modality. For some modalities, such as face and speech, we can use an *active liveness detection* working on a challenge-and-response principle—during the biometrics acquisition the user might be asked to turn head, smile, or speak a particular sentence. For other biometrics, for example, fingerprint, such method will not work and we need to devise a *passive liveness detection*, which searches for the specific properties of live biometric scans. For example, the fingerprints produced by the synthetic gummy finger might have smoother edges than fingerprints of the live fingers, as well as have no sweat pores. The fingerprint image-processing algorithm might look for these specific features and determine if the used finger was artificial.

Sometimes the liveness detection might require the use of separate scanner. For example, the determined intruder might simply cut off the finger of person to bypass a security system. The scanned fingerprint in this case will be practically same as coming from a live fingerprint if traditional fingerprint sensors are used. But, if the fingerprint scanner also incorporates the sensor able to analyze the chemical blood content, the liveness of the fingerprint can be easily detected.

5.3 Indexing biometric databases

As we already pointed out in Section 3.1, in addition to more widespread verification mode of operation, the biometric system can operate in other modes, for example, identification and watch list modes. These other modes might require the matching of input biometric templates to a set of N biometric templates enrolled in the database. But the biometric matching usually takes a significant time. For example, matching two fingerprint or two face templates can typically take up to 1 s. If the database contains a large number N of enrolled persons, for example, millions, matching input template to all enrolled templates will require a prohibitively large time. Therefore, to deal with large-scale biometric applications, some kind of indexing algorithm should be used in the system.

If the biometric templates are represented as fixed length feature vectors, then traditional indexing techniques in multidimensional space, such as kd-trees, can serve as a basis for biometric index. For example, in Mhatre et al. (2005) a pyramid technique was used to index hand geometry biometrics. Such techniques are most helpful when the dimension of feature vectors is rather small. If the dimension of the feature vectors is large, for example, 1000, multidimensional indexing techniques might not be effective. But, the ordered nature of biometric templates makes the distance calculation between them relatively fast and still allows their use in large-scale real-time applications. For example, an iris recognition system deployed in the watch list mode (Daugman and Malhas, 2004) is able to perform a significant number of matches, since each match consists in a fast calculation of Hamming distance between two binary iris templates.

The situation is more difficult when the biometric templates do not have fixed length feature vector presentation. Fingerprint templates usually consist of a minutia set of a variable size and with no particular order. Moreover, the coordinates of corresponding minutia in two fingerprints can differ significantly due to their translation and rotation. Therefore, the simple, euclidean-like, calculation of distance between two templates is not possible. Hence, earlier described techniques are not applicable—we are not able to perform multidimensional indexing, and we are not able to simply match every template in the database.

The construction of fingerprint indexing algorithm turned out to be a rather difficult task. Three general approaches for reducing match time exist. The first approach is to classify all fingerprints into few classes (usually five) of the Henry classification system, and perform matching of the input fingerprint only to enrolled fingerprints of the same class. Many algorithms for doing such classification were proposed, but the existence of only few classes is an inherent limiting factor for this approach. The second approach relies on representing fingerprint as a fixed length feature vector. The features are usually extracted from the orientation field of fingerprint ridges, and finding common frame of reference (e.g., core positions) might be required (Cappelli et al., 1999). The third approach tries to use minutia triplets to construct position invariant fingerprint representation, finger-prints are matched based on the number of similar triplets and the transformations between these triplets (Germain et al., 1997). The input fingerprint is still practically matched against each enrolled template, but, in contrast with second approach, does not require separate processing of orientation fields and finding reference frame. The last two approaches have better performance than first approach based on Henry classification, but still not sufficient for large scale deployment (retrieving 10% of enrolled templates has 90% probability of getting correct match).

5.4   Individuality of biometrics

Is it possible for two different persons to have almost identical fingerprints or face appearances? The research into *biometric individuality* tries to investigate this question. It is clear that biometric measurements of the same person are not absolutely identical and some variation always exists. It would be interesting to know the chances of an impostor template to be within the boundaries of this variation. The individuality research has most impact on the forensic investigations. It also defines the best possible performance of biometric systems and separate biometric modalities.

Since the introduction of fingerprints in the criminal investigation, it was important for the prosecution to prove that the latent fingerprints found on the crime scene match exactly the fingerprints of the suspect, and do not match fingerprints of any other person. The first known individuality model of Galton (1892) randomly placed minutia on a grid and calculated the probability that specific grid locations are chosen. Most subsequent models used similar designs and reported almost negligible probabilities that fingerprints of different persons would match. As a consequence, the fingerprint evidence was considered as infallible in the courts for a long time.

But, the time showed that few errors in the fingerprint matching did happen (Cole, 2005). The errors have become more visible when the DNA evidence took more central role; some fingerprint matching evidence has been overturned by the DNA evidence. The most important case occurred in 2004, when an innocent person was arrested as a suspect in Madrid terrorist bombing (Cole, 2005). The degree of the incorrect fingerprint match was exceptionally high—approximately 15 minutia were matched in two fingerprints, as well as, some third-level features—sweat pores (12 matching minutia are sometimes regarded as sufficient for the positive match by FBI). The errors might also be the result of the increased use of fingerprint databases. If we already have a suspect and match his/her fingerprints to ones left in the crime scene, the probability of positive match is indeed quite low. But, if the suspect is not known, and a multimillion database is searched for a match, it is quite possible to find few well-matching fingerprints and declare the wrong person as a suspect.

To confirm the validity of fingerprint evidence in courts, it is desirable, as in the case of DNA evidence, to derive specific probabilities that two fingerprints belong to the same person. Ideally, an automatic algorithm would be used to report exact confidence numbers, and these numbers would be statistically verified by the experiments. Unfortunately, the current performance of automatic fingerprint matchers is still inferior to the performance of human experts, and we cannot rely on them. Some recent research attempts to find a more precise fingerprint individuality models that would agree with the results of automatic fingerprint matchers. For example, Pankanti et al. (2002) consider the model that accounts for the way fingerprint matchers try to find a transformation of one minutia set into another. But the results of experiments show that constructed model still does not have required precision.

The individuality research is an active part of biometrics research. With regard to fingerprints, we expect the appearance of more advanced individuality models, which would take into account the statistical distributions of minutia and ridges, as well as nonlinear fingerprint deformations. With the proliferation of other biometrics and their "latent" recordings, for example, face, gait, speech, we expect the growth of research into their individuality as well.

5.5 Hardening of biometrics

The *two-factor authentication*, relying on biometrics and traditional random key-based authentication, is usually considered as a good approach to increase the security of the system. Indeed, it would be more difficult for intruder to obtain both means, fake biometrics and stolen key, to bypass the security of such system than the system relying on only one of those factors. Both factors can be kept separate; the authentication of the user might consist in first verifying the key and then verifying the biometrics. If the key is incorrect or the confidence of biometric match is low, the user is not authenticated.

At the same time there is a growing number of approaches trying to merge both factors together and construct the so-called *hardened biometrics* or *biohashing* methods. In such approaches, both during enrollment and matching, the biometric template is transformed using user-specific random key. The matching is performed using transformed biometrics, and significant increases in performance are usually reported. Here, we present a simple example of such technique.

Suppose the biometric template is represented as a fixed length feature vector of length N, $x_1, \ldots, x_N$, and suppose $0 \leq x_i \leq 1$ for all i. Let the user-specific key be a binary string of length N, $b_1, \ldots, b_N$. Let the biometric hardening be the following operation: $x_i \rightarrow x_i + b_i * (N + 1)$. In this case, if two different users use different keys, then there will be index j, where b_j is 0 for one user and 1 for the other. The distance between corresponding transformed features will be at least N, and the total distance between two transformed templates (e.g., assuming city–block distance) is at least N. It is also easy to see that the distance between any two templates transformed using the same key will be less than N. So, apparently the presented hardening algorithm is able to achieve 0 FAR−0 FRR error rates: genuine users, utilizing same key, will have matching distance between templates always less than N, and impostor users, utilizing different keys, will have matching distance always bigger than N. The hardening transformations might be more complex and deal with nonfixed biometric templates, but the essence remains the same—biometrics of different users have different transformations and transformed templates have greater separation for impostors.

Does biometric hardening give any advantage over separate use of biometrics and keys in two factor authentication systems? If we assume that genuine matches are always performed using same keys, and impostor matches always use different keys, the separate use of keys and biometrics can easily be made to have 0 FAR and 0 FRR—the matching should only compare keys and discard biometric matching scores. So, the claim of superior performance in hardened biometric systems is easily achieved when keys and biometrics are used separately. The interesting case would be if intruder steals the key of legitimate user and tries to be authenticated using this key. In separate key-biometrics system, the performance in this case will be exactly the performance of original biometric system. For hardened system, we have some transformation that is applied to two templates of different persons; it is very doubtful that such transformation will result in better performance. If it were so, why would not we use transformed biometric templates instead of original templates for original biometric matcher?

Thus, by considering different scenarios, hardened biometrics is expected to have worse performance than separate use of keys and biometrics in two-factor authentication systems (Kong et al., 2006). Another point against biometric hardening is hiding of proper security analysis, which might involve the probabilities of either key or biometrics to be compromised. If deployed system will attempt to set acceptance thresholds so that claimed 0 FAR−0 FRR performance is achieved, it will completely rely on keys (to make 0 FRR, we have in general to accept any biometric match). The intruder with stolen key will be accepted by the system in this case.

It might be difficult for biometric system buyers to determine whether the claims of superior performance are results of improving matching algorithms or the results of hardening. Consequently, despite having worse performance and decreased security, it is possible that hardened biometric systems will be increasingly deployed in the future.

Note that cancelable biometrics (Section 5.1) is also a two-factor authentication system, and due to the effect described in this section, a superior performance for such systems might be claimed. To correctly estimate the performance of cancelable biometric system, we need to assume that intruder is able to steal the user-specific key. When the templates of different users use the same key, the transformation applied to these templates is the same, and we expect the reduced matching performance of corresponding cancelable templates.

5.6 *Performance of biometric matchers and quality control*

Owing to large commercial interests in the biometrics field there is a great number of reports claiming almost ideal performances of developed biometric systems. It is practically impossible to verify such reports—the systems might include expensive and difficult-to-obtain sensors and evaluations might be performed on privately collected data. The system's performance evaluation might also be distorted by the use of hardening, which as we discussed can elementarily make any biometric matcher to appear to have ideal performance.

The competitions using publicly available data and well-defined performance evaluation criteria provide a good way to compare the performance of different matching algorithms. Fingerprint verification competitions (FVC), face recognition vendor test (FRVT), and iris challenge evaluation (ICE) are the examples of such competitions. The testing protocols usually include multiple performance criteria for evaluating biometric matchers. For example, FVC competitions report EER, TER, and FRR rates corresponding to different FAR levels (1%, 0.1%, 0.01% FAR). This is reasonable approach to performance evaluation—as we saw in Section 3.2, a single number is not sufficient for comparison, and few selected numbers give an adequate replacement for comparisons of ROC curves.

As the results of recent competitions show (Phillips et al., 2007), modern biometric matchers have achieved good progress. Though, the human visual system is well adapted for the task of face recognition, automated face matchers can have better performance than humans. Another conclusion of the experiments is the importance of good quality biometric scanners and standardized acquisition procedures. For example, the face recognizers perform best on high-resolution face images taken under controlled illumination conditions.

The quality control during biometric scanning can be a decisive factor in the deployment of biometric system. The large-scale iris recognition system (Daugman and Malhas, 2004) deployed in UAE reportedly did not produce any errors during its entire operation. But the same iris-matching algorithm had only average performance in ICE 2006 competition. This might be explained by the poor quality of some iris images in the ICE 2006 database. The quality control in the production biometric system might be able to detect the presence of such bad images and require additional scanning attempts.

6 Conclusion

The area of biometrics includes multiple topics and is currently under intensive study by many scientists and companies. In this chapter, we reviewed the major topics of biometrics research. Some research topics have reached a maturity stage and are interesting mainly from implementation point of view. For example, multiple solutions have been proposed for fingerprint matching, and the problem consists in the proper combination of these solutions rather than in developing new algorithms. But, still there are topics that do not have ready solutions and present challenges. Cancelable biometrics, indexing, and biometrics individuality are among such topics.

References

Ashraf, B., S. Lucey, T. Chen (2008). Learning patch correspondences for improved viewpoint invariant face recognition, in: *IEEE International Conference on Computer Vision and Pattern Recognition (CVPR)*, Anchorage, AL, USA.

Berry, J., D.A. Stoney (2001). History and development of fingerprints, in: H.C. Lee, R.E. Gaensslen (eds.), *Advances in Fingerprint Technology*. CRC Press, Boca Raton, FL, USA.

Blanz, V., T. Vetter (2003). Face recognition based on fitting a 3D morphable model. *IEEE Transactions on Pattern Analysis and Machine Intelligence* 25(9), 1063–1074.

Cappelli, R., A. Lumini, D. Maio, D. Maltoni (1999). Fingerprint classification by directional image partitioning. *IEEE Transactions on Pattern Analysis and Machine Intelligence* 21(5), 402–421.

Chikkerur, S., A.N. Cartwright, V. Govindaraju (2007). Fingerprint enhancement using STFT analysis. *Pattern Recognition* 40(1), 198–211.

Clancy, T., D. Lin, N. Kiyavash (2003). Secure smartcard-based fingerprint authentication, in: *ACM Workshop on Biometric Methods and Applications (WBMA 2003)*, Berkeley, CA, USA.

Cole, S.A. (2005). More than zero: accounting for error in latent fingerprint identification. *Journal of Criminal Law and Criminology* 95(3), 985–1078.

Cootes, T.F., G.J. Edwards, C.J. Taylor (2001). Active appearance models. *IEEE Transactions on Pattern Analysis and Machine Intelligence* 23(6), 681–685.

Daugman, J., I. Malhas (2004). Iris recognition border-crossing system in the UAE. *International Airport Review* (2), 49–53.

Daugman, J.G. (1993). High confidence visual recognition of persons by a test of statistical independence. *IEEE Transactions on Pattern Analysis and Machine Intelligence* 15(11), 1148–1161.

Davida, G., Y. Frankel, B. Matt (1998). On enabling secure applications through on-line biometric identification, in: *Proceedings of the IEEE 1998 Symposium on Security and Privacy*, Oakland, CA.

Delac, K., M. Grgic, S. Grgic (2005). Independent comparative study of PCA, ICA, and LDA on the FERET data set. *International Journal of Imaging Systems and Technology* 15(5), 252–260.

Farooq, F., R.M. Bolle, T.-Y. Jea, N. Ratha (2007). Anonymous and revocable fingerprint recognition, in: R.M. Bolle (ed.), *IEEE Conference on Computer Vision and Pattern Recognition, 2007. CVPR '07*, pp. 1–7.

Galton, F. (1892). *Fingerprints*. McMillan, London.

Germain, R.S., A. Califano, S. Colville (1997). Fingerprint matching using transformation parameter clustering. *Computational Science and Engineering, IEEE [see also Computing in Science & Engineering]* 4(4), 42–49.

Jea, T.-Y., V. Govindaraju (2005). A minutia-based partial fingerprint recognition system. *Pattern Recognition* 38(10), 1672–1684.

Juels, A., M. Sudan (2002). A fuzzy vault scheme, in: *IEEE International Symposium on Information Theory*, Lausanne, Switzerland.

Kittler, J., M. Hatef, R.P.W. Duin, J. Matas (1998). On combining classifiers. *IEEE Transactions on Pattern Analysis and Machine Intelligence* 20(3), 226–239.

Kong, A., K.-H. Cheung, D. Zhang, M. Kamel, J. You (2006). An analysis of biohashing and its variants. *Pattern Recognition* 39(7), 1359–1368.

Maltoni, D., D. Maio, A.K. Jain, S. Prabhakar (2003). *Handbook of Fingerprint Recognition*. Springer-Verlag, New York.

Mhatre, A., S. Chikkerur, V. Govindaraju (2005). Indexing biometric databases using pyramid technique, in: *Audio and Video-based Biometric Person Authentication (AVBPA), 5th International Conference, Lecture Notes in Computer Science*, Vol. 3546. Springer, Berlin, pp. 841–849.

Pankanti, S., S. Prabhakar, A.K. Jain (2002). On the individuality of fingerprints. *IEEE Transactions on Pattern Analysis and Machine Intelligence* 24(8), 1010–1025.

Phillips, P.J., W. Todd Scruggs, A.J. OToole, P.J. Flynn, K. W. Bowyer, C. L. Schott, M. Sharpe (2007). FRVT 2006 and ICE 2006 largescale results. Technical Report NISTIR 7408, NIST.

Scheirer, W.J., T.E. Boult (2007). Cracking fuzzy vaults and biometric encryption, in: T.E. Boult (ed.), *Biometrics Symposium, 2007*, Baltimore, MD, USA, pp. 1–6.

Sim, T., S. Baker, M. Bsat (2003). The CMU pose, illumination, and expression database. *IEEE Transactions on Pattern Analysis and Machine Intelligence* 25(12), 1615–1618.

Tulyakov, S., F. Farooq, P. Mansukhani, V. Govindaraju (2007a). Symmetric hash functions for secure fingerprint biometric systems. *Pattern Recognition Letters* 28(16), 2427–2436.

Tulyakov, S., V. Govindaraju (2006). Utilizing independence of multimodal bio-metric matchers, in: *International Workshop on Multimedia Content Representation, Classification and Security*, Istanbul, Turkey.

Tulyakov, S., V. Govindaraju, C. Wu (2007b). Optimal classifier combination rules for verification and identification systems, in: *7th International Workshop on Multiple Classifier Systems*, Prague, Czech Republic.

Tulyakov, S., C. Wu, V. Govindaraju (2007c). Iterative methods for searching optimal classifier combination function, in: *First IEEE International Conference on Biometrics: Theory, Applications, and Systems, 2007. BTAS 2007*, Washington, DC, USA, pp. 1–5.

Turk, M., A. Pentland (1991). Eigenfaces for recognition. *Journal of Cognitive Neuroscience* 3(1), 71–86.

Chapter 3

Database Recovery in Information Warfare Scenario

Brajendra Panda and Prahalad Ragothaman

Computer Science and Computer Engineering Department, University of Arkansas,
Fayetteville, AR 72701, USA

Abstract

System invasion has become a common phenomenon especially after the concept of information sharing paved its way into the technical and business world. Databases have become one of the prime targets of attackers. Once a database is attacked, the damage would spread to unaffected parts of the database when valid transactions read damaged data and update clean data based on the value read. Therefore, it is necessary to develop faster and accurate damage assessment and recovery (DAR) techniques to bring a damaged database back to consistent state as soon as possible.

The database log is the primary resource for DAR after an attack on the corresponding database. DAR methods designed to restore databases from information attacks require that transaction logs must store all operations to identify the trail of damage and that the logs must not be purged. Therefore, the logs can grow massively and the DAR process would be extremely slow due to the high volume of data to be accessed from the log.

In this chapter, we present methods to segment a log based on transactions that have read-from relationships with other transactions in the segment. Once a malicious transaction is identified, our damage assessment mechanism accesses the corresponding segment to determine the set of affected transactions. The recovery protocol then uses this list to maintain the consistency of the database. This eliminates the requirement of accessing operations of all transactions in the log. We offer techniques for dividing the log into several segments based on three different methods, namely, based on the number of committed transactions, time, and space. We also discuss a hybrid log segmentation method that reduces the time taken to perform damage assessment while still segmenting the log fast enough so that no intricate computation becomes necessary.

1 Introduction

To sustain in the fast changing technological world, organizations need to share information with others. Computers are probably the most powerful information sharing devices in today's world and thanks to the Internet to make the process of information sharing even faster and easy. Unfortunately, the Internet has also attracted a large number of malicious users who have used it to break into systems and render them inconsistent and unstable. It is extremely difficult to find and close all security flaws in the system. Hackers are always in search of new ways to prevail over the system security. There are many methods to protect a system from such attacks, but savvy hackers always find newer ways to break into a system. Hence, the next best thing would be to detect the attack and bring the system back to a consistent state as soon as possible. But these methods do not detect an intrusion as soon as it occurs. In fact, in most cases, an attacker enters the system and accesses data as a valid user. Thus, in case of attacks on databases, any update performed by the attacking transaction is made permanent when the malicious transaction commits. Therefore, the damage can spread to other parts of the database through legitimate users as they update fresh data after reading any damaged data (Ammann et al., 1997; Graubart et al., 1996). In course of time, the system may become so unstable that we have to shut the entire system down to bring it back to a consistent state. This is highly unacceptable in time critical database systems where valid users must have access to data at all times. Intrusion detection techniques are beyond the scope of this chapter and will not be discussed here. The next best solution to the problem is to design fast and efficient damage assessment and recovery (DAR) algorithms to be used during the post-intrusion detection scenario.

Traditional recovery techniques were designed to recover a database after system failures. For this purpose, a log that stores all write operations of every transaction is used. After a system failure, the log is scanned from the end till the last checkpoint and all those active transactions whose effects were saved into the database are undone and those transactions that were committed but whose effects were not saved into the database are redone. Also in the traditional logging mechanism, read operations are not stored and the log is periodically purged to free up disk space. However, for recovery of databases after an attack by a malicious transaction, it is required that both read and write operations of transactions are stored in the log and the log is never purged. This causes the log to grow to astronomical proportions and scanning such a log will become a very tedious and slow process. This will lead to a prolonged denial-of-service. A solution is to devise methods that read only parts of log and skip as much as possible while guaranteeing that the sections skipped do not contain any affected transactions. This is done by log segmentation. Segmenting the log based on transaction dependency (Panda and Patnaik, 1998) and data dependency (Tripathy and Panda, 2001) achieves this goal. However, these approaches use intricate computation and slow down transaction processing although achieving faster DAR. This chapter intends to strike a balance between log segmentation overhead and time needed for DAR. We offer to segment the log based on the number of committed transactions, time, and space. We also discuss a hybrid log segmentation method that reduces the time taken to perform damage assessment while still segmenting the log fast enough so that no intricate computation is necessary. To the best of our knowledge, these types of methods have not been used before.

The rest of the chapter is organized as follows. In Section 2, we discuss the motivation for this research. The log segmentation methods are presented in Section 3. Section 4 offers the corresponding DAR techniques. Sections 5 and 6 discuss the hybrid log segmentation mechanism and the corresponding DAR algorithms, respectively. Section 7 concludes the chapter.

2 Motivation

Traditional database recovery mechanisms as discussed by Bernstein et al. (1987), Elmasri and Navathe (1994), Gray and Reuter (1993), and Korth et al. (1997), to cite a few, have their scope confined to system failures. They are designed to flush out all effects of all non-committed transactions while ensuring that effects of all committed transactions are saved in the stable storage. For this kind of recovery, the vitality of read operations does not exist. Recovery is possible only from the before and after images of data items. However, as required for defensive information warfare purposes (Ammann et al., 1997), after the detection of an attack, effects of all transactions reading directly or indirectly from the malicious transaction have to be undone along with that of the malicious transaction. Then, all legitimate transactions must be re-executed to reflect the consistent state of the database. Hence, to establish read-from relationships, all read operations of transactions need to be stored in the log and the log cannot be purged. Jajodia et al. (1999) have proposed several guidelines for trusted recovery. Ammann et al. (1997) followed a transaction dependency approach that uses relationships among transactions to identify and repair damage in the database. Reordering transactions for efficient recovery has been discussed by Liu et al. (2000). Panda and Giordano (1999) adopted a data dependency approach to recover from malicious attacks. In their method, they define a data item as dependent on another data item if the former was calculated using the value of the latter. Therefore, if the value of a data item were determined to be corrupt, all data items that are dependent on this value would also be regarded corrupt. An advantage of this approach is that it considers blind-writes, that is, updating data items without reading them, which refresh damage automatically. Furthermore, this approach also considers a transaction as affected only after the transaction reads a damaged data. Thus, all updates made by a transaction before it read a damaged data are regarded as unaffected. This results in recovery of less number of data items leading to a faster recovery.

All of aforementioned approaches scan a sequential log file, which is very huge. To expedite the DAR process, techniques of segmenting the log using the transaction dependency approach and the data dependency approach have been proposed by Panda and Patnaik (1998) and Tripathy and Panda (2001), respectively. These methods avoid scanning too many unaffected transactions during the damage assessment period. In transaction dependency-based log segmentation, all transactions that are dependent on one another are stored in one segment. So, a log is divided into multiple segments, and during DAR, only one of these segments needs to be accessed. However, using the data dependency-based segmentation, each segment contains only dependent operations, and, therefore, a transaction's operations may be stored in multiple segments. So, during DAR, few of these segments will be accessed as opposed to a major portion of the log. Both these methods reduce denial-of-service since data items in unaffected segments can be made available to active transactions as soon as the damage assessment is performed.

A drawback in these approaches is that there is a chance of a segment growing too large because too many transactions (or data items in case of data dependency-based segmentation) may be dependent on one another. Different segments have a chance of merging into one segment and ultimately it could result in one huge segment, as big as the log itself. This defeats the purpose of log segmentation. Another drawback in both these approaches is the amount of system resources used in building the segments. In real time, segmenting the log based on transaction dependency and data dependency involves usage of valuable system resources when execution of operations of transactions must be given higher priority. In an ideal scenario, a database is not attacked very frequently. Hence, having simple algorithms to build the segments and designing efficient algorithms to assess damage is necessary.

As stated earlier, here we present techniques to segment the log based on the number of committed transactions, time, and space. A fixed number of transactions will form a segment in the first approach. In the second method, a new segment will be formed with all committed transactions after a set time has elapsed. In the third approach, a segment will be built with all the committed transactions after they have used up a set size of disk space. The three schemes mentioned also vouch for the fact that no segment will grow out of proportion since we are enforcing constraints on their sizes (Ragothaman and Panda, 2002). The algorithms to implement this approach will be relatively simple and easy.

However, the trade off in using the segmentation techniques mentioned earlier is that, in trying to make log segmentation a simple and fast process, damage assessment becomes intricate. To strike a balance, we then propose a hybrid log segmentation method that will reduce the time taken to perform damage assessment while still segmenting the log fast enough so that no intricate computation is necessary (Ragothaman and Panda, 2003). While performing damage assessment, we re-segment the log based on transaction dependency. Thus, during repeated damage assessment procedures, we create new segments with dependent transactions in them so that the process of damage assessment becomes faster when there are repeated attacks on the system.

3 Log segmentation

As stated earlier, we have developed methods of segmenting the log so that the segments are limited from growing out of proportion. A segment is formed after a certain condition such as a fixed number of committed transactions, a specified time window, or the space occupied by the committed transactions is satisfied. Our model is based on the following assumptions: (1) transaction operations are scheduled in accordance with the rigorous two-phase locking protocol as defined in Elmasri and Navathe (2000), (2) read operations are also recorded in the log file, (3) intrusion is detected using one of the intrusion detection techniques and the ID of the attacking transaction is available, (4) the log is never purged, and (5) blind-writes are not allowed. Next, we define a few data structures that are used in the algorithms.

Tuft: It is a group of transactions that adheres to any one of the three models presented. The transactions in the *tuft* are stored in the chronological order of their commit time. A *tuft* is denoted by Γ_i, where i denotes the *tuft* number.

Read_items: It is a table that consists of two fields—the *tuft* number and a list of all the data items that were read by all the transactions in that *tuft*.

Tuft_table: It is a table that lists transaction number and the corresponding *tuft* in which the transaction's operations are stored.

To implement the algorithms, a temporary log file is maintained. The temporary log file is the system-generated log that stores all necessary operations of transactions. The operations of the transactions in the temporary log file are considered to build the *tufts*. During checkpoint, the following steps take place: no new transactions are considered, all active transactions are completed, the modified database buffers are saved into the stable storage, an end-checkpoint record is added to the last *tuft* after the last transaction, the temporary log file is deleted, and then execution of new transactions resume. The methods of segmentation are discussed later with the help of examples. Algorithms to implement these approaches are also provided.

3.1 Log segmentation based on number of committed transactions

In this approach, a fixed number of committed transactions are grouped together to form a *tuft*. Consider the following piece of history, H, in the temporary log file. T_i represents the start of transaction i, and c_i represents the commit record of transaction i. Individual operations of the transactions are not shown for simplicity.

$$H : T_1 \ T_5 \ c_1 \ T_7 \ c_7 \ T_9 \ c_5 \ T_{10} \ T_{12} \ c_{12} \ T_{15} \ T_2 \ c_{10} \ T_{13} \ c_9 \ T_6 \ T_8 \ c_{15} \ c_2$$
$$T_4 \ c_8 \ c_4 \ T_{18} \ c_{18} \ c_6 \ c_{13}.$$

Let us assume that five committed transactions form a *tuft*. Thus, the *tufts* are

$$\Gamma_1 = \{T_1, T_7, T_5, T_{12}, T_{10}\}, \ \Gamma_2 = \{T_9, T_{15}, T_2, T_8, T_4\}, \text{ and}$$
$$\Gamma_3 = \{T_{18}, T_6, T_{13}\}.$$

It has to be observed that the transactions are considered in the order of their commit sequence. Doing so ensures that the partial order among the transactions is maintained in the *tufts*. A lemma to prove this is provided later. The variables that are used to implement the algorithm for this approach are provided in the following text.

Transactions_in_tuft is a variable that holds the number of transactions that make a *tuft*.

Transaction_count is a variable that holds the number of transactions that are recorded into the *tuft* so far.

Algorithm 1.

1. Initialize $i = 1$
2. Create *tuft* Γ_i. Add a record for Γ_i in the *read_items* table; *transaction_count* $= 0$
3. if(*transaction_count* $! =$ *transactions_in_tuft*)
   3.1. Read the next committed transaction, T_j, from the temporary log file and store the operations of T_j in Γ_i. Add a new record in the *tuft_table* for T_j
   3.2. Add the read_set of T_j in the *read_items* table against *tuft* Γ_i.
   3.3. Increment *transaction_count*.
   3.4. Go to step 3.
4. Else
   4.1. Increment i.
   4.2. Go to step 2.

The process of segmenting the log is much simpler than the log segmentation algorithms based on either transaction dependency approach or data dependency approach. Also, we do not run the risk of segments growing too large. We can be rest assured that a segment, a *tuft* in this case, will definitely end once a fixed number of transactions commit. If the algorithm, at step 3.1, does not find any committed transactions to store into the *tuft*, it will wait until a transaction commits and then proceed with the rest of the steps in the algorithm.

3.2 Log segmentation based on a time window

For this protocol, we assume that the commit time of each transaction is also stored along with the commit record of the transaction. Using this method, all transactions that committed in a particular window of time will form a *tuft*. To explain the idea, let us consider a piece of log from the temporary log file. Commit time (assume in AM) of each transaction shown next to the commit record of that transaction.

$$H : T_1 \; T_5 \; c_1[9:05] \; T_7 \; c_7[9:07] \; T_9 \; c_5[9:12] \; T_{10} \; T_{12} \; c_{12}[9:15] \; T_{15}$$
$$T_2 \; c_{10}[9:16] \; T_{13} \; c_9[9:16] \; T_6 \; T_8 c_{15}[9:23] \; c_2[9:25]$$
$$T_4 \; c_8[9:40] \; c_4[9:42] \; T_{18} \; c_{18}[9:43] \; c_6[9:43] \; c_{13}[10:10].$$

The operations of each individual transaction and operations of aborted transactions are not shown for simplicity. Let us assume that the time allotted to build a *tuft* is 5 min. Let us also assume that this algorithm started at 9:00 AM. Thus, all transactions that committed between 9:00 AM and 9:05 AM, both times non-inclusive, must form a *tuft*. The next window of time will begin at 9:06 AM and end at 9:10 AM and so on. If no transaction committed in a particular window of time, that *tuft* will be used for the committed transactions that occur in the next window of time. The *tufts* and their transactions for the history given earlier are shown in the following.

$$\Gamma_1 = \{T_1\}, \; \Gamma_2 = \{T_7\}, \; \Gamma_3 = \{T_5, \; T_{12}\}, \; \Gamma_4 = \{T_{10}, \; T_9\},$$
$$\Gamma_5 = \{T_{15}, \; T_2\}, \; \Gamma_6 = \{T_8, \; T_4, \; T_{18}, \; T_6\}, \; \Gamma_7 = \{T_{13}\}$$

As in the previous model, here too we do not have to worry about a *tuft* growing too big. The *tuft* will certainly end when the time slice ends. The number of transactions in a *tuft* is not known unlike the previous method. Nor is the size of each *tuft*. A regulation on the size of the *tuft* can be enforced and this method is discussed in Section 3.3.

As mentioned earlier, we assume that *tuft* Γ_1 will be created at 9:00 AM. Hence, Γ_3 will be created at 9:11 AM. With respect to *tuft* Γ_3 from the aforementioned example, we will define a few necessary data structures that are required in the algorithm to implement this approach.

Tuft_end_time is the variable that holds the time at which the current *tuft* must end.

Time_of_last_creation is the variable that holds the time when the most recent *tuft* was built.

Current_time is the variable that stores the time at that moment. It has to be noted that *current_time* will be called only once and the same time will be used through one iteration of the algorithm.

Period_of_creation is the variable that holds the time period after which the next *tuft* must be built.

Commit_time(T_i) is the time at which transaction T_i committed.

When the procedure starts, *tuft_end_time* is initialized to *current_time* plus the *period_of_creation*. *Time_of_last_creation* is initialized to the *current_time*. All those transactions that have their commit time between the *time_of_last_creation* and *tuft_end_time* will form a *tuft*. When the *tuft* ends, the window is advanced to the next time slice by adding the *period_of_creation* to the *tuft_end_time* and setting the *time_of_last_creation* to the *tuft_end_time*.

Algorithm 2.

1. Initialize $i = 1$; *tuft_end_time = current_time + period_of_creation; time_of_last_creation = current_time*;
2. Create *tuft* Γ_i; add a new record for Γ_i in the *read_items* table.
3. WAIT UNTIL (*current_time > = tuft_end_time*)
   3.1. Read all transactions, T_j, from temporary log where (*commit_time(T_j) > time_of_last_creation*) and (*commit_time(T_j) < = tuft_end_time*) and record their operations into *tuft* Γ_i. Add a new record for T_j in the *tuft_table*.
   3.2. Add the read_set of T_j to the *read_items* table against *tuft* Γ_i.
   3.3. Increment *i*.
   3.4. *time_of_last_creation = tuft_end_time*
   3.5. *tuft_end_time = tuft_end_time + period_of_creation*
   3.6. Go to step 2.

3.3 Log segmentation based on fixed size tuft

In this approach, the size of the *tuft* is kept constant. Operations of committed transactions are added to the *tuft* until there is no more space for the next committed transaction to fit into it. It is assumed that the size of a *tuft* is bigger than the largest transaction. If a committed transaction does not fit into the current *tuft*, we close the *tuft* and create a new one. We do not allow the transactions to span from one *tuft* to another. This will result in wastage of disk space in this approach. But if we do allow the transactions to span, damage assessment will be more complicated. This will be evident when we present the damage assessment model in Section 4. A few necessary variables and data structures used in the algorithm to implement this approach are shown in the following:

Sizeof(i) returns the size of *i*.
Tuft_size is the size of the *tuft*.
Var is a variable that has units as bytes.
T_{lar} is the largest transaction in terms of size.
Space_available(i) contains the space available in *i*.

Algorithm 3.

1. $i = 1$; *tuft_size* $= sizeof(T_{lar}) + var$;
2. Create *tuft* Γ_i; *space_available*$(\Gamma_i) = tuft\_size$; Add a new record for Γ_i in the *read_items* table.
3. Read next committed transaction, T_k, from temporary log file.
4. if *sizeof*$(T_k) <= $ *space_available*(Γ_i)
   4.1. Store the operations of T_k in Γ_i.
   4.2. Add the read_set of T_k to the *read_items* table against *tuft* Γ_i.
   4.3. Add a record for the transaction T_k in the *tuft_table*.
   4.4. *space_available*$(\Gamma_i) = $ *space_available*$(\Gamma_i) - $ size_of(T_k)
   4.5. Go to step 3.
5. Else
   5.1. Increment *i*.
   5.2. Create *tuft* Γ_i; *space_available*$(\Gamma_i) = tuft\_size$; Add a new record for Γ_i in the *read_items* table.
   5.3. Go to step 3.

3.4 Correctness of the models

This section provides a discussion on the correctness of all three log segmentation approaches presented earlier. We intend to prove that the transactions in the *tufts* maintain the same partial order as they did when the scheduler scheduled them. We will also provide a brief discussion to show that the log maintained by using any of the models discussed earlier is adequate to recover the database to a consistent state in case of system failures.

Lemma. Transactions in the *tufts* maintain the same partial order among them as scheduled by the scheduler.

Proof. Consider two transactions, say T_j and T_i, from any two *tufts* say Γ_k and Γ_l (where $l > k$), respectively. Let us assume that transaction T_j is dependent on transaction T_i. As mentioned earlier, the scheduler follows the rigorous two-phase locking protocol to schedule the transactions. From the models, it is clear that the transactions are recorded into *tufts* in a chronological order, that is, they are stored into the *tufts* according to their commit sequence. If T_j is dependent on T_i, then there should be a partial order existing between these two transactions. The rigorous two-phase locking protocol does not allow any transaction to gain a conflicting lock on a data item over which another active transaction has already gained a lock. Only after the active transaction that holds the conflicting lock on the data item commits, another transaction can gain a lock on that data item. In this case, it has to be noted that T_j appears before T_i, which means that the former committed first. Also if T_j is dependent on T_i, there is no way that T_j might have committed before T_i because T_i will not release the locks that it is holding on data items until it commits. This argument can be extended to any two transactions from any two *tufts* or to two transactions appearing in the same *tuft*. Thus, partial order among the transactions is maintained in the *tufts*. This proof holds true for *tufts* created by any one of the three models discussed earlier.

A combination of all transactions in all *tufts* and all transactions in the temporary log file (if any) is equivalent to a conventional log that would be generated by the system had there been no segmentation. This shows that in case of a media failure, the log maintained by any one of our approaches will be adequate to recover the database to a consistent state.

4   Damage assessment based on foregoing log segmentation model

Damage spreads in a database when valid transactions directly or indirectly read data items written maliciously by attacking transactions and then update other data items. Damage assessment is the process of identifying all those data items written by transactions that read damaged data written either by malicious transactions or by other affected transactions. This process is often executed by denying service of the system to other valid transactions. Other valid transaction must not be kept waiting for long while damage assessment is done. Thus, this process has to be done as efficiently as possible and open the system for other transactions. Next, we present the damage assessment procedure for our model.

4.1   Damage assessment procedure

The damage assessment model presented in this section holds good for segmented logs developed by any one of the three methods proposed earlier. It is assumed that the intrusion is detected and all the attacking transactions are known before the start of damage assessment. When an attack is detected, the following steps take place: (1) no new transactions are accepted; (2) all active transactions are completed, any updates made by these transactions are saved to the database, and the *tufts* updated accordingly; and (3) the temporary log file is deleted. Thus, the temporary log file can be completely ignored during damage assessment. Some of the variables and data structures used in this algorithm are as follows:

affected_items: This list contains data items that were written either by a malicious transaction or by a transaction that read a data item written by a malicious transaction.

affected_transactions: This list contains all malicious transactions and those transactions that read malicious data items.

The process of damage assessment starts by identifying all malicious transactions. The *tuft* in which the first malicious transaction, say T_m, is stored is obtained by looking up in the *tuft_table*. All transactions that appear in all of the *tufts* before the one in which T_m appears can be safely ignored because they are not affected. No valid transaction that read a data item written by T_m and appearing in one of the *tufts* before the one in which T_m is present will be affected because it would have committed earlier than T_m. The data items that were written by T_m are stored into the *affected_items* list. The same procedure is carried out for any malicious transaction that we encounter further in the process of damage assessment.

Each of the transactions that appear in the same *tuft* as transaction T_m is scanned to check if it is affected. The read_set of the transactions is intersected with the *affected_items*. If the result is not a null set, then that transaction is affected because it has read a data item written by a malicious transaction. The transaction number is added to the *affected_transactions* list and its write_set is appended to the *affected_items* list.

After all the transactions in the same *tuft* are scanned, the subsequent *tufts* are scanned to look for malicious and affected transactions. If a malicious transaction is present in the subsequent *tuft*, the write_set of the malicious transaction is added into the *affected_items* list. The *affected_items* list is intersected with the *read_items* list of the corresponding *tuft*. If the result is not a null set, it means that the *tuft* is affected and one or more of the transactions in that *tuft* has read data item(s) written by a malicious transaction. All the transactions in that *tuft* are scanned to determine which of the transactions have read an affected data item. This is done by intersecting the *affected_items* list and the read_set of each of the transactions in that *tuft*. If the result is not a null set, it means that the transaction is affected. The transaction's write_set is appended to the *affected_items* list and the transaction number is added to the *affected_transactions* list. This process is done until the process is through with all the *tufts*.

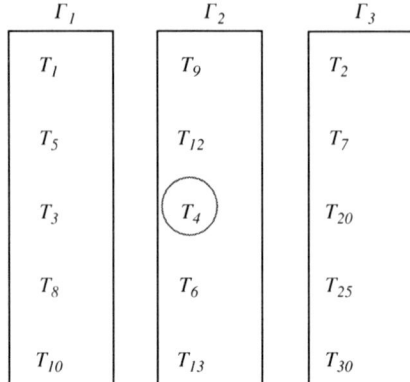

Fig. 1.   Tufts that were created using one of the methods previously described.

Table 1
The *read_items* table

Tuft	Read_items
1	p, q, s, b
2	x, y, z, a, e, b
3	z, x, c

Figure 1 and Table 1 offer an example to explain the damage assessment model. Let T_4 be the first attacking transaction and let the operations of the transaction T_4 be $r_4[b]$, $w_4[x]$, $w_4[z]$ c_4. From the *tuft_table*, it can be determined that transaction T_4 is present in Γ_2. Γ_1 is certainly not affected because none of the transactions appearing in Γ_1 can be dependent on T_4 or any of the other transactions in Γ_2. The data items that transaction T_4 wrote (x and z) are appended to the *affected_items* list. Each transaction that appears after T_4 is scanned and checked to see if it is affected. This is accomplished by intersecting the read_set with the *affected_items* list. If the result is not a null set, then the transaction is affected.

The *affected_items* is intersected with the *read_items* from the next *tuft*, Γ_3. Since data items x and z appear in the result, it means that one or more of the transactions in Γ_3 have been affected. Thus, all transactions in Γ_3 are scanned to check if any of them are affected. The following algorithm enumerates the damage assessment procedure.

Algorithm 4.

1. Let the first attacking transaction be T_i
2. Set *affected_items* = {}
3. Using the *tuft_table*, determine the *tuft* number, say Γ_k, where transaction T_i is stored
   3.1. Append the write_set of transaction T_i into the *affected_items* list

3.2. For each transaction (say T_j) appearing after T_i in *tuft* Γ_k

    3.2.1. If T_j is a malicious transaction then append the write_set of transaction T_j to the *affected_items* list

    3.2.2. Else

        3.2.2.1. Call procedure *assess_damage*(T_j)

3.3. For each *tuft* Γ_l where $l > = k + 1$

    3.3.1. if(*read_items*(Γ_l) $\cap$ *affected_items* ! $= \phi$)

        3.3.1.1. Call procedure *assess_damage*(T_j) on every transaction, say T_j, from the beginning of the *tuft*

    3.3.2. For each malicious transaction appearing in *tuft* Γ_l

        3.3.2.1. Append the write_set of the next malicious transaction, say T_m, to the *affected_items* list

        3.3.2.2. For each transaction, say T_n, appearing after T_m in *tuft* Γ_l

        3.3.2.3. Call procedure *assess_damage*(T_n)

    3.3.3. Increment l

Procedure *assess_damage*(T_j)

1. Obtain the read_set and the write_set of the transaction T_j

    1.1. If T_j is not a malicious transaction

        1.1.1. If(*read_set* (T_j) $\cap$ *affected_items* ! $= \phi$)

            1.1.1.1. Enter the *write_set* of the transaction T_j into the *affected_items* list

            1.1.1.2. Enter the transaction number in the *affected_transactions* list

    1.2. Else

        1.2.1. Append the write_set of transaction T_j to the *affected_items* list

In case of multiple attacks, we assume that all malicious transactions have been detected through one of the intrusion detection techniques. These malicious transactions may be present in many *tufts*. While scanning the *tufts* for dependencies (step 3.3.2 of Algorithm 4), we also determine if there are any malicious transactions present in that *tuft* using the *tuft_table*. If there are malicious transactions present, we perform the same steps as we did with the first malicious transaction. While doing so, there are chances that some of the good transactions have read data items written by multiple malicious transactions and those good transactions may have already been appended to the *affected_transactions* list. We check to see if they are already present in the list and add them only if they are not present.

4.2 Performance analysis using simulation

We simulated the scenario using the C programming language. A sample log was generated in accordance to the rigorous two-phase locking

Table 2
Values of parameters used in simulation

Total number of transactions	500
Total number of data items	5000
Maximum data items accessed by a transaction	40
Attacker ID varies with increments of 100	50–450

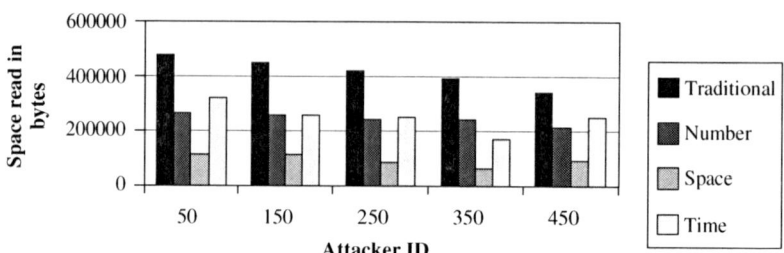

Fig. 2.   Comparison of traditional damage assessment approach and damage assessment
using the segmented log.

protocol. Inter-leaving of transactions was allowed. This was accomplished
by starting a new transaction after a certain random number of data items
were accessed by previous active transactions. To reduce complexity,
aborted transactions were not considered. A random number determined
whether the transaction must perform a read, a write, or a read and write
operation. When multiple transactions were active, the program randomly
picked one of the active transactions and performed the transaction's
operations. Programs were written to segment the log based on each of the
three methods described earlier. A program to assess damage assuming
an attacker ID was also written and affected transactions were obtained.
Table 2 presents the parameter values used in the simulation. Comparison
analysis of damage assessment using unsegmented log and that using a
segmented log is shown in Fig. 2, which confirms that having a segmented
log greatly improves performance. In that, significantly less number of bytes
are read during damage assessment.

5   Hybrid log segmentation

In the log segmentation method discussed in Section 3, the size of each
segment is kept under control and running the risk of a segment growing
too big is avoided in all three approaches. Also, each of these methods uses
very little computation while segmenting the log. However, a significant
amount of computation has to be done to determine the dependencies

among the segments during damage assessment. In scenarios where attacks are quite frequent, neither of these methods may yield the fastest solution to recover a database.

In this section, we present a hybrid method of log segmentation. We propose to further segment a log already segmented based on any of the three approaches described earlier based on transaction dependency approach as described in Panda and Patnaik (1998). We shall do the re-segmentation while assessing damage during subsequent attacks on the database. By doing so, we intend to achieve a significant improvement in terms of time required during damage assessment while still keeping the log segmentation algorithm simple enough so that the time for execution of transactions is not hindered.

Our model is based on the same assumptions presented in Section 3.

A list of definitions that are helpful in understanding the research and the algorithms is as follows:

Dependent Transaction: Transaction T_j is said to be dependent on transaction T_i if T_j read one or more data items that were last written by the committed transaction T_i.

Read_items list: This is a list of all the data items that were read by all the transactions in a segment. (Note that the data structure, *read_items*, used in Section 3 is a table rather than a list.)

Write_items list: This is a list of all the data items that were written by all the transactions in a segment.

Affected_items list: This is a list of all the data items that were written either by a malicious or by an affected transaction.

Affected Transaction: A transaction is said to be affected if it updates the value of a data item using the value of another data item that was previously written by either a malicious or another affected transaction.

Size-controlled segment: This is a segment that was created using one of the three approaches described in Section 3. In other words, we choose to call a *tuft* as a size-controlled segment.

Size-un-controlled segment: This is a segment that was created using transaction dependency.

The log segmented based on any of the three approaches described earlier can be pictorially represented as shown in Fig. 3.

Re-segmenting the log begins after an attack is detected and the attacking transaction is known. The process is done during the damage assessment phase. Let us assume that an attack was detected in Γ_2. It has been

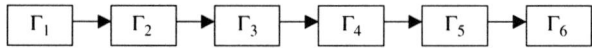

Fig. 3.   Log segments before re-segmentation.

shown that scanning of transactions in Γ_1 is unnecessary because none of the transactions in Γ_1 read a data item written by any of the transactions present in Γ_2. Rigorous two-phase locking protocol ensures this. The attacking transaction in Γ_2 is determined using the *tuft_table*. All transactions in all the segments until the last affected segment, that is, the segment that has the last affected transaction in it, are scanned. A new segment is started with the first malicious transaction in it. To determine the dependency among transactions, we intersect the "write" set of the malicious transaction with the read_set of the transaction to be scanned. There are two cases, as discussed in the following, depending on the results of the intersection.

5.1 The result is not a null set

The transaction is affected. That particular transaction is stored in the newly formed segment that contains the malicious transaction and other affected transactions. The data items that were written by the transaction are appended to the *affected_items* list. Thus, all malicious and affected transactions will be present in one segment at the end of the damage assessment phase and all affected data items in the *affected_items* list.

5.2 The result is a null set

This means that the transaction did not read any affected data. The "read" and the "write" sets of the transaction are stored in a new *read_items* list and *write_items* list, respectively. We can be sure that the transaction is not dependent on any other transaction in any of the other size-un-controlled segments that were formed. Hence, a new segment is created and the operations of the transaction are stored in it.

During subsequent scanning of transactions, the "read" items of that transaction is intersected with all the *write_items* lists and *affected_items* list available to determine whether there is a dependency between the transaction and the segments. By doing so, it is checked whether the transaction read a data item that was previously written by another transaction. If the result of all the intersections is a null set, it means that transaction is completely independent of all other transactions scanned so far. A new segment is created and the operations of that transaction are stored in it. Also, a new *read_items* list and a *write_items* list is started as in the previous case and the "read" set and the "write" set of the transaction are stored into the respective lists.

If on the contrary, the result of the intersection of the "read" set of the transaction with two or more *write_items* lists is not a null set, it means that the transaction is dependent on two or more transactions that are present in two different segments. In such a case, those two segments are merged and

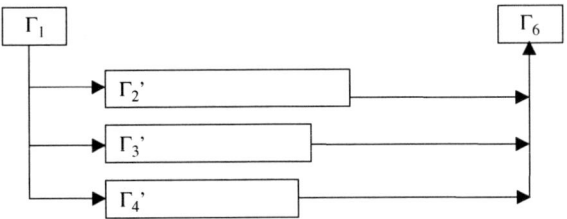

Fig. 4.   Log segments after re-segmentation.

the operations of the current transaction are stored in the merged segment. The *read_items* list and the *write_items* list are also merged and the "read" set and the "write" set of the transaction are stored into the appropriate lists.

If the transaction is dependent on only one of the segments that have been formed, it is added to the end of the segment upon which it is dependent. The "read" set and the "write" of the transaction are stored into the appropriate lists. Thus, one or more size-un-controlled segments will be present in parallel between Γ_1 and the last affected segment. Each size-un-controlled segment will have its own *read_items* list and a *write_items* list. A pictorial representation of a re-segmented log is shown in Fig. 4.

Some segments may be larger or smaller than others depending on how many transactions are present in that segment. Each of the newly formed segments Γ_2', Γ_3', and Γ_4' will contain transactions that are dependent on one another. When an attack is detected, only the segment containing the malicious transaction has to be scanned since all affected transactions would be present in that segment alone. All other size-un-controlled segments can be safely avoided. An algorithm for log re-segmentation follows:

Algorithm 5.

1. Determine the position of the attacking transaction using the *tuft_table*. Let us assume that the transaction, say T_i, is present in Γ_i.
2. Set *affected_items* = write_set(T_i); *read_items* = read_set(T_i).
3. Start new segment Γ_i'.
4. For each transaction, say T_j, that appears after the attacking transaction T_i, in Γ_i until the last transaction in the last affected *tuft*, say Γ_j, where $j > i$
   4.1. If (*affected_items* $\cap$ read_set(T_j) != ϕ)
      4.1.1. Add T_j to Γ_i'; Add the write_set of T_j to *affected_items*; Add read_set(T_j) to *read_items*.
   4.2. Else
      4.2.1. Intersect the write_set of T_j with all available *read_items* list. If none are available, start a new size-un-controlled segment, add the operations of T_j in the segment, start a

new *read_items* list and a *write_items* list and add the read_set and write_set of T_j into the respective lists. Continue from step 3.

4.2.1.1. If the result of all the intersections is a null set

4.2.1.1.1. Start a new size-un-controlled segment, say Γ_j', and add the operations of T_j.

4.2.1.1.2. Start a new *read_items* list and a *write_items* list and add the read_set and the write_set of T_j into the respective lists.

4.2.1.2. If the result of the intersection is not a null set with only one of the segments

4.2.1.2.1. Add the operations of T_j into that segment.

4.2.1.2.2. Update the appropriate *read_items* list and the *write_items* list.

4.2.1.3. If the result of the intersection is not a null set with more than one of the segments

4.2.1.3.1. Merge the segments into one single segment.

4.2.1.3.2. Add the operations of T_j into the merged segment.

4.2.1.3.3. Merge the appropriate *read_items* list and *write_items* list and add T_j's read and write items into the respective lists.

As it is evident in the aforementioned method, there is the risk of having to manage a segment that is too large because various segments might get merged to form one big segment. Eventually, this segment might end up being as big as the log itself. To avoid this scenario, a new method to segment the log in a hybrid manner is proposed. In this approach, pointers are provided to link the information flow from one segment to another instead of merging the segments together. Thus, after subsequent damage assessment on the database, the log can pictorially be represented as shown in Fig. 5.

Let us consider the segments as shown in Fig. 3. Assume that an attack was detected in Γ_2. As mentioned earlier, none of the transactions that are present in Γ_1 need to be scanned as they are not affected. Damage assessment is carried out as mentioned earlier and all the cases hold true here too. Let us assume that the first set of parallel segments are formed and they are named as Γ_2', Γ_3', and Γ_4'. During subsequent scanning of transactions from other size-controlled segments, it is assumed that a transaction read data items that were written by transactions from two different size-un-controlled segments making that transaction dependent on

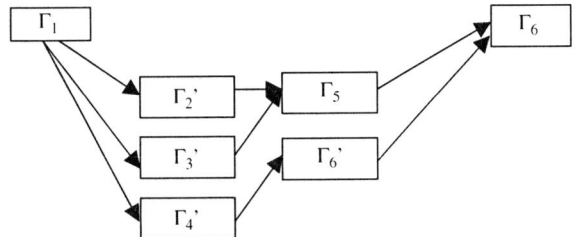

Fig. 5.   A newer method to segment the log in a hybrid manner.

two different segments. From Fig. 5, it is evident that a transaction present in Γ_5' read data items written by transactions in Γ_2' and Γ_3'. Thus, pointers are established from these two segments to Γ_5' to show that there is an information flow from both Γ_2' and Γ_3' onto Γ_5'. Thus, during subsequent damage assessment procedures, the pointers can be checked and the information flow can be obtained. An algorithm to segment the log using the new hybrid log segmentation approach is as follows:

Algorithm 6.

1. Determine the tuft, say Γ_i, where attacking transaction, say T_i, is present.
2. Set *affected_items* = write_set(T_i); *read_items* = read_set(T_i); Start new segment Γ_i'.
3. For each transaction, say T_j, that appears after the attacking transaction T_i, in Γ_i until the last transaction in the last affected *tuft*, say Γ_j, where $j > i$
   3.1. If (*affected_items* ∩ read_set(T_j) ! = ϕ)
        3.1.1. Add T_j to Γ_i'; Add the write_set of T_j to *affected_items*; Add read_set(T_j) to *read_items*.
   3.2. Else
        3.2.1. Intersect the write_set of T_j with all available *read_items* list.
        3.2.2. If none are available, start a new size-un-controlled segment, add the operations of T_j in the segment, start a new *read_items* list and a *write_items* list and add the read_set and write_set of T_j into the respective lists. Continue from step 3.
              3.2.2.1. If the result of all the intersections is a null set
                       3.2.2.1.1. Start a new size-un-controlled segment, say Γ_j', and add the operations of T_j.
                       3.2.2.1.2. Start a new *read_items* list and a *write_items* list and add the read_set and the write_set of T_j into the respective lists.

3.2.2.2. If the result of the intersection is not a null set with only one of the segments
    3.2.2.2.1. Add the operations of T_j into that segment.
    3.2.2.2.2. Update the appropriate *read_items* list and the *write_items* list.
3.2.2.3. If the result of the intersection is not a null set with more than one of the segments
    3.2.2.3.1. Establish pointers between the two segments.
    3.2.2.3.2. Retain the *read_items* list and *write_items* list as it is.

6 Damage assessment using the re-segmented log file

There are two cases to consider during damage assessment process when an attack is detected after re-segmentation. They are explained based on the segments shown in Fig. 5.

Case 1. An attack is detected in Γ_1 or in any of the size-controlled segments that were ignored when damage assessment was done the first time.

The operations of all the transactions from the point of attack in Γ_1 until the point where the size-un-controlled segments start are scanned. The "write" set of the first malicious transaction in Γ_1 is added to the *affected_items* list. The *affected_items* list is then intersected with the "read" set of transactions that appear after the malicious transaction in all the *tufts* until the size-un-controlled segments start. The log gets re-segmented with all dependent transactions in one segment. Cases similar to those described in Section 5 hold good here too. Thus, new sets of parallel size-un-controlled segments are formed. Dependency between each of the newly formed size-un-controlled segments and the existing size-un-controlled segments is then established. It has to be noted that the segments will not be merged as described in Section 5. Instead, pointers will be established to determine information flow. An algorithm to assess damage for the case discussed is as follows:

Algorithm 7.

1. Let the first attacking transaction in Γ_1 be T_i. Add the write_set of T_i to the *affected_items* list. Start a new size-un-controlled segment, say Γ_1' and add the operations of T_i in Γ_1'.
2. For every transaction that appears after T_i, say T_j, until the last transaction before the size-un-controlled segment starts, do

2.1. If (*affected_items* ∩ read_set(T_j) ! = ϕ)

    2.1.1. Add write_set(T_j) to *affected_items*; Add the operations of T_j to Γ_1'.

2.2. Else

    2.2.1. Intersect the read_set of T_j with all available *read_items* lists that were formed for the newly created size-un-controlled segments.

    2.2.2. If none are available, start a new size-un-controlled segment and add the operations of T_j to that segment. Start new *read_items* list and *write_items* list and update them accordingly.

        2.2.2.1. If the result of all the intersections is a null set

            2.2.2.1.1. Start a new size-un-controlled segment and add the operations of T_j.

            2.2.2.1.2. Start a new *read_items* list and a *write_items* list and add the read_set and the write_set of T_j into the respective lists.

        2.2.2.2. If the result of the intersection is not a null set with only one of the segments

            2.2.2.2.1. Add the operations of T_j into that segment.

            2.2.2.2.2. Update the appropriate *read_items* list and the *write_items* list.

        2.2.2.3. If the result of the intersection is not a null set with more than one of the segments

            2.2.2.3.1. Establish appropriate pointers between segments.

            2.2.2.3.2. Record the "read" items and the "write" items in the appropriate lists.

Case 2. An attack is detected in any of the size-un-controlled segments.

In this case, all the size-controlled segments that appear before the segment in consideration and all other size-un-controlled segments that were formed with the current segment can be safely ignored, as there would be definitely no dependency between those segments. Thus, the damage assessment process begins by scanning each transaction after the first malicious transaction in the current segment. This is followed by checking every size-controlled segment and size-un-controlled segment that appears after the first scanned segment until the last affected segment in the log file. With the help of pointers from one segment to another, we can determine the information flow and thus know what segments need to be scanned after the current one. If there are pointers from a segment leading to two different segments, both the segments have to be scanned after the current segment is scanned. Similarly, if two different pointers from two different segments lead to one single segment, then that segment must be scanned twice while assessing damage. If the result is not a null set, it means that segment is affected and one or more transactions in that segment have read a data item that was previously written by a malicious or affected transaction. An algorithm for this case is as follows:

Algorithm 8.

1. Identify the size-un-controlled segment where the malicious trans-action is present. Let us assume it is Γ_i'. All other size-un-controlled segments parallel to Γ_i' can be ignored. Identify the malicious transaction, say T_i, in Γ_i.
2. Append the write_set of T_i and all other transactions in the same segment to the *affected_items* list.
3. For each segment, say Γ_j, that appears after the current segment until the last affected segment, do
   3.1. If (*affected_items* $\cap$ *read_items*(Γ_j) ! $= \phi$)
      3.1.1. If Γ_j is a size-un-controlled segment
         3.1.1.1. Merge Γ_i' and Γ_j.
         3.1.1.2. Merge the respective *read_items* list and *write_items* list.
         3.1.1.3. Append the *write_items* list to the *affected_items* list.
      3.1.2. If Γ_j is a size-controlled segment then for each transaction, say T_k in Γ_j
         3.1.2.1. If (*affected_items* $\cap$ *read_items*(T_k) ! $= \phi$)
            3.1.2.1.1. Append operations of T_k to Γ_i'.
            3.1.2.1.2. Append the read_set and write_set of T_k to appropriate *read_items* list and *write_items* list.
      3.1.3. Else
         3.1.3.1. Intersect the read_set of T_k with all available *write_items* lists of size-un-controlled segments that were recently created.
         3.1.3.2. If the result of the all the intersections is a null set or if no size-un-controlled segments were recently formed
            3.1.3.2.1. Create a new size-un-controlled segment with the operations of T_k in it.
            3.1.3.2.2. Start a new *read_items* list and a *write_items* list and add the read_set and write_set of T_k to the appropriate list.

3.1.3.3. If the result of the intersection is not a null set with only one segment

3.1.3.3.1. Append the operations of T_k and its read_set and write_set to the segment, the *read_items* list and *write_items* list respectively.

3.1.3.4. If the result of the intersection is not a null set with more than one segment

3.1.3.4.1. Establish pointers between the appropriate segments.

In the case when an attack is detected in any of the size-controlled segments that appear after all the size-un-controlled segments, the scenario is similar to that described earlier.

7 Conclusions

Every computer system that is networked is vulnerable to information attacks. Although retaliation to these attacks is virtually impossible, immediate attention must be paid for database survivability. Quick and efficient recovery of the system is vital for an organization whose information resources have been attacked. The log file, the only source where past transaction information is stored, is accessed to accurately determine all affected transactions and damaged data items that are required to be recovered. However, since log file is a sequential file stored in secondary storage, log access time significantly dominates DAR methods. Log segmentation helps in reducing the process. A log file can be segmented by either transaction dependency-based approach or data dependency-based approach. However, these approaches consume ample resources and slow down transaction execution considerably. Particularly in situations where attacks are infrequent, this is undesirable. The second problem with these methods is that the segments can become too large due to dependency relationships among various segments. This defeats the purpose of log segmentation.

In this chapter, we focused on producing segments quickly enough without having to consume too much system resources. In the process, we also ensured that the size of each segment was under control and did not grow to humongous proportions. We achieved this by enforcing constraints on the size of the segment, such as number of committed transaction, space occupied by committed transactions, and a fixed time window for transactions to commit and form a segment. We have provided necessary damage assessment algorithm, which can be used on the log file that was segmented using any of the three approaches described. The result of the damage assessment process is a list of all the malicious and affected transactions.

Using this information, we can use any of the previously proposed approaches to carry out the recovery process.

We have also presented a technique for re-segmenting an already segmented log based on transaction dependency for much faster damage assessment and hence recovery. We have overcome the shortcomings of the previous methods where we observed that damage assessment would be more time consuming when compared to other log segmentation approaches such as transaction dependency and data dependency while still being much faster had there been no segmentation at all. The model that we have presented here will work best in scenarios where attacks are more frequent. The segmented log will be re-segmented again based on transaction dependency, thus limiting damage to only one segment. The process of re-segmenting is done while performing damage assessment and thus system resources will not be wasted. Different cases were observed while re-segmenting and assessing damage using the re-segmented log. Each case was discussed in detail and algorithms were provided to handle the cases separately.

Acknowledgments

This work has been supported in part by US AFOSR under grant F49620-01-10346. We are thankful to Dr. Robert L. Herklotz for his support, which made this work possible.

Glossary

Damage assessment: The process of determining the set of data items affected by the attack.

Recovery: Bringing the database to a consistent state.

Transaction dependency: A relationship that shows which transactions have read data values written by a particular transaction.

Log segmentation: The process of dividing the log file into multiple segments.

Malicious transaction: The transaction that changes data items in the database in an unauthorized way.

Affected transactions: The set of transactions that have read damaged data.

References

Ammann, P., S. Jajodia, C.D. McCollum, B. Blaustein (1997). Surviving information warfare attacks on databases, in: *Proceedings of the 1997 IEEE Symposium on Security and Privacy, May*, IEEE Press, Oakland, CA, pp. 164–174.

Bernstein, P., V. Hadzilacos, N. Goodman (1987). *Concurrency Control and Recovery in Database Systems*. Addison-Wesley, Reading, MA.

Elmasri, R., S.B. Navathe (1994). *Fundamentals of Database Systems*. 2nd ed. Addison-Wesley, Menlo Park, CA.

Elmasri, R., S.B. Navathe (2000). *Fundamentals of Database Systems.* 3rd ed. Addison-Wesley, Menlo Park, CA.

Graubart, R., L. Schlipper, C. McCollum (1996). Defending database management systems against information warfare attacks. Technical Report, The MITRE Corporation.

Gray, J., A. Reuter (1993). *Transaction Processing: Concepts and Techniques.* Morgan Kaufmann, San Mateo, CA.

Jajodia, S., C.D. McCollum, P. Amman (1999). Trusted recovery. *Communications of the ACM* 42(7), 71–75.

Korth, H.F., A. Silberschatz, S. Sudarshan (1997). *Database System Concepts.* 3rd ed. McGraw-Hill International Edition, New York, NY.

Liu, P., P. Ammann, S. Jajodia (2000). Rewriting histories: recovering from malicious transactions. *Distributed and Parallel Databases* 8(1), 7–40.

Panda, B., J. Giordano (1999). Reconstructing the database after electronic attacks, in: S. Jajodia (ed.), *Database Security XII: Status and Prospects.* Kluwer Academic Publishers, Norwell, MA.

Panda, B., S. Patnaik (1998). A recovery model for defensive information warfare, in: *Proceedings of the 9th International Conference on Management of Data, December,* Hyderabad, India, pp. 359–368.

Ragothaman, P., B. Panda (2002). Modeling and analyzing transaction logging protocols for effective damage assessment, in: *Proceedings of the 16th Annual IFIP WG 11.3 Working Conference on Data and Application Security, July,* King's College, University of Cambridge, UK.

Ragothaman, P., B. Panda (2003). Improving damage assessment efficacy in case of frequent attacks on databases, in: *Proceedings of 17th Annual IFIP WG 11.3 Working Conference on Data and Application Security, August,* Estes Park, CO.

Tripathy, S., B. Panda (2001). Post-intrusion recovery using data dependency approach, in: *Proceedings of the 2nd Annual IEEE Systems, Man, and Cybernetics Information Assurance Workshop, June,* West Point, NY.

Suggested readings

Patnaik, S., B. Panda (2003). Transaction-relationship oriented log division for data recovery from information attacks. *Journal of Database Management* 14(2), Special issue on Data and Information Security.

Sobhan, R., B. Panda (2002). Reorganization of database log for information warfare data recovery, in: M. Olivier, D. Spooner (eds.), *Database and Application Security XV.* Kluwer Academic Press, Norwell, MA, pp. 121–134.

Yalamanchili, R., B. Panda (2004). Transaction fusion: a model for data recovery from information attacks. *Journal of Intelligent Information Systems* 23(3).

Part II
Incentive Mechanisms and Web Security

Chapter 4

Incentive Mechanisms for Internet Security

Manoj Parameswaran

Operations & Management Information Systems (OMIS), Santa Clara University, Santa Clara, CA 95053, USA

Andrew B. Whinston

Information, Risk and Operations Management (IROM), The University of Texas, Austin, TX 78712, USA

Abstract

Security problems in general, and email spam in particular, are growing faster than the Internet itself and threatening its role as a critical infrastructure. Technical solutions, regardless of how good they are, may by themselves be inadequate to address these problems, which are also the result of distorted incentives and organizational structure of the Internet. A combination of incentive systems, public policy, insurance systems, reputation, and audit systems is required to ensure technology is deployed optimally to minimize these problems. This chapter proposes such an institutional change in the Internet. In the process, it describes an analytical model using game theory to coordinate incentives by implementing a certification scheme for service providers that emphasizes feasibility. In addition, the chapter explores implications of the mechanism in the context of current technical approaches, and extends the use of economic mechanisms to security in general, and to additional institutional frameworks for insurance, audit, and reputation. The chapter addresses issues related to public policy, law, social computing, and cyber warfare in the context of this novel approach of tackling security from the viewpoint of coordinating incentives.

1 Introduction

Various types of communications and distribution channels are converging toward internet protocol (IP); and numerous formats of information exchange and service delivery are converging toward the web interface; and e-mail is on the verge of becoming the legitimate communication tool for business transactions. However, the Internet faces a crisis in terms of security problems in general and spam in particular, and many are raising concerns that the infinite promise of the Internet may not be realized.

Waves of malicious activity in the form of viruses, worms, trojans, spam, phishing, hacking attacks, DDoS attacks, spyware, and adware have beset the Internet in recent years (Weaver and Paxson, 2004), rendering surfing a harrowing experience for many, and usage of the Internet a severe headache for organizations. Information security has become a priority investment in public and private organizations (mi2g, 2004); security technologies are being continually refined and more and more information security personnel hired. Nevertheless, the attacks and malicious activity in general are predicted to rise in scope and viciousness, and many organizations have started talking of futility in the defensive efforts. Combined with the perceptions that web surfing is hurting productivity, business leaders have been contemplating giving up on the Internet altogether, unless it could be significantly revamped (Talbot, 2006). As for individual users, in a survey by the Pew Internet and American Life Project, 22 percent of respondents reported reducing their use of e-mail because of spam, and 67 percent labeled the act of being online "unpleasant and annoying" (Pew, 2005).

E-mail spam in particular has become a serious problem. A study that aggregated information from a variety of sources including Google, BrightMail, Jupiter Research, and Gartner put the level of spam in 2006 as at 40% of all e-mail. Furthermore, spam cost U.S. corporations 8.9 billion dollars per year; 28% of users ended up replying to spam e-mail; 16% of all e-mail address changes were due to spam. Many practitioners contend that such numbers can be misleading, as it relates number of spam messages to number of legitimate mails, despite the fact that the two bear no relation to each other. Nevertheless, the cost imposed on resources for routing and filtering at the backbone, service providers (SPs) and corporate infrastructure does depend on the percentage of all mail that constitute spam. An overwhelming majority of spam gets filtered out, leading to user-level perception that the problem is exaggerated by aggregate statistics. However, by the time they get filtered out, the spam messages have already consumed valuable network and computing resources. Furthermore, the better the spam filters get, the higher the volume of spam injected into the network, as spammers are well aware of filtering effectiveness ratios, and release sufficient volumes to achieve their target number of delivered messages.

Daily tracking information provided by one spam-filter company shows more than 90% of received e-mail being blocked as spam each day. An overwhelming majority of spam messages relate to pharmacies and prescription drugs. Country-wide stats indicate that United States is the leading source by far, and frequently mentioned sources such as Russia or

China generate much less spam than United States. However, these numbers are significantly skewed by the fact that a majority of spam is generated by bots in the United States, which are zombie computers compromised and taken over by offshore hackers. According to Spamhaus, among the top ten sources of spam are such large SPs as Verizon, XO Communications, and Internap, as of early 2008. These sources have changed over time; in 2005, the sources were predominantly from Asian countries.

Obfuscation of identity by spammers has reduced the effectiveness of reputation analyses methods used by spam filters that depend on historic information. Botnets and cheap domain registrations are utilized to generate multiple sources for spam that aids obfuscation. Security software vendors have had to resort to improved techniques such as domain name validation, and profiling and prediction based on correlating multiple messages to counter the threat. However, spammers are quick to adapt to such techniques and invent new workarounds; further, they merely increase the volume of spam to exploit the fact that a percentage of spam still gets through.

The factors behind this increased spread of malicious activity are many, and most of them are bred by the phenomenal success of the Internet itself, and sustained by its inherent open and decentralized nature. The rapid growth of the Internet has transformed the nature of the Internet community and the prevalent culture over it from its early days of productive collaboration. Today, a much larger number of malicious hackers and spammers have easy access to information and tools for their malicious activity. Information on newly discovered vulnerabilities propagates quickly and coordinated attacks to exploit them commence in very short timeframes. Furthermore, with availability of inexpensive computers off the shelf, every user becomes a security administrator for an Internet node, a role most are not sufficiently informed to perform well. Combined with prevalence of insecure operating systems and broadband connectivity, this leads to the spread of large-scale intrusions into such machines as well as many of them being hijacked to act as zombie slaves that launch further malicious activity at the behest of a remote manipulator (Huang et al., 2006; Talbot, 2006). The consequence of all these activities is a heightened perception of the Internet as an insecure environment, which could become seriously harmful to its adoption for beneficial uses. As Ropeik and Gray (2002) pointed out, perceived risk may lead users to make irrational choices to stay away from specific environments.

2 Are technical solutions adequate?

Research and development in security technology has been making tremendous progress in keeping pace with the threats even as new ones emerge. Although a significant part of security technologies is about proactive prevention of attacks, much of the time, individual solutions are reacting to newly devised attacks. Is it sufficient to trust the rapid progress in security technologies, and assume that participants will deploy the best solutions, moving the Internet to a secure environment?

If we examine the data for sources of spam, the top ten SPs list has always included prominent network providers each year. The fact is that SPs and institutions have no direct incentive to control for spam that may originate from their network and impact others, and their investments are usually prompted by the incentive to provide better service for their own customers. The technical solutions need to be supplemented by the right institutional and incentive structure for optimal deployment, and the current environment does not ensure that available solutions are used to the best effect.

As new security solutions are developed, more sophisticated spamming techniques are developed as well. Indeed, the Internet itself allows the information needed to develop more sophisticated attacks spread quickly. The virtual communities of attackers are highly efficient at disseminating new "exploits" far and wide. Thus, technological solutions are not permanent in their impact and it is an ongoing battle. It is not sufficient to install the currently available best fix for the problem and resort to refinements in response to detection of new types of spam; it is necessary to create a framework where security assessment and investment are done on a dynamic basis; where the objective is to maintain a required level of security through a rapidly changing network environment. We need sustainable ways of deploying the security technologies. It may be necessary to bring on institutional changes that will supplement technology to ensure that technological defenses are arrayed optimally by most users and providers at any time.

The Internet is a decentralized, open network, where malicious activity originates in one part of the network, and impacts another. Today, in most cases, the controls—such as those deployed by Internet service providers (ISPs), enterprises as well as individual users—are primarily deployed at the destination. Although there is an increasing trend among retail ISPs and mail SPs to check outgoing traffic for spam, there is still no incentive structure to ensure that most providers find it in their interest to optimally control outgoing traffic.

Addressing the above points would require that an institutional structure that strongly motivates participants to control attacks at their origin, as well as to target maintaining security on a dynamic basis. The decentralized organizational structure of the Internet does not provide for this. A key issue in Internet security is that there are no clear lines of accountability; this derives from both the decentralized way datagram routing is implemented as well as the decentralized organizational structure. It is important to introduce some organizational mechanism that induces participant networks to voluntarily accept some degree of accountability, without interfering with the decentralized protocols. Introducing a degree of accountability can in turn lead to users getting some measure of predictability as to their security levels.

3   Incentive mechanisms and economics

A novel way of tackling the spam issue is to view the Internet as an economic system where participants act in tune with their incentives, and may be induced to respond in specific ways by imposing an incentive structure. Viewed thus, problems such as that of security, or piracy can be viewed as incentive problems where the right incentives in conjunction with appropriate tools from technology can address some of the fundamental issues arising from the organizational structure of the Internet.

Viewing spam (and other malicious activity) as an incentive problem, we see that the global, open nature of the Internet facilitates a large and growing community of spammers who stand to gain by malicious activity. Most SPs do not actively seek to exclude such customers from service. Nor do most providers seek to examine outgoing traffic to identify and eliminate spam. SPs lack any incentive to do so, as the impact tends to be to the rest of the network. SP efforts are focused on protecting their own customers and networks. So long as technical solutions are not perfect, and the spammers have incentive to profit from exploiting the open network, whereas network providers and organizations lack sufficient incentives to limit spam originating from their networks, the battle is likely to be ongoing. Since the volume of spam increases each year, this ongoing confrontation is not necessarily maintaining a stable level of user benefits and productivity. As the figures for losses caused by spam keep increasing year by year, it may be argued that the ongoing battle is not being won. The only way to win it would be to achieve perfection in technologies used to filter spam, or to change the current incentive structure so that participants in the Internet act toward collective benefit.

What is needed is an infrastructure that integrates economic, political, and legal aspects and overlaps with existing technology as well as motivating development of new technologies to manage risks better. In particular, appropriate incentives, policies, and laws could aid technology in enhancing security. Fundamental issues with the design and interconnection policies of the Internet infrastructure contribute to the vulnerability to generation and dissemination of new attacks. Instead of relying exclusively on technology solutions in the context of the current policy framework, the implications of a possible altered framework that could relate interconnection to security need to be considered. Policy changes, rather than protocol changes, are needed. Today, most of the research and development investments in Internet security are focused on technology (Walfish et al., 2005), for example. Allocating some of these investments into policy can enhance the advantages gained by technology solutions, as well as reduce the need for technology investments over the long run. Deploying policies that emphasize security can render the impact of technology solutions more durable.

Viewing the Internet as an economic system focuses attention on the interdependence and incentives of participating economic agents, including SPs, users, and purveyors of malware and spam. Internet security problems can be understood in terms of economic concepts, such as externality, liability, and moral hazard. Although this is a useful insight, we need to go further and explore whether economic concepts can help us frame a pragmatic solution to alleviate security-related risk. Such a solution should seek to influence some of the economic factors that govern the actions and interdependence of the participants. In the process, we may also draw from public policy and law, which have also dealt with the need to control socially harmful actions in various communities by some of their members.

3.1   Assigning responsibility in a practical way

In taking this view, it is important to recognize certain features of the Internet. First, as distinct from the legal approach to controlling crime, the information infrastructure has no clear delineation of jurisdiction, or corresponding enforcement powers. To illustrate by an analogy, with traditional criminal behavior such as bank theft, assigning the liability to the perpetrators and expecting the police to apprehend them are considered reasonable ways to reduce crime. Prosecution of a crime is focused on the perpetrator, precisely because the scope of jurisdiction, and the powers of investigation, enforcement, verification, and punishment are well defined and can be vested into formal institutions and policies. With the Internet, the analogy is to view the crackers as the liable entity to be apprehended and punished. The analogy breaks down since the cracker could be in a foreign jurisdiction that does not recognize the laws of the country that suffered the attack of the crackers. (Even with co-operation among governments, prosecution of such crimes can be hard and expensive.) Of course, this assumes that the crackers could be identified which could be impossible.

The assignment of liability to the perpetrators is not a practical way of looking at the Internet security problem. Instead we need to identify appropriate participants to be assigned responsibility and given proper incentives. The SP is the ideal candidate as the entity to assume liability for the actions of its customers. Since the SP itself does not carry out any attack, but only transports traffic from customers some of whom may be crackers, it appears unreasonable to place blame on SPs. It is common practice for public policy and law to make allowances for aspects of practical deployment of enforcement policies while formulating them. Accordingly, it may be seen that controls are sometimes applied at those nodes in organizational or community hierarchies that have the highest ability to influence the targeted criminal activity. Even a bank that does not lock its vaults may face some legal liability for a bank robbery. Lichtman and Posner (2004) proposed that ISPs must bear some liability for cyber-security. In the case of the Internet, the SP is best positioned to detect malicious activity; hence, they would be the practical choice for taking on the responsibility for controlling malicious activity originating from their customers. The intention should not be to advocate legal sanctions, rather, to answer the growing call to action for incentive-based trust in the cyber-infrastructure (Thomas and Amon, 2007).

It would also be reasonable to assume that SPs would not voluntarily accept responsibility that might make them liable for criminal actions they did not commit. Thus, we need to show that a case can be made for SPs to voluntarily accept liability. In other words, we need to show that a significant number of SP's may find it in their interest to subscribe to a framework that makes them responsible for security problems originating from their networks. We denote the providers that subscribe to such a policy framework as being "certified."

4 Certification of service providers

To make certification an incentive for an ISP to accept liability, all of the certified SPs' traffic (once identified) should be carried to other certified SP's without any (additional) reduction in performance for inbound filtering. In contrast, traffic from a noncertified SP may be blocked or significantly slowed down by certified SPs (for careful screening). Thus, customers of a certified SP would obtain better service quality compared with customers of a noncertified SP and should be willing to pay a higher price for the service. Certification signals quality, and attracts more discerning customers who can lead to higher revenues for the provider. For any certified provider, processing of inbound traffic can now focus on the noncertified, which can lead to more efficient investments. With tight controls in place that discourage users from violating security policies, such a provider is also likely to retain a customer base that is more security conscious. Over time, that may render investments in monitoring outgoing traffic more efficient as well. Our theoretical results show such a framework can indeed improve overall security and lower risk.

However, the value to customers of a certified SP depends, in general, on how many other SPs decide to become certified. If most providers remain uncertified, customers lose value by the loss of service quality in communications with the uncertified users. With a significant number of certified SPs and discerning users, this framework can lead to a more secure certified network, which is not isolated from the uncertified part. Also, the more networks are certified, the higher the share of network traffic that gets a higher quality of service (QoS).

Certified providers are liable to other certified providers for any malicious traffic originating from their network, and consequently must carefully screen their outgoing traffic and security practices of users. In deciding whether to be certified or not, an SP has to consider how many other providers are expected to choose certification and how capable it is in monitoring its own users and their traffic so as to minimize penalties. The latter decision is one that can be based on private information that the SP possesses but the former information has to be an estimate or conjecture. The willingness to pay on the part of the user for higher levels of security is also private information, and hence unknown to the SP.

4.1   Service providers as focus of accountability

The key idea of certification of providers is to assign liability to those SPs who in turn voluntarily accept it. There are various factors that suggest this approach could work. First, although many of the SPs are very large companies with millions of customers, they are still in a good position to carefully monitor their customers' outgoing traffic. For an SP that has accepted responsibility there is a strong incentive to monitor users and also to write contracts with customers that hold them responsible both financially and possibly in terms of reputation. Even without explicit liability many organizations already monitor the behavior of their computing environments to ensure that it is not used explicitly or otherwise to cause damage or in violation of laws. Second, to take the example of spam, agencies monitoring spam activity report that spammers are not isolated to offshore or obscure networks, and the SPs they belong to can often be easily identified. Statistics from such agencies list some of the better known SPs also as hosting spammers. Assigning incentive and liability can stimulate these providers into action in controlling such activity. Third, a certification scheme brings in some degree of predictability to a world of uncertainty, in that the certification status of another network signals the degree to which they are prone to security problems, and the degree of risk involved in communicating with them. Fourth, such a scheme allows more directed and efficient investments in focusing more on the higher-risk traffic, and in enhancing screening at the source network before traffic loads up the backbone and spreads to multiple destinations. Fifth, the provider–customer relationship being more direct, screening can lead to more effective enforcement.

4.2   A certification mechanism for service providers

The design of the mechanism is informed by the following considerations:
First, SPs represent the most feasible and effective points in the network where the locus of responsibility and controls can be placed. The notion is to decentralize security coordination to agents who have a coherent,

autonomous network, have access to resources and information to implement coordination policies, and have some value in implementing such coordination. In the context of security, SPs can filter incoming and outgoing traffic, monitor security practices, and enforce restrictions and offer service differentiation at different security levels. Accordingly SPs are the locus of deploying security measures.

Second, it is not feasible for a central agency to enforce security policies on providers, nor to correctly identify the security profiles of all providers. Responsibility has to be decentralized so that providers make the optimal investments in security, based on their own information about the security profile of their traffic. However, providers are commercial entities, and decentralization will work only by making it financially attractive for them to participate. Accordingly, we design a decentralized incentive and reputation system, which allows providers to signal their security profile to users and other providers, with built-in incentives that ensure that providers choose to join only if it is profitable to them. Providers tend to vary in the amount of spam their networks generate, they will normally not signal such information. Users and other providers would stand to gain by being able to choose based on the security profile of a provider. When a provider gets certified, it is signaling that it is confident in the security measures deployed and the profile of its user base.

Third, the primary focus of filtering by most providers is on inbound traffic as their responsibility is to their own customers, and not to the general welfare of the Internet. This leads to inefficient controls. Spam has already wasted network resources by the time it arrives at a destination network; spam and its sources are easier to detect and control at the source rather than at the destination; and bulk distributions spread out to multiple destinations from a single source, leading to wasteful effort in inbound filtering at multiple networks. We address this issue by tying incentives to control of outbound spam, specifically by making providers financially accountable for spam originating from their domain.

Fourth, the mechanism must be feasible to be deployed incrementally, without necessarily requiring global participation; it should not entail changes in fundamental protocols or routing or architecture; it should not entail changes in ownership or interference in provider operations; although it should facilitate differentiation of different security classes of providers, it should not lead to a disconnect of the Internet. Accordingly, the mechanism we outline involves no ownership changes, or new protocols, or changing routing practices; it creates a new institution in the certification authority (CA), but its role is coordination and monitoring rather than being an active part of the network itself. It will require sender identification protocols, which is a trend already in force.

Fifth, spam is an obvious subject to address with ISP collaboration. Currently, many ISPs view outgoing spam as an externality that is not to their advantage to solve.

As certification signals an ISP's ability to minimize spam and its commitment to do so, ISPs would have reputational incentive to be certified, thus turning an economic externality into an opportunity for competitive advantage.

Maintaining that reputation would in turn provide incentive for ISPs to find and implement effective mechanisms to suppress spam with minimal false positives.

4.3   Framework

The mechanism consists in introducing a reputation/certification scheme for Internet providers. Participation by providers is voluntary, based on cost-benefit analysis. A CA is a new institution to coordinate the certification scheme. The providers that choose to join pay a subscription fee, and are called *certified providers*, and those that do not, are called *noncertified providers*. Certified providers will be bound to pay compensation to remote providers that receive malicious traffic originating from their users. They will also be bound to pay compensation to their own customers who receive malicious traffic, regardless of the source.

Under such a system with voluntary subscription to certification, certified providers tend to degrade ("degrade" can range from delaying the traffic to blocking it altogether, the notion being to provide an inferior service quality for uncertified traffic) all incoming traffic from uncertified providers, and do not control incoming traffic from other certified providers. For outgoing traffic, certified providers will filter all outgoing traffic to other certified providers to minimize penalty payments, but will not filter outgoing traffic to uncertified providers. Noncertified providers, on the other hand, will only filter incoming traffic. The analytical results discussed by Zhao et al. (2006) and Parameswaran et al. (2007) further explain these strategies. The net result is a partial grouping of the Internet into a certified and a noncertified network, where, in the former, certified domains exchange "secure" traffic and attract more security conscious users who still have access to the entire Internet. In the latter part of the network, users are subject to more risk-prone traffic, and are getting a lower QoS access to the certified domains. The partial fragmentation will not undermine global connectivity. The QoS received by the uncertified networks would be less. The certification mechanism provides incentives for controlling *both* incoming and outgoing traffic.

4.3.1   CA

The CA is the institution that sets the subscription fee at a level to induce an optimal number and class of providers to join. The CA does not directly engage in filtering or enforcement, nor is it a network provider. Subscription fee does not imply that the CA has to be a for-profit entity.

It is merely the device used to screen providers into different groups based on their security profile. A higher subscription fee can only attract providers with well-secured traffic, as others would not find it profitable. *The CA is not to be confused with certificate authorities used in encryption schemes.*

Besides managing certificates, the CA also maintains a reputation system—certification itself is a reputation system—storing and publicizing reputation information about providers. The CA can also set up distributed dummy mail servers as honey pots to trap spam and monitor source providers, as a means of calibrating security levels that providers can use as guidelines in certification choices. The CA can also potentially use such information to monitor certified providers; however, the mechanism is designed such that a certified provider would stand to lose heavily if it let its security policies lapse. The CA's role is not to monitor or police SPs.

The CA may be a nonprofit agency, or a for-profit organization. There are feasible examples of both models in the current coordination of the Internet. A nonprofit agency leads to *superior* results in our model.

It is important to note that the division into certified and uncertified networks does not imply fragmentation: every user has the choice to switch to a different class of provider, and every provider has the choice to reverse its certification decision; also, we visualize some users and providers maintaining presence in both classes. What the framework does is to provide a less risky environment for the value-conscious users.

The segregation is not an active division of the network, rather, only in reputations, and perceived functionality. Nor is the division into a private, closed-off network; the proposal's focus is on the public Internet.

4.3.2 Issues

For the provider, the additional cost of outbound control is compensated by elimination of the need for filtering traffic from other certified providers, the potential blocking of uncertified traffic, the efficiency gains in reduction of spam, and the ability to charge a premium to users. Furthermore, outbound control measures will be more effective, and in the long run less expensive. Computational overhead of outbound control is compensated partially by the lack of inbound control; you are dealing with a much smaller volume of traffic. Also, there is an inherent tradeoff with the gain in security.

A key issue is whether a significant number of providers will sign up. Note that the CA can set the fee depending on the distribution of different classes of providers so as to induce an optimal number to join. If a group of providers decided to stay uncertified, they will gradually start losing customers due to eroding value of communications. The system builds a continuous pressure on providers to get certified.

Attacks against outbound filtering are likely to be limited in effectiveness: as both the CA and SPs would be monitoring the filtering performance, such attacks would be detected quickly, before they can subvert the reputation system. Any large-scale failure of certified providers would simply lead users to switch to other mail providers temporarily, and will not be catastrophic. Certified SPs could be targets for attacks: but certification itself indicates that these providers are capable of defending against such attacks, so their effectiveness may be limited; and the insurance scheme is also meant to address such possibilities.

Any attack whose source is identified will lead to the certified source provider being held liable, regardless of whether it was initiated by a human customer, or a zombie node. This is important because today remotely directed zombies constitute a major source of attacks (Huang et al., 2006). Insurance or performance bonds could smooth out SP payouts due to such liability.

Our model assumes that providers cannot continue to be profitable without making security investments at all; as in today's network environment users will simply defect. In such investments, we also assume outbound control investments as being more efficient, reflecting the aforementioned reasoning and expert opinion. We assume that providers try to maximize profits from users, net of their compensation payments, cost of security, and cost of subscription. We also assume that users gain the most value by being able to communicate with the most number of other users, and lose value for each spam message received.

5 Model

The analytical model assumes that SPs may belong to a "high" or "low" type. The relative extent of malicious traffic originating from high types is low, and the low types tend to have a higher share of malicious activity in their outgoing traffic. Note that the analytical model for certification can be applied to a continuum of types; the simplification into two discrete types is for ease of exposition, and is in line with common practice in similar game theoretical models. The type of each SP is not known, and part of the intention of the mechanism design is revelation of this information. The distribution of types is assumed to be known. The distribution of ISPs' types is exogenously given and is common knowledge. A customer stands to gain by communicating with all other customers. ISPs can implement two types of controls, controls at inbound traffic and those at outbound traffic. An ISP can choose to invest in either or both. We assume that investing in outbound filtering is more efficient, and use quadratic cost functions. For mathematical details of the signaling game and proofs, see appendix and Parameswaran et al. (2007) and Zhao et al. (2006).

In this mechanism, ISPs voluntarily choose whether to subscribe to the CA. The CA charges a subscription fee for each ISP. Certified ISPs must pay compensation proportional to the quantity of spam received to their customers and other certified ISPs.

In this setting, SPs must make strategy choices on whether to subscribe to certification, in addition to pricing their services accounting for both the subscription and penalty dues. Each provider chooses strategies for controlling inbound and outbound traffic based on its beliefs about the distribution of types in the Internet, and the respective payoffs expected from each strategy (Mas-Colell et al., 1995). All providers that belong to the same type adopt similar strategies.

The CA can induce three mutually exclusive and collectively exhaustive scenarios: only high-type ISPs subscribe to the CA; all ISPs subscribe to the CA; and no ISP subscribes to the CA. We use backward induction to solve the game, and discuss preliminary results later.

5.1 *Separating scenario: only high-type SPs subscribe to the CA*

Certified providers screen all outbound traffic to other certified providers, to minimize penalties. They have no incentive to control for the outbound traffic toward uncertified providers. Certified providers also do not engage in filtering inbound traffic from other certified providers, as certification insures them against any potential loss. Results show that certified providers block all traffic from noncertified providers. The uncertified providers have no incentive in controlling outbound traffic, but they do invest in inbound control due to observability of the investment (see Fig. 1).

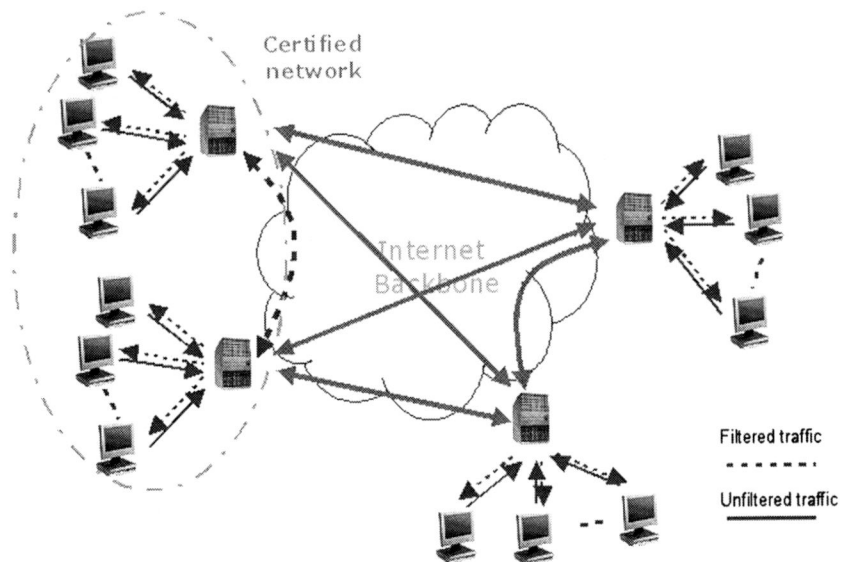

Fig. 1. The certification program for ISPs.

5.2   Pooling scenario: all ISPs subscribe to the CA

Every SP invests in outbound control, since all traffic goes to certified providers. Since all sources are bound to pay compensation, no provider invests in inbound control. The primary focus of investment is shifted from ingress to egress, thus rendering control measures far more effective.

5.3   Pooling scenario: no ISP gets certified

If customers and ISPs believe that no ISP subscribes to the CA, the pricing and investment strategies are the same as when no CA exists. This outcome is dominated by previous two scenarios.

5.4   Equilibrium

With a profit maximizing CA, different equilibria may be shown to exist depending on the proportion of high type providers in the network. Note that the model can accommodate a nonprofit maximizing CA without any loss of the potential welfare gain (reduced overall spam); such a CA would set subscription fees to induce optimal subscription levels (which may mean inducing separation) in a way to maximize welfare. The case of profit maximizing CA is explored to demonstrate that the CA can be a private entity, similar to domain name administrators, and that the model is not dependent on a benevolent agent running certification.

The certification mechanism yields higher social surplus—signifying less net losses due to security problems—compared to the regular Internet, when all providers subscribe. When only the high types subscribe, this comparison depends on the actual proportion of high providers in the system. It can be shown that the mechanism leads to imporved security in all cases.

6   A divided Internet?

Certification and deliberate degradation of traffic from noncertified users raises the question of creating a digital divide between certified and uncertified networks. A related issue is if only a small number of providers were certified, they may not be able to afford to degrade all uncertified traffic, which would affect most of their users. A critical mass is crucial, but can the system get there from a cold start? This is an issue that needs experimental research.

It is also important to note that large SPs currently actively filter user traffic, and engage in blocking or differentiating based on the types of traffic. Many do this in response to piracy concerns; but more importantly, the entry of SPs into content provision and converged local loop services (triple play) have started momentum toward tiered service and selective filtering, further emphasized by interference from government agencies in various countries. Some degree of discrimination and segregation already happen; and as spam becomes a grave issue, outright blocking of some networks as well as large-scale defections by customers could lead to further rifts in the network. Having an organized incentive-based reputation and certification system would allow blocking and divisions to be transparent, systematic, predictable, thus, giving users sufficient choice and ability to connect to their peers using alternate providers if necessary.

7 Insurance

Cyber-insurance has been touted as a market-based solution to managing IT security. It is suggested that cyber-insurance can reduce Internet risk faced by IT-intensive industries and has the potential to improve system benefits (Kesan et al., 2005; Schneier, 2002; Yurcik and Doss, 2002). Current research focuses on the impact of cyber-insurance markets on corporate IT security investment (Böhme, 2005; Kesan et al., 2005, Ogut et al., 2005). Insurance can be introduced as a further incentive for certification, since insurance can mitigate the liability incurred by certified providers. Certification makes a provider eligible for group insurance, where the certified SPs together form the group. As penalty payments by any individual certified provider triggers insurance payoffs and consequent rise in premiums, there will be community pressure on individual providers to invest in security practices that minimize problems in outgoing traffic. In effect, such pressure acts as an additional incentive. In a system that faces losses due to hazardous incidents, such incidents may arise from inherent randomness, or by systematic malicious activity. Randomness could be due to human errors in configuration or software glitches, for example. Incentives from certification and insurance can drive investments to eliminate systematic malicious activity within the certified network, but not entirely eliminate the risk of liability payments. Insurance will be used to cover the residual risk, which ideally should only be that from the random incidents. A potential issue cited in relation to group insurance schemes is the possibility of moral hazard leading to individual participants free-riding on the community; that is, the availability of insurance possibly diluting incentives for investment against security incidents. Remedial measures may be taken by designing optimal deductibles as suggested by Rothschild and Stiglitz (1976) and Shavell (1979).

We have developed a group insurance model for SPs working in conjunction with the certification mechanism. A group insurance model will pool premiums from certified providers, and will cover liabilities according to clearly defined scope of what is covered; this will lead to peer pressure on certified providers to keep premiums in check, quantification and monitoring efforts from insurance organization to standardize assessment of types and extent of damage, and will in turn provide users with protection from damage as insurance from SPs cascade to the user level. Insurance companies will require assessments for use of standard Internet security measures before approving customers, and reassessments as part of the adjustment process before approving claims. Such assessment and adjustment can be aided by the certification mechanism, which will provide ongoing information relevant to those processes, calibrated by independent third parties.

8 Incentive mechanisms in the context of technical antispam

8.1 Review of technical approaches

The following discussion focuses only on aspects of technical antispam approaches relevant to this chapter. In the following, *sender* refers to the node that sends mail, and *author* refers to the individual that is sending mail.

A possible classification of antispam techniques is in terms of what entity is the focus of filtering: thus, we can identify three trends—content filtering, sender authentication, and digital signature-based methods. Challenge-response systems may be identified as a fourth category.

8.1.1 Filtering approaches
8.1.1.1 Content filtering.
Here, the focus is the message itself, which is analyzed for likelihood of its being spam, and approved, rejected or quarantined accordingly. Though some content filtering tools analyze only the message headers, today the majority of them analyze the message body as well.

Traditional filtering tools use a large collection of rules to assign scores to messages. Many of the rules are based on occurrence of suspicious words in the mail, or in the headers. If the cumulative score from rules exceeds a threshold, the message is classified as spam. In such tools, the values and weights of scores assigned by rules, the aggregation formulae, and choice of thresholds may vary, and use some form of trial-and-error. Objections have been raised as to the potentially arbitrary and subjective nature of scoring and ranking, further complicated by the secrecy of such formulae.

A spam filter can generate false negatives and false positives. A false negative is a spam message that was classified as legitimate, and false positive is a legitimate mail that was classified as spam. The former is expected to happen as no spam filter is known to operate with perfect accuracy, and the cost incurred is not significant if the numbers are very low. However, in the case of false positives, even one can prove costly to the user. Some developers think of reducing false negatives as improving the filtering algorithm's effectiveness, whereas addressing false positives as removing bugs in the program (e.g., see Paul Graham).

As filters try to improve their rejection rate of spam, false positives also tend to increase; this is especially true of rule-based systems. As the number of rules mount, the potential for innocuous messages that happened to contain certain expressions to be tagged as spam increases, and the author may be tagged as "spammy." Further, rules may frequently involve generalizations: for example, residential or university computers may be given higher likelihood scores for being "spammy." A particular problem in spam is the presence of "zombie" nodes, which are nodes that have been hijacked by remote hackers, and are running code in the background waiting for remote commands. Zombie nodes are heavily used to originate spam. If a class of nodes is thought to be more likely to be zombie nodes, users sending legitimate messages from such nodes may end up scoring high in spam likelihood.

Spammers have been known to innovate message generation to elude such filters, and most of the time, the new rules put in are in response to increased bulk mail of specific types getting through the filter. This leads to a situation where the filter software is essentially reacting to spammers.

8.1.1.2 Bayesian content filtering.   Here, the Bayes' rule is used to estimate the probability of a message being spam based on the occurrence of specific words in the message. The software uses legitimate and spam messages to refine the probabilities, and may use a training set at the outset. Its ability to learn leads to improved performance, and the lack of human intervention in determining what scores and weights are to be assigned to individual words eliminates the subjective aspect. Some such tools allow the user to refine the filtering by indicating errors it made, as well as providing keywords or addresses which definitely indicate legitimate mail (or spam). Such filters improve performance, reduce rule-based lookup operations, reduce false positives, and most importantly, the user-level customization defeats generalized spamming strategies.

To realize its full potential, Bayesian filters will need to operate at the individual customization level, rather than for each domain or sender. The effectiveness of the technology depends on where it is deployed, by who, and to filter what type of messages. An incentive system can direct the locus of deployment effectively.

8.1.1.3 Locus of deployment.   Content filtering is deployed by e-mail SPs and some ISPs, primarily for received mail. Very few are known to do such filtering for mail originating from their domain. Organizations invest in enterprise level content-filtering tools. The more sophisticated individual users deploy content filters at their mail client. Some mail clients bundle content filtering. In all these cases, the primary focus is received mail, and the objective is to minimize the number of spam messages showing up in the inbox, with some also emphasizing elimination of false positives. An added emphasis on filtering outgoing mail would significantly reduce incidence of spam.

8.1.2 Sender authentication

In sender authentication, the focus of filtering is the mail server that is sending the mail.

Blacklists: The oldest form of sender authentication was to use blacklists of known spammer domains, with lists such as domain name service blacklist (DNSBL). With the increased use of fake addresses, rapid changing of addresses, and excessive use of zombies and relay services, the reliability of this method in isolation was rendered limited. Blacklists are today used in conjunction with content filtering tools. There are public blacklists as well as private blacklists.

Whitelists: A whitelist is a collection of sender addresses (or author addresses if the list is deployed by individual users) authorized as legitimate senders. A whitelist allows mail to be passed through without filtering, reducing overhead and chance of false positives. Whitelists are also used in conjunction with other methods. With relay services and Trojans and other malware using legitimate users' mail clients to send spam, the effectiveness of whitelists by themselves is limited.

8.1.2.1 Designated sender schemes.
Sender authentication methods focus on the headers of the message in trying to authenticate the sender instead of focusing on the contents of the message to identify if it is spam. Spammers frequently use fake addresses, leading to the notion that authentication can filter out a significant number of them. The domain designates specific nodes as authorized mail senders, and publishes this information. When mail is received purportedly from such a domain, the receiver can compare the originating node address with the list of designated senders, and reject the mail if sender is not authenticated. When DNS records are used by domains to publish such information, two advantages are gained: the responsibility of advertising who are authenticated senders is decentralized to each mail SP; and mail receiving node can verify sender before actual message is received (since the headers will be transmitted prior).

Various early efforts such as designated mail protocol (DMP) and reverse MX consolidated into sender policy framework (SPF), currently the best-known sender verification protocol that uses DNS. Some companies that use or support SPF are AOL, Earthlink, Sophos, Symantec, Brightmail, Ciphertrust, MailArmory, and MailFrontier. Microsoft's Caller ID initially developed separately, but then the two converged (Sender ID), so that domains have to advertise only one time instead of once for each protocol. Sender ID verifies sender's IP address against that of the listed owner of the domain the mail is coming from. CSV is another such protocol.

SPF follows the open-source model, whereas Sender ID follows a more proprietary model. Both SPF and Sender ID require significant additions to the DNS at sender domains to identify which nodes are authorized to send mail from that domain, and also additions to mail servers to verify sender identity. Since DNS was designed with an entirely different intent, some observers object to its being used this way, in particular, the use of XML.

8.1.2.2 Locus of deployment. For sender authentication methods in general, deployment is by e-mail SPs, usually for received mail. Google uses both SPF and DomainKeys, and Yahoo! Uses DomainKeys, whereas Microsoft uses Sender ID. Today, many of the leading ISPs advertise authenticated sender information to their DNS records. Some individual users add their own digital signatures to mail.

8.1.3 Digital signatures

The main alternative besides these, DomainKeys from Yahoo!, is an encryption-based scheme. DKIM is also an example of a digital signature based scheme. These are frequently classified as part of sender authentication schemes, but they authenticate the messages as well. The message is signed with the digital signature, whose public key may be retrieved from the sending domain, and used to verify it. So long as the private key is not compromised, this can rule out spoofing, forging or relay services and can authenticate author and message.

Although the sender authentication schemes like SPF and CSV make an authentication decision before the message is transmitted, signature-based methods (DomainKeys, Sender ID) must receive the message first, as you need to get the signed message to verify it.

In practice today, although a consensus is yet to emerge about the choice of a specific sender authentication and digital signature method and there are criticisms of each method, both providers and vendors have started using a combination of them, and reported numbers show significant ability to catch spam as well as other malicious traffic. However, overall numbers still show rising spam percentages. Since zombie machines are the favored sources of spam, a spammer can potentially use a compromised node in a trusted domain to send spam.

8.1.4 Challenge–response schemes

Challenge–response schemes involve each mail leading to a challenge mail sent to the sender, which requires a relatively effortless response, but one which becomes expensive when done in bulk numbers. Each valid response leads to the sender being added to a whitelist at the receiver, avoiding further challenges. These systems find very limited deployment and face criticism both from technical and social viewpoints. In general, challenge-response (C-R) systems could work if all participants meticulously followed all its recommended steps; but in practice, that is unlikely to ever happen, and meanwhile, C-R is likely to significantly degrade the value of e-mail as a service, its immediacy, convenience, reach, and simplicity. C-R systems that use return path information can lead to backscatter, which supports the case for filtering outgoing mail.

> *Greylists*: Rule-based scoring systems frequently end up with messages that are suspected, but not certain of, being spam. In such cases, the sender is greylisted and the mail rejected temporarily, to be accepted if the sender resends it. Spammers are unlikely to resend the same message. Greylists are very similar to challenge–response and can cause similar loss of utility.

8.2   Incentive issues related to technical approaches

As mentioned earlier, most deployments are focused on filtering incoming mail. At present, the incentive structure is that the customer is who you cater to, and if the customer is receiving the least spam, the provider gains reputation, and customer retention. ISPs as well as organizations could potentially filter outgoing mail as well, as well as take far more active measures to control outgoing spam. Such control can reduce load on the network, computational cost of filtering, and significantly shrink the scope of free operations of the spammer. For example, providers could actively track zombie nodes in their network and initiate cleanup, help customers secure their machines, actively engage in removing "spammy" customers, or engaging in limited blocking such as Port 25 blocking, mine outgoing mail for patterns such as bulk sending or sudden spikes, sample and audit outgoing mail, limit forwarding of mail in terms of the number of steps and type of headers used.

It is significant to note that statistics for the last few years show alarming increase in total spam, whereas filter vendors claim significant improvement in performance. On the one hand, we have statistics that show more than 90% of all e-mail as being spam, and on the other hand, filter vendor statistics of close to 99% filtering. That clearly indicates that while inboxes may be showing less spam, there is much more spam traveling the core networks. If such spam (and spammers) were to be actively controlled at the origin domain, they would not travel and clog up the network, only to be filtered out at the destination. But the fact is that there is no direct incentive to the SP in what is largely perceived as a social benefit. Meanwhile, the spammers and content-filtering industry generate revenues, and enterprises, users, and network providers lose wealth in security investments, lost value of e-mail and congestion.

The fact that spam filtering industry has incentives that are almost in sync with spamming community in that the worse the spam problem gets, the more organizations are forced to invest in spam filters, is of interest. If spam were to disappear overnight, this billion dollar industry would lose its reason for existence. Proponents of reliable sender verification have been known to argue that the industry favors content filtering as being more lucrative.

Some related issues of sender authentication include intellectual property and market power issues, with some providers taking proprietary routes toward sender identification, which is also an indirect way of "hijacking" e-mail and making it a private product. Indeed, a strong motivation for an incentive scheme is to preclude the possibility of some organizations and SPs moving to a fragmented network, where they deploy their own secure e-mail that has evolved into a proprietary product.

8.3 Implications of certification on technical approaches

Sender authentication schemes can work very effectively if certain requirements are met: a significant number of senders must participate in the authentication scheme and advertise designated senders; and such providers must ensure that outgoing spam from these senders is strictly controlled. Leading mail SPs have been using sender authentication information in spam filtering. However, in the absence of the latter requirement, such schemes are subject to forged identities. The recipient provider would still need to expend resources in exhaustive filtering of mail from authenticated domains. Even some of the proponents of authentication schemes have been quoted as saying their overall effectiveness in reducing spam is limited.

On the other hand, if the providers participating in authentication were to filter outgoing spam to set standards, multiple benefits can ensue. The congestion on the network will be eased; spammers will need to switch providers and will eventually find fewer and fewer choices; and recipient domains will need to do less filtering. However, there is no incentive for these providers to engage in outgoing spam control. United States is the second highest source of spam in the world, and among the top ten of all network providers in generation of spam are some very well known and large providers.

This is where the certification scheme comes in. It provides incentives to certified providers to control outgoing spam, and ties such control to penalties for actual spam received at remote domains. The design of the incentive system ensures that the provider finds it in its interest to participate voluntarily, and only the providers who do not have a prohibitive cost of controlling outgoing spam are likely to sign up. More importantly, certification takes much stronger steps than authentication schemes: it introduces a partial segregation where the ability of customers of noncertified providers to communicate is limited. In turn, this represents a significant impact on revenues of providers, as well as utility to customers, motivating providers even more strongly to stay certified, and for spam-conscious customers to switch to certified providers. The same type of seeding effect can work to incrementally propagate such a scheme. Thus, certification requires the provider to: participate in a sender authentication scheme, commit to minimizing outgoing spam, commit to a set of prescribed security policies, including expelling spammers, port blocking, actively engaging in zombie cleanups and content filtering, and paying penalties when other certified domains receive spam from the certified provider. Thus, certification can effectively leverage sender authentication schemes: it gives strong and well-defined incentives for providers to join, and ensures participation actually reduces spam, not just forged identities. The strict requirement to control outgoing spam can lead to certified providers not filtering mail received from other certified providers; so in effect, the focus of investment is shifted to outbound spam control as against inbound and the providers are not substantially increasing their security investment. For uncertified mail, strict filtering will still be deployed. Thus, certification may be viewed as encasing sender authentication and content filtering schemes into a formal incentive structure that is sustainable and decentralized.

Viewed from the perspective of the economic model, certification requires two criteria to be met for its feasibility: a sufficient number of providers getting certified, and an ability to verify sender identity. In the absence of the former, the loss of value to the noncertified user is not significant in being cut off from only a small number of users; this would depend on a few large providers initially signing up and creating a seeding effect. Sender authentication mechanisms nicely complement certification in providing the ability for sender verification.

The certified provider may reject or filter (according to the optimal strategy indicated) all mail from uncertified providers; and for mail purportedly from certified domains, it will verify the sender, and reject all mail failing this step. All legitimate mail from certified domains is accepted without further filtering. Means such as greylisting, challenge–response, and spam filtering in general, impose a delay on mail, robbing legitimate mail of its value. In this context, certification is important, as certified mail may proceed with minimal delay and filtering.

Filtering would use a combination of techniques listed earlier for maximum effectiveness. Meanwhile, such a provider also continually filters its outgoing mail, and works to follow prescribed policies for securing its own network and customers. The CA may mediate advertising of designated sender and public key information, and engage in audits of certified providers for outgoing spam, and security profiles of their customers.

A standard criticism goes thus: if a provider is willing to be certified, that implies it accepts the risk of that certification being revoked. Which in turn implies that the provider will try to prevent this from happening, by blocking its customers who generate spam, as outgoing spam is what will lose the provider their certification. So the provider is demonstrating a willingness to block its spammers. If that willingness existed, the provider could simply block these spammers, and there would be no spam problem that makes certification necessary. However, a certification scheme ties an economic incentive to motivate such willingness to block spam, and takes that further by relating spam sent to penalties incurred. That is also a more realistic approach than a blanket revocation of certification (unless of course some threshold is breached). In other words, what such arguments claim is that the provider has no incentive to block its own spammers, which is true. And therein lies the need to furnish just such an incentive scheme, which can complement the technological protocol, and make participation in it more than a nominal exercise.

9 Reputation and audit

Incentive systems for providers may devise and employ some form of reputation for providers that indicate their historic performance in proportion of outgoing mails being spam. Such schemes would need an incentive structure that can collect reliable historic information, generate accurate and trusted reputations, and can provide incentives to providers to improve and sustain their reputations. Furthermore, providers should have incentives to use the reputation measure of other providers in making choices about filtering mail received from them, implying that use of such measures should lead to palpable improvements in spam filtering performance.

Some form of technological implementations of reputations (without any associated incentive structure) is used by some filtering tools and services, third party audit services, and by some e-mail SPs. SenderScore is an example of a system that determines and assigns reputation scores to domains. Google uses its own reputation scoring system in mail filtering, and claims significant improvement in performance due to its use. In a broad sense, black and white lists may be said to be crude reputation systems. The statistical rule engines used in content filtering software may also include dynamically updated reputation lists. Evaluating the probability of a mail being spam based on reputation should ideally be done after sender authentication, since we need to be confident of sender identity before we can use the corresponding reputation for a given sender. So also, content filtering as well as other schemes like greylisting or challenge–response may follow this stage, with one obvious approach being to subject only those mails which have not already been clearly ruled out as spam or legitimate to further steps of evaluation. Users should have the option to mark false negatives and positives so as to improve the reputation computations; but this feature should anyway be present as a way to improve performance of filtering tools in general, over time.

Reputation systems used in practice do not give any incentives for domains to improve their reputation. The incentive structure anchored around certification can be extended to incorporate a reputation system as well. In a crude sense, certification by itself is a reputation system, as certified providers are signaling higher security and investments, in effect, a higher reputation than the uncertified providers. However, that is a binary classification that is not rich enough. What it does have is an incentive system that motivates sustaining high reputations and penalizes loss of reputation.

The certification system can add a score-based reputation measure for certified providers. This measure can be based on data about received mail aggregated across other certified providers, and data from honeypots (dummy nodes set to receive and analyze mail, set up to entrap spam) and random sampling set up by CA or its designated agents. If historic information were to be collected from providers, incentives for truthful revelation will also be an issue. The CA can conduct random audits to monitor such information. A better solution may be for the authority to audit outgoing mail from providers. Such an audit system, properly designed, can address incentive issues, generate reputation scores, and also aid in arbitration of penalty settlement in the original certification scheme.

Since the certification system provides incentives for individual certified providers to minimize their outgoing spam, and requires deployment of prescribed policies to control outgoing spam, a reputation system anchored on certification will have providers working to maintain and improve their reputation, and the likelihood of disparity among their customers in spamming behavior is reduced. Further, the penalties, and certification status itself, could be made contingent on reputation scores, providing direct incentives for improving reputations.

The CA can publish reputation scores of certified providers, which will serve for effective use of the scores in mail filtering, and since the authority is trusted, this public information will signal quality of individual providers to customers and other providers alike. Loss of reputation can lead to defections and loss of value, and act as an incentive for providers to maintain reputation.

Problems with mail forwarding and list mails can be addressed with technological workarounds just as in the case of sender authentication: by following best practice policies in writing headers, and utilizing systems like the sender rewrite scheme, all in conjunction with whitelists of legitimate forwarders.

A potential problem with a reputation system can be that a domain that has built up a good reputation and is going out of business may have a strong incentive for spamming behavior in the last period as the effect on its reputation may matter no more, and gains from spamming may be a strong incentive. One solution is to introduce a market for trading reputations, which allows exiting players to trade reputations for gains rather than exploit them.

A combination of certification, insurance, reputation, and audit can form the basis for a well laid out incentive structure that induces voluntary participation, and collective welfare improvement. Deploying technological solutions within such a framework is essential to ensure maximum effectiveness of such solutions, and to provide a sustainable basis for rolling out newer and improved filtering tools. In particular, it can get providers to filter outgoing spam, which is where the content filtering tools become most effective in their impact on overall spam, and where filtering should focus.

10   Social computing and security

Social Computing is rapidly becoming a major portion of the Internet, and for many regular users, their primary or most frequent way of interacting with the Internet. Networks like MySpace, FaceBook, LinkedIn, or YouTube have come to be where most user activity is concentrated. They are domains of trust that, once breached can be highly vulnerable to malicious activity including spamming.

Both network and social issues related to security affect social computing. Network security issues are similar to what happens elsewhere in the Internet, with some qualifying aspects. Social online networks create a partition within the Internet; although the communities are not closed in technological or social sense, frequently, generalized tools for security miss out on addressing them or their specific traits.

Being highly decentralized, and easy to access, social online networks present high risk of spamming and other malicious activity. Exchange of multimedia and active content is a highlight of many such communities, and members of the community trust other members in accessing such content, even though in many cases members may be using online identities and for all practical purposes, anonymous. The ability to inject spurious content, or compromise user nodes into becoming zombies, is significant. These platforms bring in their own viral aspects to information dissemination, which can aid the spammer. Indeed, white hackers have been known to inject spurious content into networks that engage in piracy or other suspect activity to corrupt and degrade their performance.

In effect, the Web 2.0 tools used by social online networks create client side computing environments, which are insecure and could play a significant role in two ways. First, the cracker can use this to access and manipulate the user computer; and second, the platform can be used to initiate attacks directed at other nodes. Potentially, a multimedia page from

MySpace may be acting as the launch pad for a zombie node, and the high degree of community interaction may see this page being visited by many in a short time.

The threat of such client-side code can also extend to the servers hosting social networks, as the client code is given permission to access server resources. However restricted that access is, it in effect is a door opened to the public domain to access the server, and that is all that is required for resourceful attackers. To make matters worse, the code used at the client may be open source script, and authentication for server access by the code minimal.

We can see that security problems at social online networks involve both potential losses to the networks themselves, and to the Internet in general by way of attacks originating or disseminating through these communities. Both types of risks are amplified by relatively high proportion of less security-aware users, focus on trust and sharing of content, and presence of active content. This increase in risk is due to what are defining traits of social computing; so the remedy is to provide additional mechanisms to manage this risk. This should be the responsibility of the platform provider.

If providers differ in their level of investment in security for social networks, users are likely to observe the resulting difference in security, and may switch. Providers would prefer to be able to signal their commitment level and security profile to potential users; and users would prefer to be able to choose providers that match their security requirements. Certification of mail SPs may be extended to social computing networks, where certified status implies that a minimum required set of policies are put in place, and zombies and malicious code are actively cleaned up. Moreover, such providers commit to being responsible for any malicious code their members may get through using their system, as well as malicious code originating from their platform and arriving at other domains. Since social computing is dependent on network effects, the threat of being cut off from other networks is a strong incentive for participation.

In social computing, certification of providers can have associated, equally important benefit. Today, the biggest question about these platforms is how their anonymity allows criminals to masquerade under innocuous identities and target unsuspecting victims; the presence of a large number of children and teenagers making this an urgent concern for parents and communities. It is not surprising that crime is present in these networks; they are social environments, and society's phenomena show up there, albeit in an exaggerated way, because some of the controls and limitations of conventional society are absent online.

The communities have been concerned enough that some schools have banned *MySpace* access and parents have tried to filter it; however, both bans and filters continue to be easily defeated. It is not just young users who are at risk; adults are targeted for identity thefts or confidence tricks.

Certification of providers can require them to put in stringent safeguards to monitor, prevent, and respond to any criminal activity. Although this goes beyond the domain of technology-related issues, the introduction of an incentive system based on certification provides a vehicle for assigning incentives to address an equally important problem of social crime as well.

11 Cyber espionage and cyberwarfare

Military leadership in the United States (and presumably elsewhere) have now set a high priority on defending cyberspace from threats to national security. The USAF already treats cyberspace on par with air and space as a domain where it seeks dominance (Grant, 2008). Discussions mention activity originating from specific countries targeting America's military and industrial infrastructure. In February 2007, defense officials stated that these attacks had reached force-on-force, full-campaign levels. In April 2007, the highly wired country of Estonia that uses the cyber-infrastructure for many of the governance operations (possibly much more so than any other country), suffered a denial-of-service attack that lasted long and crippled critical infrastructure. Tensions with Russia immediately preceding this event led to many observers suggesting the attack originated from Russia. In most such attacks, it is hard, if not impossible to prove participation or complicity by other governments. So defense becomes the first priority. According to the Frontline documentary, "the critical infrastructure of the United States—including electrical power, finance, telecommunications, health care, transportation, water, defense and the Internet—is highly vulnerable to cyber attack. Fast and resolute mitigating action is needed to avoid national disaster" (see Cyberwar, www.pbs.org).

From the early days of the Internet, espionage activities have existed. Moonlight Maze is a name denoting a top-secret forensic investigation by the federal government into some outsider systematically stealing information from Pentagon systems, including ARPANET nodes with a high degree of sophistication. Reports suggest that the source was traced to a mainframe computer in the former Soviet Union, but that was not sufficient information to assign responsibility to either specific individuals or institutions. Today, attacks can include phishing, which would attempt to make targets yield sensitive information by appearing to be legitimate probes, such as contractual discussions. Targets may be industrial or military. Traditional warfare has always included dissemination of misleading information; the Internet allows such activities to be conducted with more ease, from remote locations, and with increased effect. For example, the echo chamber effect of Internet can be leveraged by injecting false news stories into legitimate news agencies.

Complicating the issue is the fact that modern armed forces increasingly use the cyber-infrastructure in waging operations; this may include launching missiles from remote locations using coordinates that are electronically transmitted, harnessing sensor data from enemy terrain for use as operational information, and using online maps and social software to chart operations of patrols. Ability to interfere with any such system can allow a potential opponent to disastrously alter operational plans. The lack of any concept similar to sovereign borders makes it hard to impose any international laws of conduct in cyberspace.

Organized, systematic attacks are now prevalent not only in international politics but also in private business as well, according to the SANS institute. Organizations are known to hire hackers to steal information from other organizations, often counterparts in some ongoing negotiations (Hines, 2008). It is further noted that the awareness and defense levels of industries are fairly low to nonexistent to effectively counter such incursions. Frequently, it is federal law enforcement agencies investigating trails of attackers they track that find stolen data from industry and inform concerned businesses that their data may have been stolen, by then it is too late. Many such attacks into United States come from offshore, lesser known, domains. Thus, cyber-warfare is not merely among nations of the world, it is also among corporations of the world; a terrifying prospect for businesses that increasingly digitize their data and put it in cyberspace. In both circumstances, even when large corporations or the U.S. federal government deploy massive resources to track down, prevent, and prosecute attacks, identification or prosecution of responsible individuals or agencies has not taken place. Most investigations stop at being able to track originating domains, or nodes. So efforts evolve into hacker-against-cracker, prevention, and counter-offensives. Indeed, in the general context of Internet security, investigations into some of the notorious attacks such as Nimda, Slammer, or CodeRed have never been resolved as to the identity of the attacker, despite enormous amount of damage inflicted. Thus, on the one hand, it becomes more critical for sound operation of economies and nations to have some predictable degree of security; on the other hand, they are only able to track originating providers at best, and engaging in a shadow warfare. In this context, it makes sense to consider identifying and segregating offending providers, and doing so through a voluntary certification system that targets the real reason why ISPs are operating networks—their revenues—makes it a more feasible system than detection and enforcement. The provider either squelches local malicious activity, or its certified peers block it; in both cases, the certified users get predictable levels of security, an essential requirement for both businesses and governments.

12 Public policy and law

Legal approaches have been sought in United States and the European Union to combat spam. Today, Internet law, spam, and security are a key focus issue among legal scholars. The CAN-SPAM Act of 2003 (Federal Trade Commission (FTC), 2005), enforced by the FTC is the primary legal instrument for spam control in the United States. CAN-SPAM requires messages in bulk distributions to have an opt-out address and a postal address.

CAN-SPAM is criticized both on general counts of effectiveness of legislation in controlling spam, and on specific aspects of the law itself, including the lack of requiring marketers to obtain permission before sending out bulk distributed messages. Further, antispam activists contend that opt-out solutions are not effective or economically viable on the part of recipients. Some call for opt-in solutions, where bulk mail is allowed only if the user has at some point indicated willingness to receive mail.

Some reports indicate that the CAN-SPAM Act of 2003, has not had a significant influence on spam, with the rate of spam going up, and the percentage of mail that is CAN-SPAM compliant being very low (Grant, 2004). A small number of enforcement cases have come to court, and a larger number of suits have been brought forth by ISPs, based on the act.

For any legislation, the feasibility and willingness for enforcement is the key to its effectiveness. In the case of spam in particular, this dependency on enforcement becomes critical as law by itself does not provide any motivation for spammers to be compliant. Enforcement is hard to do, as tracking down the identity of spammers is difficult. Investigators on forensic trails of spam are frequently able to track down source domains or providers, and occasionally the source node, but not the actual perpetrator. So it is hard to find culprits or prosecute cases.

The complexity of resolving jurisdictional issues and the difficulty of legal steps against spam were illustrated by the E360 Insight vs Spamhaus Project case, where E360 complained of Spamhaus including its name in a list of potential spammers, and sought damages for blocking its mail. The court awarded the damages and instructed Spamhaus not to block E360 traffic in the future. Though what occasioned the judgment was defaulting by Spamhaus, it is interesting to note that blocking spam was construed as blocking free speech and obstructing commercial activity. E360 went further in asking the court to direct Internet Corporation for Assigned Names and Numbers (ICANN) to revoke the Spamhaus domain name for nonpayment. Spamhaus had argued that being located in the United Kingdom it was not subject to jurisdiction; and ICANN indicated it has no authority to revoke the domain name. However, ICANN operates from the United States, and potentially can be subject to judgments by U.S. courts. The tension between jurisdiction over cyberspace and nations has only been getting worse, with a recent judgment actually admitting that technology has far outpaced jurisprudence. The net effect is that passage of legislation or empowerment of agencies to enforce may not be sufficient to fight spam. In a broad sense, neither technology, nor law, by themselves can completely stop spam in the near future; for technology, some level of unattainable perfection or dramatic transformation of protocols may be required; for law, it is not conceivable that cyber law and conventional law will come to resolve ambiguities and conflicts in the near future; if ever, given the decentralized and distributed nature of the Internet. Technology, law, and institutionalized incentives will need to go hand in hand: the incentives prompt appropriate deployment of technology, reducing spam; technology aids enforcement of law; and law aids sustainability of the incentive structure. In a sense, legislation and enforcement may be seen as being a type of incentive structure; and economic incentives complement them. Although the law may not be able to reach across national boundaries, or migrate its definitions of free speech or contracts or legitimate commerce to cyberspace easily, economic incentives can impact around the global network. In this respect, it is important to note that in an incentive structure, the key economic impact is not threat of penalties, rather threat of inferior service or disconnect, and losses caused by that.

One aspect of legislation and enforcement is noteworthy: the difficulty of tracking down a spammer and proving spamming activity in a court of law. What can be tracked down and proved is the origin domain, and corresponding SP. This adds to the case for providers to be certified, with certification entailing responsibility. Although even the provider may have difficulty tracking down the spammer, the provider can filter out spam originating from its domain. The problems of legislation involve not only issues of adapting conventional legal concepts to cyberspace, but also the existence of boundaries of jurisdiction, and property rights. The former become significant when spam or other problems originate offshore; even when the origin country, and possibly even the specific node can be identified, there is no legal recourse as per international or national law to ascribe blame to someone or to prosecute them. Once again, the comparison with SPs is interesting: although national or regional jurisdiction is neither clearly defined nor enforceable over the Internet, the network providers do have authority and control over their networks; a fact well recognized in the early design of the Internet in designating administrative domains, and giving each the responsibility for handling traffic inside their networks. Providers being the locus of authority and capacity for enforcement, it is rational to assign responsibility for spam control and enforcement with them.

13 Incentives for users

Since spamming behavior of individual users vary within domains, and the economic gains from sending spam accrue to individual users rather than the domains that send them, it is logical to consider extending incentive systems to the user level. However, this is very difficult to deploy as a direct incentives-for-users system, as it is a hard problem to identify and hold individual users accountable, due to fake and dynamic identities, zombie nodes, automated software, offshore accounts, etc. It would also be hard to tie penalties or other economic incentives directly to users and enforce them. The ideal incentive structure would be expulsion from the domain and legal prosecution. Law enforcement agencies do pursue spam vigorously; but, prosecution has proved difficult. In this respect, the most feasible solution is delegating responsibility to the agency most capable of enforcement of users, that is, the SPs, as discussed earlier, becomes the sensible approach. This is precisely the rationale for focusing certification and reputation systems on providers. The provider that does not control outgoing spam is anyway gaining a share of the surplus as subscription from such customers, at a high social cost. The provider can deploy a wide variety of strategies including outgoing mail filtering to control spammers, as well as work toward minimizing zombie activity, as discussed earlier. Thus, rather than explicitly devise a user-level incentive system whose results may be imperfect and come at prohibitively high cost, it is more attractive to let the incentives propagate to the users through the providers. In turn, that will motivate migration of spammers to lower reputation, uncertified providers, which would make it easier to filter spam as well as make it less economically attractive to send spam in the first place.

14   Other approaches

It is widely recognized that the source of the spam problem relates to how spammers stand to make economic gains at relatively low cost, and if their costs could be raised and their gains curtailed, the problem could be effectively addressed. Some other approaches using economic incentives have been proposed. The most notable among them suggests that each mail arriving in the inbox demands the user's attention and time, which have inherent value. To command this value, the mail sender must make a micropayment for the mail to be certified legitimate. The argument is that the micropayments will not unduly tax the regular users, but will add up to a significant cost for bulk mailers. Such a system would require micropayment tracking and settlement mechanisms and universal subscription to be effective.

15   Economic mechanisms in the context of security in general

Incentive systems anchored around trusted third parties like CA can extend their scope to controlling malicious activity in general, besides spam. Most malware cause damage by propagation over the Internet, and arrive from remote domains. The same logic as used in certification can be used to motivate providers to filter outgoing traffic for presence of malware, as well as imposing secure configurations on their users and using active blocking strategies. Indeed, a major share of malware will be cut off by the spam control infrastructure, since most malware today travel through e-mail, and most content filters check for malware as well. Filtering at the source can limit the spread of malware, and thus significantly reduce the overall costs. The pertinent issue is assessment of sources and damages in the incentive structure, which can be more tricky with malware than with mail. However, these are not intractable issues, and provider-level control of all outgoing traffic, as well as provider responsibility for their customers' secure usage, can significantly reduce malicious activity on the Internet.

Web spam is emerging as a significant issue, with fraudulent web pages taking over the role of e-mail messages. Once again, the web pages are hosted by domains, which may be required to monitor them as part of certification requirements. In general, given that the public network is an environment of multiple interacting economic agents who engage in both socially beneficial and harmful activity, an incentive-based organizational structure is essential to complement technological controls against malicious activity. And such manipulation of incentives can attack the problem of security at its origin, and will be far more effective than technologies acting alone. It is essential that the community of Internet users, providers and standards organizations recognize the significance of the role incentives must play in Internet security.

Acknowledgment

The authors would like to acknowledge National Science Foundation for support of this research (under NSF grant numbers 0831338 and 0830852).

References

Böhme, R. (2005). Cyber-insurance revisited. Workshop on the Economics of Information Security (WEIS). Available at http://www.infosecon.net/workshop/pdf/15.pdf

Cyberwar, Frontline Program on PBS. Available at http://www.pbs.org/wgbh/pages/frontline/shows/cyberwar/

Federal Trade Commission (FTC) Document. (2005). Final rules for CAN-SPAM. Available at http://www.ftc.gov/os/2005/01/050112canspamfrn.pdf

Grant, G. (2004). Is the CAN-SPAM law working? *IDG News Service, PCWorld Magazine* (January 13). Available at http://www.pcworld.com/article/id,114287-page,1/article.html

Grant, R. (2008). The dogs of web war. *AirForce Magazine* 91(1). Available at http://www.afa.org/magazine/jan2008/0108dogs.asp

Hincs, M. (2008). Cyber-espionage moves into B2B. *InfoWorld* (January 15). Available at http://www.infoworld.com/article/08/01/15/Cyber-espionage-moves-into-B2B_1.html

Huang, Y., X. Geng, A.B. Whinston (2006). Defeating DDoS attacks by fixing the incentive chain. Forthcoming in *ACM Transactions on Internet Technology.*

Kesan, J.P., R.P. Majuca, W.J. Yurcik (2005). The economic case for cyberinsurance, in: A. Chander, L. Gelman, M.J. Radin (eds.), *Securing Privacy in the Internet Age (peer-reviewed)*. Stanford University Press, Stanford.

Lichtman, D., E. Posner (2004). Holding Internet Service Providers Accountable, U Chicago Law & Economics, Olin Working Paper No. 217. (Also in Regulation, Winter 2004–2005.)

Mas-Colell, M., M.D. Whinston, J.R. Green (1995). *Microeconomics Theory*. Oxford University Press, New York, NY.

mi2g (2004). Silently Preparing for the $100 billion cyber-catastrophe risk. *News Alert*, February 16.

Ogut, H., S. Raghunathan, N.M. Menon (2005). Information Security Risk Management through Self-Protection and Insurance. Working paper, 2005. Available at http://server1.tepper.cmu.edu/ seminars/docs/Menon_CyberInsuranceOct27-2005.pdf

Parameswaran, M., X. Zhao, A.B. Whinston, F. Fang (2007). Reengineering the internet for better performance. Forthcoming in *IEEE Computer*. Available at http://crec.mccombs.utexas.edu/

Pew Internet and American Life Project (2005). Survey report on email spam. Available at http:// www.pewinternet.org/pdfs/PIP_Spam_Ap05.pdf

Ropeik, D., G. Gray (2002). *Risk: a practical guide for deciding what is really safe and what is really dangerous in the world around you*. Houghton Mifflin, Boston, MA.

Rothschild, M., J. Stiglitz (1976). Equilibrium in competitive insurance markets: an essay on the economics of imperfect information. *The Quarterly Journal of Economics* 90(4), 629–649.

Schneier, B. (2002). Computer security: it's the economics, stupid. *Conference Papers in Proceedings of the 1st Annual Workshop on Economics of Information Security*. Available at http://www.cl.cam. ac.uk/users/rja14/econws/18.doc

Shavell, S. (1979). On moral hazard and insurance. *The Quarterly Journal of Economics* 93(4), 541–562.

Talbot, D. (2006). *The Internet is Broken*. MIT Technology Review. Cover story, December 2005/ January 2006.

Thomas, R.C., P.D. Amon (2007). Incentive-Based CyberTrust—A Call to Action, Working Paper, Meritology. Available at http://meritology.com/resources/Incentive-based%20Cyber%20Trust% 20Initiative%20v3.5.pdf

Walfish, M., H. Balakrishnan, D. Karger, S. Shenker (2005). DOS: fighting fire with fire, in: *Proceedings of HotNets, Fourth Annual Workshop on Hot Topics in Networks, November*, College Park, MD, USA.

Weaver, N., V. Paxson (2004). *A Worst-Case Worm. The Third Annual Workshop on Economics and Information Security (WEIS04)*. Digital Technology Center, University of Minnesota.

Yurcik, W., D. Doss (2002). CyberInsurance: a market solution to the internet security market failure. Conference Papers in: *Proceedings of the 1st Annual Workshop on Economics of Information Security*. Available at http://www.sims.berkeley.edu/resources/affiliates/workshops/econsecurity/econws/53.pdf

Zhao, X., F. Fang, A.B. Whinston (2006), A Certification Scheme for Internet Security. Working Paper CREC, The University of Texas, Austin, TX. Available at Crec.bus.utexas.edu

Appendix (Parameswaran et al., 2007; Zhao et al., 2006)

A1 Model setup

There are N ISPs. Each ISP has n subscribed customers. We assume ISPs have two types on the basis of the ratio of the amount of potential malicious traffic to that of legitimate traffic originating from their respective customers. We refer to ISPs that send out little malicious traffic as high-type (good) and use q_h to denote the ratio of the amount of malicious traffic to that of legitimate traffic. Those ISPs who send out a large amount of malicious traffic are of low type and the ratio is q_l.

$$q_h < q_l.$$

The distribution of ISPs' types is exogenously given and is common knowledge. $\Pr(q = q_h) = \delta$ and $\Pr(q = q_l) = 1 - \delta$. A customer stands to gain by communicating with all other customers. A customer's valuation of a unit of legitimate traffic is V. We normalize the expected amount of unidirectional legitimate traffic between two customers to 1. Each customer incurs a cost, v, for a unit of malicious traffic. ISPs charge a flat access fee, p, to each customer. Thus, a customer's expected utility can be defined as $2NnV - Nnv(\delta q_h + (1 - \delta)q_l)$.[1]

ISPs can implement two types of controls, controls at inbound traffic and those at outbound traffic. An ISP can choose to invest in either or both. By investing $C_1(x)$ in controls at inbound traffic, an ISP can successfully identify a unit of malicious traffic with probability $x \in [0, 1]$ among inbound traffic. For simplicity, we assume that the probability for a unit of legitimate traffic to be erroneously marked as being malicious is 0.

$$C_1'(x) > 0; \quad C_1''(x) > 0.$$

Similarly, if an ISP invests in controls at outbound traffic, the investment needed to achieve similar degree of effectiveness, x, is $C_2(x)$.

$$C_2'(x) > 0; \quad C_2''(x) > 0.$$

$C_1(x)$ and $C_2(x)$ are the same for all ISPs. In addition, we assume $C_1(x) > C_2(x)$, $C_1'(x) > C_2'(x)$ for every $x \in [0, 1]$. That is, to reach a given level of effectiveness, the investment required in controls at inbound traffic is more than that at outbound traffic. We characterize investment cost functions as $C_1(x) = 1/2\,\alpha x^2$ and $C_2(x) = 1/2\,\beta x^2$.

$$\alpha > \beta.$$

$1/\alpha$ (or $1/\beta$) reflects the efficiency of controls.

In our mechanism, ISPs self-select whether to subscribe to the CA. The CA charges a subscription fee, t for each ISP. Certified ISPs must pay a compensation to the tune of s to their customers and other certified ISPs who received a unit of malicious traffic originating from their networks.

---

[1] The customer's utility should be $2(Nn - 1)V - Nnv(\delta q_h + (1 - \delta)q_l)$. Since N and n are much greater than 1, we simplify it to be $2NnV - Nnv(\delta q_h + (1 - \delta)q_l)$. In the rest of the chapter, we make the similar simplification.

We make the following assumptions:

Assumption 1. $\alpha \geq MvE[q]$

Assumption 2. $2MV - MvE[q] < 0$

Assumption 3. $VM + VM(1 - \delta) - MvE[q] + \dfrac{1}{2\alpha}(MvE[q])^2 > 0$

Assumption 4. $s = v$

The first assumption implies that controls at inbound traffic are less efficient than those at outbound traffic. Assumption 2 is used to ensure that ISPs cannot make a profit if they do not invest in traffic controls. This assumption reflects the reality that the problem of Internet security is so drastic that people decline to use the Internet in the absence of controls. Assumption 3 is used to ensure that low-type ISPs can make a profit by investing in controls at inbound traffic even though high-type ISPs completely block inbound traffic from low-type ISPs. Assumption 3 also implies that all ISPs can make a profit if they invest in controls at inbound traffic. Assumption 4 implies that the compensation paid to an ISP for a unit of malicious traffic is equal to the loss that the malicious traffic causes. It is fair to let ISPs be completely responsible for the loss they cause.

A2 Benchmark case

This is the base case, without the CA. A customer's willingness to pay by subscribing to ISP i's service is

$$u_{ib} = 2NnV - Nnv(1 - x_{ib})E[q] \tag{A.1}$$

Here b denotes the benchmark case. The first term of Eq. (A.1) is a customer's expected values of the communication with all Internet users. The second term is a customer's expected loss from malicious traffic. x_{ib} represents the effectiveness of ISP i's controls. By investing $C_1(x_{ib})$ in controls at inbound traffic, the malicious traffic can be detected with probability x_{ib} and the inbound malicious traffic can be reduced by $100x_{ib}$ percent in a customer's expectation. A customer's expected value is independent of her ISP's type, but affected by all ISPs' types in the network. Thus, we drop subscript i in Eq. (A.2). The price that ISPs charge is equal to the customers' willingness to pay $p_b = u_b$. We can write down an ISP's profit as follows:

$$
\begin{aligned}
\pi_b &= p_b n - C_1(x_b) \\
&= 2MV - Mv(1 - x_b)E[q] - C_1(x_b) \tag{A.2}
\end{aligned}
$$

Proposition 1. In the benchmark case, (1) ISPs' optimal investment is $x_b^* = 1/\alpha M v E[q]$; (2) ISPs' optimal price is $2NnV - NnvE[q] + 1/\alpha(NnvE[q])^2 n$; and (3) The system surplus, S_b, is

$$\left(2MV - MvE[q] + \frac{1}{2\alpha}(MvE[q])^2\right)N.$$

For all proofs, see Parameswaran et al. (2007) and Zhao et al. (2006).

A3   *The network with the certification authority deployed*

We investigate the network with the CA deployed. The CA can induce three mutually exclusive and collectively exhaustive symmetric scenarios: only high-type ISPs subscribe to the CA; all ISPs subscribe to the CA; and no ISP subscribes to the CA. We use backward induction to solve the game. We first identify the optimal strategies of ISPs' in each scenario and then analyze the CA's pricing strategy that leads to this scenario, respectively. Finally, we derive the equilibria.

A3.1   *Separating scenario: only high-type ISPs subscribe to the CA*

(1) Certified ISP's strategy

Lemma 1. In the separating scenario, a certified ISP's optimal strategies are as follows: (1) it completely blocks the inbound traffic from noncertified ISPs; (2) the optimal investment is

$$x_j^{s*} = \min\left\{1, \frac{1}{\beta}Mv\delta q_j\right\} = \begin{cases} \frac{1}{\beta}Mv\delta q_j & \text{if } \beta > Mv\delta q_j \\ 1 & \text{otherwise} \end{cases};$$

and (3) the optimal price is $p^s = (V\delta + V)Nn$.

(2) Noncertified ISPs' strategies

Lemma 2. In a separating outcome, a noncertified ISP's optimal strategies are as follows: (1) the optimal investment is $\hat{x}^{s*} = 1/\alpha M v E[q]$; and (2) the optimal price is

$$\hat{p}^s = VNn + V(1 - \delta)Nn - NnvE[q] + \frac{1}{\alpha}(NnvE[q])^2 n.$$

(3) The CA's strategies

Proposition 2. When $\beta \geq Mvq_h\delta$, there exists a range of values for t that are feasible to the separating scenario in which only high-type ISPs will subscribe to CA. The optimal fee, t^{s*}, for the CA to induce the separating outcome is

$$MV(2\delta - 1) + Mvq_l(1 - \delta) + \frac{1}{2\beta}(Mvq_h\delta)^2 - \frac{1}{2\alpha}(MvE[q])^2.$$

A3.2   Pooling scenario: all ISPs subscribe to the CA

(1) ISPs' strategies

Lemma 5. In a pooling scenario, the optimal strategies of a certified ISP with type q_j are as follows: (1) the optimal investment in controls at outbound traffic is

$$x_j^{p*} = \min\left\{1, \frac{1}{\beta}Mvq_j\right\} = \begin{cases} \frac{1}{\beta}Mvq_j & \text{if } \beta > Mvq_j \\ 1 & \text{otherwise} \end{cases};$$

and (2) certified ISPs' optimal price is $p^{p*} = 2VNn$

(2) The CA's strategies

Proposition 3. There exists a range of t feasible to the pooling scenario that all ISPs subscribe to the CA. The optimal fee for the CA to induce the pooling outcome is

$$\begin{cases} t \leq VM - Mvq_l + MvE[q] + \frac{1}{2\beta}(Mvq_l)^2 - \frac{1}{2\alpha}(MvE[q])^2 & \text{if } \beta \geq Mvq_l \\ t \leq VM - \frac{1}{2}\beta + MvE[q] - \frac{1}{2\alpha}(MvE[q])^2 & \text{if } \beta < Mvq_l \end{cases}$$

A3.3   Pooling scenario: no ISP gets certified

If customers and ISPs believe that no ISP subscribes to the CA, the pricing and investment strategies are the same as those in the benchmark case. And in this case, the CA's profit is zero. This outcome is dominated by previous two scenarios.

A3.4   Equilibrium

Proposition 4. When $\beta > Mv\delta q_h$, a marginal δ_1 exists. When the proportion of high-type ISPs is higher than δ_1, the separating scenario is the equilibrium outcome. Otherwise, the pooling scenario is the equilibrium outcome.

Proof. Define $\Delta_i = \pi_i^p - \pi_i^s$, $i \in \{1, 2\}$.

(1) When $\beta > Mvq_l$:

The CA's profit in the separating outcome is

$$\pi_1^s = \left(MV(2\delta - 1) + Mvq_l(1 - \delta) + \frac{1}{2\beta}\left(Mvq_h\delta\right)^2 - \frac{1}{2\alpha}(MvE[q])^2 \right)\delta$$

The CA's profit in the pooling outcome is;

$$\pi_1^p = VM - Mvq_l + MvE[q] + \frac{1}{2\beta}\left(Mvq_l\right)^2 - \frac{1}{2\alpha}(MvE[q])^2$$

$$\Delta_1 = \pi_1^p - \pi_1^s$$

$$= \left(\begin{array}{c} MV - Mvq_l + MvE[q] + \frac{1}{2\beta}(Mvq_l)^2 - \frac{1}{2\alpha}(MvE[q])^2 \\ -\left(MV(2\delta - 1) + Mvq_l(1 - \delta) + \frac{1}{2\beta}(Mvq_h\delta)^2 - \frac{1}{2\alpha}(MvE[q])^2 \right)\delta \end{array} \right)$$

(2) When $Mvq_h\delta < \beta < Mvq_l$:

The CA's profit in the separating outcome is

$$\pi_2^s = \left(MV(2\delta - 1) + Mvq_l(1 - \delta) + \frac{1}{2\beta}\left(Mvq_h\delta\right)^2 - \frac{1}{2\alpha}(MvE[q])^2 \right)\delta$$

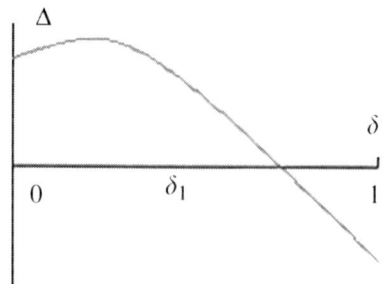

Fig. A.1. The relation between Δ_1 and δ.

The CA's profit in the pooling outcome is

$$\pi_2^p = VM - \frac{1}{2}\beta + MvE[q] - \frac{1}{2\alpha}(MvE[q])^2$$

$$\Delta_2 = \pi_2^p - \pi_2^s$$

$$= \left(\begin{array}{c} VM - \frac{1}{2}\beta + MvE[q] - \frac{1}{2\alpha}(MvE[q])^2 \\ -\left(MV(2\delta - 1) + Mvq_l(1 - \delta) + \frac{1}{2\beta}(Mvq_h\delta)^2 - \frac{1}{2\alpha}(MvE[q])^2 \right) \delta \end{array} \right)$$

The relation between Δ_i and δ can be demonstrated in Fig. A.1.

Thus, when $\delta \geq \delta_1$, the CA makes a higher profit in the separating outcome. Thus, it will induce the separating equilibrium in this scenario. Otherwise, it will induce the pooling equilibrium in which all the ISPs subscribe to the CP.   QED

Rao & Upadhyaya, Eds., *Handbooks in Information Systems, Vol. 4*
Copyright © 2009 by Emerald Group Publishing Limited

Chapter 5

Autonomic Computing and Information Security

Hina Arora, T.S. Raghu and Ajay Vinze
W. P. Carey School of Business, Arizona State University, Tempe, AZ 85287, USA

Abstract

Increasing complexity of IT infrastructures imposes cognitive challenges on security professionals in monitoring and safeguarding information. The dynamic nature of exploited security vulnerabilities calls for better decision and intelligence support to improve the effectiveness of IT security experts. This chapter critically reviews and summarizes the current frameworks and mechanisms that provide decision support for information security. Promising recent developments in computational and economic approaches to enhance the ability of IT architectures to self-correct and self-manage are described. Directions for future research in this decisional context and potential possibilities for system development are presented.

1 Introduction

In July 2001, the Code Red 2 worm infected over 350,000 computers in a 14-hour period (CAIDA Website). At the peak of the infection, over 2000 computers were being infected every minute. The 2001 strain of the worm was weak and was therefore controlled easily. But had the strain been more potent, data on all 350,000 of the computers could have been seriously compromised. The speed and extent of the 2001 attack clearly demonstrated the need for prevention and detection mechanisms to fix security vulnerabilities.

Investments in IT security are ultimately business decisions. A recent IT Security research report released by COMPTIA, which surveyed over 1000 organizations, found that nearly 20 percent of the IT budget is spent on IT security-related expenses (COMPTIA Information security spending on the rise, 2007). The security-related portion of IT budget has steadily increased from about 12 percent in 2004. The top measures used to monitor

IT security include intrusion detection systems, traffic monitoring tools, patch and configuration management systems, and various other monitoring tools (CSO Magazine, 2005). Interestingly, many of these systems require intervention by security personnel and are labor intensive. A key factor driving this is the need for audit and tracking by security professionals of the log files generated by various Enterprise systems and servers.

A recent survey by the Computer Security Institute (CSI) indicated that over 87 percent of the respondent organizations had implemented some form of security audit (Gordon and Loeb, 2002). Although periodic audit of system logs is essential to IT security practice, the costs of implementing effective audit processes are often prohibitive given the complexity of today's corporate infrastructure. Even a medium sized firm would have hundreds of systems and databases exposed to internal and external threats. The cognitive load on IT security professionals in sifting the audit trails can therefore be extremely high.

The number of information security professionals worldwide was estimated at 1.5 million in 2006, an increase of 8 percent from 2005 (Carey, 2006). Many industry analysts project continued growth in demand for security professionals for the near future. Personnel costs are estimated to account for over 40 percent of IT security budget. The constantly changing nature of security threats requires that a significant portion of security budget be spent on continuing education as well. Given that IT departments are under constant pressure to cut their budgets, it has become extremely critical to better manage IT security investments.

To reduce the need for manual intervention in managing IT security, decision support technologies are needed for detection and recovery processes. Detection processes include monitoring and anomaly detection in transactional data on the IT and communications infrastructures. Massive amounts of data and complex correlations between logs are hard for humans to handle. Therefore, vast amounts of data in system logs go uninspected. Recovery mechanisms can also be time consuming in complex IT infrastructures, which means that zero or low latency worms and viruses can bring down an infrastructure before corrective actions can be carried out.

Autonomic computing systems (ACSs) can potentially enhance decision support and intelligent sense and respond mechanisms and increase the productivity of IT security professionals. ACSs are self-managing systems that are intended to reduce human involvement in system management and configuration (Chess et al., 2003; Kephart and Chess, 2003). They rely on high-level system policies delineated by system administrators to ensure the smooth functioning of IT systems (Kephart and Walsh, 2004). While autonomic computing (AC) is a term associated with a related initiative inside IBM to build self-managed systems, the technology concept is generally embraced by other major IT firms. Other terms that denote the same concept includes "Adaptive Enterprise," "Dynamic Systems Initiative," and "Proactive Computing." A common underlying theme under these initiatives is the need to deal with the growing complexity of today's computer networks and IT infrastructures. The main objective of this chapter is to describe how AC framework in the context of IT security applications can be further enhanced with epidemiological disease models that capture the spread of worms and viruses in computing networks and predict their behavior, thereby aiding in response tactics.

This chapter will critically review and summarize the current frameworks and mechanisms that provide decision support for information security. The AC approach for decision support will be described, and its viability in multiple decisional contexts will be illustrated. These base principles will then be extended with epidemic models to analyze the spread of worms and viruses. The chapter concludes by highlighting promising recent developments in computational and economic approaches to enhance the ability of IT architectures to self-correct and self-manage. Directions for future research in this decisional context and promising possibilities for system developments are presented.

2 Trends in IT security threats

Malware describes malicious software including viruses, worms, and Trojan Horses. Computer viruses, much like their biological counterparts, attach themselves to a host (files, boot sector, etc.) and then look for a way to replicate and spread to other hosts. They can spread to other computers only if the infected file is transferred to another computer for instance through email, where the virus makes use of the computer users' address book for email addresses of new hosts. Worms do not attach themselves to a host but, instead, exist in active memory as standalone programs. They can replicate themselves over computer networks by cloning themselves and using system transmission capabilities to transfer from machine to machine. Trojan Horses do not replicate and do not attach themselves to hosts. They disguise themselves as useful programs and often provide backdoor access to private data on computers.

Most organizations use three forms of security control against Malware. Preventive controls offer the first of line of defense. These include methods such as authentication, authorization, firewalls, anti-virus software, encryption, and so on. Detective controls are used to detect security breaches that have circumvented preventive controls. These include intrusion detection systems and log analyses. Corrective controls are used to fix successful security breaches. This includes an organized patch management system to fix the vulnerabilities and install the latest security patches and programs.

The use of these controls gives rise to two prevalent security models. The first one is the time-based model of security that focuses on the relationship between preventive, detective, and corrective controls. In this model, a security measure is said to be effective if the time it takes an attacker to break in is greater than the total time it takes the organization to detect and respond to the attack. Security investments are based on which of these parameters can best be brought under control with a particular investment. The second one is the defense-in-depth model that employs multiple layers of preventive, detective, and corrective controls. This model strives to avoid having a single point of failure. Redundancy increases effectiveness because if one procedure fails or is circumvented, another may function as planned. This gives more time to the organization for detection and response.

Viruses and worms spread exponentially. Earlier strains of viruses and worms used to take some time to get off the ground or, in other words, spread the infection to say the first 10,000 hosts. However, even this time lag is fast diminishing due to more recent techniques such as hit-list, permutation, and topology scanning, where the worm can specifically target a list of highly vulnerable computers very quickly (Staniford et al., 2002). This leaves users and system administrators everywhere the overwhelming task of disinfecting the computers that have already succumbed, while at the same time, coming up with a strategy of saving as many vulnerable computers as possible, in a very short period of time. The time required to design, develop, and test a security update is limited by human cognition and can take days to achieve: far too slow to have a significant impact on an actively spreading worm (Moore et al., 2003). During the Code Red 2 epidemic for instance, it took 16 days for most hosts to eliminate the underlying vulnerability, and thousands had not patched their systems up even six weeks later. Given the huge economic losses associated with network downtimes in today's information economy, the inability to contain the spread of viruses and worms that cripple computing networks can have serious consequences. The direct costs of recovering from Code Red 2, for instance, have been estimated to be over $2.6 billion.

Virus and worm containment response times can be minimized by automating as much of the detection, analysis, and security update phases as possible. Automated response requires data gathering and analysis capabilities to detect new strains of worms and viruses. Simulation and modeling capabilities are required to predict the extent of the threat and how it is likely to spread. These capabilities also help with designing an appropriate security patch or response measure. The automated system should also have a knowledge base that can be used to look for suggested response measures and that can be updated with information on the new strain of virus or worm. An effective and efficient automated response therefore requires the capability of monitoring large amounts of data, analyzing it, planning a course of action, and executing or recommending it. The AC paradigm lends itself to building such automated self-healing systems.

3 Autonomic computing

AC has been suggested as a new paradigm to deal with the ever-increasing complexity in today's systems (Kephart and Chess, 2003). Autonomic systems are composed of self-managed elements. Self-management requires that the system be self-configuring (capable of goal-driven self-assembly with the help of a central registry), self-optimizing (especially with respect to resource allocation), self-healing (the system as a whole should be capable of dealing with the failure of any constituent part), and self-protecting (against undesirable system behavior due to bugs or unanticipated conditions and against system penetration by attackers). Each autonomic element consists of an autonomic manager (AM) and a set of managed components (Fig. 1). The AM continuously monitors the managed components, analyzes the data they generate, plans actions if required, and executes them (the monitor–analyze–plan–execute (MAPE) model) to achieve the self-management aspects of the system (Kephart and Chess, 2003).

The AM relies on high-level system policies to guide its goals (White et al., 2004). A policy is a representation, in a standard external form, of desired behaviors or constraints on behavior. High-level system policies refer to high-level objectives set by the administrators for the autonomic systems, while leaving the task of how they are achieved to the AMs. At least three forms of policy have been identified: action policies, goal policies, and utility policies (Kephart and Walsh, 2004). Action policies are typically of the form IF (condition) THEN (action). Autonomic elements employing these policies must measure and/or synthesize the quantities stated in the condition and execute the stated actions whenever the

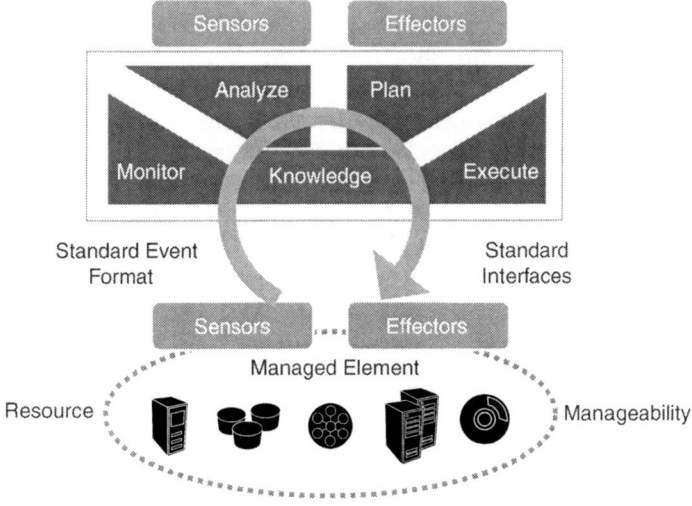

Fig. 1. Autonomic computing architecture and MAPE cycle.

condition is satisfied. Goal policies describe the conditions to be attained without specifying how to attain them. Goal policies are more powerful than action policies because they can be specified without requiring detailed knowledge of that element's inner workings. Autonomic elements employing goal policies must possess sufficient modeling and planning capabilities to translate goals into actions. Utility policies specify the relative desirability of alternative states either by assigning a numerical value or by a partial or total ordering of the possible states. Utility functions are even more powerful than goal policies because they automatically determine the most valuable goal in any given situation. Autonomic elements employing utility policies must possess sufficient modeling and planning capabilities to translate utilities into actions.

The AM also assumes the existence of a common knowledge base that it continuously uses and modifies according to its experiences and policies (Kephart and Walsh, 2004). For instance, when considering utility policies, the decision problem is essentially one of choosing values of decision variables so as to maximize the utility function. Since the relation between the decision variables and process outcomes is oftentimes dynamic and non-stationary, the agent continuously learns about the process outcomes and updates its knowledge repository.

AMs can be used to gather data, synthesize information, and distribute it. The managers would rely on their knowledge base and high-level policies to decide on what to gather, how to synthesize, and whom to distribute to. Every element can be a consumer and a provider of information, thus enabling AMs to communicate actions in response to events.

4   Sharing event information

Effective analysis of event data in a surveillance system will require the data to be reported in a consistent manner between the AM and the managed element. Since managed elements are typically heterogeneous and distributed, the only way to reliably interpret the data, correlate it with events from other diverse sources, and respond effectively is to use a common event format with a canonical vocabulary. This can be accomplished by modeling events using the Common Base Event (IBM Autonomic Computing, 2003), which standardizes the format and content of events and provides the foundation for AC. The Common Base Event is based on a structured "3-tuple" format and includes information on the impacted or impacting component, the observing component, and the situation or event (see Table 1 for an example of a Common Base Event).

More recently, the Organization for the Advancement of Structured Information Standards (OASIS) approved a related Web Services Distributed Management (WSDM) standard for exchanging event information

Table 1
Example of a CBE in the security context

Field name	Example data	Description
Version	1.0.1	The version of the CBE format that is being used
creationTime	2005-09-01T01:02:03.456Z	The time that the event was detected
Severity	1	The severity of the event from the point of view of the entity that is reporting it
globalInstanceId	C1F2ACFE…	A unique value that identifies the event instance such as a GUID (Globally Unique Identifier)
sourceComponentId	[source identifier]	Identifies who was affected by the situation
Location	[source location]	Identifies the location of the source
locationType	[source location type]	The type of location
reporterComponentId	[reporter identifier]	Indicates who reported the event
Location	[reporter location]	Identifies the location of the reporter
locationType	[reporter location type]	The type of location
Situation	…	The event that has occurred (contains information in the next three rows)
categoryName	ReportSituation	Category of the type of event that is being reported
situationType	STATUS	Provides additional information associated with each event category
ResoningScope	EXTERNAL	Defines whether the source of the event is internal or external
ExtensionName	ReportableBreach	Extensions are used to provide information that is specific to a situation. There must be a canonical definition for these data
ExtendedDataElement[0]	name='BreachCategory' type='string' values='worm'	The first entry in this extension
ExtendedDataElement[1]	name='BreachName' type='string' values='CodeRedv2'	The second entry in this extension
ExtendedDataElement[..]	…	Additional extended data elements could be used

in distributed environments (OASIS, 2006). The scope of the standard is quite broad and can be used to manage network and wireless devices, consumer electronic devices, web services, and computers.

The event-based approach can enable event message distribution, consumption, and filtering to be automated in the AC architecture. Common examples of events would include component failure, activity completion, resource depletion, start or stop event, interrupt, and connection failure.

While standard message structures to exchange event information is essential to the creation of an autonomic environment, real value of event standardization is in the analysis and correlation of events. Large-scale event information can be mined for managing systems resources (Li et al., 2005). Rule-based event triggers for specific actions can also be specified in an autonomic environment (Li and Parashar, 2004).

5   Autonomic computing for IT security

Research uses of AC architectures in IT security have begun to emerge in the past few years. In this section, we present a brief overview of some of the studies that have attempted to use the autonomic paradigm in IT security contexts.

A progenitor of the autonomic security system idea appeared in White et al. (1999), which described a security "immune system." The immune system approach automates many of the tasks performed by system administrators. Traditionally, when a virus attacked, the virus would be manually captured and forwarded to an antivirus company. A human expert would analyze it using various analysis tools to come up with a virus definition with instructions on how to detect and remove the virus. The users would then download the definition update from the server and install it on the infected computer. With the immune systems approach, every step of this process is automated. The antivirus software on the users' machine uses a host of heuristics to identify infected files. The infected file is sent to the analysis center, where the virus is made to spread in a protected environment and automatically analyzed. The updated definitions are sent to the reporting machines and to any other machines registered to receive automatic updates. Decisions are deferred to human experts only in cases where the virus is not automatically identifiable. It is also possible to use predictive data mining approaches to automatically find patterns in executable files (Schultz et al., 2001). The data mining approach can create new rule sets that can be distributed periodically to subscribing hosts.

Signature-based and data mining approaches have to overcome scalability problems of cooperation. Without sufficient information on the type of worms or viruses, effective generation of rules through data mining approaches can be difficult. Attacks on the Internet require collective actions from multiple organizations for rapid mitigation of the risk. To address this problem, Nojiri et al. (2003) proposed a peer-to-peer architecture for addressing large-scale worm attacks. Although the initial results are encouraging, their analysis points to the need for classifying propagation behaviors to device different strategies for fast and slow spreading worms. Agosta et al. (2006) approach autonomic enterprise security system using a similar collaborative framework. End hosts use the Intel Active Management and Virtualization Technologies to regulate themselves (self-defending). The end hosts collaborate to and detect network-wide anomalies (distributed detection and inference). If an anomaly is detected, a central feedback-based security system is triggered to mount an automated response (adaptive feedback). The central system is more effective than *ad-hoc* per-device control approaches, since system-wide information and policy can help target the most effective control points. In this manner, new threats are detected and isolated or treated autonomically, with minimal intervention from the network administrators.

The biological analogy of viruses and worms has inspired approaches that mimic the human immune system. For example, Hofmeyr and Forrest (2000) suggest a biologically inspired network monitoring system called the Lisys. The Lisys system is essentially an anomaly detection system, which is trained to distinguish between good and bad network traffic. The inspiration for this system comes from human immune cells called lymphocytes that learn to distinguish between elements of the body (self) and pathogens (non-self). Lisys is a detection system and therefore little is said about response measures. ACSs on the contrary are self-healing systems and, therefore, integrate detection and response under a common framework. For a review of research and systems implementing artificial immune system inspired methods and algorithms, see Aickelin et al. (2004).

Like in most other anomaly detection systems, the attacker can evade the system by making anomalous connections infrequent enough to keep the anomalous behavior well below the activation threshold of the detection system. Decreasing the activation threshold would put more strain on the attacker, but it would also require more resources at the organization to cope with the higher number of false positives that would result.

This in fact is a well-known challenge with intrusion detection systems. The probability of detection and the probability of false positives are related as shown by the receiver-operating characteristics (ROC) curves in Fig. 2 (Trees, 2001). The implication of the high false alarm rate is rather bleak—higher detection rates can only be achieved by accepting higher false-positive rates. Higher false positives will require organizations to spend more resources analyzing the alarms, resulting in higher cost. It appears that ACSs can potentially decrease the cost of investigations even in the presence of high false alarm rates.

In a game theoretic analysis of the economic benefits from AC, Arora et al. (2006) demonstrated that a partially configured ACS has clear economic benefits even when malicious attack frequency is low. If most of the detection and preventive measures can be automated, then the organizations could afford to incur higher false-positive rates to achieve higher detection rates, at a lower cost.

The AC paradigm is only a framework. Tools, techniques, and models are required to build the monitoring, analysis, planning, and execution phases of the framework. Additionally, immune systems analogy can be

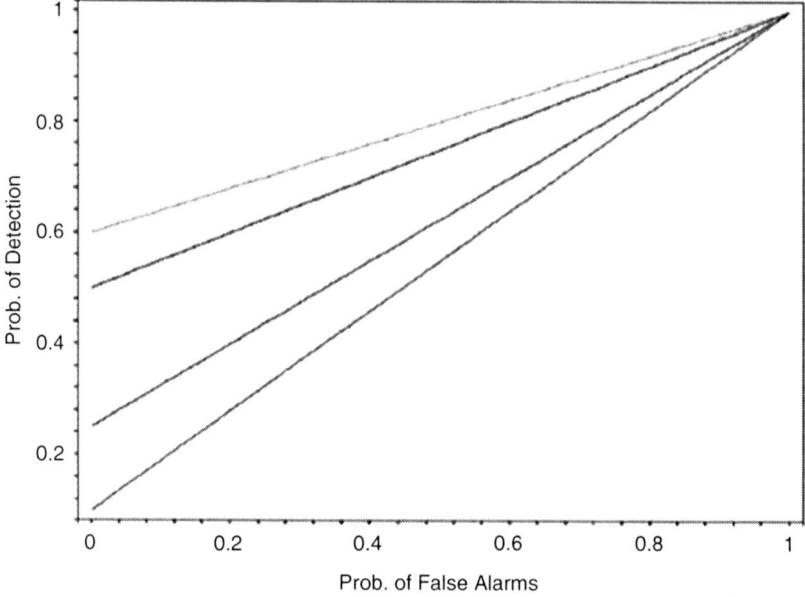

Fig. 2.   ROC curves.

logically extended to epidemiological models. Much like public health agencies respond to contagious diseases through their knowledge of how a disease spreads through a community, autonomic responses can be designed to contain the spread of viruses and worms by taking appropriate actions adapted from epidemiological models. Section 6 surveys models that can be used in the analysis and planning phases of the MAPE cycle.

6   Epidemiological disease models

Epidemics are best described by the SEIR model (Anderson and May, 1982). The SEIR model is a classic epidemiological model that captures the spread of an epidemic in a homogeneous population. This model describes four discrete states of an epidemic: susceptible, exposed, infectious, and recovered (Fig. 3). Infectious individuals spread the disease to the (non-immune) susceptible population. Those in the susceptible population to which the disease is transmitted become exposed, and after a period of time, the incubation (or latent) period, they become infectious. Individuals remain infectious for a period of time, the infectious period, and then recover (with immunity). Timely intervention in the form of immunization (to reduce the number of susceptibles), quarantine (to reduce the number of contacts with the infected), and treatment (to help the infected recover) can help contain the epidemic. A set of differential equations models the spread

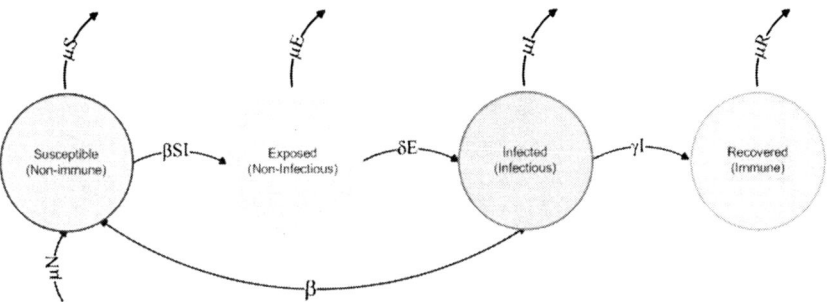

Fig. 3.   The SEIR model.

Table 2
Notation definitions

N	Total population size
μ	Birth/death rate
$s(t)$	Fraction of susceptible population at time t
$e(t)$	Fraction of exposed population at time t
$i(t)$	Fraction of infected population at time t
$r(t)$	Fraction of recovered population at time t
β	Average number of *adequate* contacts (contacts that will lead to an infection)
$1/\delta$	Average latent period
$1/\gamma$	Average infectious period

of the disease (see Table 2 for notation definitions):

$$\frac{ds(t)}{dt} = \mu - \beta\, s(t)\, i(t) - \mu s(t)$$

$$\frac{de(t)}{dt} = \beta\, s(t)\, i(t) - \delta\, e(t) - \mu e(t)$$

$$\frac{di(t)}{dt} = \delta e(t) - \gamma i(t) - \mu i(t)$$

$$\frac{dr(t)}{dt} = \gamma i(t) - \mu\, r(t)$$

$$s(t) + e(t) + i(t) + r(t) = 1$$

The spread of viruses and worms in computing networks are analogous to the spread of diseases in human populations (Fig. 4; count of dead in Fig 4(a), shown in black color, is similar in shape to the infected hosts in Fig 4(b)). Computers with software vulnerabilities constitute the *susceptible* population. They get *infected* when successfully attacked by a virus or a

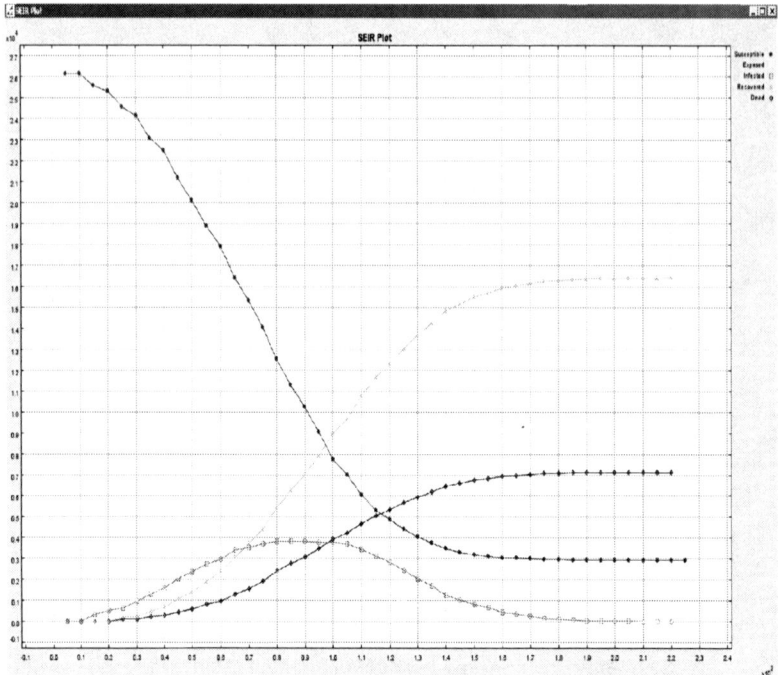

Fig. 4a.   SEIR plot for a smallpox epidemic.

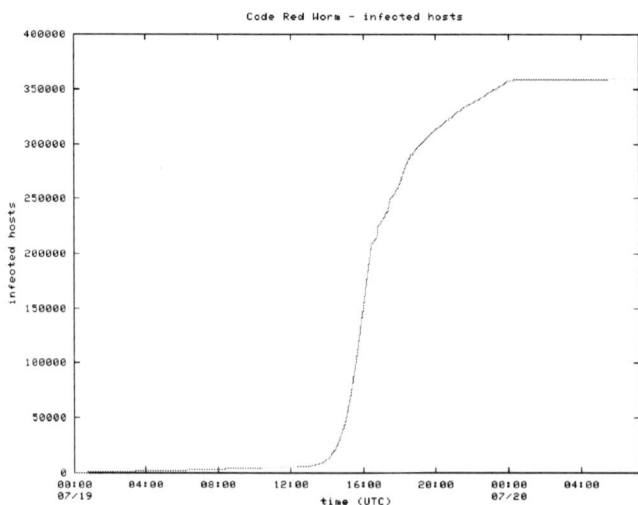

Fig. 4b.   Infected hosts plot for Code Red Worm (from http://www.caida.org/research/
security/code-red/coderedv2_analysis.xml).

worm. They *recover* when the virus or worm is removed. They recover with immunity if they are updated with the latest security patch. Three potential interventions can be used to mitigate security threats (Moore et al., 2003): prevention (reducing the susceptible population through better software design), treatment (disinfecting the computer with virus and worm detection tools and update it with the latest security patches), and containment (through the use of firewalls, filters, and blacklists).

Mathematical models help with the development of intervention policies. They also help in predicting the course of an epidemic, which can aid in planning for intervention resource requirements (Kephart and White, 1991). Variations of the SEIR model have therefore been used extensively in understanding the spread of worms and viruses through computing networks. These models change one or more of the stages of the disease propagation stages thereby changing the underlying mathematical properties.

The susceptible-infected-susceptible (SIS) model (Kephart and White, 1991) assumes that susceptible computers get infected and become susceptible again soon after they are cured of an infection. Another approach that utilizes an SIR model (Zou et al., 2002) assumes that susceptible computers get infected and recover with immunity soon after they are cured of an infection. The SIR model can be more realistic when compared to SIS model, since once an infected computer is patched or cleaned, it is more likely to be immune to that particular strain of worm or virus.

The traditional SEIR model is a homogeneous model that considers the spread of the disease through the population as a whole. It does not consider the individual or the discrete nature of the links between individuals. This basic model has therefore also been extended to include the heterogeneous nature of epidemics by imposing the SIS model on a directed graph topology (Kephart and White, 1991). The traditional SEIR model also assumes that the infection rate is a constant. In reality, however, the infection rate is dependent both on preventive, treatment, and containment measures taken by users and on the slow down of the infection due to network congestion caused by the rampant propagation of the worm or the virus. The SIR model has therefore been extended to include a time-varying infection rate (Zou et al., 2002), resulting in a more accurate epidemic model.

7 Network-based epidemiological models

Networks are the means by which viruses and worms spread. Therefore, it is natural to consider the impact of network structure on virus propagation. It is possible to investigate computer epidemiological models within the context of the network structure of the connected hosts. Analysis of the Internet topology suggests that the Internet is a scale-free network (Barabasi and Albert, 1999). Scale-free networks are characterized by the

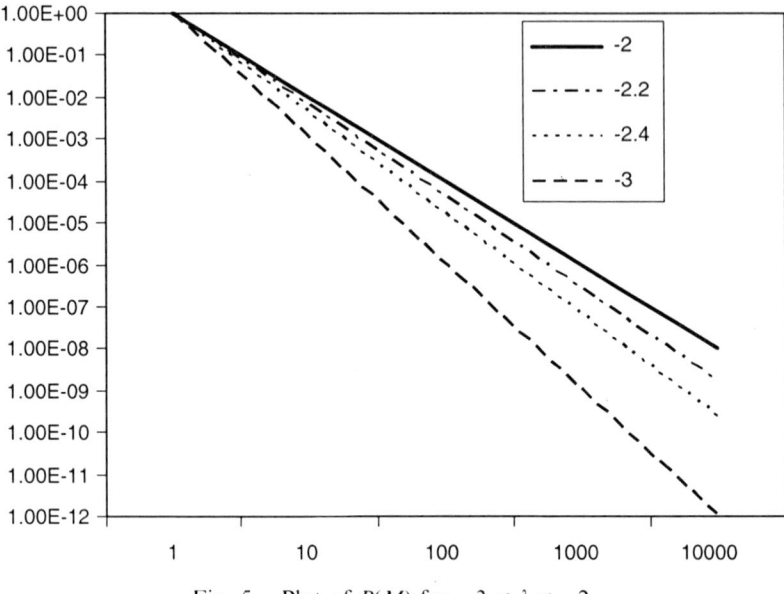

Fig. 5. Plot of $P(M)$ for $-3 \leq \lambda \leq -2$.

power law distribution that states that the probability that a particular node connects to M other nodes in the network is given by the relation, $P(M) = M^{-\lambda}$. Empirical studies have shown that the pattern of linkages of the WWW is characterized by a power law distribution with $\lambda \approx -2$ (see Fig. 5). A key implication is that a very small percentage of hosts on the Internet would have a large number of connections and a large percentage of hosts would have very few connections. This type of network would be extremely vulnerable to attacks especially when nodes with the highest number of connections are targeted first.

Network-based models can further refine epidemiological models of virus and worm propagation. For example, Pastor-Satorras and Vespignani (2001) show an interesting contrast in the results when scale-free network model of the Internet is utilized. Traditional epidemiological models (Kephart and White, 1991) have shown that an epidemic threshold (i.e., infection rate) point exists below which a virus or worm would quickly die out without spreading. However, most viruses end up affecting a few hosts and persist over a long time period at a very low level. Pastor-Satorras and Vespignani (2001) simulated the SIS model in a scale-free network environment and showed that viruses can spread even when the infection rate is close to zero, that is, the threshold point does not exist. This refinement of the epidemiological model shows that network topology is an important element in the modeling of virus propagation on the Internet. In Dezso and Barabasi (2002), they exploit the scale-free property to demonstrate that a policy that targets hubs for "vaccinations" can potentially eliminate the virus threat in a cost-effective fashion. Refinement of these ideas under different network topologies has the potential to create the rules and policies necessary to create effective AMs.

8   A model for autonomic Malware containment

Epidemiological models based on the SEIR model and the environments created by scale-free networks point to the need for collaborative arrangements between organizations and, in turn, computer networks. Staniford et al. (2002) suggested the establishment of a "Cyber-Center for Disease Control" (CDC), a cyber equivalent of the Centers for Disease Control and Prevention in the United States. The CDC will be responsible for the following. The CDC should have the ability to identify outbreaks. This will involve the deployment of sensors and the development of communication mechanisms for gathering and coordinating distributed field information. The field data should be analyzed for any suspect applications and the associated threat potential in terms of the extent of damage they are likely to cause. Once the outbreak is identified, the CDC should provide rapid analysis of new pathogens. This will involve an understanding of how they spread and what they do. This can be achieved with the help of analysis and simulation tools and a knowledge base that contains information on previous worms. Once the pathogen is identified, the CDC should provide infected computers with the signatures, describing how the Malware can be detected and terminated or isolated. The treatment process should be automated as much as possible. The CDC should also proactively devise detectors for detecting worms as they propagate.

All of the aforementioned tasks should be automated as much as possible, since any analysis involving human administrators will be too slow to match the pace of a rapidly propagating worm. To contain the epidemic, the automated system should cure the Malware faster than it can spread. The AC paradigm along with the SIER model is a compelling candidate to build a CDC. The MAPE cycle lends itself naturally to the monitoring of field information and traffic patterns, the analysis of such patterns to detect Malware, and a knowledge base that is continuously updated with the latest strains of viruses and worms. The knowledge base along with the SEIR model can be used to determine the potency of the Malware strain and the extent of damage they are likely to cause. The SEIR model can also be used to determine how the epidemic is most likely to spread and what maybe the best possible course of action to combat the epidemic.

One approach to building an autonomic "Cyber-Center for Disease Control" system could be as shown in Fig. 6. As initial information about worm or virus appears over the network and begins to affect the hosts at level 1, the information can be collected through the sensors of the AMs at level 2. Level 2 hosts can take local actions to limit the spread of the

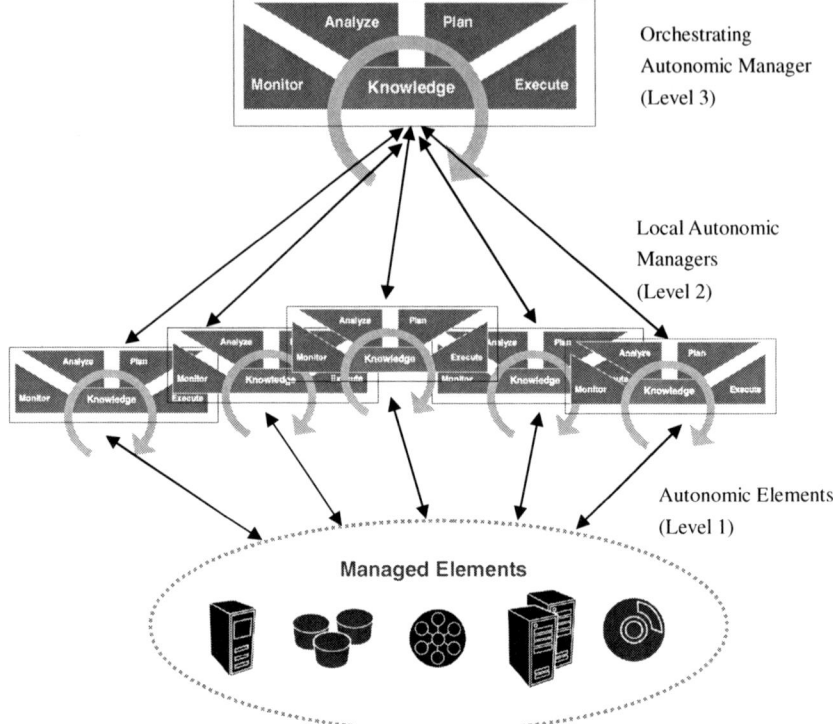

Fig. 6. Autonomic Cyber-Center for Disease Control.

attack while simultaneously communicating with the central AM (as well as other level 2 managers). The exchange of information between AMs can be in the Common Base Event format. It would also be possible to share updates to the knowledge base to AMs and autonomic elements at all levels. Continuous sharing of event information will allow AMs to update their strategies based on the level of disease propagation and the states of the various hosts under their purview. Response steps can also be tailored to the type of network topologies within each subnetwork.

9 Conclusions

IT security threats are ultimately the result of intentional actions of hackers and malicious insiders. The economic and psychological incentives of the hackers have to be considered in any response strategy and autonomic IT security system design. Recent research in the area of IT security, epidemiology, and scale-free networks is beginning to provide the necessary knowledge base needed to build ACSs that can self-configure and self-heal. The autonomic approach shows great potential in reducing the cognitive burden of IT security professionals.

Although isolated autonomic management systems can still create business value within organizations, there is great potential in creating a centralized autonomic security environment of the kind proposed in this chapter. Like public health epidemics, computer viruses and worms spread through connections and proximity. Just as Centers for Disease Control closely coordinates with various local public health organizations to monitor, track, and analyze communicable diseases, a network of AMs with local controls can potentially alleviate security threats on the Internet.

10   Discussion questions

1. Review the different types of hacker attacks. Discuss how disease spreading models can be useful in each such attack scenario.
2. While using an autonomic approach can be immensely beneficial, one still is required to define the business level objectives and actions for the security system. Model the action space for an autonomic system in the IT security context. What are the informational requirements and dependencies (if any) associated with the action space?
3. Briefly describe the responsibilities and processes required to efficiently run a "Cyber-Center for Disease Control."

References

Agosta, J.M., J. Chandrashekar, D.H. Dash, M. Dave, D. Durham, H. Khosravi, H. Li, et al. (2006). Towards autonomic enterprise security: self-defending platforms, distributed detection, and adaptive feedback. *Intel Technology Journal*. Available at http://www.intel.com/technology/itj/2006/v10i4/4-security/1-abstract.htm

Aickelin, U., J. Greensmith, J. Twycross (2004). Immune system approaches to intrusion detection – a review, in: G. Nicosia, V. Cutello, P.J. Bentley (eds.), *Artificial Immune Systems: Lecture Notes in Computer Science*, LLC, Springer-Verlag, New York, pp. 316–329.

Anderson, R.M., R.M. May (1982). Directly transmitted infections diseases: control by vaccination. *Science* 215(4536), 1053–1060.

Arora, H., B.K. Mishra, T.S. Raghu (2006). Autonomic-computing approach to secure knowledge management: a game-theoretic analysis. *IEEE Transactions on Systems, Man and Cybernetics, Part A* 36(3), 487–497.

Barabasi, A.L., R. Albert (1999). Emergence of scaling in random networks. *Science* 286, 509–512.

CAIDA Website. Available at http://www.caida.org/research/security/code-red/coderedv2_analysis.xml

Carey, A. (2006). Global information security workforce study, IDC (ISC) Sponsored Study. Available at http://www.isc2.org/uploadedFiles/Industry_Resources/workforcestudy06.pdfAlso. Accessed on March 30, 2009.

Chess, D.M., C.C. Palmer, S.R. White (2003). Security in an autonomic computing environment. *IBM Systems Journal* 42(1), 107–118.

COMPTIA Information security spending on the rise (2007). COMPTIA Survey Reveals, Press Release. Available at http://www.comptia.org/pressroom/get_pr.aspx?prid=1286. Accessed on October 31, 2007.

CSO Magazine (2005). E-crime watch survey – survey results. Available at http://www.csoonline.com/info/ecrimesurvey05.pdf. Accessed on October 31, 2007.

Dezso, Z., A.L. Barabasi (2002). Halting viruses in scale-free networks. *Physical Review E* 65, 055103.1–055103.4.

Gordon, L.A., M.P. Loeb (2002). The economics of information security investment. *ACM Transactions on Information and System Security* 5(4), 438–457.

Hofmeyr, S., S. Forrest (2000). Architecture for an artificial immune system. *Evolutionary Computation* 7(1), 1289–1296.

IBM Autonomic Computing (2003). Automating problem determination: a first step toward self-healing computing systems. *IBM Technical Library*. Available at http://www.ibm.com/developerworks/library/specification/ws-cbe/

Kephart, J.O., D.M. Chess (2003). The vision of autonomic computing. *IEEE Computer* 36(1), 41–50.

Kephart, J.O., W.E. Walsh (2004). An artificial intelligence perspective on autonomic computing policies. *Fifth IEEE International Workshop on Policies for Distributed Systems and Networks* 3–12.

Kephart, J.O., S.R. White (1991). Directed-graph epidemiological models of computer viruses. *IEEE Symposium on Security and Privacy* 343–359.

Li, T., F. Liang, S. Ma, W. Peng (2005). An integrated framework on mining log files for computing systems management. *Proceedings of the Eleventh ACM SIGKDD International Conference on Knowledge Discovery and Data Mining*, Chicago, IL, pp. 776–781.

Li, Z., M. Parashar (2004). Rudder: a rule-based multi-agent infrastructure for supporting autonomic grid applications. *Proceedings of the Internal Conference on Autonomic Computing*, New York, NY, pp. 278–279.

Moore, D., C. Shannon, G.M. Voelker, S. Savage (2003). Internet quarantine: requirements for containing self-propagating code. *22nd Annual Joint Conference of the IEEE Computer and Communications Societies* 3, 1901–1910.

Nojiri, D., J. Rowe, K. Levitt (2003). Cooperative response strategies for large scale attack mitigation. *Proceedings of the DARPA Information Survivability Conference and Exposition*, Washington, DC, pp. 22–24.

OASIS (2006). An introduction to WSDM, committee draft, February 24. Available at http://www.oasis-open.org/committees/tc_home.php?wg_abbrev=wsdm. Accessed on November 1, 2007.

Pastor-Satorras, R., A. Vespignani (2001). Epidemic spreading in scale-free networks. *Physical Review Letters* 86, 3200–3203.

Schultz, M.G., E. Eskin, E. Zadok, S.J. Stolfo (2001). Data mining methods for detection of new malicious executables. *IEEE Symposium on Security and Privacy* p. 38.

Staniford, S., V. Paxson, N. Weaver (2002). How to own the Internet in your spare time. *Proceedings of the 11th USENIX Security Symposium*, San Francisco, CA, pp. 149–167.

Trees, H.V. (2001). *Detection, Estimation and Modulation Theory—Part I*. Hoboken, NJ, Wiley.

White, S.R., M. Swimmer, E. Pring, W. Arnold, D. Chess, J.F. Morar (1999). Anatomy of a commercial-grade immune system. *Proceedings of the Ninth International Virus Bulletin Conference*, September/October, Vancouver, BC, Canada, pp. 203–228.

White, S.R., J.E. Hanson, I. Whalley, D.M. Chess, J.O. Kephart (2004). An architectural approach to autonomic computing. *IEEE Proceedings of the International Conference on Autonomic Computing*, Vancouver, BC, Canada.

Zou, C.C., W. Gong, D. Towsley (2002). Code red worm propagation modeling and analysis. *Proceedings of the 9th ACM Conference on Computer and Communications Security*, Washington, DC, pp. 138–147.

Rao & Upadhyaya, Eds., *Handbooks in Information Systems, Vol. 4*

Chapter 6

Policy Management for the Semantic Web

Bhavani Thuraisingham

Department of Computer Science, The University of Texas at Dallas, 2601 N. Floyd Road, Richardson, TX 75080, USA

Abstract

Semantic web technologies provide support for machine-understandable web pages. In addition, these technologies provide support for web services as well as information integration. It is critical that these technologies are secure. Recent work on semantic web has focused on policy management and enforcement. In particular, policies for confidentiality, privacy, and trust (CPT) management have been proposed. In this chapter, we review the various developments and discuss approaches for policy management for the semantic web.

1 Introduction

Recent developments in information systems technologies have resulted in computerizing many applications in various business areas. Data has become a critical resource in many organizations, and therefore, efficient access to data, sharing the data, extracting information from the data, and making use of the information have become an urgent need. As a result, there have been many efforts on not only integrating the various data sources scattered across several sites, but extracting information from these databases in the form of patterns and trends has also become important. These data sources may be databases managed by database management systems, or they could be data warehoused in a repository from multiple data sources.

The advent of the World Wide Web (WWW) in the mid-1990s has resulted in even greater demand for managing data, information, and knowledge effectively. There is now so much data on the web that managing it with conventional tools is becoming almost impossible. New tools and techniques are needed to effectively manage this data. Therefore, to provide interoperability as well as to ensure machine-understandable web pages, the concept of semantic web was conceived by Tim Berners-Lee who heads the World Wide Web Consortium (W3C) (Berners-Lee et al., 2001).

As the demand for data and information management increases, there is also a critical need for maintaining the security of the databases, applications, and information systems. Data and information have to be protected from unauthorized access as well as from malicious corruption. With the advent of the web, it is even more important to protect the data and information as numerous individuals now have access to this data and information. Therefore, we need effective mechanisms to secure the semantic web technologies. In particular, we need effective policy management and enforcement techniques for semantic web technologies. Policies will include those for confidentiality, privacy, and trust (CPT) management.

This chapter describes policy management for the semantic web technologies. In Section 2, we describe confidentiality issues including securing eXtensible Markup Language (XML), Resource Description Framework (RDF), and Web Ontology Language (OWL), which are key semantic web technologies. In Section 3, we describe trust management. Privacy management is discussed in Section 4. Integrity and data quality issues are discussed in Section 5. Policy engineering, which is about tools for managing policies, is discussed in Section 6. Our current research on developing a policy framework will be discussed in Section 7. Section 8 concludes the chapter.

2   Confidentiality management and the semantic web

2.1   Overview

In this section, we discuss confidentiality management for the semantic web. Note that we use confidentiality and security interchangeably. We first provide an overview of security issues for the semantic web and then discuss some details on XML security, RDF security, and secure information integration, which are components of the secure semantic web. As more progress is made on investigating these various issues, it is hoped that appropriate standards would be developed for securing the semantic web. Security cannot be considered in isolation. That is, there is no one layer that should focus on security. Security cuts across all layers and this is a challenge. For example, the semantic web technology stack that includes XML, RDF, ontologies, and rules technologies has to be secure.

We also need to examine the inference problem for the semantic web. Inference is the process of posing queries and deducing new information. It becomes a problem when the deduced information is something the user is unauthorized to know. With the semantic web, and especially with data mining tools, one can make all kinds of inferences. Recently, there has been some research on controlling unauthorized inferences on the semantic web. We need to continue with such research (see, e.g., Farkas and Huhns, 2002; Thuraisingham, 2007b, 2008).

The organization of this section is as follows. XML security is discussed in Section 2.2. RDF security is discussed in Section 2.3. Ontologies and security are discussed in Section 2.4. Finally, secure query processing for the semantic web is discussed in Section 2.5. More details of securing the semantic web are discussed by Thuraisingham (2007a).

2.2 XML security

Various research efforts have been reported on XML security (see, e.g., Bertino et al., 2002). We briefly discuss some of the key points. The main challenge is whether to give access to entire XML documents or parts of the documents. Bertino et al. have developed authorization models for XML. They have focused on access control policies as well as on dissemination policies. They also considered push and pull architectures. They specified the policies in XML. The policy specification contains information about which users can access which portions of the documents. In the work by Bertino et al. (2002), algorithms for access control as well as computing views of the results are presented. In addition, architectures for securing XML documents are also discussed. Bertino et al. (2004) go further and describe how XML documents may be published on the web. The idea is for owners to publish documents, subjects to request access to the documents, and untrusted publishers to give the subjects the views of the documents they are authorized to see.

W3C is specifying standards for XML security. The XML security project (see http://xml.apache.org/security) is focusing on providing the implementation of security standards for XML. The focus is on XML-Signature Syntax and Processing, XML-Encryption Syntax and Processing, and XML Key Management. W3C also has a number of working groups including XML Signature working group (see http://www.w3.org/Signature/) and XML encryption working group (see http://www.w3.org/Encryption/2001/). While the standards are focusing on what can be implemented in the near-term, much research is needed on securing XML documents.

2.3 RDF security

RDF is the foundation of the semantic web (RDF Primer). Whereas XML is limited in providing machine-understandable documents, RDF handles this limitation. As a result, RDF provides better support for interoperability as well as searching and cataloging. It also describes contents of documents as well as relationships between various entities in the document.

Whereas XML provides syntax and notations, RDF supplements this by providing semantic information in a standardized way.

The basic RDF model has three types: resources, properties, and statements. Resource is anything described by RDF expressions. It could be a web page or a collection of pages. Property is a specific attribute used to describe a resource. RDF statements are resources together with a named property plus the value of the property. Statement components are subject, predicate, and object. So, for example, if we have a sentence of the form "John is the creator of xxx", then xxx is the subject or resource, property or predicate is "Creator," and object or literal is "John." There are RDF diagrams very much like say ER diagrams or object diagrams to represent statements. It is important that the intended interpretation be used for RDF sentences. This is accomplished by RDF schemas. Schema is sort of a dictionary and has interpretations of various terms used in sentences.

More advanced concepts in RDF include the container model and statements about statements. The container model has three types of container objects, and they are bag, sequence, and alternative. A bag is an unordered list of resources or literals. It is used to mean that a property has multiple values, but the order is not important. A sequence is a list of ordered resources. Here, the order is important. Alternative is a list of resources that represent alternatives for the value of a property. Various tutorials in RDF describe the syntax of containers in more detail.

RDF also provides support for making statements about other statements. For example, with this facility, one can make statements of the form "The statement A is false" where A is the statement "John is the creator of X." Again one can use object-like diagrams to represent containers and statements about statements. RDF also has a formal model associated with it. This formal model has a formal grammar. For further information on RDF, we refer to the excellent discussion in the article by Antoniou and van Harmelen (2003).

Now to make the semantic web secure, we need to ensure that RDF documents are secure. This would involve securing XML from a syntactic point of view. However with RDF, we also need to ensure that security is preserved at the semantic level. The issues include the security implications of the concepts resource, properties, and statements. That is, how is access control ensured? How can statements, properties, and statements be protected? How can one provide access control at a finer grain of granularity? What are the security properties of the container model? How can bags, lists, and alternatives be protected? Can we specify security policies in RDF? How can we resolve semantic inconsistencies for the policies? How can we express security constraints in RDF? What are the security implications of statements about statements? How can we protect RDF schemas? These are difficult questions and we need to start research to provide answers. XML security is just the beginning. Securing RDF is much more challenging (see also Carminati et al., 2004).

2.4 Security and ontologies

Ontologies are essentially representations of various concepts to avoid ambiguity. Numerous ontologies have been developed. These ontologies have been used by agents to understand the web pages and conduct operations such as the integration of databases. Furthermore, ontologies can be represented in languages such as RDF or special languages such as OWL.

Now, ontologies have to be secure. That is, access to the ontologies has to be controlled. This means that different users may have access to different parts of the ontology. On the contrary, ontologies may be used to specify security policies just as XML and RDF have been used to specify the policies.

2.5 Secure query and rules processing for the semantic web

The layer above the secure RDF layer is the secure query and rules processing layer. While RDF can be used to specify security policies (see, e.g., Carminati et al., 2004), the web rules language being developed by W3C is more powerful to specify complex policies. Furthermore, inference engines are being developed to process and reason about the rules (e.g., the Pellet engine developed at the University of Maryland). One could integrate ideas from the database inference controller that we have developed (see Thuraisingham et al., 1993) with web rules processing to develop an inference or privacy controller for the semantic web.

The query-processing module is responsible for accessing the heterogeneous data and information sources on the semantic web. Researchers are examining ways to integrate techniques from web query processing with semantic web technologies to locate, query, and integrate the heterogeneous data and information sources. We need to examine the security impact of query processing.

3 Trust management and the semantic web

3.1 Overview

This section focuses on trust management and the semantic web. Trust has been discussed in a great deal in developing secure systems. Much of the early focus was on trusting the software to develop high assurance systems. For example, in designing say a multilevel system that has to be evaluated at say A1 level according to the Trusted Computer Systems Evaluation criteria (TCSEC), the software has to go through a formal verification process to ensure that there are no covert channels. Such software is called trusted software. However, during the past 10 years or so, when data and applications security received prominence, the focus was on trusting the individuals or processes acting on behalf of the individuals. Here, we had to determine the trust that had to be placed on the individuals. Furthermore, the data also had to be assigned say trust values. That is, data could have a high trust value if it is emanated from a trustworthy individual.

The organization of this section is as follows. Trust management including trusting individuals as well as data is discussed in Section 3.2. Semantic web technologies for trust management are the subject of Section 3.3. Trust management for semantic web technologies is discussed in Section 3.4. Note that trust and risk have a relationship between them. That is, if a person is not trustworthy and if you have to give him/her some data, you are taking a risk. Therefore, some of the developments on correlating trust and risk and the use of semantic web technologies for this correlation are discussed in Section 3.5. For completion, we discuss digital rights management (DRM) and its relationship to the semantic web in Section 3.6.

3.2   Trust management

Before we discuss aspects of trust management and describe the relationship to semantic web, we need to determine what is meant by trust. Trust has been defined by philosophers and it relates to the amount of value that one would place on another. This value will depend on whether the person can keep secrets or carry out safe activities, among others. Based on the trust that is placed on a person, the data that is emanating from that person would also be assigned a trust value. We address data trust later. First, we focus on trusting an individual. We can extend the arguments to include not only an individual but also a group of individuals or even a web site or an organization.

As stated earlier, work on trust initially focused on amount of verification or testing that has to be carried out to ensure that the software meets the specification. If the software has a Trojan horse, then it is not trusted. If the software is trusted, then depending on the techniques used to trust the software (e.g., formal verification vs. testing), one could then determine the assurance that is placed on the software. Later on, with the prominence of data security, trust was assigned to individuals or organizations. In such cases, two approaches were used to define trust: one was based on credentials and the other was based on reputation. Both schools of thought have received attention in the research community working on trust.

Bertino and her team have conducted extensive research in credential-based trust management. The idea here is to exchange credentials between individuals, and depending on the type of credentials, trust is established between two parties. Credentials are obtained initially through some credential authority. Therefore, if John wants to see Jane's personal data, he has to present Jane with his credentials that were given to him by a credential authority. Other noted research on credential-based trust management is the work by Winslett et al. and Winsborough et al. among others. Numerous articles on credential-based trust management have appeared in the Proceedings of conferences such as *ACM SACMAT* and *IEEE POLICY* (see also Bertino et al., 2003; Winsborough and Li, 2004; Yu and Winslett, 2003).

In the reputation-based systems, trust is assigned based on the reputation that one gets based on his past behavior. For example, if Jane applies for a position as a teacher, then those who have heard about Jane will discuss her reputation such as she is not reliable and misses classes a great deal of the time. If this is the case, then Jane's reputation as a teacher is not good and so Jane will not be trusted to be given the job. We use reputation all the time in our daily lives. That is, we trust an individual or an organization based on its reputation. It is usually very hard to improve the reputation. It however does not take much to ruin the reputation and as a result to decrease the trust value. Reputation-based trust systems are discussed in Shmatikov and Talcott (2004).

The third type of trust is to determine the confidence value that one places on the data. In other words, how much do you trust the data? To give an answer, we need to determine who has produced the data? Who has accessed the data? Has the data gone through an organization that is untrustworthy? We will discuss data trust when we address data quality and data provenance in Section 5.

Once trust values are assigned, what does it take to manage trust? This involves exchanging data depending on the trust values as well as increasing and decreasing trust values based on credentials received or subtracted or the reputation that has changed. For example, if John is entrusted with some critical data and if it is known that John has misused the data, the trust value will be decreased. There is research on formalizing the notion of trust and performing operations on trust. Algebras for trust management are also being developed. One important aspect of trust management is trust negotiation. Here, two parties may negotiate with each other the trust values and the data to be shared among them. Trust negotiation is an active research area in trust management (Winsborough and Li, 2004).

3.3 Semantic web for trust management

What is of interest to us is the use of semantic web technologies for trust management and negotiation. Although several trust policy languages have been developed, a notable system that takes advantage of XML for policy representation is the system developed at the University of Milan and Purdue University by Bertino and her group. The system developed is called Trust-X and is based on XML. A trust policy language based on XML is used by Trust-X. It is a credential-based system (Bertino et al., 2004).

Although XML is a suitable policy language, it suffers from the drawbacks in that it cannot adequately represent semantics. For example, statements such as A trusts B only if B does not trust C or A trusts B and B trusts C does not mean that A trusts C. It is difficult to express such statements in XML. Note that unlike XML, RDF can express class-subclass relationships, and languages such as OWL can represent relationships such as Union and Intersection. Therefore, we need rich policy languages to represent trust. Furthermore, since the 9/11 commission report, the environment is migrating from a need to know to a need to share environment. Therefore, it is important to represent trust relationships in such an environment. We need policy languages to represent statements of the form "in emergency situations, one need to share all the data and then determine the consequences of data sharing with respect to trust." Finin et al. are investigating the use of language such as REI for the need to share environments (Kagal et al., 2003).

The advantage of using semantic web-based policy languages is that one could use reasoning capabilities based on descriptive logic to reason about trust statements and make inferences about trust that are not explicitly specified. Reasoning engines such as JENA and PELLET are also being explored for representing and reasoning about semantic web-based policy specifications. The Policy Aware Web project being carried out at MIT is also developing specification languages and reasoning engines for trust policies.

Note that one of the layers of the semantic web is the logic, proof, and trust layer. This type of trust is different from trust as discussed in this section. The trust layer for the semantic web is essentially about reasoning the trustworthiness of statements. For example, how much trust do you place on statements such as "John and James are best friends." Trusting this statement depends on the source of the statement. We will discuss this type of trust when we discuss data quality and data provenance in Section 5. We also revisit this aspect in Section 3.4.

While there is lot of research now on specification of policy languages, the advantage of semantic web languages is that we can utilize the reasoning tools being developed to reason about the policies so that we can check for the consistency of the policies. We also want to ensure that trust policies do not divulge sensitive information that is classified or private. Research along these lines is been carried out by Bertino and her group (Squicciarini et al., 2006).

3.4 Trust management for the semantic web

In Section 3.3, we discussed the application of semantic web technologies for trust management. Essentially, the idea here is to use languages such as XML, RDF, and OWL to specify policies and reason about policies based on descriptive logic. In this section, we discuss how trust management techniques may be applied for the semantic web. Note that the semantic web is a collection of technologies that give us machine-understandable web pages. Therefore, the challenge here is how do we trust the reasoning that is carried out to obtain machine-understandable web pages? Furthermore, do we trust the web pages that are produced?

As we have stated in Section 3.3, one of the layers of the semantic web is the logic, proof and trust layer. Here, we need technologies to reason about say the accuracy of the web pages. Do we trust the data that is produced? Do we trust the decisions that are made by say the agents that carry out the activities on behalf of the user? Trusting the web pages will also determine who produced the web pages. If the agents who produced the web pages are highly trustworthy, then we may place higher trust on the results. We will discuss this aspect in Section 5.

The other aspect is trusting the agents that make use of semantic web technologies such as XML and RDF-based data and carry out the activities. Do we trust the answers produced by the agents? Do these agents carry out trust negotiations between them? The problem is then reduced to the problem we discussed in Section 3.3. That is, trust established between agents is essentially the trust that is established between the people as discussed in Section 3.3. This trust may depend on credentials or based on reputation. For example, in providing a travel service, the agent has to make reservations, paper hotels, as well as make arrangements for the client to participate in tours. The agent who acts on behalf of the client will read the web pages in XML or RDF and then contact the agent that is acting on behalf of the airlines and hotels. The trust that the first agent places on the other may depend on the credential or the reputation that the travel agent has.

Therefore when we discuss trust, there are two major aspects. One is the trust placed on the data and the other is trust placed on the agents. The trust placed on the data will depend on the trust placed on the agent. Similarly, an agent that consistently produces trustworthy data can be regarded to have a higher trust value.

3.5   Trust and risk management

As stated by Celikel et al. (2007), "to manage risks in data sharing, we need to have a thorough understanding of the underlying risk factors." First of all, although trust and risk are related, they are not one and the same. For example, the more you trust someone, the more you share the data with that person. However, there is also the situation that a hospital A trusts hospital B, but A does not share data with B as B's systems are not secure. One could argue that since B's computers are not secure, then B cannot be trusted. In some cases, sharing data with untrustworthy parties may not be risky. For example, a hospital may share its data with a drug company to find a cure, even though the hospital does not trust the company. Here again, one could argue that the hospital places some trust that the company will find a cure for the disease even if it may not use the data appropriately. However, if the data is not sensitive data, then sharing it may not be an issue. Therefore, one can treat trust and risk to be interrelated but different concepts.

Although different models for the relationship between trust and risk have been proposed, the exact relationship between trust and risk in data-sharing applications is yet to be made clear (Bohnet and Zeckhauser, 2004). What we need is an appropriate model to specify trust and risk relationships. As stated by Celikel et al., "trust is one, but not the only factor that affects risk." Our research is involved with understanding trust and risk and developing a risk-based trust model. Celikel et al. state that "in order to create a trust based risk model, we need to capture all the risks associated with trust misjudgments." Furthermore, he states that cost-benefit analysis has to be carried out to share the data even if the risks are high (Celikel et al., 2007). Some initial research in this area is being carried out by Finin et al. at the University of Maryland, Baltimore County. We also need to develop an inference engine that can infer trust and risk based on existing values. For example, what are the risks involved in sharing the data? What happens if we do not share the data? What happens if we share the data even if it is risky?

3.6   Digital rights management

A digital rights management (DRM) system is composed of information technology components and services along with corresponding law, policies, and business models that enable controlled distribution of content and associated usage rights. The different DRMs must interoperate and International Standards Organization (ISO) standards are being specified for interoperation. The relationship between rights management and the semantic web is the ontologies. An example of such as ontology is the copyright ontology. Copyright ontology is a semantic approach that uses web ontologies. It is based on OWL. The copyright ontology conceptualization is divided into three parts: creation model, rights model, and action model.

The creation model defines the different forms a creation can take, which are classified depending on three points of view: abstract, object, and process. The rights model follows the World Intellectual Property Organization (WIPO) recommendations to define the rights hierarchy. It includes both economic and moral rights. The most relevant rights in the DRM context are economic rights as they are related to productive and commercial aspects of copyright. Example rights include reproduction, distribution, public, performance, fixation, communication, transformation and economic rights. Action model corresponds to the primitive actions that can be performed on the concepts defined in the creation model and which are regulated by the rights in the right model. Implementations of DRM model have used OWL descriptive logic (DL) and Pellet Logic Reasoner (further details can be obtained from the work by García and Gil, 2006).

3.7 Reputation-based systems

Trust may be established using what is called a reputation network. As stated in Golbeck et al. (2003), a reputation-based network is a distributed, web-based social network. Reputation rating inferred from one user to another. Individuals are connected to each person they rated and results in a large interconnected network of users. The only requirement is that the individuals should assert their reputation ratings for one another in the network. Individuals will be controlling their own data. Data is maintained in a distributed fashion. Data can be stored anywhere and integrated through a common foundation

The FOAF (Friend-Of-A-Friend) RDF primer project illustrates the relationship between the semantic web and the reputation networks. An ontological vocabulary is used for describing people and their relationships. This is extended by providing a mechanism describing the reputation relationships and allows people to rate the reputation or trustworthiness of another person.

Algorithms are being developed to infer reputations. As stated in (Golbeck et al., 2003), recommendations are made to one person (source) about the reputation of another person (sink). Trust and reputation literature contains many different metrics. These metrics are categorized according to the perspective used for making calculations. For example, global metrics calculate a single value for each entity in the network. Local metrics calculate a reputation rating for an individual in the network. In global system, an entity will always have the same inferred rating. In local system, an entity could be rated differently depending on the node the inference is made for.

Example of a reputation system is TrustMail. It is a message scoring system and adds reputation ratings to the folder views of a message. It helps sort messages accordingly by the user after he sees the reputation ratings. It highlights the important and relevant messages.

4 Privacy and the semantic web

4.1 Overview

As we have stated, while confidentiality is about the web site or system releasing data/information only to those who are authorized according to the policies, privacy is about a person determining what information should be released about him. Therefore, if the web sites privacy policies are not acceptable to this user, then he/she can decide whether he/she wants to give the information to the web site.

Note however that while privacy has been discussed a great deal even at the congressional levels, not everyone agrees with this definition. For example, I teach at the Armed Forces Communication and Electronics Association in Washington DC in Data Mining, National Security and Privacy at the unclassified level. The students who take my courses mainly work for the Department of Defense and Intelligence agencies. For them, privacy is not the same as one feels about releasing say his or her medical records. It is my understanding that the Federal Bureau of Investigation's (FBI) idea of privacy is to ensure that the personal information of US citizens does not get into the wrong hands. Even to other agencies, FBI will release private information only if the agency is authorized to get that information. In a way, privacy becomes more or less like confidentiality for such organizations.

Much work has been carried out on privacy including specification and enforcement of privacy policies, developing techniques for privacy preserving data mining, and specifying standards for privacy. In this chapter, interest in privacy is with respect to the semantic web. One of the significant developments with W3C is the specification of standards that a web site can use to specify its privacy polices. This standard is called Platform for Privacy Preferences (P3P). Another challenge for the semantic web is to ensure that private information is not released as a result of semantic web mining.

The organization of this section is as follows. In Section 4.2, we discuss privacy management in general. In Section 4.3, we discuss semantic web technologies (such as XML and RDF) for specifying privacy policies. Protecting the private information such as private web pages will be discussed in Section 4.4. P3P will be discussed in Section 4.5. Privacy problem through inference including privacy constraint processing will be discussed in Section 4.6. Privacy preserving semantic web mining is the subject of Section 4.7.

4.2   Privacy management

Social scientists have studied privacy for several years, and policy specialists have developed privacy policies for agencies and corporations. However, it is only recently that security specialists have started focusing on privacy. Furthermore, the Terrorism Information Awareness program at DARPA together with the focus on data mining has resulted in efforts on privacy preserving data mining and privacy preserving data management. Today, privacy is an important area of information security. However, it has been difficult to give a precise definition of privacy as each organization and agency has a different view.

So the question is what is privacy? The general notion is that a person should decide what personal information should be released about him or her. Such a definition was fine before we had tools for data analysis and data mining and the WWW. Through such tools, it may now be possible for someone to infer private information about another person. Therefore, we need to perhaps redefine the notion of privacy. On the contrary, some organizations want to control personal information about the community and decide who they should release the personal information to. That is, as stated earlier, my understanding is that the FBI has information about various individuals; they will determine whether to release the information to say Central Intelligence Agency (CIA). Initially, I argued that this is essentially ensuring confidentiality and not privacy. However, after working more on privacy issues and reading about the subject, I now believe that there can be no universal definition of privacy. Privacy has to be defined by an organization. That is, one organization may define privacy policies as policies protecting its sensitive information. Another organization may define privacy policies to be those that are specified by those who work for the organization as to what information can be released by them. Therefore, whether privacy policies are a subset of confidently policies or whether they are separate policies is left to an organization to determine (Sweeney, 2002).

Our interest also lies in the relationship between privacy, confidentiality, and trust. In our work, we have made the following assumption. Trust is established between say a web site and a user based on credentials or reputations. When a user logs into a web site to make say a purchase, the web site will specify what its privacy policies are. The use will then determine whether he wants to enter personal information. That is, if the web site will give out say the user's address to a third party, then the user can decide whether to enter this information. However before the user enters the information, the user has to decide whether he trusts the web site. This can be based on the credential and reputation. If the user trusts the web site, then the user can enter his private information if he is satisfied with the policies. If not, he can choose not to enter the information.

We have given a similar reasoning for confidentiality. Here, the user is requesting information from the web site; the web site checks its confidentiality policies and decides what information to release to the user. The web site can also check the trust it has on the user and decide whether to give the information to the user. As stated in Section 2, one can also determine the quality of the data based on the trust placed on the user or on the web site.

More details on specific aspects of privacy and the semantic web will be discussed in the following several sections. In particular, applying semantic web technologies for privacy management, privacy issues for the semantic web, P3P, privacy problem that occurs through inference, and privacy preserving semantic web mining will be discussed.

4.3   Semantic web applications for privacy management

The major contributions of semantic web technologies for privacy management are in specifying policies in semantic web technologies. These policies could be specified in XML, RDF, OWL, or related semantic web languages. Another contribution is the P3P. The W3C community has come up with a framework for web sites to specify privacy policies. This framework is called P3P. We will discuss P3P in Section 4.5.

As in the case of trust management, one needs to decide the appropriate language to specify privacy polices. XML is becoming a popular language for this purpose. Even the P3P standards initially focused on using RDF for privacy policy specification and switched to XML. However, if one needs to represent the semantics of the privacy policies and reason about privacy then RDF or OWL would be more appropriate.

In specifying privacy policies, one also needs to determine whether sensitive or private information could be leaked. Therefore, appropriate confidentiality or privacy policies may be enforced on the original privacy policies themselves. Therefore, we may want to control access to various parts of the privacy policy specifications that describe the policies.

4.4   Privacy for semantic web

Privacy for the semantic web is essentially about ensuring that private information is not divulged through the usage of the semantic web. Note that semantic web is a collection of representation and reasoning technologies. Therefore, the goal is not to reveal private information. For this, we need to ensure that privacy policies are enforced properly on XML and RDF documents as well as OWL ontologies. Furthermore, the goal of the reasoning engines that are developed based on descriptive logics are such that private information cannot be inferred by deduction.

Privacy for semantic web technologies has received little attention. Bertino et al. have investigated privacy for XML and also examined aspects of privacy violations that result from trust management based on their Trust-X system (Squicciarini et al., 2007). Finin et al. are examining privacy for their research on semantic web, although their research is focusing mainly on trust management. In our investigation of CPT for the semantic web, we have privacy enforcement based on both what we call the basic system and the advanced system (Thuraisingham, 2007b, 2008). Note that the advanced system consists of a privacy engine that will focus on privacy violations through inference. In Section 4.2, we discussed CPT for a general web environment. With the semantic web, the idea is for the machine to examine the web pages and determine whether any private information is revealed. Furthermore, in an ordinary web, the web site will display its privacy policies to the user and the user determines whether to enter his/her private information. However with semantic web technologies, the web site will examine the privacy policies and the use preferences and give advice to the user as to whether he/she should enter his private information. As we have stated earlier, one of the significant developments of privacy and semantic web lies in the P3P. This will be discussed in Section 4.5.

4.5 Platform for privacy preferences

P3P is an emerging industry standard that enables web sites to express their privacy practices in a standard format. The format of the policies can be automatically retrieved and understood by user agents. It is a product of W3C (www.w3c.org). As we have stated, the main difference between privacy and security as considered in many domains is the following. User is informed of the privacy policies enforced by the web site. User is not informed of the security (or confidentiality) policies in general. When a user enters a web site, the privacy policies of the web site are conveyed to the user. If the privacy policies are different from user preferences, the user is notified. User can then decide how to proceed.

Several major corporations are working on P3P standards including Microsoft, IBM, HP, NEC Nokia, and NCR. Several web sites have also implemented P3P. Semantic web group has adopted P3P. Initial version of P3P used RDF to specify policies. Recent version has migrated to XML. P3P policies use XML with namespaces for encoding policies. P3P has its own statements and data types expressed in XML. P3P schemas utilize XML schemas. XML is a prerequisite to understanding P3P. P3P specification released in January 2005 uses catalog shopping example to explain concepts. P3P is an international standard and is an ongoing project.

Note that P3P does not replace laws. P3P works together with the law. What happens if the web sites do not honor their P3P policies? Then, appropriate legal actions will have to be taken. Today, XML is the technology to specify P3P policies. Policy experts will have to specify the policies. Technologies will have to develop the specifications. Legal experts will have to take actions if the policies are violated.

4.6 Privacy problem through inference

We have conducted extensive research on the inference problem for secure databases. Much of our work focused on security constraint processing, which has now come to be known as policy management. Policies included those for content- and context-dependent constraints as well as dynamic- and event-based constraints. For example, the ship's mission becomes classified after the war begins (Thuraisingham and Ford, 1995). We have since adapted this approach for privacy constraint processing where security levels would now become privacy levels (public, private, semipublic, etc.) and the security constraint becomes a privacy constraint such as names and healthcare records taken together becomes private. It should be noted that with this approach, we are assuming that privacy and confidentiality are one and the same. Now, this agrees with say FBI's notion of privacy where it has to protect the private information of US citizens. But this is not consistent with medical privacy where in this context privacy is specified by an individual. That is, an individual determines the information he has to keep private. In this case, the privacy controller is managed by the individual. That is, the client will determine that if it gives out say its genetic information, then an insurance company can figure out the illnesses it may be prone to. Therefore, the privacy controller will guide the client what information to release about itself.

We have designed and developed a privacy controller. Here, data represented using semantic web technologies such as XML, RDF, and ontologies are augmented with inference engines. These engines may carry out rule processing or utilize ontology-based reasoning to deuce new data from existing data. If the new data is private, then it can give advice to the client as to what information should be kept private. Note that under the FBI scenario, the privacy controller is essentially the confidentiality controller (which we have called the inference controller), and therefore, it acts on the server side and determines what information it has to release to the client (such as the CIA).

4.7   Privacy preserving semantic web mining

In (Clifton et al., 2002), an overview of privacy preserving data mining is provided. The idea is as follows. Using the data mining tools, even the naïve users can make unauthorized inferences that could be highly sensitive or private. Furthermore, the goal is to hide the private data such as disease of a particular person while giving out general trends and associations. That is, we could give out the information that "people living in California are more prone to asthma" without giving out the fact that John has asthma. Privacy preserving data mining techniques work with perturbed or randomized data without revealing the actual data (Agrawal and Srikant, 2000).

Recently, there have been reports on semantic web mining. There are two aspects here. One is to mine the data on the web represented using semantic web technologies such as XML, RDF, and OWL. Note that much of the work has focused on mining relational data. More recently, there is work on mining unstructured data such as text, audio, images, and video. The challenge is to mine the databases that store and manage XML and RDF documents. The other aspect is to mine the XML and RDF documents without revealing the actual data but giving out correlations and trends. The former is an aspect of data mining, whereas the latter is an aspect of privacy preserving data mining. There is yet a third aspect and that is to use ontologies to help the mining process. For example, the data mining tool may need clarifications about the meaning of a web page. Here, ontologies expressed in OWL may be used to clarify the concepts to facilitate the mining process.

5 Integrity management and the semantic web

5.1 Overview

In this section, we will discuss integrity management for the semantic web. Integrity includes several aspects. In the database world, integrity includes concurrency control and recovery as well as enforcing integrity constraints. For example, when multiple transactions execute at the same time, the consistency of the data has to be ensured. When a transaction aborts, it has to be ensured that the database is recovered from the failure into a consistent state. Integrity constraints are rules that have to be satisfied by the data. Rules include "salary value has to be positive" and "age of an employee cannot decrease over time." More recently, integrity has included data quality, data provenance, data currency, real-time processing, and fault tolerance.

In this section, we will discuss integrity with respect to semantic web technologies. For example, how do we ensure the integrity of the data and the processes? How do we ensure that data quality is maintained? Some aspects of integrity are already being investigated by the researchers and some other aspects are yet to be investigated. The organization of this section is a follows. In Section 5.2, we discuss aspects of integrity. Semantic web technologies for integrity management are discussed in Section 5.3. Integrity for the semantic web is discussed in Section 5.4. Closely related to integrity is data provenance and this is discussed in Section 5.5.

5.2 Integrity, data quality and data provenance

As stated in Section 5.1, there are many aspects to integrity. For example, concurrency control, data recovery, data accuracy, real-time processing, data authenticity, data completeness, data currency, data quality, data provenance, fault tolerance, and integrity constraint enforcement are all aspects of integrity management. In this section, we will examine each aspect of integrity.

Concurrency control: In data management, concurrent control is about transactions executing at the same time and ensuring consistency of the data. Therefore, transactions have to obtain locks or utilize time stamps to ensure that the data is left in a consistent state when multiple transactions attempt to access the data at the same time. Extensive research has been carried out on concurrency control techniques for transaction management both in centralized and in distributed environments (Bernstein et al., 1987).

Data recovery: When transactions abort before they complete execution, the database should be recovered to a consistent state such as its state before the transaction started execution. Several recovery techniques have been proposed to ensure the consistency of the data.

Data authenticity: When the data is delivered to the user, its authenticity has to be ensured. That is, the user should get accurate data and the data should not be tampered with. We have conducted research on ensuring authenticity of XML data during third party publishing (Bertino et al., 2004).

Data completeness: Data that a user receives should not only be authentic but also be complete. That is, everything that the user is authorized to see has to be delivered to the user.

Data currency: Data has to be current. That is, data that is outdated has to be deleted or archived and the data that the user sees has to be current data. Data currency is an aspect of real-time processing. If a user wants to retrieve the temperature, he has to be given the current temperature, not the temperature that is 24 h old.

Data accuracy: The question is how accurate is the data? This is also closely related to data quality and data currency. That is, accuracy depends on whether the data has been maliciously corrupted or whether it has come from an untrusted source.

Data quality: Is the data of high quality? This includes data authenticity, data accuracy, and whether the data is complete or certain. If the data is uncertain, then can we reason with uncertainty to ensure that the operations that use the data are not affected? Data quality also depends on the data source.

Data provenance: This has to do with the history of the data. That is, from the time the data originated such as emanating from the sensors until the present time such as when it is given to the general. The question is who has accessed the data? Who has modified the data? How has the data traveled? This will determine whether the data has been misused.

Integrity constraints: These are rules that the data has to satisfy, such as the age of a person cannot be a negative number. This type of integrity has been studied extensively by the database and the artificial intelligence communities.

Fault tolerance: As in the case of data recovery, the processes that fail have to be recovered. Therefore, fault tolerance deals with data recovery as well as process recovery. Techniques for fault tolerance include check pointing and acceptance testing.

Real-time processing: Data currency is one aspect of real-time processing where the data has to be current. Real-time processing also has to deal with transactions meeting timing constraints. For example, stock quotes have to be given at within say 5 min. If not, it will be too late. Missing timing constraints could cause integrity violations.

In Sections 5.3 and 5.4, we will explore the relationships between integrity management and semantic web technologies.

5.3 Semantic web for integrity management

In Sections 2–4, we discussed the use of semantic web technologies to specify policies for CPT. For example, in Section 2, we discussed the use of XML and RDF to specify confidentiality policies. In Section 4, we illustrated how semantic web technologies may be used to specify privacy policies. Specifying trust policies was discussed in Section 3. In this section, we will discuss the use of semantic web technologies for integrity management.

Like CPT, semantic web technologies such as XML may be used to specify integrity policies. Integrity policies may include policies for specifying integrity constraint as well as policies for specifying timing constraints, data currency, and data quality. Note that there are many other applications of semantic web technologies to ensure integrity. For example, to ensure data provenance, the history of the data has to be documented. Semantic web technologies such as XML are being used to represent say the data annotations that are used to determine the quality of the data or whether the data has been misused. That is, the data captured is annotated with metadata information such as what the data is about, when it was captured, and who captured it. Then as the data moves from place to place or from person to person, the annotations are updated so that at a later time the data may be analyzed for misuse. These annotations are typically represented in semantic web technologies such as XML, RDF, and OWL.

Another application of semantic web technologies for integrity management is the use of ontologies to resolve semantic heterogeneity. That is, semantic heterogeneity causes integrity violations. This happens when the same entity is considered to be different at different sites and therefore compromises integrity and accuracy. Through the use of ontologies specified in say OWL, it can be expressed that ship in one site and submarine in another site are one and the same. Semantic web technologies also have applications in making inferences and reasoning uncertain or miming. For example, the reasoning engines based on RDF, OWL, or say Rules may be used to determine whether the integrity policies are violated. We have discussed inference and privacy problems and building inference engines in the works by Thuraisingham (2005) and Thuraisingham (2007a). These techniques have to be investigated for violation integrity policies.

5.4 *Integrity for the semantic web*

Note that in Section 2 we discussed third party publications of XML documents while maintaining consistency and completeness. This is one aspect of integrity management for semantic web technologies. The ideas expressed in our work could be extended for RDF and related documents. Note also that XML, RDF, and OWL documents have to be current, they have to be of high quality, and they have to satisfy say the integrity constraints. That is, all of the integrity issues that we discussed in Sections 5.2 and 5.3 have to be addressed for documents represented in XML and RDF. This is one aspect of integrity for the semantic web.

As we have discussed in Section 5.3, annotations that are used for data quality and data provenance are typically represented in XML or RDF documents. These documents have to be accurate, complete, and current. Therefore, integrity has to be enforced for such documents. Another aspect of integrity is managing databases that consist of XML or RDF documents. These databases have all of the issues and challenges that are present for say relational databases. That is, the queries have to be optimized and transactions should execute concurrently. Therefore, concurrency control and recover for XML and RDF documents become a challenge for managing XML and RDF databases. This is yet another aspect of integrity for semantic web documents.

The actions of the agents that make use of the semantic web to carry out operations such as searching, querying, and integrating heterogeneous databases have to ensure that the integrity of the data is maintained. These agents cannot maliciously corrupt the data. They have to ensure that the data is accurate, complete, and consistent. Finally, when integrating heterogeneous databases, semantic web technologies such as OWL ontologies are being used to handle semantic heterogeneity. These ontologies have to be accurate and complete and cannot be tampered with.

In summary, for the semantic web technologies to be useful, they have to enforce integrity. Furthermore, semantic web technologies themselves are being used to specify integrity policies.

5.5 *Inferencing, data quality and data provenance*

Some researchers feel that data quality is an application of data provenance. Furthermore, they have developed theories for inferring data quality. In this section, we will examine some of the developments keeping in mind the relationship between data quality, data provenance, and the semantic web.

Data quality is about accuracy, timeliness, and dependability (i.e., trustworthiness) of the data. It is however subjective and depends on the users and the domains. Some of the issues that have to be answered include the creation of the data, That is, where did it come from and why and how was the data obtained? Data quality information is stored as annotations to the data and should be part of data provenance. One could ask the question as to how we can obtain the trustworthiness of the data. This could depend on how the source is ranked and the reputation of the source. Note that we discussed reputation in Section 3.

As we have stated, researchers have developed theories for inferring data quality (Pon and Cardenas, 2005). The motivation is due to the fact that data could come from multiple sources; it is shared and prone to errors. Furthermore, data could be uncertain. Therefore, theories of uncertainty such as statistical reasoning, Bayesian theories, and Dempster Schafer theory of evidence are being used to infer the quality of the data. With respect to security, we need to ensure that the quality of the inferred data does not violate the policies. For example, at the unclassified level, we may say that the source is trustworthy, but at the secret level, we know that the source is not trust-worthy. The inference controllers that we have developed could be integrated with the theories of interceding developed for data quality to ensure security.

Next let us examine data provenance. For many of the domains including medical and healthcare, as well as defense where the accuracy of the data is critical for life therein activities, we need to have a good understanding as to where the data came from and who may have tampered with the data. Data provenance is information that helps determine the derivation history of a data product, starting from its original sources. Provenance information can be applied for data quality, auditing, and ownership, among others. By having records of who accessed the data, data misuse can be determined. Usually, annotations are used to store the prevent information of the Darla. The challenge is to determine whether one needs to maintain coarse-grained provenance data or fine-grained provenance data. For example, in a coarse-grained situation, the tables of a relation may be annotated, whereas in a fine-grained situation, every element may be annotated. There is of course the storage overhead to consider for managing provenance. XML, RDF, and OWL have been used to represent provenance data, and this way, the tools developed for the semantic web technologies may be used to manage the provenance data.

6 Policy engineering

6.1 Overview

One of the major challenges with policy research is the generation, specification, and the management of policies. This area has come to be known as policy engineering. This is similar to software engineering that deals with the specification and management of software and to data engineering that deals with the definition and management of data. In this section, we will focus on policy engineering as it relates to the semantic web.

The organization of this section is as follows. Now that we have discussed various aspects of policies including CPT and integrity, we will revisit semantic web policies in Section 6.2. Much of our discussion on policies has been obtained from the works of Bonatti and his team (Bonatti and Olmedilla, 2005; Bonatti et al., 2006). In Section 6.3, we discuss policy generation and specification. We utilize some of our earlier research on security constraints generation and specification to deal with policy engineering. In Section 6.4, we will discuss the consistency of policies. Evolution of policies including policy reuse is discussed in Section 6.5. Integration of policies is discussed in Section 6.6. Visualization of policies is discussed in Section 6.7. Our work on policy engineering with respect to the semantic web is influenced by the discussions we have had with Tim Finin and his team at the University of Maryland at Baltimore County as well as the developments with ontology engineering as discussed by Antoniou and van Harmelen (2003).

6.2   Revisiting semantic web policies

In this section, we provide a broad discussion of policies as discussed in the works by Bonatti et al. (2004), Bonatti et al. (2005), Bonatti et al. (2006), and Blaze et al. (1998).

6.2.1   Policies

There are various types of policies that enhance security, privacy, and usability of distributed services. Bonnati and his team have stated that the different policies should be integrated into a single framework. These policies include not only access control but also privacy policies, business rules, quality of service, and others. Access control policies protect any system open to the Internet. Privacy policy protects the user while they are browsing web and accessing web services. Business policy specifies the condition that applies to specific customer of web services. Other policies specify constraints related to quality of service. All these policies make decisions based on the information of the peer/user involved in the transaction. For example, age, nationality, customer profile, identity, and reputation may all be considered both in access control decisions and in determining which discounts are applicable. These kinds of policies need to be integrated to provide a common infrastructure that can be used for decision making and interoperability. Policies can be harmonized and synchronized. There are also policies that require the events to be logged and are called provisional policies.

Policies specify actions to be executed along with the decision process. Policies in these context act as both decision support system and declarative behavior system. An effective approach to policy specification could give common user a better control on the behavior of their own system. Achievement of this goal depends on policies' ability to interoperate with rest of the system. Policies make decisions based on properties of the peers interacting with the system. These properties may be strongly certified by cryptographic techniques or may be reliable to some intermediate degree with lightweight evidence gathering and validation.

6.2.2 Policy framework

A flexible policy framework should try to merge these two forms of evidence to meet the efficiency and usability requirements of web applications. Trust negotiation, reputation models, business rules, and action specification languages have to be integrated into a single framework. Automated trust negotiation (ATN) plays an important role in trust management. The semantic web is a large, uncensored system to which anyone may contribute. This raises the question of how much credence to give each source. We cannot expect each user to know the trustworthiness of each source. This is where trust management plays an important role in establishing the trustworthiness of each source.

6.2.3 Trust management and negotiation

As we have discussed in Section 3, two major approaches to managing trust exists and they are policy-based and reputation-based. In policy-based trust management approach, strong security mechanisms are used to regulate access of user to web services. Strong security mechanisms include signed certificates and trusted certification authorities (CAs). Access decisions are based on this mechanism with well-defined semantics that provides strong verification and analysis support. Policy-based approach helps in making a decision about the "trustworthiness" of the requester and determines whether the service/resource is allowed or denied to the requester. Reputation-based trust relies on a "soft computational" approach to the problem of trust. In this approach, trust is computed based on the local experience and the feedback given by the other entities in the network. For example, online buyers and sellers rate each other after each transaction. The ratings pertaining to a certain seller (or buyer) are aggregated by web sites reputation system into a number reflecting seller (or buyer) trustworthiness as judged by the web page community.

The reputation-based approach has been favored for environments such as peer-to-peer or semantic web. The existence of certifying authorities cannot always be assumed, but a large pool of individual user ratings is often available. Another common approach is to make requester to commit to contract/copyrights by clicking on the "accept" button. To make decisions in real-life scenarios, a combination of these approaches is needed.

For example, transaction policies must handle expenses of all magnitudes, from micro payments to credit card payments of a thousand euros or even more. The cost of the traded goods or services contributes to determine the risk associated to the transaction and hence the trust measure required.

Strong evidence is generally harder to gather and verify than lightweight evidence. Sometimes, a "soft" reputation measure or a declaration in the sense outlined earlier is all one can obtain in a given scenario. Success of trust management depends on the ability of the system to balance trust level and risk level for each task. The following are two important research directions related to the area of trust. How should different forms of trust be integrated? How many different forms of evidence can be conceived? Access control presents difficult problems in a distributed environment. This problem becomes severe when resources and subject requesting it belong to different security domains.

Common access control mechanisms provide authorization decisions based on the identity of the requester, which is ineffective. ATN solves this ineffectiveness.

Attribute credentials are exchanged to establish trust among strangers who wish to share a resource. ATN is an approach to regulate the exchange of sensitive attribute credentials by using access control policies. In ATN, peers are able to automatically negotiate credentials according to their own declarative, rule-based policies.

Some of the challenges include how negotiations take place between peers? Web server asks for credentials from the client requesting resource. The client in turn asks for server credentials to determine the validity of the server. Both are in symmetrical situation. Each peer decides how to react to incoming request based on local policy. Local policy is a set of rules written in logic programming. Requests are formulated based on the rules from the policies. Several factors are taken into account while formulating requests. More details on trust management can be found in the policy work of Bonnati and his team (Bonatti et al., 2004).

6.2.4 *Cooperative policy enforcement*

This involves both machine-machine and human-machine interaction. Machine-machine interaction is handled by the various negotiation mechanisms as discussed earlier. Human-machine interaction is more problematic than expected. Most users lack the technical expertise to tailor existing policies to match their own needs, causing easy access to their protected resources. Such lack of knowledge on the part of the users also affects privacy protection. Most users are not able to personalize their information release policies to suit their needs. To make the user understand the meaning of responses better, we bring in cooperative policy enforcement (CPE). This gives users the reasons for negative responses and suggestions for how to avoid such responses in the future.

Greater user awareness and control on policies are the main objectives of CPE. Policies are made user-friendly by using rule-based policy specification language such as controlled natural language and advanced explanation mechanisms. Several novel aspects are described in CPE including tabled explanation structure and suitable heuristics for focusing explanations; heuristics are generic, that is, domain-independent combination of tabling techniques and heuristics yields a novel method for explaining failure.

Query answering is conceived for the following categories of users: users who try to understand how to obtain access permissions, users who monitor and verify their own privacy policy, and policy managers who verify and monitor their policies. Find the right tradeoff between explanation quality and the effort for instantiating the framework in new application domains. Second generation explanation systems prescribe a sequence of expensive steps, including the creation of an independent domain knowledge base expressly for communicating with the user. This would be a serious obstacle to the applicability of the framework.

6.2.5 Natural language policies

Policies should be written by and understandable to users, to let them control behavior of their system. Policies should be formulated based on rules and stated in simple language. The inherent ambiguity of natural language is incompatible with the precision needed by security and privacy specifications.

6.2.6 Next Steps

In summary, policies represent single body of declarative rules used in many possible ways, for negotiations, query answering, and other forms of system behavior control. Transparent interoperation based on ontology sharing will determine the success of trust negotiation. Users have better understanding and control over the policies that govern their systems with the help of CPE and trust management. Policies will have to handle decisions under a wide range of risk levels and performance requirements.

6.3 Policy generation and specification

The first step in policy engineering is generating the policies. The application specialist will specify the application. Together with the policy expert, they will come up with the appropriate policies to enforce for the application. This is essentially the policy generation phase. Once the policies are generated, the next step is to come up with a language to specify the policies.

The application specialization will likely specify the policies in natural language. The policy expert will work the application specialist to refine the policies. However, the policy expert and the application specialist may not have a clear picture of the data. Therefore, based on the policies and the data, the policies will have to be refined further. This will be done with the help of a data engineer.

Note that in the case of ontology engineering, one of the challenges is to generate the ontologies automatically. That is, from the various data sources, the concepts that will form the ontologies have to be generated. For this, data mining has been used. That is by mining the data, concepts and subsequently ontologies are generated. Now, these ontologies may be used to aid in the policy generation phase.

Once the policies are generated, the next step is to come up with a language to specify the policies. For this, we can use the various semantic web technologies such as XML, RDF, and OWL. There are also several other policy languages that have been generated based on XML and RDF such as the REI system developed at UMBC or the XML-based languages developed at the University of Milan and Purdue University.

6.4   Policy consistency

Once the policies are generated and specified in a language, they have to be refined and also made consistent. We have developed theorem provers in the past for secure systems based on the NTML logic that we developed (Thuraisingham, 1991). More recently, Jim Hendler and his group at University of Maryland (now at RPI) have developed a system called Pellet that is the reasoning system. Furthermore, reasoning systems such as JENA have been developed for RDF. These systems have to be examined for policy consistency. Research in this direction has been carried out by UMBC, UMD, and MIT in the policy aware web project.

One of the challenges with reasoning systems is scalability. For example, we can build reasoning systems that can reason about a few policies. However in the real world, especially with multiple databases, there are numerous policies that have to be handled. Furthermore, the policies may have semantic and syntactic heterogeneity. That is, policy consistency has to be ensured as part of policy integration and interoperability. We will discuss this aspect Section 6.6. We also have to develop ontologies that will specify the meaning of policies so as to facilitate policy consistency.

6.5   Policy evolution and reuse

Policies, like ontologies, will continue to change. For example, when an administration changes, which is often the case, new policies maybe enforced and old policies removed. Furthermore, policies may be modified.

Therefore, an organization needs to ensure that policy changes occur in a smooth fashion.

When policies change, an organization could throw away the old policies and generate a new set of policies from scratch. That means the organization has to go through the policy generation, specification, and consistency checking phases. On the contrary, the organization may reuse as many policies as possible and introduce additional policies. Furthermore, the organization may want to minimize the number of policies that are modified. This is called policy evolution and reuse.

There is a strong analogy between software evolution and reuse as well as ontology/data evolution and reuse. There is still a debate between software reuse and re-developing the software. For example, in the case of legacy applications, do we migrate them to new platforms or do we throw the legacy applications and develop new applications.

Up to a certain point, reusing and evolution works. However, when the changes that have to made are massive, it would be better to re-develop them. In the case of ontologies, we have found that ontology reuse is of immense help. For example, we have developed several geospatial anthologies. However, we have used the ontologies that have been developed by others in many cases and built on top of them. Now, unlike software engineering, ontology engineering is a newer field and therefore reuse may help. But as the field gets more mature, then there may be a challenge as to whether to reuse the ontologies and build on them or to develop new ontologies.

Policy reuse is even newer than ontology reuse. It is only recently that policy engineering is evolving as a field. Therefore, we need more research on determining how to evolve policies and reuse policies.

6.6 Policy integration and interoperability

Until this point, we have more or less assumed that policy engineering is with respect to one organization. As we will see in Section 7, organizations work together and form coalitions. Data from multiple organizations and sources have to be integrated. Ontologies are being developed for data integrity. Interoperability issues arise due to heterogeneity. We could have semantic as well as syntactic heterogeneity for data. Ontologies are being used for handling heterogeneity. In Section 7, we will discuss secure data interoperability using semantic web technologies. While much of the focus has been on data interoperability and integration, the heterogeneous policies have to be integrated. Therefore, in this section, we will focus on policy interoperability.

Our recent research has focused on policy interoperability for geospatial technologies. We have developed geospatial ontologies that could be used to handle semantic as well as syntactic heterogeneity with respect to policies. For example, policies P1 and P2 below show two policies that are semantically heterogeneous (Policy P1 specifies that only an administrator with certain resolution at or above specific alert level can access the map region represented by an array of latitude/longitude coordinate pairs. Policy P2 specifies if a manager is at a specific location, she can access all census data including highways, streets and addresses for zip code 79900). In a coalition environment, these heterogeneities have to be resolved to develop global policies. We have developed algorithms that determine the types of heterogeneities and resolve the differences using ontologies and then integrate them to develop a global policy.

Note that policy integration is not new. Our initial work on policy integration was carried out within the context of secure federated data management (Thuraisingham, 1994). This was well before the development of semantic web technologies. However today, we have policy languages that are based on XML, RDF, and OWL. Furthermore, ontologies show a lot of promise to resolve semantic differences. For the first time, we have a good handle on data heterogeneity. Therefore, it is time to examine policy interoperability using semantic web technologies.

6.7 *Policy management, visualization and mining*

While policy generation, specification, consistency checking, reuse, and interoperability are all major aspects of policy engineering, we would like to add one other major aspect and that is policy data management. This encompasses many aspects including policy querying and updating, policy visualization, and policy mining. In this section, we will discuss policy management.

The set of policies can be stored in a database and managed in the same way we manage the data. Therefore, query languages are needed to query the policies. Note that for policies represented in XML, we can use languages such as XML-QL or XQuery, and for policies represented in RDF, we can use RQL. Policies also have to be updated and we can use the policy query language to update the policies.

Policies can be quite complex and difficult to understand. Therefore, graphical resonating languages such as Unified Modeling Language (UML) diagrams have been used for policy representation and merging policies. Furthermore, visualization tools have been developed to visualize the policies and subsequently merge policies.

Finally, policies can be mined to extract the nuggets and better understand them. Note that one aspect of policy mining is role mining for role-based access control. Here, the user activities are mined so that consistent set of roles can be defined. Policy mining may go beyond role mining to determine the usage policies as well as role-based policies.

7 Some recent research on policy management for semantic web

We have started a research project with the University of Maryland, Baltimore County (Finin et al.), the University of Texas at San Antonio (Sandhu et al.), and the W3C group at the Massachusetts Institute of Technology (Kagal et al.) and are developing a semantic framework for policy management for assured information sharing. In this project, we are first applying role-based access control to OWL, and the resulting model is called ROWLBAC (Finin et al., 2008). We are now investigating the integration of Sandhu' UCON (Usage Control) model with semantic web technologies. Our policies are those for information sharing among organizations and coalitions.

A coalition consists of a set of organizations, which may be agencies, universities, and corporations that work together in a peer-to-peer environment to solve problems such as intelligence and military operations as well as healthcare operations. Coalitions are usually dynamic in nature. That is, members may join and leave the coalitions in accordance with the policies and procedures. A challenge is to ensure the secure operation of a coalition. We assume that the members of a coalition, which are also called its partners, may be trustworthy, untrustworthy, or partially (semi) trustworthy.

Various aspects of coalition data sharing are discussed in the Markle report (Vatis, 2003). However, security including CPT, integrity, release, and dissemination has been given little consideration. Much of the earlier work on security in a coalition environment has focused on secure federated data sharing. Thuraisingham (1994) was one of the first to propose multilevel security for federated database systems. Discretionary security was proposed in (Olivier, 1996). We have carried out an initial investigation of policy management for assured information sharing in the work by (Thuraisingham, 2007b, 2008).

Our research is essentially focusing on applying semantic web technologies for secure data sharing. While confidentiality is our major focus, our techniques can be applied to privacy and trust as well. In a coalition, the policies enforced by the component organizations through the local agencies have to be integrated at the coalition level. Each organization may export security policies and data to the coalition. The component systems may have more stringent access control requirements for foreign organizations. The challenge is to ensure that there is no security violation at the coalition level.

8 Summary and directions

Section 2 has provided an overview of the semantic web and discussed security standards. We first discussed security issues for the semantic web. We argued that security must cut across all the layers. Next, we provided some more details on XML security, RDF security, secure information integration, and trust. If the semantic web is to be secure, we need all of its components to be secure. We also described some of our research on access control and dissemination of XML documents. Much research needs to be done. We need to continue with the research on XML security. We must start examining security for RDF. This is more difficult as RDF incorporates semantics. We need to examine the work on security constraint processing and context-dependent security constraints and see if we can apply some of the ideas for RDF security. Finally, we need to examine the role of ontologies for secure information integration. We have to address some hard questions such as how do we integrate security policies on the semantic web? How can we incorporate policies into ontologies?

In Section 3, we have discussed trust management and its relation with the semantic web. We first discussed aspects of trust management including defining trust and also describing trust negotiations. Then, we discussed enforcing trust within the context of the semantic web. Furthermore, we also discussed the use of semantic web technologies for specifying trust policies. Next, we discussed related concepts including risk-based trust management, DRM, and reputation networks. Trust management is a fledging research area and several researchers including Bertino at Purdue University, Berners Lee at MIT, Finin at UMBC, and Winslett at UIUC among others are conducting extensive research on this topic. For example, Finin and his team at UMBC have pioneered techniques for specifying and reasoning about trust using a language called REI. We are collaborating with UMBC on trust management in a need to share environment, although numerous trust negotiation approaches have been proposed, we need research on evaluating these approaches and determine which approaches are appropriate and under what context. Therefore, although much has been done on trust management during the past decade, much still remains to be done for specific applications and domains.

In Section 4, we have discussed the various notions of privacy and provided an overview of privacy management. Then, we discussed the semantic web technology applications for privacy management. Privacy for the web was discussed next. This was followed by a discussion of the standard P3P. Finally, we discussed privacy violations through inference and privacy preserving semantic web mining. Much of the discussion in this section is in the early stages of research. We have not attempted to discuss the correct definition of privacy. Our goal is to illustrate the connection between the privacy management and the semantic web. As we have mentioned, the semantic web technologies are useful in the specification of privacy policies. Furthermore, data represented by XML and RDF could be mined and privacy violated as a result.

In Section 5, we have provided an overview of data integrity that includes data quality and data provenance. We discussed the applications of semantic web technologies for data integrity as well as discussed integrity for semantic web technologies. Finally, we provided an overview of the relationship between data quality and data provenance. Data provenance and data quality, although important, are only recently receiving attention. This is due to the fact there are vast quantities of information on the web and it is important to know the accuracy of the data and whether the data be copies or plagiarized. We also need to have answers to questions such as who owns the data. Has the data been misused? Therefore, data provenance is important to determine the security of the data. Semantic web technologies provide a way to represent and store data quality and provenance data. As we make progress with these technologies, we will have improved solutions for data quality and data provenance management. Essentially, data quality and data provenance are part of data security, and semantic web technologies are very useful to manage data quality and data provenance information.

Finally, in Section 6, we have discussed several aspects of policy engineering including policy generation and specification, policy consistency and completeness, policy reuse and evolution, policy integration, and policy management including policy visualization and mining. Like software engineering, data engineering, and ontology engineering, policy engineering is critical for the effective management of policies. The University of Maryland at Baltimore County is leading the direction for policy engineering. The research by Bertino, Bonatti, and Winslett is also showing a lot of policy engineering. Although some progress has been made on policy engineering with languages such as REI and reasoning systems such as Pellet, there is a lot to be done. One of the directions that UMBC is working is developing a policy workbench and a middleware to integrate the various policy engineering tools. This is an important direction to pursue. We also need to develop a research program for policy engineering. The discussions in this section have provided some of the challenges that need to be addressed.

Standards play an important role in the development of the semantic web. W3C has been very effective in specifying standards for XML and RDF. We need to continue with the developments and try as much as possible to transfer the research to the standards efforts. We also need to transfer the research and standards to commercial products. The next step for the semantic web standards efforts is to examine security, privacy, quality of service, integrity, and other features such as secure query services. As we have stressed in our work, security and privacy are critical and must be investigated while the standards are being developed.

References

Agrawal, R., R. Srikant (2000). Privacy-preserving data mining, in: *SIGMOD Conference*, Dallas, TX, pp. 439–450.
Antoniou, G., F. van Harmelen (2003). *A Semantic Web Primer*. MIT Press, Cambridge, MA.

Berners-Lee, T., J. Hendler, O. Lassila (2001). The semantic web. *Scientific American*, May.

Bernstein, P.A., V. Hadzilacos, N. Goodman (1987). *Concurrency Control and Recovery in Database Systems*. Addison-Wesley, Reading, MA.

Bertino, E., B. Carminati, E. Ferrari, B.M. Thuraisingham, A. Gupta (2004). Selective and authentic third-party distribution of XML documents. *IEEE Transactions on Knowledge and Data Engineering* 16(10), 1263–1278.

Bertino, E., S. Castano, E. Ferrari, M. Mesiti (2002). Protection and administration of XML data sources. *Data and Knowledge Engineering* 43(3), 237–260.

Bertino, E., E. Ferrari, A. Cinzia Squicciarini (2003). X-TNL: an XML-based language for trust negotiations, in: *Policy*, Springer, Heidelberg, pp. 81–84.

Blaze, M., J. Feigenbaum, M. Strauss (1998). Compliance checking in the policymaker trust management system, in: *Financial Cryptography*, Springer, Heidelberg, pp. 254–274.

Bohnet, I., R. Zeckhauser (2004). Trust, risk and betrayal. *Journal of Economic Behavior & Organization* 55, 467–484.

Bonatti, P.A., C. Duma, N.E. Fuchs, W. Nejdl, D. Olmedilla, J. Peer, N. Shahmehri (2006). Semantic web policies: a discussion of requirements and research issues, in: *ESWC*, Springer, Heidelberg, pp. 712–724.

Bonatti, P.A., D. Olmedilla (2005). Driving and monitoring provisional trust negotiation with metapolicies, in: *Policy*, Los Alamitos, CA (IEEE), pp. 14–23.

Bonatti, P.A., D. Olmedilla, J. Peer (2005). Advanced policy queries. Technical Report I2-D4, Working Group I2, EU NoE REWERSE. Available at http://www.rewerse.net

Bonatti, P.A., N. Shahmehri, C. Duma, D. Olmedilla, W. Nejdl, M. Baldoni, C. Baroglio, et al. (2004). Rule-based policy specification: State of the art and future work. Technical Report, Working Group I2, EU NoE REWERSE. Available at http://rewerse.net/deliverables/i2-d1.pdf

Carminati, B., E. Ferrari, B.M. Thuraisingham (2004). Using RDF for policy specification and enforcement. *DEXA Workshops*, pp. 163–167.

Celikel, E., M. Kantarcioglu, B.M. Thuraisingham, E. Bertino (2007). Managing risks in RBAC employed distributed environments, in: *OTM Conferences*, Vilamoura, Portugal, (2), pp. 1548–1566.

Clifton, C., M. Kantarcioglu, J. Vaidya (2002). Defining Privacy for Data Mining, Purdue University (see also Next Generation Data Mining Workshop, Baltimore, MD, November).

Farkas, C., M.N. Huhns (2002). Making agents secure on the semantic web. *IEEE Internet Computing* 6(6), 76–79.

Finin, T.W., A. Joshi, L. Kagal, J. Niu, R.S. Sandhu, W.H. Winsborough, B.M. Thuraisingham (2008). ROWLBAC: representing role based access control, in: *OWL, SACMAT*, NY, NY (ACM), pp. 73–82.

García, R., R. Gil (2006). An OWL copyright ontology for semantic digital rights management. *OTM Workshops*, (2), 1745–1754.

Golbeck, J., B. Parsia, J. Hendler (2003). Trust networks on the semantic web, in: *Proceedings of Cooperative Information Agents 2003*, August 27–29, Helsinki, Finland.

Kagal, L., T.W. Finin, A. Joshi (2003). A policy based approach to security for the semantic web, in: *International Semantic Web Conference*, Sanibel Island, FL, pp. 402–418.

Olivier, M.S. (1996). Integrity constraints in federated databases, in: *DBSec*, Chapman and Hall, Boca Raton, FL, pp. 43–57.

Pon, R.K., A.F. Cardenas (2005). Data quality inference, *IQIS*, 105–111.

RDF Primer. Available at www.w3.org/TR/rdf-primer/

Shmatikov, V., C. Talcott (2004). Reputation-based trust management. Navigating Computer Science Research through Waves of Privacy Concerns: Discussions among Computer Scientists at Carnegie Mellon University. *ACM Computers and Society*. Available at http://www.cs.utexas.edu/~shmat/shmat_rtm.pdf

Squicciarini, A.C., E. Bertino, E. Ferrari, F. Paci, B.M. Thuraisingham (2007). PP-trust-X: a system for privacy preserving trust negotiations *ACM Transactions on Information and System Security* 10(3), 1–50.

Squicciarini, A.C., E. Bertino, E. Ferrari, I. Ray (2006). Achieving privacy in trust negotiations with an ontology-based approach. *IEEE Transactions on Dependable Security and Computing* 3(1), 13–30.

Sweeney, L. (2002). k-Anonymity: a model for protecting privacy. *International Journal of Uncertainty, Fuzziness and Knowledge-Based Systems* 10(5), 557–570.

Thuraisingham, B. (2005). *Database and Applications Security: Integrating Data Management and Information Security*. CRC Press, Boca Raton, FL.

Thuraisingham, B. (2007a). *Building Trustworthy Semantic Webs*. CRC Press, Boca Raton, FL.

Thuraisingham, B.M. (1991). A nonmonotonic typed multilevel logic for multilevel secure database/ knowledge-based management systems, in: *CSFW*, Los Alamitos, CA (IEEE), pp. 127–138.

Thuraisingham, B.M. (1994). Security issues for federated database systems. *Computers & Security* 13(6), 509–525.

Thuraisingham, B.M. (2007b). Confidentiality, privacy and trust policy enforcement for the semantic web, in: *Policy*, Hershey, PA, pp. 8–11.

Thuraisingham, B.M. (2008). Assured information sharing: technologies, challenges and directions, in: *Intelligence and Security Informatics*, 1–15.

Thuraisingham, B.M., W. Ford (1995). Security constraints in a multilevel secure distributed database management system. *IEEE Transactions on Knowledge and Data Engineering* 7(2), 274–293.

Thuraisingham, B.M., W. Ford, M. Collins, J. O'Keeffe (1993). Design and implementation of a database inference controller. *Data and Knowledge Engineering* 11(3), p. 271.

Vatis, M. (Ed.) (2003). Creating a trusted network for homeland security. Markle Report, New York.

Winsborough, W.H., N. Li (2004). Safety in automated trust negotiation, in: *IEEE Symposium on Security and Privacy*, Los Alamitos, CA (IEEE), pp. 147–160.

Yu, T., M. Winslett (2003). A unified scheme for resource protection in automated trust negotiation, in: *IEEE Symposium on Security and Privacy*, May, Oakland, CA, pp. 110–122.

Part III
Human-Centric Aspects of Security

Chapter 7

Social Engineering in Phishing

Markus Jakobsson

Palo Alto Research Center, 3333 Coyote Hill Dr, Palo Alto, CA 94304, USA

Christopher Soghoian

Indiana University at Bloomington, 901 E. 10th St., Bloomington, IN 47408-3912, USA

Abstract

Social engineering is a term that is used to describe psychological tricks aimed at making victims agree to things they would not have done normally. Phishing is the theft of user credentials, such as passwords, social security numbers, PINs, and answers to security questions. Starting to become prevalent around 2003, it is a crime that is now on everybody's lips. This is mostly due to its commonality, which in turn is fueled by the low costs of perpetrating the crime and the unlikelihood for attackers to be traced. The typical structure of a phishing attack involves some initial communication—normally in the form of an e-mail—that indicates to the recipient that he or she needs to log in, verify credentials, or otherwise transact in a way that requires credentials to be entered. What makes different phishing attacks different is the degree of targeting of the victim that is used, and the psychological twist used to make him or her enter the credentials. For a better understanding of the targeting of phishing attacks, also referred to as *spear phishing*, we refer to the book on phishing by M. Jakobsson, S. Myers (eds.) (2006). *Phishing and Counter-measures: Understanding the Increasing Problem of Electronic Identity Theft*, Wiley-Interscience, Hoboken, NJ, USA.

We discuss the psychological aspects of phishing next; when reading this material, please keep in mind that the same insights will hold to a very large extent when discussing other types of online crimes. A good example of one is *crimeware* (see Jakobsson and Ramzan, 2008), which may use social engineering of different kinds to make user machines get infected.

Click fraud may also soon use social engineering techniques, and other types of online crime may soon follow suit. Of course, social engineering exists beyond the Internet as well, and has existed there probably as long as human civilization has. In this chapter, we only focus on the type of social engineering that is used in typical online crime; for a more general overview of social engineering, we refer the reader to the excellent book on the topic (Mitnick and Simon, 2002).

In this chapter, we discuss the importance of understanding psychological aspects of phishing, and review some recent findings. Given these findings, we critique some commonly used security practices and suggest and review alternatives, including educational approaches. We suggest a few techniques that can be used to assess and remedy threats remotely, without requiring any user involvement. We discuss some approaches to anticipate the next wave of threats, based both on psychological and technical insights. Finally, we conclude with a case study on the threats to the online political donation system posed by phishing. We apply the concepts discussed throughout this chapter and use them to examine the core vulnerabilities and risks in such online donations and propose a number of mitigation and harm reduction techniques.

1   What will consumers believe?

Take a brief look at the following three URLs: www.accountonline.com, www.democratic-party.us and www.wachovia.pin-update.com. Can you tell which ones (if any) correspond to legitimate service providers? Assuming you can, do you think the average Internet user can tell, too? (Note that the content on the associated pages will not help. If any of these URLs were owned by phishers, they would make sure that the page contents would match the domains.)

In fact, most people have no idea how to tell a good URL from a bad one. A recent study (Jakobsson and Ratkiewicz, 2006) showed that regular people are not the least suspicious of so-called cousin-name domains. These correspond to URLs that are "semantically correct"—like www. democratic-party.us looks like it should belong to the Democratic Party. Similarly, most people do not identify subdomain attacks—these are attacks in which the subdomain is used to semantically defraud. Like www.wachovia.pin-update.com has nothing to do with Wachovia. Part of the problem is that people are people, not string-matching machines. We are just not very good at remembering things verbatim, but we are pretty decent at making sense of cues. Which is what gets us into trouble. But that's not all. The problem is made worse by companies that register and use domains that have nothing, in particular, to do with their brand. Like www.accountonline.com, which belongs to CitiBank, and is used to access credit card accounts.

Many types of online crime rely on making a victim take an action by convincing him to do so. To understand security vulnerabilities, it is therefore very important to understand what people will fall for, or, in other words, what kinds of deceptive material they will find believable.

There are several reasons why it is important to understand what consumers will find believable. First of all, it is crucial for service providers to know their vulnerabilities (and those of their clients) to assess their exposure to risks and the associated liabilities. Second, recognizing what the vulnerabilities are translates into knowing from where the attacks are likely to come; this allows for suitable technical security measures to be deployed to detect and protect against attacks of concern. One example of this kind of prediction of future phishing techniques can be seen in the case study of political phishing risks later in this chapter.

Understanding consumers' risks to deception also allows for a proactive approach in which the expected vulnerabilities are minimized by the selection and deployment of appropriate e-mail and web templates, and the use of appropriate manners of interaction. There are reasons for why understanding users is important that are not directly related to security: Knowing what consumers will believe—and will not believe—means a better ability to reach the consumers with information they do not expect, whether for reasons of advertising products or communicating alerts. Namely, given the mimicry techniques used by phishers, there is a risk that consumers incorrectly classify legitimate messages as attempts to attack them. Being aware of potential pitfalls may guide decisions that facilitate communication.

Although technically knowledgeable, specialists often make the mistake of believing that security measures that succeed in protecting *them* are sufficient to protect average consumers. For example, it was for a long time commonly held among security practitioners that the widespread deployment of secure sockets layer (SSL) would eliminate phishing once consumers become aware of the risks and nature of phishing attacks. This, very clearly, has not been the case, as supported both by real-life observations and by experiments (Wu et al., 2006). This can not only be ascribed to a lack of attention to security among typical users (OUT-LAW News, 2004; Whitten and Tygar, 1999), but also to inconsistent or inappropriate security education (Emigh, 2006)—whether implicit or not. An example of a common procedure that indirectly educates user is the case of lock symbols. Many financial institutions place a lock symbol in the *content portion* of the login page to indicate that a secure connection *will be* established as the user submits his credentials. This is to benefit from the fact that users have been educated to equate an SSL lock with a higher level of security. However, attackers may *also* place lock icons in the content of the page, whether they intend to establish an SSL connection or not. Therefore, the use of the lock symbol in the content part of the page dilutes the importance of the true SSL lock symbol. To many users, it is not clear exactly where the lock symbol needs to be placed to signal security.

Educating consumers that the lock must appear in the address bar or the chrome of the web page and raising their awareness of phishing does not eradicate the problem. It has been shown that the typical computer user is unable of distinguishing a valid certificate from one that is invalid or self-signed (see, e.g., Stamm and Jakobsson, 2006; Whalen and Inkpen, 2005), and that he may not even detect the absence of indicators that a connection is SSL secured. The latter statement is supported by a recent study (Jakobsson and Ratkiewicz, 2006) that showed that while users often detect the *presence* of *incorrect* information, they almost never detect the *absence* of *correct* information.

1.1 Experimental assessments of consumer psychology

(Fogg et al., 2001, 2003) conducted a study with over 2500 subjects and investigated how different elements of web sites affect people's perception of credibility and laid down guidelines for the credible perception of web sites. Dhamija et al. (2006) recently studied how computer users fall victims to phishing attacks based on a lack of understanding of how computer systems work, due to a lack of attention, and because of visual deception practiced by the phishers. Their research involved finding out what indicators of security people are looking for while judging a web site as fake or authentic, and their study provides a quantitative measure of how these aspects manifest themselves in people's susceptibility to attacks. In their user survey, they noted that 23% of subjects completely overlooked browser-based security clues such as the address bar, the status bar, and the SSL lock icon, and that 40% of subjects made the wrong security decision. We report on extensions of their study in which the thought process leading to security decisions is also analyzed, and the importance of design issues is quantified.

To understand what typical computer users react to, and why, we performed two in-lab user studies (Jakobsson et al., 2007b). Subjects in both of these studies were shown e-mails and web pages, and were asked to rate these in terms of their likely authenticity. Subjects were shown both legitimate stimuli and stimuli that corresponded to attempts to deceive, and asked to rate these on a scale from 1 (very phishy) to 5 (very likely to be legitimate).

It is clear that studies of these kinds are bound to introduce a bias, as subjects know that they are being tested on their ability to detect phishing. Therefore, their awareness is heightened. However, we argue that such studies are still useful to obtain insights into *relative* appearances of security: One can compare the reactions to different stimuli in studies of this kind. We believe that to determine what makes e-mails and web pages believable (as opposed *to what extent* they are believed), in-lab user studies are probably better suited than naturalistic experiments (e.g., Finn and

Jakobsson, 2007; Jagatic et al., 2007; Jakobsson and Ratkiewicz, 2006). This is due to the fact that naturalistic experiments typically cannot test a sequence of stimuli for each subject, which increases the required sample size dramatically. Therefore, in spite of the fact that naturalistic experiments can offer bias-free results, in-lab experiments may still be preferable. The exit interview of the study we report on provided an opportunity to determine what approaches might have been more suitable, based on the answers given by subjects.

In a first study (Jakobsson et al., 2007), a qualitative approach was taken in which subjects *spoke their thoughts aloud* as they rated stimuli. In an exit interview for the study, we also asked subjects what would have made them react differently to stimuli they found noteworthy.

Guided by the ratings given to different stimuli, we reviewed the recordings for clues of why stimuli were interpreted as they were. We also attempted to determine what caused subjects to make up their minds about the trustworthiness of stimuli. Typically, this decision was made right before a classification was performed. We took note of pivotal observations appearing to inform the decisions of subjects. Having collected a large number of pivotal observations, we then interpreted these in the context of the quantitative ratings to find a likely implication. The implications, in turn, correspond to conclusions about how subjects make decisions of trust. Many of these conclusions support already held beliefs, whereas some highlight aspects that are not common knowledge, and some even contradict commonly held beliefs.

In a second study a quantitative approach was taken instead, in which two large groups of subjects—totaling close to 400 subjects—were shown sequences of stimuli such that the stimuli shown to each group were near identical. The differences in the ratings of near-identical stimuli were used to assess the importance and impact of the differences between such related stimuli. This way, we could simply test the impact of minor design differences, whether these are actually in use or simply held a promise to be of relevance. Such differences related to the design and presentation of material, the inclusion of various types of trust indicators, and various personalization aspects.

The conclusions from the two studies are presented below. When reading the conclusions, it is important to keep in mind that these were made in the context of subjects who knew that they were being evaluated on their abilities to detect phishing attampts; therefore, they describe the *abilities* of the subjects rather than the *habits* of the subjects. This means that some of these observations may not hold in a real-life setting, unless the users in question are on the lookout for potential attempts to attack them.

1. *Spelling and design matter*: The number one aspect that subjects consider is the design and spelling of messages. Several phishing e-mails were dismissed based on spelling alone. Subjects rarely paused

to notice third-party endorsements—let alone alter their judgment—in the presence of a gross grammatical error. Many subjects were suspicious of e-mails that were not signed by a person (Jim Smith) but instead by a position only (e.g., Account manager, PayPal). Similarly, subjects criticized e-mail messages that instructed them not to reply. Some legitimate providers (such as Keybank) were given a low rating due to "unprofessional design." In the case of Keybank, subjects cited the absence of the institutional name on the login page, along with the fact that the fields for user name and password were of different length. The presence of copyright information and legal disclaimers, typically at the bottom of the stimulus in small print, enhanced trust for many subjects quite dramatically. Subjects argued that phishers do not need legal disclaimers, and do not care about copyright infringement. Therefore, phishers are not likely to include such texts in messages, the argument was.

2. *People look at URLs*: It was found that subjects looked carefully at URLs of web pages, and on the URLs obtained by mouse-over in e-mails. Subjects were good at detecting IP addresses as being illegitimate URLs, but were not highly suspicious of inauthentic URLs that were well-formed, such as www.chase-alerts.com. However, subjects were good at detecting syntactically peculiar addresses, such as www-chase.com. (Although this is a well-formed URL, most subjects did not know this, and treated it much like a spelling error.)

   A recent naturalistic study (Jakobsson and Ratkiewicz, 2006) found that the yield of a simulated attack more or less doubled when the URL shown at mouse-over and in the address bar was believable; this supports that URL viewing *is* used for real security decisions, in clear contrast to what is often believed. If we compare the results of Jakobsson and Ratkiewicz (2006)—which corresponds to a naturalistic study—to those in Jakobsson et al. (2007)—which are in-lab studies—then we see evidence that the reliance of mouse-over is greater in the in-lab experiment. This supports that the security *abilities* of typical users differ from their security *habits*, and we confirm that subjects behave differently when they *know* that they are participating in an experiment.

   It was found that subjects favor short URLs. Jakobsson et al. (2007) showed that a page with URL https://www.accountonline.com/View?DocId = Index&siteId = AC&langID = EN was considered significantly *less* trustworthy (with $p < 0.004$) than a page whose URL was http://www.attuniversalcard.com. Here, the *contents* of these two pages were identical, and the first page was actually SSL protected, but was still given a lower rating.

3. *Too much emphasis on security can backfire*: Some stimuli were criticized for their overwrought concerns about online security. An example of this is the IU Credit Union web site shown in Fig. 1;

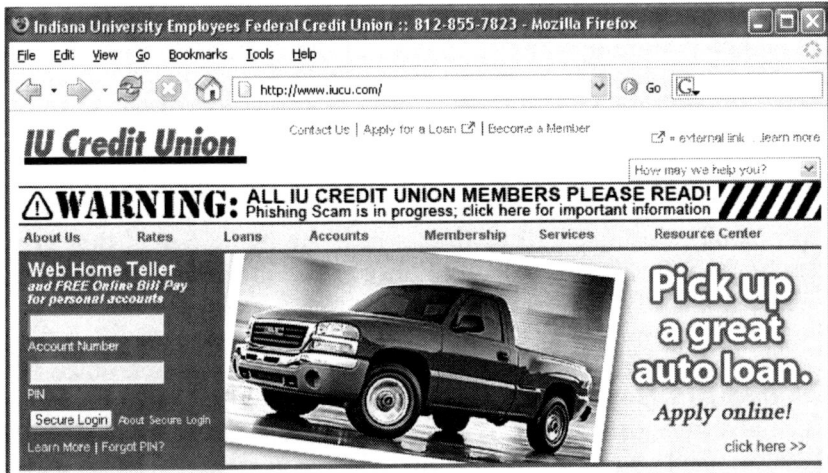

Fig. 1. The top part of the actual web page of Indiana University Credit Union. No subjects noticed that the URL was incorrect—www.IUCU.com as opposed to the real www.IUCU. org—but many felt that the site probably was not legitimate, citing the unusual emphasis on security as their reason. Lower down on the same page, phishing was mentioned again.

this is a legitimate web site, but with a very strong attention to phishing. Subjects did not like that this web site said "phishing attack in progress" in three different locations. Some commented that "phishing" is too obscure a term for a financial institution to use in their communications – the phrase "identity theft" was offered as a plausible substitute. In Jakobsson et al. (2007), it was established that if the focus on security was downplayed, then there was a significant increase in trust ($p < 0.022$).

4. *Third-party endorsements depend on brand recognition*: Several stimuli included a range of third-party endorsements, from well-established brands like Verisign to made-up endorsements like *Safe Site*. We found that endorsements from Verisign were taken with the most gravity. Almost every subject mentioned Verisign by name as a positive factor in their trust evaluation. BBBOnLine and TRUST-e endorsements had no significant effect. Made-up endorsements evoked consistent criticism.

Some subjects noticed third-party endorsements on stimuli they clearly believed to be phishing, and deduced that the graphics could be rendered on any page. One subject observed "Probably now that I see all these [stimuli], I should not believe in Verisign," but later dismissed a web page because "it's not Verisign protected, but it says something which I've never seen, 'TRUST-e'. I don't know, so probably I wouldn't go in this account." No other third-party endorsement was mentioned by name as a prerequisite for trust.

5. *People judge context before authenticity*: Subjects often decided whether a stimulus was legitimate or not based on the content, as opposed to the signs of authenticity. In particular, any stimuli that offered a monetary reward were considered phishy, independently of whether it was authentic or not. Likewise, e-mails that requested passwords upfront were considered phishy, whereas e-mails that only appeared to contain information were considered safe. The latter is a problem, as users could be drawn to a site by an e-mail that appears to be for information only, and once at the site, asked for credentials. Having already made a trust decision (for the e-mail), we believe that the user is now less likely to be critical of the web page material.

   We note that the observation that people judge relevance before authenticity may pose a problem to companies that rely on surveys or on advertising that is likely to be considered phishy by recipients.

6. *Personalization creates trust*: A high degree of personalization increases the trustworthiness of stimuli, whether e-mail or web pages. Thus, the more personal information is present, the more likely did the subject find that the stimulus was authentic. This suggests that data mining could be a troublesome new aspect of phishing. One subject said that the presentation of ZIP code and mother's maiden name would enhance trust in an e-mail message. Yet, this data could be gathered by an attacker using geolocation software (such as IP2Location) and publicly available databases (see Griffith and Jakobsson, 2005, for a recent study on the security of mother's maiden names).

   Many financial service providers attempt to authenticate themselves to their clients by including information of the last few digits of the account number of the client. However, no legitimate service providers use the first few digits of an account number as an authenticator, as these digits typically are identical for large numbers of their clients, and so, can be anticipated by an attacker. Subjects did not realize this, and some found it comforting with an e-mail stating it was intended for a user whose account starts with 4546. Many subjects insisted that presence of the last four digits is more trustworthy, but did not penalize a message for using the first four digits. Some commented that they did not like to see the prefix in isolation, but preferred it to be formatted with the others starred out, for example, 4546-****-****-****.

7. *E-mails are very phishy, web pages a bit, phone calls are not*: Overall, e-mail stimuli were considered more phishy than web stimuli to participants in the study. Many subjects said that following links from e-mail was a risky activity, and that they consciously avoid the practice. Since very few admit to follow links given in phishy e-mails, it could be assumed that their exposure to phishy web pages is inherently more limited. Many participants said that they would try to independently verify e-mail contents by calling the institution

directly. Few participants specified how they would obtain the correct phone number and, therefore, could expose themselves to fraudulent customer service numbers. We note that most systems prompt users to dial in their account number and zip code before speaking with a representative, which trains consumers to be ready to give out identifying information and credentials when initiating a phone call to a financial institution. Several participants also said that e-mail is an inappropriate alert medium for urgent matters, such as password changes and account lock-outs, and expected a phone call from the institution. A strategy using automated phone messages may increase an attack's potency. For example, a voicemail alerting potential victims to the imminent receipt of an e-mail may improve the consecutive e-mail message's apparent legitimacy.

8. *Padlock icons have limited direct effects*: Large padlock graphics were effective at drawing attention to specific portions of the stimulus. By themselves, they did not cause any subject to express an improvement in trust. Small padlock icons in the content body were never commented on by subjects. Their ineffectiveness was supported by the nearly identical rating distributions of two Chase web pages that differ only by the presence of the SSL-post padlock icon in the login area. One of the pages was the real Chase login page, and the other one was a slight modification of the same in which the padlock graphics was removed.

   The SSL padlock at the bottom of a browser frame enhanced trust in many subjects, however two subjects lost trust when mouse-over revealed a made-up certification authority, *Trust Inc.*

   Most users were confused by the presence of a favicon[1] padlock in the browser's address bar. We were surprised by this result because we hypothesized that the address bar contents would be more trusted since web servers have limited control over its appearance.

9. *Independent channels create trust*: If a stimulus suggested that the subject could call to verify the authenticity of the e-mail/web page, then the very existence of this possibility strengthened the trust the subjects had in this stimuli. Subjects stated that they would not call the number to verify the authenticity, but "someone else would."

10. *People recognize common attacks*: Subjects were better at detecting potential attacks that were of commonly occurring types than structurally similar attacks using different language. This suggests that while people may become better at recognizing phishing, they are no less vulnerable to attacks that use different deceit approaches. Therefore, as soon as a new psychological twist is developed, there is reason to believe that it will become successful.

---

[1]The favicon is the small logo used in the address bar by many organizations. This logo can be set to a lock, to make it appear that the page is SSL secured.

1.2   Educational efforts

Although educational efforts designed to reach typical computer users can help change the way consumers react to phishing, there are also inherent limitations in what can efficiently be communicated, given the complexity of the problem and the relative lack of interest in active involvement on behalf of typical users. Although "phishing IQ tests" (Sonic WALL Phishing IQ Test II, 2007) have been proposed as a way to measure the efficacy of phishing education, recent studies (Akavipat et al., 2007) suggest that they fail to measure the ability to recognize threats. However, they do show that exposure to traditional phishing education raises the level of concern among consumers—at least in the short run.

There is an abundance of efforts attempting to educate consumers of the risk of phishing, spanning the spectrum between popular articles (such as Shanahan, 2006) and books (e.g., Arata, 2004). Most of these efforts are traditional, and are believed among security researchers to have rather limited impact. There are some recent efforts to develop non-traditional methods to educating consumers, with promising efforts based on computer games by Kumaraguru et al. (2007), and an effort using a cartoon format by Srikwan and Jakobsson (2007, 2008); an example of the latter effort is shown in Figs. 2 and 3. Common to both of these efforts is the attempt to

Fig. 2.   This cartoon strip intends to increase the understanding of URLs, which is a difficult topic to teach. Typical computer users do not understand the difference between domains and sub-domains, and are easily fooled by cousin-name attacks, as supported by (Jakobsson and Ratkiewicz, 2006). Reprinted with permission. See www.SecurityCartoon.com for more material.

Fig. 3. This cartoon strip shows how easily readers can be updated about recently occurring threats. When the message does not depend on the medium, one can achieve a high degree of adaptability of the educational message to a changing threat. This strip was developed in response to a wave of malware attacks occurring in the late spring of 2007, where the recipient of the e-mail was enticed to download content on the premises that it was a postcard from a friend. Reprinted with permission. See www.SecurityCartoon.com for more material.

relate the educational message to the audience in a manner that encourages the audience to learn more. The comic approach relies heavily on analogies and on reviewing common threats in a way that the reader can relate to.

The educational efforts have several goals. First of all, they aim to raise awareness of the problem, and various expressions of the problem. It is important that people can identify not only current attacks, but also variations of these. This is emphasized by the rapid speed of online fraud evolution. Second, educational efforts aim to enable typical consumers to perform good security decisions, and know their limits. Fear appeal is often not a suitable approach, as the goal is not to make the consumer avoid being engaged in online commerce, but rather, to do so in an appropriate and secure manner.

2 Some emerging attacks and their mitigation methods

To defend against new types of deceit, we believe it is best to anticipate the threats, whether by studying existing attacks on other brands, or by employing people in charge of "being" the attacker—that is, trying to think a step ahead all the time. Once the likely threats have been established, these may be countered by designing user interfaces in a way that promotes security; by pre-emptively registering domains that could benefit attackers; and by other approaches that limit the freedom to attackers.

Here, we present some strategies we believe may be useful to mitigate deceit-based attacks; this is, in no way an exhaustive list of defenses, but rather, is intended to illustrate some potentially helpful approaches.

2.1 Mitigating side-channel threats

Our experimental data suggests that the use of side-channels, such as regular telephony, may increase the yield of attacks. Assume for a moment that an attacker can make an educated guess about the likely banking affiliation of a given user (see Section 3 or Jakobsson et al., 2007a for a description of how this might be done), or simply is lucky to pick the right one. Consider then an attack in which each potential victim receives a sequence of e-mails appearing to come from his or her bank, each e-mail being a notification of some fictitious transaction, and in which the phone number to call in case of questions has been changed to one that the attacker controls. Most banking clients are used to interacting with an automated system when calling their bank, and, according to informal surveys, most people would feel that since they initiated the call (and "know" whom them are calling), it is reasonable for them to enter credentials to get to speak to a person. Although this in essence is structurally the very same attack as users are becoming weary of when it is perpetrated on the Internet alone, it has two new twists: First, the attack e-mails (the "lures") do not demand that the user acts, but rather, are purely for his or her information. Second, instead of relying on a recipient visiting a web site, the attack is based on getting victims to place a phone call. Apart from the fact that people appear more willing to give out information when they feel they initiated the transaction, this hypothetical attack benefits from the fact that takedown—while becoming reasonably fast for web sites—is not likely to be very fast at all for phone numbers. How is an attack like this best avoided? We believe that the answer to this question is to avoid training clients to call the number indicated in the e-mail if they have questions, but rather, always ask clients to use the number on the back of their credit card, ATM card, on a recent statement, or one that they look up themselves. Doing so will not *stop* an attack of this type, but will at least avoid *helping* the attacker.

2.2 An eye on mutual authentication

Clients of financial institutions are used to have to authenticate themselves to obtain service. As a result of the rising tide of phishing attacks, they are also becoming used to financial institutions providing some authenticating information *to them*. This is commonly done by stating the last few digits of an account, but there are efforts to deploy methods that offer better security guarantees, for example, by presenting user-specific images to clients after having verified their IP addresses, cookies, and other partially identifying information. Although both approaches offer some security benefits, we argue that neither is bullet-proof.

As described in Section 1, few subjects distinguished between authentication based on the *last* few digits of an account number and the *first* few. The latter, clearly, offer a less meaningful manner of authentication, as large batches of accounts (if not all) have the same first few digits for a given issuer or financial institution. Since the last *first* digits do not provide a meaningful way of authentication and typical computer users do not notice one approach being switched for the other, then authentication using the *last* four digits arguably invites abuse by training clients to accept a form of authentication that is easily abused. Similarly, stating the e-mail address to which the account is registered clearly does not provide any degree of authentication, but offers the *perception* of authentication to clients, which makes it dangerous to do—whether it is intended for authentication or not.

Another approach is to use a user-specific image to authenticate to the client, as is done by Bank of America's SiteKey (Bank of America, 2007). This is a promising approach, but preliminary experiments support that attackers could still use deceptive approaches in which the images are switched. Namely, subjects found the following message believable: "Due to the Americans with Disability Act (ADA), we are replacing all images with high-contrast images. Your new image is presented below. To acknowledge this change, please log in at www.bankofamerica.image-update.com at your earliest possible convenience, and check the box indicating that you agree to using the displayed image. Before logging in, please verify that the image is the same as what is presented below."

Although, attacks that involve the deceptive switching of authenticators are possible when bank-chosen authenticators are used, there are also distinct drawbacks associated with allowing users to provide the authenticators during a setup phase. Apart from the increased burden carried by clients and the associated support calls, there is also the problem of poorly chosen authenticators. For example, if users select the images later used to authenticate the bank to them, many may choose a picture of their favorite musician, which significantly reduces the overall entropy of the set of authenticators. One way to approach the problem is to use information that means something to the client, but which the client does not have to explicitly select and provide. We suggest that an alternative approach would be to use the billing address of the client as a means for authentication. The benefits of this approach are that it is very difficult for attackers to associate physical addresses and e-mail addresses on a large scale. Given potential privacy concerns of consumers, however, one could use *part* of the address only, instead of the full address. Still, this is not a panacea: An attacker may simply send spoofed e-mails in which the address-based authentication is absent (see Jakobsson and Ratkiewicz, 2006). Clearly, the authentication has to be made prominent enough that its absence is noticed. Also, one must remember that attackers may attempt a two-round attack, the first phase of which involves tricking the victim to give out his mailing address. Still, this increases the burden on the attacker in comparison to one-round attacks.

2.3   Domain-based attacks

There are many ways to keep up with the threats and anticipate the next wave of attacks. First of all, history shows that after a new type of attack has been successfully launched against one brand, it is soon launched on other brands as well. For example, in the spring of 2006, an attack targeting Chase customers involving a request to fill a survey became common. In the late spring the same year, similar attacks targeting WaMu started to appear. There is evidence suggesting that the second round of attacks were not performed by the same attacker, but by a copycat. One such piece of evidence was that, whereas, the attacks on Chase involved sites hosted at sites with deceptively named cousin names, such as *chase-rewards.com*, the web pages involved in the WaMu attack instead had URLs that were based on plain IP addresses. This is known (Jakobsson and Ratkiewicz, 2006) to be substantially less effective, but requires less sophistication on behalf of the attacker. Although the reason could have been that all suitable cousin domains have been pre-emptively registered by WaMu, this is not the case: We registered *wamu-rewards.com* at the onset of the attacks (and have, half a year later, still not been asked to transfer the domain.) One way of keeping up with the threats—and lower the expected yield of copycat attacks—would be for brands to pre-emptively register all suitable cousin-name domains relating to the psychological twist of a new attack. It is commonly argued that this is infeasible, as there is a near-endless number of possible domains; however, there is a fairly limited number of domain names that *closely match* the structure and concept of a given attack. In the case of the survey-based attack, each brand not yet affected by this particular attack could have monitored all the domains used by the attacker on Chase, substituted the term "chase" with their own name, and registered the resulting domain. This requires no particular effort, given that most financial institutions run honeypots in the first place. Requiring only slightly more effort, each brand could set out to also register all cousin names that are related to the psychological twist, as determined by people observing the first attack.

A second way to benefit from pre-emptive registration of cousin-name domains is to register domains that match existing or potential services or features that are or have been offered by the brand or its competitors. For example, Chase offers an alert service in which notifications are sent to clients who opt in to this service. The clients are sent with an apparent sender of *Chase@alerts.Chase.com*. We registered *alerts-chase.com* and *chase-alerts.com*; the domains were later requested by and transferred to Chase. These domains were registered since, presumably, they could otherwise have been used by an attacker who sent out legitimate-looking notifications corresponding to fictional transactions, adding a line such as "For more details on this transaction, log in to see your alerts at www.alerts-chase.com." Although this format would be slightly different than the actual notification (in which no link is given), it is believed that very few recipients would notice the difference, or care about it if they did notice.

Although, it is more difficult to anticipate attacks based on legitimate advertising campaigns, this is still meaningful. For example, an attacker might register *switch-to-citi.com* and use this in an apparent effort to have the recipient open an account with Citibank. An example of how such an e-mail lure might look is shown in Fig. 4. This type of attack has the side benefit (as far as the attacker is concerned) that he does not have to target people who *are* clients of Citibank, but rather, people who are *not*. This, arguably, makes his e-mail believable to a larger group of potential victims. The attacker could use this either in concert with an existing advertisement campaign, or independently of the same. He would be able to offer very nice enticements for people who agree to make the switch (which is made simply by "transferring" a small amount from an existing bank account). This highlights why phishers often have higher click-through rates than legitimate providers of advertisements. Fraudsters can offer much nicer enticements than legitimate service providers, as they are not tied to their word.

As a third example of a domain-based attack, it is known that the time just around the acquisition of a competitor increases the vulnerability to attacks, as do any other big changes that can be observed by consumers. As the acquisition is announced, it makes sense to register domains that might otherwise be taken advantage of, such as domains that are the concatenations of the names of two financial institutions, and slight variations of these, for example, *bankone-becomes-chase.com*. It also makes sense to protect domain names that correspond to functional changes that become apparent to consumers. For example, assume that the financial institution using six-digit PINs is acquired by a financial institution using four-digit PINs. It is imaginable that clients of either institution would be requested to change their PIN. We pre-emptively registered *PIN-update.com* and related domains, anticipating that these could be used in such an attack, potentially using the name of the attacked brand as a subdomain.

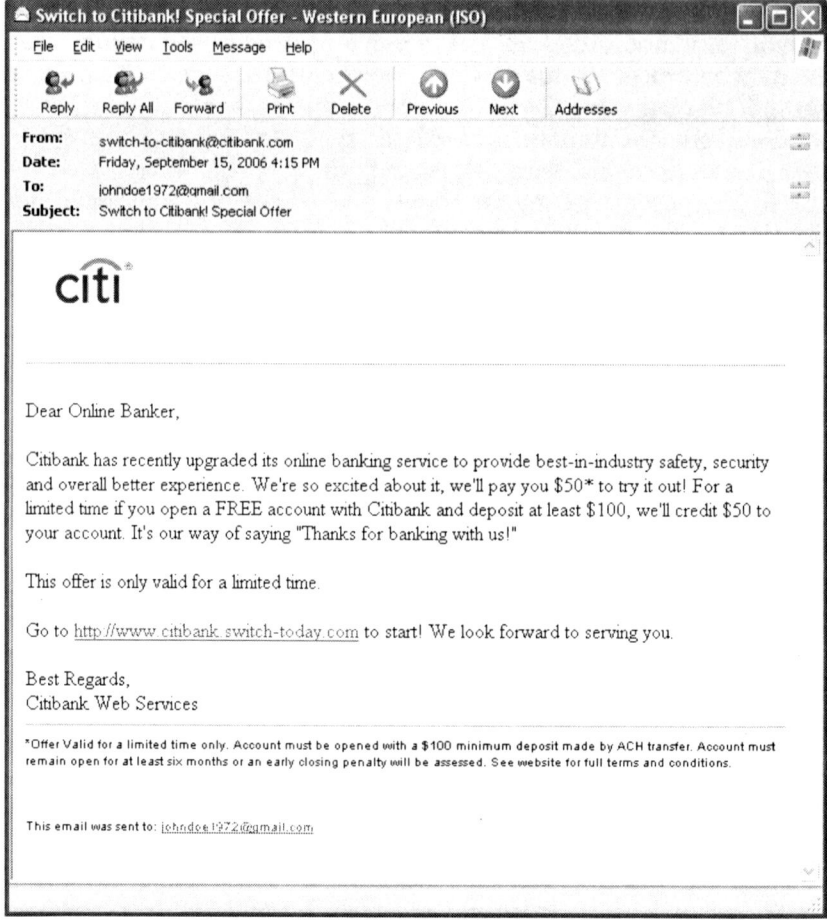

Fig. 4. A stimulus demonstrating how phishers might devise deceit approaches to take advantage of advertising campaigns, and to target large group of users. Note that this e-mail is relevant to all users who *are not* clients of the impersonated brand, as opposed to those who *are*. If a recipient follows a link, he may be asked to give information relating to his current bank, in order to initiate a transfer of funds to the account he is led to believe he is opening. The stimulus is synthetic, that is, has not occurred in the wild.

3   Server-side security

Although client-side tools like spam filters and antivirus software have obvious benefits, we have argued extensively that there are also good reasons not to rely entirely on clients and their machines for their security. Users may fail to see warnings or signs of fraud, and may be duped into installing software that circumvents their malware protection or which plainly performs keylogging, screen scraping or other actions associated with spyware. It has been estimated (Markoff, 2007) that 11% of all networked computers run botnet software, and a larger portion still are affected by various forms of malware. Therefore, it is important to complement client-side countermeasures with server-side techniques. We review some such techniques herein.

3.1 Remote-harm diagnostics

Most phishing attacks today are based either on luring users to enter credentials on sites mimicking legitimate sites, or on installing spyware (such as keyloggers) on their machines. There are many efforts to prevent such threats. Remote-Harm Diagnostics (or RHD) is a recently proposed technique to detect when such an attack has already been performed. Its aim, in other words, is to detect client exposure to phishing and malware attacks *after the fact* and to mitigate the harm that these attacks cause Internet users. The use of reactive defenses is not intended to replace proactive measures, but to provide a second line of defense.

Broadly speaking, RHD involves a web server learning whether a client browser has initiated dangerous Internet connections. Such connections can include browsing of known phishing sites as well as browsing that is indicative of malware infection. Note that for some malware, evidence of infection is best obtained *indirectly*, for example, by detecting whether the client has been directed to certain ad-bearing web sites or has been attacked by *other* malware relying on similar vulnerabilities. This is an important observation, as it suggests that one can potentially detect the presence of sophisticated malware that takes direct action to erase its tracks.

Depending on the information that an RHD-enabled server gleans about suspected malware and on the transactional relationship between the server and a client, the server or its administrators can initiate defensive action on behalf of the client/user. For example, an Internet bank might reject transactions conducted by customers through clients with probable malware infections, and might take additional measures like contacting vulnerable customers by mail or telephone.

It is worth pointing out that RHD requires no user involvement and no client-side software. In other words, the method relies exclusively on server-side implementation. The advantages of this approach are that the system is transparent to users and avoids the complications and burden of user-mediated software installation. Furthermore, it does not stoke the dangerous habit in users of downloading potentially troublesome executables or patches from the Internet.

The basis for RHD system is a web-browser feature that is referred to as *URL probing*. Most web browsers are configured to retain what is called a *history*, a list of the URLs visited by a user in the recent past—typically the last nine days. Thus, a server can ascertain the presence of a particular URL in the browser of a visiting client. For example, a server can determine if a visiting client has browsed the site www.xyz.com in the past few days. It is important to note that URL probing only reveals information in the case of *exact matching*. For example, if a client has visited www.xyz.com/nihil, a server will not learn this fact by probing the client's browser history for the URL "www.xyz.com."

> **Example.** *downloader.trojan.* As an example of how an RHD system might work, let us consider a Trojan program that is subject to drive-by installation, namely the executable referenced by the antivirus community as *downloader.trojan.* This Trojan, released in 2002, is relatively old. Computers that lack up-to-date virus protection, however, are still vulnerable. This Trojan used to have the ability to install itself from a web site without the user's permission, making use of a security flaw in the Internet Explorer browser. Recent browser versions require user consent for the program to install. However, as Edelman (2007) has pointed out, there are deceptive ways of making users install software. Having been installed, this piece of malware downloads and installs other programs from other web sites without the user's knowledge, and adds bookmarks (also referred to as *favorites*) to the user's browser.

There are two strategies for an RHD system to perform URL probing to detect the presence of *downloader.trojan* on a client. The sensor can attempt to detect browsing behavior that may have resulted in infection by the Trojan, or else it can search for browsing behavior characteristic of existing infection. In particular, the sensor can probe for

1. *Browser visits to malware-installing sites*: The server checks to see if the user has visited any sites that are known to attempt to install the Trojan. Note that this may work only for a short time subsequent to infection, namely the length of time that the user's browser retains entries (usually nine days).
2. *Browser visits that imply malware infection*: The server checks to see if the user has visited sites that match the Trojan's *signature*—that is, sites that the Trojan, once installed, causes a client to visit and/or bookmark. The presence of a cluster of such sites is indicative of infection.

A naïve deployment of either approach would involve the RHD server harvesting highly specific information about user browsing habits. However, this raises considerable privacy concerns. Although acknowledged traces of malware might not be privacy-sensitive for users, some of the URLs associated with malware are also sites that receive actual user-originated traffic (as opposed to traffic resulting from malware infection). This is particularly so in the case of *downloader.trojan*, which bookmarks large numbers of sites with pornographic content. However, as described in Juels et al. (2007) it is possible to deploy an RHD system that filters data on the client machine and returns only a binary result. For example, we can design an RHD system that returns only a rough "positive" or "negative" classification of the perceived probability of infection of a given client by *downloader.trojan*, and no information about which sites reside in the client's browser history. Therefore, if a user has not been infected by a given piece of malware, but has visited sites that happen to be part of the footprint of the malware piece, then a diagnostic should return the response "no infection," and not "partial match." However, if the user's browser has evidence of visits/bookmarks to *all* the sites corresponding to a footprint, then it is safe to assume that the user's machine has been infected. (Moreover, even if this were not the case for a small set of users, it would not be stigmatizing for them to be incorrectly classified as having been exposed malware. This is a very unlikely event, though, given the typical sizes of footprints.)

It is worth pointing out that RHD is a heuristic technique that only works for users that keep browser history (which is a large portion of the Internet users). It is also worth noting that the same tactics can be used for information collection carried out by attackers, which of course does not lessen its use for good purposes.

3.2   Takedown vs. take-home

One way to determine the likely success rates of various phishing attacks, learn the demographics of vulnerable clients, and provide educational feedback to apparent would-be victims of attacks is to change from takedown of offending sites to what we may call "take-home." Take-home works by having all traffic to a phishing site forwarded to an external site that the attacked brand controls, whereas takedown works by removing access to the phishing site. The external site that receives the redirected traffic would be hosted at the impersonated domain, and therefore, it would receive any cookies that were previously set, since these are automatically[2] released to the site. This helps build an understanding of who is vulnerable to attacks. It also allows the number of accesses to be counted as a function of time; this allows the financial institution to determine what phishing campaigns are the most threatening, and estimate the likely number of actual victims before take-home was initiated. (See Jagatic et al. (2007) for information on the time-dependency of the yield of a given phishing attack for an example of how partial information of number of accesses can help estimate previous accesses and compromises.) In addition, the site may

---

[2]If cache cookies (Juels et al., 2006) are used instead of conventional cookies, then they would not be automatically sent by the client computer, but would have to be requested from the client computer by the server of the site that traffic is redirected to.

inform the visitor of the risks of phishing, how to avoid it, and of the commitment to security of the financial institution.

A passive version of take-home would simply monitor accesses to graphics, and detect instances where logos and other images are accessed by a party at a given IP address, but where the supporting html documents are not downloaded from the same party. This is an indication of an attack in which the phisher provides a web page in which credentials are requested, but in which graphics are not stored on the machine controlled by the server but taken directly from the site of the brand. Again, this can be used to estimate the number of victims in ongoing attacks, and to determine the identities and demographics of the clients who visited the site.

3.3   Sticky cookies

A conventional computer cookie is a piece of information stored in a specially designated cache in a web browser. Cookies can include user-specific identifiers, or personal information about users (e.g., this user is over 18 years). Service providers typically employ cookies to personalize web pages. For example, when Alice visits the web site X, the domain server for X might place a cookie in Alice's browser that contains the identifier that uniquely identifies Alice. When Alice visits X again, her browser releases this cookie, enabling the server to identify Alice automatically. However, many users (and some software packages) regularly clear their cookies, which frustrates efforts to distinguish legitimate access from attacks.

A cache cookie (Juels et al., 2006), by contrast, is not an explicit browser feature. It is a form of persistent state in a browser that a server can access in unintended ways. There are many different forms of cache cookies; they are byproducts of the way that browsers maintain various caches and access their contents. Their main benefit is that they are "sticky"—they are harder to remove, and are not cleared along with conventional cookies. Like conventional cookies, they can store identifiers who allow servers to recognize repeat visitors. This allows for better recognition of users, which can be used for purposes of mutual authentication. This is meaningful in the context of approaches such as SiteKey (Bank of America, 2007). Another way to authenticate the service provider to the client would be to automatically fill the user name in a form. If consumers become accustomed to have a web site autofill their user name, then they may become suspicious of sites that do not. Of course, this is a double-edged sword, as the absence of the user name will be the typical experience of roaming users (who use different computers for different accesses to a legitimate site). Also, it does not address the problem of users who choose their e-mail address as their user name, or any other information that is easily guessed by an attacker.

3.4 Avoiding automated configuration of attacks

As demonstrated in Jakobsson et al. (2007), it is possible for attackers to determine the banking affiliation of a given potential victim with a reasonable success probability, without even interacting with the human user. This is achieved by inspection of the browser history of the potential victim, concluding that a person banks with a given institution if he or she has visited their web site recently. The attack demonstrated in Jakobsson et al. (2007) assumes two rounds of interaction: A first round, in which the affiliation is inferred by a web site that the user visits, and a second round in which an appropriately configured e-mail is sent to the user. The attack can also be performed in one round, by combining the two rounds described earlier (Jackson, C. personal communication). This can be done by an attacker who would send out e-mails that contain a large selection of logos and other graphics, where these images are stacked in an order that depends on the contents of the browser history. This would be done in a manner so that the graphics of a visited site shows up on top of the other images (thereby suitably hiding the latter.) This would cause the e-mail to appear to originate exactly from the institution the recipient is banking with. We note that the one-round version of the attack only appears to work against people reading their e-mail using webmail; these people, though, are currently a majority of computer users. Countermeasures to this attack are described in (Jakobsson and Stamm, 2006; Jackson et al., 2006), whether on the server side or client side.

4 Anticipating threats from strengths and weaknesses

The way phishing attacks will be carried out in a few years is likely to be affected by the strengths and weaknesses of current countermeasures, including law enforcement efforts, technology deployment, and education. We argue that it is possible to further anticipate trends by building hypotheses of likely developments. We give two examples of how we believe this can be done.

4.1 Better detection of spoofed messages

Assume that general spoof detectors[3] will become increasingly successful at blocking attempts at spoofing. We argue that if this happens, then phishers will come to rely more on real domains that they control, and that

---

[3]Examples of spoof detectors include Domainkeys (Yahoo and Inc., 2007), SenderId (Corp, 2007), and antispoof toolbars (such as Chou et al., 2004; Cloudmark, Inc., 2007; eBay, Inc., 2007; EarthLink, Inc., 2007; GeoTrust, Inc., 2007; Google, Inc., 2007a). Also see Zhang et al. (2007) for an analysis of these toolbars.

they increasingly mount attacks based on cousin domains (e.g., switch-to-citi.com) and subdomains (e.g., bankofamerica.image-update.com and jpm.organchase.com). To proactively defend against attacks in such a scenario, brands can register domains that appear suitable for phishing.

If spoof detection tools become increasingly powerful, we also have to consider the possibility that attackers take another approach that is not based on impersonating brands. One likely approach would be malware-based, for example, a keyloggger. This could be installed either by methods involving deceit (see, e.g., Edelman, 2007; Stamm and Jakobsson, 2006) or using technical vulnerabilities. To counter this threat, brands can make an effort to assure that clients have up-to-date antivirus software. The latter has to be done in a careful manner, though, to avoid that clients become so focused on anti-malware initiatives that they can be deceived to download "patches and updates" supplied by an attacker impersonating the financial institution. Namely, a client who worries too much about malware and having up-to-date antivirus software may be deceived to install software that while claiming to be a countermeasure against spyware is, in fact, the spyware itself. That has become increasingly common as of recent.

4.2   Faster ISP takedown

Takedown is one of the most potent countermeasures against phishing attacks today. As the speed of takedown increases, phishers are likely to mount attacks that defeat this measure. One such attack, referred to as a *Distributed Phishing Attack* (Jakobsson and Tsow, 2006), uses per-victim personalization of Web hosting, and hosts web sites on machines controlled by the phisher. In a distributed phishing attack, takedown of an individual server only prevents a small number of victims (or one in the extreme case) from responding with their credentials, as different sets of potential victims are pointed to different sites. The web sites can be hosted on botnets, whose recent commoditization has made it practical to deploy thousands of fraudulent Web hosts to collect personally identifying information from their victims. Such machines could be home routers and access points, which—while not able to serve large amounts of traffic (which would not be needed)—do have near-constant connectivity. See Stamm et al. (2006), Tsow (2006), Tsow et al. (2006) for a discussion of such threats.

The use of botnets as hosts for phishing web pages will to a large extent require URLs that are IP addresses. To avoid detection of this, phishers may use spoofing tricks for the address bar (Raskin, 2006). This can be accomplished by using JavaScript to create a new browser window without the address bar (a browser feature), which accesses the phishing site. The phishing site could use JavaScript and cascading style sheets (CSS) to create a frame which hovers at the top of the page (where the real address bar used to be), and which looks like a real address bar. It is even possible for a cleverly written spoofed address bar to have buttons that work, and to accept keyboard input. Of course, the phisher may display *any* URL in the spoofed address bar, regardless of the URL actually being visited. Another approach would be to use a pharming attack (see Meiss, 2006; Stamm et al., 2006, for examples of new breeds of such attacks).

5 Case study: political phishing

Internet-based donations to political candidates are now a vital part of any successful campaign. Tens of millions of dollars are raised each year, primarily in sub 100-dollar amounts from individuals around the country. Politicians have exempted their own campaign donation solicitation e-mails from federal antispam legislation, and their campaigns encourage risky behavior by teaching users that it is ok to click the "donate" button on an unsolicited e-mail that arrives from a candidate. Although not yet a major problem, fraudulent web sites that masquerade as genuine campaign sites aiming to defraud donors are a significant threat on the not-so-distant horizon. These political phishing sites are easy to create, and extremely difficult for users to detect as not authentic. We discuss threats against online campaign donation systems, and discuss the unique factors that make this type of online commerce particularly vulnerable to fraud-based attacks. Finally, we propose a realistic and cost-effective solution to the problem.

5.1 *The importance of online campaign donations*

Over the past few years, online campaign donations have increasingly become a significant portion of the overall campaign fundraising process. Hillary Clinton's presidential campaign raised over eight million dollars online during the third quarter of 2007, more than one year before the 2008 presidential election (Stirland, 2007). During the 2004 election, John Kerry set the single-day online campaign donation record, raising over three million dollars on June 30, 2004 (Justice, 2004). More than half of Democrats gave online in 2004; double the percentage of Republicans. Furthermore, over 80% of the contributions by people aged 18–34 were made over the Internet (Edsall, 2006).

Tens of millions of dollars of campaign donations are now raised annually through the Internet. This logically means that hundreds of thousands of consumers have shown a willingness to hand over their credit card numbers in response, in many cases, to unsolicited donation request e-mail messages from the candidates. Although this is no doubt good for the politicians, this kind of behavior is very risky, and could easily be taken advantage of by phishers.

The very success of a campaign donation solicitation depends on impulsive reactions by the potential donors. Millions of e-mail messages are regularly sent off to possible benefactors (Fig. 5), typically in response to some act committed by the opposing party. Donors are made to feel shocked, repulsed or alarmed and then urged to donate money to help to combat the evil of the day. This strategy is aimed at producing impulsive reactions on the part of the donor. From the perspective of the political campaigns, giving now is far preferable to give later.

The problem with this approach is that unlike an impulsive purchase on Amazon.com, a political donation does not result in the sale of a physical good. Other than a thank-you e-mail, the donor typically does not receive

   Christopher Soghoian <csoghoian@gmail.com>

What good is a judge?
1 message

Howard Dean <democraticparty@democratic-party.us>   Tue, Jul 03, 2007 at 7:59 PM
To: csoghoian@gmail.com

THE
DEMOCRATIC PARTY

Dear Concerned Citizen,

Yesterday, despite overwhelming public opposition, President Bush commuted the sentence of Scooter Libby, the former White House Chief of Staff to Vice President Cheney who was convicted by a jury of lying about a matter of national security. As yet another example of the elitist attitude that defines Republicans in Washington, he shamelessly put partisan loyalties before the fundamental American value of fair and equal justice under the law.

ENOUGH IS ENOUGH

Contribute now to help us change things in Washington in 2008

★ Contribute ★

We can't stand for this, and that's why we're doing something to change it. We may not be able to change the President's decision, but we are fighting back -- we're working day and night to take back the White House in 2008 so that we can put an end to just this type of nonsense. Contribute now to help us change things in Washington:

http://www.democratic-party.us

Fig. 5.   A synthetic example of a political phishing e-mail demonstrating the ease with which an attacker can falsify the header information and content to look as though the e-mail came from a political party. Although, a legitimite e-mail from the Democratic Party would come from *democrats.org*, this synthetic phishing e-mail lists *democratic-party.us* as its source, a web site that was registered by the authors of this chapter and is not connected to the official Democratic Party. This example shows the power of cousin-domain attacks, and in particular, against political campaign web sites (Friedrichs, 2008).

anything after submitting their donation. This means that it is very difficult for some to confirm after-the-fact who they donated to, or to learn that they may have been scammed. There have been some recent efforts to spread consumer awareness of security threats with user education (Srikwan and Jakobsson, 2007). However, in this chapter we focus instead on more direct methods enabling campaign donation sites to safely establish user trust.

5.2 *The problem of domain names*

US consumers each have, on average, four credit cards (Experian, 2007). Although customers may open and close cards over time, the names of the major banks for the most part stay the same (barring mergers and aquisitions). For those consumers who check their online bank and credit cards on a regular basis, it is quite possible for customers to memorize the web site address of the bank sites that they login to regularly. More importantly, these web site addresses stay the same. Although banks overhaul the layout of their web sites from time to time, the address stays the same. Citibank's web site, www.citibank.com was located at the same address in 2003, 2005, 2007, and will most likely still be accessible at the same location in 2009. Banks spend significant sums of money in establishing well-known and trusted brands. It is simply not in their best interest to change their name every few years.

Contrast this to the political system in the United States where candidate brand turnover can be very high. Candidates for particular public offices change on a regular basis, as successful politicians seek to advance their careers. Someone who solicits campaign donations for a House of Representatives run in 2004 may very well come back to solicit donations in 2006 as a potential Senator. Furthermore, for every politician who wins an election, there is typically at least one other opposing candidate who lost the very same race. The logical side effect of this is that even if a candidate successfully wins and retains the same office year after year, the opposing political party will typically replace the candidates that lost with someone else more likely to win.

Although some political campaigns select Internet domain names that can be reused in the future, many others do not do so. Examples of this include domain names tied to a specific political office (Dennis Kucinich's www.dennis4president.com), and those tied to an election being held in a specific year (Fred Thompson's www.fred08.com and Rudy Giuliani's www.joinrudy08.com). In addition to having to print new stationary in preparation for future elections, candidates also have to work to spread knowledge of their new domain name. The time and money spent on making the public aware of JoeSmith08.com will be wasted when Joe Smith runs for re-election in 2012. On top of all of these problems, it is often not possible for campaigns to purchase all of the alternative possible domain names for a candidate. Other individuals on the Internet often snap up alternative, and quite reasonably sounding domain names.

This leads to a state of confusion for the voter, where it is simply not possible to reasonably predict or confirm the location of the official web site for a politician's campaign. Should a potential donor visit joinrudy08.com, or rudygiuliani.com, barack.com or barackobama.com, fredthompson.com or fred08.com? If a user clicks on a web advertisement that takes them to hillary08.com, how can they be sure that they are at her official campaign web site? Although some of the alternative domains are purchased by fans, others can be purchased by those who oppose the candidates. Examples of this include gwbush.com and whitehouse.com, both of which at one time or other, hosted content which the politicians they targeted certainly did not appreciate (Raney, 1999; Swartz, 1998).

5.3   Political phishing

The previous two sections discussed the importance of the online fundraising channel to political campaigns, and the fact that it is almost impossible for a potential donor to know which domain name points to the official web site for a candidate. Building on this, we now explore potential attacks against the online fundraising process in which phishers create fake, yet believable campaign web sites with realistic looking domain names. These web sites would then be used to lure users into submitting their credit card numbers and other financial information. Were such phishing sites to become common, donors could lose confidence in the online political donation system and stop giving.

5.4   Drawing users in

The most obvious technique for drawing in potential phishing victims to a fake political campaign web site is e-mail. This is currently the dominant technique used in other phishing scams, and is ideal for political deceit. Many US banks have spent significant money and time trying to educate users against clicking on links and in responding to e-mails from anyone claiming to be their bank. The opposite is true for political candidates, who increasingly turn to e-mail lists to reach potential voters, and depend on impulsive user reactions to trigger donations. The importance of unsolicited e-mail messages to the political campaigns that send them can be inferred from the fact that Washington politicians made sure to exempt their own contribution requests from the CAN-SPAM Act, which bans most forms of unsolicited commercial e-mail (McCullagh, 2003).

Phishers often have no way of knowing which bank a potential victim has accounts with. Thus, in cases where e-mails are blindly being sent out to millions of addresses, phishers will often masquerade as one of the major

US banks (Citibank, Chase, Bank of America, etc.). The logic behind this is simple: a random victim is more likely to be a customer of one of the major banks than a small regional financial firm, and thus phishing as one of the financial market leaders will provide a phisher with the most bang for his buck.

Political phishing does not suffer from the problem of hundreds of different banks, or even the 5 or 6 largest firms. For the most part, in the United State, there are just two political parties: The Democrats and Republicans. A phisher has at least a 50/50 chance of guessing the correct political party for a potential victim. By using more advanced user reconnaissance techniques such as invasive browser sniffing (Jakobsson and Stamm, 2006) or browser-based timing attacks (Felten and Schneider, 2000) to learn which news and political web sites a user visits, it might be possible to guess a victim's political affiliation with a higher rate of success.

5.4.1 Social phishing

Although e-mail is currently the dominant method of luring users to phishing sites, there are several other promising strategies. Jagatic et al. have demonstrated that users are particularly vulnerable to deceit-based attacks when the phishers take advantage of knowledge of the victim's social group (Jagatic et al., 2007). Thus, one potential avenue of attack could be fake grassroots groups on social networking sites such as Facebook.

Detailed records of political donations, including contributor name, city, state, zip code, and principal place of business are published online by the Federal Election Commission (2007). Through the use of online telephone books, social networking sites and personal home pages, it may be possible to link a donation record to an online identity and e-mail address. This information, especially when combined with knowledge of a person's employer, could be used to execute highly targeted and accurate phishing attacks (Fig. 6).

5.4.2 Phishing via advertisements

Web-based advertisements, both those using graphics, text, and more complicated flash-based content have been used to spread malware and trick users. One example of this is a September 2007 incident in which malicious flash advertisements were served millions of times on a number of high-profile web sites, all of which were serving ads placed by an advertising company owned by Yahoo (Goodin, 2007). In a previous incident, a malicious flash advertisement was able to infect over a million users of the popular social networking site MySpace users with a Trojan (Krebs, 2006). Google's popular text-based advertising network has also been used to spread malware, although doing so did at least require that the user click on the ads (whereas the flash ads silently installed the malware without any user interaction). A report in April 2007 indicated that criminals were

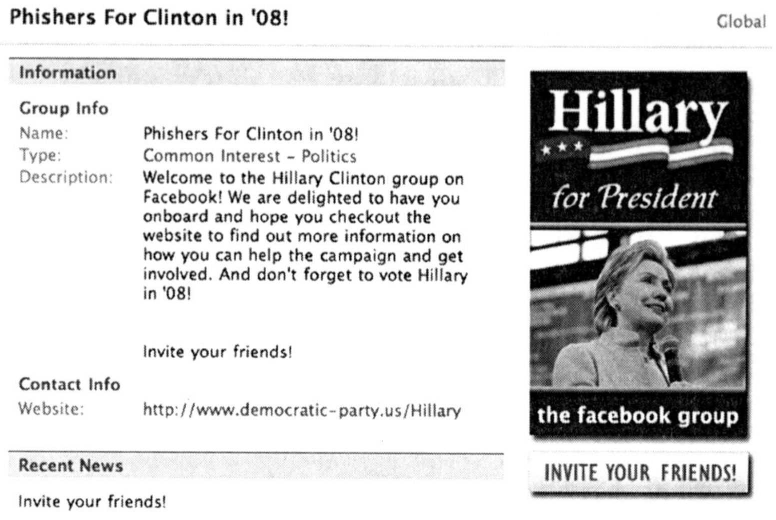

Fig. 6. A synthetic example of a malicious political interest group located at a popular social networking site. The group page contains a prominent link to another malicious political phishing web site. The figure demonstrates the ease with which an attacker can use branded images taken from the legitimate candidate's web site to lend credibility to the attacker's own site.

purchasing Google text for legitimate web sites such as the Better Business Bureau. Users clicking on the ads would be taken to an intermediate web site, which would attempt to silently install password-stealing malware, before then taking the user to the actual Better Business Bureau web site (Krebs, 2007). Using one or more of these techniques, it should be possible for phishers to place advertisements for politics-related keywords (such as the names of the candidates), which would take unwitting users who click to a phishing site masquerading as a campaign donation web site (Fig. 7).

5.5   The problem of web site authentication

The previous section listed three methods with which a phisher could draw traffic to a political phishing web site. Section 2 explained why users simply cannot be expected to know which domain names are the authentic and official web sites for the politicians they are interested in. We now discuss why key anti-phishing technologies, including two-factor authentication, that have been widely deployed in the Internet banking market will not be able to protect political web sites.

Consumers typically have ongoing relationships with their banks. This provides both entities, the bank and the consumer, with additional means

Fig. 7. A synthetic example of an attack using text advertisements placed on a search engine to direct users to a political phishing web site. This demonstrates the ease with which advertising networks can be used to lay the groundwork for more sophisticated attacks. The official web site of the Republican Party is www.gop.org and Fred Thompson's 2008 Presidential campaign site is www.fred08.com. However, the text advertisements in this synthetic attack sent users to www.support-gop.org/Fred08, a domain name registered by the authors of this chapter. This further demonstrates the power of cousin-domain attacks.

with which to verify each other. Users who are tricked to provide their login details to a web site masquerading as their bank may become wise to the fraud when the fake web site does not display their valid account number, balance or recent transactions. Recent advances in two-factor authentication technology have also provided customers with methods to detect web sites masquerading as their banks. Schemes such as Bank of America's SiteKey system provide a way for the bank's web site to prove to the user that it is authentic. These authentication technologies can be bypassed with deceit augmented man-in-the-middle attacks (Soghoian, 2007), but this at least raises the bar for the attacker.

Many donors do not have an ongoing financial relationship with political candidates. This makes it very difficult for a candidate's web site to prove its authenticity to the user, and consequently, provide few signals for users to detect when a site is not authentic. From the perspective of the user, if the site looks legitimate, it probably is (Fig. 8).

The easiest way for an attacker to make a phishing page look authentic is to simply clone the content of the original web site. Web cloning tools

Show Dick Cheney Just How Strong We Are

During a press interview in Tokyo, the vice president said, "'I think if we were to do what Speaker Pelosi and Congressman Murtha are suggesting, all we will do is validate the al-Qaida strategy... The al-Qaida strategy is to break the will of the American people ... try to persuade us to throw in the towel and come home, and then they win because we quit."

Donate to the Democratic Party and show Dick Cheney that his insults only make us stronger.

This page is a simulated phishing attack. It is not dangerous, but is meant to raise awareness of the dangers of phishing and new deceit tactics. Click here to read more about phishing and political phishing. Click here to send this site to a friend.

Contributor	Amount
first name last name	○ $50 ○ $75 ○ $250 ○ $2,500
	○ $25 ○ $100 ○ $1,000 ○ Other: $
address	
	Secure Paypal Donation 🔒

Fig. 8. A synthetic example of a political phishing web site. The majority of the content has been taken wholesale from the legitimate candidate's web site, which will make it exceedingly difficult for normal users to determine that the web site is fraudulent.

such as the ScrapBook extension for the Firefox web browser (Murota Laboratory—Tokyo Institute of Technology, 2006), or the Macintosh application Web Devil (Chaotic Software, 2007) allow attackers to create a working local copy of a remote political campaign web site, which the attacker can then modify, upload to a server, and make available online with a fake, but authentic-sounding domain name.

As the attacker controls and can edit the local cloned copy of his new political phishing site, it is possible for him to enhance the original content to optimize it for phishing. One example of this would be to expand the payment options accepted by the web site, as most political campaign web sites only permit credit cards donations, to accept PayPal and electronic checks (Fig. 9).

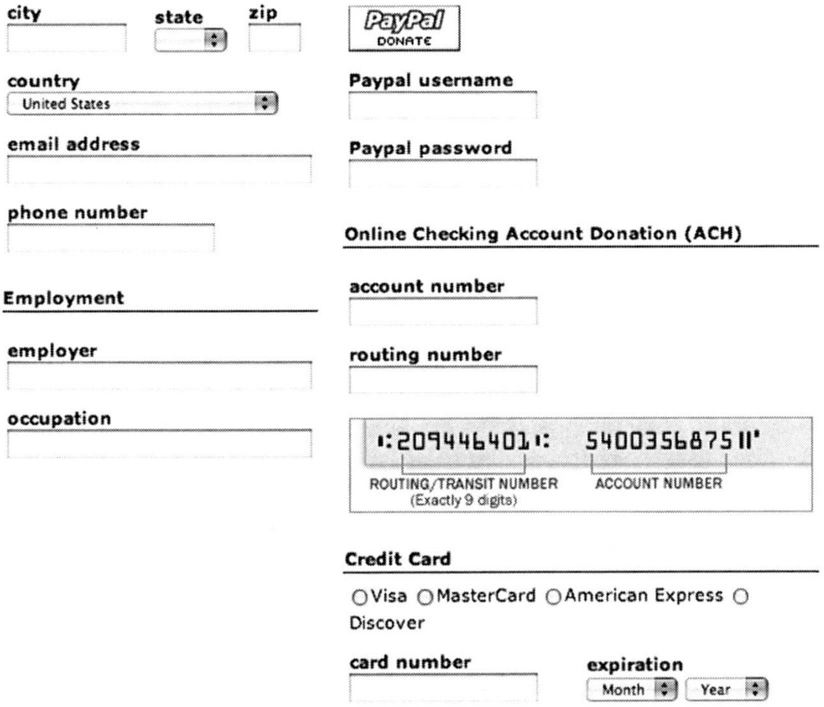

Fig. 9. A synthetic example of a political phishing web site. Its content has mostly been copied wholesale from the original legitimate candidate's web site, yet has been "upgraded" to accept PayPal and electronic checks. These are two forms of financial information that are far more valuable to phishers than credit cards, yet that are not typically asked for by legitimate campaign sites.

5.6 Fixing the political phishing problem

Earlier sections of this chapter explained the factors that could make political phishing a major problem in the future. The large amounts of money being collected by political campaign sites, users giving their financial information to untrusted web sites and the practical issues preventing users from being able to safely differentiate legitimate and fake political campaign web sites. We now explore potential solutions to this problem.

5.6.1 Consolidation at the back end

It simply does not make good business sense for each candidate to pay to re-invent the technology necessary for a campaign web site. Most political candidates' web sites share enough common features that code reuse makes far more sense. As a result, a small number of companies have been able to dominate the niche market of political campaign software, with one single company providing its software to more than two-thirds of the federal democratic political campaigns in 2004 and 2006 (National Geographical and Political Software, 2007). These companies provide turn-key solutions for candidates, permitting one or two tech staff members to install and deploy a sophisticated campaign web site without too much work.

Thus, while a potential donor can visit one of the hundreds of different political candidates' campaign web sites, most of the sites will be running the same back-end software that will be sending credit card transactions through the very same processing firm.

5.6.2 Restricted domain names

One proposed solution to the problem of phishing sites is to create top-level domain names exclusive to specific markets. An exclusive .bank domain was proposed by an Internet security researcher in 2007 (Hypponen, 2007) whereas a similar scheme for political domains was proposed in the Trademark Cyberpiracy Prevention Act, a bill introduced to Congress in 1999, but which failed to pass. That law would have created a second-level domain name under .us, like .politics.us or .elections.us, exclusively for use by politicians (McCullagh, 2001).

The main problem with the proposal for a restricted domain for political candidates, was that administering the domain and verifying applicants is a major task, one which the Federal Election Commission, the logical choice for such a job, was unwilling to take on. "Given the large number of federal, state, and local candidates and officeholders, compiling and maintaining a complete list of all persons who are eligible would likely be a sizable undertaking ... The commission does not have the resources to assume responsibility for a task of this magnitude," the FEC said in a March 2000 letter to the Commerce Department. The most the FEC was willing to do, was to compile a list of links to "the official web sites of all current federal candidates" and campaign committees (McCullagh, 2001).

5.6.3 Consolidation at the front-end

From a security standpoint, it is far better for candidates to join forces and share one common, trusted brand for their online campaign donations. The current situation in which money, time and other resources are spent creating brand awareness for new campaign web sites each election cycle is both inefficient and also makes it extremely difficult for users to begin to trust any one site. Campaign web sites simply churn too fast for users to establish trust relationships with them (Fig. 10).

One example of the success of brand consolidation is the highly successful Democratic fundraising web site ActBlue. The site is popular with left-wing bloggers and netroots organizations and is used to funnel campaign donations for multiple candidates through a single brand. In addition to being used by third-party political organizations and activists, it has recently been adopted by high-profile political candidates such as

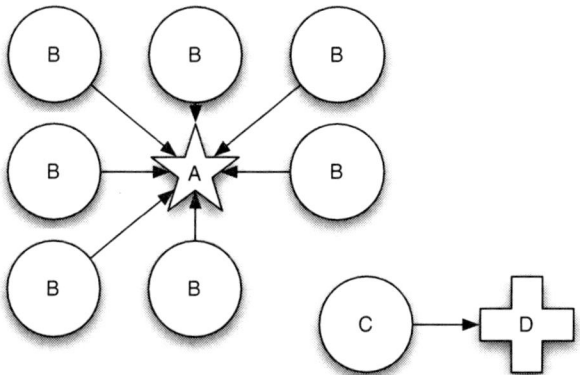

Fig. 10. The figure depicts the currently used infrastructure for online campaign contributions, and an attack on the same. Potential donors are sent to the payment aggregator (A) by different campaign web sites (B). At the same time, a malicious web site (C) sends traffic to a malicious payment aggregator (D), which may be a spoofed version of A. The core of the problem is that the campaign web sites often have a very low URL recognition among donors, and that donors will make a security decision already while on the supposed campaign web site, and therefore be vulnerable to attack by D.

John Edwards, as their official campaign fundraising platform. Users who visit the official Edwards web site and click on one of the many "donate" links and buttons will be redirected to a web page located on the ActBlue web site. ActBlue has raised over $29 million since its launch in 2004 (ActBlue—The online clearinghouse for Democratic action, 2007). A similar Republican centralized donation web site, RightRoots, was launched in early 2007, although it has yet to achieve ActBlue's level of success.

ActBlue has rapidly become a major source of funding for Democratic candidates, and widely popular among liberal netroots activists and bloggers. However, it is still unknown to the general public and to the millions of voters who already give money via official campaign web sites. To establish a major brand identity, companies typically spend millions of dollars on an advertising campaign. Although major political candidates certainly spend millions, their primary goal is not to establish web site brand identity, but to spread recognition and positive feelings for that candidate. It is unlikely that the candidates or anyone else would spend the money required to make ActBlue or RightRoots household names. To do so would simply be an inefficient use of limited campaign funds.

The optimal solution would be for candidates to leverage existing and well-known brands that consumers already associate with safe and trustworthy online financial transactions. Luckily, these already exist in the form of online payment systems such as PayPal and Google Checkout.

5.6.4   Leveraging the existing trusted online payment networks

We propose that PayPal and Google Checkout, the two market leaders in online payment, should create verified political candidate donation sites (Figs. 11 and 12). Under such a system, the payment companies would permit political campaigns to create fundraising pages hosted within the *paypal.com* and *checkout.google.com* branded domains. Before allowing a site to go live, the companies would require the campaigns to submit documentation proving their official candidate status, and would verify that the individuals registering for the sites be authorized to act on behalf of the campaigns. Ideally, the payment web sites would establish a consistent URL structure, which would further assist potential donors in verifying that sites are authentic. Examples of such URLs could include www.paypal.com/candidates/president/Hillary and *checkout.google.com/politics/senate/Webb*.

The major online payment firms already process hundreds of millions of dollars in transactions per year, and do so safely and securely. These companies have spent significant sums in establishing well-known, trusted brands, and in getting users to sign up for accounts. By using one or more

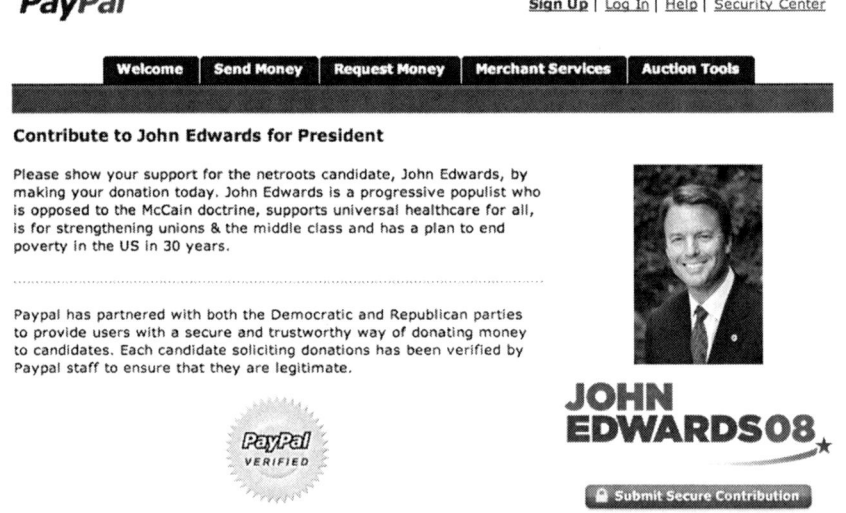

Fig. 11.   A synthetic example of a legitimate political campaign donation web site hosted by Paypal, and branded extensively with its logos. Were political phishing to become a major threat, a site similar to the one pictured would do much to encourage user trust in online political donations. The use of a strongly branded service, such as PayPal, as a starting point for donations has the benefit of increased URL recognition among users. It also benefits from the security features made possible with pre-established relationships between the user and the payment portal (such as PayPal's Security Key), and could leverage the financial service providers' existing anti-fraud measures that political candidates and their existing payment clearing houses may not have access to.

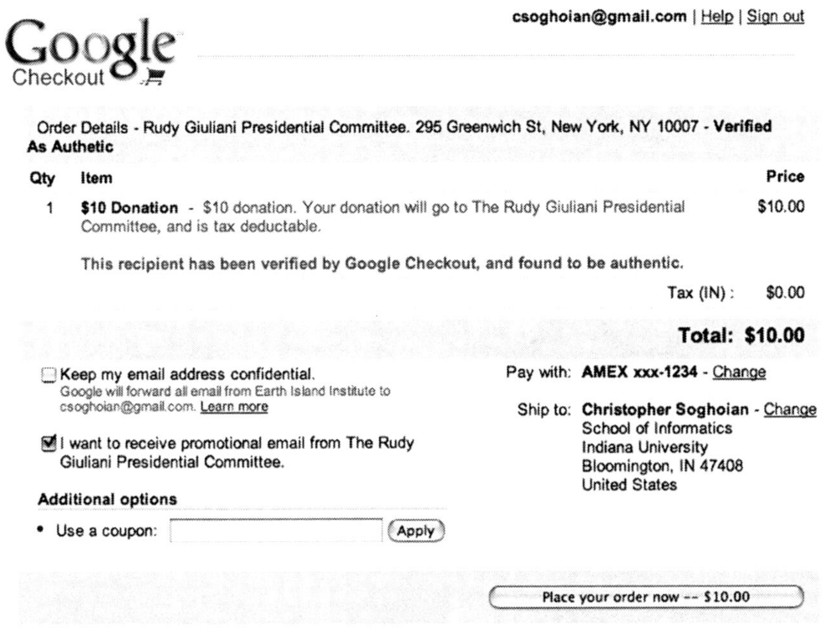

Google
Checkout

Order Details - Rudy Giuliani Presidential Committee. 295 Greenwich St, New York, NY 10007 - **Verified As Authetic**

Qty	Item	Price
1	**$10 Donation** - $10 donation. Your donation will go to The Rudy Giuliani Presidential Committee, and is tax deductable.	$10.00

This recipient has been verified by Google Checkout, and found to be authentic.

Tax (IN) : $0.00

Total: $10.00

☐ Keep my email address confidential.
Google will forward all email from Earth Island Institute to csoghoian@gmail.com. Learn more

☑ I want to receive promotional email from The Rudy Giuliani Presidential Committee.

Additional options

• Use a coupon: [   ] (Apply)

Pay with: **AMEX xxx-1234** - Change

Ship to: **Christopher Soghoian** - Change
School of Informatics
Indiana University
Bloomington, IN 47408
United States

(Place your order now -- $10.00)

Fig. 12. A synthetic example of an in-progress political donation to a candidate using the Google Checkout payment system. In the figure, Google attests to the fact that the political candidate has been verified to be legitimate. Such a system would do much to enable users to know that their donations really are going to their chosen candidates, something that is currently not possible.

of these online payment firms, political campaign will be able to take advantage of the significant economies of scale that PayPal and Google will bring, in terms of existing infrastructure, resources, and technical expertise (Fig. 13).

Political campaigns that switch to a Google or PayPal-hosted solution will find the transaction time for donations that will be significantly reduced. This is mainly due to the fact that many customers leave their credit card details on file with the major online payment processors. Thus, for a donor who already has a PayPal account, giving money to a candidate would no longer require that she type in her name, address, or credit card information. In addition to reducing the work required to donate, this may result in an increase in donations, as donors will have less time to second-guess their donation in the time that they would normally be typing in their credit card information. Such a system, while not completely "one click," would definitely result in a more streamlined and user-friendly donation process.

Both PayPal and Google have significant experience in dealing with phishers and other forms of fraud online. PayPal is a frequent target of phishing attacks, while "click fraud" against Google's advertising system is

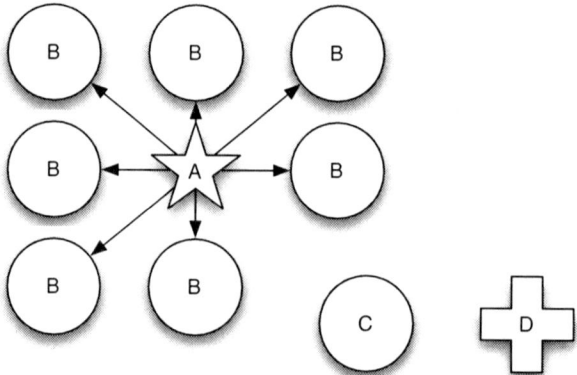

Fig. 13. The figure depicts our proposed structure for online donations. Here, a small number of payment aggregators (A) with high brand name and URL recognition allow users to access campaign web sites (B) and transfer money to the corresponding campaigns. The malicious payment aggregator (D) has a harder time attracting traffic than in Fig. 4. This setting, therefore, is similar to the typical phishing attack today on financial institutions.

major concern for many in the industry. As a result, both companies have teams of researchers, engineers, and operations staff working in the areas of security and fraud. By using these online payment firms, political campaigns will be able to take advantage of the antifraud expertise that the companies possess—a resource they do not currently have access to.

Shifting to the major payment processing companies would provide the campaigns with a number of benefits in terms of security for their donors' financial information. Under the current system of candidates hosting their own donation software, or using niche back-end software suppliers, the possibility exists that donor credit card information can be lost or stolen. Insiders, either in the political campaigns themselves or technical staff managing the web servers can steal data, or insert backdoors into the software code. In the event of an incident of accidental data loss, or data theft by hackers, it is quite likely that consumers would blame the candidates for the loss of their financial data and any associated risk of identity theft. By using a company with a trusted and well-known brand to process transactions, the campaign will benefit twofold: First, donors' credit card information will be transmitted directly to PayPal or Google, and as such, there will be no opportunity for campaign insiders to steal the data, nor for hackers to break in later and steal it from the campaign servers. Second, in the event that Google or PayPal get hacked or lose data, the public will most likely blame the payment companies and not the political candidates. It will be Google's brand that suffers, not the politician's.

Finally, the political campaigns should be able to shift to using Google Checkout or PayPal without having to pay any additional costs. Owing to the massive number of transactions that the firms process, they are able to offer extremely low transaction fees. As a result, political campaigns would not see an increase in fees, and could actually save money. ActBlue charges campaigns 3.95% of the gross contribution amount to cover the credit card processing costs. In contrast, Google Checkout charges merchants 2% plus $0.20 per transaction (Google, Inc., 2007b) whereas PayPal charges approximately 1.9% plus $0.30 cents per transaction, for the transaction levels that most major candidates would achieve (PayPal, 2007).

Acknowledgments

Many thanks to Sid Stamm for helpful feedback on earlier versions of the chapter. Thanks to Sukamol Srikwan, Alex Tsow, Ankur Shah, Eli Blevis, Youn-kyung Lim, Ari Juels, and Jacob Ratkiewicz for permitting extensive citations of material of theirs.

References

ActBlue—The online clearinghouse for Democratic action (2007). Available at www.actblue.com/

Akavipat, R., V. Anandpara, A. Dingman, C. Liu, D. Liu, K. Pongsanon, H. Roinestad, M. Jakobsson (2007). Phishing IQ tests measure fear, not ability, in: *USEC Lecture Notes in Computer Science*, Springer, Berlin. Available at http://www.springerlink.com/content/2921154865166k77/

Arata Jr., M. J. (2004). Preventing identity theft for dummies. For dummies, illustrated edition (July 30). ISBN-10: 0764573365, ISBN-13: 978-0764573361.

Bank of America (2007). SiteKey. Available at www.bankofamerica.com/privacy/sitekey. Accessed on January 8.

Chaotic Software (2007). Web Devil. Available at www.chaoticsoftware.com/ProductPages/WebDevil.html

Chou, N., R. Ledesma, Y. Teraguchi, J.C. Mitchell (2004). Client-side defense against web-based identity theft, in: *NDSS*, The Internet Society, San Diego, CA.

Cloudmark, Inc. Available at www.cloudmark.com/desktop/download/. Accessed on January 8, 2007.

Dhamija, R., J.D. Tygar, M. Hearst (2006). Why phishing works, in: *CHI '06: Proceedings of the SIGCHI Conference on Human Factors in Computing Systems*. ACM Press, New York, pp. 581–590.

EarthLink, Inc. (2007). EarthLink Toolbar. Available at www.earthlink.net/software/free/toolbar/. Accessed on January 8.

eBay, Inc. (2007). Using eBay Toolbar's Account Guard. Available at pages.eBay, com/help/confidence/account-guard.html. Accessed on January 8.

Edelman, B. (2005). How VeriSign Could Stop Drive-By Downloads, February 22. Available at www.benedelman.org/news/020305-1.html. Accessed on January 12, 2007.

Edsall, T.B. (2006). Rise in Online Fundraising Changed Face of Campaign Donors. *The Washington Post*, page A03, March 6.

Emigh, A. (2006). Mis-education, in: M. Jakobsson, S.A. Myers (eds.), *Phishing and Countermeasures: Understanding the Increasing Problem of Electronic Identity Theft*. Wiley-Interscience, Hoboken, NJ, USA, pp. 260–273.

Experian. National Score Index (2007). Available at www.nationalscoreindex.com/

Federal Election Commission (2007). Campaign Finance Disclosure Data Search. Available at www.fec.gov/finance/disclosure/disclosure_data_search.shtml

Felten, E.W., M.A. Schneider (2000). Timing attacks on web privacy, in: *CCS '00: Proceedings of the 7th ACM Conference on Computer and Communications Security*. ACM Press, New York, pp. 25–32.

Finn, P., M. Jakobsson (2007). Designing and conducting phishing experiments. *IEEE Technology and Society Magazine, Special Issue on Usability and Security.*

Fogg, B.J., J. Marshall, O. Laraki, A. Osipovich, C. Varma, N. Fang, J. Paul, A. Rangnekar, J. Shon, P. Swani, M. Treinen (2001). What makes web sites credible?: a report on a large quantitative study, in: *CHI '01: Proceedings of the SIGCHI Conference on Human Factors in Computing Systems.* ACM Press, New York, pp. 61–68.

Fogg, B.J., C. Soohoo, D.R. Danielson, L. Marable, J. Stanford, E.R. Tauber (2003). How do users evaluate the credibility of web sites?: a study with over 2,500 participants, in: *DUX '03: Proceedings of the 2003 Conference on Designing for User Experiences.* ACM Press, New York, pp. 1–15.

Friedrichs, O. (2008). Cybercrime and the electoral system, in: M. Jakobsson, Z. Ramzan (eds.), *Crimeware*, Chapter 10.

GeoTrust, Inc. (2007). Trustwatch toolbar. Available at toolbar.trustwatch. com/tour/v3ie/toolbar-v3ie-tour-overview.html. Accessed on January 8.

Goodin, D. (2007). Yahoo feeds Trojan-laced ads to MySpace and PhotoBucket users. *The Register*, September 11. Available at www.theregister.co.uk/2007/09/11/yahoo_serves_12million_malware_ads/

Google, Inc. (2007a). Google Safe Browsing for Firefox. Available at www.google.com/tools/firefox/safebrowsing. Accessed on January 8.

Google, Inc. (2007b). Google Checkout Fees. Available at checkout.google. com/seller/fees.html

Griffith, V., M. Jakobsson (2005). Messin' with texas: deriving mothers' maiden names using public records, in: *Applied Cryptography and Network Security (ACNS)*, Springer, Berlin, pp. 91–103. Available at http://www.springerlink.com/content/j0ctulfq9x2kwq4n/

Hypponen, M. (2007). 21 solutions to save the world: masters of their domain. *Foreign Policy* (May/June). Available at www.foreignpolicy.com/story/cms.php?story_id = 3798

IP2Location. Available at http://www.ip2location.com

Jackson, C., A. Bortz, D. Boneh, J.C. Mitchell (2006). Protecting browser state from web privacy attacks. in: L. Carr, D.D. Roure, A. Iyengar, C.A. Goble, and M. Dahlin (eds.). *Proceedings of the 15th international conference on World Wide Web, WWW 2006, Edinburgh, Scotland, UK, May 23–26, 2006*, ACM, New York, NY, pp. 737–744.

Jagatic, T.N., N.A. Johnson, M. Jakobsson, F. Menczer (2007). Social phishing. *Communications of the ACM* 50(10), 94–100.

Jakobsson, M., T. Jagatic, S. Stamm (2007a). Phishing for clues: Inferring context using cascading style sheets and browser history. Available at browser-recon.info. Accessed on January 8.

Jakobsson, M., Z. Ramzan (2008). *Crimeware: Understanding New Attacks and Defenses.* 1st ed., Addison-Wesley Professional, (April 16), ISBN-10: 032150195, ISBN-13: 978-0321501950.

Jakobsson, M., J. Ratkiewicz (2006). Designing ethical phishing experiments: a study of (ROT 13) rOnl query features. in: L. Carr, D.D. Roure, A. Iyengar, C.A. Goble, and M. Dahlin (eds.). *Proceedings of the 15th international conference on World Wide Web, WWW 2006, Edinburgh, Scotland, UK, May 23–26, 2006*, ACM, New York, NY, pp. 513–522.

Jakobsson, M., S. Stamm (2006). Invasive browser sniffing and countermeasures. in: L. Carr, D.D. Roure, A. Iyengar, C.A. Goble, and M. Dahlin (eds.). *Proceedings of the 15th international conference on World Wide Web, WWW 2006, Edinburgh, Scotland, UK, May 23–26, 2006*, ACM, New York, NY, pp. 523–532.

Jakobsson, M., A. Tsow (2006). Making takedown difficult, in: M. Jakobsson, S.A. Myers (eds.), *Phishing and Countermeasures: Understanding the Increasing Problem of Electronic Identity Theft.* Wiley-Interscience, Hoboken, NJ, USA, pp. 461–467.

Jakobsson, M., A. Tsow, A. Shah, E. Blevis, Y.-K. Lim (2007b). What instills trust? A qualitative study of phishing, in: *Usable Security (USEC'07)*, February 15–16, Hilton Tobago Resort Lowlands, Scarborough, Trinidad/Tobago.

Juels, A., M. Jakobsson, T.N. Jagatic (2006). Cache cookies for browser authentication (extended abstract), in: *Proceedings of the 2006 IEEE Symposium on Security and Privacy*, IEEE Computer Society, Washington, DC, USA, pp. 301–305.

Juels, A., M. Jakobsson, J. Ratkiewicz (2007). Remote-harm diagnostics. Available at http://ravenwhite. com/files/rhd.pdf

Justice, G. (2004). Clicking into the Kerry Coffers for a one-day online record. *The New York Times,* July 2.

Krebs, B. (2006). Hacked ad seen on MySpace Served Spyware to a million. *The Washington Post — Security Fix,* July 19. Available at blog.washingtonpost.com/securityfix/2006/07/myspace_ad_served_ adware_to_mo.html

Krebs, B. (2007). Virus writers taint Google ad links. *The Washington Post — Security Fix,* April 25. Available at blog.washingtonpost.com/securityfix/2007/04/virus_writers_taint_google_ad.html

Kumaraguru, P., Y. Rhee, A. Acquisti, L.F. Cranor, J. Hong, E. Nunge (2007). Protecting people from phishing: the design and evaluation of an embedded training email system, in: M.B. Rosson, D.J. Gilmore (eds.), *CHI.* ACM, New York, NY, USA, pp. 905–914.

M. Corp. Senderid (2007). Available at www.microsoft.com/mscorp/safety/technologies/senderid/ default.mspx. Accessed on January 8.

Markoff, J. (2007). Attack of the zombie computers is growing threat. *The New York Times,* January 7.

McCullagh, D. (2001). Satirists didn't steal election. *Wired News,* January 19. Available at www. wired.com/politics/law/news/2001/01/41293

McCullagh, D. (2003). Bush OKs spam bill-but critics not convinced. *CNET News.com,* December 16. Available at www.news.com/2100-1028-5124724.html

Meiss, M. (2006). Race pharming, in: M. Jakobsson, S.A. Myers (eds.), *Phishing and Countermeasures: Understanding the Increasing Problem of Electronic Identity Theft.* Wiley-Interscience, Hoboken, NJ, USA, pp. 133–136.

Mitnick, K., W.L. Simon (2002). *The Art of Deception: Controlling the Human Element of Security,* Wiley Books, pp. 368. ISBN 978-0-7645-4280-0.

Murota Laboratory—Tokyo Institute of Technology (2006). Scrapbook Firefox Extension, December 15. Available at amb.vis.ne.jp/mozilla/scrapbook/

National Geographical and Political Software (2007). Our clients. Available at www.ngpsoftware.com/ clients

OUT-LAW News (2004). Staff reveal passwords for a chocolate bar, April 20. Available at http:// www.out-law.com/page-4469

PayPal (2007). Transaction fees for domestic payments—United States. Available at www.paypal.com/ us/cgi-bin/webscr?cmd = _display-receiving-fees-outside

Raney, R.F. (1999). Bush campaign asks government to go after critical web site. *The New York Times,* May 21.

Raskin, A. (2006). Simulated browser attack, in: M. Jakobsson, S.A. Myers (eds.), *Phishing and Countermeasures: Understanding the Increasing Problem of Electronic Identity Theft.* Wiley-Interscience, Hoboken, NJ, USA, pp. 89–101.

Soghoian, C. (2007). A deceit-augmented man in the middle attack against Bank of America's SiteKey Service. *Slight Paranoia,* April 10. Available at paranoia.dubfire.net/2007/04/ deceit-augmented-man-in-middle-attack.html

Sonic WALL Phishing IQ Test II. Available at www.sonicwall.com/phishing/. Accessed on January 8, 2007.

Srikwan, S., M. Jakobsson (2007). Available at www.securitycartoon.com—a consumer security awareness campaign based on cartoons.

Srikwan, S., M. Jakobsson (2008). Using cartoons to teach internet security. *Journal of Cryptologia* 32(2), 137–154.

Stamm, S., M. Jakobsson (2006). Social malware. Experimental results available at www.indiana.edu/ ~phishing/verybigad/

Stamm, S., Z. Ramzan, M. Jakobsson (2006). Drive-by pharming. Indiana University Technical Report, TR641, December. Available at www.cs.indiana.edu/pub/techreports/TR641.pdf

Stirland, S.L. (2007). Scoop: Clinton raised $8 million online in 3Q. *Wired News—Threat Level,* October 2. Available at blog.wired.com/27bstroke6/2007/10/scoop-clinton-r.html

Swartz, J. (1998). Government parasites—"stealth" web pages feed off addresses. *San Francisco Chronicle,* June 3.

Tsow, A. (2006). Phishing with consumer electronics—malicious home routers. *Models of Trust for the Web, a workshop at the 15th International World Wide Web Conference (WWW2006)*, May 22–26.

Tsow, A., M. Jakobsson, L. Yang, S. Wetzel (2006). Warkitting: the drive-by subversion of wireless home routers. *Journal of Digital Forensic Practice* 1(3 Special Issue: Phishing and Online Fraud, Part II), 172–192.

Whalen, T., K.M. Inkpen (2005). Gathering evidence: use of visual security cues in web browsers, in: *GI '05: Proceedings of Graphics Interface 2005*. School of Computer Science, University of Waterloo, Waterloo, Ontario, Canada, pp. 137–144. Canadian Human-Computer Communications Society.

Whitten, A., J.D. Tygar (1999). Why Johnny can't encrypt: a usability evaluation of PGP 5.0, in: *8th USENIX Security Symposium*. USENIX Association, Berkeley, CA, USA, pp. 169–184.

Wu, M., R. Miller, S. Garfinkel (2006). Do security toolbars actually prevent phishing attacks? in: *Proceedings of CHI*, ACM, New York, NY, USA.

Yahoo, Inc. (2007). Domainkeys. Available at antispam.yahoo.com/domainkeys. Accessed on January 8.

Zhang, Y., S. Egelman, L. Cranor, J. Hong (2007). Phinding phish: evaluating anti-phishing tools, in: *NDSS '07: Proceedings of the 14th Annual Network and Distributed System Security Symposium*, The Internet Society, San Diego, California, USA.

Rao & Upadhyaya, Eds., *Handbooks in Information Systems, Vol. 4*

Chapter 8

Human-Centered Security

Vidyaraman Sankaranarayanan

Microsoft Corporation, One Microsoft Way, Redmond, WA 98052, USA

Shambhu Upadhyaya

Computer Science and Engineering, University at Buffalo, Buffalo, USA

Kevin Kwiat

Air Force Research Laboratory, 525 Brooks Road, Rome, NY 13441, USA

Abstract

The human factor has long been viewed as the weakest link in the security chain. In this chapter, we examine the current manifestations of the weak human factor and present three different views on users. We then discuss the application of design principles from a user centric perspective, taking into account environmental issues and user preferences. In this context, threat modeling and risk analysis/estimation are studied, with principles that are specific to user centric design. We then present some new paradigms that have been proposed recently to incorporate the user in the security loop in a meaningful manner, and elicit cooperation from noncompliant users. Lastly, we investigate the assessment techniques for a user centric security mechanism and point to some recent developments in simulations for the same.

---

1 Introduction

Computer Systems today are made up of a variety of heterogeneous components, each fulfilling a well-defined set of roles or providing some services. This statement generically applies to almost all the systems we see around us today. Even desktop systems can be considered as a collection of components that provide some service to the user. Security design and correct operation are critical and hence designers have worked toward ensuring the security of the system either from a component point of view or from a functional point of view.

In this scheme of things, the human factor is an interesting and important aspect, and perhaps the most ignored one too. A fundamental process and the common denominator to most systems is the interaction between the system and the user. It is this interaction that is responsible for the functioning of the system; and in most cases, regardless of the goal of the system, this very interaction, according to Schneier (2000), is the greatest risk. The variable and often unpredictable factor in this interaction is the user. It is this user who has earned the label of a *Weak Human Factor*. The weak human factor does not always cause an attack by itself; rather, the actions of users are the starting point for some attacks, and in some cases, the users themselves may launch the attacks. This chapter looks into the security of a system with the inclusion of the human factor. We shall begin with a brief history of Human–Computer Interaction (HCI) system design philosophy and how it has affected security design. Our first step is to investigate the current state of affairs as regard to the effect of human factors on computer security. We then investigate a probable cause as to why this state of affairs has come about and the recent advances aimed toward addressing this problem. These approaches include standardized security design principles, threat assessment and risk mitigation, among others, as an approach to address the problem. We examine the design principles of these approaches and related models and algorithms. Security mechanisms that specifically consider the human factors will also be covered. Finally, as is usual in any software development, we look into testing the security of these systems, and examine the unique challenges that researchers face when they try to evaluate these systems.

1.1 A brief history

Conventional wisdom and decades of established design practice have user transparency as the basic principle of system design: all subsystems must be transparent to the users. The concept of transparency originated in the ideology of user-entered design in the HCI domain, where the initial focus has been ease of usage. The concept was mainly centered around the fact that the user must get the task done as easily as possible, without even being aware of the interaction between the subsystems that is required for the completion of the task. With the development of information systems, the types and functionalities of the constituent subsystems became varied. The ideology of transparency has proliferated to all these subsystems, not as a result of careful consideration, but more due to familiarity in the design process and an attitude among designers that it was a logical path to follow.

This design principle has been applied to the security subsystems as well. However, the security subsystems are a class apart from most other systems in that they have a negative requirement. Basically they exist to protect the system and in the normal course of activity, do not produce any tangible deliverable (except in certain specialized circumstances). However, their very existence (and their requirements) institutes certain procedures in the system that is not strictly a required process in the normal workflow of the system. The simple act of requiring a password to enter into a system is an example of such a process, which, in the absence of a threat to the system, is strictly not part of the workflow, though it is so ingrained into systems today that it (authentication in general) is part of any workflow. Such processes required for the security of the system are regarded (or have come to be regarded) by users as a performance block or an impediment to their routine functioning. And hence users tend to ignore or bypass these "performance blocks." The main problem with the security design is not ignorance; rather it is the preconceived ideas on the design methodology. There are, however, different viewpoints on the problem of the weak human factor, apart from simply the bad design methodology followed today. Consider these illustrations

- *Weak passwords*: This example, by far, has been the one that is well studied and by now is self-explanatory in its manifestation and effect. Users prefer to choose simple and often blindingly obvious passwords that are susceptible to automated password crackers. Technological solutions that force users to choose complex passwords result in the password being written down in a convenient place, often stuck on the user's console, or very "securely" stored under the keyboard. Although biometric solutions like fingerprint readers exist, they are expensive to deploy and simple to deceive.
- *Social engineering attacks*: These attacks take the form of shoulder surfing, e-mail phishing, etc. Users often fall prey to these attacks due to ignorance. Addressing these attacks often involves more than just technical solutions. Till date, educating users about these attacks remains the state-of-the-art technique.
- *Failure to install security updates on time*: Users often resort to delaying or ignoring the best practices relating to security updates unless forced to, either in the form of a system compromise or through a forced update by the system administrator. By security updates, we do not mean only the ubiquitous Microsoft Windows and Office Security Updates. Many other products also require updates, some of which, unlike operating system upgrades, are not enforced by the system administrator.
- *Inappropriate usage of organizational resources*: Users usually have reasonable protection when they are inside the perimeter of the organization. However, they use their computational devices

(company Laptops) inappropriately—like installing games, allowing family members to surf the Internet, connecting new untested devices inside the office, etc., thereby bypassing organizational perimeter controls.

These scenarios are illustrative of many facets of the user. They bring out the characteristics of the typical user that has earned them the adage of the *Weak Human Factor*. The reasons for the weak human factor are many, and cannot usually be generalized, since the scenarios are widely spread over, as are the attack vectors. For example, Phishing attacks and weak passwords are both a manifestation of the weak human factor, yet the attack vectors are almost completely different. Although this problem has been slow to proliferate, it is now receiving the attention it deserves due to a variety of reasons. The primary reason is that in the chain of components (or subsystems) that make up present day systems, the human factor has become the *weakest link*. Needless to say, the security of a system is only as strong as its weakest link, and attackers have been quick to exploit the weak human factor. Not only are systems hacked into due to security vulnerabilities, but the human factor is also used as a stepping-stone to gain entry into systems. This is done by exploiting even arcane security vulnerabilities in conjunction with the weak human factor. As an example, we consider phishing e-mails and investigate their evolution and usage in exploiting a system.

1.2   An example: phishing e-mails

Phishing e-mails are cleverly crafted e-mails that are sent to bulk mailing lists. They appear to be from a financial institution, such as Citibank, PayPal or eBay. The success of this attack relies solely on the huge number of e-mail recipients and the popularity of the financial institution that is being masqueraded. Their template is usually standard across all the recipients of the e-mail: the recipient, in our case the user, is advised to verify his account details due to a "security problem." The users are directed to the financial institutions' web site where such "verification" can be performed. However, the link provided in the e-mail leads users to a fraudulent web site that looks exactly like the original web site, and harvests the information provided by the users and redirects them to the legitimate web site, with a message of "account unlocked" or something similar. Let us examine the various stages of evolution of the phishing attack.

Stage 1: E-mails are crafted by non-English speakers; most of them are misspelled and expose the nonprofessional nature of the communication. The evolution in these e-mails is evident by professional looking e-mails today.

Stage 2: The links in the e-mails are obfuscated; sometimes the links appear to be genuine due to cross browser scripting attacks or International Domain Name (IDN) vulnerabilities. Basically, the evolution here is in terms of exploiting browser vulnerabilities.

Stage 3: Although an isolated incident, the fraudulent web sites now have an secure socket layer (SSL) certificate, something that users are educated to trust as being "secure." So now, users are not only fooled by the correct-looking link, they also have the "yellow lock" which they have been educated to trust as being secure. This is a giant leap for phishers, since SSL certificates are implicitly trusted.

Stage 4: Finally, phishing e-mails are no longer for direct financial gain; they have been used to gain access into a company server.[1] A certain brokerage company used a Microsoft IIS web server for providing access to their clients. One such client received a mail from the company asking him to log on to the server for some "interface redesign test." Surprisingly, *the link in the e-mail was not fraudulent; in fact it pointed exactly to the brokerage company's domain*. The client therefore logged into the server, found the experience normal, and logged off. The problem was the link provided contained a predefined session ID. The attacker was making use of the "session fixation" vulnerability in Microsoft IIS and was able to remotely login *exactly* when the client activated the session ID.

Such evolution is representative of one certainty; the weak human factor can no longer be ignored. Not only are the attack vectors unpredictable as in other situations, it is possible for the user to act as a stepping-stone to other attacks. Security researchers and system administrators alike have realized the importance of integrating the notion of system security with human-centered security, and by doing so, have taken a human-centric view of system security as opposed to only a technological view of system security.

2 Human-centered security

The threat posed by legitimate users in an organization has appropriately been labeled as "The Enemy Within" (McAfeeCorporation, 2005) in a recent survey by McAfee Corporation (http://www.mcafee.com). We can divide the user broadly into two different categories:

- *Type I—A legitimate user*: This category of users includes legitimate and authorized users of the system. These users log into the system and execute workflow processes according to their roles. According to the

---

[1]This case study was presented in the 2006 NYS cyber-security symposium by Mr. Belani of Mandiant.

McAfee Survey (McAfeeCorporation, 2005), such users are varyingly labeled as "The Security Softie", "The Gadget Geek", or "The Squatter". Although they do not have any stated intentions to disrupt the system, their actions nonetheless endanger the system. For example, these users do not have any idea of the threat model of the system and hence, may not implement the best practices suggested by the organization.

- *Type II—A legitimate, but malicious user*: Similar to Type I users, users in this category are legitimate, that is, they possess authorized credentials to log into the system. However, their goal is to disrupt the system, either through a self-inflicted cataclysmic system compromise or through slow poisoning attacks like leaking confidential information about the organization to its competitors. According to the Survey (McAfeeCorporation, 2005), such users are labeled as "The Saboteur."

2.1 The three prisms

We mentioned in the previous section that the human factor has become the weakest link in the security chain. But there are schools of thought (that the authors also agree with) that state that terming the human factor the weakest link somehow offloads the responsibility of bad system design on the users. Human-centered security, however, is a more holistic approach and needs to be approached as such: bad system design is only part of the equation. We can view the problem from three different, not necessarily disjoint, prisms, called *Bad Design, User Ignorance* and *Non-Compliant Users*.

The first prism *Bad Design*, as the name suggests, consists of badly designed systems, with a lack of foresight on usage scenarios. Password-based systems fall under this category. Open Simple Mail Transport Protocol (SMTP) relays, with a lack of authentication, also falls under these categories. It can be (correctly) argued that such instances are not bad design in the same manner as described earlier, where transparency is prioritized more than awareness.

Bad Design. Open SMTP relays are the cause of spam and phishing e-mails that consume bandwidth and cause huge financial losses.

Also, usage/threat scenarios could not have been predicted (who would have thought of spam when TCP/IP was invented? Even when spam was beginning, nobody thought of phishing e-mails!) when these technologies/systems were developed. Nevertheless, such systems can be viewed through the prism of bad system design. Toward such issues, better system design could (almost) solve the problem. The concept of *usable security* also falls under this category. This consists of systems that may be technically sound, in that "correct" usage of the system according to the vendor guidelines will result in a secure system, but do not offer a "correct" interface for using and implementing vendor guidelines. These systems may also not give appropriate cues to the user that indicates the current state of the system.

Ignorance Prism. Social Engineering attacks, like phishing e-mails, calls from support desk requesting user's password, exploit naïve user's.

The second prism is that of user *Ignorance*. Any threat vector that exploits user ignorance may be viewed through this prism. For example, phishing e-mails exploit user ignorance (or naivety). Although technical solutions can be built to address these problems, their primary cause is not bad design. Social engineering attacks also fall under this category.

Non-Compliance Prism. Users tunnel connections through port 80 to evade firewall-blocking rules in their companies.

The third prism is that of user *Non-Compliance* with the security policies and best practices in the organization, despite knowledge of the requirements and proper communication. Users in an organization may bring in electronic gadgets and install software on their machines for working with them. Despite security policies that prevent certain actions, users may willfully evade them, not to penetrate the system, but to obtain functionality that may not be available otherwise. This too forms part of the weak human factor, and is perhaps the most difficult one to address.

Let us first examine the challenges that researchers and designers face when dealing with the weak human factor. In any system, users perform *actions* toward fulfilling their roles. The notion of *actions* is an abstract one that can be generalized to most, if not all, systems. Actions can be split in the following manner:

Action Type I: The fundamental user actions required for the workflow. These fundamental actions are defined by the user's role in the environment. For example, a graphics designer will need to use some photo-/video-editing software. In addition, a device like a tablet may need to be connected to the computer via the Universal Serial Bus (USB) interface for rendering hand sketches.

Action Type II: Ancillary actions required for the fundamental actions to work, for example, exploring the hard drive is a prerequisite for most job roles. In addition, connecting USB devices, burning images onto a CD may be in this list for a graphics designer.

Action Type III: These are actions that are not predefined like Actions types I and II. These actions are the ones that users normally execute without any restrictions, since they do not fall under the purview of "restricted objects." They might have the potential to disrupt the working of the system, or may be inimical to the individual. Examples of such actions include clicking on a potential phishing link in an untrusted/unsigned e-mail.

For those actions that are relevant to the security of the system, there exists an *easy* or an *efficient* manner of performing them. For example, choosing a password is an (one time) action that users have to perform when registering into the system. The *easy* way is to choose a password that is easy to remember (and hence easy to guess/crack). The *effective* way, however, is to choose a complex password that is tough to remember. Similar is the situation with security updates; it is *easy* to ignore them while it is *effective* to update the system. For reasons that are mostly context- and domain-specific, users prefer to perform only the easy action, and not the efficient one. In the case of passwords, it is simply because users may not wish to go the extra mile to remember complex passwords; in the case of security updates, users may not want any interruption to their normal workflow. Viewing the interaction between the user and the system as a set of easy vs. efficient actions, where the easy action is most often the inefficient one, provides us a global view to look into this issue. *Thus the main challenge for human-centered security schemes is to ensure that users perform the effective action with awareness of the consequences of their actions.* Viewing these actions under the three prisms provides us one methodology to address the human factor related security issues.

2.2   What is a human-centered security scheme?

Before we delve into the vagaries of the human nature and present design methodologies for securing a system, we must first define what exactly we mean by "human-centered security" and state very clearly the end goal of having such a system. Although there is no consensus in the community on what human-centered security is, there have been a variety of works done on addressing the weak human factor. These works and the goals they (seek to) accomplish can guide us toward a working definition. We can start by defining human-centered security as a security mechanism that takes into account the weak human factor (consciously or unconsciously). Consider the oft-quoted example of weak passwords. Users initially are educated about the hazards of using weak passwords. Although such user awareness programs are still conducted in organizations, they are not considered as a security scheme *per se*. The next stage, and in fact the first technical measure, is to force users to choose a complex password when establishing an account. This merely results in users writing down their passwords, which is clearly not a desirable result. Organizations now use a complex form of two-factor authentication, which is basically a combination of a password (what you know) and a biometric ID, like a fingerprint (what you are) or a Secure ID token (what you have). Thus two-factor authentications can be considered as a security scheme that addresses a manifestation of the weak human factor.

Consider the issue of security updates or phishing e-mails. Users are initially educated to update their machines and not respond to phishing e-mails. Next, security updates are forced on machines by the system administrators. Phishing e-mails are either filtered at the e-mail server or addressed by client-side solutions, mostly browser-based, that check on a domain to verify its authenticity. However, consider the nature of the threat. Although the threat model remains the same, that is, an attack that exploits the weak human factor, the attack vectors are vastly different and mostly unpredictable. But all the security schemes that address phishing e-mails or weak passwords or unpatched systems aim at the same final end goal, which is user awareness, or more generally, *a user culture that prioritizes security over immediate performance gains or "comfort level."* Even two-factor authentications require a certain level of awareness from the users side to not lose their security token (SecureID). Similarly, solutions that address phishing e-mails require awareness from users and a need for their response to potential false positives. Thus, we arrive at a working definition of a human-centered security scheme.

Any security scheme that inculcates a user culture which prioritizes security over immediate performance gains or 'comfort level' is a *human centered security scheme.*

User culture is perhaps the determining factor that decides the security state of the system, and thus it is appropriate that human-centered security must eventually aim at inculcating such culture in the users. This definition may be used to evaluate the systems, which fall under the first prism of bad design: does the security scheme (in addition to proper design) inculcate a culture of security in users? The second prism of user ignorance is directly related to this definition and requires no further exposition. The third prism of noncompliance is also directly related: if there were a user culture that prioritizes security, users would be more inclined to forgo performance gains over maintaining security.

3 Analysis, design principles, models, solutions, and algorithms

3.1 Human-oriented perspective

Examining the security issues of a system from a human-oriented perspective is similar to the abstraction of events affecting the user and the actions that a user performs, either in response to these events or as part of fulfilling his role. The approach toward a defensive mechanism is also similar; user actions have to be categorized as easy or inefficient (and notwithstanding whether they are rooted in ignorance or negligence). To gain additional insight into the human-oriented perspective, let us consider the situation from an attacker's point of view. The primary motive of the attacker notwithstanding (financial in the case of phishing e-mails, system access in the case of social engineering attacks, etc.), the core weakness that is exploited is the users' ignorance or lack of awareness toward the potential consequences of an inefficient action. A suggested requirement to address such issues is to have an ethnographer perform a study of the organization. Ethnographers study the interaction between users and computer systems within the organizational context that is determined by the organizational norms, rules, procedure, ethos, culture, etc. Their study can be analyzed for understanding the security issues of the weak human factor from a sociological, psychological, and even a systems' design perspective.

3.2   Human factors in designing security

When designing a system that takes into account the human factor, it is instructive to investigate the characteristics of the user at different levels. The first level is user operation/interaction, more commonly known as HCI. There have been extensive studies to improve the quality of HCI toward increasing performance of the system. The second level at which user characteristics may be accounted for are cognitive, psychological, cultural, and sociological factors. Although these user characteristics have been individually (and extensively) studied, it is interesting to know the utility and implications of such factors toward the design of a system from a security viewpoint. Mental models of users have been used to study the usability of interfaces in HCI. Usability, as defined by ISO 9241, *is the effectiveness, efficiency, and satisfaction with which specified users achieve specified goals in a particular environment.* As is typical in most high-level definitions, the standards specify only the performance expectations and not the specific elements that are required to extract these goals. However, these mental models are so much important to security design, since (a) they are representative of what the users expect from the system and (b) they are indicators of how users will react to a stimulus from the system. Hence mental models of users, when interpreted appropriately, are an important indicator for security designers. This should come as no surprise, since security and usability are closely tied together, and as we have aforementioned, the ideology of transparency (and greater usability) has hurt security. The second level of user characteristics like cognitive, psychological, cultural, and sociological factors is more difficult and tedious to determine. Surveys and questionnaires, focus groups and interviews, etc., are used to determine these factors. Their validity unfortunately, is usually circumspect, since any properly worded survey can be used to prove almost any point. The results of surveys and "sponsored" studies must be perused deeply before using them in any kind of system design. Focus groups and interviews, particularly those conducted by academic organizations *without commercial influence, by means of sponsoring, etc.,* are perhaps more reliable. Even in those cases, a study of the interview questions, target group, and relevant experience of the group members, must be looked into.

There are three types of lies - lies, damn lies, and statistics

Mark Twain

However, when such studies are validated, their results could prove *invaluable* to security designers and practitioners alike. One such study relates to the importance users give to moral values. Another study relates to the importance users attach to different work-related values. The results from such studies can be used by human-centered security schemes, *since their eventual goal is to inculcate a user culture.*

3.3 Threat modeling and risk analysis

As a first step to addressing the weak human factor, security designers must create a threat model for their system. Such a threat model must be specific to the particular systems, and not generic. For example, a commercial organization might account for phishing e-mails in their threat model, whereas a military unit might not have any conception of an e-mail in their work scenario. Thus the threat model relates to all manifestations of the weak human factor of that particular system. Once a threat model is ready, the next step is to try and resolve the issues through a technically feasible solution. For example, if a system breach due to weak passwords is a possibility, then two-factor authentications must be instantiated. If e-mail borne viruses are an issue, either a virus scanner must be installed at the e-mail server or client end or all incoming mails with suspicious attachments must be flagged for users. Note that according to our definition of a human-centered security scheme, they do not strictly try to inculcate a security conscious user culture, although they might do so through warnings in e-mails, etc. As we have seen before, the attack vectors for this threat are entirely unpredictable; hence these technical solutions, as we see, can only go to a certain extent to solve the problems. It may also not be economically feasible for an organization to implement all these techniques. A combination of these two-factors leads us to the notion of risk analysis of an action/situation and a tradeoff as a means to address the problem. The nature of the tradeoff is of course dependent on the particulars of the system and the risk involved in that particular context. For example, in scenarios where high security is a requirement, usability might occupy a lower spot of the priority list. Therefore, users might have to perform two-factor authentication for certain critical operations. Security updates might be applied immediately even at the cost of interrupting the user's workflow. Irrespective of the mechanism used to detect threats, the very act of threat modeling and risk analysis for the particular system under consideration is an important step.

3.4   Risk mitigation

Once a risk analysis has been performed, the next step is to either address the threats behind them or, if the cost of doing so were too high, attempt to mitigate the risks with a recovery plan for worst-case scenarios. This approach is standard for most of the security risks; however, applying it to the weak human factor has its challenges. A part of the analysis of the weak human factor included the classification of actions as easy or effective. Although such a view is indispensable, it is often not practically feasible for a number of reasons.

- Judging a user action accurately as easy or inefficient may not be possible in certain domains.
- Not all user actions have a simple categorization; actions that were deemed effective in a certain context might be inefficient in a different context.
- Users may have to perform certain actions to ensure proper workflow.

Consider the scenario where a user may not deploy security updates on his desktop since the workflow is interrupted; however, a developer or an admin may not deploy the update if it affects a business process adversely. This action of (not) applying security updates is hence a context-specific issue and cannot always be tagged as easy/effective. This is also an example of an action that is required for some workflow. Thus we arrive at a situation where users have to be allowed to perform actions regardless of their categorization. In such situations, risk mitigation lends itself as a solution that quantifies the tradeoff between a potential security threat and the perceived benefits of an action. Within the confines of a human-centered security scheme, risk mitigation usually implies a decision on the part of the system to either allow a user action or initiate other procedures. Various user characteristics can be used as an input to such a decision engine. If the system has a trust-monitoring engine, users may be allowed to operate based on their trust level. In a group interview/survey/questionnaire, a user may have demonstrated a greater awareness of security issues and an ability and willingness to implement security processes. Such a user may be allowed to take potentially risky actions, in the expectation that his domain knowledge offsets the knowledge of the security mechanism.

3.5 Design principles for systems

Design principles for addressing the human factor are mostly centered on the user interface (apart from just good security design). Ka-Ping Yee has summarized the design principles for user interaction in terms of derivatives/descendants of well-established principles. These principles (Yee, 2002) are given in Table 1.

These principles are applicable to most interactive systems, although the specific means of implementation will depend on the application domain and the context. A brief listing is mentioned here: the reader is encouraged to read the work (Yee, 2002) for a greater detail of the *actor-ability state* introduced by the author. The principle of least privilege, path of least resistance, appropriate boundaries, explicit authorization, visibility, trusted path, etc., are the commonly know design principles that are yet to see "correct" application. The problems of proper implementation are manifold, since the very notion of security also depends on the perspective of the implementer. For example, consider the notion of a trusted path. From a technical standpoint, a trusted path is a "Mechanism by which a person using a terminal can communicate directly with the trusted computing base (TCB). Trusted path can only be activated by the person or the TCB and cannot be imitated by untrusted software." A trust path, among others, can be used to assure appropriate boundaries; but it also

Table 1
Secure interaction design principles

Path of least resistance	Match the most comfortable way to do tasks with the least granting of authority
Active authorization	Grant authority to others in accordance with user actions indicating consent
Revocability	Offer the user ways to reduce others' authority to access the user's resources
Visibility	Maintain accurate awareness of others' authority as relevant to user decisions
Self-awareness	Maintain accurate awareness of the user's own authority to access resources
Trusted path	Protect the user's channels to agents that manipulate authority on the user's behalf
Expressiveness	Enable the user to express safe security policies in terms that fit the user's task
Relevant boundaries	Draw distinctions among objects and actions along boundaries relevant to the task
Identifiability	Present objects and actions using distinguishable, truthful appearances
Foresight	Indicate clearly the consequences of decisions that the user is expected to make

Source: Yee (2002).

takes away a degree of control from the end user. Although this may help in terms of security, such measures have far reaching implications on consumer rights and user privacy, a dimension that was not even accounted for while designing these systems. Thus, while design principles can be generic, their implementation for certain scenarios are not straightforward.

Let us examine the translation of these design principles through the prism of *easy vs. effective* actions. The first guideline for security designers is that any security mechanism that is human centered must ensure that the system is secure in the face of any inefficient action of the user. Situations where the user has to be allowed to perform inefficient actions in the interests of the system have to be dealt with separately. Second, users have to be aware of the repercussions of their actions, that is, a feedback mechanism that informs the user of the potential effects of his actions must be present. If users still persist in their inefficient actions, then it may safely be said that their actions are rooted in negligence. Third, when a determination has been made to the effect that the inefficient action is rooted in negligence (or ignorance), the security mechanism must adaptively take a suitable action that ensures the security state of the system. Details on the adaptive actions are dependent on the domain of the system and are out of scope of this chapter. Lastly, the mechanism must deliver events to the user in a trustworthy manner, that is, users must be able to trust the external *events* affecting them (and hence the system). It is desirable for events to be tagged as trustworthy or suspicious. Tagging e-mails as spam and phishing are examples in the current situation, but the concept of tagging must be generalized to those *events* that affect the system the most.

3.6   Security measures that consider human factors

The three prisms through which we may look at the human factor also lend themselves to objectively evaluating any security measure that considers/addresses the human factor. As a solution to weak passwords, two-factor authentication has been introduced. This scheme is a classic example of addressing the problem of *Bad Design*. Next, consider the evolution of security updates in the Microsoft Windows Operating System (from Windows XP SP2). Initially, updates had to be manually installed by the user. A pull-mechanism was later introduced where every system could check either on a local Software Update Service (SUS) or on the Microsoft updates web site. Users were asked if they wanted to download updates. If installed, the system requested to be restarted every 5 min. This security mechanism can be considered to address the second and the third prism, viz. *user ignorance* and in part, *non-compliance*. Informing the user of the updates dispelled *user ignorance*. *Non-compliance* to restart the machine was addressed by a frequent restart reminder. This brings out important points, that is, do users need to be inconvenienced in some form or other to ensure that a noncompliant user adheres to the system policy? Was the restart reminder intended to just be a reminder or was it geared toward those users who refused to restart their machines?

Consider the act of launching executables on a host machine. Again, we choose Windows XP SP2 as an example. Executables that are downloaded from the Internet can be digitally signed, in which case the Operating system shell verifies the digital signature and presents a dialog to the user with the appropriate message. If the executable is not signed, users are asked each time to confirm to the execution, unless they specifically choose to *unblock* it. This security measure guards against users unknowingly launching an executable that may be malicious. Thus it can be looked through the second prism of *user ignorance*. Although there are many other measures, in general, any security measure that follows the Least User Privilege (LUP) and secure-by-default design may be said to address the human factor.

In this context, the Windows Vista operating system introduces a user account control (UAC) (Russinovich, 2007) to help address the weak human factor. Although the LUP principle had been known, application developers mostly wrote their software assuming that the user was running under administrative credentials. This gradually has lead to most users always running under administrative credentials to ensure their programs ran properly. Thus, it was easy for virus writers to exploit the system given a foothold in the system. This foothold could be easily established by exploiting the weak human factor (e.g., the ILOVEYOU virus). The User Account Control (UAC) in Windows Vista introduces a privilege separation for even administrative users, called *Integrity*. Most processes run at Medium Integrity Level, which disables any modification to critical system files. Thus, system stability is theoretically maintained even if the user inadvertently launched a (new) virus that had no signatures to match against. Thus, the UAC may be considered the next step in the evolution of *practical* security mechanisms that address the weak human factor. When a process requires administrative access, the user is asked whether to allow or disallow execution, with appropriate context-specific information. The UAC and other similar technologies are a step in the right direction.

However, the core problem of naïve users has not been addressed. This has been the main criticism against measures such as UAC—a very frequent interruption to the workflow. Although opinion is divided whether a user will have many UAC interruptions during a typical workday, it is conceivable for a naïve user to allow (even) a virus to execute with administrative credentials. The reasoning is that users will blindly allow programs that appear to require administrative credentials to execute as their default action to UAC prompts, or users may simply disable the UAC warnings. Let us examine this aspect from the viewpoint of the operating system (OS) vendor; poorly coded applications blindly require administrative credentials, which is the fault of the application developer. However, due to the existing state of affairs, it is simply not feasible for a complete overhaul of the system. Too many legacy applications would simply break and the disruption to the workflow, although not formally estimated, might be too huge to bear with. There exists a school of thought, often expressed in the New Security Paradigms Workshop (NSPW) series (http:// www.nspw.org/), that an unsettling and perhaps revolutionary change in the security landscape is required for a provocative and permanent solution to the problem of human-centered security. In Section 4, we mention some of these approaches and their practical feasibility.

4   New paradigms

A New Security Paradigm may be defined as a doctrine that defines security design and implementation with a new set of core principles that are possibly and completely incompatible with the existing computation model. We mention a synopsis of a few paradigms that relate to the human factor in security.

4.1   QoS throttling

We start off with a promising paradigm that has already found expression, albeit unconsciously, in many practical scenarios. Traditionally, security and quality of service (QoS) have been perceived as only orthogonally achievable goals. The enforcement of security is thought to be a performance obstacle, and guaranteeing QoS is thought to require the relaxation of security mechanisms. This paradigm elicits user cooperation with the security mechanisms in place by gracefully throttling the quality of service returned to an end-user as the security of the system degrades. However, it rewards users who cooperate with the security subsystem with a better QoS. The approach enjoys two main benefits: It encourages legitimate users to cooperate with security mechanisms as well as deters rogue users by proportionally degrading QoS in light of suspected security breaches.

The idea of degrading performance in case of observed security problems is not new. The graded QoS model is similar to the per-message quality-of-protection parameter introduced by Linn (1993) to manage the level of protection provided by a security mechanism. Irvine and Levine (2000) define security as a constructive dimension of QoS rather than an obstacle. Frameworks like Gonzalez and Sawicka (2002) rely on modeling user dynamics in terms of sociological issues, but ultimately rely on effective tools and policies to educate users and elevate risk perception. This concept of consciously elevating risk perception, thereby highlighting the effects of accidents has been suggested by Gonzalez (Gonzalez and Sawicka, 2002), but has not been further investigated or brought into the technical realm. A model called "safe staging" byWhitten and Tygar (2003) applies QoS degradation to legitimate users, where the system restricts the rights of Java applets (the service quality) in response to users' demonstrated understanding of the security implications. As users become more familiar with the security issues, the service quality is increased. In the area of network security, a server may gradually start dropping connections or reducing the QoS to stop a Denial of Service (DoS) attack or delay the propagation of Worms. This mechanism is applied in cases where there is no *absolute certainty* that there is an attack (malicious traffic in the case of a DoS and improper user activity in our case). Degrading performance is done for two reasons: Delaying the attack (if there is one in progress) and not stopping or hindering legitimate activity/traffic due to a false alarm.

4.2 Trusting user's actions

In Section 2.1, we defined the types of actions and their impact on the system security. However, determining if the actions of the user are in conformance with the systems overall functioning is a difficult task, particularly since not all user actions over time are black-and-white as choosing a strong password vs. a weak one. Additionally, actions initiated by users can be evaluated differently depending on the current security state at which the system resides. Since each system has its own problems, user actions are usually varied and as a result, it is not always possible for a monitoring mechanism to decide if the action taken by the user is in the interests of the system. The work on a Compensatory Trust Model (CTM) (Vidyaraman and Upadhyaya, 2006) builds a trust model for evaluating and updating the trust of users actions. Note that this is not the same as trusting a user; an untrusted user is a malicious user, who, upon detection or suspicion, demands some kind of proactive action. However, a user whose actions are not trusted may be classified as either an ignorant or a noncompliant user. The CTM builds on the action profiles of users and evaluates the effectiveness of the actions toward maintaining the system security. The trust measure is representative of the systems trust in the users' actions. The model can be applied to evaluate the trustworthiness of users and the efficiency of their actions toward maintaining the security level of the system. The parameters can be assigned such that the trust level updates are as granular or as coarse as required by the system. The model evaluates the users' actions continuously and provides the monitoring mechanism with a basis to allow or disallow an action, which, while permitted by the security policies in the system, is not clearly favorable or detrimental to the system. The intuition for the trust assignment framework is derived from a game-theoretic formulation by Green (2005), where the user and the system are modeled as playing a virtual game. Each user is assigned an initial trust score, which is updated dynamically on every action. The initial trust scores are assigned depending on the context of the application domain. Trust updates are performed through a model called "compensatory transfer" where for each effective action, the user is assigned a trust value equal to the "best claim for compensation" (Green, 2005). A claim of compensation is the difference between the benefits of the alternate action and the selected effective action by the user.

4.3   Insider threat

Throughout this chapter, we have focused on the weak human factor only from the legitimate, but ignorant or noncompliant user's viewpoint. The notion of a malicious insider is not completely within the purview of the weak human factor *per se*, but it does warrant a mention in terms of its threat vector and the mechanisms, current and new, to address them. An insider, for characterization purposes, may be a *malicious* insider or a *masquerading* insider. A malicious insider is a legitimate user who misuses his privileges inside the organization; for example, a disgruntled employee may be leaking trade secrets to a competitor. A masquerading insider, however, occupies the position of a legitimate user and operates under his credentials. A janitor or a co-employee operating on an open terminal of an employee who has just taken a coffee break is a classic example.

The classical procedure to detect masquerading insiders is to profile all legitimate users during their operations. The profiles may consist of monitoring their immediate actions, like mouse movements (MacAoidh et al., 2007) and keyboard typing characteristics (Gunetti and Picardi, 2005), or their network bandwidth usage and browsing characteristics (Grcar et al., 2005), etc. Once a profile is established, anomaly detection algorithms are used to detect any variations in their profiles, thereby detecting a masquerader. Masquerading insiders are a threat that can be overcome in high-security places by the use of appropriate technology, like fingerprint-sensitive input mechanisms. The malicious insider threat is more difficult to tackle, and requires constant monitoring and detection through possible deviation of workflow patterns, as opposed to profile violations. However, a typical workflow cannot be completely defined in terms of granular actions performed by a user, and thus, this area is still a topic of research.

A relatively new paradigm that attempts to address the malicious insider threat is the concept of user intent encapsulation (Upadhyaya et al., 2005) and remote chatterbox queries (Foster et al., 2006). Consider a typical desktop system: although a user may have access rights over a number of executables, he typically uses only a subset of them in his work. For example, the three browsers Internet Explorer, Mozilla Firefox, and Opera may be installed on the system, but the user may prefer only Internet

Explorer. Thus user intent (Upadhyaya et al., 2005) can be loosely interpreted as a set of executables he intends to use, as opposed to all the executables he has access rights over. An intrusion in a system may thus be detected when the user deviates from his stated intent beyond a statistically specified threshold. When such a deviation occurs, users are considered to be in the suspect region. Unfortunately, due to the vagaries and the inadequacies of workflow process specification, the number of users in the suspect region may be very huge. The remote chatterbox system (Foster et al., 2006) is the new paradigm proposed to better understand user motives. Basically, a chatterbox system is an Artificial Intelligence chatbot, like ELIZA (Weizenbaum, 1966) or ALICE (The Artificial Intelligence Foundation, 2008) that are programmed to make offers or ask questions to users in the suspect region. Depending on the responses of the users, an evaluation engine decides if the user's actions are in conformance with their stated intent or if a human monitor should take over the AI bot. The value of the AI bot lies in emulating a human user's responses/questions to the suspect user. Needless to say, such a bot might be deemed too intrusive or interruptive to the workflow process of the user. But this is the price we pay for security, and in some sense this could be tied in with the notion of QoS degradation, where QoS is defined not only as the interactive response a user receives from the system, but also the smoothness of his workflow, without any interruptions.

5 Assessment and evaluation

Evaluating a security mechanism that is targeted toward the weak human factor is difficult, given that our definition of human-centered security is one that inculcates a proper user culture. After all, how does one measure the effect on user culture? This problem is compounded by the fact that the user base in an organization is a fluid one. Let us consider the example of two-factor authentication; this scheme attempts (and succeeds to a good extent) to address the problem of weak passwords. Apart from the rationale to deploy it from a cost-benefit analysis let us examine the guidelines security designers have to follow to evaluate the scheme from a human angle. In two-factor authentication, users have a token generator, usually a device that generates random numbers based on the timestamp and a pre-programmed seed. First and foremost, since the users are now "allowed" to have weak passwords, can they be tricked into giving their token number through a social engineering attack? Second, do users still need to be persuaded to use and remember strong passwords? Is two-factor authentication supposed to solve the weak password's problem or unauthorized login's problem? These questions can give us some insight into the generic evaluation criteria for other similar security mechanisms.

Some of the *ad hoc* evaluation questions are listed later. These are meant to be guidelines, not strict design criteria.

- What is the security scheme meant to address?
- Can the new scheme be circumvented by users leaking information?
- Does the scheme fit it culturally? Does it attempt to inculcate a security culture?

Other methods of evaluation involve user experience investigation, user involvement in the design and evaluation phase and finally, an upcoming field of user simulation. Another evaluation technique relates to user involvement in the design phase. Although this strictly is not an evaluation technique, the security mechanism design is performed with the cognizance of the user community on the threat model. This technique has its advantages and disadvantages: however, users are aware of what is expected of them, and in some contexts, this leads to a greater awareness of the user community of the threat model. However, users are not designers, and the results of involving them in the design phase are not completely justified.

5.1 User experience investigation

Once the security scheme has been designed, user experience evaluation has been suggested by many security practitioners as an evaluation technique for human-centered security schemes. In this process, the security scheme is usually deployed in a limited setting, preferably among a limited set of the actual users of the system. At the end of an evaluation phase, a feedback, usually in the form of directed questionnaires, is solicited from the test subjects. Based on their evaluation, the security mechanism process is modified appropriately to reflect the users' preferences. Unfortunately, this mode of evaluation has been largely ineffective due to many reasons. Primary among them is the fact that users typically want to get their job done with minimum interruption, and usually prefer a greater application level QoS instead of conforming to security-related processes. Added to this is the fact that security-related schemes (like host-based firewall security) usually leave the crucial decision (like allowing a program to accept incoming connections) to the user. This frequent decision making is an impediment to the user, and is representative of a spectrum of application level QoS degradation. Note that, although the concept of QoS was originally defined for digital multimedia, we use the term in the context of application level QoS that is directly perceived by the user. Added to this is the fact that every legitimate product that requires access to the Internet instructs the user to "Answer 'Yes' to all security questions that pop up." Hence user experience evaluation, while being a good first step, is inadequate due to the plethora of evolving test conditions.

5.2   Penetration testing

The most promising evaluation technique appears to be a recently mooted scheme which involves a "social engineering" twist on a well-known technique, viz. penetration testing, also known as pen tests. A Social Engineering pen test attempts to evaluate a human-centered security scheme by attempting to exploit users to compromise resources. For example, a pen test would call users and claim to be from tech support and ask them for their passwords for a maintenance check. In situations where two-factor authentications are used, a pen test would go further, asking for the one-time token which users are assigned to. Similar experiments were carried out independently, where users of large corporate organizations were given free CD's supposedly with promotional Valentines Day material (Sturgeon, 2006). Despite a clear warning on the packaging of the CDs, users still ran the program on the CD, expecting some promotional material. Instead they were informed of the hazard of running unauthorized programs from untrusted sources. In a similar case, users "found" free USB drives (Stasiukonis, 2006) and inserted them in their computers and voluntarily ran a program (that was disguised as a jpeg image). These pen tests are examples of generic social engineering flaws. Other similarly designed tests could be used in the evaluation of human-centered security schemes. Social Engineering pen tests have a major advantage of shock value. Once a test is successful, users usually remember the "bad experience" and are more vigilant toward similar attacks in the future. However, they also have the capacity to leave a bad taste, and in some cases, may lead to a negation of the core work values the users are expected to follow. Such was the case in a social engineering test among the cadets of the West Point Military Academy. An e-mail was sent to all cadets asking them to visit a web site and enter personal details. Since the e-mail was signed by an authority figure, almost all cadets complied. Later when they were told about the fraudulent nature of the e-mail, those interviewed said they "felt betrayed." Their military values of "Obey first, ask questions later" seemed to have been the primary reason for such obedience. Although the cadets may never fall prey to such an e-mail again, the value of the social engineering test is circumspect in such situations.

5.3   Simulation techniques

Another methodology for evaluation is the concept of simulation to evaluate the effectiveness of a human-centered security scheme. However, using simulation for human factor testing is in its nascent stage. In its current state, such simulation techniques cannot be used to test against social engineering attacks. But they can be used to determine the effectiveness of host-based security mechanisms. The simulation methodology starts off with real user activity. User's actions on systems are actively monitored based on different parameterization. For example, users' mouse movements and keyboard strokes, their mode of operation (keyboard vs. mouse), issuing commands (menu driven or shortcuts driven), and their responses to dialog boxes (default, very fast vs. slow thoughtful and slow, etc.) are measured. From these user profiles, statistically similar user profiles are generated that mimic the relevant characteristics of the user. These user profiles are then "played out" on the security mechanism under question, and the effect on a workflow is measured. Although the exact metrics depend on the workflow, such simulation gives an idea of user responses to the security mechanism (and hence an extrapolation can be made toward their tendency to disagree or hate the mechanism under question).

6 Conclusion

All in all, we are at odds with ourselves in the crucial area of human-centered security. As users we want convenience and performance. We do not like to be interrupted with frequent questionnaires, even if it is for our own good. The UAC in Windows Vista is a classic example, where users are interrupted for most of the actions taken by installing applications. A simple act such as creating a directory in a restricted area may result in two interruptions. Although such restrictions and interruptions are useful from a security point of view, their utility is revealed only in certain rare circumstances. This is due to the inherent negative nature of security requirements: systems must *not* be compromised; data must *not* be read in transit, etc. However, such interruptions cause users to devise workarounds for the security mechanisms, thus rendering them incapable of addressing the threat vectors they were supposed to address.

The situation is further compounded by the fact that users are not confined to one workspace or to a single role. Security is often quoted not in terms of protecting devices, but in terms of content in various devices in various contexts, operated by the same user under different environment roles. Such a complex notion in current organizations have led to the notion of context-based dynamic security policies that specify access control for objects based on roles. Thus the same user has different permissions depending on his or her context. These dynamic security policies are a good step forward to insure against potential vulnerabilities that may be caused by the weak human factor.

Security schemes to counteract threats that exploit the weak human factor are aplenty. However, as with many other schemes, they are reactive, not proactive. Consider the example of phishing e-mails. E-mail filters and browser plug-in's or add-on's are available today to address phishing e-mails; however, they are aimed at mitigating the threats themselves, not at educating the users to recognize such fraudulent e-mails (and hence inculcate a user culture of security). Therefore, they are not, according to the definition adopted in this chapter, a human-centered security scheme.

As defined in this chapter, a human-centered security scheme is one that inculcates a user culture of security. As it stands, the definition borders on the sociological and psychological effects of a cyber-security scheme on users. Therefore, evaluation of a strictly computer-related security scheme must now encompass domains other than just computers. This raises a fundamental problem for evaluation, and more importantly, for a scheme to proclaim itself as a human-centered security scheme. Toward evaluation, social engineering penetration tests seem to be a practical and representative technique. Simulation, although not without its merits, it is still in the nascent stage. However, the definition of a human-centered scheme could be changed so as to restrict ourselves to the computer domain. However, such a definition would not serve the end purpose, which is to strengthen the human factor in an *attack and technology agnostic* manner. Finally, the manifestation of the human factor depends not only on the prism through which we look through a system, but also on the application domain and the context within the application domain. Therefore, it is likely that as technologies evolve and as new systems are brought into place, the manifestation will also change. Thus the defenses need to be as versatile as the innovative attacks. It remains to be seen if a completely automated solution is possible, or if a human-in-the-loop will be required to react to this ever-changing threat.

7   Questions for discussion

1. What is Usable Security?
2. What is the principle of least privilege? How does it help in security?
3. What are the secure interaction design principles? Describe them with an example.
4. What is an insider threat and how it can be mitigated?
5. Is QoS throttling an effective mechanism to improve human factor security?

Acknowledgment

This work was supported in part by U.S. Air Force Research Laboratory Grant No. 200821J.

References

Foster, K., J. Johnson, K. Kwiat (2006). *Reverse Social Engineering: Countering the Insider Attack by Simulating a Human Overseer, 2006 Summer Simulation Multiconference*, Calgary, Canada.

Gonzalez, J.J., A. Sawicka (2002). A Framework for Human Factors in Information Security, in: *Proceedings of the 2002 WSEAS International Conference on Information Security* (ICIS'02).

Grcar, M., D. Mladenic, M. Grobelnik (2005). *User Profiling for Interest Focused Browsing History, 7th International Multi-conference on Information Society IS'05*, Ljubljana, Slovenia.

Green, J. (2005). Compensatory transfers in two-player decision problems. *International Journal of Game Theory* 33(2), 159–180.

Gunetti, D., C. Picardi (2005). Keystroke analysis of free text. *ACM Transactions on Information and System Security* 8, 312–347.

Irvine, C., T. Levine (2000). Quality of security service, in: *Proceedings of the 2000 Workshop on New Security Paradigms*. ACM Press, Ballycotton, County Cork, Ireland.

Linn, J. (1993). *Generic Security Service Application Program Interface, IETF Request for Comments*, September.

MacAoidh, E., M. Bertolotto, D. Wilson (2007). Implicit profiling for contextual reasoning about user's spatial preferences, in: *Proceedings of the 2nd International Workshop on Case Based Reasoning and Context-Awareness*, Belfast, Northern Ireland, pp. 177–184.

McAfeeCorporation (2005). *The Enemy Within*. Available at http://www.theregister.co.uk/2005/12/15/mcafee_internal_security_survey/

Russinovich, M. (2007). *Inside Windows Vista User Account Control*. Available at http://www.microsoft.com/technet/technetmag/issues/2007/06/UAC/, *TechNet Magazine*.

Schneier, B. (2000). *Secrets and Lies: Digital Security in a Networked World*. Wiley, New York.

Stasiukonis, S. (2006). *Social Engineering, the USB Way*. Available at http://www.darkreading.com/document.asp?doc_id = 95556&WT.svl = column1_1, *Dark Reading*, Secure Network Technologes Inc.

Sturgeon, W. (2006). *Proof: Employees don't care about security*. Available at http://software.silicon.com/security/0,39024655,39156503,00.htm, *Silicon.com*

The A. L. I. C. E. Artificial Intelligence Foundation (2008). Available at http://www.alicebot.org

Upadhyaya, S., K. Kwiat, R. Chinchani, K. Mantha (2005). Encapsulation of owner's intent—A new proactive intrusion assessment paradigm, in: V. Kumar, J. Srivastava, A. Lazarevic (eds.), *Managing Cyber Threats: Issues, Approaches and Challenges*. Springer, New York, NY, pp. 221–245.

Vidyaraman, S., S. Upadhyaya (2006). A trust assignment model based on alternate actions payoff, in: *Proceedings of the 4th International Conference on Trust Management (iTrust '06)*, Volume 3986, Pisa, Italy, pp. 339–353.

Weizenbaum, J. (1966). ELIZA: a computer program for the study of natural language communication between man and machine. *Communications of the ACM 9*, 36–45.

Whitten, A., J.D. Tygar (2003). *Safe staging for computer security, HCI and Security Systems Workshop, CHI*, Ft. Lauderdale, Florida.

Yee, K. (2002). User interaction design for secure systems, in: R.H. Deng, S. Qing, F. Bao, J. Zhou (eds.), *Proceedings of the 4th international Conference on Information and Communications Security (December 09–12, 2002)*. Lecture Notes in Computer Science, Vol. 2513. Springer, London, pp. 278–290.

Suggested reading and online resources

http://usablesecurity.com

New Security Paradigms Workshop. Available at http://www.nspw.org
   a. Archive of Paper: http://portal.acm.org/toc.cfm?id = SERIES101&type = series&coll = portal&dl = ACM&CFID = 39021985&CFTOKEN = 82529791

Security and Usability, by Lorrie Faith Cranor; Simson Garfinkel, Print ISBN-13: 978-0-596-00827-7

The Risks Digest. Available at http://catless.ncl.ac.uk/Risks

User-centered security, Zurko, M.E., R.T Simon (1996). Available at http://doi.acm.org/10.1145/304851.304859

Chapter 9

An Exploration of the Design Features of Phishing Attacks

Jingguo Wang

Information Systems and Operations Management, College of Business,
The University of Texas at Arlington, Arlington, TX 76019, USA

Rui Chen

Department of Information Systems and Operations Management, Miller College of Business,
Ball State University, Muncie, IN 47306, USA

Tejaswini Herath

Finance, Operations and Information Systems, Faculty of Business, Brock University,
St. Catharines, Ontario L2S 3A1, Canada

H. Raghav Rao

Management Science and Systems, School of Management, State University of New York at
Buffalo, Buffalo, NY 14260-4000, USA

Abstract

Phishing is a growing phenomenon, which has not only caused billions in losses, but also has eroded consumer confidence in online transactions. To develop effective countermeasures, we need to understand how phishing e-mails exploit human vulnerabilities. We develop a framework to explore phishing from the perspective of victims. The framework helps understand different features that are utilized by phishers in designing e-mails and websites. We further explore the design patterns of phishing attacks. We collect 195 phishing records from the antiphishing work group website. Using content analysis and two-step cluster analysis, we examine those attacks for the presence of design features identified through our framework. We find that phishing attacks in different time periods present different character-istics, and the quality of phishing attacks have advanced consistently over time. Finally, on the basis of the location of the phishing hosts, we group the phishing attacks into four groups: USA, Asia, Europe, and South America. We find interesting patterns among the phishing attacks worldwide and pinpoint the major similarities and differences.

---

1 Introduction

Phishing is a new form of deception appearing over the Internet in recent years. In a typical phishing scheme, a phisher sends a forged e-mail to a recipient, falsely mimicking a legitimate establishment in an attempt to scam the recipient into divulging personal information such as personal name, bank account and passwords, credit card numbers, social security numbers, and other sensitive information. In most of the cases, the e-mail will request the user to visit a web site to fill in the information. Different from many other types of deception widely carried out through use of rich media such as face-to-face conversations or telephone communication, phishing e-mail lacks the availability of dynamics of face-to-face interaction. Phishers only rely on e-mail/website to deceive the targeted consumers. Garfinkel and Cranor (2005) provided an excellent description of phishing examples.

Phishing has caused billions of dollars in losses. Although estimates of losses due to phishing vary, Gartner estimated that phishing attacked 57 million Americans in 2003 and based on responses from 5000 online adults reported that phishing e-mails successfully deceived more than half of the recipients (Litan, 2004). Phishing also erodes the consumer's trust in online communication and transactions. The erosion drives the consumer from an online business (such as an online bank) to more expensive and labor-intensive channels, such as telephone call centers or "bricks and mortar" branch offices. Fighting phishing is an urgent task for the health of e-commerce (Garrity et al., 2004).

Phishing is a form of cognitive hacking. It manipulates a user's perception and relies on the user's changed actions to carry out attacks (Cybenko et al., 2002). In this study, we look at various features presented in phishing attacks to understand how phishing exploits human vulnerabilities through so called "interface illusions," in which a criminal attacks people via user interfaces (Levy, 2004). Guided by the elaboration likelihood model (ELM) (Petty and Cacioppo, 1986) and research in e-commerce, we first develop a framework and identify a set of features which are used by phishers to exploit consumers' vulnerabilities. We then explore the design patterns of the phishing e-mails collected from the antiphishing work group (APWG) (http://www.antiphishing.org) using content analysis and cluster analysis. Finally, we group the phishing attacks based on their hosting location into four groups: USA, Asia, Europe, and South America. On the basis of the analysis, we identify the major similarities and differences.

The contribution of this study is threefold. First, we examine the users' information processing and decision-making process during phishing attacks through theory informed approaches (e.g., activity theory and ELM). Second, we identify a set of phishing design features employed for deception purpose, which provide the research community with an opportunity for further development of attack taxonomy and antiphishing instruments. Third, we design and carry out content analyses to study the evolution of phishing attacks. Using the phishing design framework, we provide a comprehensive and vivid illustration of the phishing phenomena along with greater details on development trends and patterns than the prior phishing research offers. Last, we find interesting patterns among the phishing attacks worldwide and we pinpoint the major similarities and differences among phishing website hosted in USA, Asia, Europe, and South America. Although recently, new vectors such as spyware/adware or other malware are also used in phishing attacks, we focus on phishing that uses e-mail/webmail as the attack vector.

This chapter is organized as follows. In Section 2, we introduce the relevant theoretical foundations and explore the phishing design features. We introduce our research methodology for the exploration of the design pattern of phishing attacks in Section 3 and discuss evolvement of phishing in Section 4. In Section 5, on the basis of the traced-back IP address of hosting website, we group the hosts into four: Asia, USA, Europe, and South America. We compare the differences in their design patterns using statistical analysis. Finally, we conclude the chapter with the discussion of avenues for future research in Section 6.

2   Design features in phishing attacks

In a classical phishing attack, a phisher first sets up a spoofed website and then sends an e-mail bait to a group of targeted consumers. Recipients read bait, and might click the spoofed link presented in the e-mail following the instructions of the bait. The link leads to the spoofed website mimicking a legitimate establishment that might be of the recipients' interest. Some recipients enter personal information and fall victim. Activity theory provides a general framework for us to understand the phishing process (Fig. 1). Activity theory describes human activity in terms of elements such as an *actor* who is using a *tool* to manipulate an *object* such as users via executing a *plan* (Nardi, 1996). The *actor* goes through a *process* to achieve

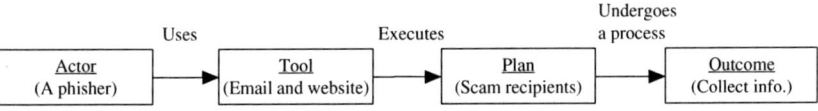

Fig. 1.   The activity theory framework.

a certain *outcome*. In our case, the actor is the phisher. The tool is e-mail and website (user-interface). The objective of a phisher is to manipulate and scam recipients into divulging personal information, such as personal identity, financial accounts, etc. The process is sending out the e-mails to a target population and luring the recipients release their personal information. The potential outcome of a phisher is to obtain the recipient's information and gain the financial benefits. E-mail recipients are active agents in the process of making choices on clicking the spoofed link and further entering their personal information. The phisher may do all that is possible to lure recipients to release their information. In this study, we make an effort to understand how recipients might be influenced by forged e-mails and websites via different design features based on previous studies in psychology and e-commerce.

2.1   An elaboration likelihood model (ELM) perspective

Dual-process theories expounded in prior psychology research have examined the role of influence in shaping human perception and behavior. The theories postulate two sets of processes underlying human reasoning: a process that is associative, automatic, unconscious, parallel, and fast based on heuristic cues, and a process that is rule-based, controlled, conscious, serial, and slow based on effortful processing of judgment-relevant information (Schneider and Shiffrin, 1977; Shiffrin and Schneider, 1977). Dual-process theories also specify conditions under which each of the two alternative processes are likely to be invoked. We take the perspective of the ELM (Petty and Cacioppo, 1986), one of the often used dual-process theories, to understand how phishing might explore human vulnerabilities. We consider that the underlying influence process in phishing (via cues in phishing e-mail/website) and the recipients information process can be directly related to ELM (Bhattacherjee and Sanford, 2006; Petty and Cacioppo, 1986).

The flow of phishing attack initiates at the moment a conned e-mail reaches the target population. As the recipient examines the persuasive arguments and the heuristic cues conveyed, he or she may be influenced or persuaded to give out valuable information and fall victim to the attack. ELM posits two basic routes for persuasion: the central route and the peripheral route. The routes differ in the amount of thoughtful information processing or "elaboration" needed. The central route involves message elaboration. In this route, a recipient carefully thinks about issue-related arguments contained in the phishing e-mail and inspects all available information. In the phishing context, such arguments may refer to the description of a dramatic event/scenario, response actions requested in the e-mail and its justification, potential benefits of following the instruction in the e-mail and the potential cost of not acting as requested. The peripheral route processes the message without any active thinking about the attributes of the issue, and requires less cognitive efforts. The recipients rely on a variety of cues to make quick decisions, such as the appearance of e-mail/web page, rather than the content in the message. In summary, the central and peripheral routes differ in at least two aspects: first, different types of information processed (message-related arguments via heuristic cues); second, the cognitive effort involved in information processing (higher in the central route than in the peripheral route). The central and peripheral routes of attitude change are typically operationalized in ELM using the argument quality and peripheral cue constructs, respectively. Note that ELM does not imply that people persuaded via the central or peripheral routes will experience different outcomes.

The recipients may vary widely in their motivation and ability to elaborate the e-mail, which in turn moderate how a given influence impacts the attitude formation (Petty and Cacioppo, 1986). ELM captures the ability and motivation to elaborate in terms of levels of elaboration likelihood. The recipients that experience high elaboration likelihood are more likely to be persuaded via the central route, and the recipients that experience low elaboration likelihood are more likely to be persuaded via the peripheral route. If recipients view an e-mail as being important and relevant, they are more likely to elaborate the content, and inspect the content. If the recipient thinks the message is not such important or relevant, he may just rely on cue-based heuristics for framing his/her perceptions. By examining the peripheral cues (e.g., e-mail and website appearance), the recipient forms his attitudes and may still be persuaded without carefully examining the quality of the argument. Although a phisher may not be able to anticipate the ability of an individual recipient, he may manipulate the relevance of a phishing message applying more contextual information (Jakobsson, 2005). Although recipients' motivation and ability are critical to their attitude formation, in this research we will only consider the features that are purposely presented in phishing attacks to scam the recipient into divulging private information. Message relevance and recipients' ability are beyond the scope of study.

ELM posits that the central route and peripheral route together account for all the changes in persuasive communication (Petty and Cacioppo, 1986). When it is applied in the phishing context, however, we find that the ELM may be insufficient to capture the dynamics of recipient's propensity unless it recognizes the media embedded in the phishing scenario. Consumers consider Internet involves more uncertainty and risk compared with the traditional communication channels. Consumers' risk perception serves as additional sources of influence; and they may even offset the favorable propensity changes from argument quality or information credibility. An individual who is persuaded by the phishing e-mails may not necessarily submit his or her sensitive information over the Internet, in case he or she perceives high levels of risk. Consequently, we argue that, in addition to the influences from central/peripheral route, perceived risk may have an impact on the recipient's propensity.

Table 1
Key design features of phishing attacks

Dimensions	Number of features	Features
E-mail argument quality	7	Event, impact, urgency, courtesy, justification, response action requested, penalty
E-mail title	3	Impact, urgency, company name
Message appearance	8	Authentic looking e-mail sender, e-mail signatory, personalization, media type, typo, third party icon for trustworthiness, copyright, company logo
Website appearance	5	Consistent links, consistent appearance theme, third party icon for trustworthiness, copyright, company logo
Assurance mechanisms	7	Third party icon for assurance, antifraud/privacy statement, SSL padlock, general security lock, help link/feedback mechanisms, authentication mechanisms, https link

2.2   The key features in phishing attacks

In this section, we employ ELM along with research in e-commerce to identify the key features that play roles in the phishing attacks. We further examine interdependencies among the involved entities as well as their interactive dynamics. By synthesizing and extending the related work into a coherent body, we identify key design features as summarized in Table 1. In this study, we will explore the design features of phishing attacks. We will examine the effects of those features empirically in our future study.

2.2.1   Message argument quality: central route of persuasion

ELM literature suggests that the message argument quality affects the attitude change of the message recipient. The argument quality refers to the persuasive strength of arguments embedded in an informational message (Bhattacherjee and Sanford, 2006). Arguments presented with these features are stronger in the persuasion effectiveness and are the primary drivers of message acceptance. Information quality also impacts the customer's willingness to pay (or fall for the scam) (Chung et al., 2006).

We use a grounded approach to generate the measurement from data since there are no existing measurements for argument quality in phishing e-mails. We employ a computer-aided text analysis tool called CATPAC™ to investigate the underlying components (patterns) of e-mail content. CATPAC is a self-organizing artificial neural network computer program, which is optimized for analyzing text. It is able to identify the most important words in a text and determine their patterns of similarity

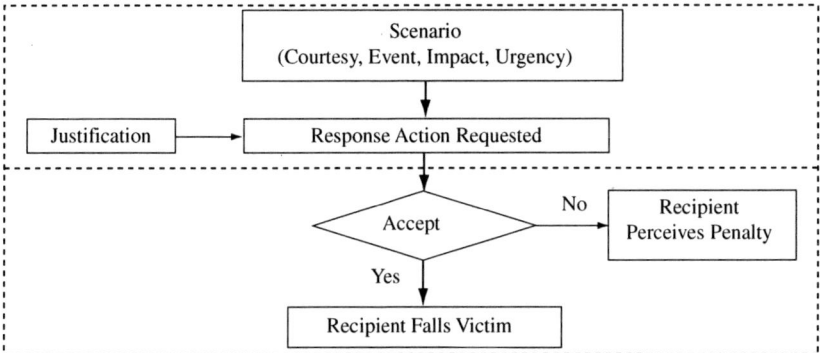

Fig. 2.   Argument quality measurement framework.

(TerraResearch, 1993; Woelfel, 1993). As CATPAC does not require precoding or linguistic assumptions, it has been widely used in the text analysis research (Gay and Hembrooke, 2002; Kim et al., 2005a). On the basis of the CATPAC analysis results, we identified seven argument components: event, impact, justification, response action requested, penalty, urgency, and courtesy. Figure 2 demonstrates the interactions among the components and the roles they play to convey a strong influence on persuasion. These seven components are consistent with the prior research findings discussed and they systematically contribute to the quality of the argument as a coherent group. Any argument with missing features, justification for example, may be perceived as flaw of logic and fail to convey strong persuasion consequently.

2.2.2   Message and website appearance: peripheral route of persuasion

Perceived credibility of the message plays a major role in the peripheral route to impact persuasion (Petty and Cacioppo, 1986). At its simplest, credibility can be defined as "believability" (Wathen and Burkell, 2002). The appearance and the background credentials of the e-mail/website have a persuasive impact regardless of how the message itself argues. In this section, we examine the e-mail heuristic cues that may contribute to the perceived credibility of information presented in phishing attacks.

Among others, the source (sender) credentials have long been recognized for their impact on perceived credibility (Schneider and Shiffrin, 1977; Shiffrin and Schneider, 1977). It is suggested that *reputation* and *legitimacy* are two pivotal credentials for effective communication. The words from a reputable authority may be perceived as of higher credibility than to those from an unknown identity. For communication media such as e-mails, the features such as *designation of the signatory, company logo, and copyright* may be manipulated to enhance the credentials of the messenger senders and to improve the perceived credibility of the e-mail consequently. The *third party icon for trustworthiness* (such as "FDIC Member", "Trust.*e*") also presents a high level of business integrity and reputation of the seal receivers. The icons, therefore, serve as effective artifacts to convey the credibility of the sender as well as that of the information (Hu et al., 2003).

Credibility of message also considers the message formation and layout, suggesting that the e-mail is well-written, well-produced, and well-organized. In contrast with well-presented e-mail, poorly presented e-mails such as one with *typos* (including grammar errors) may detract from the credibility of the source. Furthermore, IS literature finds that rich-media content improves data quality and perceived credibility (Kim et al., 2005b). The e-mails presented in rich html format with pictures and animations, therefore, may lead to a greater level of perceived credibility than those written in plain text.

Recent studies have identified personalization as an influential component in communication (Tam and Ho, 2005). When the personalization (tailoring) matches the preference of the recipient, he or she may perceive higher credibility of the information. In the context of e-mail communication, we therefore argue that the personalization (e.g., using the recipient's name) may enhance the information credibility perceived.

On the basis of the earlier discussion, eight features are proposed to measure the information credibility (or lack of it) presented in the phishing e-mails. They include *authentic looking sender e-mail address, e-mail signatory, personalization, e-mail media type, lack of typos, third party icon for trustworthiness, copyright*, and *company logo*.

After evaluating the phishing e-mail in terms of its content and peripheral cues, the recipient may follow the links given in the e-mail and visit the phishing website. Through the manipulation of website designs, the phishers may enhance the credibility and deceive the victims through such cues as *third party icon for trustworthiness, copyright*, and *company logo* consistent with the e-mail body (Kim et al., 2005a; Wathen and Burkell, 2002). As the website visitors have already viewed and read the e-mail, it is important for both media (i.e., e-mail and website) to remain consistent. A recipient would expect to witness the same visible URL and appearance themes between the e-mail and website. Appearance themes may include page layout, color scheme, and font types. A lack of consistency during information process may greatly reduce the perceived information credibility. We summarize these features for Website as *consistent links, consistent appearance themes, third party icon for trustworthiness, copyright*, and *company logo*.

2.2.3 E-mail title: motivation

ELM suggests that the effects of argument quality and information credibility are moderated by the recipient's motivation. The psychology literature defines motivation as "an internal state or condition, sometimes described as a need, desire, or want, that serves to activate or energize behavior and give it direction" (Kleinginna and Kleinginna, 1981). For a communication channel such as e-mail, subject line (e-mail title) is identified as a motivating factor for e-mail comprehension (Mackenzie, 2000). With regard to the motivation effect, however, a detailed measurement for e-mail title is missing in prior literature. Following a grounded approach, for e-mail argument quality, we identified three measurements for the title based on the CATPAC analysis that include (1) *urgency* which portrays the emergency of the situations, (2) *impact* which depicts the threats and potential losses of one's personal interest, and (3) *company name* which may be stated in the e-mail titles to draw reader attention.

By describing an emergency situation, the *urgency* attracts user attentions. By conveying the sense of threat and loss, the *impact* may successfully raise the cognitive needs for motivation and also introduce a high level of relevance. Meanwhile, the *company name* of reputable business entities may arouse favorable affective needs for motivation and encourage the recipient to process the e-mail with more effort. The proposed measurements, therefore, are consistent with and supported by the motivation research findings.

2.2.4 Assurance mechanisms: decision making under risk

IS research suggests that online users are skeptical about Internet as a secure channel and they worry about the potential risks from attacks, losing private information, and losing monetary information (Lee and Rao, 2007). This perceived risk may discourage individuals to submit sensitive information (such as credit card number and SSN) over the Internet. In the context of phishing attacks, such perceived risks are even more salient since the recipients are requested to give out their information and to submit online. Counter-risk approaches, therefore, may be exploited by the phishers to reduce the perceived risks by the potential victims. In line with the e-commerce findings, we expect that the perceived risk may have a negative impact on the recipient's propensity to release requested information.

Studies have proposed information assurance mechanisms, which may address the risk concerns. Extending these into the phishing phenomenon, we summarize seven *assurance mechanisms*, which may reduce the perceived risks involved in the attacks. The mechanisms include: *third party icon for assurance (security and privacy)*, *antifraud/privacy statement*, *SSL padlock*, *general security lock*, *help link/feedback mechanism*, *authentication mechanism*, and *Https links*. These components represent the typical information assurance mechanisms that have been widely exercised in e-commerce nowadays. The presence of these features, therefore, may help the recipients lower the perceived risks involved in giving out sensitive information during phishing attacks.

Typical information that is requested in the attacks may be described as (1) personal information such as *date of birth*, (2) nonfinancial information which refers to online service accounts rather than real banking accounts, (3) financial information which refers to credit card, debit card, and banking accounts, (4) social security numbers, and (5) other information which could not be otherwise categorized. Besides those, we are also interested in studying the targeted industry. As industries of different types may vary in their information assurance practices and in the types of information involved with customers, we wish to examine whether such differences hold in phishing attacks. We identify four industry types in this study: (1) financial service (banking and credit card), (2) retail and auction, (3) ISP, and (4) miscellaneous.

3 Methodology

In this section, we discuss our methods for data collection. We employ content analysis. The data collected will be used in the statistical analysis presented in Sections 4 and 5.

3.1 Sample

We collected the samples of phishing records from the phishing archive maintained by the APWG. APWG is the leading organization in fighting e-mail frauds and phishing. It provides comprehensive information on phishing statistics, attack documentations, and business solutions. When we carried out the study, 210 phishing e-mail records spanning from September 2003 to July 2005 were kept in its archives. Each record contains the related phishing e-mail, phishing website, and a brief summary. The phishing archive provides a representative sample set within which the general phishing themes and patterns are reserved. The bias of the sample set, though inevitable, is recognized as a limitation of this study.

3.2 Content analysis

To extract the desired information from multiple data formats such as text and images, we employed both human- and computer-based coding in content analysis. A codebook and corresponding code sheet were developed for human-based coding. The computer software VBPro (http://www.textanalysis.info/VBPRO.pdf) was used with custom dictionaries for computer-based coding. The first two dimensions presented in Table 1 (e-mail argument quality and e-mail title) were computer coded, whereas the next three dimensions (message appearance, website appearance, assurance mechanisms) and information requested were human coded.

Two graduate students who were unaware of the research questions were hired to perform human-based coding. This practice allows blind coding and thus reduces the biasing effect of coder knowledge of variables extraneous to the content analysis (Neuendorf, 2002). We captured the coding protocol into a codebook and corresponding code spreadsheet. The codebook defined the features and gave coding instructions. The coding options for each item were designed to be mutually exclusive for validity and reliability concerns.

We developed the coding protocol through multiround revisions in accordance with the coder training process. The coders were first instructed to fully understand the coding protocols. Next step involved a consensus building among the coders. The feedback from the coders was obtained to update the codebook and the code sheet accordingly. Next, a pilot coding was carried out and the Cohen's κ (Krippendorff, 1980) indicating the intercoder reliability was above 0.76 for each individual coding item. The coding codebook was revised for the inconsistencies. The Cohen's κ in final coding was above 0.81 for each coding item. As Kappa is an overly conservative test for reliability, the results of over 0.81 is considered as an excellent agreement, given the fact that many of the items, with only two options, have chance agreements at 0.5 (Benerjee et al., 1999).

For computer-based coding, we employed VBPro, a powerful content analysis program, to process the dataset with word as the unit of analysis. A set of custom dictionaries were developed to precisely measure the features of interest. Owing to the lack of research in phishing, we were not able to find related dictionaries and had to build them. We constructed dictionaries based on the findings from CATPAC analysis. These dictionaries were then screened by a panel of seven experts from academia, FBI, and industry. The dictionaries were modified and finalized with keywords that are closely related to the features under investigation. A sample of custom dictionary keywords is illustrated in Table 2. The computer-coding analysis is based on a single keyword and raises possibility of false errors since the analysis ignores the contexts where the keywords are

Table 2
Example of custom dictionaries

Dimensions	Features	Example keywords
E-mail title	Urgency	Important, warning, prompt, immediately, instant
	Impact	Account, card, record, data, service
	Company name	*The list of names of all companies in the sample*
E-mail argument quality	Event	Fraud, unauthorized, compromised, hijacked, misappropriate
	Impact	Account, card, record, data, service
	Justification	Security, safety, law, protect, reward
	Response action	Update, verify, click, confirm, fill
	Penalty	Limited, block, terminate, suspend, restricted
	Urgency	Important, warning, prompt, immediately, instant
	Courtesy	Thank, apologize, dear, please, sincerely

presented. It is a limitation that is common to computer-based content analysis studies.

Fifteen phishing records were eliminated from the study as they are not properly achieved and had more than 5 features (out of 35) that cannot be exactly coded. The missing data in the rest of the records were replaced with the most frequently occurring values in the corresponding features. We, therefore, had 195 valid phishing records for final analysis. 127 of these were targeted at the financial services sector, 43 targeted the retail and auction industry, whereas 23 targeted ISPs.

4   Evolution analysis of phishing attacks

In this section, we analyze the evolution of phishing attacks in terms of its design patterns and changes. This study is enabled by two-step cluster analysis (Bapna et al., 2006; Okazaki, 2006), which discovers three clusters in the entire sample size with each cluster representing phishing attacks in a different era.

4.1   Cluster analysis

The two-step cluster analysis starts with a precluster phrase where sequential clustering approaches are employed to build a modified cluster feature (CF) tree (Zhang et al., 1996). The goal of preclustering is to reduce the size of the matrix that contains distances between all possible pairs of sample cases. During the construction of CF tree, each case may be emerged to the existing preclusters or may create a new precluster, using a likelihood distance measure as the similarity criterion. Upon the completion of the precluster phrase, standard hierarchical clustering algorithm such as agglomerative (Johnson, 1967) is performed on the preclusters to group them into desired number of clusters. In our study, we use SPSS v13 and employ the clustering criteria of Schwarz's Bayesian inference criterion (BIC) (Schwarz, 1978), a well-known and default criteria, to calculate the cluster number automatically by finding the largest increase in distance between the two closest clusters in each hierarchical clustering stage. In addition, we standardized the continuous variables and treated the outliers with noise handling in the clustering process.

As in Table 3, three clusters are identified through two-step cluster analysis. Interestingly, the compositions of each cluster, in terms of the occurrence year and industry, are quite different from one another. In the whole sample, 10% occurred in 2003, 68% in 2004, and 22% in 2005. If the clusters are uniformly drawn from the whole sample, a distribution of the occurrence year in each cluster would be expected to be similar. However, the results demonstrated that the three clusters are represented in

Table 3
Composition of three clusters

Cluster	Number of e-mails	Year composition			Industry composition			
		2003 (%)	2004 (%)	2005 (%)	Financial service (%)	Retail and auction (%)	ISP (%)	Other (%)
The whole sample	195	10	68	22	65	22	12	1
1 (maps to early-stage)	40 (20%)	35	55	10	75	10	10	5
2 (maps to mid-stage)	81 (42%)	4	77	19	30	47	23	0
3 (maps to late-stage)	74 (38%)	4	65	31	99	1	0	0

Note: Grayed cells represent individual cluster compositions that are greater than those in the whole sample composition. For example, composition of 2005 is 31% in Cluster 3, which is greater than that (22%) in the whole sample.

different years. In cluster 1, 35% occurred in 2003, together with 55% in year 2004, accounting for 90% of the cluster. In cluster 2, there is a dominant percent for year 2004 (77%), which is far above 68% in the whole sample. In cluster 3, 31% occurred in 2005, which is greater than 22% as in the whole sample. And years 2004 and 2005, accounts for 96% of that cluster.

Because of the way the clusters congregate in terms of year composition and time spanning of the clusters, we use the following names for the three clusters hereafter: "early-stage" for cluster 1 which primarily consists of phishing attacks occurred in 2003 and 2004, "mid-stage" for cluster 2 which primarily consists of attacks in 2004, and "late-stage" for cluster 3 which primarily consists of attacks in the 2004 and 2005. The sample clusters, therefore, in general reveal the evolution of the phishing attack.

We observed that the distributions of the target industry across the three clusters are quite different. The early-stage (cluster 1) has a strong interest in the financial service industry, the middle-stage (cluster 2) shifts the interest toward retail and auction and ISP, and the late-stage (cluster 3) returns to the financial service as their major target. This trend suggests the financial service as the most threatened industry. The shift of target industry between financial service and retail and auction and ISP may also indicate that phishers are altering their targets to avoid an increased public awareness and to raise their perceived benefits, resulted by the excessive attacks in the selected industries. We discuss other results in detail in the following subsections. An overview of the findings is presented in Table 4.

Using the design framework developed earlier, we investigated the design patterns and changes in the three clusters. An illustration of the findings is

Table 4
Summary of discussion

Cluster	Major occurrence year	Attack quality				Target industry	Information focus
		E-mail/ website feature presence	Assurance mecha-nism	E-mail content	E-mail title		
Early-stage	2003, 2004	Low	Low	Low	Low	Financial service	Nonfinancial account
Mid-stage	2004	Medium	Medium	Medium	Medium	Retail and auction, ISP	Everything
Late-stage	2004, 2005	High	High	High	High	Financial service	Nonfinancial account, financial

presented in Fig. 3. We discuss the detailed findings in the rest of this section.

4.2 Information requested

Spoofing people to give out information is the ultimate goal of the phishing attacks. The information requested in the attacks may vary over time. In this section, we explore the three clusters to examine the trend of the requested information and to learn the patterns embedded.

Figure 3(a) compares the three clusters through the five types of information requested. For example, in *personal information*, among the whole sample of 195 phishing records, 41% of the attacks requested this specific type of information. When the individual clusters are concerned, however, 8% attacks in the early-stage, 68% attacks in the middle-stage, and 30% attacks in the late-stage requested this information, respectively.

As we can see from Fig. 3(a), overall the early-stage cluster requests much less information except for the nonfinancial account. The middle-stage cluster has high proportions for each type of requested information. The late-stage cluster is much more focused and it concentrates on the *nonfinancial account information* and *financial information*. This is also in line with the target industries for late-stage cluster attacks.

4.3 E-mail and website appearance

The e-mail message appearance features are examined across the three clusters and the results are illustrated in Fig. 3(b). Among the eight features, seven are categorical values, whereas the eighth typo is continuous.

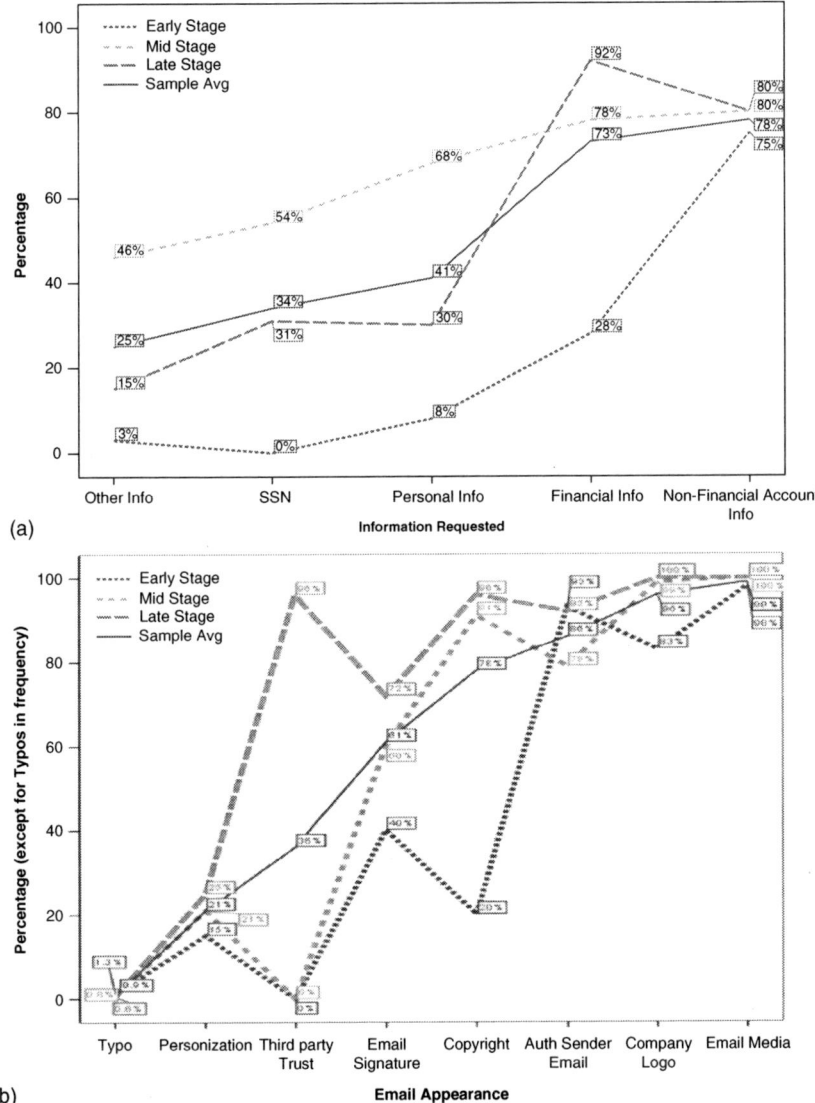

Fig. 3. Features comparison in difference dimensions

Consider the feature, *authentic looking sender e-mail* as an example. 86% of the attacks presented this feature in their phishing e-mails in the whole sample, 93% in early-stage cluster, 79% in mid-stage cluster, and 92% in late stage. The number of typo is a reverse measurement of the message appearance. In the whole sample, the average number of typos reaches 0.88, which means that there is almost one typo in every phishing e-mail. It is worthy to mention that typos may exist, which are rendered invisible,

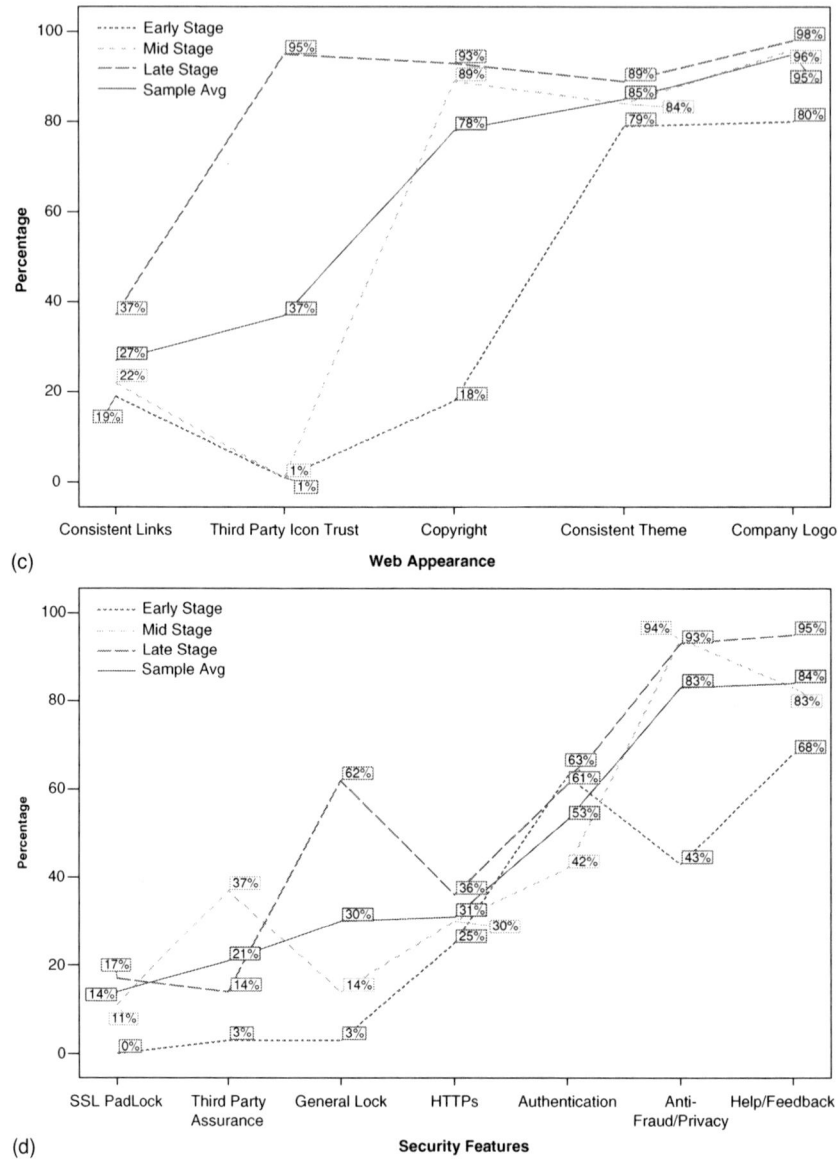

Fig. 3.   (Continued)

through appropriate HTML design techniques, to the e-mail recipients. They are injected into the e-mails so as to elude spam or phishing filters. They are discarded in this research due to the zero-impact on information processing of the recipients. Nevertheless, further research on typos may be

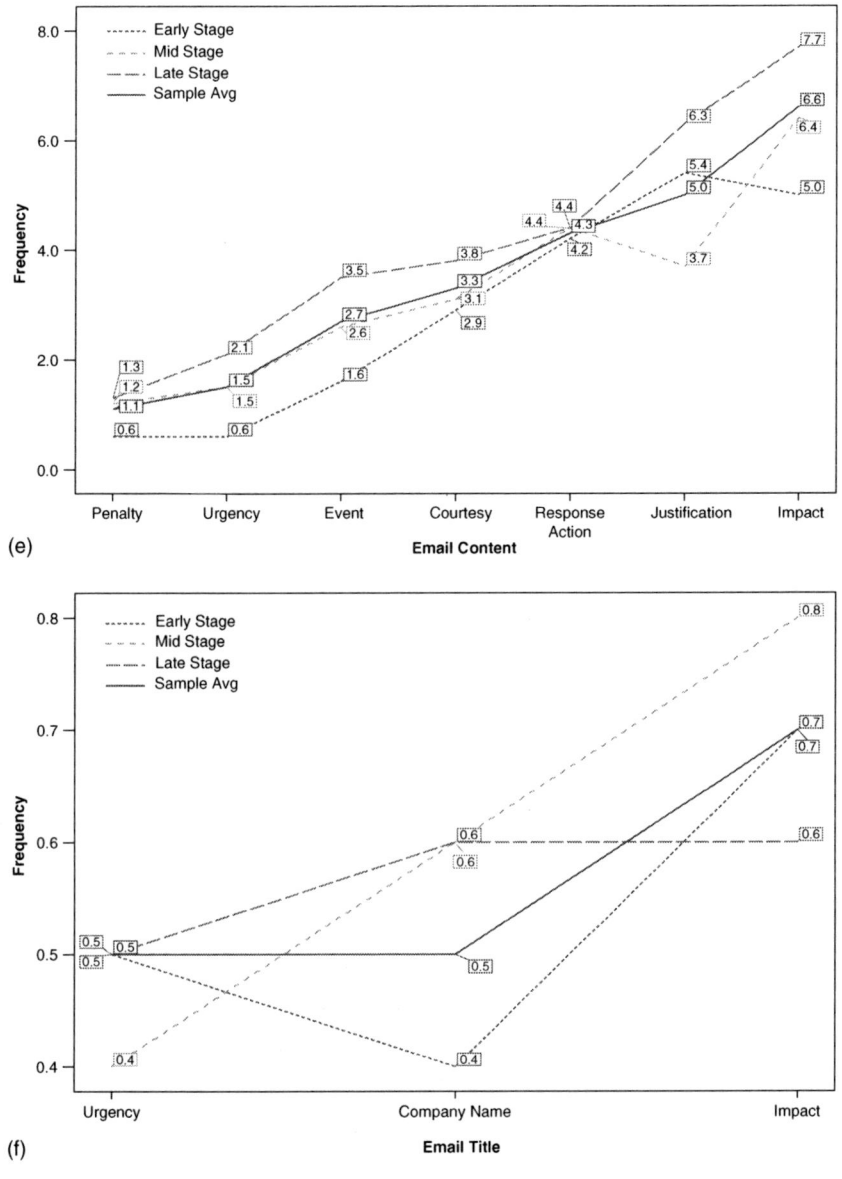

Fig. 3. (Continued)

important for the development of effective phishing filters. Fig. 3(b) shows that the early-stage cluster has the lowest percent of desirable features presented in e-mail appearance, and highest of the number of typos. The mid-stage cluster presents a great improvement over the early-stage cluster.

However, the late stage is even better crafted. It outranks the mid-stage in seven out of eight features. The late-stage also has better features than the whole sample. The sharp difference in the use of message features suggests that the attacks realized the importance of e-mail and website appearance, and improved those features consistently. The presence of website features demonstrates the similar patterns (Fig. 3(c)).

4.4   Assurance mechanism features

The three phishing clusters differ greatly in the features of assurance mechanisms (Fig. 3(d)). Generally speaking, the early-stage cluster has the lowest percentage of e-mails/website featured with the assurance mechanisms. It, however, has a highest level presence of the authentication mechanisms than that of the whole sample. This may be because that the cluster requests the relative high level of nonfinancial account information. Each authentication procedure presents an opportunity for the phishers to harvest the user accounts. The mid-stage cluster demonstrates an improvement over the early-stage cluster in other features than authentication. It has two of eight features above the presence percentage of the sample, whereas the late-stage cluster has six features. It demonstrates that phishers consistently have an intension to take advantage of assurance mechanisms over the time.

4.5   E-mail content

Unlike the previous analysis, the e-mail content analysis reveals the frequency of the words used in the e-mail composition. With the information on the average word usage among the entire sample, we found that the phishing e-mails highly value the importance of *impact*, for which about 6.60 words are used to describe the impact. The phishing attacks also values the roles of *courtesy*, *justification*, and *response action*. Surprisingly, we found that the penalty is not well utilized in the phishing e-mails. This may suggest that the phishers are expecting that the individuals are willing to cooperate with requests from the "legitimate looking" companies.

The analysis results are illustrated in Fig. 3(e). The three clusters have similar patterns. The early-stage cluster used the least amount of the words except for the *justification*. The mid-stage cluster presents a higher level of manipulation on the keywords. It has three out of seven features that have a frequency above that of the sample average, whereas the late-stage cluster is most effective and have all seven features with a frequency above that of the sample average.

4.6   E-mail title

Owing to the fact that the e-mail title is short in length with only two to five words in most cases, the analysis of the e-mail title does not reveal too much new findings on the cluster patterns. We found similar patterns across the three clusters (Fig. 3(f)). The early-stage cluster has a lowest level of all title features and the levels are all below the sample average. Both the mid- and late-stage have two features above the sample average. However, the late-stage is better than the mid-stage in two out of three features. Within the whole sample, the usage frequencies of the three features are all below one, which may suggest further improvement to the custom dictionary and new features to be identified.

5   Host-based analysis of global attack difference

Recent literature suggests that cyber crimes committed from different regions across the world would differ due to differences in regulative, normative, and cognitive legitimacy as well as hacking skills relative to the availability of economic opportunities (Kshetri, 2006). Other differences such as language skills, technology skills, and cultural influences may also play a role in a way how a criminal activity is carried out. In general, drawing from insights of cultural studies, "cultural criminology" stream of research has considered various influences of culture on image, representation, and style of crime (Ferrell, 1999).

We examine whether the attacks worldwide are homogeneous in attack design. To do this, we categorized the attack records into geographic groups based on their corresponding hosts (i.e., web server) of phishing websites. We are aware of the fact that several phishers mount their attacks from hijacked legitimate websites, but we have not considered that aspect in our analysis. Although this is a limitation, we also believe that the exercise conducted in this chapter has useful implications with regard to the forensic process. We believe the findings in this chapter will help forensic analysts to comprehend regional development patterns in phishing attacks and to recognize their similarities and differences.

Prior research suggests that USA and Asia are among the top regions where phishing attacks are initiated (Wolfer, 2005). Studies have also found that Europe and South America are becoming more and more active in the online phishing and other cyber crimes recently (Weiss, 2006). Accordingly, we consider the attack origins as USA, Asia, Europe, and South America, attempting to explore their attack design similarities and differences. The categorization process was facilitated through the analyses (www.ip2location.com) of IP addresses of the phishing website that were used in the attacks. Despite the typical criticisms that website hosts may include offshore providers and zombie networks, the above categorization process is followed by antiphishing research leaders, such as APWG, as the best known approach so far. After leaving out 32 records with unknown sources (such as missing data or hijacks), we categorized USA (67 cases), Asia (60 cases), Europe (20 cases), and South America (16 cases).

Among the design features, 24 out of 35 are recorded in our data set using nominal value. These design features are message appearance (other than "typo"), website appearance, assurance information, and information requested. The rest of the design features, mainly e-mail argument and e-mail title, are recorded using ratio values. For design features of nominal values, we conducted χ^2 tests using SPSS v13. χ^2 test is able to detect whether the attack regions and attack designs are dependent on each other, that is, whether the attack design patterns are homogenous across the four attacks regions. Once we found that the attack regions significantly differ on a particular design feature, we conducted additional Z tests. It is noticed that each design feature may be implemented using a variety of options. For example, phishers may choose from different options, for example, "no visible https link," "visible https link with false looking address," and "visible https link with true looking address" in designing *Https Link* feature (Chandrasekaran et al., 2006; Drake et al., 2004; Fette et al., 2007). The Z test allows us to examine the four attack regions on each one of the design options for a given design feature under question. As in Fig. 4, the Z test compares two groups (the attack regions in this study) with their proportions of utilizing one specific design option. To facilitate our discussion, we compare Asia, Europe, and South America with USA as it has been well known as the world leader in high technology development and its related crimes. By comparing with USA (one tail Z test), we are interested to explore whether the phishers worldwide have grown as mature as those in USA.

Meanwhile, we employed analysis of variance (ANOVA) and multi-variate analysis of variance (MANOVA) to examine the phishing designs whose data is recorded by ratio values. ANOVA is used to analyze the design feature of e-mail typo, whereas MANOVA is exercised on e-mail argument quality and e-mail title dimensions. MANOVA provides several advantages over ANOVA test such as it protects against type I error of multiple ANOVA. For phishing designs on which the four attack regions significantly differ, we conducted additional *post hoc* analysis (Scheffe and

$$z_1 = \frac{\hat{p}_1 - \hat{p}_2}{\sqrt{\dfrac{\hat{p}_1(1 - \hat{p}_1)}{n_1} + \dfrac{\hat{p}_2(1 - \hat{p}_2)}{n_2}}}$$

where $\hat{p}_1,\ \hat{p}_2$ are the proportions of group 1 and 2 respectively while n_1 and n_2 are the two corresponding group size.

Fig. 4. Z test for homogeneity of group proportions.

Tukey), which compares all pairs of the attack regions to explore their similarities and differences for given design features.

5.1   E-mail message appearance

The e-mail message appearance dimension consists of design feature such as authentic looking e-mail sender, e-mail signatory, personalization, media type, typo, third party icon for trustworthiness, copyright, and company logo. For these design features (except typo), the χ^2 test found that the four attack regions marginally differ in their use of copyright feature (Table 5).

To find any patterns that were embedded, we conducted a follow-up Z tests. As illustrated in Table 6, 89.55% of all Phishing attacks originated in USA are designed with copyright information appearing in the phishing e-mails, whereas only 10.45% of them do not. The Z test indicated that, compared with USA, Asia, Europe, and South America attacks represent significantly lower proportions of e-mails designed with copyright information. That is, 78.33% of Asian phishing e-mails, 70% of European e-mails, and 68.75% of South American e-mails are designed with copyright information shown up. As copyright information is likely to enhance the recipient's perception of e-mail authenticity, the results suggest that phishers in USA are more sophisticated in crafting e-mails.

The higher use of copyright in e-mails from USA can be explained by the fact that intellectual property laws are stricter in USA than in the other

Table 5
χ^2 test for e-mail copyright

	Value	df	p-value (two-sided)
Pearson χ^2	6.589	3	.086*
Likelihood ratio	6.703	3	.082
Linear-by-linear association	6.059	1	.014
Number of valid cases	163		

*Significant at 0.1 level.

Table 6
Homogeneity of group proportion test for copyright

Design option/region	USA (%)	Asia (%)	Europe (%)	South America (%)
Without copyright information	10.45	21.67**	30**	31.25**
With copyright information	89.55	78.33**	70**	68.75**

**Significant at 0.05 level.

regions of the world. Intellectual property literature suggests that USA is a world leading nation in protecting intellectual property rights and USA has established a rich volume of related regulations including Copyright Act and US Digital Millennium Copyright Act (Analytics, 2005). USA also dominates the world economy with respect to trade in copyright-based goods and it plays a dominant role in developing worldwide intellectual property regulations such as WTO Trade-Related Aspects of Intellectual Property Rights (TRIPs) agreement (Canada, 2003). The use of copyright has therefore become an accepted social norm in the society of USA; phishers are therefore more likely to add copyright signs when they are crafting phishing designs.

For e-mail typo (ratio value), the ANOVA test reveals that the four attack regions differ significantly on the number of typos appeared in the phishing e-mails (Table 7). *Post hoc* analysis found that there is no significant difference between USA and the other three attack regions. The differences mainly stems from the fact that Asia (0.47 typo per e-mail) has a significantly lower number of typos than Europe (1.95 typo per e-mail). Studies have shown that Asia has a much larger population practicing English than European countries (Wikipedia, 2007). As most of the European countries (e.g., Russia and Romania) in our data sample do not have English as their first language, the observed discrepancy in typo numbers is consistent with the known differences in English levels.

5.2   Website appearance

The website appearance dimension includes design features of *consistent links*, *consistent appearance theme*, *third party icon for trustworthiness*, *copyright*, and *company logo*. The χ^2 analysis found that the four regions follow similar design patterns.

5.3   Assurance mechanisms

Assurance mechanisms consist of following design features: third party icon for assurance, antifraud/privacy statement, SSL padlock, general

Table 7
ANOVA test for e-mail typo

	Sum of squares	df	Mean square	F	Significance
Between groups	35.141	3	11.714	2.631	.052**
Within groups	708.000	159	4.453		
Total	743.141	162			

**Approximately significant at 0.05 level.

security lock, help link/feedback mechanisms, authentication mechanisms, and https link. The χ^2 analysis found that the four attack regions follow similar design patterns.

5.4   Information requested

The information requested dimension consists of *personal information, nonfinancial account information, financial information, social security number (SSN)*, and *other information* such as mother's maiden name. The χ^2 test found that the four attack regions marginally differ in their requests of SSN (Table 8).

The follow-up Z test reveals the following analysis results. As in Table 9, 28.36% of phishing e-mails from USA requested SSN information. Compared with USA, Asia and Europe have marginally higher proportions of e-mails requesting SSN. On the contrary, South America phishers have a marginally lower proportion in this regard. These findings suggest that both Asian and European phishers may be more aggressive than those in USA, in part because they reside in countries where phishing-related regulations are less mature. The findings also suggest that South American attackers are likely to be less aggressive in their pursuit of extremely sensitive information such as SSN; they are more focused on other types of information (e.g., credit card number) that can be quickly and easily cashed in.

Table 8
χ^2 test for SSN

	Value	df	*p*-value (two-sided)
Pearson χ^2	6.917	3	.075*
Likelihood ratio	7.425	3	.060
Linear-by-linear association	.026	1	.871
Number of valid cases	163		

*Significant at 0.1 level.

Table 9
Homogeneity of group proportion test for SSN

Design option/region	USA (%)	Asia (%)	Europe (%)	South America (%)
SSN not requested	71.64	58.33*	55*	87.50*
SSN requested	28.36	41.67*	45*	12.50*

*Significant at 0.1 level.

5.5 E-mail argument

E-mail argument quality consists of design features such as *event, impact, urgency, courtesy, justification, response action requested,* and *penalty.* The MANOVA test found that the four attack regions share similar design patterns except their use of penalty in the phishing e-mails (Table 10).

The follow-up *post hoc* test revealed that there is no significant difference between USA and the rest (Asia, Europe, and South America) in terms of their e-mail *penalty* design. Rather, Asia (1.52 penalty keywords per e-mail) significantly differ from South America (0.5 penalty keywords per e-mail) when e-mail penalty is concerned. The fact that Asian culture has a high use and tolerance of punishment may account for the preceding difference (Kwok and Tam, 2005). This belief is consequently reflected in the phishing attacks.

5.6 E-mail title

The e-mail title dimension consists of design features such as company name, urgency, and impact. The MANOVA test found that the four attack regions significantly differ in their design of impact feature (Table 11).

The follow-up *post hoc* tests revealed that there is significant difference between USA (0.82 impact keywords per e-mail title) and South America (0.38 impact keywords per e-mail title) in their utilization level of impact keywords in e-mail title design. This difference is consistent with the fact that openness is a typical personality in USA. The phishers may therefore tend to explicit the impact information more frequently than the others.

Table 10
MANOVA test for e-mail argument quality

Source	Dependent variable	Type III sum of squares	df	Mean square	F	Significance
Country	Courtesy	16.259	3	5.420	1.462	.227
	Event	47.987	3	15.996	1.925	.128
	Impact	46.930	3	15.643	.791	.501
	Urgency	5.346	3	1.782	.700	.553
	Justification	100.212	3	33.404	1.536	.207
	Response act	39.721	3	13.240	1.807	.148
	Penalty	16.009	3	5.336	2.393	.070*

*Significant at 0.1 level.

Table 11
MANOVA test for e-mail title

Source	Dependent variable	Type III sum of squares	df	Mean square	F	Significance
Country	Company name	.349	3	.116	.358	.783
	Urgency	.652	3	.217	.542	.654
	Impact	3.286	3	1.095	2.856	.039**

**Significant at 0.05 level.

6 Conclusion

In this chapter, we understand phishing based on ELM and studies in e-commerce. Key features in phishing attacks are identified. We found that the quality of the crafted e-mails and websites (user-interfaces) are improving over the time. The current research is explorative in nature and lays the foundation for the future research effort to leverage the findings in this chapter. Several future research streams are suggested as follows.

We found that there was at least one typo in every phishing e-mail in our sample and there were significant differences in number of typos per e-mail among the four regions evaluated in this study. Our intuition tells us that perhaps the typos may be due to the language differences existing in countries from which the phishing attacks are carried out. Also, the corporate e-mails will most probably be cautious about typo and grammatical errors in their communication. It would be interesting to analyze if there are differences in normal e-mails and phishing e-mails in future.

The evolutionary nature of phishing attacks has also resulted in enrichment of the phishing attack design framework. For example, new phishing e-mails have incorporated emerging attack designs such as "Re:" in the title of some SPAM e-mail, which increases message relevance and helps elude e-mail filters.

An investigation into the human factors with their impacts on the individual's tendency toward acceptance of the phishing persuasion calls for an experiment-based study. A theoretical development of how various factors of the phishing e-mail and websites influence persuasion process can be developed based on the framework introduced in this chapter. Factors such as motivation, ability/skills (it is likely that e-mail recipients have become wiser over time), and risk perceptions are likely to affect elaboration and persuasion. ELM posits the moderating role on the effects of central and peripheral routes of persuasion on the attitude formation. In a similar vein, recipient awareness regarding phishing e-mail as well as recipient's risk perception can be evaluated. These related inquiries can be investigated in laboratory experiments. In addition to the role of motivation considered by ELM, role of awareness and risk perception can be evaluated in the extended framework.

It is also worthy of mention that, although conventional wisdoms such as "cultural criminology" may still be existent, the results of this chapter show that differences, even if they exist are no longer significant across the globe and hence will prove less helpful for forensic analysis. The attacks worldwide are evolving toward a high level of homogeneity in most parts. Although the findings may be biased to certain extent, it certainly highlights the pending challenges to the forensic research in the new era of Internet.

7   Suggested questions

1. Discuss the new trends in phishing attacks with the help of information available on current Internet statistics, cyber threats, and internet crimes.
2. Discuss various approaches recommended to fight phishing attacks such as phishing-fighting software tools available in market as well as techniques promoted by awareness campaigns.

Acknowledgment

The research of H. Raghav Rao was supported in part by NSF under grant 0548917 and 0705292. The usual disclaimer applies.

References

Analytics, C. (2005). Intellectual property. Caslon Analytics.

Bapna, R., P. Goes, A. Gupta, Y. Jing (2006). User heterogeneity and its impact on electronic auction market design: an empirical exploration. *MIS Quarterly* 28, 21–43.

Benerjee, M., M. Capozzoli, L. McSweeney, D. Sinha (1999). Beyond kappa: a review of interrater agreement measures. *Canadian Journal of Statistics* 27, 3–23.

Bhattacherjee, A., C. Sanford (2006). Influence processes for information technology acceptance: an elaboration likelihood model. *MIS Quarterly* 30(4), 805–825.

Canada, I. (2003). *Assessing the Economic Impacts of Copyright Reform on Performers and Producers of Sound Recordings in Canada*. Report Commissioned by Industry Canada. Available at http://www.ic.gc.ca/eic/site/ippd-dppi.nsf/vwapj/towes_final_e.pdf/$FILE/towes_final_e.pdf. Accessed on April 02, 2009.

Chandrasekaran, M., K. Narayanan, S. Upadhyaya (2006). Phishing email detection based on structural properties, in: *NY State Security Symposium*. Albany, New York.

Chung, M., J. Moon, B. Yoo, Y. Choe (2006). Paradox of information quality: do consumers pay more for premium product information on E-commerce sites? in: The Twelfth Americas Conference on Information Systems, Acapulco, Mexico.

Cybenko, G., A. Giani, P. Thompson (2002). Cognitive hacking: a battle for the mind. *IEEE Computer* 35, 50–56.

Drake, C.E., J.J. Oliver, E.J. Koontz (2004). Anatomy of a phishing email, in: *First Conference on Email and Anti-Spam (CEAS)*, Mountain View, CA.

Fette, I., N. Sadeh, A. Tomasic (2007). Learning to detect phishing emails, in: *The 16th International Conference on World Wide Web (WWW '07)*, Banff, Alberta, Canada.

Ferrell, J. (1999). Cultural criminology. *Annual Review of Sociology* 25, 395–418.

Garfinkel, S., L.F. Cranor (2005). What is Phishing. O'Reilly Media, Inc. Available at http://www.oreillynet.com/pub/a/network/2005/10/25/what-is-phishing.html. Accessed on April 02, 2009.

Gay, G., H. Hembrooke (2002). Collaboration in wireless learning networks, in: *The 35th Hawaii International Conference on System Science*, Hawaii, HA.

Garrity, E.J., J. O'Donnell, Y.J., Kim, G.L. Sanders (2004). Measuring consumer shopping oriented web site success: a motivation-based model, in: *2004 IRMA International Conference*, New Orleans, LA, USA, pp. 74–77.

Hu, X., Z. Lin, H. Zhang (2003). Trust promoting seals in electronic markets: an exploratory study of their effectiveness for online sales promotion. *Journal of Promotion Management* 9, 163–180.

Jakobsson, M. (2005). Modeling and preventing phishing attacks, *Financial Cryptography and Data Security*, pp. 73–89.

Johnson, S.C. (1967). Hierarchical clustering schemes. *Psychometrika* 2, 241–254.

Kim, D.J., Y.I. Song, S.B. Baynov, H.R. Rao (2005a). A multidimensional trust formation model in B-to-C e-commerce: a conceptual framework and content analyses of academia/practitioner perspectives. *Decision Support Systems* 40, 143–165.

Kim, Y.J., R. Kishore, G.L. Sanders (2005b). From DQ to EQ; understanding data quality in the context of e-business systems. *Communications of the ACM* 48, 75–81.

Kleinginna, P.R., Jr., A.M. Kleinginna (1981). A categorized list of motivation definitions with suggestions for a consensual definition. *Motivation and Emotion* 5, 263–291.

Krippendorff, K. (1980). *Content Analysis: An Introduction to its Methodology*. Sage, Beverly Hills, CA.

Kshetri, N. (2006). Pattern of global cyber war and crime: a conceptual framework. *Journal of International Management* 11, 541–562.

Kwok, S.-M., D.M.Y. Tam (2005). Child abuse in Chinese families in Canada. *International Social Work* 48, 341–348.

Lee, J.K., H.R. Rao (2007). Perceived risks, counter-beliefs, and intentions to use anti-/counter-terrorism websites: an exploratory study of government-citizens online interactions in a turbulent environment. *Decision Support Systems* 43(4), 1431–1449.

Levy, E. (2004). Interface illusions. *IEEE Security & Privacy* 2, 66–69.

Litan, A. (2004). Phishing attack victims likely targets for identity theft. Gartner Group, May.

Mackenzie, M. L. (2000). The classification, storage and retrieval of electronic mail-two exploratory studies, in: *ASIS Annual Meeting*, Chicago, IL.

Nardi, B. (1996). *Context and Consciousness: Activity Theory and Human Computer Interaction*. Cambridge, MIT Press.

Neuendorf, K.A. (2002). *The content analysis guidebook*. 1st ed. Sage, Thousand Oaks.

Okazaki, S. (2006). What D W know about mobile internet adopters—a cluster analysis. *Information & Management* 43, 127–141.

Petty, R.E., J.T. Cacioppo (1986). *The elaboration likelihood model of persuasion*. Vol. 19 Academic Press, New York.

Schneider, W., R.M. Shiffrin (1977). Controlled and automatic human information processing: I detection, search, and attention. *Psychological Review* 84, 1–66.

Schwarz, G. (1978). Estimating the dimension of a model. *The Analysis of Statistics* 6, 461–464.

Shiffrin, R.M., W. Schneider (1977). Controlled and automatic human information processing: II perceptual learning, automatic attending and a general theory. *Psychological Review* 84, 127–190.

Tam, K.Y., S.Y. Ho (2005). Web personalization as a persuasion strategy: an elaboration likelihood model perspective. *Information Systems Research* 16, 271–291.

TerraResearch (1993). *Galileo CATPAC: User Manual and Tutorial*. The Galileo Company, Amherst, NY.

Woelfel, J. (1993). *Galileo CATPAC: User Manual and Tutorial*. The Galileo Company, Amherst, NY.

Wathen, C.N., J. Burkell (2002). Believe it or not: factors influencing credibility on the web. *Journal of the American Society for Information Science and Technology* 53, 134–144.

Weiss, R. (2006). Sopranos in cyberspace. Check Point Software Technologies Ltd.

Wikipedia (2007). List of countries by English-speaking population.

Wolfer, B. (2005). Phishing attacks dampen online consumer trust. *The Epoch Times*, p. 8.

Zhang, T., R. Ramakrishnon, M. Livny (1996). BIRCH: an efficient data clustering method for very large databases, in: *ACM SIGMOD Conference on Management of Data*, Montreal, Canada, pp. 103–114.

Online resources

Anti-Phishing Working Group—http://www.antiphishing.org/

Indiana University—http://www.indiana.edu/~phishing/

Security Focus—http://www.securityfocus.com/infocus/1745

Suggested readings

Abad, C. (2007). The economy of phishing: a survey of the operations of the phishing market. Cyber Crime, the AVIEN Guide to Managing Malware in the Enterprise, Syngress.

Harley, D., A. Lee (2007). Phishing phodder: is user education helping or hindering, in: *Virus Bulletin Conference, September*, Vienna, Austria.

Mitnick, K., W. L. Simon, S. Wozniak (2002). The art of deception: controlling the human element of security. Wiley, Indianapolis, IN.

Mustaca, S. (2006). Present and future phishing techniques. *Virus Bulletin*.

Part IV
Security, Privacy and Access Control Theory

Rao & Upadhyaya, Eds., *Handbooks in Information Systems, Vol. 4*
Copyright © 2009 by Emerald Group Publishing Limited

Chapter 10

Identification and Access Management and Data Privacy ☆

Sateesh S. Kannegala

IBM India Software Lab, Block D2, MD2-A-101, Manyata Business Park, Bangalore 560 045, India

Abstract

Proliferation of information and decentralization of data have driven the identity and access management technologies. Various studies estimate the size of this market to be around $4.5 billion by 2012. The ease of conducting transactions on the net and the growing availability of bandwidth have paved the way for organizations and governments to provide services increasingly on-line. Governments are adopting digital technologies as the primary means of providing identity to their citizens. Apart from the issues of scaling, this has raised concerns of identity theft and privacy. In this chapter, we explore several aspects of digital identity, access management, and privacy.

1 Introduction to identification and access management

The world is moving away from classical paper transactions to the more convenient electronic transactions in the increasingly networked world. Fundamental to electronic transaction in a networked world is the ability to identify entities on the network and establish a trust relation—the digital identity. This digital identity forms the basis for all other security measures required to successfully conduct any transaction over the net.

Services are provided on the net based on digital identity, and transactions worth billions of dollars are conducted. Businesses and governments are offering an increasing number of services on the net. Governments have

---

☆ This work is not original and should not be interpreted as such. The references to the sources are only a sampling of the work being done in this area. There are numerous other sources that have been left out and the omission is by no means a reflection on the importance of their contribution.

always grappled with issues related to identity and privacy and have always been at the forefront of public policy (Identity Management, The National Electronic Commerce Coordinating Council, http://www.ec3.org/downloads/workgroups/2002/id_management.pdf). The ease of access and the increased use of networks and digital technologies accentuate the problems related to identity management and access controls. On the one hand, there is the need to protect citizen's freedom while protecting privacy and on the other is the responsibility of providing law and order, institutional efficiency, and national security. Today, the issues are more acute because of easy access to network and the ease of doing transactions on the net. With the ever-increasing ease of doing transactions on the net, there is a growing demand for services to be available on the net.

Identification has to precede any transaction and access rights of the identity established. The paper-based identification systems that have evolved over centuries now need to be transformed into the increasingly network-based digital identification systems. Establishing identity in the traditional world was quite straightforward. However, the digital world opens up new possibilities and thus new opportunities and challenges.

Traditional practices associated one identity per person. There was one person who represented herself. The identity was established by either some biological trait, such as fingerprint, or a signature or a combination. However, in the digital world, a user is often represented by a computer or a process running on a machine. Identity is a context-dependent concept and users need to create different digital identities for different contexts. Establishing such identities often requires providing personal information to entities that are unknown to the user.

The large number of identities that a user is thus associated with results in the need for the user to remember a large number of identity-related information. Often, even the user ID associated with different digital identities may not be the same. Single sign-on (SSO) solutions provide a partial answer to this. SSO is one form of identity consolidation.

The other side of this coin arises from the difficulty in correlating different digital identities with a given person (identity disambiguation). This is especially useful for law enforcement agencies, governments, banks, and so on. For example, when a single person opens different bank accounts with no apparent connections with them, it becomes important to correlate these and link it to the single person to whom it belongs. For an introduction of this side of the identity consolidation, see, for example, non-obvious relationship analysis (Jeff Jonas, 2007; http://idmashup.org/schedule/conferencesession.2006-06-13.8355598228/conferencefile.2006-06-17.0445782133/download).

There are many issues arising out of the advances in technology. Users are faced with a literal explosion of identity-related information. Whereas managing this explosion and the related problems poses one type of challenge, the risk associated with sharing personal and private information is another side of the same problem. The service providers are faced with the same problem of managing an explosion of identity-related information. Enterprises often reorganize themselves and re-aggregate into different groups. This is made easier with the advent of virtualization. Virtual domains are frequently created with new relationships. Establishing the trust relations among these domains becomes an important challenge.

Requirements arising out of regulatory compliance also influence the direction in identity and access-related issues. There is an evermore increasing need to be vigilant of the activities of individuals in an organization. This can be particularly tricky in regard to issues of privacy. For example, the task of providing reliable and secure service to customers involves recording and maintaining meaningful logs. Often these logs could include sensitive information. Balancing the need to provide secure and reliable service with requirements of privacy can be quite tricky.

The need for business partners to collaborate over the net brings on the additional dimension of sharing identity information across trusted domains. This has driven the need for and the standards in federated identity management.

Identity and access management includes authentication, user provisioning, password management, enterprise SSO, federation, enterprise access management, virtual and meta-directory services, and auditing. Often, non-repudiation (the ability to prove that the transaction was actually conducted by a given identity) becomes an important component of access management.

Several studies (World Identity and Access Management Markets, F607-74) place the world identity and access management market at several billion dollars by 2012. Among the factors influencing this market are the need for different authentication for different users, access, and privilege rights and proliferation of information that is no longer completely centralized on corporate networks and expand beyond the enterprise, creating the need for a federated identity model.

Section 1.1 examines identity and access management (IAM) from the perspective of different stakeholders, namely the enterprise, the end user, and governments. Section 1.2 explores the "lifecycle" of identity. This section explores the need for creating identities and how they get created to how they get used and terminated. This is followed by more details on provisioning of identity and the issues involved in this activity in Section 1.3. Security context forms the theme of Section 1.4. Attempts to define comprehensive framework for achieving the goals of giving the control back to the end users form the main theme of Section 1.5. Higgins framework is discussed in greater detail in Section 1.5.

Section 2 focuses on issues arising out of privacy concerns. We explore efforts to address the concerns arising out of privacy. Privacy is complicated by the difficulty in arriving at a common understanding of what privacy really means and entails in terms of policies and technology. Section 2.1

introduces the attempts made by the Organization of Economic Cooperation and Development (OECD). This is followed by a discussion in Sections 2.2 and 2.3 of attempts to implement privacy principles in databases. Section 3 concludes with a short discussion of the state of identity and access management and privacy today.

1.1 IAM—perspectives

Identity and access management refers to the infrastructure to manage disparate identities needed by (i) employees to perform their roles, (ii) business partners to conduct businesses with one another on the net, (iii) customers to transact on the net with enterprises, and (iv) governments to maintain reasonable information on the citizens necessary for good governance. In this section, we will look at identity and access management from the perspective of different players, that is, (i) governments, (ii) private industry, and (iii) the user. We will also take a look at IAM from the perspective of its potential vulnerabilities.

Once the identity of a user is established, access decisions to objects stored in a machine need to be computed based on the privileges of the identity accessing the object and the sensitivity of the information being accessed. There are three types of access models that are in vogue—discretionary access control, mandatory access control, and role-based access control (Ferraiolo et al., 2007).

In the discretionary access control model, access permissions are determined by the owner and are expressed in the form of access control matrix. This is the most common model deployed in UNIX systems where the access controls are explicitly determined by stating who can do what operations (such as read, write, and execute) on an object. In this model, the decision of who can access what is with the owner of the object.

Mandatory access control relies on not only the privileges of the process accessing the object but also a label that determines the sensitivity of the data. The access permissions depend on the "level" of clearance of the process accessing the data and the "sensitivity" of the data as determined by the label. In military context, for example, the sensitivity label can take the form "Top Secret," "Secret," "Confidential," "Unclassified," and so on. The level of clearance is determined typically by the rank, such as General, Captain, and Lieutenant, of the person accessing the information.

In the enterprise context, access permissions are typically decided based on the roles a person plays in the organization. This entails granting accesses to multiple applications required to perform a role. Ferraiolo et al. (2007) provides a convenient framework for managing access permissions in this context. As the role of the person changes, the corresponding access permissions need to change as well.

Although the underlying infrastructure to support various access models exists, access permissions may need to be computed at a stage before this.

For example, when a user accesses a resource through the web, the same process will serve the request for all the users. In this case, the person's access rights need to be computed before the process is invoked to access the information sought by the user. This is typically achieved by deploying a policy engine that is configured to implement the policy of an organization. When a user attempts to access an application, the policy engine checks the access policy for the application and implements it. Furthermore, usually the infrastructure also provides for non-repudiation. Non-repudiation is a set of protocols to ensure that the initiator of the transaction cannot deny that the transaction was initiated by him/her. Refer to Fig. 1 for a generic architecture that incorporates these.

Without an IAM solution, enterprises lose control over who is doing what. Enterprises in this situation are always in the reactive mode. They are forced to respond to incidents and with little that they can do about controlling the damage.

It is almost imperative today to have some IAM solution that aids regulatory requirements. It is important to be able to track all transactions and be able to report who did what, when and why, and whether they had the authority to perform that transaction. IAM solutions should provide the ability to track and report any suspicious activity. In fact, immediate corrective actions are also possible with good IAM solutions in place.

While it is important to ensure tracking activities, it is equally important to be sensitive to privacy concerns. It is technically easy to collect, store, and use private data of individuals, making it easy to track and control activities, but unless there are good privacy policies, it might be difficult to pay attention to violation of privacy.

Let us now take a closer look at IAM from the perspective of consumers of IAM solutions.

1.1.1 Enterprise perspective

Enterprises today have become increasingly distributed, geographically diverse units working together. A large number of employees choose to work from home offices. Constant changes in organizations due to mergers, acquisitions on the one hand and work force changes on the other bring in a different dimension to IAM. Integration and consolidation of identities and access rights across organizations can be a challenge. Changes in business directions often require appropriate changes in access permissions.

These characteristics determine the nature of the requirements for IAM solutions from the enterprise perspective. Following issues are among the top ones that need to be addressed.

    (i) A literal explosion of identity-related data
    (ii) Distributed nature of enterprises and geographical and national diversity
    (iii) Multiple sources of data
    (iv) Regulatory requirements and their implication

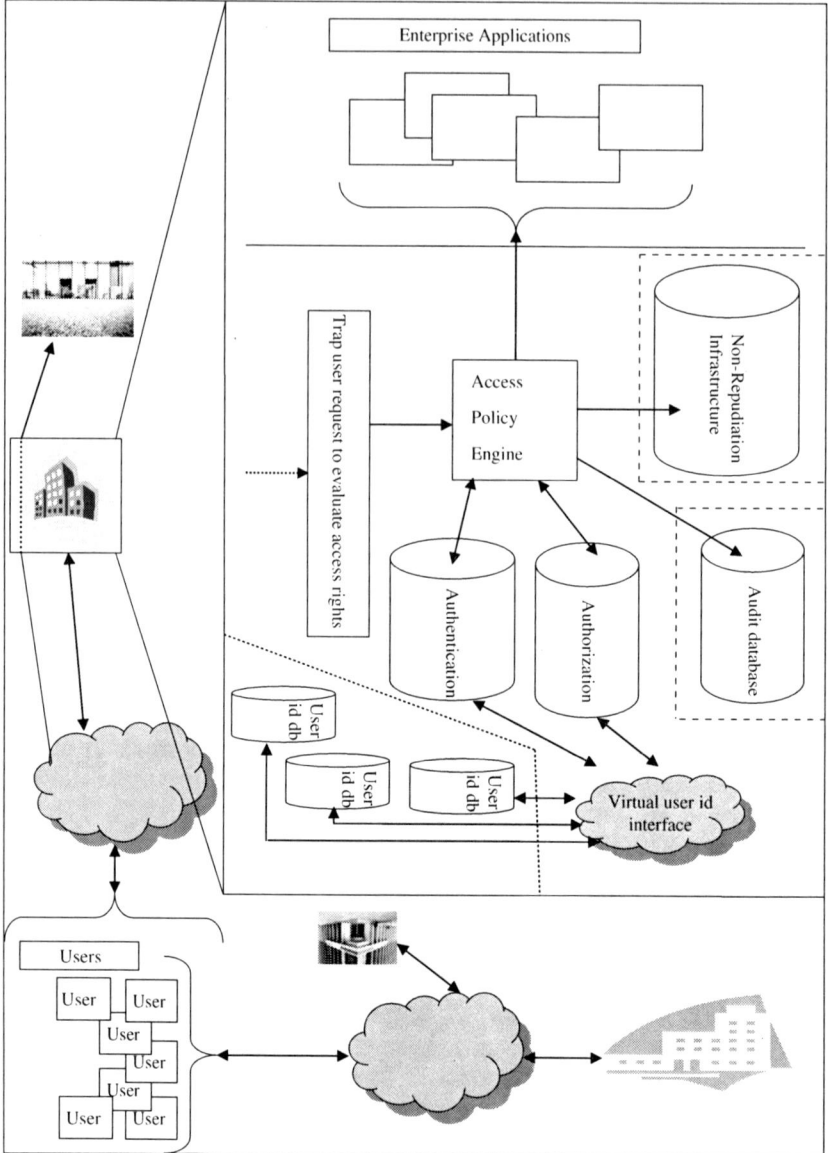

Fig. 1. A schematic architecture of enterprise IAM.

(v) Conducting business on the net with business partners
(vi) Increasing number of customers choosing to transact on the net
(vii) Constantly changing business requirements
(viii) Mergers and acquisitions resulting in re-organization
(ix) Employee attritions, new employees, role changes, and so on
(x) Privacy-related issues

Figure 1 gives a high-level depiction of a possible architecture for achieving some of the aforementioned goals. Provisioning of identities is not depicted in Fig. 1; refer to Fig. 3 for more details on identity provisioning. Identity provisioning applications typically address issues arising out of granting accesses based on the roles played by people. These applications are used in creating accounts on systems needed for executing a role.

1.1.2 User perspective

From the user perspective, digital identity poses a different set of challenges. The user needs a simple way of establishing an identity without having to remember complicated long passwords and multiple user identities. The user has to deal with multiple passwords, with the associated complications of password management. Frequently, the user has to deal with multiple user identities. The user needs a simple mechanism with a password that is easy to remember to establish the identity. But, it is also necessary that the mechanisms used for establishing the identity are robust and trusted. The risk of identity theft is quite real. Given the many identities that a typical user has to deal with makes it very complicated.

Identity theft is the fraud of a miscreant stealing identity information belonging to a victim and using that information to pretend to be the victim. With this, the perpetrator can obtain loans, credit cards, open new bank accounts and steal from existing ones, and so on. This financial fraud often goes undetected for considerable lengths of time. The size of losses due to identity theft is difficult to estimate, but is put at several billion dollars. Identity theft is one of the fastest growing criminal activities.

Phishing is a simplistic trick used by perpetrators in stealing identities. They use a fake website or e-mail that looks very similar to that of an organization such as a bank or a financial institution. This site invites the user to login as would the original site. The information thus provided goes to the perpetrator and not the intended institution. This information is then misused.

The other dimension to this problem is the fact that the way identity information is maintained and used in different countries are different. See the official websites maintained by the UK government (http://www.identity-theft.org.uk/) and the Department of Justice in the United States (http://www.usdoj.gov/criminal/fraud/websites/idtheft.html) for examples of this problem. These two websites provide information on what is identity theft as well as the steps to be taken to prevent identity theft and what to do if you have been a victim. This information depends on the country of citizenship and how identity information is collected, maintained, and used.

Since establishing digital identity often involves sharing personal information, privacy concerns play an important role. The user maybe required to provide personal and private information. Indiscriminate use of such information is potentially dangerous. The user naturally expects adequate protection of privacy.

The issues that a typical user faces include the following:

    (i) Dealing with multiple user identities with different contexts and the consequent difficulty in managing the information
   (ii) Password management
  (iii) Minimizing the risk of identity theft
   (iv) Controlling the information shared with organizations
    (v) Privacy

1.1.3   Government

Many governments have undertaken projects to issue "digital identities" to citizens. Governments traditionally have been involved in debates over conflicting policy requirements of citizen privacy, civil liberty, and freedom on the one hand and efficient governance, national security, and law and order on the other. Improved technological capabilities have reopened the debate. Apart from this, the governments play a crucial role in the directions in IAM through regulations. The regulatory requirements enforced by the governments influence the development in technologies. For example, Sarbanes Oxley has introduced organizations.

Purely from the technical point of view, the need for scaling the existing systems to accommodate ever larger number of identities brings on new technological challenges. This is especially so in some emerging economies with very large populations, such as China and India. Furthermore, in some cases, the complications are compounded by the need of maintaining the information in more than one language.

1.2   Identity life cycle

In its broadest sense, digital identity management starts at the time the identity is provisioned. This is the process of creating an on-line account. In the simplest case, the user creates an account for him/herself. Such self-registration process is sufficient in many cases. The user creates an identity and provides other required information to establish the identity. An identity is established in a given context. In that context, the identity has to be unique. Often, this forces the user to choose a user ID that may not be the same as the other IDs she/he has set up in other contexts. Given a large number of contexts in which a user creates such identities, remembering the contexts and the associated identity becomes a nightmare.

The existence of many identities associated with a single individual creates yet another challenge. There are situations in which it is important to associate the multiple identities with the person to whom they belong. Such correlation among multiple digital identities is needed in identifying and rewarding loyal frequent customers and also serves as a tool in fighting anti-social activities. Analyzing different digital identities to establish if they belong to a single individual is the art of identity resolution or identity disambiguation. Identity resolution takes information from different sources and arrives at conclusions about the individual to whom these identities belong. For an interesting discussion of identity resolution using non-obvious relationship analysis, refer Jeff Jonas, http://idmashup.org/schedule/conferencesession.2006-06-13.8355598228/conferencefile.2006-06-17.0445782133/download.

Let us now look at a typical scenario in an enterprise. A new employee joins the organization and has a specific role to play in that organization. The demands of the role dictate the systems on which an account for this employee should exist. It also determines the level of access the employee should be given to that system.

Figure 2 is a depiction of the kind of accesses a new employee may need to perform the job.

1.3 Identity provisioning

Identity provisioning is the first step in the life cycle of a digital identity. In this section, we will look at various aspects of identity provisioning.

1.3.1 Creation of accounts

Account creation is the first step in the provisioning process. Most organizations have policies in place that determine (a) the necessary accesses to perform a role, (b) the level of access necessary to perform the role, and (c) the kind of authentication required to establish the identity of

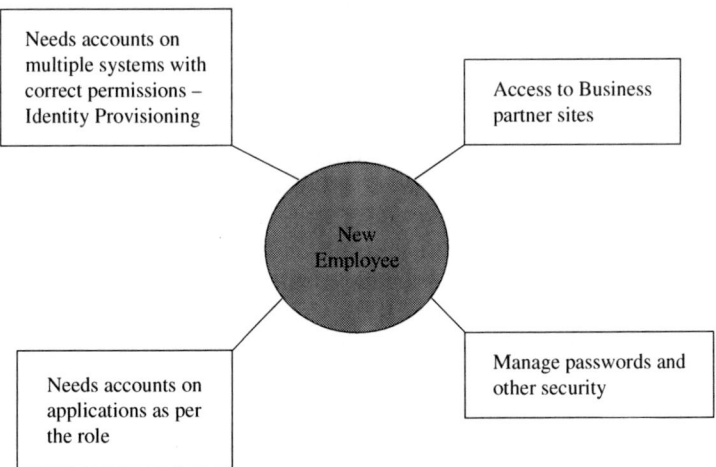

Fig. 2.   Typical needs of a new employee.

the person accessing the system. Policies also cover the approvals required to create the accounts. The heterogeneity of systems (many different platforms, a variety of applications, different authentication mechanisms, etc.) in the organization adds an extra level of complexity.

Provisioning policies typically include statements about what level of automation is possible. For example, self-registration is often enough to provide access to non-confidential information (this would typically apply to people outside the organization). However, creating access with more privileges may need intervention and approvals. While the accounts are being created, the users maybe required to provide personal information. It is important to have clearly defined privacy policies that cover privacy aspects of an account.

Tools are available to automate identity provisioning. However, tools alone may not be sufficient. When there is a need for approvals before an account can be created as per the policy, sophisticated workflow tools and policy engines can help aid the process of provisioning. Figure 3 is a schematic of the steps involved in identity provisioning.

1.3.2   Access to business partner sites

In the course of performing a role, an employee often needs access to information on business partner sites. This access maybe in the form of a login to the partner site. Such login would assume that the necessary accounts in the partner site have been created.

Employee may need access to sites of service providers outside the organization. For example, the employee might need to access information on health insurance from an insurance provider. Such access may not necessarily need a separate authentication and security context creation in the service provider's site. This access can be achieved by using federation. Standards for federation of identity is discussed in Section 1.4.

1.3.3   Manage accounts and passwords

Passwords are an essential part of establishing an identity. From the perspective of the enterprise, passwords are the key to accessing information. Enterprise policies on passwords typically address the need for strong passwords and frequent changing of passwords. However, a typical user with multiple accounts finds it extremely inconvenient to remember the details of all the accounts. It is not practical to remember a large number of identity-related information. Storing or writing down such information introduces vulnerabilities. A combination of enterprise SSO and federated identity management provides a convenient solution to this.

1.3.4   Migration of accounts

When an employee's role in the organization is changed, the accounts and the permissions need to be appropriately altered. Provisioning tools can also be used for automating these processes where possible.

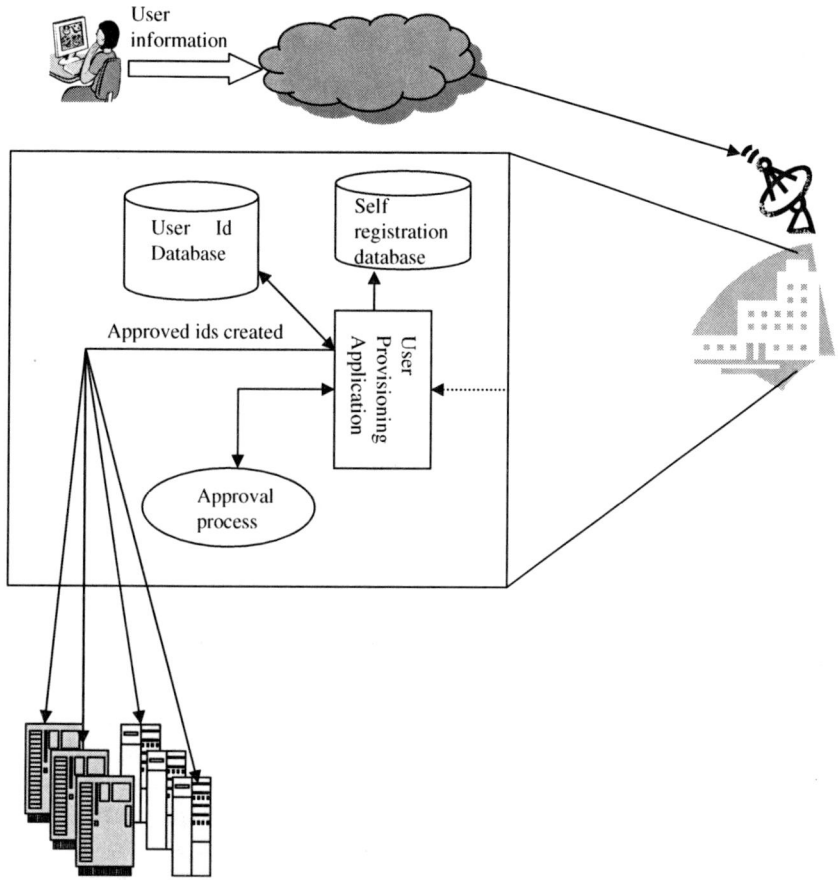

Fig. 3. Schematic illustrating the process of identity provisioning.

During acquisitions and mergers, large-scale migration of accounts becomes inevitable. Without the aid of tools to achieve such reconciliations and identity consolidations, the process would be quite unmanageable.

1.3.5 Termination of accounts

This typically happens when an employee separates from the organization. Many accounts may have been created over the time the employee was a part of the organization. All these accounts need to be terminated properly. Terminating these accounts has a considerable financial implication of freeing up software licenses associated with that user. Accounts not terminated properly also opens up the vulnerability of unauthorized accesses by these account holders.

1.4   Security context

The term "security context" is used to describe the collection of security-related attributes of a process that is executing on behalf of a user. This consists of the user ID, the authentication mechanism, and other security-related information. This is all the more important in the context of regulatory requirements introduced by HIPAA, Sarbanes Oxley, BASEL II, and other similar regulations. It is important not only in determining the authority of the process to initiate the request but also in auditing the tasks executed.

In the digital world, the "identity" that is capable of executing a transaction is usually a process that represents a person. Formally, digital identity is defined by Higgins (http://www.eclipse.org/higgins) as "A Digital Identity is the 'runtime' representation of identity information about a person, group thing or concept. A Digital Identity is in Higgins analogous to a security token used in an identity exchange. It is often digitally signed by an issuer. The issuer maybe the 'source' of the claims being made in the Digital Identity, but the source maybe another person, group, etc." Digital identity often translates into the representation of the role a person or a system is attempting to play. It is a collection of identity information and attributes that define the role. This information is used in making access decisions and determines the capability of the identity. This identity is established each time for a specified period of time. Such a session determines the security context in which that identity is acting.

Identity information typically consists of the user information and an authenticator (Camp, 2004) and information pertaining to time. The authenticator depends largely on the process of authentication. It is important to realize that there is no one-to-one mapping of the digital identity and a person associated with that ID. There can be many digital identities associated with a single person depending on the purpose for which the identity is being established. However, a digital ID is never associated with more than one person. It is a one-to-many relation.

Figure 4 represents a generic architecture showing the flow of information as it relates to a user attempting to access a resource.

The user request for access to applications or resources comes in with information that is used for authenticating the user. In reference to Fig. 4, the following sequence of events typically occurs before access to a resource is granted.

(a) User request is checked against IAM policy—if the resource requested is not protected, access is granted. If not the flow continues with the next step.
(b) User login status is checked and if there is no active session, the user is requested information to establish identity.

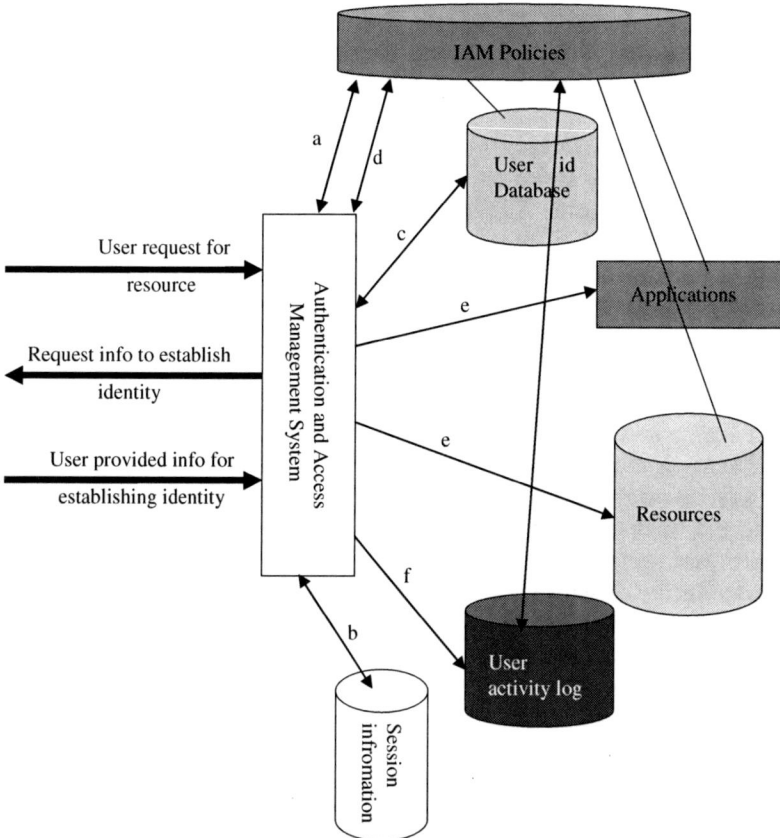

Fig. 4. Generic access architecture.

(c) User-provided identity information is used to establish the identity of the user.
(d) Once the identity is established, the policies are checked for authorization of the user to access the application/information.
(e) Access is granted or denied based on the policy for access to the application or the resource and the user-provided information.
(f) This user activity is logged into the user activity database for the purposes of audit trail.

Most of the older systems were designed assuming that the information required in making authentication, authorization, or other security decisions were available in a centralized database. Data today is mostly distributed and in disparate sources. This poses a challenge with dispersed data. This necessitates a common interface where all the necessary information is consolidated. Refer to Fig. 1 for a schematic that illustrates this point.

A number of security standards have evolved to deal with different aspects of security. Notable among these are Security Assertion Markup Language (SAML), Web Services Security (WSS), and eXtensible Access Control Markup Language (XACML) (see http://www.oasis-open.org/specs/index.php for SAML and XACML and WSS; Harold Lockhart, Demystifying security standards, http://oreilly-test.bea.com/pub/a/2005/10/security_standards.html). These standards use XML and are suitable for large-scale distributed systems.

SAML provides standards for expressing user attributes authentication and authorization information. It also provides protocols for requesting and receiving these. SAML is ideally suited to execute identity federation. SAML 2.0 is an OASIS standard that incorporates standards for communication between SAML authorities, detailed description of authentication methods, and enhanced ability to protect privacy.

XACML is a standard developed for expressing access control policies. Legacy systems depended largely on simple Access Control Lists (ACLs) to make access decisions. ACLs were often embedded in the applications and were not easily discoverable. This made access control decisions difficult to derive. XACML can be used to make access decisions based on any available information such as the content or other attributes like time, date, and location. Combining these with the information about parties making the request, necessary access control decisions can be made more easily (Sjöholm et al., 2008).

WSS (http://docs.oasis-open.org/wss/2004/01/oasis-200401-wss-soap-message-security-1.0.pdf) is a specification that provides the user mechanisms to build higher level security protocols (also see Li and Pahl, 2003). WSS supports various security models such as PKI, Kerberos, and SSL. The specification provides mechanisms to send security tokens as a part of the message, message integrity, and message confidentiality. These are used as building blocks in conjunction with other extensions to web services and application-specific protocols to accommodate various security models and technologies. WS-Trust (http://docs.oasis-open.org/ws-sx/ws-trust/200512/ws-trust-1.3-os.

html) uses these base mechanisms and defines additional primitives and extensions for security token exchange to enable the issuance and dissemination of credentials within different trust domains. With its support for PKI, Kerberos, SSL, and so on, WSS can be used to establish the authentication mechanisms that exist in these models.

1.4.1   Authentication mechanisms

SAML, XACML, and WSS standards provide a means of managing the security information but are silent about how the actual authentication takes place. The most basic and traditional methods of verifying the claim of identity depended largely on user ID password, where the user's knowledge of the password attests the identity.

Simple username password authentication is insufficient, especially, when authenticating to a remote system on the network. The password, even if it is encrypted, can be captured in transit and can be used in replay attacks.

Authentication is the process of verifying the identity of a person or a process. Different authentication mechanisms can be used to distinguish various possible levels of authentication. Usually, authentication is achieved by a combination of one or more of (i) "something you know"—typically a password or PIN, (ii) "something you possess"—for example, a credit card, an ATM Card, or a hardware device, and (iii) "something you are"—usually biometric evidence such as fingerprints and retina print. Authentication levels can be based on which combinations of the mechanisms have been used and the strength of the mechanisms used to achieve authentication. For any process of authentication, systems typically depend on user databases. Most often, this is an LDAP or an RDBMS.

There are robust authentication protocols built especially for use in the network where data is potentially at risk of being captured by anyone snooping on the net. Kerberos is one such protocol designed to achieve authentication of an identity without disclosing the password (see http://www.ietf.org/rfc/rfc4120.txt, for a detailed discussion of Kerberos Network Authentication Protocol). Also see Cervesato et al. (2005) for a discussion on using kerberos for Cross realm authentication.

There are other authentication mechanisms used for authentication over the network, notably SSL (see, e.g., http://docs.sun.com/source/816-6156-10/contents.htm). See Gupta et al. (2002) for a discussion of comparative performance of SSL based on the cryptographic technique. Another way of reducing the risk of password capture while authenticating over the net is to change the passwords frequently. This is achieved by using a SecureID infrastructure (for an example of a commercial product implementing this, see http://www.rsa.com/node.aspx?id = 1156).

1.5   Higgins

The information about people on the net is growing without control. When organizations seek information about users, concerns about privacy seems to take a back seat. There is a growing awareness that the user must be able to control the information she shares with anyone.

Higgins (http://www.eclipse.org/higgins) is an open source Internet identity framework designed to integrate identity, profile, and social relationship information across multiple sites, applications, and devices. Higgins is not a protocol, it is a software infrastructure to support a consistent user experience that works with all popular digital identity protocols, including WS-Trust, OpenID, SAML, XDI, LDAP, and so on.

Higgins recognizes the fact that in different contexts in which identities are created, different types of personal information are to be shared.

Higgins framework provides the user the ability to control the information she provides in creating an identity in a given context.

Higgins addresses five major areas in the following:

- Provide a consistent user experience based on card icons for the management and release of identity data.
- Empower users with more convenience and control over personal information distributed across external information silos. Provide a single point of control over multiple identities, preferences, and relationships.
- Provide an Application Programming Interface (API) and data model for the virtual integration and federation of identity and security information from a various sources.
- Provide plug-in adapters to enable existing data sources including directories, communications systems, collaboration systems, and databases each using differing protocols and schemas to be integrated into the framework.
- Provide a social relationship data integration framework that enables these relationships to be persistent and reusable across application boundaries. It organizes relationships into a set of distinct social contexts within which a person expresses different personas and roles.

For more details, please see Higgins charter page (http://www.eclipse.org/higgins/higgins-charter.php) on the website.

2 Privacy

Protection of privacy of the individual users is a fundamental issue with far-reaching consequences. With the ever-increasing speed and ability to collect and store personal data, data privacy has become a great matter of concern.

Privacy is the "Right to be left alone." In its simplest form, privacy is the right of individuals to determine what information about them they are willing to share with others and how others use this information.

The surprising fact is that privacy had not been considered on par with other fundamental rights. The concept of privacy has evolved to where it is today largely due to the opinion of courts in litigations.

For example, see Center for Democracy & Technology site (http://www.cdt.org/privacy/guide/protect) for an extensive introduction to privacy and related issues.

Analysis of behavior patterns on the Internet shows that privacy concerns are an inhibitor to the acceptance of electronic commerce. The first step toward making electronic transactions an acceptable means of electronic commerce is obviously through public awareness of privacy policies.

Transparency about how the personal data collected is used goes a long way in creating the comfort.

Technologies to meet the needs of businesses have grown with little consideration for the needs of the individuals who use these technologies. This has effectively eroded the ability of the user to control the flow of personal information. The user has little say in how the personal information collected for one purpose is shared among businesses. This is often at the bottom of an inherent mistrust of the Internet technologies for electronic commerce.

Technology alone, however, is insufficient to address all the issues involved in privacy. Societal pressure, sanction, and so on play a role as well. Yet another dimension of the problem is that the Internet respects no international borders. Data flows occur freely and almost instantaneously across national borders. This requires an international body to provide high-level guidelines to bring about common understanding among nations in dealing with issues of privacy.

Major international bodies such as OECD (http://www.oecd.org) and the United Nations (UN) have taken steps to establish guidelines to deal with issues of data privacy. The UN adopted "guidelines concerning computerized personal data files." These guidelines provide the orientation to member states for enacting laws on how to handle personal data.

Recognizing the need to have a common understanding among member and non-member nations, the commission recommended certain principles that guide nations to formulate policies for privacy. Section 2.1 discusses the highlights of the recommendation. For the full text of the recommendation, see http://www.oecd.org/document/18/0,3343,en_2649_34255_1815186_1_1_1_1,00.html.

2.1 OECD guidelines

The goal of OECD recommendations is to maintain free flow of information across national boundaries while ensuring that nations determine the policies suitable to them. The transborder flow of information is crucial for building confidence in performing electronic transactions involving different nations. The guidelines fall under two major groups: national and international.

2.1.1 National

The guidelines provide principles based on which privacy policies are to be developed. The following are the gist of the principles:

1. *Collection limitation*: This principle states that there should be a limit to the collection of personal data; personal data should be collected by lawful and fair means and where possible with the consent of the subject.

2. *Data quality*: The data collected should be relevant and necessary for the purpose for which the data is collected. The purpose should be kept up-to-date.
3. *Purpose specification*: The purpose for the collection of personal data should be mentioned before collecting the data and should only be used in fulfilling the stated purposes.
4. *Use limitation*: Personal data should not be disclosed, except as agreed with the subject or for law enforcement purposes.
5. *Security safeguards*: Personal data should be provided reasonable protection against modification, loss or unauthorized access, use, or modification.
6. *Openness*: There should be openness about developments, policies, and practices with regard to personal data.
7. *Individual participation*: Individual should have the right to obtain information about personal data pertaining to her. If such information is denied, the individual should have the right to the reasons why it is denied and be able to challenge them.
8. *Accountability*: The data controller (the authority who is charged with dealing with personal data) should be accountable for effecting the aforementioned principles.

2.1.2 *International*
1. Member countries should take into consideration the implications of domestic processing and re-export of personal data.
2. Transborder flow of data between borders should be made secure and uninterrupted.
3. Member countries should refrain from restricting transborder flows, except when it compromises its domestic legislation.
4. Member countries should not enact legislation, or develop policies and practices, in the guise of protecting privacy and liberty, that would create obstacles to transborder flow of personal data.

Other sections of the OECD recommendations deal with implementation of the principles and international cooperation. Refer to OECD guidelines (http://www.oecd.org) for a detailed set of all the recommendations.

2.2 *Technical initiatives*

There have been many initiatives to address the needs of privacy in sharing personal information. We have already seen Higgins (http://www.eclipse.org/higgins) as an example of a platform that provides the user control over the information that is being shared. Some of the initiatives in this direction include Platform for Privacy Preferences (P3P) (http://www.w3.org/P3P/). P3P is an initiative of the W3 Consortium. The (P3P) project enables websites to express their privacy practices in a standard format that can be retrieved automatically and interpreted easily by user agents. P3P user agents will allow users to be informed of site practices (in both machine- and human-readable formats) and to automate decision-making based on these practices when appropriate. Thus users need not read the privacy policies at every site they visit.

Proxies and firewalls are usually useful in controlling the information flow between machines. Such proxies can be used for achieving anonymization. Some other useful technologies include system cleaners that can be used to clean up the trail of sites visited and the cache stored in computers that can potentially be misused.

2.3 Hippocratic databases

Agrawal et al. (2002; http://www.cse.ust.hk/vldb2002/program-info/program.html) presented a paper in VLDB conference that attempted to create a comprehensive privacy aware database. The paper identifies key technical issues and provides a design for a database that includes the Hippocratic Oath as a key design principle. Hippocratic Oath has guided physicians and medical doctors for centuries in the area of privacy of the information they are privy to: "WHATEVER IN CONNECTION with my professional practice or not in connection with it I may see or hear in the lives of my patients which ought not be spoken abroad, I will not divulge, reckoning that all such should be kept secret." See, for example, Hippocratic Oath (http://members.tripod.com/nktiuro/hippocra.htm) for a translation of the original oath. Hippocratic databases are databases inspired by the oath and include the tenets of Hippocratic Oath in the design of the databases.

Databases are at the heart of information storing and management. With the ever-increasing amounts of data collected for various reasons, concerns about the misuse of such information are also rising. Database systems with lax security make it difficult to control either accidental violations of privacy or violations due to a lack of concern or plain illegal actions.

The solution to privacy concerns is not technological alone. We have seen attempts to understand and address the issues and concerns in different forums in different directions, such as legal, national, and international. The solution to the problems of privacy, especially those that exist due to poorly designed technologies, will have to come from technologies designed with due consideration for the concerns of privacy.

The fundamental requirement of database systems is the ability to access and manage large amounts of persistent data efficiently. Typical database systems support a high-level language for the ease of accessing and manipulating the data and defining the structure of the data. They also provide for the accuracy of the data stored in them and provide for controlling access to the database. Database systems are typically not sensitive to issues of privacy (Wahlstrom and Quirchmayr, 2007).

Statistical databases do share the goal of not compromising sensitive information. However, they fall short of the broader goals of Hippocratic databases. Similarly, secure databases do share some common attributes. Hippocratic databases may use some of the techniques used in secure databases.

The original paper on Hippocratic databases went on to create a straw-man design for the database. This design was based on 10 fundamental principles. These principles were derived from various privacy legislations and inspirit incorporated the OECD guidelines on data privacy.

The principles in summary are the following:

(a) *Purpose specification*: any personal information stored in the database will also store the purpose for which the data was collected.
(b) *Consent*: Any personal data collected should have the consent of the data provider.
(c) *Limited collection*: The personal information collected should be the minimal required to accomplish the purpose of collection.
(d) *Limited use*: The database will only run queries consistent with the purpose for which they were collected.
(e) *Limited disclosure*: The personal data stored will not be communicated outside unless the consent of the donor is explicitly obtained.
(f) *Accuracy:* The data in the database should be accurate and up to date.
(g) *Safety*: Information will be safeguarded against theft and other misuse.
(h) *Openness*: The donor of the information shall be able to access all the information provided by her.
(i) *Compliance*: The owner should be able to verify compliance to the above principles.

3 Summary

In summary, this chapter has attempted to expose the reader to the importance of identity and access management and privacy in the emerging world. While the issues faced by various players in the field were high-lighted, we have only suggested generic and high-level architectures to address these. It is important to realize that easy access to networks and new technologies have now opened our horizons beyond what we were able to do before. However, with it come challenges that need to be addressed. Security measures introduce extra steps that tend to be inconvenient to the user. A balance between this inconvenience and the ease of an open free, environment should be the goal of these measures. There are always concerns of privacy and these are addressed by many initiatives in the direction of user-centric security. We saw Higgins as an example of this. Databases where information persists for a long time are particularly sensitive to privacy concerns. We saw the initiatives OECD has taken in the direction of addressing privacy and some technical advances in the area of databases.

With various issues that concern security and privacy, identity and access management is an area that will constantly evolve and will always remain an important component in the future of how we interact, conduct business, and belong to a "society."

Acknowledgment

I gratefully acknowledge the guidance given by my colleague Yoshinobu Ishigaki, IBM, Japan.

References

Agrawal, R., J. Kiernan, R. Srikant, Y. Xu (2002). Hippocratic databases. Very large data bases, in: *Proceedings of the 28th International Conference on Very Large Data Bases*, Hong Kong, China, pp. 143–154.

Camp, J.L. (2004). Technology and society magazine. *IEEE* 23(3), 34–41.

Cervesato, I., A.D. Jaggard, A. Scedrov, C. Walstad. (2005). Specifying Kerberos 5 CrossRealm authentication, in: *Proceedings of the 2005 workshop on Issues in the Theory of Security*, Annual Symposium on Principles of Programming Languages, Long Beach, CA, pp. 12–26.

Ferraiolo, D., R. Kuhn, R. Sandhu (2007). RBAC standard rationale: Comments on "a critique of the ANSI standard on role-based access control." *Security & Privacy, IEEE* 5(6), pp. 51–53.

Gupta, V., S. Gupta, S. Chang, D. Stebila (2002). Performance analysis of elliptic curve cryptography for SSL, in: *Proceedings of the 1st ACM Workshop on Wireless Security*, Workshop on Wireless Security, Atlanta, GA, USA, pp. 87–94.

Jonas, J. (2007). Identity resolution: 23 years of practical experience and observations at scale, in: *Proceedings of the 2006 ACM SIGMOD international conference on Management of data*, International Conference on Management of Data Archive, Chicago, IL, USA, p. 718, ACM, New York, NY, USA.

Li, C., C. Pahl (2003). Security in the web services framework, in: *Proceedings of the 1st International Symposium on Information and Communication Technologies*, ACM International Conference Proceeding Series, Vol. 49, pp. 481–486.

Sjöholm, A., L. Seitz, B. Sadighi (2008). Secure communication for ad-hoc, federated groups, in: *Proceedings of the 7th Symposium on Identity and Trust on the Internet*, ACM International Conference Proceeding Series, Vol. 283, pp. 48–58.

Wahlstrom, K., G. Quirchmayr (2007). The motivation and proposition of a privacy-enhancing architecture for operational databases, in: *Proceedings of the fifth Australasian Symposium on ACSW frontiers*, Vol. 68, Ballarat, Australia. Session: Fifth Australasian Information Security Workshop (AISW) (Privacy Enhancing Technologies), ACM International Conference Proceeding Series, Vol. 249, pp. 173–182.

Rao & Upadhyaya, Eds., *Handbooks in Information Systems, Vol. 4*
Copyright © 2009 by Emerald Group Publishing Limited

Chapter 11

Children's Online Privacy: Issues with Parental Awareness and Control ☆

France Bélanger and Robert Crossler

Department of Accounting and Information Systems, Virginia Tech, Blacksburg, VA 24060-0101

Janine Hiller

Department of Finance, Insurance, and Business Law, Virginia Tech, Blacksburg, VA, 24061-0221

Michael Hsiao and Jung-Min Park

Bradley Department of Electrical and Computer Engineering, Virginia Tech, Blacksburg, VA 24060-0111

Abstract

As children increasingly use the Internet, there have been mounting concerns about their privacy online. As a result, the U.S. Congress enacted the Children's Online Privacy Protection Act (COPPA) in 1998 to prohibit web sites from collecting information from children under 13 years of age without verifiable parental consent. Unfortunately, few technologies and tools are available for parents to provide this consent. Further, our research demonstrates that very few parents are even aware of the laws and technologies available to protect their children's privacy online. In addition to exploring parental awareness of laws and technologies associated with protecting children's privacy online, this research explored factors that would influence the usage of technologies and techniques for parental control, using a focus group research methodology. The results of the content analysis of the data are used to propose an emergent framework of factors that impact use of privacy protection tools and techniques by parents. Three categories of factors are identified: awareness factors (laws and risks), behavioral adoption

☆ An earlier and condensed version of this work was presented at the 2007 AMCIS Conference in Keystone, CO.

factors (social influence, behavioral control, and trust), and technology adoption factors (ease of use, net benefits, and relative advantage).

---

1 Introduction

A paramount concern of individuals using the Internet is the protection of their privacy, especially their children's privacy. As a group, children use the Internet more than any other demographic set in the USA: 65% of children between the ages of 10 and 13 use the Internet (NTIA, 2002). Further, 12% of 8- to 10-year-olds and 21% of 11- to 14-year-olds spend an hour or more every day on the Internet (Roberts et al., 2005). A major issue is that with even the simple promise of a small prize, children can be easily convinced to share personal information (Turow, 2001). With estimates suggesting that 77 million children are going to use the Internet (Kawamoto, 2004), and with the escalating threat of insidious child predators and phishing scams in recent years, effective protection of children's privacy in cyberspace is a pressing issue.

In 1996, a Federal Trade Commission (FTC) survey of web sites found that 86% of web sites collected information from children, yet only 30% had privacy policies, and a mere 4% asked for parental consent to do so. Two years later, the number of web sites collecting information from children increased to 89%, whereas 42% stated a privacy policy; yet less than 11% required some form of parental consent. During this period, the FTC brought legal action against the practices of specific web sites who were misleading children while collecting information. Geocities, Kids.com, and Liberty Financial Investors all were subjects of action by the FTC for misleading and deceptive practices. In reaction to the documented and widespread collection of information from children and related abuses identified by the FTC, in 1998 the U.S. Congress enacted the Children's Online Privacy Protection Act (COPPA). COPPA took effect in 2000 and gave the FTC jurisdiction to adopt regulations pursuant to the act.

COPPA prohibits web sites from collecting information from children under 13 years without verifiable parental consent and requires web sites to give parents notice of their information practices and inform them of how they will use the collected information. Although, in its original regulations implementing COPPA the FTC stated that its rule regarding parental consent was only temporary to allow time for technology to develop, no such technology has emerged. After several periods of comments, the FTC stated in March 2006, "the Commission conclude[d] that more secure electronic mechanisms and infomediary services for obtaining verifiable parental consent are not yet widely available at a reasonable cost" (FTC, 2006).

According to the Center for Democracy and Training (CDT), a privately funded policy group, despite the work of the FTC the protection of children online is still a serious issue (Harbour, 2006). To deal with privacy concerns on the Internet, the FTC advocates parents stay aware of what children are doing online by placing computers in open areas and using the Internet with their children (Harbour, 2006). However, it appears that parents are not heeding the advice of the FTC since 10% of 8- to 10-year-olds and 21% of 11- to 14-year-olds have Internet access in their bedrooms (Roberts et al., 2005). This raises the question as to why parents are not doing more to protect their children's online privacy. The purpose of this research is to answer this question by investigating parental awareness of laws and technologies associated with protecting children's privacy online, and usage of technologies and techniques for parental control.

2 Literature review and overview

2.1 General technologies for online privacy protection

Online privacy protection has taken two paths: (1) a technical platform (known as P3P) that allows users to set privacy preferences for automatic implementation and (2) the creation of self-regulatory "seals" of approval designed to impart trustworthiness to users. Both of these approaches were developed initially to address adult concerns about online privacy; therefore, their inherent limitation is the failure to address the more complex and more pressing need of protecting children who lack the sophistication to protect themselves.

The Platform for Privacy Preferences (P3P) created by the World Wide Web Consortium was developed to create a machine readable, common vocabulary for identifying privacy practices. P3P allows users to setup a set of privacy preferences that are then compared with a web site's privacy policy and provides feedback to the user that allows them to make better decisions on what type of personal information to release (Reagle and Cranor, 1999). This solution to online privacy protection was believed to have a great future. However, a recent technical report prepared for the FTC studying the use of P3P reports that, in general, the error rate for P3P implementation was unacceptably high, many policies were out of date, and that "it may be necessary to explore the possibilities of third-party P3P policy certification, auditing, or other measures to ensure that P3P policies are trustworthy" (Cranor et al., 2003).

Privacy seals are one type of trust seals that emerged with the growth of online resources. There are several seal programs that businesses can participate in to show their commitment to security (e.g., VeriSign), trustworthiness (e.g., TRUSTe and BBBOnLine), or privacy (e.g., BBBOn-line Privacy). For example, TRUSTe states to consumers: "When you see the TRUSTe seal, you can be assured that you have full control over the uses of your personal information to protect your privacy." Once joining the program, the business is allowed to post the third-party "seal" indicating their participation. Although seals are supposed to reassure users of web sites, studies have shown that even experienced Web users are less familiar with privacy and security seals than with the underlying concepts and technology that web sites employ, such as cookies and encryption (Cheskin, 1999). In general, only 25% of consumers seem to recognize seal features on web sites (Harris, 2001).

2.2   COPPA compliant solutions

Current solutions for meeting COPPA requirements are primarily based on seal programs, rather than technical solutions, as far as gaining parental trust. Four entities have received FTC approval as safe harbors for providing a methodology for meeting the requirements of the law: PRIVO, Children's Advertising Review Unit (CARU), ESRB Privacy Online, and TRUSTe. A safe harbor means that there are standards and procedures that have been approved by the FTC, and if a business is a member of and goes through the processes of and adopts the standards of this system, they will be assumed to have met the requirements of the law. The approved programs, generally, comprise a standard agreement to use particular means to obtain a parent's consent, providing notice, payment of fees, audits, and participation in online dispute resolution processes. The web site can then post a children's privacy seal, which indicates compliance and certification. Seals are designed to stimulate trust and increase use. However, researchers find that consumers do not view seals as effective or important (Bélanger et al., 2002; Cranor et al., 2003; Livingston, 2003; NTIA, 2002).

Considering the number of children who are online, it is surprising that no widely acceptable technical solution for verifiable parental consent has emerged in the years since COPPA was enacted. In fact, in comments to the FTC, the Motion Picture Association stated, "No widely and economically feasible verification technology even appears to be on the near horizon" (FTC, 2002). The P3P technology described earlier does not specifically address children's privacy as it does not incorporate technology for parental consent. Further, a study of children's web sites shows that only 3% of the web sites used P3P, and the privacy policies in these web sites were no better than web sites not directed toward children. As a result, the report's authors concluded that, "Given the US regulatory requirements for children's web sites, we believe it would be useful to examine the privacy practices of children's web sites in more detail in future studies" (Cranor et al., 2003).

2.3   Problem definition

For many years Congress has struggled with how to protect children online, especially as it concerns inappropriate content. The CDT criticizes laws requiring monitoring or filtering of Internet activity by web sites because of free speech and privacy concerns, and alternatively recommends the education and empowerment of parents to protect their children online (CDT, 2007). Similarly, COPPA seeks to empower parents with the legal means to protect their children's online privacy by requiring consent before web sites may collect children's personal information. Effective parental supervision, however, will depend on knowledge and technological facility. It is the goal of this research to explore the current state of parental awareness of laws and technologies, and use of tools and techniques to protect their children online. The findings are used to develop a preliminary framework of the salient factors and their inter-relationships that affect future use of a privacy protection tool. We also provide recommendations for educating parents.

3   Research approach

The goal of this research is to explore the factors that explain parents' practices regarding the use of technologies and tools to protect their children's privacy online. Given the lack of in-depth literature on this topic and of frameworks to guide the research, we conduct exploratory research with the use of focus groups consisting of parents with at least one child between the ages of 5 and 13. Focus groups provide a desirable approach to gaining insights into a research domain where limited research has been previously published or as part of a larger scale research effort (Krueger, 1994). Focus groups often allow researchers to get deeper into the topic of interest by providing more background information about the circumstances of the answer (Krueger, 1994).

3.1   Respondents

To select participants for this research, our sampling strategy included several different sources. We contacted church groups in different geographical areas, sporting (soccer) associations, and several parent–teacher associations (PTAs) from different areas. Parents from these groups were invited to participate without knowledge of focus group details (to avoid self-selection bias) except that it was related to the privacy of their children on the Internet. Four focus groups were conducted in total, one group was formed with parents belonging to a soccer association, one group with parents belonging to a PTA, and two groups each from church

Table 1
Respondent demographics

Demographic ($n = 18$)	Range	Average
Age (years)	29–48	38.6
Work experience (years)	8–26	16.6
Experience using computer (years)	6–27	16.7
Number of children	1–10	4
Number of computers at home	0–3	1.6
	Categories	Count
Gender	Male	4
	Female	14
Education	High school	5
	Two-year college	3
	Bachelor	5
	Graduate	5

groups (from two different geographical areas). Each focus group had between three and six people. After the fourth focus group was conducted no new ideas were coming from the sessions, so we concluded that saturation had been reached. We collected data from a total of 18 parents. Table 1 presents general demographics of the respondents.

The respondents had a variety of occupations (homemakers, laborers, artists, salespeople, real estate agents, supervisors, teachers, accountants, consultants, and loan officers). The ages ranged from 29 to 48 years. We had more females than males in the sample. Of the respondents, 11 browsed the web every day, 2 several times a week, 4 once a week, and 1 once or twice a month. Twelve of the parents' children browsed the web more than several times a week, three once a week, two once a month, and one never.

3.2   Focus group procedures

Before conducting the focus groups, a protocol was developed, tested, and modified several times. During the focus group sessions, parents were invited to sign a consent form and answer simple demographic questions on paper. They were then presented with the context of the study, asked an icebreaker question, and then asked questions from the protocol targeted at the research questions. Two researchers attended the focus groups, which were recorded. One of the researchers moderated the discussion and probed for further details on the answers provided when appropriate. The sessions lasted on average 60 min. The recorded focus group sessions were then transcribed into text files, which were imported into the Atlas.ti qualitative analysis software for data analysis.

3.3 Focus group coding

The first step in the analyses of the focus group data involved the development of coding categories. An initial list of categories was developed from the focus group protocol and knowledge gained during the focus group sessions (Miles and Huberman, 1994). The list was revised several times. Once the team agreed on the list of categories, two independent coders were trained on the Atlas.ti software and then asked to code one focus group session each. The unit of analysis for this coding was the individual. The coders then met with one of the researchers to compare their coding and discuss differences until agreement was reached on the categories, meanings, and future coding procedures. The coders then coded the remaining transcripts for the focus group sessions using a revised coding template, which was designed to provide structure but also flexibility in the coding for new or unexpected findings (Miles and Huberman, 1994). The inter-rater agreement between the two coders was 75.1%, which is a satisfactory level of agreement. Appendix provides a description of the final coding categories used in this chapter. The Atlas.ti software was then used to obtain tabulated results for each construct and subcategory.

4 Findings

The analysis of the data resulted in several findings. This section examines the awareness that parents exhibited on (1) the laws that protect their children, (2) the tools available to protect children's privacy online, and (3) the activities their children perform while online. The following sections will focus on risks and parental control. The final set of results focus on factors that would make parents use a privacy protection tool.

4.1 Parental awareness

4.1.1 Legal awareness
Results indicate that parents are not aware of COPPA and the legal requirement of web sites to gain parental consent for collecting personally identifiable information. None of the respondents indicated any knowledge of COPPA. As one individual suggested, parents will try to see if laws are available only if a problem occurs:

> *I think there should be, but I'm not aware … when the problem doesn't come I don't do it, but when the problem does come I do some research …*

Of all the respondents present, when asked about any laws pertaining to children on the Internet, two parents had very vague knowledge of some aspects of the laws. None of the parents knew where to report fraudulent web activity (i.e., to the Federal Trade Commission, FTC).

> *I was just thinking the laws about becoming a predator and the laws that are associated with that. So that's basically what I was thinking about the laws. Other than that …*

4.1.2   Tools and technology awareness

As discussed in the beginning of this chapter, there are four safe harbor programs approved by the FTC for COPPA compliance. We asked respondents to rate their level of knowledge of those programs. As shown in Table 2, parents are not aware of the safe harbor means or seals used by web sites to convey their compliance.

Although not aware of the laws and the FTC approved compliance programs, some of the parents at least recognized some other seals or tools (not specifically privacy-protecting tools) available to them for online protection. In particular, some recognized VeriSign and Net Nanny as demonstrated in Table 3. VeriSign provides security measures for sharing sensitive information, and Net Nanny is content filtering software. Few are familiar with P3P or AT&T Privacy Bird. AT&T Privacy Bird is a web browser plug-in that communicates to the user the differences between his/her privacy settings and the policies of a web site. The users can then decide for themselves if they want to continue using the site (Cranor et al., 2006).

Table 2
Awareness levels of FTC approved trust seals ($n = 18$)

Ratings	PRIVO	ESRB	CARU	TRUSTe
Never heard of it	17	17	18	16
Vaguely heard of it	1	1	0	2
I know about this but do not use it	0	0	0	0
I have used it once	0	0	0	0
I use it regularly	0	0	0	0

Table 3
Awareness levels: distribution of respondents ($n = 13$)

Ratings	P3P	AT&T Privacy Bird	Net Nanny	VeriSign
Never heard of it	12	11	6	9
Vaguely heard of it	1	2	5	3
I know about this but do not use it	0	0	1	0
I have used it once	0	0	0	0
I use it regularly	0	0	1	1

Overall, it appears that few parents are aware of privacy protection tools or practices available to protect their children's privacy online.

So I know that there are some safety features that we can implement that we haven't.

I just vaguely heard about it somewhere, I don't even know where. Just had a conversation or something ...

4.1.3 Online activities awareness

Finally, regarding what children do online, most parents admit to know only some of the web sites children go to. None of them knew if merchants do anything to protect their children's privacy online. When asked about whether they believe their children were asked to provide information, most said they believe so, and a few respondents provided examples. Several parents indicated their children were instructed to put the parent's e-mail in when asked.

A lot of the motocross ones just for instance you have to put your own email address before it will show you anything.

I think that she likes to go the American girl website and I think on that they ask for their age or that type [of] thing.

I tell him to put mine. I mean for that he asks though but they won't give him [any] information until there's an email address.

Many of the parents lamented the fact that so many web sites their children visit require an e-mail address before the children can access the information they are seeking on those web sites.

4.2 Perceived risks

Parents were asked what dangers they believe their children faced on the Internet. Although we left the question open ended, four of the parents specifically mentioned predators on the Internet. The other major category that emerged from the focus group data for the perceived risks was concerns about children sharing information online. These concerns were often voiced more toward predators, again, then toward their children's privacy in general. Many of the parents identified MySpace as a particularly troublesome web site. MySpace is a social networking site that allows individuals to post commentary and pictures.

... like a blog and she's just going ahead and typing all this stuff ... I was like you can't do this type of stuff. She was telling everything that happened that day. At school, who she talked to, you know the neighborhood she lived in. I mean if someone wanted to target that child she was wide open. It just freaked me out.

That's the problem with MySpace.

4.3   Parental control

Parents were asked how they control what their children do online and what tools they use to protect their privacy. Responses varied significantly, but we found several key themes. We discuss two main control mechanisms used by parents: technologies and tools and techniques.

4.3.1   Technologies and tools

Several parents use passwords as a means to "protect" their children online. Four respondents stated that their computers are password protected, preventing their children from using the computers without their knowledge.

> *My wife and I, and one of us has to physically logon to the computer for our kids to use it. So we already know where we've been and where they've been.*

Other parents stated that they use some form of logging software, meaning that they look at which web sites their children have visited. At least two parents mentioned warning their children about their ability to see which web sites they have visited (although acknowledging to us they did not necessarily have the skills to). Another parent says he looks at the cookies from the web sites his children have visited. One parent mentioned the name of the software used: Content Protect.

> *We actually use a program called 'Content Protect' that actually is password protected and when they go in there, they have to put a password in that actually identifies at least who is online. That program actually records everything that happens. It can record all their IMs. It records what websites they see. It also can restrict them as to what timeframes they can be on the Internet. [It] still doesn't automatically protect them from identifying themselves and we've had some discussions with our older ones particularly about [putting] identifying information on, so that they are aware of the dangers that exist with that.*

When this parent was asked how he found out about this tool, it became clear the parent made an extra effort to find tools when he became aware of threats.

> *I was concerned about what my kids [accessed] online so ... So I just started doing web searches [to see] what tools are out there to be able to do that. I felt for me Content Protect was the best tool. I did look at Web Nanny [Net Nanny] as well ...*

Overall, few parents knew or used tools beyond password protection. As one parent explained, it is often the effort to install and manage the software that prevents them from using it. Other times, the parents do not have technical expertise to do this. As seen in the second quote, one parent believed that Norton Antivirus would protect their children from bad content on the Internet.

> *Web Nanny [Net Nanny]. We've used it before. And [when we switched to a] different computer it didn't get loaded. [I] don't know what happened to it.*

We have the virus scan and things like the protection that is supposedly with the computer and upgraded the security like Norton.

4.3.2 Techniques

Although not often using technologies and tools, parents do use various techniques that are not computer-related to have some level of control over their children's activities and privacy online. Five of the 18 respondents suggested that the computers are in plain view in their home, limiting what children would do. However, as one parent suggested, that is often not considered enough.

We [have] 2 laptops and 2 desktops and 2 desktops are in 1 room so that I can watch and those are the ones I allow the kids to get on.

I would agree parental supervision and software but there needs to be more because [with] 5 children I can't be everywhere.

The real issue for many of the parents is that they do not actually control what their children do online, but they rely on trusting that their children will do the right things, according to parental instructions. A surprising number of respondents indicated that while they trust their children they somehow know that they should not.

When my daughter wants to use the computer, she asks me and tells me the purpose. Usually I think she will only do what I have consented to. Right now it's OK, but in the future I'm afraid that once she finds something that's interesting or that makes her very very excited ... I would lose control ... And I can't promise that she won't let out any information that I don't want her to let out. So although I just told her not to give her personal information ... I don't know for sure if she won't in the future.

Trust I guess. Our computer is downstairs. But again we can always back into her room and check it. I know all her passwords and to get online for her email or anything like that.

We're just too trustworthy I think. We just expect our kids to walk that line.

4.4 Usage factors

As part of the research, we are interested in establishing requirements for a tool that would provide parents with more control over their children's online privacy. As a result, we asked parents what would make them start to use a tool that would protect their children's privacy online. The 18 parents combined made 37 statements specifically discussing such usage factors. The analysis of these comments revealed several key factors, as illustrated in Table 4.

Table 4
Privacy protection tool usage factors

	Parents will use a privacy protection tool if	Number of comments	Percentage of comments
1	... it requires little effort (easy to use)	16	43
2	... it is easy to modify its settings	5	14
3	... it is needed because the regulations in place protect their child	3	8
4	... log files are available (but can be turned on and off)	3	8
5	... it gives them more control over the consent they give for web sites their children visit	2	5
6	... it is efficient to use (cost–benefit)	2	5
7	... it provides a list of pre-approved web sites (convenience)	2	5
8	... it gives them more control over their children's privacy	1	3
9	... they believe that others they know are using it	1	3
10	... it is also implemented in schools	1	3
11	... it is downloadable (cannot be lost)	1	3
	Total	37	

5 Discussion

COPPA was passed with the intention to protect children by granting parents legal rights to control the information flows from their children to commercial web sites. Education and technology are meant to empower these parental rights (Harbour, 2006). Our findings, however, illustrate that parents are unaware of the laws, regulations, and technologies available to protect their children's privacy online.

The results from the focus groups provide insights into what causes parents to use techniques or technological tools to protect their children's privacy. The emergent model from the data analysis consists of technology adoption factors, behavioral adoption factors, and awareness factors that lead to privacy protection behaviors, both technological and non-technological. Figure 1 summarizes the findings of this study, presenting an emergent model of factors important in the use of privacy protection tools and techniques by parents to protect their children's privacy in online environments. The following section describes this emergent model in further detail, giving examples from the focus groups to explain how each construct fits in the model.

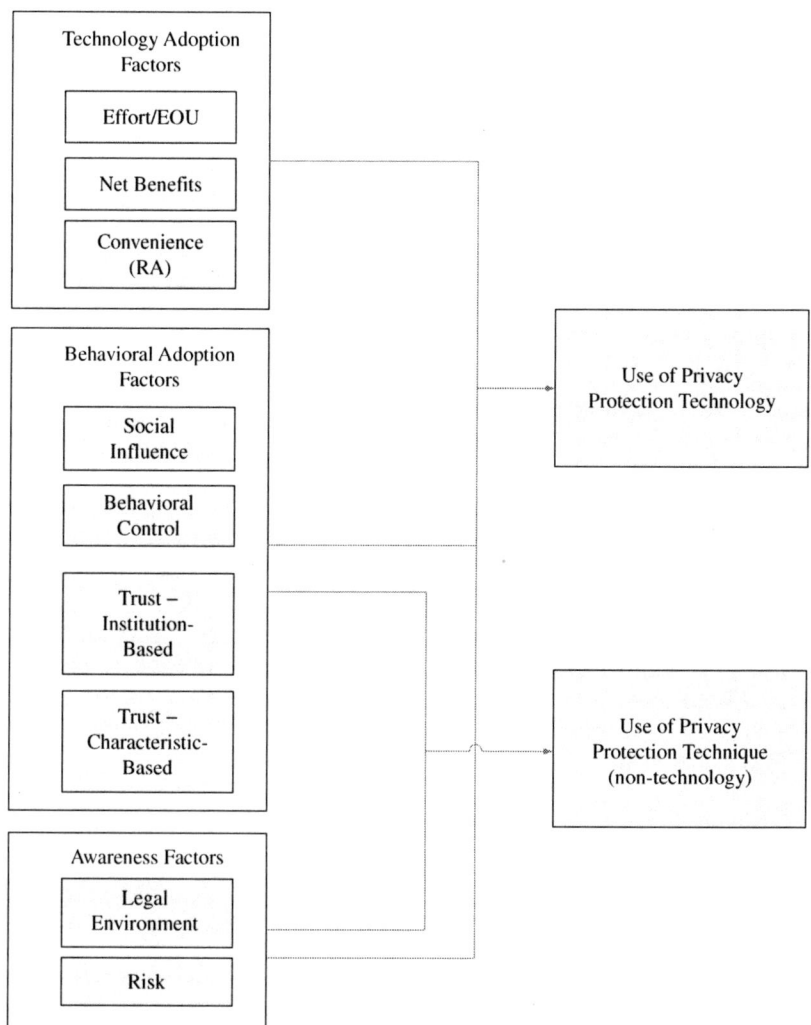

Fig. 1.   Emergent privacy protection model.

5.1   *Privacy protection behaviors*

There were two privacy protection behaviors that were identified as being used by parents—technological and non-technological. Most parents do not currently use privacy protection technologies, which consist of software and hardware solutions to protect privacy. However, our findings did show that parents had varying techniques for trying to control their children's privacy, which we refer to as privacy protection techniques. Our proposed model, therefore, contains usage of both technological tools and techniques for protecting children's privacy.

5.2   Technology adoption factors

Technology adoption models regularly show that several factors lead to use of a technology (Venkatesh et al., 2003). In the course of our focus groups a number of technology adoption factors emerged—effort/ease of use, net benefits, and relative advantage. In the proposed model, these technology adoption factors are expected to impact use of privacy protection technologies and tools, but not use of privacy protection techniques (non-technology based).

5.2.1   Effort/ease of use

Parents commented many times that for them to use a tool to protect their children's privacy it needed to be easy to use (mentioned 16 times) and easy to modify when needed (mentioned 5 times). Examples of these comments are provided later. Again, this is consistent with several technology adoption models, such as the Technology Acceptance Model (Davis, 1989) or the Unified Theory of Acceptance and Use of Technology UTAUT (Venkatesh et al., 2003). Effort or ease of use is defined in these models *as the degree of ease associated with the use of the privacy protection tool* (Venkatesh et al., 2003).

Yeah same reason we forget to use everything else. [We] work with multiple computers [and] it's too hard to keep up with stuff.

I think only if it isn't working or if it is too difficult to get into on a regular basis it just becomes a nuisance.

There are many features of a privacy protection tool needed to ensure it is easy to use by parents. For example, error messages have to be clear and not overwhelming for parents; there should be few clicks required for parents to both install and make use of the tool, and there should be no further action required after initial installation unless the parents want to change their policies. More features should be implemented by looking at the field of Human–Computer Interaction (HCI), where research on making systems easy to use abounds.

5.2.2   Net benefits

Parents indicated the benefit of using a technology to protect their children's privacy was impacted by the cost of acquiring that technology. If a privacy protection tool would be made available for free, they thought it was an easy decision to choose to use it. Although cost could be considered a factor by itself, the idea of cost versus features is better captured by the net benefits construct, which captures the balances of positive and negative impacts of the technology (DeLone and McLean, 2003).

R4: I think you'd have to compare the cost to what else is out there. And the features to what else is out there.

F1 (facilitator): What if it's free?

R4: I think at that point it's a slam dunk. I mean if it's free ...

Since parents are concerned about the costs/benefits of a privacy protection tool, it would be important to make such a tool available at limited costs, if possible. Further, beyond acquisition, the support provided for this tool needs to be cost effective/beneficial as well. To accomplish this, it is first necessary that the software is designed as simply as possible. In doing so, it should eliminate the need for most technical support. In addition to this, we also recommend that the FTC find a way to require children's web sites to provide a support mechanism. A privacy protection tool that helps merchants to be COPPA compliant should be worth providing them the financial support necessary to offer technical support to users who are trying to use the privacy protection tool since such a tool would ensure they are complying with COPPA and not subject to potential fines.

5.2.3 Convenience/relative advantage

Parents indicated that whatever additional software they added to their computer should not cause added steps to the login process as that would not be better than what they were previously doing. They also mentioned that the software would have to have certain features, such as log files that can be turned off (so children would not see the logs of their parents' activities), lists of pre-approved web sites (so they would spend less time approving web sites at first), and a downloadable product (so they could get it again easily if they "lost it"). These convenience factors can be represented by the relative advantage construct, which refers to *the perception that a new innovation is better than what was used before it* (Moore and Benbasat, 1991; Venkatesh et al., 2003).

At least something you can download. I lost the software for the other somewhere.

The relative advantage of using a privacy protection tool needs to be thought of as both over the current state of practices (re: using no tools), as well as over existing tools. For example, using a privacy protection tool needs to provide an advantage over having computers in the same room or having parents present when children are using the Internet. It also needs to provide an advantage over such tools as AT&T Privacy Bird and "seal" programs.

5.3 Behavioral adoption factors

Behavioral adoption describes why people perform certain behaviors (Fishbein and Ajzen, 1975). Three behavioral adoption factors became apparent during our focus groups social influence, behavioral control, and trust. Behavioral adoption factors are expected to impact both the use of privacy protection technologies and the use of privacy protection techniques.

5.3.1 Social influence

Parents in our focus groups indicated that one way to get them to use a privacy protection tool or technique would be through the influence of others. This is consistent with prior research where social influence is predicted to affect technology usage. Social influence can be defined as *the degree to which an individual perceives that others who are deemed important to him or her believe that he or she should use the privacy protection tool* (Venkatesh et al., 2003).

> *If this was something like the don't drink, don't smoke, don't talk to strangers ads that came on TV or that was distributed through schools. Or the schools have educational websites that they let the kids go to during rainy days at recess. If this was something that the kids got excited about and were like hey! Like McGruff or Smokey the Bear or anything else. Mom dad this [tool] I heard about it at school we really need to put it on the computer. What better way to get us to do it.*

There are several "types" of social influences that could be considered for ensuring that parents use a privacy protection tool. First and foremost, parents might be influenced by other parents who find the tool or technique useful. For this to happen, however, parents must be made aware of both the tool and who uses it. This could be a good role for PTAs. It could also be that parents are influenced by schools. If a privacy protection tool or technique becomes widely implemented in schools, and parents become aware of this, they may be more prone to use them as well.

5.3.2 Behavioral control

The behavioral control construct refers to the internal and external constraints on a person's behavior and encompasses self-efficacy (Taylor and Todd, 1995; Venkatesh et al., 2003). Self-efficacy is the confidence a person has in their ability to use technology to complete a certain task (Compeau and Higgins, 1995; Venkatesh et al., 2003). In the case of this study, self-efficacy is the confidence parents have in their ability to use software to protect their children's privacy. When asked if they used any software to protect their children's privacy or filter the web sites they visited, parents often indicated that they wanted to but did not know how. However, parents indicated their desire for control over both their children's privacy and the consent they give to web sites (see Table 4).

> *No, but I want to. As she gets older I want to. I don't know how to though.*

Self-efficacy has been shown in prior research to influence use intentions. Fortunately, self-efficacy can be increased with proper training. As a result, it is recommended that parents be trained on both computer-related topics and topics specifically related to the privacy protection tool that could be used to protect Children's Online Privacy. As self-efficacy is improved, parents will have a higher sense of behavioral control, and will be more likely to use the privacy protection tool.

5.3.3   Trust

In the study, trust appeared to impact use of privacy protection tools and techniques in two very different ways. On the one hand, parents indicated that they trusted their children, and therefore did not feel the need to use privacy protection tools and techniques. On the other hand, parents indicated that they needed to trust the software to watch what their kids were doing. Two types of trust can then be considered important to the use of privacy protection tools. Institution-based trust refers to *an individual's perceptions of the institutional environment, including the structures and regulations that make an environment feel safe* (McKnight et al., 2002). In this case, this would refer to the privacy protection tool and its ability to meet regulations. Characteristic-based trust (CBT) refers to *one's belief in the integrity and ability of the trustee* (McKnight et al., 2002). In this case, this would involve the trust of the parent in his child to be aware and capable of dealing with the threats to their own privacy.

> *Software[and computers] in general. [T]here's always a way around things [or] a glitch in something. I have a hard time trusting something [or] any other mechanism to watch what my kids are doing. I have a hard time trusting it to do what it says it does.*

Institution-based trust may increase by utilization of an already recognized brand, for example, VeriSign or Microsoft, as a trusted third party (TTP). The association of a well-known company with a children's privacy tool may help parents accept that it is a trustworthy program. To address characteristic-based trust we recommend increased parental education concerning the necessity of communication with their children regarding Internet usage and privacy. We also recommend increased information dispersion for parents about how they can review history and logs to trace children's actions on their personal computers.

5.4   Awareness factors

As previously discussed, parents are not aware of the laws or risks relating to children's privacy. Without an understanding of either of these aspects, it is unlikely that parents would take necessary measures to protect their children's privacy. The results from the focus groups confirm this as both awareness and usage were low. As such, awareness is a necessary determinant of both use of privacy protection technology and use of privacy protection techniques.

To educate parents and make them aware of the laws and risks relating to children's privacy, we provide two recommendations. First, although the FTC currently has resources to inform parents of the importance of their children's privacy, our research shows that the parents are not aware of this information. Similar to the approach the Virginia Legislature has taken, we recommend the dissemination of Internet safety information through the public schools. Under Virginia Code Section 22.1–70.2, each school superintendent must have a plan for integrating Internet safety instruction into the curriculum. The Virginia Department of Education issued guidelines for meeting this requirement, which include a major emphasis on the education of parents, as well as children. It states that "Although a school's legal responsibility does not extend to home Internet use, school leaders can help prevent tragic situations by ensuring parents and students are well-informed." Secondly, we recommend the use of a multimedia approach including television, radio, billboards, and the Internet to raise the awareness of parents. The campaign could be similar to the antismoking campaigns that raise awareness about the dangers of smoking; the recommended campaign could achieve an increased parental awareness about the dangers to children on the Internet.

6 Conclusion

As the number of children using the Internet continues to grow, protecting their privacy becomes an ever more pressing issue. Parents have a key role to play in ensuring children are protected. Yet, as demonstrated in this study, few parents are aware of the laws and technologies available to perform this. This study proposes an emergent framework as a result of focus groups conducted with parents. The framework can serve as a starting point to explore factors that can help to ensure that parents are aware of the privacy protection laws and technologies, and use appropriate tools for their children in the online environment.

7 Questions for discussion

1. Is it possible for parents and educators to take interest in technologies to protect children's online privacy and make it happen?
2. How can the government encourage web sites to become COPPA compliant? To adopt technologies that enforce COPPA?
3. What is the role of industry self-regulation in protecting children's privacy online? What is the ethical responsibility of businesses to protect children?

4. What is the best way to educate parents and educators about children's online privacy rights? What is the best way to educate parents and educators about tools available to protect children's privacy online?
5. How is children's privacy different from adult's privacy?
6. Should COPPA be extended beyond children under the age of 13? Why or why not?
7. What strategies would you recommend to parents about discussing online privacy with their children?
8. In the case of children's online privacy, it is often the case that their information is either voluntarily disclosed or finagled by self-serving individuals on social networking web sites. Please discuss how web sites might go about balancing the protection/collection of information from minors while maintaining the functionality and privacy needs that an adult subscriber requires.

Acknowledgment

This research is supported in part by NSF grant CNS-0524052. The authors would like to thank Karthik Channakeshava and Kaigui Bian for their work on this project.

Glossary

AT&T Privacy Bird: A web browser addition that communicates to the user the differences between his/her privacy settings and the policies of a web site.

Atlas.ti: Software to conduct qualitative analysis of data collected.

Behavioral control: The internal and external constraints on a person's behavior.

Characteristic-based trust (CBT): One's belief in the integrity and ability of the trustee.

Children's Advertising Review Unit (CARU): An FTC approved children privacy trust seal.

Children's Online Privacy Protection Act (COPPA): Prohibits web sites from collecting information from children under 13 years without verifiable parental consent.

Cookies: A small text file stored on a personal computer that contains information browsers use, such as userIDs, passwords, and other information the user has entered on web sites.

Effort or ease of use: The degree of ease associated with the use of the privacy protection tool.

Entertainment Software Rating Board (ESRB) Privacy Online: A non-for-profit self-regulatory organization. An FTC approved children privacy trust seal.

Focus group: A methodology that uses small groups of four to six individuals who are asked questions to gain insights into a research topic.

Institution-based trust (IBT): An individual's perceptions of the institutional environment, including the structures and regulations that make an environment feel safe.

MySpace: A social networking web site that allows individuals to post pictures and commentaries.

Net benefits: The balances of positive and negative impacts of the technology.

Net Nanny: Content filtering software, which allows parents to control which web sites kids visit.

Platform for Privacy Preferences (P3P): Created by the World Wide Web Consortium. Used to create a machine readable, common vocabulary for setting up a set of privacy preferences that are then compared with a web site's privacy policy to provide feedback to the user who can decide what type of personal information to release.

Privacy: The ability of the individual to control information about oneself.

Privacy policy: Statement located on an organization's web site describing its policies regarding privacy of the users, including which information is collected, how, and with whom it is shared (or not).

Privacy seals: A type of trust seal that indicates a web site follows a set of privacy practices. Once joining the program, the business is allowed to post the third-party "seal" indicating their participation.

PRIVO: Privacy Vaults Online, Inc. has a proprietary technology platform. An FTC approved children privacy trust seal.

Relative advantage: The perception that a new innovation is better than what was used before it.

Safe harbor: Exists when an organization follows the standards and procedures approved by the FTC and is therefore assumed to have met the requirements of the law.

Self-efficacy: Confidence a person has in their ability to use technology to complete a certain task.

Social influence: The degree to which an individual perceives that others who are deemed important to him or her believe that he or she should use the privacy protection tool.

TRUSTe: An independent nonprofit organization. An FTC approved children privacy trust seal.

VeriSign: A company based in California that provides a variety of security and telecom services ranging from digital certificates to downloadable digital content for mobile devices.

References

Bélanger, F., J. Hiller, W.J. Smith (2002). Trustworthiness in e-commerce: the role of privacy, security, and site attributes. *Journal of Strategic Information Systems* 11(3/4), 245–270.

CDT (2007). *Child Safety and Free Speech Issues in the 110th Congress*, p. 10. Center for Democracy and Technology, Washington DC.

Cheskin (1999). Ecommerce trust study. Cheskin Research and Studio Archetype/Sapient. Available at http://www.cheskin.com/cms/files/i/articles/17__report-eComm%20Trust1999.pdf. Accessed on March 25, 2009.

Compeau, D.R., C.A. Higgins (1995). Computer self-efficacy: development of a measure and initial test. *MIS Quarterly* 19(2), p. 189.

Cranor, L.F., S. Byers, D. Kormann (2003). An analysis of P3p deployment on commercial, government, and children's web sites as of May 2003. Technical Report Prepared for the 14 May 2003 Federal Trade Commission Workshop on Technologies for Protecting Personal Information, AT&T Labs-Research, Florham Park, NJ.

Cranor, L.F., P. Guduru, M. Arjula (2006). User interfaces for privacy agents. *ACM Transactions on Computer-Human Interaction* 13(2), p. 135.

Davis, F.D. (1989). Perceived usefulness, perceived ease of use and user acceptance of information technology. *MIS Quarterly* 13(3), 319–340.

DeLone, W.H., E.R. McLean (2003). The Delone and Mclean model of information systems success: a ten-year update. *Journal of Management Information Systems* 19(4), p. 9.

Fishbein, M., I. Ajzen (1975). *Belief, Attitude, Intention and Behavior: An Introduction to Theory and Research.* Addison-Wesley Publishing Company, Reading, MA.

FTC (2002). Children's online privacy protection rule: final rule amendment. *Federal Register Rules and Regulations, 16 CFR Part 312*, April 17.

FTC (2006). Retention of rule without modification. Available at http://ftc.gov/os/2006/03/P054505 COPPARuleRetention.pdf. Accessed on January 19, 2007.

Harbour, P.J. (2006). Prepared Statement of the Federal Trade Commission before the Subcommittee on the Oversights of the Committee on Energy and Commerce. Washington, DC, June 28, p. 9.

Harris (2001). Why some companies are trusted and others are not: personal experience and knowledge of company more important than glitz. *Harris Interactive*, June.

Kawamoto, D. (2004). VeriSign works to id kid surfers. *Cnet News.* Vol. 2004.

Krueger, R.A. (1994). *Focus Groups: A Practical Guide for Applied Research*. 2nd ed. SAGE Publications, Inc, Thousand Oaks, CA.

Livingston, S. (2003). Children's use of the Internet: reflections on the emerging research agenda. *New Media & Society* 5, 147–166.

McKnight, D.H., V. Choudhury, C. Kacmar (2002). Developing and validating trust measures for e-commerce: an integrative approach. *Information Systems Research* 13(3), 334–359.

Miles, M.B., A.M. Huberman (1994). *Qualitative Data Analysis: An Expanded Sourcebook*. Sage Publications, Thousand Oaks, CA.

Moore, G., I. Benbasat (1991). Development of an instrument to measure the perceptions of adopting an information technology innovation. *Information Systems Research* 2(3), 192–222.

NTIA (2002). A nation online: entering the broadband age. *Economics and Statistics Administration* 6 (February). Available at http://www.ntia.doc.gov/ntiahome/dn/index.html. Accessed on February 25, 2004.

Reagle, J., L.F. Cranor (1999). The platform for privacy preferences. *Association for Computing Machinery. Communications of the ACM* 42(2), p. 48.

Roberts, D.F., U.G., Foehr, V. Rideout (2005). Generation M: media in the lives of 8–18 year olds. A Kaiser Family Foundation Study, p. 145.

Taylor, S., P.A. Todd (1995). Understanding information technology usage-a test of competing models. *Information Systems Research* 6(2), 144–176.

Turow, J. (2001). Privacy Policies on Children's Websites: Do They Play by the Rules? The Annenberg Public Policy Center of the University of Pennsylvania Report Series No. 38, March.

Venkatesh, V., M. Morris, G. Davis, F. Davis (2003). User acceptance of information technology: toward a unified view. *MIS Quarterly* 27(3), 425–478.

Suggested readings

Cantos, L., L. Fine, N. Porcelli, S.E. Selby (2001a). FTC approves first COPPA "safe harbor" application. *Intellectual Property & Technology Law Journal* 13(4), p. 24.

Cantos, L., J. Linn, N. Porcelli, S. Selby (2001b). FTC announces settlements with three Web sites charged with violating COPPA. *Intellectual Property & Technology Law Journal* 13(7), p. 22.

Cranor, L.F. (2003). P3P: making privacy policies more useful. *IEEE Security and Privacy* 1(6), 50–55.

Davis, J.J. (2002). Marketing to children online: a manager's guide to the children's online privacy protection act. *S.A.M. Advanced Management Journal* 67(4), p. 11.

Parke, R.D., D.B. Sawin (1979). Children's privacy in the home: developmental, ecological, and child-rearing determinants. *Environment and Behavior* 11(1), 87–104.

Online resources

Article about Xanga.com fine. Available at http://www.ftc.gov/opa/2006/09/xanga.shtm

Fact Sheet 21: Children's Online Privacy. Available at http://www.privacyrights.org/fs/fs21-children.htm.

FTC website on COPPA. Available at http://ftc.gov/privacy/privacyinitiatives/childrens.html

Kidz Privacy. Available at www.ftc.gov/bcp/conline/edcams/kidzprivacy/

Researchers' website. Available at http://www.pocket.ece.vt.edu/

Appendix. Description of relevant coding categories

Construct	Subcategory level 1	Subcategory level 2	Description
Parental awareness	Laws	COPPA	Parents are aware (coded positive) or not aware (coded negative) of the COPPA law
		Other	Other laws parents are aware of related to Internet and privacy
	Risks	Predators	Awareness of parents of risk to children on Internet related to predators
		Sharing info	Awareness of parents of risk to children on Internet related to them sharing information
	Child activities	Positive/negative	Parents are aware (coded positive) or not aware (coded negative) of what their children do on the Internet
		Partial	Parents partially aware of what children do on the Internet
		Sharing info	Parents are aware of children sharing their information
	Support		Parents were provided with support or information about how to control what their children do on the Internet
	Tools		Parents are aware of tools to protect their children online
Parental control	Computer in view		Parents control what children do by having computer in view
	No control	Trust	Parents do not control children use of Internet but trust them
	No control		Parents do not control children's use of Internet
	Software		Parents use software to control web sites children have access to
Consent	Yes/no		Parents have provided (not provided) some form of consent for their children to visit certain web sites

Usage Factors

Parents will use a privacy tool if they believe that

Effort		... using it requires little effort (easy to use)
Convenience	Registration	... the registration process is easy
	Modification	... it is easy to modify its settings
Control	Parental consent	... it gives them more control over the consent they give for web sites children visit
	Privacy	... it gives them more control over their children's privacy
	Web sites visited	... the web sites their children visit are trustworthy
Trustworthiness	Privacy tool	... it is trustworthy
Tech support		... technical support is available to help them
Social influence		... other parents they know are using it
Regulations	Protect child	... the regulations in place protect their child
	Enforcement	... it enforces the regulations in place
Efficiency		... it is efficient to use
Other desirable characteristics		... other characteristics of a privacy tool that are desirable to parents

Rao & Upadhyaya, Eds., *Handbooks in Information Systems, Vol. 4*
Copyright © 2009 by Emerald Group Publishing Limited

Chapter 12

Usable Mandatory Access Control for Operating Systems

Ninghui Li, Ziqing Mao and Hong Chen

Department of Computer Science and Center for Education and Research in Information Assurance and Security, Purdue University, 305 N. University Street, West Lafayette, IN 47907-2107, USA

Abstract

Modern operating systems primarily use discretionary access control (DAC) to protect files and other operating system resources. DAC mechanisms are more user-friendly than mandatory access control (MAC) systems, but are vulnerable to Trojan horse attacks and attacks exploiting buggy software. However, existing MAC systems for operating systems are difficult to use. We identify several principles for designing usable access control systems and introduce the usable mandatory integrity protection (UMIP) model that adds usable MAC to operating systems.

1 Introduction

Today's computer systems support multiple users and are connected to the Internet. Therefore, today's operating systems need to use access control mechanisms to protect both system resources and user data. Modern commercial off the shelf operating systems use discretionary access control (DAC) to protect files and other operating system resources. According to the Trusted Computer System Evaluation Criteria (TCSEC, 1985) (often referred to as the Orange Book), DAC is "a means of restricting access to objects based on the identity of subjects and/or groups to which they belong. The controls are discretionary in the sense that a subject with a certain access permission is capable of passing that permission (perhaps indirectly) on to any other subject (unless restrained by mandatory access control)."

It has been known since early 1970s that DAC is vulnerable to Trojan horses. A Trojan horse, or simply a Trojan, is a piece of malicious software that in addition to performing some apparently benign and useful actions, also performs hidden, malicious actions. Such Trojans may come from email attachments, removable media such as USB thumb drives, or files downloaded from the Internet. By planting a Trojan, an attacker can get access to resources the attacker is not authorized under the DAC policy, and is often able to abuse such privileges to take over the host or to obtain private information. DAC is also vulnerable when one runs buggy programs that receive malicious inputs. For example, a network-facing server daemon may receive packets with corrupted data, a web browser may visit malicious web pages, and a media player may read malformed data stored on a shared drive. An attacker can form the input in a way to exploit the bugs in these programs and take over the processes running them, for example, by injecting malicious code. In essence, a buggy program that takes malicious input can become a Trojan horse.

This vulnerability of DAC is a key reason that today's computer hosts are easily compromised. Host compromise, in turn, leads to a number of other serious computer security problems today. Computer worms propagate by first compromising vulnerable hosts and then propagating to other hosts. Compromised hosts may be organized under a common command and control infrastructure, forming botnets. Botnets can then be used for carrying out attacks such as phishing, spamming, and distributed denial of service. To effectively counter these threats, one needs to address the root cause of these threats, namely, the vulnerability of end hosts.

There are a lot of research efforts trying to improve or supplement the existing DAC mechanisms to make end hosts more difficult to be compromised. Most approaches add some form of mandatory access control (MAC), for example, Janus (Goldberg, 1996), DTE Unix (Badger et al., 1995a,b), Linux intrusion detection system (LIDS, see http://www.lids.org/), LOMAC (Fraser, 2000), systrace (Provos, 2003), AppArmor (see http://www.novell.com/linux/security/apparmor/ for Apparmor application security for Linux; Cowan et al., 2000), and security-enhanced Linux (SELinux) (NSA, see http://www.nsa.gov/selinux/). Several of these systems are flexible and powerful. Through proper configuration, they could result in highly secure systems. However, they are also complex and intimidating to configure, making them difficult to be used by end users.

In this chapter, we tackle the problem of enhancing DAC mechanisms to be able to defend against threats posed by Trojan horses and buggy software. While doing so, we identify several principles for designing usable access control mechanisms in general. Our focus is the usable mandatory integrity protection (UMIP) model, which was designed following these principles.

2   Literature review/overview of the field

We now provide an overview of various access control mechanisms in operating systems.

2.1 Unix access control

Perhaps the best-known DAC mechanism is the DAC system in the Unix family of operating systems (including Linux, Solaris, OpenBSD, and others). This DAC mechanism has many intricate details. Because of the space limit, we can cover only the features that are most relevant to its security and usability.

Three most important concepts in this DAC system are users, subjects, and objects. From the computer's point of view, each account is a user. Each user is uniquely identified by a user id. There is a special user called root; it has user id 0. A user can be a member of several groups, which contains a set of users as its members. Every group has a numerical id call group id. Each subject is a process; it issues requests to access resources. Many protected resources are modeled as files, which we call objects. Users can configure the DAC system to specify which users are allowed to access the files. For nonfile privileges, the access policy is generally fixed by the system. In most systems, only the root user has these privileges. In the descriptions later, we use subjects and processes interchangeably, and objects and files interchangeably. We dissect the UNIX DAC system into two components: the policy specification component and the enforcement component.

The policy component determines which users are allowed to access what objects. Each object has an owner (which is a user) and an associated group. In addition, each object has 12 permission bits. These bits are

- three bits for determining whether the owner of the file can read/write/execute the file,
- three bits for determining whether users in the associated group (other than the owner) can read/write/execute the file,
- three bits for determining whether all other users can read/write/execute the file,
- the SUID (set user id) bit, the SGID (set group id) bit, and the sticky bit. Only the SUID bit is relevant for our discussions later.

The file owner, group, and permission bits are part of the metadata of a file, and are stored on the inode of a file. The owner of a file and the root user can update these permission bits, which is the discretionary feature. In most modern UNIX-based systems, only the root can change the owner of a file.

The policy component specifies only which users are authorized, whereas the actual requests are generated by subjects (processes) and not users. The enforcement component fills in this gap; it tries to determine on which users' behalf a process is executing. Each process has an effective user id (euid), which determines the access privileges of the process. The first process in the system has euid 0 (root). When a user logs in, the process's euid is set to the id corresponding to the user. When a process loads a binary through the *execve* system call, the new euid is unchanged except when the binary file has the SUID bit set, in which case the new euid is the owner of the file.

The SUID bit is needed for two reasons. First, the granularity of access control using files is not fined-grained enough. For example, the password information of all the users is stored in the file /etc/shadow. A user should be allowed to change her password; however, we cannot allow normal users to write the shadow file, as they can then change the passwords of other users as well. To solve this problem, the system has a special utility program (*passwd*), through which a user can change her password. The program is owned by the root user and has its SUID bit set. When a user runs the *passwd* program, the new process has euid root and can change /etc/shadow to update the user's password. Note that this process (initiated by a user) can perform anything the root user is authorized to do. By setting the SUID bit on the *passwd* program, the system administrator (i.e., the root user) trusts that the program performs only the legitimate operations. That is, it will authenticate a user and change only that user's password in /etc/shadow. Any program with SUID bit set must therefore be carefully written so that they do not contain vulnerabilities to be exploited.

Second, nonroot users often need to use the nonfile privileges. For example, a user may need to mount a CD, which requires a nonfile privilege that is available only to the root user. This requires the mount utility program to be owned by root and has the SUID bit set.

2.2   Trojan horses and buggy programs

Recall that in UNIX access control, when a process loads a new binary file, the euid remains unchanged by default. This means that when a user runs a program, the resulted process can do anything the user is allowed to do. If the program is created by an attacker, that is, is a Trojan horse, then the security objective of DAC protection may be violated, as this amounts to giving the user's account to the attacker.

DAC is also vulnerable when one runs buggy programs that receive malicious inputs. For example, a network-facing server daemon may receive packets with corrupted data, a web browser might visit malicious web pages, and a media player can read malformed data stored on a shared drive. An attacker can form the input in a way to exploit the bugs in these programs and take over the processes running them, for example, by injecting malicious code. In essence, a buggy program that takes malicious input can become a Trojan horse.

2.3   Windows access control

In the Microsoft Windows family of operating systems, the privileges of a process are determined by the access token the process possesses. When a user logs in, either locally or remotely, the operating system will create an access token for the user's processes. The token includes a security id (SID) representing the user, and several SIDs representing the user's groups. When a process attempts to access some resource, the operating system will decide if the access is granted based on the access token of the process.

A problem with this access control mechanism is that the user's processes are given the full privileges when the user is logged in. Given the popularity of windows system in end-user desktops, the users are often the administrators of their system. To make it easy for users to perform tasks such as installing software or changing system settings, the common practice is that the users are often logged in to an account with administrative privileges. As a result, if an attacker is able to launch a Trojan horse attack, or exploit some programs of the user, the attacker is able to acquire virtually all the privileges. Then the attacker can change the critical part of the operating system and take over the system silently.

To provide enhanced security for users, Windows Vista features a access control mechanism called user access control (UAC). In UAC, when an administer logs in, the user is granted two access control tokens instead of just one: an administrator access token that has full privileges and a standard user access token. When the user performs normal tasks, for example, browsing the web, reading emails, only the standard user access token is involved in access control decisions. When the user wants to perform some administration tasks, for example, install a program or a driver, Vista will prompt to ask for user's consent and the administrator access token is used afterwards. Therefore, the user is alerted when the privileges are used, and a Trojan cannot just take over the system silently. This mechanism requires a user to be able to correctly tell whether extra privileges is required for a particular activity and not to blindly enter the password each time it is prompted to do so. This feature has also caused significant inconvenience, as a user is often required to enter the password.

2.4 Security-Enhanced Linux (SELinux)

SELinux is a security mechanism in Linux that has been developed to support a wide range of security policies. The development originated from the National Security Agency. SELinux was first implemented as kernel patches and currently it is implemented using the Linux security module (LSM) framework. The architecture of SELinux separates policy decision-making logic from the policy enforcement logic. SELinux policies include features as type enforcement, role-based access control, multilevel security, etc. We discuss the architecture of SELinux and some policies in this section.

In SELinux, every subject (process) and object (resources like files, sockets, etc.) is given a security context, which includes a type. Every process has a domain, which is a kind of types, and every object (e.g., files) has a type. All processes with a same domain are treated identically. The objects (resources) are categorized into object security classes. Each object security class represents a specific kind of object (e.g., regular files, folders, TCP sockets). For every object security class, there is a set of access operations that can be performed (e.g., the operations to a file include read/ write/execute, lock, create, rename, getattr/setattr, link/unlink). All objects with the same type and the same class are treated identically. When an access attempt is made by a process, the enforcement part will decide whether to grant this access based on the security context of the process, the security context of the object being accessed, and the object security class of the resource. To have fine-grain control of the accesses, there are several types of rules in the policy:

- A TE access vector rule defines what *operations* a process with a particular *domain* can perform on an object of a particular security *class* with a particular *type*. For example, the following rule

      allow sshd_t sshd_exec_t:file {read execute entrypint;}

  says a process with the sshd_t domain can perform three operations on a file with the sshd_exec_t type: read, execute, and entrypoint. The meaning of read and execute is the same as in standard UNIX. The entrypoint operation means that the sshd_exec_t type is a legitimate entrypoint for the sshd_t domain, that is, a process is *allowed* to enter sshd_t domain by executing a file with sshd_exec_t type.

  An access vector can also start with auditallow, auditdeny, or dontaudit, in addition to allow. Operations are denied unless there is an explicit allow rule. When an access request is granted, it is not logged unless it is authorized by an auditallow. And when an access request is denied, it is logged unless it is authorized by a dontaudit rule.

- A TE transition rule for a process defines which new domain a process should enter after executing a program, based on the current process domain and the type of the program. For example, the flowing rule

      type_transition initrc_t sshd_exec_t:process sshd_t;

  says when a process with the initrc_t domain executes a program with the sshd_exec_t type, the process should transit to the sshd_t domain. The domain transition can occur only if two additional conditions are met: (1) the initrc_t domain is allowed to execute files of the sshd_exec_t type; and (2) the sshd_exec_t type is a legitimate entrypoint for the sshd_t domain. Both conditions are specified by access vector rules.

- A TE transition rule for an object defines the type of a newly created object. For example, the following rule

      type_transition sshd_t tmp_t:{dir file} sshd_tmp_t;

says when a process with the sshd_t domain creates a file or a directory in a directory with the tmp_t type, the newly created file or directory should be with the sshd_tmp_t type.

SELinux policies are complex and intimidating to configure. For example, SELinux has 29 different classes of objects, hundreds of possible operations, and thousands of policy rules for a typical system. The SELinux policy interface is daunting even for security experts. Although SELinux makes sense in a setting where the systems run similar applications, and sophisticated security expertise is available, its applicability to a more general setting where additional configuration by local system administrators is unclear.

2.5   AppArmor

AppArmor is an access control system that confines the access permissions on a per program basis. It tries to follow the least privilege principle. For every protected program, AppArmor defines a list of permitted accesses, including file accesses and capabilities. The list for a program is called the program's profile. And the profiles of all protected programs constitute an AppArmor policy. A program's profile contains all possible file reads, file writes, file executions, and capabilities that may be performed by a protected program. Under AppArmor, a process that executes a protected program can only perform accesses in the program's profile.

By following the least privilege principle, AppArmor makes local and remote exploits more difficult. Consider a system that runs an FTP server using the root account. If an attacker exploits a vulnerability in the server and injects her own code, under normal Linux DAC protection, the attacker is able to gain full privileges in the system. The attacker can, for example, install a rootkit by loading a kernel module. However, if the system is protected by AppArmor, there will not be a kernel module loading capability in the FTP server's profile, because a FTP server would not need that. Then even if the attacker controls the server process, she cannot directly install a rootkit.

Following is an excerpt from a profile for passwd (see http://packages. ubuntu.com/gutsy/base/apparmor-profiles for AppArmor profiles package). The profile guarantees that if a local user exploits this setuid root program, the user cannot get full privileges of root.

```
1. . . .
2. /usr/bin/passwd {
3. . . .
4. capability chown,
5. capability sys_resource,
6. /etc/.pwd.lock w,
```

7. /etc/pwdutils/logging r,
8. /etc/shadow rwl,
9. /etc/shadow.old rwl,
10. /etc/shadow.tmp?????? rwl,
11. /usr/bin/passwd mr,
12. /usr/lib/pwdutils/lib*.so* mr,
13. /usr/lib64/pwdutils/lib*.so* mr,
14. /usr/share/cracklib/pw_dict.hwm r,
15. /usr/share/cracklib/pw_dict.pwd r,
16. /usr/share/cracklib/pw_dict.pwi r,
17. }

In the profile, there are 2 rules for capabilities (lines 4 and 5) and 11 rules for file accesses (lines 6–16). A file rule consists of a file name and one or more permitted access modes. There are 9 access modes in total: read mode, write mode, link mode, and six other modes for executing the file (for details of these access modes, please refer to Apparmor application security for Linux).

A profile can be created using AppArmor utilities. One can run a program in the "learning mode." In this mode, all the requests of a program are permitted and logged. The user makes the program perform as many accesses as possible. Later the user can use the logs to create the profile of the program. For each access, an AppArmor utility asks the user whether to allow the access; and if the access is a file access, the user can choose to generalize the access by using wildcards in the permitted filename (globbing).

AppArmor also provides finer-grain access control than process level, by the "ChangeHat" feature. ChangeHat-aware programs can use this feature to have part of a program using a different profile. For more details, please refer to Apparmor application security for Linux.

AppArmor identifies a number of programs that, when compromised, could be dangerous, and confine them by a policy. If a program has no policy associated with it, then it is by default not confined, and if a program has a policy, then it can access only the objects specified in the policy. This approach remains vulnerable to Trojan horse attacks. As most programs, such as shells, obtained through normal usage channels are unconfined, a user would mostly operate in an unconfined environment, and the execution of a Trojan horse program will not be subject to the control of the system.

3   Problem definition and technical solution

3.1   Design principles for usable access control systems

Although it is widely agreed that usability is very important for security technologies, how to design an access control system that has a high level of usability has not been explored much in the literature. In this section, we present six principles for designing usable access control systems. Some of these principles challenge established conventional wisdom in the field, because we place an unusually high premium on usability. These principles will be illustrated by our design of the UMIP model, which will be presented later.

Principle 1. *Provide "good enough" security with a high level of usability, rather than "better" security with a low level of usability*

Our philosophy is that rather than providing a protection system that can theoretically provide very strong security guarantees, but requires huge effort and expertise to configure correctly, one should aim at providing a system that is easy to configure and can greatly increase the level of security by reducing the attack surfaces. Sandhu (2003) made a case for good-enough security, observing that *"cumbersome technology will be deployed and operated incorrectly and insecurely, or perhaps not at all."* Sandhu also identified three principles that guide information security, the second of which is *"Good enough always beat perfect."* (The first one is *"Good enough is good enough"* and the third one is *"The really hard part is determining what is good enough."*) He observed that the applicability of this principle to the computer security field is further amplified because there is no such thing as "perfect" in security, and restate the principle as *"Good enough always beats 'better but imperfect'."*

There may be situations that one would want stronger security guarantees, even though the cost of administration is much more expensive. However, to protect the most vulnerable computers on the Internet, that is, computers that are managed by users with little expertise in system security, one needs a protection system with a high level of usability.

One corollary following from this principle is that *sometimes one needs to trade off security for simplicity of the design.* Later we discuss five other principles, which further help achieve the goal of usable access control. The following five principles can be viewed as "minor" principles for achieving the overarching goal set by the first principle.

Principle 2. *Provide policy, not just mechanism.*

Raymond discussed in his book (Raymond, 2003) the topic of *"what UNIX gets wrong"* in terms of philosophy, and wrote *"perhaps the most enduring objections to Unix are consequences of a feature of its philosophy first made explicit by the designers of the X windowing system. X strives to provide 'mechanism, not policy'. [...] But the cost of the mechanism-not-policy approach is that when the user can set policy, the user must set policy. Nontechnical end-users frequently find Unix's profusion of options and interface styles overwhelming."*

The mechanism-not-policy approach is especially problematic for security. A security mechanism that is very flexible and can be extensively configured is not just overwhelming for end users, it is also highly error-prone. Although there are right ways to configure the mechanism to enforce some desirable security policies, there are often many more incorrect ways to configure a system. And the complexity often overwhelms users so that the mechanism is simply not enabled.

This mechanism-not-policy philosophy is implicitly used in the design of many MAC systems for operating systems. For example, systems such as LIDS, systrace, and SELinux all aim at providing a mechanism that can be used to implement a wide range of policies. Although a mechanism is absolutely necessary for implementing a protection system, having only a low-level mechanism is not enough.

Principle 3. *Have a well-defined security objective.*

The first step of designing a policy is to identify a security objective, because only then can one make meaningful tradeoffs between security and usability. To make tradeoffs, one must ask and answer the question: if the policy model is simplified in this way, can we still achieve the security objective? A security objective should identify two things: what kind of adversaries the system is designed to protect against, that is, what abilities does one assume the adversaries have, and what security properties one wants to achieve even in the presence of such adversaries. Often times, MAC systems do not clearly identify the security objective. For example, achieving multilevel security is often identified together with defending against network attacks. They are very different kinds of security objectives. History has taught us that designing usable multilevel secure systems is extremely difficult, and it seems unlikely that one can build a usable access control system that can achieve both objectives.

Principle 4. *Carefully design ways to support exceptions in the policy model.*

Given the complexity of modern operating systems and the diverse scenarios in which computers are used, no simple policy model can capture all accesses that need to be allowed, and, at the same time, forbid all illegal accesses. It is thus necessary to have ways to specify exceptions in the policy model. The challenges lie in designing the policy model and the exception mechanisms so that the number of exceptions is small, the exceptions are easy and intuitive to specify, the exceptions provide the desired flexibility, and the attack surface exposed by the exceptions is small. Little research has focused on studying how to support exceptions in an MAC model. As we will see, much effort in designing UMIP goes to designing mechanisms to support exceptions.

Principle 5. *Rather than trying to achieve "strict least privilege," aim for "good-enough least privilege."*

It is widely recognized that one problem with existing DAC mechanisms is that it does not support the least privilege principle (Saltzer and Schroeder, 1975). For example, in traditional UNIX access control, many operations can be performed only by the root user. If a program needs to perform any of these operations, it needs to be given the root privilege. As a result, an attacker can exploit vulnerabilities in the program and abuse these privileges. Many propose to remedy the problem by using very fine-grained access control and to achieve strict least privilege. For example, the guiding principles for designing policies for systems such as SELinux, systrace, and AppArmor is to identify all objects a program needs to access when it is not under attack and grants access only to those objects. This approach results in a large number of policy rules. We believe that it is sufficient to restrict privileges just enough to achieve the security objective; and this enables one to design more usable access control systems.

Principle 6. *Use familiar abstractions in policy specification interface.*

Psychological acceptability is one of the eight principles for designing security mechanisms identified by Saltzer and Schroeder (1975). They wrote *"It is essential that the human interface be designed for ease of use, so that users routinely and automatically apply the protection mechanisms correctly. Also, to the extent that the user's mental image of his protection goals matches the mechanisms he must use, mistakes will be minimized. If he must translate his image of his protection needs into a radically different specification language, he will make errors."* This entails that the policy specification interface should use concepts and abstractions that administrators are familiar with. This principle is violated by systems such as systrace, which uses system call parameters to describe permissions, and SELinux, which uses hundreds of operations on dozens of object classes to describe permissions.

3.2   The UMIP model (an overview)

We now introduce the UMIP model, which was guided by the principles identified in Section 3.1. Although the description of the UMIP model in this section is based on our design for Linux, we believe that the model can be applied to other UNIX variants with minor changes.

Following Principle 3, we now identify the security objective of our policy model. We aim at protecting the system integrity against network-based attacks. We assume that network server and client programs contain bugs and can be exploited if the attacker is able to feed input to them. We assume that users may make careless mistakes in their actions, for example, downloading a malicious program from the Internet and running it. However, we assume that the attacker does not have physical access to the host to be protected. Our policy model aims at ensuring that under most attack channels, the attacker can get only limited privileges and cannot compromise the system integrity. For example, if a host runs privileged network-facing programs that contain vulnerabilities, the host will not be completely taken over by an attacker as a bot. The attacker may be able to exploit bugs in these programs to run some code on the host; however, the attacker cannot install rootkits. Furthermore, if the host reboots, the attacker does not control the host anymore. Similarly, if a network client program is exploited, the damage is limited. We also aim at protecting against indirect attacks, where the attacker creates malicious programs and wait for users to execute them, or creates/changes files to exploit vulnerabilities in programs that later read these files.

The usability goals for UMIP are twofold: First, configuring a UMIP system should not be more difficult than installing and configuring an operating system. Second, existing applications and common usage practices can still be used under UMIP. Depending on the needs of a system, the administrator of the system should be able to configure the system in a less secure, but easier-to-use manner. Another constraint that we have for UMIP is that it can be implemented using an existing mechanism (namely the Linux security modules framework).

3.3   The basic UMIP model

An important design question for any operating system access control system is: What is a principal? That is, when a process requests to perform certain operations, what information about the process should be used in deciding whether the request should be authorized. The traditional UNIX access control system associates each process with an effective user id (euid) and treats the euid as a principal. As many operations can be performed only when the euid is 0, many daemon programs need to run with euid being 0 and many programs owned by the root user are designated setuid. When privileged programs contain bugs, they can be exploited so that attackers can use the privileges to damage the system.

As using just the euid is too coarse-granulated, a natural extension is to consider both euid and the current program that is running in the process as a principal. The thinking is that, if one can identify all possible operations a privileged program would do and only allows it to do those, then the damage of an attacker taking over the program is limited. However, this design is also insufficient. Consider a request to load a kernel module that comes from a process running the program insmod with euid 0. As loading a kernel module is what insmod is supposed to do, such access must be allowed. However, this process might be started by an attacker who has compromised a daemon process running as root and obtained a root shell as the result of the exploits. If the request is authorized, then this may enable the installation of a kernel rootkit, and lead to complete system compromise. One may try to prevent this by preventing the daemon program from running certain programs (such as shell); however, certain daemons have legitimate need to run shells or other programs that can lead to running insmod. In this case, a daemon can legitimately run a shell, the shell can legitimately run insmod, and insmod can legitimately load kernel modules. If one looks at only the current program together with euid, then any individual access needs to be allowed; however, the combination of them clearly needs to be stopped.

The preceding analysis illustrates that, to determine what the current process should be allowed to do, one has to consider the parent process that created the current process, the process who created the parent process, and so on. We call this the *request channel*. For example, if insmod is started by a series of processes that have never communicated with the network, then this means that this request is from a user who logged in through a local terminal. Such a request should be authorized, because it is almost certainly not an attacker, unless an attacker gets physical access to the host, in which case not much security can be provided anyway. On the other hand, if insmod is started by a shell that is a descendant of the ftp daemon process, then this is almost certainly a result from an attack; the ftp daemon and its legitimate descendants have no need to load a kernel module.

The key challenge lies in how to capture the information in a request channel in a succinct way. The domain-type enforcement approach used in SELinux and DTE Unix can be viewed as summarizing the request channel in the form of a domain. Whenever a channel represents a different set of privileges from other channels, a new domain is needed. This requires a large number of domains to be introduced.

The approach we take is to use a few fields associated with a process to record necessary information about the request channel. The most important field is one bit to classify the request channel into high integrity or low integrity. If a request channel is likely to be exploited by an attacker, then the process has low integrity. If a request channel may be used legitimately for system administration, then the process needs to be high integrity. Note that a request channel may be both legitimately used for system administration and potentially exploitable. In this case, administrators must explicitly set the policy to allow such channels for system administration. The model tries to minimize the attack surface exposed by such policy setting when possible.

When a process is marked as low integrity, this means that it is potentially contaminated. We do not try to determine whether a process is actually attacked. The success of our approach depends on the observation that with such an apparently crude distinction of low- and high-integrity processes, only a few low-integrity processes need to perform a small number of

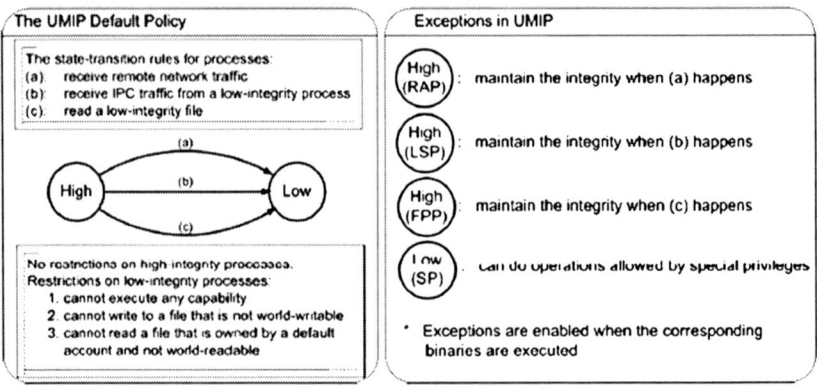

Fig. 1.   The summary of the UMIP model.

security critical operations, which can be specified using a few simple policies as exceptions.

Basic UMIP model: Each process has one bit that denotes its integrity level. When a process is created, it inherits the integrity level of the parent process. When a process performs an operation that makes it potentially contaminated, it drops its integrity. A low-integrity process by default cannot perform sensitive operations.

Figure 1 gives an overview of UMIP. In the default policy, a high-integrity process may drop its integrity to low in one of three ways, and a low-integrity process is limited in its access privileges. This default policy is then extended with exceptions to support existing software and system usage practices. There are two classes of exceptions that can be specified for programs. Exceptions of the first class allow a program binary to be identified as one or more of: remote administration point (RAP), local service point (LSP), and file processing program (FPP). Such exceptions allow a process running the binary to maintain its integrity level when certain events that normally would drop the process's integrity occur. Exceptions of the second class give a program binary special privileges (e.g., using some capabilities, reading/writing certain protected files) so that a process running the program can have these privileges even in low integrity. In the rest of this section, we describe the UMIP model in detail. Section 3.4 discusses contamination through network and inter-process communications. Section 3.5 discusses restrictions on low-integrity processes. Section 3.6 discusses contamination through files. In Section 3.7, we discuss how the design principles in Section 3.1 are applied in designing UMIP. Comparison of UMIP with closely related integrity models is given in Section 3.8. We describe an implementation of UMIP for Linux in Section 3.9 and the evaluation in Section 3.10.

3.4   Dealing with communications

When a process receives remote network traffic (network traffic that is not from the localhost loopback), its integrity level should drop, as the program may contain vulnerabilities and the traffic may be sent by an attacker to exploit such vulnerabilities. Under this default policy, system maintenance tasks (e.g., installing new softwares, updating system files, and changing configuration files) can be performed only through a local terminal. Users can log in remotely, but cannot perform these sensitive tasks. Although this offers a high degree of security, it may be too restrictive in many systems (e.g., in a collocated server-hosting scenario).

In the UMIP model, a program may be identified as a *RAP*. The effect is that a process running the program maintains its integrity level when receiving network traffic. If one wants to allow remote system administration through, for example, the secure shell daemon, then one can identify /usr/sbin/sshd as a remote administration point. (Note that if a process descending from sshd runs a program other than sshd and receives network traffic, its integrity level drops.) Introducing RAP is the result of trading off security in favor of usability. Allowing remote administration certainly makes the system less secure. This is an example of applying Principle 1, providing good enough security.

If remote administration through sshd is allowed, and the attacker can successfully exploit bugs in sshd, then the attacker can take over the system, as this is specified as a legitimate remote administration channel. However, note that in this case the attack surface is greatly reduced from all daemon programs, to only sshd. Some daemon programs (such as httpd) are much more complicated than sshd and are likely to contain more bugs. Moreover, firewalls can be used to limit the network addresses from which one can connect to a machine via sshd, whereas one often has to open the httpd server to the world. Finally, techniques such as privilege separation (Brumley and Song, 2004; Provos et al., 2003) can be used to further mitigate attacks against sshd. The UMIP model leaves the decision of whether to allow remote administration through channels such as sshd to the system administrators.

We also need to consider what happens when a process receives interprocess communications (IPC) from another local process. UMIP considers integrity contamination through those IPC channels that can be used to send free-formed data, because such data can be crafted to exploit bugs in the receiving process. Under Linux, such channels include UNIX domain socket, pipe, fifo, message queue, shared memory, and shared file in the tmpfs file system. In addition, UMIP treats local loopback network communication as a form of IPC. When a process reads from one of these IPC channels, which have been written by a low-integrity process, the integrity level of the process drops, even when the process is a RAP.

Similar to the concept of RAP, a program may be identified as a LSP, which enables a process running the program to maintain its integrity level after receiving IPC from low-integrity processes. For example, if one wants to enable system administration and networking activities (such as web browsing) to happen in one X Window environment, the X server and the desktop manager can be declared as LSPs. When some X clients communicate with network and drop to low integrity, the X server, the desktop manager, and other X clients can still maintain high integrity.

3.5   Restricting low-integrity processes

Our approach requires the identification of security critical operations that would affect system integrity so that our protection system can prevent low-integrity processes from carrying them out. We classify security-critical operations into two categories, file operations and operations that are not associated with specific files.

Examples of nonfile administrative operations include loading a kernel module, administration of IP firewall, modification of routing table, network interface configuration, rebooting the machine, ptrace other processes, mounting and unmounting file systems, and so on. These operations are essential for maintaining system integrity and availability, and are often used by malicious code. In modern Linux, these operations are controlled by capabilities, which were introduced since version 2.1 of the Linux kernel. Capabilities break the privileges normally reserved for root down into smaller pieces. As of Linux Kernel 2.6.11, Linux has 31 capabilities. The default UMIP rule grants only two capabilities CAP_SETGID and CAP_SETUID to low-integrity processes; furthermore, low-integrity processes are restricted in that they can use setuid and setgid only in the following two ways: (1) swapping among effective, real, and saved uids and gids; and (2) going from the root account to another system account. (A system account, with the exception of root, does not correspond to an actual human user.) We allow low-integrity processes to use setuid and setgid this way because many daemon programs need to perform these actions and doing so does not compromise our security objective. Note that by this design, a low-integrity process running as root cannot set its uid to a new normal user.

It is much more challenging to identify which files should be considered sensitive, as a large number of objects in an operating system are modeled as files. Different hosts may have different softwares installed, and hence have different sensitive files. The list of files that need to be protected is quite long, for example, system programs and libraries, system configuration files, service program configuration files, system log files, kernel image files, images of the memory (such as /dev/kmem and /dev/mem), and so on. We cannot ask the end users to label files, as our goal is to have the system configurable by ordinary system administrators who are not security experts. Our novel approach here is to utilize the valuable information in existing DAC mechanisms.

3.5.1. Using DAC info for MAC

All commercial operating systems have built-in DAC mechanisms. For example, UNIX and UNIX variants use the permission bits to support DAC. Although DAC by itself is insufficient for stopping network-based attacks, DAC access control information is nonetheless very important. For example, when one installs Linux from a distribution, files such as /etc/passwd and /etc/shadow would be writable only by root. This indicates that writing to these files is security critical. Similarly, files such as /etc/shadow would be readable only by root, indicating that reading them is security critical. Such DAC information has been used by millions of users and examined for decades. Our approach utilizes this information, rather than asking the end users to label all files, which is a labor intensive and error-prone process. UMIP offers both read and write protection for files owned by system accounts. A low-integrity process (even if having effective uid 0) is forbidden from reading a file that is owned by a system account and is not readable by world; such a file is said to be *read-protected*. A low-integrity process is also forbidden from writing to a file owned by a system account and is not writable by world. Such a file is said to be *write-protected*. Finally, a low-integrity process is forbidden from changing the DAC permission of any (read- or write-) protected file.

3.5.2. Exception policies: least privilege for sensitive operations

Some network-facing daemons need to access resources that are protected. Because these processes receive network communications, they will be low integrity, and the default policy will stop such access. We deal with this by allowing the specification of policy exceptions for system binaries. For example, one policy we use is that the binary "/usr/sbin/vsftpd" is allowed to use the capabilities CAP_NET_BIND_SERVICE, CAP_SYS_SETUID, CAP_SYS_SETGID, and CAP_SYS_CHROOT, to read the file /etc/shadow, to read all files under the directory /etc/vsftpd, and to read or write the file /var/log/xferlog. This daemon program needs to read /etc/shadow to authenticate remote users. If an attacker can exploit a vulnerability in vsftpd and inject code into the address space of vsftpd, this code can read /etc/shadow file. However, if the attacker injects shell code to obtain a shell by exploiting the vulnerabilities, then the exception policy for the shell process will be reset to NULL and the attacker loses the ability to read /etc/passwd. Furthermore, the attacker cannot write to any system binary or install rootkits. Under this policy, an administrator cannot directly upload files to replace system binaries. However, the administrator can upload files to another directory and login through a remote administration channel (e.g., through sshd) and then replace system binary files with the uploaded files.

When a high-integrity process loads a program that has an exception policy, the process has special privileges as specified by the policy. Even when the process later receives network traffic and drops integrity, the special privileges remain for the process. However, when a low-integrity process loads a program that has an exception policy, the process is denied the special privileges in the policy. The rationale is as follows. Some network administration tools (such as iptables) must perform network communications and will thus drop its integrity, so they need to be given capability exceptions for CAP_NET_ADMIN. However, we would not want a low-integrity process to invoke them and still have the special privileges. On the other hand, some programs need to invoke other programs when its integrity is low, and the invoked program needs special privilege. For example, sendmail needs to invoke procmail when its integrity is low, and procmail needs to write to the spool directory that is write-protected. We resolve this by defining executing relationships between programs. If there is an executing relationship between the program X to the program Y, then when a process running X executes Y, even if the process is in the state of low integrity, the process will have the special permissions associated with Y after executing. In the example, we define an executing relationship from sendmail to procmail and give procmail the special permission to write to the spool directory.

Our approach does not provide strict least privilege, as our default policy allows high-integrity processes to access any resource and low-integrity process to access files that are not sensitive, whereas no high-integrity process needs to access *all* resources and no low-integrity process needs to access *all* nonsensitive resources. Rather, our approach aims at achieving good-enough least privilege (Principle 5). Allowing these accesses does not affect our objective of protection against network attackers, whereas it greatly simplify the specification of policies, because one does not need to figure out exactly what resources a high-integrity process needs to access.

Also our approach provides several exception mechanisms (RAP, LSP, and exception policies) to allow the specification of different levels of trust in programs. These exception mechanisms are carefully designed to balance the usability goal and the security goal (Principle 4). The trust placed on a RAP program is greater than that placed on one with exception policies.

3.6 Contamination through files

As an attacker may be able to control contents in files that are not write-protected, a process's integrity level needs to drop after reading and executing files that are not write-protected. However, even if a file is write-protected, it may still be written by low-integrity processes, due to the existence of exception policies. We use one permission bit to track whether a file has been written by a low-integrity process. There are 12 permission bits for each file in a UNIX file system: 9 of them indicate read/write/execute permissions for user/group/world; the other three are setuid, setgid, and the sticky bit. The sticky bit is no longer used for regular files (it is still useful for directories), and we use it to track contamination for files. When a low-integrity process writes to a file that is write-protected as allowed by an exception, the file's sticky bit is set. A file is considered to be low integrity (potentially contaminated) when either it is not write-protected, or has the sticky bit set.

When a process reads a low-integrity file, the process's integrity level drops. We do not consider reading a directory that was changed by a low-integrity process as contamination, as the directory is maintained by the file system, which should handle directory contents properly. When a file's permission is changed from world-writable to not world-writable, the sticky bit is set, as the file may have been contaminated while it was world-writable.

A low-integrity process is forbidden from changing the sticky bit of a file. Only a high-integrity process can reset the sticky bit by running a special utility program provided by the protection system. The requirement of using a special utility program avoids the problem that other programs may accidentally reset the bit without the user intending to do it. This way, when a user clears the sticky bit, it is clear to the user that she is potentially raising the integrity of the file. The special utility program cannot be changed by low-integrity processes, so that its integrity level is always high.

Similar to the concept of RAP, we introduce file-processing programs (FPP). A process running an FPP maintains its integrity level even after reading a low-integrity file. Programs that read a file's content and display the file on a terminal (e.g., vi, cat) need to be declared to be FPP.

We observe that our approach for handling file integrity is different from existing integrity models (such as Biba, 1977), in which an object has one integrity level. The integrity level of an object can be used to indicate two things (1) the importance level of the object as a container (i.e., whether the object is used in some critical ways); and (2) the quality (i.e., trustworthiness, or, alternatively, contamination level) of information currently in the object. These two may not always be the same. When only one integrity level is used, one can keep track of only one of the two, which is problematic. Consider, for example, the system log files and the mail files. They are considered to be contaminated because they are written by processes that have communicated with the network. However, it is incorrect not to protect them, as an attacker who broke into the system through, say, httpd, would be able to change the log.

UMIP handles this by using a file's DAC permission to determine the importance level of the file, and using the sticky bit to track the contamination level. Even if a file has the sticky bit set (i.e., considered contaminated), as long as the file's DAC permission is not writable by the world, a low-integrity process still cannot write to the file (unless a policy exception exists). In other words, the set of write-protected files and the set of contaminated files intersect. This way, files such as system logs and mails are protected. This is different from other integrity models such as Biba, where once an object is contaminated, every subject can write to it. UMIP's design reduces the attack surface.

3.7 Design principles in UMIP

We now briefly examine how the design of UMIP illustrates the principles identified in Section 3.1. Principle 1 is to provide good enough security with a high level of usability. In UMIP, usability concerns are twofold. First, the protection system must allow normal usage practices and applications to be used. This motivates the introduction of exception mechanisms that trade off security for usability. Second, policy configurations should be user friendly. This motivates the design of allowing default accesses and using path names for file access exceptions. Principle 2 requires providing policy, not just mechanism. Following this principle, in UMIP we use an existing mechanism (namely, LSM) and focus on designing a policy model to achieve the security objective laid out in the beginning of Section 3. Principle 3 requires having a well-defined security objective. UMIP aims at preventing remote attackers from taking over a system, rather than claiming to offer comprehensive protection. Principle 4 emphasizes the importance to design exceptions, whereas a major part of the work in developing the UMIP model is in designing the exception mechanisms. Principle 5 promotes good-enough least privilege, rather than strict least privilege and is reflected in our design of default policy plus exceptions, as discussed in Section 3.5. Finally, following Principle 6, UMIP uses files and capabilities in policy specifications, rather than exposing kernel data structures in the policy specification interface.

We believe that using DAC information is one key to the usability of UMIP. This makes deployment and installation of new software easy, as no labeling process is needed. This also uses concepts that users are already familiar with.

3.8 Comparison with other integrity models

The UMIP model borrows concepts from classical work on integrity models such as Biba (1977) and LOMAC (Fraser, 2000). Here we discuss UMIP's novel features.

The Biba (1977) model has five mandatory integrity policies (1) the strict integrity policy, in which the integrity labels of subjects and objects never change and a subject cannot read objects of lower integrity or write objects of higher integrity; (2) the subject low-water mark policy, in which a subject is allowed to read objects of lower integrity, but its integrity level drops after such reading; (3) the object low-water mark policy, in which an object can be written by a subject of lower integrity, but the object's integrity level drops after the writing; (4) the low-water mark integrity audit policy, which allows all reading and writing accesses, but requires the integrity levels of both subjects and objects to drop after such accesses; (5) the ring policy, which allows a subject to read low-integrity objects while maintaining its integrity level, reflecting trust in the subject's ability to process low-integrity inputs. LOMAC (Fraser, 2000) is an implementation of the subject low-water mark policy for operating systems. Each object is assigned an integrity level. Once assigned, an object's level never changes. It aims at protecting system integrity and places emphasis on usability. Compared with Biba and LOMAC, UMIP has the following novel features.

First, UMIP supports a number of ways to specify some programs as partially trusted to allow them to violate the default contamination rule or the default restrictions on low-integrity processes in some limited way. This enables one to use existing applications and administration practices, whereas limiting the attack surfaces exposed by such trust.

Second, in UMIP a file essentially has two integrity level values: whether it is protected, which reflects the file's importance level, and whether it is contaminated, which reflects the quality of information currently stored in the object. The former is determined by the DAC permission, and does not change unless the file's permission changes. The latter is tracked using the sticky bit for protected files, and may change dynamically. The advantages of our approach are explained in Section 3.4.

Third, UMIP allows low-integrity files to be upgraded to high integrity. (This feature also exists in LOMAC.) This means that low-integrity information (such as files downloaded from the Internet) can flow into high-integrity objects (such as system binaries); however, such upgrade must occur explicitly, that is, by invoking a special program in a high-integrity channel to remove the sticky bit. Allowing such channels is necessary for patching and system upgrade.

Fourth, UMIP offers some confidentiality protection, in addition to integrity protection. For example, low-integrity processes are forbidden from reading files owned by a system account and not readable by the world.

Finally, UMIP uses DAC information to determine integrity and confidentiality labels for objects, whereas in LOMAC each installation requires manual specification of a mapping between existing files and integrity levels.

3.9   An implementation under Linux

We have implemented the UMIP model in a prototype protection system for Linux, using the LSM framework. The basic design of our protection system is as follows. Each process has a security label, which contains (among other fields) a field indicating whether the process's integrity level is high or low. When a process issues a request, it is authorized only when both the Linux DAC system and our protection system authorize it. A high-integrity process is not restricted by our protection system. A low-integrity process *by default* cannot perform any sensitive operation. Any exception to the above default policy must be specified in a policy file, which is loaded when the module starts.

3.9.1.   The policy specification

The policy file includes a list of entries. Each entry contains four fields (1) a path that points to the program that the entry is associated with; (2) the type of a program, which includes three bits indicating whether the program is a RAP, LSP, and FPP; (3) a list of exceptions; and (4) a list of executing relationships, which is a list of programs that can be executed by the current program with the exception policies enabled, even if the process is low integrity. If a program does not have a corresponding entry, the default policy is that the program is not an RAP, a LSP or an FPP, and the exception list and the executing relationship list are empty. An exception list consists of two parts, the capability exception list and the file exception list, corresponding to exceptions to the two categories of security critical operations. A file exception takes one of the four forms as shown in Table 1.

The authorization provided by file exceptions includes only two levels: read and full. We choose this design because of its simplicity. In this design, one cannot specify that a program can write a file, but not read. We believe that this is acceptable because system-related files that are read-sensitive are also write-sensitive. In other words, if the attacker can write to a file, then he can pose at least comparable damage to the system as he can also read the file. A policy of the form "(*d*, read, R)" is used in the situation that a daemon or a client program needs to read the configuration files in the directory *d*. A policy of the form "(*d*, full, R)" is used to define the working directories for programs.

Table 1
The four forms of file exceptions in UMIP

Syntax		Meaning
(f, read)	f is a regular file or a directory	Allowed to read f
(f, full)	f is a regular file or a directory	Allowed to do anything to f
(d, read, R)	d is a directory	Allowed to read any file in d recursively
(d, full, R)	d is a directory	Allowed to do anything to any file in d recursively

3.10   Evaluation

We evaluate our design of the UMIP model and the implementation under Linux along the following dimensions: usability, security, and performance.

3.10.1.   Usability

One usability measure is transparency, which means not blocking legitimate accesses generated by normal system operations. Another measure is flexibility, which means that one can configure a system according to the security needs. A third usability measure is ease of configuration. Several features of UMIP contribute to a high level of usability: the use of existing DAC information, the existence of RAP, LSP, and FPP, and the use of familiar abstractions in the specification of policies. To experimentally evaluate the transparency and flexibility aspects, we established a server configured with Fedora Core 5 with kernel version 2.6.15, and enabled our protection system as a security module loaded during system boot. We installed some commonly used server applications (e.g., httpd, ftpd, samba, svn) and have been providing services to our research group over the last few months. The system works with a small and simple policy specification as given in Table 2. With this policy, we allow remote administration through the SSH daemon by declaring sshd as RAP.

3.10.2.   Security

Most attack scenarios that exploit bugs in network-facing daemon programs or client programs can be readily prevented by our protection system. Successful exploitation of vulnerabilities in network-facing processes often results in a shell process spawned from the vulnerable process. After gaining shell access, the attacker typically tries downloading and installing attacking tools and rootkits. As these processes are low integrity, the access to sensitive operations is limited to those allowed by the exceptions. Furthermore, if the attacker loads a shell or any other program, the new process has no exception privileges.

In our experiments, we use the NetCat tool to offer an interactive root shell to the attacker. We execute NetCat in "listen" mode on the test machine as root. When the attacker connects to the listening port, NetCat spawns a shell process, which takes input from the attacker and also directs output to him. From the root shell, we perform the following three attacks and compare what happens without our protection system with what happens when our protection system is enabled.

1. *Installing a rootkit*: Rootkits can operate at two different levels. User-mode rootkits manipulate user-level operating system elements, altering existing binary executables or libraries. Kernel-mode rootkits manipulate the kernel of the operating system by loading a kernel

Table 2
Sample policy

Services and path of the binary	Type	File exceptions	Capability exceptions	Executing relationships
SSH Daemon /usr/sbin/sshd	RAP			
Automated update: /usr/bin/yum	RAP			
/usr/bin/vim	FPP			
/usr/bin/cat	FPP			
FTP server /usr/sbin/vsftpd	NONE	(/var/log/xferlog, full)	CAP_SYS_CHROOT	
		(/etc/vsftpd, full, R)	CAP_SYS_SETUID	
		(/etc/shadow, read)	CAP_SYS_SETGID	
			CAP_NET_BIND_SERVICE	
Web server /usr/sbin/httpd	NONE	(/var/log/httpd, full, R)		
		(/etc/pki/tls, read, R)		
		(/var/run/httpd.pid, full)		
Samba server /usr/sbin/smbd	NONE	(/var/cache/samba, full, R)	CAP_SYS_RESOURCE	
		(/etc/samba, full, R)	CAP_SYS_SETUID	
		(/var/log/samba, full, R)	CAP_SYS_SETGID	
		(/var/run/smbd.pid, full)	CAP_NET_BIND_SERVICE	
			CAP_DAC_OVERRIDE	
NetBIOS name server /usr/sbin/ nmbd	NONE	(/var/log/samba, full, R)		
		(/var/cache/samba, full, R)		
Version control server /usr/bin/ svnserve	NONE	(/usr/local/svn, full, R)		

Service		Capability	File accesses
Name server for NT /usr/sbin/winbindd	NONE		(/var/cache/samba, full, R) (/var/log/samba, full, R) (/etc/samba/secrets.tdb, full)
SMTP server /usr/sbin/sendmail	NONE	CAP_NET_BIND_SERVICE /usr/sbin/procmail	(/var/spool/mqueue, full, R) (/var/spool/clientmqueue, full, R) (/var/spool/mail, full, R) (/etc/mail, full, R) (/etc/aliases.db, read) (/var/log/mail, full, R) (/var/run/sendmail.pid, full)
Mail processor /usr/bin/procmail	NONE		(/var/spool/mail, full, R)
NTP daemon /usr/sbin/ntpd	NONE	CAP_SYS_TIME	(/var/lib/ntp, full, R) (/etc/ntp/keys, read)
Printing daemon /usr/sbin/cupsd	NONE	CAP_NET_BIND_SERVICE CAP_DAC_OVERRIDE	(/etc/cups/certs, full, R) (/var/log/cups, full, R) (/var/cache/cups, full, R) (/var/run/cups/certs, full R)
System log daemon /usr/sbin/syslogd	NONE		(/var/log, full, R)
NSF RPC service /sbin/rpc.statd	NONE		(/var/lib/nfs/statd, full, R)
IP table /sbin/iptables	NONE	CAP_NET_ADMIN CAP_NET_RAW	

module or manipulating the image of the running kernel's memory in the file system (/dev/kmem).

We use two methods to determine whether a system has been compromised after installing a rootkit. The first method is to try to use the rootkit and see whether it is successfully installed. The second method is to calculate the hash values for all the files (content, permission bits, last modified time) in the local file system before and after installing the rootkit. For the calculation, we reboot the machine using an external operating system (e.g., from a CD) and mount the local file system. This ensures that the running kernel and the programs used in the calculation are clean. A comparison between the hash results can tell whether the system has been compromised.

We tried two well-known rootkits. The first one is Adore-ng, a kernel-mode rootkit that runs on Linux Kernel 2.2/2.4/2.6. It is installed by loading a malicious kernel module. The supported features include local root access, file hiding, process hiding, socket hiding, syslog filtering, and so on. Adore-ng also has a feature to replace an existing kernel module that is loaded during boot with the Trojaned module, so that adore-ng is activated during boot. When our protection was not enabled, we were able to successfully install Adore-ng in the remote root shell and activate it. We were also able to replace any existing kernel module with the Trojaned module so that the rootkit module would be automatically loaded during booting. When our protection system was enabled, the request to load the kernel module of Adore-ng from the remote root shell was denied, getting an "operation not permitted" error. We got the same error when trying to replace the existing kernel module with the Trojaned module. When trying to use the rootkit, we received a response saying "Adore-ng not installed." We checked the system integrity using the methods described earlier. The result showed that the system remained clean.

The second is Linux rootkit family (LRK). It is a well-known user-mode rootkit and replaces a variety of existing system programs and introduces some new programs, to build a backdoor, to hide the attacker, and to provide other attacking tools. When our protection was not enabled, we were able to install the Trojaned SSH daemon and replace the existing SSH daemon in the system. After that we successfully connected to the machine as root using a predefined password. When our protection was enabled, installation of the Trojaned SSH daemon failed, getting the "operation not permitted" error. The system remained clean.

2. *Stealing the shadow file*: Without our protection system, we were able to steal /etc/shadow by send an e-mail with the file as an attachment, using the command "mutt –a /etc/shadow alice@haker.net </dev/null." When our protection was enabled, the request to read the shadow file was denied, getting an error saying "/etc/shadow: unable to attach file."

Table 3
The performance results of Unixbench 4.1 measurements

Benchmark	Base	Enforcing	Overhead (%)	SELinux (%)
Dhrystone	335.8	334.2	0.5	
Double-precision	211.9	211.6	0.1	
Execl throughput	616.6	608.3	1	5
File copy 1K	474.0	454.2	4	5
File copy 256B	364.0	344.1	5	10
File copy 4K	507.5	490.4	3	2
Pipe throughput	272.6	269.6	1	16
Process creation	816.9	801.2	2	2
Shell scripts	648.3	631.2	0.7	4
System call	217.9	217.4	0.2	
Overall	446.6	435.0	3	

3. *Altering user's web page files*: Another common attack is to alter web files after getting into a web server. In our experiment, we put the user's web files in a sub directory of the user's home directory "/home/Alice/www/." That directory and all the files under the directory were set as not writable by the world. When our protection was enabled, from the remote root shell, we could not modify any web files in the directory "/home/Alice/www/." We could not create a new file in that directory. Our module successfully prevented user's protected files from being changed by low-integrity processes.

3.10.3. Performance

We have conducted benchmarking tests to compare performance overhead incurred by our protection system. Our performance evaluation uses the Lmbench 3 benchmark and the Unixbench 4.1 benchmark suites. These microbenchmark tests were used to determine the performance overhead incurred by the protection system for various process, file, and socket low-level operations.

We compare our performance result with SELinux. The performance data of SELinux is taken from Loscocco and Smalley (2001). For most benchmark results, the percentage overhead is small ($\leq 5\%$). The performance of our module is significantly better than the data for SELinux (Tables 3 and 4).

4   Discussions

In this chapter, we identified six design principles for designing usable access control mechanisms. We have also introduced the UMIP model, a

Table 4
The performance results of lmbench 3 measurements

Microbenchmark	Base	Enforcing	Overhead (%)	SELinux (%)
syscall	0.6492	0.6492	0	
read	0.8483	1.0017	18	
write	0.7726	0.8981	16	
stat	2.8257	2.8682	1.5	28
fstat	1.0139	1.0182	0.4	
open/close	3.7906	4.0608	7	27
select on 500 fd's	21.7686	21.8458	0.3	
select on 500 tcp fd's	37.8027	37.9795	0.5	
signal handler installation	1.2346	1.2346	0	
signal handler overhead	2.3954	2.4079	0.5	
protection fault	0.3994	0.3872	−3	
pipe latency	6.4345	6.2065	−3	12
pipe bandwidth	1310.19 MB/s	1292.54 MB/s	7	
AF_UNIX sock stream latency	8.2	8.9418	9	19
AF_UNIX sock stream bandwidth	1472.10 MB/s	1457.57 MB/s	9	
fork+exit	116.5581	120.3478	3	1
fork+execve	484.3333	500.1818	3	3
for+/bin/sh-c	1413.25	1444.25	2	10
file write bandwidth	16,997 KB/s	16,854 KB/s	0.8	
page fault	1.3288	1.3502	2	
UDP latency	14.4036	14.6798	2	15
TCP latency	17.1356	18.3555	7	9
RPC/udp latency	24.6433	24.8790	1	18
RPC/tcp latency	29.7117	32.4626	9	9
TCP/IP connection cost	64.5465	64.8352	1	9

simple, practical MAC model for host integrity protection, designed using these principles. The UMIP model defends against attacks targeting network server and client programs and protects users from careless mistakes. It supports existing applications and system administration practices, and has a simple policy configuration interface. To achieve these, we introduced in UMIP several novel features in integrity protection. UMIP categorizes the processes into two integrity levels, high and low. When a process performs an operation that makes it potentially contaminated, it drops its integrity. One novel feature of UMIP is that, unlike previous MAC systems, UMIP uses existing DAC information to identify which files are to be protected. Although the basic UMIP policy achieves the security goal, many existing applications will not be able to run and many common practices for using and administering the system will become impossible. We thus need to extend the basic UMIP policy to balance the functional requirements, the security goal, and the simplicity of the design (for usability). UMIP introduces several concepts to model programs that are partially trusted; these programs can violate the default integrity policy in certain limited, well-defined ways. We found that only a small number of exceptions and settings need to be specified for our environment.

5 Questions for discussion

1. Why is DAC vulnerable to the Trojan horse attacks? Is there a way to enhance DAC to be resilience to Trojan horses?
2. Generally, what are the differences between MAC and DAC? Is it valid to say that MAC can provide better security properties than DAC? What are the advantages and limitations of both MAC and DAC? How are COTS operating systems applying MAC and DAC, respectively?
3. The default policy in the UMIP model strictly partitions the subjects and objects into two sets, high- and low-integrity; no information flow between the two sets is allowed. Certainly such a policy does not work. Give some examples to explain why such information flow cannot be avoided. UMIP introduces exception policy to enable administrator to explicitly allow some kinds of information flow between high- and low-integrity. Why is the exception policy designed in that way? Are there alternative ways? How to compare different ways of specifying policy to allow certain information flow? What are the criteria?
4. Can we compare the different MAC systems, such as SELinux, AppArmor, LOMAC, and UMIP in some way? What are the attack channels exposed by those systems? What kinds of security assumption do those systems make? Are those assumptions valid in real-world applications? Is there a way to validate the assumptions somehow?

References

Badger, L., D.F. Sterne, D.L. Sherman, K.M. Walker, S.A. Haghighat (1995a). A domain and type enforcement UNIX prototype, in: *Proceedings of the USENIX Security Symposium, June*, Salt Lake City, UT, USA, pp. 127–140.

Badger, L., D.F. Sterne, D.L. Sherman, K.M. Walker, S.A. Haghighat (1995b). Practical domain and type enforcement for UNIX, in: *Proceedings of the IEEE Symposium on Security and Privacy, May*, Oakland, CA, USA, pp. 66–77.

Biba, K.J. (1977). Integrity considerations for secure computer systems. Technical Report MTR-3153, MITRE, April.

Brumley, D., D. Song (2004). PrivTrans: automatically partitioning programs for privilege separation, in: *Proceedings of the USENIX Security Symposium, August*, San Diego, CA, USA.

Cowan, C., S. Beattie, G. Kroah-Hartman, C. Pu, P. Wagle, V.D. Gligor (2000). Subdomain: parsimonious server security, in: *Proceedings of the 14th Conference on Systems Administration (LISA 2000), December*, New Orleans, LA, USA, pp. 355–368.

Fraser, T. (2000). LOMAC: low water-mark integrity protection for COTS environments, in: *2000 IEEE Symposium on Security and Privacy*, *May*, Oakland, CA, USA, pp. 230–245.

Goldberg, I., D. Wagner, R. Thomas, E.A. Brewer (1996). A secure environment for untrusted helper applications: confining the wily hacker, in: *Proceedings of the USENIX Security Symposium*, *June*, San Diego, CA, USA, pp. 1–13.

Loscocco, P., S. Smalley (2001). Integrating flexible support for security policies into the Linux operating system, in: *Proceedings of the FREENIX track: USENIX Annual Technical Conference*, *June*, Boston, MA, USA, pp. 29–42.

Provos, N. (2003). Improving host security with system call policies, in: *Proceedings of the 2003 USENIX Security Symposium*, *August*, Washington, DC, USA, pp. 252–272.

Provos, N., M. Friedl, P. Honeyman (2003). Preventing privilege escalation, in: *Proceedings of the 2003 USENIX Security Symposium*, *August*, Washington, DC, USA, pp. 231–242.

Raymond, E.S. (2003). *The Art of UNIX Programming*. Addison-Wesley Professional, Upper Saddle River, NJ, USA.

Saltzer, J.H., M.D. Schroeder (1975). The protection of information in computer systems. *Proceedings of the IEEE* 63(9), 1278–1308. September.

Sandhu, R. (2003). Good-enough security: Toward a pragmatic business-driven discipline. *IEEE Internet Computing* 7(1), 66–68. January.

Trusted Computer System Evaluation Criteria (1985). Department of Defense 5200.28-STD, December.

Suggested readings

Skoudis, E., T. Liston (2006). *Counter Hack Reloaded: A Step-by-Step Guide to Computer Attacks and Effective Defenses*. Prentice Hall PTR, Upper Saddle River, NJ, USA.

Skoudis, E., L. Zeltser (2003). *Malware: Fighting Malicious Code*. Prentice Hall PTR, Upper Saddle River, NJ, USA.

Online resources

Novell AppArmor Project Page. Available at http://www.novell.com/linux/security/apparmor/

Security-Enhanced Linux Project Page, from National Security Agency. Available at http://www.nsa.gov/selinux/

UMIP Project Page. Available at http://www.cs.purdue.edu/homes/ninghui/projects/osac.html

Rao & Upadhyaya, Eds., *Handbooks in Information Systems, Vol. 4*

Chapter 13

Optimistic Fair Exchange

N. Asokan

Nokia Research Center, Itämerenkatu 11-13, 00180 Helsinki, Finland

Matthias Schunter

IBM Research GmbH, Zurich Research Laboratory, Säumerstr. 4, CH-8803 Rüschlikon, Switzerland

Abstract

How do two mutually distrusting parties exchange digital items in such a way that either both parties get the items they expect or neither gets new information about these items beyond what they already knew? This is the essence of the fair exchange problem. In this chapter, we will first look at different types of fair exchange and survey various fair exchange protocols. In particular, we will discuss a particular "optimistic" approach that is optimized for the common case that the parties involved in the exchange are usually interested seeing the exchange completed rather than attempting to cheat. We will then examine practical application scenarios and give an outlook on future research directions.

1 Introduction

Imagine you are a buyer on the popular Internet auction site eBay. You notice a nice antique vase up for auction. You have always wanted such a vase. So you place a bid of $100 and are delighted to learn later that you won the auction. Now comes the problem. If you send $100 to the seller, there is no guarantee that you will get your vase. You can try insisting that you will pay on delivery. But now imagine that you are the seller. You may not want to ship your antique vase to a stranger unless you are guaranteed to get paid for it.

Now, if the seller is your friend, or if it is a reputed antique dealer you already know, you would not hesitate to send the money first. The problem arises when the two parties involved do not have grounds for trusting each other. What you would need is a protocol to exchange the payment and the vase between mutually distrusting parties in such a way that either both parties receive what they expect or neither party does. Cryptographers refer to such protocols as *fair exchange* protocols. They are needed whenever two mutually distrusting participants want to exchange electronic items while requiring fairness. Additional examples include receipts for payments, exchange of signatures under a contract, or sending secret messages while obtaining a receipt.

In this chapter, we will first look at different types of fair exchange and survey various fair exchange protocols. We will then examine practical application scenarios and give an outlook on future research directions.

2   Types of fair exchange

The most general type of fair exchange is a barter of one item for another. Suppose two parties A and B want to participate in a fair exchange with A sending an item I_A and B sending an item I_B. The exchange is fair if either A gets I_B and B gets I_A or neither party gets anything valuable. For now, let us not worry about precisely defining what is meant by "anything valuable."

Unlike in common parlance, the phrase "fair exchange" does not imply that the items being exchanged have comparable values. For example, fair exchange protocols cannot and do not attempt to ensure that your antique vase is indeed worth $100. Instead, they merely ensure that whatever was agreed between the parties is exchanged fairly, so that if one party gets the item it expects, then the other party also gets the item it expects.

There have been attempts to design generic protocols for fair exchange as we will see later. Still, it is useful to look at some specific types of exchanges because it is possible to design particularly effective protocols that are limited in their applicability to a certain type of exchanges only. Here are some specific types of fair exchange (we will have a closer look at the corresponding protocols in Section 6):

- *Fair purchase*: One party, say A, is the buyer and the other party, B, is the seller. I_A is a specific amount of money. I_B is some item of value. The eBay example we saw earlier is an instance of fair purchase: I_A is $100 and I_B is the antique vase. From A's point of view, a fair purchase protocol must guarantee that either she receives the vase or B receives no money. From B's point of view, the same protocol must guarantee that either he receives $100 or A does not receive the vase. As we noted earlier, whether $100 is a fair price for the vase is not the concern of the fair purchase protocol.

- *Contract signing*: Both parties have agreed on a contract text. I_A is A's signature on the contract text, and I_B is B's signature on the same contract text. Each party wants a digital signature of the other party, which we shall call "the peer," on the contract text, which can be used to prove that the peer committed to the contract. A fair contract signing protocol must ensure that either each party receives its peer's signature or neither of them receives any information that can help them forge the other peer's signature.

- *Certified mail*: One party, say A, sends a message *m* to the other party, B, which is the recipient. I_A is a mail message. I_B is a signed receipt from the recipient, which can be used to prove that the recipient had access to *m*. Optionally, the recipient may also want the sender's signature on *m*, which can be used to prove that the sender did in fact send *m*. A's requirement for a fair certified mail protocol is that either A gets the receipt or B does not learn any part of A's message. B's requirement for the same fair certified mail protocol is that either B gets A's complete message *m* or A does not receive any information that can help her forge B's signature on the receipt for *m*.

- *Fair exchange of secret digital data*: I_A and I_B are digital data items with unique descriptions, so that given a digital item and description it can be unambiguously verified whether the item fits the description. For example, the description can be the hash of the data computed using a cryptographic hash function. A protocol for fair exchange of secret digital data must ensure that either each party gets the item it expects or neither party learns any additional information about the respective items beyond their descriptions.

Certified mail can be used to build a fair contract signing protocol by simply defining a valid contract to be a signed message and its receipt. Clearly, a protocol for the fair exchange of secret data can be used to build protocols for both fair contract signing and certified mail.

Now we will look at the different approaches for solving the fair exchange problem. The approaches differ on whether a trusted intermediary is used and the nature of the intermediary when one is used. Although the fair exchange problem is general, most of the protocols we would look at are meant for exchanging digital information: the items of value can be digital payments, digital signatures, or secret digital data.

3 Employing a middleman: exchange through trusted third party

In real life, when you have to deal with someone whom you do not know well enough, it helps to have a trusted intermediary to act as a go-between. If you are lucky, you and your peer in the transaction will be able to find a mutually trusted intermediary. The obvious approach to design a fair exchange protocol is to use such a trusted intermediary who actively participates in the exchange.

Protocols for fair exchange using a trusted intermediary were mentioned in the research literature more than two decades ago (Rabin, 1983). The trusted third party (TTP) is actively involved in each protocol run. We denote such intermediaries as *inline* TTP. In the 1990s, a number of research publications made detailed proposals (Bahreman and Tygar, 1994; Deng et al., 1996; Zhou and Gollmann, 1996) for the certified mail case. All of them follow a general pattern: suppose **sender** wants to send a message M to **recipient** in return for a receipt R. A third party **T** facilitates the process by actively participating in the exchange transaction. The schemes differ in terms of what messages are sent and by whom. However, all three schemes (Bahreman and Tygar, 1994; Deng et al., 1996; Zhou and Gollmann, 1996) contain the same essential steps as follows:

S1   A message M is encrypted using a symmetric key K that is chosen randomly. The result is the ciphertext C.
S2   **T** gains access to K.
S3   **Recipient** issues a part or the whole of a receipt R on C.
S4   **T** makes K available to **recipient**.
S5   **T** makes receipt R available to **sender**.

In all the schemes, security is guaranteed by ensuring that

1. step S4 happens only after step S3 (that is, **recipient** can access the message if and only if he releases a receipt),
2. step S5 happens after step S2 (that is, **sender** gets the receipt only if he releases the information needed to allow recipient to get the message), and
3. if either one of step S4 or step S5 happens, then the other step also happens, or at least is feasible (that is, if one party gets the item it expects, the protocol ensures that the other party can also get the item it expects).

Now, let us look at how the message sequences of these schemes differ. The public encryption keys of **T** and **recipient** are PT and PR, respectively. The notation $E_X(Y)$ describes an encryption Y using the key X, and $\text{sign}_A(Y)$ describes a digital signature of entity A on a message Y. $h()$ is a cryptographic hash function. In the scheme by Deng et al. (1996), there are four messages:

M1   **Sender** chooses K and uses it to construct the encrypted message C (step S1). It also encrypts K using the public key of **T** (step S2). **Sender** sends these to **recipient** along with a hash of the message $h(M)$:?

   Sender $\rightarrow$ recipient: $h(M)$, $E_{PT}(K)$, $C = E_K(\text{Sender, recipient, T}, M)$

   Recipient creates a signature on $h(M)$, which serves as the partial receipt $par = \text{sign}_{\text{recipient}}(\text{sender, recipient, T}, h(M))$ (step S3).

M2   Recipient sends the partial receipt *par*, the encrypted key, and the ciphertext C to T.

Recipient $\rightarrow$ T: *par*, $E_{PT}(K)$, C

T extracts the message key K and checks whether the partial receipt issued by recipient is correct. If it is, it encrypts K using the public key of recipient.

M3   T sends the (encrypted) key to recipient (step S4).

T $\rightarrow$ recipient: sender, recipient, $E_{PR}(K)$

M4   T countersigns the partial receipt. The resulting signature serves as the receipt R. T sends the receipt to sender (step S5).

T $\rightarrow$ sender: sender, recipient, $h(M)$, $E_K(\text{sign}_T(\text{*par*}, \text{recipient}, M))$

To summarize, K is chosen by sender and sent to T. Sender also sends C directly to recipient. Recipient sends a partial receipt to T. T then sends K to recipient and the receipt R to sender. Therefore, T ensures that conditions 1, 2, and 3 are met.

In the scheme by Zhou and Gollmann (1996), unlike in Deng et al. (1996), recipient sends part of R directly back to sender. When sender submits K to T, T makes the rest of R and K publicly available. Therefore, while T ensures that conditions 2 and 3 are met, sender is responsible for ensuring that condition 1 is met.

In the scheme by Bahreman and Tygar (1994), sender and recipient always communicate through T. K is chosen by T. T sends C to recipient. When recipient sends part of R to T, T sends R to sender and K to recipient. Therefore, T is responsible for ensuring that all three conditions are met.

Although the examples we have seen so far are about certified electronic mail, you can easily imagine how the same simple idea of using a trusted intermediary is applicable to any type of fair exchange. In fact, eBay recommends that its customers use an escrow service, which is a fair exchange scheme that uses a TTP. In the eBay escrow service, the third party is an escrow server run at escrow.com and works as follows:

1. The buyer and the seller agree to the terms of the transaction, including who pays for the escrow service.
2. The buyer sends the full payment to the escrow server.
3. The seller ships the merchandise directly to the buyer.
4. The buyer can accept the merchandise or return it to the seller. Note that the buyer may open and possibly even use the merchandise before deciding that it is not acceptable.
5. If the buyer accepted the merchandise, the escrow server will forward the payment to the seller, minus its escrow service fees.

6. If the buyer returned the goods and the seller accepts them, the escrow server will return the payment to the buyer minus its fees.
7. If the seller does not accept the returned goods, the transaction is sent for arbitration administered by a suitable regional entity, such as the American Arbitration Association. How the arbitration is done is not specified.

The escrow service does not come cheap. The fee for a transaction using escrow.com can be as high as 6.3%. One reason for the high cost is that the third party needs to be actively involved in every transaction. In addition, the protocols given earlier call for a high degree of trust in the third party. In particular, the third party is not *accountable*: if it abuses the trust placed in it by favoring one participant in the exchange over the other, there is no way to prove this misbehavior.

Researchers have been pondering over how to minimize the involvement of and the level of requisite trust on third parties. Ideally, one would like no third-party involvement at all. In Sections 4 and 5, we will examine ways of doing this.

4   Being optimistic: on-demand invocation of trusted third party

Let us now step back and consider the circumstances under which an exchange takes place. At the beginning of this chapter, we used the example of eBay to illustrate why fair exchange protocols are needed. We argued that when two parties who do not already have a trust relationship between them want to carry out an exchange between them, a protocol is needed to ensure that the exchange is fair. Most of the time, however, both parties involved in an exchange transaction are interested in seeing the exchange through. In eBay or in any other typical exchange scenario, legitimate players outnumber the crooks. Successful exchanges are much more common than attempts at cheating. Would it be possible to design an exchange protocol that is optimized for this common case?

4.1   Optimistic fair exchange

This was exactly the intuition behind what is known as *optimistic protocols* for fair exchange. The phrase was coined by (Asokan et al., 1997), which also described protocols for several types of fair exchange. The essential idea in optimistic protocols is that the third party is involved only if something goes wrong. Unlike inline TTPs, it need not actively participate in every exchange transaction.[1] An early instance of this

---

[1]Note that in the work by Bahreman and Tygar (1994), this optimistic behavior is called "off-line TTP." Strictly speaking, the third party cannot be offline because it must be reachable if something goes wrong.

approach was mentioned by Even (1983), where he proposed the idea of a "center of cancellations" to be used in achieving fair contract signing. If one party did not receive a signed contract from the other party before a deadline, it can ask the center of cancellations to declare a contract void.

What can the third party do in general if one of the parties initiates a dispute? It may try to contact the other party in the exchange, the peer, and get it to complete the exchange. But if the peer is unreachable or unwilling to complete the transaction, the third party can do one of the following three things:

1. *Cancel the exchange*: If the item sent by the complaining peer is revocable (e.g., a payment or contract signature), the third party can issue a revocation token. This is what Even's center of cancellations does (Even, 1983).
2. *Issue a replacement*: The third party can issue evidence that may serve as replacement for the actual expected item (e.g., a contract signature in the form of the original promises countersigned by the third party).
3. *Take punitive action*: The third party can punish the misbehaving peer if it has some means of doing so. For example, in the work by Bürk and Pfitzmann (1989), the exchange protocol hides the identities of the peers from each other. In case of misbehavior, the third party can revoke the anonymity of the misbehaving peer.

As you can see, none of these options is particularly satisfactory. They raise two serious issues:

- *Suitability of replacements*: Evidence as replacement for the expected item is useful only if there will be some external dispute resolution. For example, promises for a contract signing exchange, countersigned by the third party, could possibly be used as evidence in an external dispute involving an arbiter. If there is no such external dispute resolution, then producing a replacement cannot count as guaranteeing fairness. At best, we can call this "weak fairness" (Asokan et al., 1997).

  It would of course be better if the third party can guarantee strong fairness. For this, there must be a way for the third party to produce the expected item itself instead of some replacement.
- *Timely completion of transactions*: Communication links can break. Devices can go offline to save power or because they are out of communication range. Suppose an honest party A completes an exchange transaction and then goes offline. Peer B now complains to the third party, which proceeds to cancel the exchange or punish A!

  What is needed is a way for each honest peer to complete the protocol when it wants, with the assurance that the end result will not change.

Let us now look at how each of these issues can be dealt with. In Section 4.2, we will examine the first problem described earlier. In Section 4.3, we will look at the issue of timely completion.

4.2   From promises to permits

We want to design an optimistic exchange protocol in which, if the third party is invoked, this third party is capable of providing the item expected by the invoker. Recall that in optimistic fair exchange, the participants first exchange promises. When the third party is invoked, the invoker sends these promises to the third party. If the third party is unable to resolve the exchange, it can only issue a replacement. How can we make it possible for the third party to provide the expected item itself, instead of just replacements?

In the first round, instead of exchanging mere promises, we want the parties to exchange *permits*. A permit should be such that it permits the third party to recover (or help recover) the expected item itself. It may be difficult to construct such magical permits for physical items such as antique vases! Fortunately, for some classes of digital items, there are techniques that can be used to make permits.

One such technique uses the concept of *verifiable escrow*. We have already looked at an example of escrow in the case of the eBay escrow service. In the case of digital data, an escrow is a secret message s deposited with the third party T along with a condition *cond* such that the third party will make s accessible if *cond* is satisfied. Suppose T has a public key PT. The escrow can be implemented as $E = E_{PT}(r, s, cond)$, where $E_{PT}()$ indicates public key encryption using the key PT, r is a random string used to make the encryption probabilistic. Suppose one player, **sender**, creates such an escrow E and sends it to the other player, **recipient**. E is verifiable if **recipient** can convince itself that (a) T will be able to decrypt E and (b) T will agree to return the plaintext s if condition *cond* is satisfied. We cannot make verifiable escrows for arbitrary secrets s. But we can make verifiable escrows for a special type of secrets known as homomorphic pre-images. In Section 4.2.1, we see a protocol for the verifiable escrow of homomorphic pre-images. After that, we will see how this can be used to make verifiable escrow of standard digital signatures such as the Rivest–Shamir–Adleman (RSA) scheme and Digital Signature Standard (DSS).

4.2.1   Verifiable escrow of homomorphic pre-images

A homomorphism is a mapping θ between two commutative groups G_1 and G_2, $\theta: G_1 \rightarrow G_2$, such that θ is one to one and there is a mapping for every element of G_2. We use the symbol "+" to denote the group operation and "−" to denote its inverse. If $\theta(s) = \delta$, then s is said to be the homomorphic pre-image of δ. We can design a protocol between A and B for the verifiable escrow of s. We require that both A and B know δ. They have also agreed on a condition *cond* and a mutually acceptable third party T. The protocol proceeds as follows.

1. A does the following. For $i = 1$ to n
   - pick a random string r_i and a random element of G_1, s_i'
   - compute an escrow E_i as follows

   $$E_i = E_{PT}(r_i, s_i', cond) \tag{1}$$

   - compute δ_i' as follows

   $$\delta_i' = \theta(s_i') \tag{2}$$

   - A computes the hash of n pairs $(E_i, \delta')_i$ using a well-known cryptographic hash function $H()$ as follows:

   $$h = H(E_1, \delta_1', ..., E_n, \delta_n') \tag{3}$$

   A sends h to B.

2. B picks a random n-bit challenge $b_1, \ldots, b_n$ (not all zero) and sends it to A.
3. A does the following. For $i = 1$ to n
   - if $b_i = 0$, set $v_i = (r_i, s_i')$
   - if $b_i = 1$, set $v_i = (E_i, s_i'' = s + s_i')$
     A sends $v_1, \ldots, v_n$ to B.
4. B does the following. For $i = 1$ to n
   - if $b_i = 0$, extract (r_i, s_i'), from v_i, use expression (1) to compute E_i with these values and the mutually agreed *cond*, and then use expression (2) to compute δ_i'.
   - if $b_i = 1$, extract E_i, s_i'', from v_i compute δ_i' as $\delta_i' = \theta(s_i'') - \delta$.
   B calculates h' as follows:

   $$h' = H(E_1, \delta_1', ..., E_n, \delta_n'). \tag{4}$$

If h' is the same as h received in step 1 above, B accepts and outputs all unopened E_i values and the corresponding s_i'' values. Otherwise B rejects.

This is verifiable escrow because B now knows that it can take any of the unopened E_i to T, and T will be able to decrypt it and return s_i' as long as condition *cond* holds. Once it receives s_i', it can recover the desired secret s as $s_i' + s_i''$. Can A cheat? A could have used random junk in place of the E_i. To be able to successfully cheat, A must still get B to accept the verifiable encryption as correct. Assuming that the hash function $H()$ is collision-resistant, this implies that in expression (4), B must use exactly the same input parameters as what A used in expression (3). A could use random junk in place of some E_i values. A can get away with these if B happens to choose

b_i to be 0 exactly for those i values for which E_i is random junk (and B chooses b_i to be 1 for all other i values). The catch is that A does not know the value of b_i when it has to compute h using expression (3). It can of course guess the value of each b_i. It has a 50% chance of getting each guess right. To cheat successfully, it has to guess every b_i correctly. The probability of successful cheating is $(1/2)^n$. For example, if n was 40, the cheating probability is less than one in a trillion.

The verifiable escrow protocol described here was first introduced by Asokan et al. (1998b) and refined by Asokan et al. (2000). Bao et al. (1998) also described an optimistic fair exchange protocol using publicly verifiable encryptions. Although verifiable encryptions are similar to verifiable escrows, there is a crucial difference, which is important for the correctness of fair exchange: verifiable escrow contains the condition for opening the escrow within it. The third party must open the escrow only if the condition is satisfied. In the case of fair exchange, the condition would describe what item is expected in exchange for the item embedded within the escrow.

4.2.2 Verifiable escrow of digital signatures

Now, let us see how we can build a verifiable escrow of RSA signatures. RSA works in a group defined by a composite number N, which is a product of two large distinct prime numbers. The public exponent e is chosen as a number relatively prime to the Euler totient of N denoted by $\phi(N)$, and the private key d is calculated so that $e.d = 1 \pmod{\phi(N)}$. A message m is signed by first applying a specified formatting algorithm to get a formatted message δ and then calculating $\delta^d \pmod N$. In our notation, G_1 and G_2 are both the same group consisting of positive integers modulo N, Z_N^*. The group operation is multiplication modulo N. The homomorphism is defined by $\theta(s) = s^e \pmod N$. Suppose we have a suitably formatted message δ and an RSA signature $s = \delta^d \pmod N$. The secret we want to escrow is the signature s, and its public description is the formatted message δ.

Similar conversions can be made for signature schemes based on discrete logarithms such as the DSS. The homomorphic inverse in this case will be the discrete logarithm. Refer the work by Asokan et al. (2000) for details on how to build verifiable escrows for number of signature schemes and an anonymous electronic cash scheme based on verifiable escrow of discrete logarithms.

Recent research has focused on using other primitives such as two-signatures (Dodis and Reyzin, 2003) or RSA-based non-interactive proofs (Nenadić et al., 2004).

4.2.3 Verifiable escrow using pre-issued coupons

In the verifiable escrow scheme in Section 4.2.1, observe that s_i' is chosen as a random element in G_1 and is therefore independent of s. This leads us to construct an efficient verifiable escrow mechanism. A can generate a random s' and send it securely to T along with its own public key PA. T will then issue a coupon in the form of a pair: $\langle C1 = E_{PT}(s', PA), C2 = \text{sign}_T(C1, \bullet') \rangle$, where $\bullet' = \bullet(s') \rangle$. When A later wants to construct a verifiable escrow E of some secret s subject to some condition *cond*, it constructs E as the following set of three values: $E = \langle C1, C2, S = \text{sign}_A(C1, C2, cond) \rangle$. E and $s'' = s + s'$ are transferred to B. To check whether this is a valid escrow, the verifier first extracts δ' from $C2$ and checks whether $\theta(s'')$ equals $\delta + \delta'$ (recall that δ is the public description of s) and then verifies the signatures in $C2$ and S. T can extract s' by decrypting $C1$.

Compared with the protocol in Section 4.2.1, this variation is efficient in terms of computation and communication. To construct a valid verifiable escrow, only one encryption (and one signature) needs to be computed and communicated. The earlier protocol required n encryptions.

In the remainder of this section, we will use the notation VE_X to denote a verifiable escrow made by the entity X. This could be either a set of three values based on pre-issued coupons as described earlier or an unopened encryption of the form $E_i = E_{PT}(r_i, s'_i, cond)$, obtained using a verifiable escrow protocol as described in Section 4.2.1.

4.3 Dealing with asynchrony

Now we turn our attention to the issue of timely completion. In Section 4.1, we already saw the timeliness issues that arise if the third party is allowed to cancel or revoke completed exchanges. Even when there is no revocation, timeliness issues remain. To discuss this, consider the following simplistic optimistic fair exchange protocol consisting of the following three flows: Suppose A and B want to optimistically exchange their signatures on a message m, using the third party T in case of exceptions. Let s_A be the secret homomorphic pre-image corresponding to A's signature on m.

A1 *Commitment of A*: A creates a verifiable escrow VE_A of s_A, with T as the third party, and the condition *cond* containing the message m and the public key PB of B to describe that the expected item is the signature of B on the same message.

A2 *Signature of B*: If B cannot verify the escrow, it quits. Otherwise, it sends its signature on m to A.

A3 *Signature of A*: If the received signature is valid, A sends its own signature to B.

If B does not receive A's signature (in message A3), it can take the verifiable escrow and its own signature to T. T will be able to verify B's signature against the condition *cond* embedded inside the escrow. If the check succeeds, T will decrypt VE_A and send the result to B, which would allow B to reconstruct s_A. If B ever does this, A will be able to obtain B's signature as well, even if it did not receive it (in message A2). Thus, fairness requirements seem to be satisfied. But what about timeliness? B can conclude the exchange at any time. If it did not receive A's commitment in message A1, it simply quits. If it did not receive A's signature (in message A3), it can decide to go to T at its convenience. However, once A sends message A1 to B, A is at the mercy of B. A cannot simply decide to quit and go home because B might go to T at some later point in time. This is the timeliness problem: We want each party to be able to unilaterally end the protocol at a time of its own choosing, without having to depend on the actions of the other party. Once a party completes an exchange this way, it should be able to "just quit and go home," knowing that the state of the exchange will not change thereafter.

The first solution that might come to mind is to impose some time limit. But suitable time limits are not easy to find: if the time limit is too short, and B is behind a slow or unreliable link, it may lose out because T will refuse to open the escrow once the time limit has passed. If the time limit is too long, A will have to wait too long before it can quit.

In realistic networks where the quality of the communication links varies widely, we cannot assume any guarantees on message-delivery times. We have to assume that messages may be arbitrarily delayed. Such a network model is called the *asynchronous model*. A protocol for optimistic fair exchange in the asynchronous network model was described by (Asokan et al., 1998a). Let us see how we can use this to exchange digital signatures between A and B. The basic exchange protocol is as follows: Let s_A and s_B be the homomorphic pre-images of their respective digital signatures that A and B want to exchange. Let δ_B be $\theta(s_B)$, the public description of s_B.

Exchange protocol (between A and B):

B1   *Commitment of A*: A creates a verifiable escrow VE_A of s_A, with T as the third party, and the condition *cond* containing δ_B as well as a transaction identifier *tid* chosen by A as a cryptographic hash of a random string *r*. A sends VE_A to B.

B2   *Commitment of B*: If B can verify VE_A, B creates a verifiable escrow VE_B of s_B, with T as the third party, and the same condition *cond* as in VE_A. B sends VE_B to A.

B3   *Signature of A*: If A can verify VE_B, A sends its own signature on *m* to B.

B4   *Signature of B*: If B receives a valid signature on *m* from A, B sends its own signature on *m* to B.

Note that the each of the last three steps specifies a condition and describes what should happen if the condition holds. If the condition does not hold, nothing changes: the party checking the condition simply continues to wait. But we want to allow a party to quit the protocol at any time. As we shall briefly discuss, when a party decides to quit the exchange while the protocol is still in progress, it needs to interact with T. To this end, there are three sub protocols: abort, A-resolve, and B-resolve, each of which consists of a single request and response. In the sub protocols, T uses two databases: a status database *status* and a content database *data*. We use the notation *status*[*tid*] and *data*[*tid*] to refer to the records in these databases corresponding to the index *tid*. We require that in each of the sub-protocols, T's processing is done atomically and sequentially: that is, once T starts processing an abort or resolve request, it completes it fully before moving on to processing another abort or resolve request.

Protocol abort (between A and T): The purpose for the abort protocol is that A can ask T never to resolve a particular exchange. Naturally, T will agree to do so only if that exchange has not already been resolved. To start the abort protocol, A sends an abort request to T. The request contains A's escrow VE_A and r. T will extract *tid* from VE_A and check if it is the hash of r. If not, T will return an error. Otherwise, T will check if there is an entry in *status* corresponding to *tid*. If there is no *status*[*tid*], T sets *status*[*tid*] to "aborted," creates an abort token of the form sign_T (VE_A, "aborted"), and sets *data*[*tid*] to this. In either case, T sends the current value of *data*[*tid*] to A.

Protocol A-resolve (between A and T): The purpose for the A-resolve protocol is to allow A to complete the exchange with the help of T. To start A-resolve, A sends a resolve request to T. The request contains B's escrow VE_B and r. T will extract *tid* from VE_B and check if it is the hash of r. If not, T will return an error. Otherwise, T will look for *status*[*tid*]. If *status*[*tid*] is "aborted," then T makes no changes to the databases. Otherwise, T sets *status*[*tid*] to "resolved," decrypts VE_B, and sets *data*[*tid*] to the result of this decryption. In either case, T sends the current value of *data*[*tid*] to A.

Protocol B-resolve (between B and T): The purpose for the B-resolve protocol is to allow B to complete the exchange with the help of T. To start B-resolve, B sends a resolve request to T. The request contains A's escrow VE_A and B's secret s_B. T will first look up *status*[*tid*] corresponding to *tid*. There are two cases:

- If *status*[*tid*] is "aborted," the return value is the abort token contained in *data*[*tid*].
- Otherwise, T will extract δ_B from VE_A and check if it is the same as $\grave{e}(s_B)$. If not, the return value is an error. Otherwise, T will decrypt VE_A and set the result as the return value. T will also set *status*[*tid*] to "resolved."

Let us now see how each party can unilaterally end the exchange at any time of its choosing. First, consider the case of B. Table 1 describes what B should do if it decides to quit at various stages in the protocol: if it decides to quit before sending its commitment (message B2) or after receiving A's signature (message B3), it can do so without any loss of fairness to itself. If it decides to quit in the interim, that is, after sending message B2 but

Table 1
Unilaterally ended exchange: prescribed actions for B

State (last message sent/received)	Prescribed action for ending the exchange
Received commitment (B1)	Just quit
Sent commitment (B2)	Run protocol B-resolve
Received signature (B3)	Just quit
Sent signature (B4)	Just quit

Table 2
Unilaterally ended exchange: prescribed actions for A

State (last message sent/received)	Prescribed action for ending the exchange
Sent commitment (B1)	Run protocol abort
Received commitment (B2)	Run protocol A-resolve (or protocol abort)
Sent signature (B3)	Run protocol A-resolve
Received signature (B4)	Just quit

before receiving a valid message B3, then B must run protocol B-resolve. If B sends the correct s_B in the resolve request, it will either receive an abort token or receive the result of decrypting VE_A, which it can use to reconstruct s_A. In either case, B can complete the protocol.

Now consider the case of A. Table 2 describes what A should do if it decides to quit at various stages in the protocol: if A decides to quit before sending its commitment (in message B1) or after receiving B's signature (in message B4), it can do so without any loss of fairness to itself. If A decides to quit after sending its commitment but before receiving a valid commitment from B (in message B2), it must run protocol abort. If A sends a valid r in the abort request, it will receive either an abort token or s_B. In either case, B can complete the protocol. If A decides to quit after receiving B's commitment (in message B2), it must run protocol A-resolve.[2] If A sends a valid r, it will get the result of decrypting VE_A, which it can use to reconstruct s_B.

Thus, we can see that each party can decide to "just quit and go home" at a time of its own choosing, regardless of the behavior of its counterpart. The only requirement is that T must be reachable. Note also that in specifying the operation of each player, we made no reference to any judgment on whether its peer has behaved maliciously. This is because in an asynchronous network setting, it is not always possible to distinguish

---

[2]Of course, A has the option of running protocol abort at this point.

between malicious peer behavior and vagaries of the network: For example, an expected message may not show up in time either because the peer intentionally did not send it or because the network lost it. That is why we allow each party to quit whenever it wants, while ensuring that its security requirements are met.

Does the protocol still guarantee fairness to each party? Take the case of A. B can get its signature in one of two ways:

- Directly from A (in message B3): in this case, A has already received VE_B, which it can use in protocol A-resolve to get s_B.
- As a result of running protocol B-resolve, in this case, B must have sent s_B to T. T would have thus set *status*[*tid*] to "resolved" and *data*[*tid*] to s_B. Thus, if A attempts to run either protocol abort or protocol A-resolve, it will get s_B.

You can use a similar reasoning to see that the protocol guarantees fairness for B as well. For detailed proofs, refer the work by Asokan et al. (2000). The aforementioned basic protocol has four message flows. It has been shown in the work by Pfitzmann et al. (1998) that this is optimal for optimistic fair exchange in the asynchronous model.

5 Avoiding the middleman

The difficulty of deploying a protocol increases with the number of different parties involved in it. Fair exchange mediated by a third party is no exception. The aforementioned protocols require that both parties of the exchange are able to agree on a third party that is trusted by both and is reachable by both when needed. Finding such a third party may not always be feasible. Let us look at attempts to do away with the third party.

5.1 Exchanging in pieces

The first approach, known as the gradual release of secrets, is to perform the exchange gradually over many rounds, exchanging one pair of secrets at a time. Even and Yacobi (1980) showed that deterministically guaranteeing fair exchange without using a third party is impossible. Thus, the guarantee provided by all gradual approaches is probabilistic: They can minimize, but not eliminate, the chances that the exchange leaves a correctly behaving party in an unfair situation.

There are a number of publications describing schemes for fair exchange using gradual release of secrets (Blum, 1983; Damgård, 1995; Even, 1983). All of them follow the same basic pattern: A and B want to exchange their respective secrets s_A and s_B. Each secret is split into n components of equal length, and each component is recognizable in that when the recipient receives the component, it can verify it as a legitimate part of the whole secret. Now the parties take turns to transfer their respective secrets component by component to their counterpart. Suppose the process is interrupted after, say, A has sent the ith component: A knows that it has $n - i + 1$ missing components and B has at least $n - i$ missing components. Therefore, the computational effort needed to recover these components by brute force can be made roughly the same, by choosing a suitably large value for n. If A and B have equal computing capabilities, then neither has a significant advantage.

There are a number of problems with this approach (Ben-Or et al., 1990). First, the protocol necessarily involves many rounds of communication, resulting in excessive communication costs. Second, the fairness guarantee relies on the assumption of equal computing capabilities. But computing capabilities can vary widely, and differences by factors of tens or hundreds are not uncommon, and hence the assumption is not valid in many situations. Third, the issue of timely completion is problematic. Ben-Or et al. (1990) give the following example to illustrate the problem: suppose A and B use this protocol to sign a contract in which A commits to buy some shares on behalf of B within a week. If the protocol is interrupted, A faces a dilemma: either buy the shares anyway and risk that B refuses to accept them or not buy the shares and risk being accused of breach of contract when B shows up with A's signature on the contract a year later. Pfitzmann et al. (1998) give a similar example of a "half-sold house."

Ben-Or et al. (1990) propose a different gradual approach to contract signing, known as the *gradual increase of privileges*. This approach also uses several rounds of communication but relies on the use of a third party in case the exchange is interrupted. In each round, A and B exchange signed statements of the form: "contract C is valid with probability p." The value of p is gradually incremented in each round. If all goes well, the contract is considered signed in the last round, when p is 1. If the exchange breaks off in the middle, either party can take the latest statement they received to a third party T. T will choose a random number p_T between 0 and 1 and will declare the contract valid if $p \geq p_T$. While this removes the assumption of equal computational capabilities, it still suffers from high communication overhead. The timely completion problem also remains. To see this, suppose when the exchange breaks, A has received signed statement with $p = p_B$ but has already sent out a signed statement with $p = p_A$. When A goes to T, suppose T picks p_T such that $p_B < p_T < p_A$. A is now at the mercy of B: if B goes to T, the contract will be deemed valid, otherwise it will remain invalid. Finally, this approach is invasive because it dictates the format of the contract.

Jakobsson (1995) proposed an interesting variation in the case of fair exchanges involving a payment. Instead of attempting to guarantee fairness, his *ripping coins* approach attempts to remove the incentive to cheat. Suppose A wants to send a payment to B in return for some item. A sends a "ripped" payment first. This is analogous to A ripping a currency bill into two and giving one piece to B: B does not yet get the money but knows that A cannot use the bill either. Now, B can send its item to A, and A can send the information necessary to complete the payment. A has no rational incentive to withhold sending the last message because it will give her no advantage. Jakobsson (1995) describes how any digital payment system in which the payment process involves sending a response to a challenge issued by the payee can be made to support rippable payments. The challenge c is computed as a cryptographic hash of a secret r chosen by the payer. During the exchange, A sends a payment with c as the challenge. In the third message, A reveals r. To claim the payment, B will have to submit both the payment message and a valid r to the bank. If A does not send r, B can still deposit the payment message: in this case, although B will not get her payment, the bank can ensure that A forfeits the amount of money specified in the payment message.

5.2   Using secure hardware tokens

Tamper-resistant hardware tokens such as smartcards have been used to address security issues in various applications such as digital payments and authentication. Therefore, it is natural to ask whether the use of tamper-resistant hardware in fair exchange protocols can avoid the need for TTPs. One attempt is described by Avoine and Vaudenay (2003), where each party has a tamper-resistant hardware token known as a "guardian angel." A guardian angel of a party is intended to guard the interests of the peer entity of that party. As discussed earlier, A and B want to exchange s_A and s_B between them. Each has its own guardian angel G_A and G_B, respectively. A and B do not trust each other, but each trusts both guardian angels to behave correctly. The guardian angels belong to a trust domain: they trust each other, and have mechanisms necessary to establish a secure communication channel between them. For example, if each guardian angel has a key pair, and the public keys of genuine guardian angels can be certified by the device manufacturers, two guardian angels G_A and G_B can use these certificates with a protocol such as Transport Layer Security (TLS) to set up an authenticated and encrypted communication channel between them. The only direct communication a guardian angel has is with its host. In other words, all communication between G_A and G_B goes through A and B, who can modify or delete messages in any way they please.

To start the fair exchange, A and B first input their secrets s_A and s_B to their respective guardian angels G_A and G_B. The guardian angels exchange the secrets between them using a secure communication channel. At this point, neither A nor B has access to the secret of its peer. The guardian angels then carry out a synchronization protocol using the same authenticated and encrypted channel. The synchronization protocol works as follows. G_A picks a secret random number C and sends it securely to G_B so that A and B do not know the value of C. Then, G_A initializes a local counter to C. On receiving C, G_B also initializes its own local counter to C and sends a message to G_A. From then on, every time one of the guardian angels receives an authenticated incoming message from its peer guardian angel, it decrements a counter and sends a reply. The messages are structured to protect against replays (e.g., each message contains the current value of the counter). If the counter reaches 0, synchronization has succeeded, and the guardian angel will reveal the secret to the host after a fixed time-out. If at any time during the synchronization no incoming message is received within a fixed time interval, the synchronization is deemed failed. The fairness guarantee to A is probabilistic: if B happens to prevent the outgoing message after the counter on G_B reaches 0, then the exchange will end unfairly for A. But as B does not know the value of C ahead of time, its chance of success depends on the probability distribution on the choice of C. The probability of B cheating can be made as small as needed, at the expense of increased communication cost.

Alternative approaches using smartcards have been described by Vogt et al. (2003), where special focus is applied to the timely delivery of items in a mobile environment, and by Park et al. (2003), where memory and computational load of the receiver is optimized.

6   Instances of fair exchange protocols

Besides the notion of generic fair exchange, there has been a wide range of publications for specific instances. Historically, research developed from simple protocols with inline TTP (80s) through gradual exchange protocols (90s) toward optimistic protocols. Recent research then focused on applying optimistic protocols to practical application scenarios.

6.1   Non-repudiation and certified mail

Certified mail is the fair exchange of secret data for a receipt. It is the most mature instance as standardized in N 1105 JTC 1/SC 27 (1995). Many protocols aim at creating non-repudiable evidence for multiple steps in the message transmission chain (Fig. 1): a sender composes a signed message (non-repudiation of origin) and sends it to the first TTP (non-repudiation of submission). The first TTP may send it to additional TTPs (non-repudiation of transport) and finally to the recipient (non-repudiation of delivery, which is a special case of non-repudiation of transport). The recipient receives the message (non-repudiation of receipt). This is sometimes done by introducing multiple trusted transactions, for example, one for time-stamping and another for non-repudiation of submission.

Fig. 1.   Framework of certified mail (N 1105 JTC 1/SC 27, 1995) players and their actions.

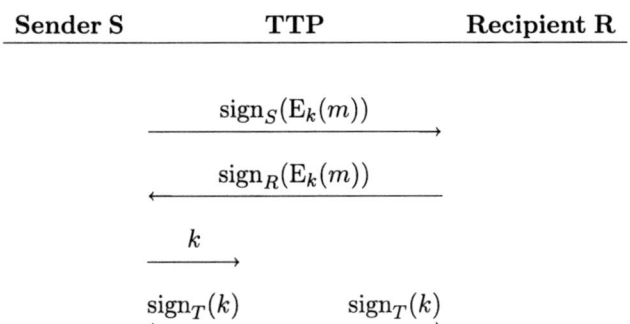

Fig. 2.   Sketch of the protocol proposed by Zhou and Gollmann (1996) (E_k denotes symmetric encryption).

Early research focused on two-party protocols (Blum, 1981; Rabin, 1981) gradually generating non-repudiation of receipt tokens in exchange of the message. Fair exchange with active participation of the TTP was proposed by Rabin (1983). A later example of a protocol using an inline TTP is the protocol proposed by Zhou and Gollmann (1996). The basic idea is that the parties first exchange signatures under the encrypted message. Then, the third party signs and distributes the key. The signature on the encrypted message together with the signatures on the key then forms the non-repudiation of origin and receipt tokens. The protocol is sketched in Fig. 2. Optimistic protocols for certified mail were proposed by Asokan et al. (1998a) and Bao et al. (1998).

6.2   Contract signing

A contract signing scheme (Blum, 1981) is used to fairly compute a contract such that even if one of the signatories misbehaves, either both or none of the signatories obtain a contract. Contract signing generalizes fair exchange of signatures: A contract signing protocol can define the format of what constitutes a valid contract. Unlike agreement protocols, contract signing needs to provide a non-repudiable proof that an agreement has been reached.

Contract signing protocols were either based on an inline TTP (Rabin, 1983), gradual exchange of secrets (Blum, 1983), or gradual increase of privilege (Ben-Or et al., 1990). The first optimistic contract signing scheme was described by Even (1983). An optimistic contract signing scheme for asynchronous networks was described by Asokan et al. (1998b).

A simple optimistic contract signing protocol for synchronous networks is sketched in Fig. 3: party **A** sends a proposal, party **B** agrees, and party **A** confirms. If party **A** does not confirm, **B** obtains its contract from the TTP.

An important extension has been the introduction of abuse-freeness (Garay et al., 1999). The "abuse" these protocols avoid is that a dishonest player may start and abort a protocol run such that no contract is produced. In this case, the agreement phase of most early protocols produces a signed proof that the peer was willing to sign a particular contract (e.g., that someone was willing to sell an item at a given price). Abuse-free protocols do not produce any evidence whatsoever. This was achieved by Garay et al. (1999) by using designated verifier proofs during the agreement phase. This guarantees that only the third party and the given peer can verify the agreement. Multi-party abuse-free optimistic contract signing protocols have been discussed in Baum-Waidner and Waidner (2000) and Mukhamedov and Ryan (2007).

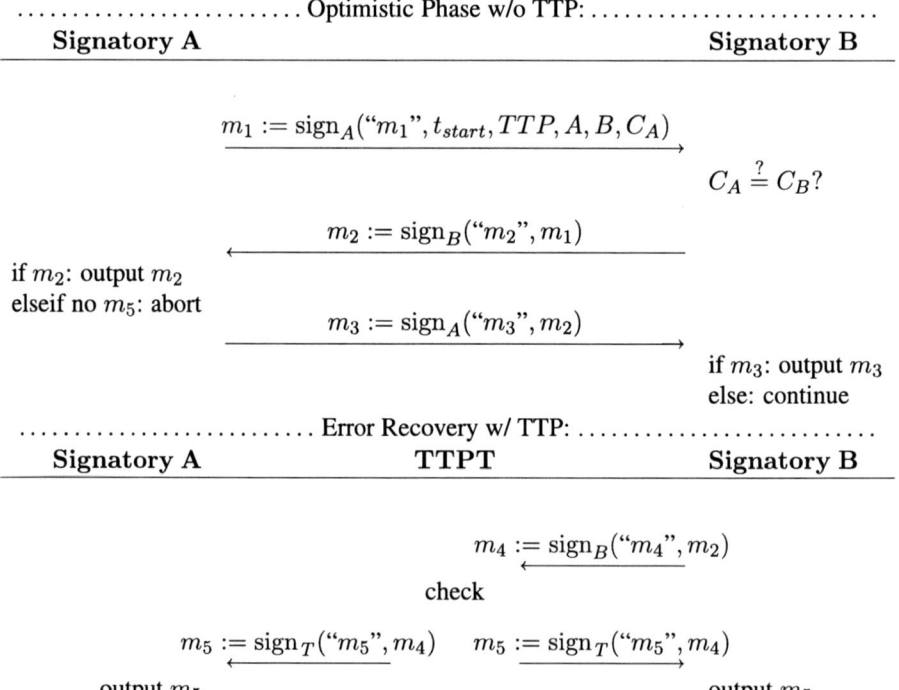

Fig. 3.   Sketch of an optimistic synchronous contract-signing protocol (Pfitzmann et al., 1998).

6.3 Fair purchase

Fair purchase aims at fairly exchanging goods for payment. Optimistic protocols for fair purchase were first outlined by Bürk and Pfitzmann (1989). The essential idea is that the exchange is divided into two rounds. In the first round, parties A and B exchange their respective *promises* to participate in the exchange. The promises describe the items being exchanged. In the second round, the actual items themselves are exchanged. If one party did not receive the item it expects, it can initiate a dispute by forwarding the promises from the first round to the TTP and ask it to resolve the dispute. In the work by Hanadate et al. (2005), an optimistic fair exchange protocol is adapted for fair value exchange (money/tickets) using smartcards. The main motivation to use fair exchange on top of tamper-resistant devices was to allow for fair and efficient recovery even if one of the players was able to break one of the smartcards.

7 Complexity of fair exchange

7.1 Number of messages and communication rounds

To assess the efficiency of a given fair exchange protocol, it is important to know a lower bound for messages and rounds needed to solve a given fair exchange problem. For contract signing, this has been analyzed by Pfitzmann et al. (1998). The results were that the round/message complexity depends on the exact model. Important parameters are synchronicity, revocability of signatures (i.e., the TTP participates in the signature verification), or whether the protocol is meant to be optimistic even if two honest players disagree.

Two patterns for optimal protocols have been identified. While message optimal protocols follow a zigzag pattern, round optimal protocols follow a pattern where both parties send messages in each of the optimistic rounds. The message-optimal protocol for the simplest model (synchronous with revocation) has two messages in two rounds. In the round-optimal protocol, both messages are sent in the same round. When using this protocol as a starting point, each increase in complexity (asynchronicity, no TTP in verification, or the requirement to be optimistic on agreement) then adds one round to the round-optimal protocol or one message to the message optimal protocol. As a consequence, for example, a synchronous protocol without revocation that is optimistic only on agreement needs either three messages (proving message optimality of the protocol depicted in Fig. 3) or two rounds with four messages. Similarly, allowing for asynchronicity requires four messages (proving optimality of Asokan et al., 1998a) or three rounds with six messages.

These results on optimal efficiency of contract signing provide a lower bound for generic fair exchanges. Furthermore, certain types of certified mail can be used to build contract signing protocols. As a consequence, these certified mail protocols cannot be more efficient. Nevertheless, we are not aware of a more detailed complexity analysis of the different fair exchange types.

7.2 *Computational complexity*

Fair exchange using an inline TTP is optimally efficient in terms of the amount of computation each party has to perform and the sizes of the messages. The protocols that were discussed in Section 3 typically involve only four messages. The messages contain a constant number of encryptions and signatures.

Approaches for optimistic fair exchange using verifiable escrow can be significantly more expensive. For example, the approach described in Sections 4.2.1 and 4.2.2 uses the cut-and-choose approach that requires n public key encryptions, where n is the security parameter (probability of successful cheating is 2^{-n}). In other words, making the protocol more secure requires increasing the number of encryptions performed by the participants.

Fortunately, it is possible to avoid the cut-and-choose approach under some conditions. One example is the use of pre-issued coupons described in Section 4.2.3: if it is permissible to contact the TTP ahead of time to obtain the coupons, verifiable escrows can be calculated using a constant number of encryptions. Since the coupon is independent of the actual item being exchanged, coupons can be obtained in bulk, long before the actual exchange happens. A second example is the use of efficient mechanisms for verifiable encryption. The cut-and-choose technique described in Section 4.2.1 is generic in the sense that it be used with any encryption algorithm. But it is possible to design much more efficient verifiable encryption schemes based on specific encryption algorithms. For example, Ateniese (2004) has proposed efficient verifiable encryption protocols for ElGamal encryption.

8 Practical applications of fair exchange

Research on foundations and core protocols for fair exchange has spawned a wide range of research into applications and adapted exchange protocols.

An important application of fair exchange is peer-to-peer (P2P) systems (Gauthier et al., 2004; Luo et al., 2006; Srivatsa et al., 2005). Given a TTP in the infrastructure, any fair exchange protocol can be used by two peers in a P2P network. Similarly, a set of peers can run a multi-party fair exchange protocol (Baum-Waidner and Waidner, 2000). As peers will frequently appear or disappear, these protocols only work if an honest majority of the initial peers remains online and none of the peers disappears in the initial agreement phase. Note that it is important to deploy asynchronous protocols in a P2P setting because synchronous protocols do not guarantee fairness if peers go offline for a while.

A particular benefit of P2P systems is that a large number of peers are present, of which the majority is usually honest. As a consequence, one can leverage the "kindness of strangers" (Franklin and Reiter, 1997), which assumes that in a randomly picked set of strangers, the average is unbiased. This enables fair exchange using an *ad-hoc* selection of peers jointly acting as a TTP.

A second important application area is e-commerce, where the main requirements are efficiency and scalability. As today's fair exchange protocols usually require a public key infrastructure (PKI), Abadi and Glew (2002) adopted certified mail to a browser-only scenario that is common in today's e-commerce, that is, the goal was to introduce an inline TTP that enables the receiver to fairly issue receipts while only running a browser.

A third application area is service-oriented architecture based on Web services. A first proposal for fair exchange using Web services has been described in the work by Maruyama et al. (2003), which describes a design and message formats to deploy asynchronous fair exchange (Asokan et al., 1998a) in a Web-services environment. Similarly, a Web-services deployment of multi-party fair exchange has been described by (Garbinato and Rickebusch, 2006). In the work by Robinson et al. (2005), an inline fair exchange protocol that provides non-repudiation in Business-to-Business Web-services transactions is proposed. The focus lies on providing multiple types of non-repudiation (including non-repudiation of submission) while not mandating interactions between sender and receiver. Similarly, Khurana and Hahm (2006) describes a secure mailing list server that utilizes fair exchange for issuing receipts.

9 Outlook and open problems

We discussed the problem of fair exchange and the various protocols proposed to solve the problem. Active research on fair exchange protocols started more than two decades ago: Protocols have evolved from fairly inefficient use of inline third parties through gradual exchange of slices toward the optimistic paradigm in which a third party is only required in case of fraud or protocol failures.

In the past few years, the increasing popularity of Internet auction services has brought the need for fair exchange into the foreground. As the predominant use of Internet auctions still is for physical items, Internet auction services take the simple approach of using an active trusted intermediary that holds payments in escrow until the physical item has been delivered and accepted. Once high-value digital items become common, we expect the used protocols to mature toward solutions that leverage optimistic fair exchange.

9.1   Open research challenges

As of today, research has resolved the basic questions of fair exchange and has provided efficient protocols that enable fair exchange on synchronous and asynchronous networks. Nevertheless, we see several important areas where further research is desirable.

Applying the "optimistic" paradigm: The first area of research is the transfer of the optimistic paradigm to other protocol types. Watanabe and Imai (2000) showed how to use an optimistic third party to improve the efficiency of an auction protocol. Another area where the optimistic paradigm can be useful is the field of practical dependability protocols (broadcast, consensus, and agreement). A first publication to this end was by Ezhilchelvan and Shrivastava (2005), which investigated fair exchange in a fail-stop failure model.[3] Similarly, we believe that the relationship between optimistic exchange and multi-party computation following the optimistic paradigm would be worth examining.

Trust management and peer-to-peer systems: Today's protocols are designed with a static setup involving a fixed set of participants in mind. While this setting is usually true for contracts, it does not necessarily hold for arbitrary exchanges: In peer-to-peer systems, groups will be built in an *ad-hoc* manner. This can include the group of semi-trusted peers that constitute the TTP. This implies three challenges for fair exchange protocols: The first challenge is that groups will be dynamic. As a consequence, it is necessary that roles (in particular the TTP) can be played by a loose assembly of players, of which a subset of players may even drop off during the protocol run. Similarly, mobile adversaries will occur, that is, parties will be dishonest in one run, while being honest in the next run.

The second challenge is that the trust relationships are unclear and that trust in heterogeneous and *ad-hoc* systems needs to be explicitly managed. Although one can assume that the majority is honest, it may be difficult to reliably identify sets of peers where this assumption holds. Protocols that allow voluntary participation are usually susceptible to large groups of malicious players "volunteering" and thus outnumbering the fewer honest volunteers.

---

[3]Note that by leveraging trusted computing (Rabin, 1983), one can implement a fail-stop model despite a potentially malicious owner.

The third challenge is the complex matrices of items to be exchanged and the even more complex exchange pattern in the multi-party case. In principle, each player can offer items to each other player. These $n \times n$ exchanges are then performed in parallel. So far, only simple instances such as certified message broadcast have been examined.

In each of these areas, research aimed at reducing the trust requirements may be worthwhile. One example is improved accountability of TTPs. Another direction would be an implementation of the TTP by means of trusted computing technology (Pearson, 2003).

Additional deployments of research results: The most common exchanges today are online auctions of physical goods. While exchanges with inline TTP can help guaranteeing fairness, today's optimistic protocols do not work in this setting. An interesting research direction would be to determine how to interconnect today's delivery services and payments with optimistic fair exchange to provide an overall service that is similar to optimistic exchange of physical items. Another area where we expect increased activity is the practical application and deployment of fair exchange protocols. While initial implementations and pilots exist, we are unaware of any large system leveraging optimistic fair exchange protocols. As with any protocol or distributed algorithm, large-scale deployment of optimistic fair exchange may uncover unexpected new problems.

Formalized security: An important area of research is the formalization and analysis of fair exchange protocols. Publications usually include at most a manual and semi-formal proof of the security of a given protocol. The manual setup of requirements and the manual proof are error-prone. Requirements as well as certain choices in the proof may be overlooked. Publications dealing with formal models and analysis of fair exchange (Chadha et al., 2005; Khurana and Hahm, 2006; Shmatikov and Mitchell, 2002) are a step in the right direction. However, further modeling and analysis are desirable.

9.2   Conclusion

Fair exchange has matured from protocols using inline TTPs through gradual exchanges toward optimistic fair exchange protocols. This trend has spawned a wide range of research into different instances of fair exchange as well as their application in practice.

Similar to other protocols, flawed fair exchange protocols have been proposed and subsequently been broken (e.g., Markowitch and Saeednia, 2003). In our experience, proper definition and use of the model as well as correct usage of the underlying cryptographic primitives are major challenges when building fair exchange protocols. In particular for efficiency analysis, minor differences in the model (e.g., optimism on disagreement) immediately change the resulting optimal efficiency.

While this has laid the foundation for practical use, substantial research challenges still remain. The two biggest challenges we see are to transfer the optimistic paradigm to other protocol classes and to show how optimistic protocols can be reliably embedded into a peer-to-peer infrastructure where a majority of players is honest, but finding actually honest players may pose a challenge. One potential avenue to reduce these trust requirements is by means of trusted computing technology (Pearson, 2003) that could enable TTPs that are run by the players.

References

Abadi, M., N. Glew (2002). Certified email with a light on-line trusted third party: design and implementation, in: *WWW '02: Proceedings of the 11th International Conference on World Wide Web.* ACM Press, New York, NY, USA, pp. 387–395.

Asokan, N., M. Schunter, M. Waidner (1997). Optimistic protocols for fair exchange, in: *Proceedings of the 4th ACM Conference on Computer and Communications Security,* April, ACM Press, Zurich, Switzerland, pp. 6, 8–17.

Asokan, N., V. Shoup, M. Waidner (1998a). Asynchronous protocols for optimistic fair exchange, in: *Proceedings of the 19th IEEE Symposium on Security & Privacy,* IEEE Computer Society Press, Oakland, CA, USA, pp. 86–99.

Asokan, N., V. Shoup, M. Waidner (1998b). Optimistic fair exchange of digital signatures, in: K. Nyberg (ed.), *Advances in Cryptology: EUROCRYPT '98, Lecture Notes in Computer Science,* Vol. 1403, Springer, Espoo, Finland, pp. 591–606.

Asokan, N., V. Shoup, M. Waidner (2000). Optimistic fair exchange of digital signatures. *IEEE Journal on Selected Areas in Communications* 18(4), 593–610.

Ateniese, G. (2004). Verifiable encryption of digital signatures and applications. *ACM Transactions on Information and System Security (TISSEC)* 7(1), 1–20.

Avoine, G., S. Vaudenay (2003). Fair exchange with guardian angels, in: *Proceedings of the 4th International Workshop on Information Security Applications-WISA, Lecture Notes in Computer Science,* Vol. 2908, Springer, Jeju Island, Korea, pp. 188–202.

Bahreman, A., D. Tygar (1994). Certified electronic mail, in: *Proceedings of the Symposium on Network and Distributed System Security,* February, Internet Society, USA, pp. 3–19.

Bao, F., R.H., Deng, W. Mao (1998). Efficient and practical fair exchange protocols with off-line TTP, in: *Proceedings of the 19th IEEE Symposium on Security & Privacy,* IEEE Press, Oakland, CA, USA, pp. 77–85.

Baum-Waidner, B., M. Waidner (2000). Round-optimal and abuse-free optimistic multi-party contract signing, in: *Proceedings of the 27th International Colloquium on Automata, Languages and Programming (ICALP), Lecture Notes in Computer Science,* Vol. 1853, Springer-Verlag, Geneva, Switzerland, pp. 524–535.

Ben-Or, M., O. Goldreich, S. Micali, R. Rivest (1990). A fair protocol for signing contracts. *IEEE Transactions on Information Theory* 36(1), 40–46.

Blum, M. (1981). Three applications of the oblivious transfer. Version 2, September 18, Unpublished manuscript, Department of Electrical Engineering and Computer Sciences, University of California at Berkeley, Berkley, CA, USA.

Blum, M. (1983). How to exchange (secret) keys. *ACM Transactions on Computer Systems* 1(2), 175–193.

Bürk, H., A. Pfitzmann (1989). Digital payment systems enabling security and unobservability. *Computers & Security* 8(5), 399–416.

Chadha, R., J.C. Mitchell, A. Scedrov, V. Shmatikov (2005). Contract signing, optimism, and advantage. *Journal of Logic and Algebraic Programming, Special Issue on Processes and Security* 64(2), 189–218.

Damgård, I. (1995). Practical and provably secure release of a secret and exchange of signatures. *Journal of Cryptology* 8(4), 201–222.

Deng, R.H., L. Gong, A.A. Lazar, W. Wang (1996). Practical protocols for certified electronic mail. *Journal of Network and System Management* 4(3), 279–287.

Dodis, Y., L. Reyzin (2003). Breaking and repairing optimistic fair exchange from PODC 2003, in: *DRM '03: Proceedings of the 3rd ACM Workshop on Digital Rights Management*. ACM Press, New York, NY, USA, pp. 47–54.

Even, S. (1983). A protocol for signing contracts. *SIGACT News* 15(1), 34–39. Winter-Spring.

Even, S., Y. Yacobi. (1980). Relations among public key signature systems. Technical Report 175, Computer Science Department, Technion, Israel, March.

Ezhilchelvan, P.D., S.K. Shrivastava (2005). A family of trusted third party based fair-exchange protocols. *IEEE Transactions on Dependable Secure Computing* 2(4), 273–286.

Franklin, M. K., M. K. Reiter. (1997). Fair exchange with a semi-trusted third party, in: T. Matsumoto (ed.), *Proceedings of the 4th ACM Conference on Computer and Communications Security*, April, ACM Press, Zurich, Switzerland, pp. 1–5, 7.

Garay, J., M. Jakobsson, P. MacKenzie (1999). Abuse-free optimistic contract signing, in: *Proceedings of Advances in Cryptology—Crypto 99, Lecture Notes in Computer Science*, Vol. 1666, Springer-Verlag, Santa Barbara, CA, USA, pp. 449–466.

Garbinato, B., I. Rickebusch (2006). Orchestrating fair exchanges between mutually distrustful web services, in: *SWS '06: Proceedings of the 3rd ACM Workshop on Secure Web Services*. ACM Press, New York, NY, USA, pp. 33–42.

Gauthier, P., B. Bershad, S. D. Gribble (2004). Dealing with cheaters in anonymous peer-to-peer networks. Technical Report 04-01-03, Computer Science and Engineering, University of Washington, January.

Hanadate, M., M. Terada, S. Nagao, T. Miyazawal, Y. Yosuke, S. Tomita, K. Fujimura (2005). P2P digital value fair trading system using smart cards, in: *Security in Pervasive Computing, Lecture Notes in Computer Science*, Vol. 3450, Springer, Boppard, Germany, pp. 18–30.

Jakobsson, M. (1995). Ripping coins for a fair exchange, in: *Advances in Cryptology: EUROCRYPT '95, Lecture Notes in Computer Science*, Vol. 921, Springer, Saint-Malo, France, pp. 220–230.

Khurana, H., H.-S. Hahm (2006). Certified mailing lists, in: *ASIACCS '06: Proceedings of the 2006 ACM Symposium on Information, Computer and Communications Security*. ACM Press, New York, NY, USA, pp. 46–58.

Luo, X., Z. Qin, J. Geng, C. Wu (2006). P2PFAIR: fair exchange in P2P sharing system without dedicated TTP, in: *Proceedings of the First International Conference on Communications and Networking in China* (ChinaCom 06), IEEE Press, Beijing, China, pp. 1–5.

Markowitch, O., S. Saeednia (2003). Cryptanalysis of the Wu-Varadhrajan fair exchange protocol. *Information Processing Letters* 87(3), 169–171. Elsevier, The Netherlands.

Maruyama, H., T. Nakamura, T. Hsieh (2003). Optimistic fair contract signing for web services, in: *XMLSEC '03: Proceedings of the 2003 ACM Workshop on XML Security*. ACM Press, New York, NY, USA, pp. 79–85.

Mukhamedov, A., M. D. Ryan (2007). Improved multi-party contract signing, in: *Proceedings of the 11th International Conference on Financial Cryptography and Data Security*, Lecture Notes in Computer Science, Vol. 4535, Springer, Scarborough, Tobago, pp. 179–191.

N 1105 JTC 1/SC 27 (1995). Information technology—security techniques—non repudiation-part 1: General model. ISO International Standard 13888-1, ISO/IEC.

Nenadić, A., N. Zhang, S. Barton (2004). Fair certified e-mail delivery, in: *SAC '04: Proceedings of the 2004 ACM Symposium on Applied Computing*. ACM Press, New York, NY, USA, pp. 391–396.

Park, J.M., I. Ray, E.K.P. Chong, H.J. Siegel (2003). A certified e-mail protocol suitable for mobile environments, in: *Proceedings of the Global Telecommunications Conference, 2003. GLOBECOM '03*, Vol. 3, IEEE, San Francisco, CA, USA, pp. 1394–1398.

Pearson, S. (ed.) (2003). *Trusted Computing Platforms*. Prentice Hall, Upper Saddle River, NJ, USA.

Pfitzmann, B., M. Schunter, M. Waidner (1998). Optimal efficiency of optimistic contract signing, in: B. Coan (ed.), *Proceedings of the 17th ACM Symposium on Principles of Distributed Computing (PODC)*, pp. 113–122.

Rabin, M.O. (1981). How to exchange secrets by oblivious transfer. Technical Report TR-81. Harvard University, Cambridge, MA, USA.

Rabin, M.O. (1983). Transaction protection by beacons. *Journal of Computer and System Sciences* 27, 256–267.

Robinson, P., N. Cook, S. Shrivastava (2005). Implementing fair non-repudiable interactions with web services, in: *Proceedings of the 9th IEEE International Enterprise Computing Conference (EDOC 2005)*, IEEE Press, Enschede, The Netherlands, pp. 195–206.

Shmatikov, V., J.C. Mitchell (2002). Finite-state analysis of two contract signing protocols. *Theoretical Computer Science, Special Issue on Theoretical Foundations of Security Analysis and Design* 283(2), 419–450.

Srivatsa, M., L. Xiong, L. Liu (2005). ExchangeGuard: a distributed protocol for electronic fair-exchange, in: *IPDPS '05: Proceedings of the 19th IEEE International Parallel and Distributed Processing Symposium (IPDPS'05)—Paper 105.2*. IEEE Computer Society, Washington, DC, USA, p. 105b.

Vogt, H., F.C. Gärtner, H. Pagnia (2003). Supporting fair exchange in mobile environments. *Mobile Networks and Applications* 8, 127–136.

Watanabe, Y., H. Imai (2000). Reducing the round complexity of a sealed-bid auction protocol with an off-line TTP, in: *CCS '00: Proceedings of the 7th ACM Conference on Computer and Communications Security*. ACM Press, New York, NY, USA, pp. 80–86.

Zhou, J., D. Gollmann (1996). A fair non-repudiation protocol, in: *Proceedings of the 17th IEEE Symposium on Security & Privacy*, IEEE Computer Society Press, Oakland, CA, USA, pp. 55–61.

Part V
Security, Privacy and Access
Control Applications

Rao & Upadhyaya, Eds., *Handbooks in Information Systems, Vol. 4*

Chapter 14

Privacy-Preserving Techniques in Wireless Sensor Networks

Sajal K. Das, Na Li and Nan Zhang

Department of Computer Science, George Washington University, Washington, DC 20052, USA

Abstract

This chapter addresses protection of privacy in wireless sensor networks (WSNs). We present a state-of-the-art survey on privacy-preserving techniques in WSNs. We discuss the privacy protection problems in detail through two categories, content- and context-oriented privacy protection, based on the different types of private information that needs to be protected. We review the existing techniques for each category, and compare their performance in terms of privacy protection, accuracy, delay time, and transmission overhead. We also point out some open challenges and issues facing this field that could guide future research directions.

1 Introduction

Privacy protection is a critical challenge in a wireless sensor network (WSN), which is a self-organized wireless network consisting of a large number of resource-limited (CPU, storage, battery power, communication bandwidth) sensors that can sense an environment, collect and process the sensed data, and (wirelessly) communicate and cooperate with each other to monitor and control the physical world. Indeed, WSNs are being deployed in a wide variety of civil and military applications, such as environment (flood, hurricane, volcano, and forest fire), habitat and agricultural monitoring, industrial process control and automation, health care and wellness management (via body sensor networks), smart environments (e.g., home, office, hospital, and airport), security and surveillance, target tracking, and so on. Consequently, a critical concern on WSNs is how to protect the privacy (Schilit et al., 2003; Soppera and Burbridge, 2004;

Walters et al., 2005) of the data being collected. For example, in Smart Health Care, patients' blood pressure, sugar level, and other vital signs are monitored and tested by sensors and then transmitted toward a central data-gathering point (i.e., *sink*) or a storage database. Such private data collected from the patients should be open only to family members, doctors, nurses, hospital or insurance personnel rather than being public. Similar is the concern in security applications dealing with personal records or sensitive information. Therefore, the system or the network must guarantee (wireless) data transmission and processing with high degree of privacy protection. Note that the privacy concern applies not only to the collected data, but also to the location and identity of the source and destination node as well as other control information about the collected data. For instance, even though eavesdropper could not decrypt data packages directly, they could track data toward the base station or back down to the data source, which makes a great menace to those two critical spots. It is important to address the privacy-protection issues in WSNs before the wide applications of WSNs are carried on and the threats to privacy spiral out of control.

A significant body of literature exists on the privacy protection in the traditional fields of wired networks, wireless networks (e.g., wireless mesh network (Wu et al., 2006) and vehicular networks (Buttyán et al., 2007; Freudiger et al., 2007). However, privacy protection in WSNs faces unique challenges:

(i) WSNs are more vulnerable due to the miniature size of sensor nodes and the very nature of wireless communication environment that may allow an adversary to launch physical attack and compromise the sensors or other components of the network. In a battlefield, for example, sensors may be captured and compromised by enemies, who may use the captured sensors to make a menace to the whole WSN.

(ii) As mentioned, a WSNs is severely constrained by various resources such as computation, storage, wireless bandwidth, and energy (battery power). An adversary may monitor such activities of sensors as the communication patterns to figure out the energy depletion or resource usage to spot the most vulnerable points in the network and then destroy them.

(iii) Mobile components of WSNs bring more challenges to privacy-preserving. In a WSN, sink could move around the network or all sensors are mobile. Mobility makes communication unstable and does not guarantee full coverage so that privacy is much easier to be threatened.

In this chapter, we present a state-of-the-art survey on privacy-preserving techniques in WSNs. Section 2 reviews some basic concepts of WSNs and also summarizes the related work on privacy protection in generic wireless networks. In Section 3, we discuss taxonomy of privacy protection problems in WSNs. Sections 4 and 5 present various privacy-preserving techniques for content- and context-oriented problems, respectively. In Section 6, we compare and evaluate the performance of different techniques based on privacy protection, application utility (accuracy), delay time, and communication overhead. In Section 7, we point out some open challenges and issues, which should shed light to future research in the field. Section 8 concludes the chapter.

2 Background

In this section, we first briefly introduce the background of WSNs, and then review the related work on privacy protection in wireless networks other than WSNs.

2.1 Wireless sensor networks

A WSN is a self-organized wireless network that consists of a few base stations (sinks) and a large number of sensor nodes deployed over a large area. Even though the size of a sensor is small, hundreds of them could cooperate to achieve tremendous tasks, such as geological environment monitoring and military target tracking. Figure 1 depicts the basic performance of WSNs. A group of sensors are assigned to monitor a target area and transmit the sensed data to the pre-assigned sink(s) by multiple-hop. As a gateway connecting the wireless sensor network with the wired backbone network, a sink is in charge of gathering data from the whole network and transmitting them to wired networks (e.g., the Internet). Collected data could be stored at databases in wired networks and available

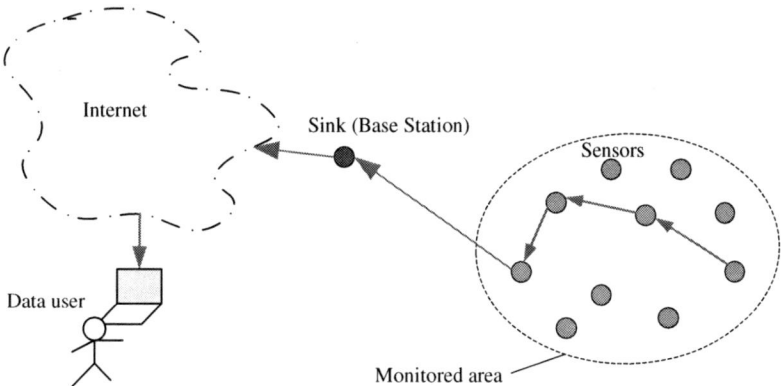

Fig. 1.   Wireless sensor network.

to users, who take advantage of those data to get service or make relative analysis.

Let us review several characteristics of WSNs which pose unique challenges to privacy-preserving techniques.

Limited resource: Limited resource, in particular energy, is one of the most challenging issues in WSN. In general, battery is the only energy source for wireless sensors. In a large deployed area (often hostile or unattended) such as a battlefield or an animal habitat, it is infeasible to recharge or change the battery for each sensor. A substantial amount of energy may be consumed by such many sensor operations as transmitting and receiving messages as well as aggregating data. Energy consumption on transmitting and receiving data is mainly determined by the communication distance, which stimulates the development of routing techniques in wireless sensor networks from one- to multi-hop communication (Heinzelman, 2000). Generally speaking, to prolong the lifetime of the network, we have to make a proper tradeoff between energy consumption and the functionality of the system.

Architecture: As shown in Fig. 2, the architecture of WSNs can be *flat* (Bi et al., 2007a) in that there is only one sink located in the center of the network, or *hierarchical* (Heinzelman et al., 2000; Xu et al., 2005) that not only provides better scalability but also facilitates the cooperation among sensors on data aggregation tasks to reduce the overall traffic load over the network. In *hierarchical* architecture based on clusters, sensors are divided into several clusters, each with a cluster head which is in charge of gathering and aggregating data within its cluster. Then, each cluster head forwards the merged data toward the base station through some other cluster heads.

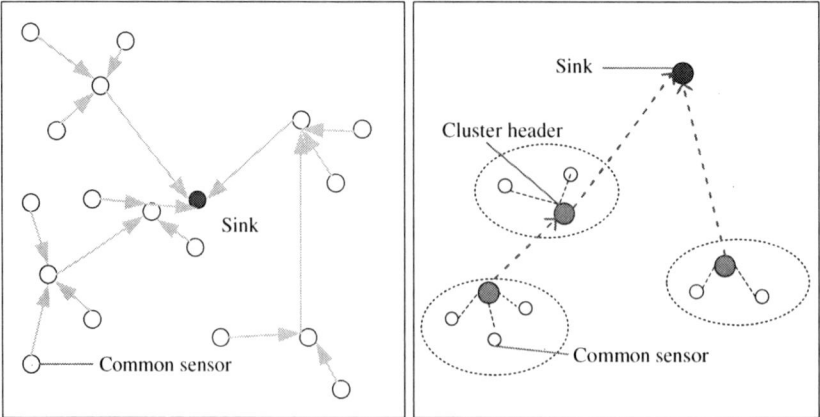

Fig. 2.   The flat and hierarchical architectures of wireless sensor networks.

Traffic pattern: By traffic pattern we refer to the distribution of traffic over the entire network. It is mainly determined by the topology of the network. Since all data are forwarded toward the base station, the pattern is approximately fixed as sandglass. Following the data flow, it is easy to track down the position of the sink and the data source. The asymmetric pattern of traffic determines heterogeneous data transmission rates and workloads of sensors. Sensor nodes closer to the sink node have the responsibility of not only transmitting data generated by themselves, but also of relaying data from nodes further away from the sink. Under that condition, even though most of the far-away sensors may have remaining energy, the network could still be dysfunctional because the sensors closer to base station already ran out of their energy, like a fence, hindering the data forwarded to the base station. This phenomenon is referred to as the "Energy Hole Problem" in WSNs, and has been extensively studied in the existing work (e.g., Li and Mohapatra, 2005). In general, the proposed solutions distribute the traffic load to multiple sinks (Chen et al., 2005; Das and Dutta, 2004; Oyman and Ersoy, 2004) and mobile sinks (Bi et al., 2007b,2009; Luo and Hubaux, 2005). Nonetheless, these solutions also make the traffic to exhibit special patterns that may be exploited by malicious entities or adversaries to compromise sensitive information, such as the locations of sinks and data sources.

2.2 Privacy protection in generic wireless networks

Various privacy protection schemes have been studied in general wireless networks. In particular, a significant body of literature exists on the protection of location privacy in wireless networks, such as mesh networks (Wu et al., 2006), vehicular networks (Buttyán et al., 2007; Freudiger et al., 2007) or WLANs (Gruteser and Grunwald, 2003; Jiang et al., 2007). A major privacy concern on vehicular networks is the disclosure of location information in the broadcast of safety messages (to nearby vehicles) and the usage of location-based services. In Freudiger et al. (2007), a mix-zone strategy is proposed in the intersection of the roads. Mix-zones are anonymized regions of the network in which mobile nodes change their identifiers to obfuscate the relationship between the entering and exiting events. Another scheme (Gruteser and Grunwald, 2003) is to introduce a trusted third party as a middleware between the users and the location-based service server, which helps to cloak user's exact locations into spatial regions so as to achieve anonymity. In Jiang et al. (2007), authors aim to obfuscate several kinds of private information which are transmitted by a mobile node. They adapted a kind of fingerprinting technique to achieve pseudonym and added silent period to the process of transmitting data so as to make targeted user mix with other users. Unlike traditional wireless networks, protecting privacy in WSN is more challenging since we have to consider its constrained resource and ability. In the following section, we address the development of privacy problems in WSN in detail.

3 Taxonomy of privacy-preserving problems

Recently efforts have been made to protect privacy in WSNs. Kamat et al. (2005) classified privacy-preserving problems in WSNs into two categories, content- and context-oriented, according to the types of private information that needs to be protected. In this chapter, we classify most of the relative literature through that standpoint and analyze in detail of the classification of privacy protection problems, content- (Carbunar et al., 2007; He et al., 2007; Shar et al., 2007) and context-oriented (Deng et al., 2004, 2005, 2006; Jian et al., 2007; Kamat et al., 2005, 2007; Xi et al., 2006). In this section, we briefly describe these two categories. Then, we present their detailed analysis in the following two sections.

Content-oriented privacy protection problem is concerned with the privacy of sensitive data values being sensed and collected by WSNs, such as location and temperature information. When attackers eavesdrop data transmission and decrypt data items in WSNs, they may directly compromise the content-oriented private information. To solve this problem, traditional studies on privacy protection focus on safeguarding data items through encryption and authentication. For example, in Shar et al. (2007) some schemes have been proposed to protect the mapping relation between the detection cells (that detect the target) and storage cells (that store the corresponding target information). Using different parameters to hash function, the privacy efficiency is gradually improved. In this chapter, we mainly consider privacy problems and corresponding solutions beyond the pure encryption. In particular, we discuss two types of privacy-preserving problems and corresponding techniques for content-oriented privacy protection, such as privacy data aggregation (PDA; He et al., 2007), which safeguards individual data in the process of data aggregation, and query privacy (Carbunar et al., 2007) in which the clients send query messages to acquire answer from target regions they are interested in. Here the location of interesting regions is regarded as private information.

Context-oriented privacy protection problem, however, is concerned with the private information beyond sensitive data values. Although it covers a wide variety of private information in the literature, we mainly focus on two types of private information, namely spatial privacy (Deng et al., 2004, 2005, 2006; Jian et al., 2007; Kamat et al., 2005; Xi et al., 2006) and temporal privacy (Kamat et al., 2007). For spatial privacy, we further discuss two subproblems, the protection of data-source identity (Kamat et al., 2005; Xi et al., 2006) and base-station identity (Deng et al., 2004, 2005, 2006; Jian et al., 2007). For an adversary, the confidence of successfully figuring out those identities is from the special traffic pattern in WSNs mentioned in Section 2. Even though an attacker could not access the data item by decryption, it could still analyze the data flow to compromise private information. Temporal privacy (Kamat et al., 2007) deals with the privacy of the time that a data point is sensed. If an adversary can deduce such temporal information along with the identity of the data source, the adversary may be able to predict the future path of a mobile target. In that case, if the target is sensitive and should be protected, the disclosure of moving path will threaten the target.

Following the taxonomical classification shown in Fig. 3; in Sections 4 and 5, we discuss content- and context-oriented privacy-preserving techniques, respectively.

4   Content-oriented problem

The objective of content-oriented privacy protection is to hide sensitive data such that no adversary can compromise the data values by eavesdropping and decrypting the observed message transmissions. The protection of content-oriented private information commonly relies on traditional cryptographic techniques such as encryption and authentication. Nonetheless, cryptographic techniques might not be able to satisfy the requirements of WSNs. In the following, we review two content-oriented privacy-preserving problems and corresponding techniques, namely private data aggregation and query privacy protection in WSNs.

4.1   Privacy data aggregation

The problem of safeguarding privacy in the process of aggregating data is discussed in He et al. (2007). Actually, the aggregation technique itself is a common method to preserve privacy; however, we have to consider the probability of attacking by semi-hostile aggregators, which perform their responsibility of aggregating data as well as being curious about private data from individual providers. He et al. (2007) designed two schemes to protect privacy in the process of aggregating data: (i) cluster-based private data aggregation (CPDA), which adds random seeds in the original data and (ii) slice-mix-aggregate (SMART), which chops one data item into pieces and rebuild data package after exchanging those pieces randomly. They focused on the sum operation in the process of aggregating data.

4.1.1   Cluster-based privacy data aggregation
This scheme is based on the clustering architecture in which the cluster heads are responsible for collecting and aggregating data from the cluster members. The aggregated data are aggregated further before being

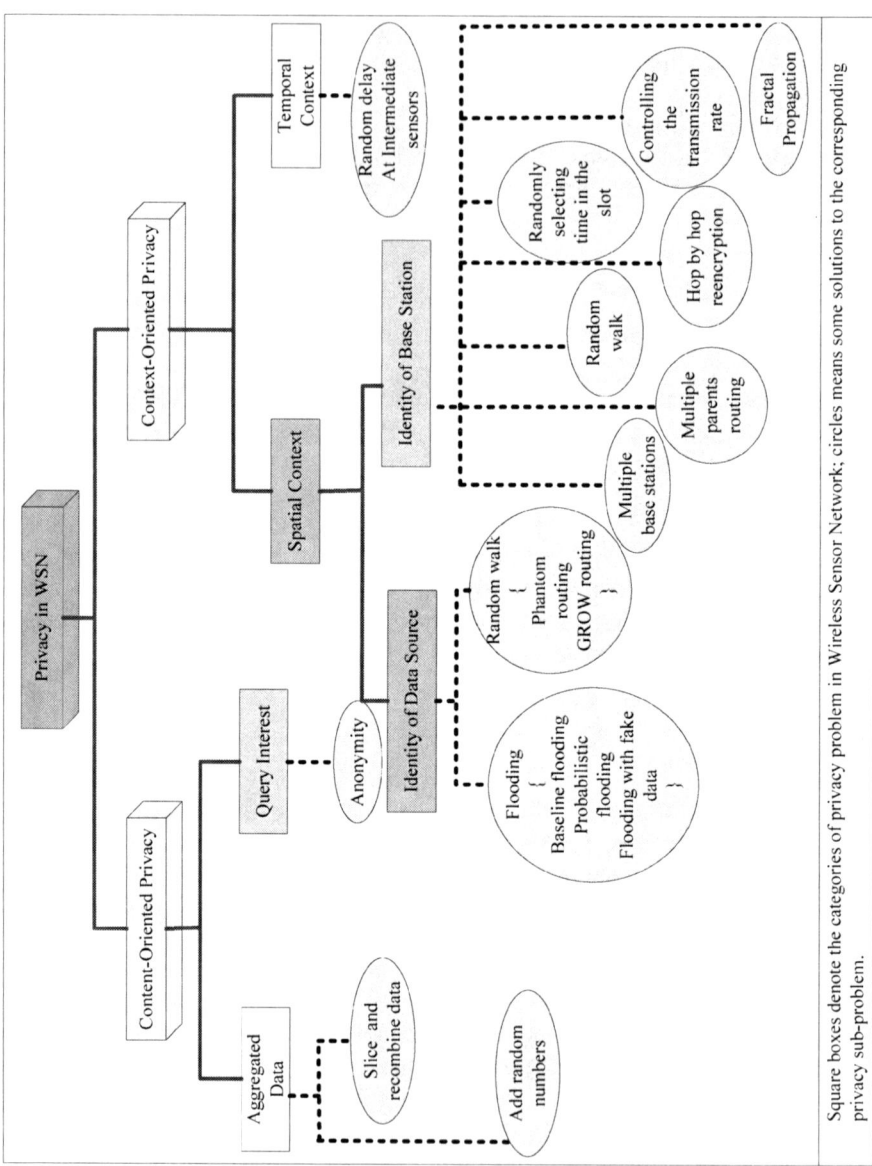

Fig. 3.   Categories of privacy problems.

Square boxes denote the categories of privacy problem in Wireless Sensor Network; circles means some solutions to the corresponding privacy sub-problem.

forwarded toward the base station. There are three main steps to implement the scheme.

First of all, the scheme constructs the clusters in the whole network. Each sensor has probability P_c to serve as a cluster head, and that value is predetermined before running the network. If a sensor becomes a cluster head, it sends *Hello* messages to its neighbors. Nodes that are not selected as cluster heads will wait for the *Hello* messages from their neighbors so as to join some cluster. After receiving the *Hello* message, a sensor sends *Join* message to acknowledge joining the cluster.

Second, the cluster heads are in charge of calculating the aggregated data. Data transmitted between each pair of sensors are encrypted by their share key.

Let us take a cluster with $n+1$ sensors as an example. The cluster head is denoted as s_0, and all other sensors are named $s_1, \ldots, s_n$, respectively. Let P_i be the private data values belonging to s_i. Each node is assigned a non-zero number, which is commonly known to all other members in the same cluster. Furthermore, each sensor s_i generates n private random numbers, $R_1^i, \ldots, R_n^i$ and calculates the following numbers

$$V_j^i = P_i + R_1^i A_j + R_2^i (A_j)^2 + \cdots + R_n^i (A_j)^n \tag{1}$$

where j is from 0 to n. Then s_i will send V_j^i to s_j, which is encrypted by the shared key between s_i and s_j. After exchanging data, every sensor s_j calculates a value F_j as follows:

$$F_j = \sum_{i=0}^{n} V_j^i = P + R_1 A_j + R_2 (A_j)^2 + \cdots + R_n (A_j)^n \tag{2}$$

where $P = \sum_{i=0}^{n} P_i$ and $R_k = \sum_{i=0}^{n} R_k^i (k \in [1, n])$. Then s_j broadcasts F_j to the cluster head s_0. s_0 could calculate the sum P according to $U = G^{-1} F$ where G^{-1} is the inverse of G:

$$G = \begin{pmatrix} 1 & A_0 & \cdots & (A_0)^n \\ 1 & A_1 & \cdots & (A_1)^n \\ \vdots & \vdots & & \vdots \\ 1 & A_n & \cdots & (A_n)^n \end{pmatrix} \tag{3}$$

and $F = (F_0, F_1, \ldots, F_n)^T$. Then $U = (P, R_1, R_2, \ldots, R_n)^T$. Here superscript X^T is the matrix transpose. So P is the first element of U. Note that matrix G is of full rank because A_i are distinct numbers. So far, cluster heads get the sum of private data from their cluster members but they could not access the privacy of their respective members separately.

Third, after data is aggregated in each cluster head, it is forwarded to the base station by multi-hop through other cluster heads. Further data aggregation across clusters is performed along the routing tree rooted at sink, which is implemented on the basis of Tiny AGgregation Protocol (TAG) (Madden et al., 2002).

4.1.2 Slice-mix-aggregate

This is a three-step scheme to preserve privacy in data aggregation. The main idea is to slice original data into pieces and recombine them randomly.

In the first step (slicing), each sensor randomly selects J neighbors within h hops to form a set S. Then it slices its data into J pieces, keeps one of those pieces for itself and sends the other $(J–1)$ encrypted pieces to $(J–1)$ sensors randomly selected from the set S.

In the second step (mixing), after a sensor receives pieces of data from some other sensors, it decrypts data using the shared key with the data sender. Each sensor waits for a while to make sure that the round aggregation data have already been sliced and received separately.

In the third step (aggregation), the intermediate sensor aggregates all pieces of data and transmits it toward the base station. Figures 4–6 illustrate these three steps. In this example, we name five sensors from s_1 to s_5, respectively. Here d_{ii} denotes the piece of data kept by s_i, d_{ij} means the piece of data transmitted from s_i to s_j and r_i means the data aggregated by s_i.

4.2 Query privacy

In Carbunar et al. (2007), the query privacy problem is proposed under the assumption that users requiring service based on WSNs are different from those building and maintaining the whole network. In general, to reduce the energy consumption, query dissemination should be constrained in a small range of the WSN. However, too obvious concentration will leak the region which clients are interested in, which is regarded as the query

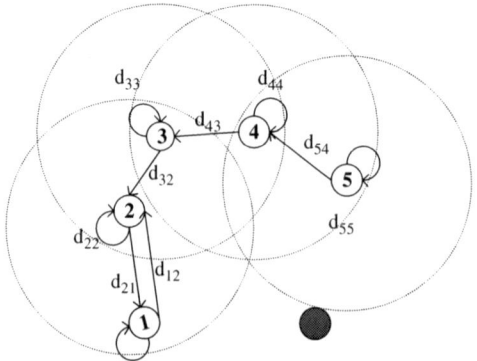

Fig. 4.   Slicing ($J = 2$, $h = 1$).

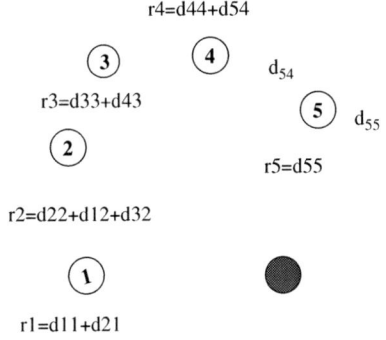

Fig. 5.   Mixing ($J = 2$, $h = 1$).

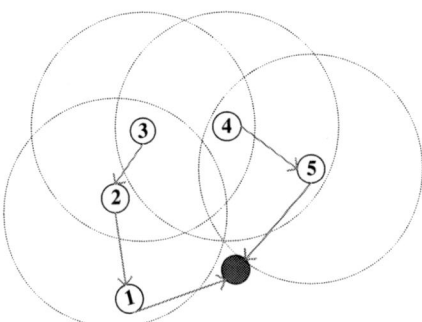

Fig. 6.   Aggregation.

privacy problem. Carbunar et al. (2007) applied transform function to fuzzy the target region which the client is interested in. The main idea is to map one region into m regions. That way, the target region of clients' interest is protected by other uninteresting regions. Carbunar et al. (2007) introduced several transform functions such as uniform, randomized, and hybrid.

In Union Transform (UT), the interesting region of each query is transformed to the set of all regions that appear in a query sequence. For instance, let (Q_1, Q_2, Q_3, Q_4) be a query sequence with target regions (0,0), (2,3), (4,2), and (1,1), respectively, where (x,y) stands for the indices of regions. Regardless of which one of those four queries is carried on, those four target regions are queried simultaneously. Figure 7 illustrates the mapping between query sequence and query regions under UT. In the Randomized Transform (RT), each query is mapped into a randomized set of regions involving the original region that users are interested in. Considering the same example as earlier, Fig. 8 shows the mapping relation under RT. Different kinds of lines stand for query regions corresponding to different

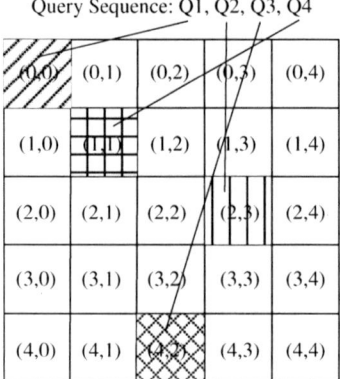

Fig. 7.   Each query maps with all target.

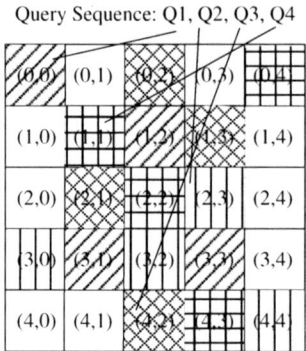

Fig. 8.   Each query randomly maps m regions in the sequence ($m = 4$).

queries. Here each query is corresponding to four regions involving the target one. Finally, the Hybrid Transform (HT) is a combination of UT and RT. This scheme is similar to the k-anonymity algorithm (Sweeney, 2002) which hides the target's identity using other ($k - 1$) similar objects so that it is difficult for the adversary to figure out the target. The cost of safe-guarding privacy in WSNs is the energy consumption on query dissemination and data collection among the uninteresting regions.

5   Context-oriented problem

In contrast to the content-oriented problem, the context-oriented privacy protection faces unique challenges because certain private information beyond the data values could be of concern. In fact, this sort of privacy involves a wide-range of subproblems. As long as the private information obtained by the adversary is not based on the content of data, it could belong to the context-oriented privacy. In this section, we give an overview of contextual privacy from spatio-temporal standpoint. We further discuss the contextual privacy on two subproblems, spatial privacy and temporal privacy. As an example, the identity of data source and base station can be regarded as two specific problems involved in spatial privacy problem. If attackers care more about the target in WSNs, they will track it based on the data traffic analysis. When the adversary pays more attention to the base station, they could destroy it directly or hinder its normal performance so that the whole network is crumpled. Consequently, protecting these two kinds of spatial privacy has to be taken into consideration. For temporal privacy, on the other hand, by correlating the data-receiving time at the base station and the hop count which a data item gets through along its routing path, the time of data generation at the source could be deduced according to the assumption that the time of relaying data at the intermediate sensors is the same. In other words, measures should be taken to protect the spatial and temporal privacy. In the following sections, we discuss them in details.

5.1 Spatial privacy

Spatial privacy deals with sensitive location and identity information. In the following, we discuss the protection of the data source and base station identity.

5.1.1 Data source privacy

Treating the identity of data source as the private information, a classic scenario called "Panda Hunter Game" is considered in Kamat et al. (2005). In this game, a large number of panda-detection sensors are deployed in the panda's habitat by the Save-Panda Organization. When sensors detect the emergence of a panda, they will report data toward the base station. In that process, the panda-hunter, as an adversary, attempts to track back along the data routing path so as to figure out the panda. On the one hand, the organization needs the panda's moving information; on the other, they should hide it against hunters. Even though a hunter could not decrypt the data item transmitted in the network, he makes a menace to the panda by analyzing the traffic flow, according to which the identity and location of the data source could be regarded as a contextual privacy.

In the literature, some solutions have been proposed to safeguard the data source privacy. In the following, we describe schemes based on flooding and random walk.

5.1.1.1   Flooding based and its variants.

Baseline flooding: This scheme assumes every sensor broadcasts data to all its neighbors, but the same data is broadcasted only once at each sensor (Kamat et al., 2005). Considering that almost all sensors participate in the data transmission by flooding, at the first glance, this scheme seems to strongly hide the data source and protect privacy. However, it guides the opposite way, since it allows the adversary to track and reach the source location within the minimum safety period. For instance, if the shortest path length between the source and sink is 10 units, then the safety period is 10 units as well. If the adversary detects the first data arriving at the sink, he could make sure the routing path of this data is the shortest path between the data source and the base station. In the later time, the attacker could track back the last forwarding sensor along the routing path so that the data source is figured out. Furthermore, the flooding consumes significant amount of energy in the whole network and hence the lifetime of the network is reduced dramatically.

Probabilistic flooding: Probabilistic flooding forces only a part of the sensors to participate in the data forwarding while other sensors only discard data messages. A forwarding probability, $P_{forward}$, is pre-set. When a sensor receives a data, it will randomly generate a value between 0 and 1. After comparing with $P_{forward}$, the sensor decides whether to transmit the data or discard it. This scheme decreases the redundant data transmission over the network, thus saving energy and reducing data collision. Moreover, this method provides a stronger privacy preserving than basic flooding, although it cannot guarantee the reception of data at the base station because of randomness.

Flooding with fake data: For much stronger protection of privacy, fake data sources and fake messages are introduced to disturb the hunter's attention to the real panda. A simple scheme called Short-lived Fake Source routing is to set a fixed probability of sending a fake message for all sensors. After a sensor receives a real message, it generates a random value between 0 and 1, which indicates whether to send the fake message. This strategy does not improve privacy protection greatly, since the lifetime of fake message is only one hop to control the number of fake data and save energy over the whole network. If a sensor receives a fake data, it just discards the fake data so that hunters could be misled by only one hop, which is not an effective scheme. An improved version of injecting fake data message is Persistent Fake Source routing strategy. The main idea is that if a sensor decides to take the responsibility of fake source, it will continue to generate fake messages so that the hunter can be misguided toward the fake source gradually.

5.1.1.2   Random walk based.

Phantom flooding: A random walk is introduced to protect the identity of the data source (Kamat et al., 2005). Initially, after leaving the data source sensor, a data item performs a random/directed walk with h hops and then carries on a regular routing (flooding or single routing). The walk is designed to distract the hunter's attention to the real data source. Even though the hunter could track back along the routing path, he could only figure out that sensor, which is the terminal node of the random/directed walk instead of the original data source. The main idea of phantom flooding is to vary routing paths for each data message so that it is more difficult for the hunter to pinpoint the panda's position. Figures 9 and 10 (Kamat et al., 2005) illustrate the two-step Phantom Flooding scheme.

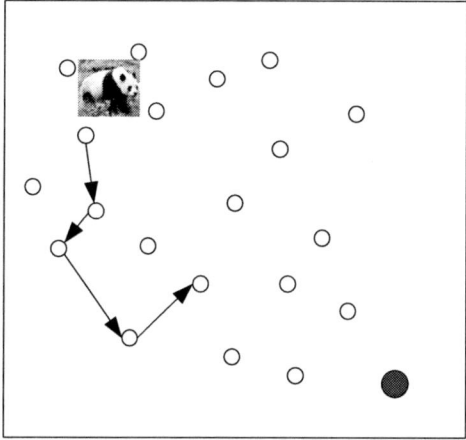

Fig. 9.   Random walk ($h = 4$).

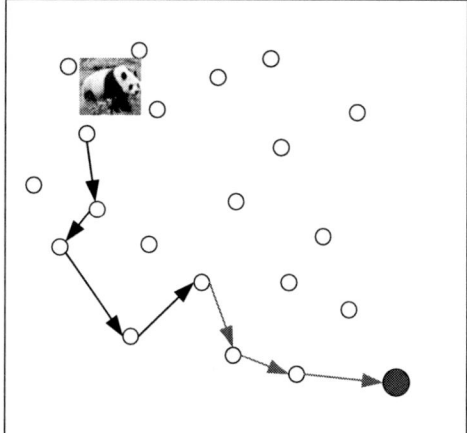

Fig. 10.   Regular routing (single routing or flooding).

Greedy random walk: To improve Phantom Flooding, a two-way Greedy Random Walk (GROW) scheme was proposed in (Xi et al., 2006). In this scheme, the sink first sets up a path through random walks along which sensors serve as receptors. Each packet from a source is then randomly forwarded until it reaches one of receptors. At that point, the packet is forwarded to the sink through the pre-established path of base station. Figures 11 and 12 illustrate this scheme.

5.1.2 Base station privacy

Another classic problem of context-oriented privacy preserving is to hide the identity of the base station. Considering the base station as a data-collecting center or a gateway that connects the WSN with the wired network, it poses significant threats to a WSN because the sink may be isolated from other sensors and loses the ability to achieve its task. Actually, if an adversary attempts to make the base station collapsed, it could perform a denial of service (DOS) attack by misleading data flow to a new destination where they could make further analysis of the data. Let us take the military scenario as an example. When sensors are deployed in the battlefield, the base station is a key center. If it is easy for the enemies to figure the base station out, they could destroy the whole network without much effort.

The precondition of launching attack to the base station for the adversary is to figure out the location of the base station. In some cases, even though the attackers could not extract any significant information about the base station directly from the data item transmitted in the network, they could figure out

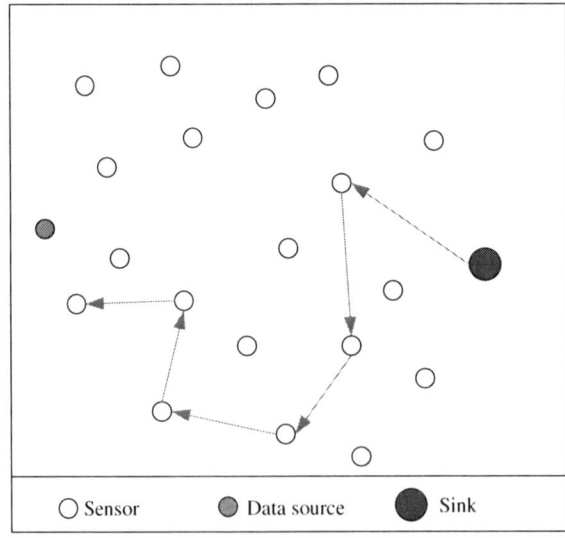

Fig. 11.   Sink builds the receptor path.

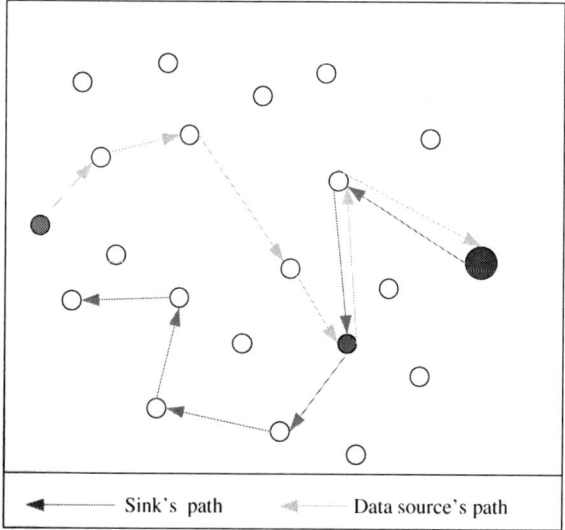

Fig. 12.   Data randomly walk, intersect with a receptor and then follow receptor path.

the base station by analyzing the traffic flow. In Deng et al. (2004, 2005, 2006) and Jian et al. (2007), some countermeasures are proposed aiming at disguising the identity of a base station against traffic analysis attack.

Actually, transmitting data toward the base station gives rise to the asymmetric data transmission pattern, which facilitates the adversary to track down the location of the base station. In Deng et al. (2004), some methods have been analyzed, which could be adopted by the adversary to figure out the sink. First of all, the basic method is to extract the location information of the base station directly from the data item. Secondly, from the time interval between receiving and sending data at each sensor, it is possible to get the parent–child relation between two sensors, which aids for the attacker to follow down the base station along the data routing path. Another clue which adversary could get from the traffic flow in the network is the higher transmission rate of sensors near the sink. The closer the sensor is to the sink, the higher the data transmission rate is. Corresponding to the possible attack aforementioned, we introduce some countermeasures as follows.

Multiple-base station: To strengthen the intrusion tolerance, multiple-path and multiple-base station are introduced as a complementary scheme against the attack to only one base station (Deng et al., 2004). Even though one of the base stations is destroyed, other ones could continue to collect data and maintain the running of the WSN. With multiple-base stations, the topology of the network consists of multiple trees with base stations as their respective roots. Initially, each base station builds the topology tree through broadcasting request (REQ) message. When a sensor first receives a REQ from some base station, it records the last-hop sensor of the message in the routing table and then rebroadcasts the REQ message to its neighbors. If the sensor receives a duplicated REQ message, it only discards it. After the construction of the topology, every sensor records its parent sensors corresponding to the multiple-base station.

Multiple-parent routing scheme: This scheme is introduced to balance the traffic load and increase the tolerance of link/node failure (Deng et al., 2005, 2006). Here the function of a multiple-path is to reduce the inflexibility of routing path to the base station. Each sensor randomly selects one of the multiple parents to transmit data toward the base station. Two methods are suggested to set up the multiple-parent routing paths. In the first method, at the beginning of running the network, the base station sends beacon message to construct the topology. The hop count from the base station is recorded in the beacon message. When a sensor receives the beacon message, it records the hop count, increases the value by one and rebroadcasts the message. A sensor selects all its neighbors with hop counts less than its hop count as its parents. In the second method, a sensor waits for a while before rebroadcasting the first received beacon message. During that short period of time, all sensors from which a sensor receives beacon messages belong to the parent set of the sensor.

Random walk: A simple random walk (Jian et al., 2007) divides the neighbors of a sensor into two lists (closer and further lists), according to the hop count from the base station (Deng et al., 2005, 2006; Jian et al., 2007). When a sensor forwards data, it randomly selects a next hop sensor from one of those two lists. In general, the random walk (Deng et al., 2005, 2006) controlling each node selects its parent as next hop toward the base station with the probability of P_r and randomly forwards data with probability of $(1 - P_r)$, which drastically reduces the probability of successfully analyzing by the adversary. Due to the probabilistic selection, it is possible that the packet travels against the base station so that more energy is consumed and the delay time is prolonged. In this sense, the scheme in Jian et al. (2007) could be regarded as a special case of the strategy in Deng et al. (2005, 2006) for $P_r = 1/2$.

Re-encryption: The confidence of the adversary to make traffic analysis is based on tracking data messages with the same data payload. To solve this problem, the re-encryption technique is proposed in Deng et al. (2004, 2006) to change the data appearance hop-by-hop, using shares key at each hop along the routing path. In other words, hop-by-hop re-encryption spatially de-correlates the packet's appearance.

Random time selection: An adversary can figure out the relationship of parent–child through the short time interval of receiving and sending data at a sensor (Deng et al., 2006). To de-correlate this specific relation, the period of time T is divided into m slots when there are one parent and $(m-1)$ children for a sensor. The parent sensor assigns time slots to its children and each sensor will transmit its data at a random time within its scheduled slot.

Controlling the same transmission rate: Another traffic analysis attack by the adversary to figure out the base station is through the asymmetric data traffic flow. The sensors close to the base station need not only to send their own data but also to relay data from sensors further away from the base station. In that case, it is easier for the adversary to figure out sensors with higher transmission rate so that the identity of the base station is disclosed. Keeping the same transmission rate among sensors is a solution. When a parent sensor has a data to send, it will not accept more data from its children until it sends the buffered data out. The children sensors monitor their parents. If a child sensor finds its parents send dummy, which means the buffer of the parent is empty, or the parent begins to transmit the child sensor's data, it will accept data from its child; otherwise, the child sensor repeats to send its old data. If a sensor does not have data to send, it will transmit dummy data to keep a global transmission rate. Obviously, this scheme protects the identity of the base station at the cost of delay time and extra energy consumption on transmitting dummy data.

Fractal propagation: Under the assumption that the attacker could not distinguish the real data from fake data, injecting fake packets into the network makes it more difficult for the attacker to extract the data transmission pattern. If a sensor detects that its neighbor is transmitting a real packet to the base station, the sensor generates a fake packet with probability P_c, and forwards it to one of its neighbors. Deng et al. (2005, 2006) introduced two fractal propagation methods. One is to control the probability P_c according to the frequency of forwarding packets. The higher the frequency, the lower the probability. The other aims at balancing the communication traffic across the whole network. The authors simulated high data-sending rate area and fake hot spots so as to mislead the adversary. Against the analysis of the transmission rate, injecting fake data, from single fake data to fake highly active area, is mainly introduced into the solutions for safeguarding the identity of the base station. The cost to protect privacy is energy consumption due to transmission of fake data over the network. Consequently, we have to decide the amount of fake data to make a proper tradeoff between energy consumption and privacy protection.

5.2 Temporal privacy

In the target-tracking scenario, when sensors detect the target, they generate and forward the corresponding data packets which indicate that the target appeared at the source at a specific time. The target will be faced with a serious threat if the adversary could associate the data source location with the specific time. The adversary could predict the target's next position and even its future moving path. The attacker's confidence depends on the assumption that the delay time (t) of data passing through each intermediate sensor along the routing path is the same. When the adversary eavesdrops the data message around the sink, he could get the arrival time z and extract the hop count h_i of the flow i. Then he could deduce the approximate time of generating that data, x', according to the equation $x' = z - hi*t$. The main idea in Kamat et al. (2007) is to locally buffer the data at the intermediate sensor for a random period of time along the routing path.

Kamat et al. (2007) discussed the case with Two-Party Single-Packet, i.e., a system with only the data source and the base station. Suppose the source sensor creates a data packet at some time X, and after locally buffering it for a random amount of time Y, it sends data to the base station. The probability that the attacker could successfully infer X from Z, where $Z = X + Y$ depends on two distributions. One depicts the likelihood of the message creation time and the other is the delay distribution, Y, used to mask X. The amount of information that the adversary can infer about X from Z is quantified by the mutual information: $I(X;Z) = H(X) - H(X|Z) = H(Z) - H(Ys)$, where $H(X)$ is the differential entropy of X. For fixed distributions of X and Y, we could calculate $I(X; Z)$. The mutual information of two random variables quantifies the mutual dependency of the two variables. The temporal privacy problem is formulated as $\min_{f_Y(y)} I(X;Z) = H(X + Y) - H(Y)$. Therefore, the goal is to design the delay distribution of Y that minimizes the information X inferred from Z.

In multi-hop WSNs, between the data source and base station, there are usually several sensors to forward the data. The total random time Y is decomposed into several random variables Y_i. The intermediate sensor i locally buffers the data for a random period of time, Y_i. The distributed delay at sensors along the routing path relieves the burden of the buffer utilization at the data source. For this purpose, a rate-controlled adaptive delaying scheme is proposed in Kamat et al. (2007) to adjust the delay distribution as a function of the incoming traffic rate and the available buffer space.

6   Comparison of privacy-preserving techniques

In this section, we compare the performance of privacy-preserving techniques in WSNs introduced in this chapter. Note that the objective of privacy protection is to hide the original sensitive information being sensed or collected by the sensors with the help of randomness or enlarging the range of target data. The negative effect brought by those schemes is the increasing difficulty to accurately rebuild the original data. Furthermore, in some cases, the cost of preserving privacy is the longer delay time, which plays an important role in the performance of time-sensitive networks. So we have to make a proper trade-off between different metrics and design an appropriate scheme according to the specific needs of applications or networks. In the following discussion, we evaluate the existing solutions.

Taking into account the characteristics of WSNs, we evaluate the existing techniques and solutions for privacy protection according to four metrics: privacy, accuracy, delay time, and transmission overhead. Privacy, referred to the effect of protecting privacy brought by schemes, is certainly an important metric to evaluate those solutions. Here accuracy covers two aspects: (i) the difference between the data rebuilt and the original data and (ii) whether useful data could arrive at the base station. If useful data could not be transmitted to the base station, we definitely lose its accuracy. The delay time includes the time of buffering and calculating the data at the intermediate sensors. Note that more time may be spent on routing under some privacy-preserving schemes than the original routing strategy. Finally, the transmission overhead measures the number of extra packets transmitted in a WSN for privacy protection. In particular duplicate data in flooding can be regarded as the transmission overhead. More transmission overhead not only consumes more energy but also wastes bandwidth and gives rise to data collision. Therefore, it may have a seriously negative influence on the quality of data transmission. Ideally, we hope to solve the privacy problem at a lower cost of all the above metrics, however, in practice, it would be hard to gain all benefits. Usually, we need to trade-off those metrics and pay more attention to some of them under specific scenarios while holding other metrics at an appropriate level. Table 1 gives an overview of various solutions to the privacy-preserving problem in WSNs. In Table 1, tags, such as <Good>, <High>, etc., we list the detailed explanation to the appropriate evaluation.

7 Open problems

Although some research has been done on privacy protection in WSNs, there are still many open research problems and issues that need to be addressed in the future work. First of all, the existing work (He et al., 2007) only addresses systems with a single mobile target (panda) in the protection of data source. An interesting open problem would be to tackle the cases with multiple mobile targets. Another open problem is how to protect the identity of mobile sinks. Mobile sinks have been proposed to relieve the "Energy Hole Problem." To guarantee the data collection toward sinks, they have to broadcast their new location, which makes it possible to be detected by an adversary. Third, re-encrypting data hop-by-hop is introduced in Shar et al. (2007) and Xi et al. (2006) to disguise the data identity with the help of random buffering to de-correlate the parent–child

Table 1
An overview of solutions

		Privacy	Accuracy	Delay time	Transmission overhead
Content PDA	CPDA	<Good> Depend on the security of share key	<High> 100% Accuracy without data loss	<Low> Calculation and aggregation time	<High> Exchange assistant data for aggregating data in the clusters
	SMART	<Good> 100% Protection for privacy	<High> 100% Accuracy without data loss	<Low> Slice and recombine data	<High> Break one data into J slices
Query	Anonymity	<Good> Depend on the parameter k in k-anonymity	N/A	N/A	<High> Data query and collection in regions not interested by clients
Context Spatial	Data Source Baseline flooding	<Bad> Easily figure out the shortest path between sink and data source	<High> 100% Data arrival	N/A	<High> Flood data over the whole network
	Probabilistic flooding (Pf)	<Good> Depend on Pf	<Median> Not 100% data arrival, depend on the probability of forwarding data, Pf	<Low> Depend on Pf	<High> Flood data based on Pf
	Flood with fake data	<Good> Dummy data injection	<High> 100% Accuracy under baseline flooding	N/A	<High> Fake data Flood data
	Phantom	<Good> A random walk from data source	<High> 100% Data arrival	<Low> One random walk, depend on the hops of the walk	N/A
	GROW	<Good> Two-way random walk	<Low> Data arrival depends on intersection of two random walk, low probability	<High> Depend on the intersection of two random walk	N/A

Base Station	Multiple-base station	<Good> Strengthen the robustness of base stations under multiple sinks	N/A	N/A	N/A
	Multiple-parent	<Good> Multiple routing paths	N/A	N/A	N/A
	Random walk	<Good> Depend on the probability of choosing parent as next hop	<Median> Depend on the probability of choosing parent as next hop	<Median> Depend on the probability of choosing parent as next hop	N/A
	Re-encryption	<Good> Reencrypt data link to link	N/A	<Median> Encryption and decryption time spent at each hop	<Low> Exchange share key between one hop sensors
	Selecting time in slot	<Good> Make parent–child relationship ambiguous	N/A	<Median> Randomly select transmission time in each slot	N/A
	Control transmission rate	<Good> Hide traffic pattern by making transmission rate the same	N/A	<High> Buffer data until parent is available	<High> Dummy data to keep the same transmission rate
	Fractal propagation	<Good> Injecting fake data	N/A	N/A	<High> Fake data and data source
Temporal	Random distribution	<Good> Destroy the deduction of approximate generation time of data	N/A	<High> Randomly buffer data at intermediate sensors	N/A

relationship between two sensors, which are intended to reduce the possibility of successfully tracking down the routing path. These schemes are effective in networks with highly dense data traffic. Nonetheless, in a sparse WSN, even if we disguise data or insert random delay when data is passing through intermediate sensors, it is still easy for an adversary to conjecture the relationship between two sensors to determine the routing path. Finally, no existing work on privacy protection in WSNs addresses the challenges with mobile sensors. Mobility will bring more challenge to privacy protection since mutual trust has to be accurately built among sensors when they communicate with each other. Furthermore, privacy protection should also be provided for such processes in WSNs as data dissemination and topology control, which should lead to more research directions.

8   Summary

In this chapter, we presented a state-of-the-art survey on privacy-preserving techniques in WSNs. We discussed the existing privacy problems in wireless sensor networks from two categories, content- and context-oriented problems. We reviewed various solutions in these two categories. For the content-oriented problem, we addressed the protection of private data and sensitive queries. For the context-oriented problem, we discussed two subproblems, spatial and temporal privacy protection, and reviewed various privacy-preserving techniques for each subproblem. Furthermore, we evaluated all discussed techniques from the viewpoint of several metrics, such as privacy, accuracy and delay as well as computational and communication overhead. Finally, we outlined some open problems for future research.

References

Bi, Y.Z., N. Li, L.M. Sun (2007a). DAR: an energy-balanced data-gathering scheme for wireless sensor networks. *Computer Communications-Network Coverage and Routing Schemes for Wireless Sensor Networks* 30(14–15), 2812–2825.

Bi, Y.Z., L.M. Sun, N. Li (2009). BoSS: a moving strategy for mobile sinks in wireless sensor networks. *International Journal of Sensor Networks.* 5(3), Available at http://cs.ua.edu/~yangxiao/IJSNet_Contents.html

Bi, Y.Z., L.M. Sun, J. Ma, N. Li, I.A. Khan, C.F. Chen (2007b). HUMS: an autonomous moving strategy for mobile sinks in data-gathering sensor networks. *EURASIP Journal on Wireless Communications and Networking* 15 pp. Available at http://www.hindawi.com/getarticle.aspx? doi = 10.1155/2007/64574

Buttyán, L., T. Holczer, I. Vajda (2007). On the effectiveness of changing pseudonyms to provide location privacy in VANET, in: *Proceedings of the European Workshop on Security and Privacy in Ad Hoc and Sensor Networks (ESAS),* Cambridge, UK, pp. 129–141.

Carbunar, B., Y. Yu, L. Shi, M. Pearce, V. Vasudevan (2007). "Query privacy in wireless sensor networks", Sensor, Mesh and Ad Hoc Communications and Networks. SECON '07, in: *4th Annual IEEE Communications Society Conference, June 18–21*, San Diego, CA, USA, pp. 203–212.

Chen, Y.Q., E. Chan, S. Han (2005). Energy efficient multipath routing in large scale sensor networks with multiple sink nodes", in: *Proceedings of the 6th International Workshop on Advanced Parallel Processing Technologies (APPT)*, LNCS 2834.

Das, A., D. Dutta (2004). Data acquisition in multiple-sink sensor networks", Abstract in ACM Mobile Communication and Communication Review. Poster version in ACM Sensys.

Deng, J., R. Han, S. Mishra (2004). Intrusion tolerance and anti-traffic analysis strategies for wireless sensor networks, Dependable Systems and Networks, *International Conference*, 28 June–1 July, pp. 637–646.

Deng, J., R. Han, S. Mishra (2005). Countermeasures against traffic analysis attacks in wireless sensor networks, in: Security and Privacy for Emerging Areas in Communications Networks (SecureComm), Greece, September, pp. 113–126.

Deng, J., R. Han, S. Mishra (2006). Decorrelating wireless sensor network traffic to inhibit traffic analysis attacks. *Pervasive and Mobile Computing Elsevier* 2(2), 159–186.

Freudiger, J., M. Raya, M. Félegyházi, P. Papadimitratos, J.P. Hubaux (2007). Mix-Zones for location privacy in vehicular networks, ACM Workshop on Wireless Networking for Intelligent Transportation Systems (WiN-ITS), Vancouver.

Gruteser, M., D. Grunwald (2003). Anonymous usage of location-based services through spatial and temporal cloaking, in: *Proceedings of the International Conference on Mobile Systems, Applications, and Services, MobiSys, May*, San Francisco, CA, USA, pp. 163–168.

He, W.B., X. Liu, H. Nguyen, K. Nahrstedt, T. Abdelzaher (2007). PDA: privacy-preserving data aggregation in wireless sensor networks, in: *The 26th IEEE International Conference on Computer Communications (INFOCOM), May*, Anchorage, AK, USA, pp. 2045–2053.

Heinzelman, W. (2000). *Application-specific protocol architectures for wireless networks*. Ph.D. thesis, Massachusetts Institute of Technology, June.

Heinzelman, W.R., A. Chandrakasan, H. Balakrishnan (2000). Energy-efficient communication protocols for wireless microsensor networks (LEACH), in: *Porceedings of the 33rd Hawaii International Conference on Systems Science*, Vol. 8, January 04–07, pp. 3005–3014.

Jian, Y., S.G. Chen, Z. Zhang, L. Zhang (2007). Protecting receiver-location privacy in wireless sensor networks, in: *The 26th IEEE International Conference on Computer Communications (INFOCOM), May*, Anchorage, AK, USA, pp. 1955–1963.

Jiang, T., H.J.Wang, Y.-C. Hu (2007). Preserving location privacy inwireless LANs, in: *MobiSys '07: Proceedings of the 5th International Conference on Mobile Systems, Applications and Services, June 11–14*, ACM Press, San Juan, Puerto Rico, 246–257.

Kamat, P., W.Y. Xu, W. Trappe, Y.Y. Zhang (2007). Temporal privacy in wireless sensor networks, in: *The 27th International Conference on Distributed Computing Systems (ICDCS), June*, Canada.

Kamat, P., Y.Y. Zhang, W. Trappe, C. Ozturk (2005). Enhancing source-location privacy in sensor network routing, in: *The 25th IEEE International Conference on Distributed Computing Systems (ICDCS), June*, Columbus, OH, USA, pp. 599–608.

Li, J., P. Mohapatra (2005). An analytical model for the energy hole problem in many-to-one sensor networks. *Vehicular Technology Conference* 4(September), 2721–2725.

Luo, J., J.P. Hubaux (2005). Joint mobility and routing for lifetime elongation in wireless sensor networks, in: *Proceedings of the 24th IEEE INFOCOM, March*, Miami, FL, USA, Vol. 3, pp. 1735–1746.

Madden, S., M.J. Franklin, J.M. Hellerstein (2002). TAG: a tiny AGgregation service for ad-hoc sensor networks, in: *Proceedings of the 5th Annual Symposium on Operating Systems Design and Implementation (OSDI)*, New York, USA, pp. 131–146.

Oyman, E.I., C. Ersoy (2004). Multiple sink network design problem in large scale wireless sensor networks, in: *Proceedings of the International Conference on Communications (ICC 2004), June 20–24*, Paris, France.

Schilit, B., J. Hong, M. Gruteser (2003). Wireless location privacy protection. *IEEE Computer* 36(12), 135–137.

Shar, M., S.C. Zhu, W.S. Zhang, G.H. Cao (2007). pDCS: security and privacy support for data-centric sensor networks, in: *The 26th IEEE International Conference on Computer Communications (INFOCOM), May*, Anchorage, AK, USA, pp. 1298–1306.

Soppera, A., T. Burbridge (2004). Maintaining privacy in pervasive computing—enabling acceptance of sensor-based services. *BT Technology Journal* 22(3), 106–118.

Sweeney, L. (2002). k-anonymity: a model for protecting privacy. *International Journal on Uncertainty, Fuzziness and Knowledge-based Systems* 10(5), 557–570.

Walters, J.P., Z.Q. Liang, W.S. Shi, V. Chaudhary (2005). *Wireless Sensor Network Security: A Survey*, Wayne State University, Detroit, MI, USA. Available at http://www.cs.wayne.edu/~weisong/papers/walters05-wsn-security-survey.pdf

Wu, T.J., Y. Xue, Y. Chi (2006). Preserving traffic privacy in wireless mesh networks, World of Wireless, Mobile and Multimedia Networks (WoWMoM), June.

Xi, Y., L. Schwiebert, W.S. Shi (2006). Preserving source location privacy in monitoring-based wireless sensor networks, in: *The 20th International Parallel and Distributed Processing Symposium (IPDPS), April*, Rhodes Island, Greece.

Xu, K., H. Hassanein, G. Takahara (2005). Relay node deployment strategies in heterogeneous wireless sensor networks: multiple-hop communication, in: *Proceedings of the IEEE SECON, September*, pp. 575–585.

Suggested readings

Bulusu, N., S. Jha (2005). *Wireless Sensor Networks: A System Perspective*. Artech House, Norwood, Mass, USA.

Cordeiro, C.D.M., D.P. Agrawal (2006). *Ad Hoc & Sensor Networks: Theory and Applications*. World Scientific Publishing Co. Pte. Ltd, 600pp.

Liu, D., P. Ning (2006). Security for wireless sensor network, in: *Advances in Information Security*, Vol. 28. Springer, New York, XII, 212pp, 83 illus., ISBN: 978-0-387-32723-5.

Xiao, Y. (2006). *Security in Sensor Networks*. AUERBACH, New York, 341pp.

Online resources

GloMoSim, A simulator for wired and wireless network systems. Available at http://pcl.cs.ucla.edu/projects/glomosim/

OMNeT++, A simulator supports the simulation of several protocols in wired and wireless network systems. Available at http://www.omnetpp.org/

Rao & Upadhyaya, Eds., *Handbooks in Information Systems, Vol. 4*

Chapter 15

Access Control and Trust Management for Emerging Multidomain Environments

Yue Zhang

University of Pittsburgh, 410 IS Building, 135N. Bellefield Ave., Pittsburgh, PA 15260, USA

James B.D. Joshi

University of Pittsburgh, 708A IS Building, 135N Bellefield Ave., Pittsburgh, PA 15260, USA

Abstract

Multidomain application environments, where distributed domains inter-operate with each other, are becoming a reality in internet-based enterprise applications. Access control to ensure secure interoperation is a crucial challenge in such environments. Different systems usually have their own access control policies and heterogeneity among different policies must be reconciled properly to ensure secure interoperation. In particular, any access permitted by the individual policy must be permitted under secure interoperation; and any access not permitted by the individual policy must be denied under secure interoperation. Trust management is another important issue in multidomain environments, as the participating domains usually do not know each other before they share information. Moreover, service or information each domain decides to share also depends on the level of trust that each has on its partners. Therefore, trust management should be integrated with access control in multidomain environment. In this chapter, we first introduce several secure interoperation approaches. These approaches assume different underlying access control models and are tailored for different multidomain scenarios. We then review work that integrates trust management with an access control framework to facilitate the overall security needs in multidomain environments.

1 Introduction

Assured information sharing is a growing concern for the rapidly increasing trend of seamless and intense information and resource sharing activities that cross organizational and geographic boundaries. Such information sharing activities have been facilitated by the rapid development in information technology (IT), the newly emerging applications, and Internet-based global information sharing activities. Emerging e/m-commerce applications, healthcare industry, e-government, grid computing environments, etc., are some examples of such environments. Ensuring the security of information and resources when they are being shared among different systems is a crucial problem. A key challenge to ensuring assured information sharing is to develop flexible and powerful frameworks that can address access control and trust management issues in an integrated, holistic way (Chuang et al., 2006).

The development of flexible access control frameworks and enforcement mechanisms to ensure secure interoperation among different systems is a daunting challenge. Consider an application involving multiple systems dealing with commerce (e.g., national credit databases), finance (e.g., stock market information systems), medicine (e.g., patient records), and defense, each having a distinct access control policy. To facilitate information exchange among such systems, some mappings among the heterogeneous policies need to be done by the system administrators. However, such mappings, even if done carefully, can result in security breaches (Gong and Qian, 1996). For example, consider the information system of a major research organization where Alice, the project supervisor, is allowed access to Bob's files, but not vice versa. Suppose that this organization has just become a subsidiary of another corporation where Charles is the Vice President for Research and Diana, his secretary, has access to his files. After the merger, it seems natural to permit Charles to allow access to Alice's project files. But if Bob is allowed access to Diana's files, there would be a security violation because now Bob would potentially have access (indirectly via Diana and Charles) to Alice's files to which he initially did not have access, as shown in Fig. 1. Although the security violation in this example may not be too difficult to spot and remove, a real-world system could have hundreds or thousands of entries in its access control list (ACL) making the task of detecting such violations among multiple interoperating systems very difficult.

Secure interoperation among independent systems that employ distinct security policies poses several challenges related to policy specification and integration, policy analysis to verify and validate the correctness of individual as well as integrated policies, and conflict resolution. The problem can be referred to as the multidomain security problem as it addresses the issue of security of an environment where multiple application domains with different security policies need to interact and share

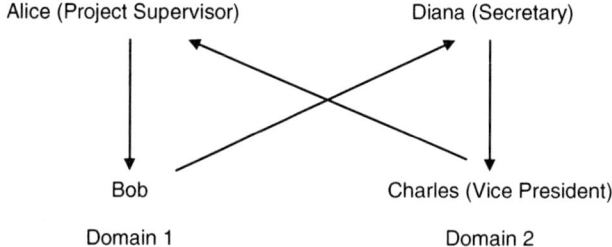

Fig. 1.   An example of security breach during interoperation.

information and resources. Although mapping is a typical way to integrate policies, it assumes use of some mathematical structures such as lattices to represent policy semantics. This may not be always possible because of other rules that may exist in a security policy. Furthermore, similar policies may employ different names as well as structures for policy entities and rules, introducing semantic heterogeneity issues during policy integration. As illustrated earlier, policy mapping could give rise to security breaches if not done carefully.

In emerging, dynamic multidomain application environments, the interacting partners may not know each other beforehand and a trust relationship may need to be established before actual sharing activities. Motivated by such a problem, effort toward developing powerful but practical trust negotiation and management approaches have become a focus of recent studies (Aberer and Despotovic, 2001; Blaze et al., 1998a,b; Damiani et al., 2002; Li et al., 2002; Winsborough et al., 2000). Little existing work, however, address the trust and access control issues in multidomain environments in an integrated way. Such a holistic, integrated approach is crucial for newly emerging dynamic multidomain application environments such as grid systems (e.g., global information grid), peer-to-peer (P2P) based applications, e-government environments, e/m-commerce environments, web services based applications, and service-oriented architectures. In essence, the multidomain security problem can be effectively addressed only by combining trust and access control issues in an integrated way as they define service access based on the perceived or established level of trust between the interacting domains.

This chapter overviews the work done in the area of access control policy integration and the integration of trust and access control issues to address problems related to multidomain security. In addition to access control and trust management, other common issues such as entity authentication, encryption techniques for communication security are also crucial. However, they are not discussed in this chapter. The chapter also does not overview access control and trust management models. They are mentioned briefly when needed. The chapter is organized as follows. In Section 2, we discuss the background and work related to the secure interoperation problem. We introduce several policy integration, and integrated trust and access control approaches in detail in Sections 3 and 4. We present the general discussion and open research problems in Section 5 and conclude the chapter in Section 6.

2   The secure interoperation problem: background

The secure interoperation problem essentially relates to ensuring trustworthiness of the interactions and protection of information, processes, and resources, as per the requirements of the interacting entities. Two key issues that need to be addressed for emerging application environments that allow information sharing among multiple security domains, each with distinct protection requirements, are

1. How to effectively and efficiently allow trust to be formed between the interacting domains if they are unknown to each other and no trust has been pre-established between them.
2. How to effectively and efficiently integrate the security policies of the interacting domains to address the specific sharing requirements of the involved domains.

Typically, a multidomain environment may be classified as a *loosely coupled* or a *tightly coupled* environment based on the level of interoperation, as illustrated in Fig. 2. In general, a *tightly coupled* environment represents a traditional federated system environment where the involved domains are assumed to completely reveal their policies, which are tightly integrated. There is typically an implicit assumption of complete trust among the involved domains. In contrast, a *loosely coupled* environment represents one where the sharing relation among domains is formed dynamically and is valid only for a transient period of time. Furthermore, the domains typically do not know each other *a priori* and hence they do not have a pre-established trust relationship. The level of sharing requirements in such an environment can be very specific and small, thus not requiring the entire security policies to be merged. With the recent growth of distributed environments such as the P2P and web services based applications, we see the loosely coupled interactions becoming more and more common. Figure 2 further indicates that emerging multidomain applications will need to integrate different types of information (multimedia and interactive content) and tasks (workflow processes), which make the access control requirements more complex. Such a highly heterogeneous environment can be projected as a melting pot for emerging technologies for grid, P2P, and mobile applications as well as workflow and multimedia-oriented systems. The issue of secure interoperation becomes very complex

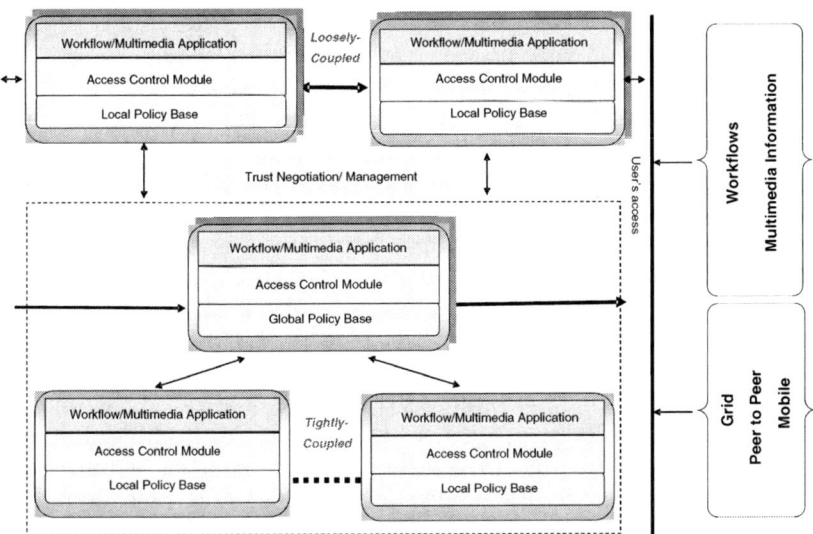

Fig. 2. Security challenges in multidomain environments.

in such emerging, dynamic multidomain environments. The importance of policy integration issues can already be seen in newly emerging multi-domain environments, for instance, in grid environments. In simple terms, grid computing can be defined as coordinated resource sharing and problem solving in dynamic multi-institutional virtual organizations (Foster et al., 2001). Several access control approaches to address the security requirements of a grid computing environment have been discussed in the literature, which include global grid forum (GGF) authorization framework (Zhang and Parashar, 2003), Shibboleth (Cornwall et al., 2005), and Sygn (Ramakrishnan et al., 2002).

Several past and current research efforts have addressed the multidomain security problem in different ways. Gong and Qian (1996) emphasized the crucial issue of access control during interoperation among multiple systems. Specifically, some policy mapping among heterogeneous access control policies is typically required to facilitate information sharing in such a way that sharing is maximized and there is no security breaches introduced by allowing interdomain accesses. They introduce the principles of *autonomy* and *security* to characterize secure interoperation in multidomain environments. Gong and Qian (1996) also analyzed various complexity issues related to the policy-mapping process. Several other researchers have also studied the secure interoperation problem on multidomain environments where each domain employs a *multilevel security* (MLS) policy (Bonatti et al., 1996, 2002; Dawson et al., 2000). Jajodia et al. (2001) proposed a language for users to specify a special access control policy and different access control policies could coexist in their system. This technology can also be used in the multidomain environment to facilitate heterogeneous access control needs (Jajodia et al., 2001). Recently, secure interoperation approaches based on *role-based access control* (RBAC) model is drawing significant research efforts because of its policy neutral characteristic, its ability to support diverse set of access control requirements, and the advantages that it provides over the traditional discretionary access control (DAC) and mandatory access control (MAC) approaches. RBAC has been shown to be inherently rich in modeling hierarchical, separation of duty (SoD), cardinality, and dependency constraints. Furthermore, RBAC has been shown to be able to express both DAC and MAC policies. Hence, RBAC is now considered possibly the most promising approach to address the secure interoperation problem in multidomain environments (Ferraiolo et al., 2001; Sandhu et al., 1996). Shafiq et al. (2005) proposed an approach to multidomain secure interoperation problem by integrating RBAC policies from multiple domains. RBAC-based policy integration assumes that each domain uses the RBAC model. Despite the use of different access control models and different algorithms, one common feature of the most of the existing approaches is that they all combine the local policies into a *global policy*, which is also termed as *meta-policy* or *mediation policy*, and then all the authorization decisions are mediated through it. Piromruen and Joshi (2005) emphasized that such an approach is only suitable for *tightly coupled* or federated environments. They introduce a different approach where the "policy mapping" is created only between the domains that provide and receive the required services from each other. However, such an approach may exacerbate the access transitivity problem illustrated in Section 3.4 if care is not taken. This approach is typically more suitable for *loosely coupled* environments where each domain dynamically requests services from some other domains for a brief time period. Shehab et al. (2005) proposed a "decentralized," cryptography-based solution called *SEcure Role mApping Technique* (SERAT) to avoid the shortcomings of a *centralized* approach in terms of complexity, response to changes, and fairness.

Trust management is crucial for facilitating information sharing especially in loosely coupled, distributed environments where the interacting entities do not have pre-established trust relationships. The existing trust management work mainly focuses on the credential-based trust negotiation where peers evaluate a trust level primarily based on credential information and some other relevant data. *PolicyMaker* (Blaze et al., 1998b) and *KeyNote* (Blaze et al., 1998a) are among the earliest such trust management systems. The *PolicyMaker* engine takes inputs such as the local trust policy, the credentials of the trustee, and a list of actions trustee wants to perform. The engine then evaluates the credentials and actions against the local trust policy to make a list of permitted actions. The *KeyNote* system is the successor of *PolicyMaker* and adds additional design goals such as standardization and ease of integration. However, both the systems are static in nature for two reasons

(1) the trust is built in the beginning of a session and cannot be changed when the information sharing activities progress and (2) the credentials of the trustee that need to be disclosed are fixed and the trustee cannot negotiate those credentials further. To address such shortcomings, the automatic trust negotiation (ATN) framework has been proposed by Winsborough et al. (2000). In ATN, each peer has a local credential access policy (CAP) to guide the trust negotiation. At first, only nonsensitive credentials are exchanged between the peers. When a peer receives some credentials from the other peer, its CAP is used to decide which sensitive credentials can be disclosed based on the credentials it has received. Using such a protocol, all the credentials that are required by the peers are exchanged. The credentials are further used to relate subjects to objects. That is, only the subjects that provide certain credentials are allowed to access the objects. Li et al. (2002) proposed a role-based trust management framework (RT), which automatically maps users to roles using the user credentials so that the users can access the permissions assigned to the roles. Another widely studied trust management approach is the reputation-based approach (Aberer and Despotovic, 2001). One good real life example of reputation-based approach is eBay. After each transaction, the buyers and sellers can rate each other and the overall reputation of a participant is computed as the sum of these ratings over a period of time. In computer systems, such reputation is usually modeled based on the probability that the peer will or will not cheat (Aberer and Despotovic, 2001). Like in eBay, the reputation of a peer is also evaluated by the previous transactions performed by that peer. Such an evaluation could be done by data mining approaches using statistical data analysis of former transactions, an approach that is also known as *servents-based trust management* since the reputation is associated with the servents in the P2P environments only (Aberer and Despotovic, 2001). Damiani et al. (2002) proposed a reputation framework where the reputation is not only related to the servents but also related to the content of the resources, called *digest*. This approach is better when the reputation of the servent itself could be compromised.

None of the approaches mentioned earlier associate trust with the current services exchanged or provided. Chandran et al. (2006) proposed an integrated framework for trust and RBAC for secure interoperation. They emphasized that trust and access control should be closely integrated to ensure secure interoperation in loosely coupled environments. In particular, the trust level established is based on the direct and indirect trust, past history, and various cost and risk factors associated with the interoperation. They use *trust tokens* and *trust tickets* to facilitate the trust negotiation and use a game theory-based approach to guide the trust/service negotiation in their framework. Lee et al. (2006) proposed a Traust model that aims to integrate the existing trust level computation model and access control model in a seamless and secure manner. They carefully design the system architecture and trust negotiation protocols to archive this.

3 Access control in multidomain environments

In this section, we briefly present the key approaches proposed to address the secure interoperation issue, especially from the perspective of the integration of access control policies from different domains to facilitate assured information sharing.

3.1 Secure interoperation and complexity issues

Secure interoperation among multiple domains can be characterized by using the principles of *autonomy* and *security*, as introduced by Gong and Qian (1996).

- Principle of autonomy: *Any access permitted in an individual system must also be permitted under secure interoperation.*
- Principle of security: *Any access not permitted in an individual system must also be denied under secure interoperation.*

To guarantee secure interoperation, both these principles need to be enforced in a system during policy integration. However, there exist several computational issues related to the secure interoperation problem (Gong and Qian, 1996).

Assume that each local domain uses an ACL to capture the authorizations that subjects have over objects. An ACL contains a set of entity pairs of form (e_1, e_2), which indicates that entity e_1 can access (objects owned by) entity e_2. An ACL can be easily represented by a directed graph $G<V, A>$, where each node in V indicates an entity and each arrow in A indicates the access right. For example, ACL_1 {(*Eve, Alice*), (*Alice, Bob*)} and ACL_2 {(*Charles, Fred*), (*Diana, Charles*)} can be represented in Fig. 3(a) (each node is named by the first letter). We say that an access (u, v) is legal in G if and only if there is a directed path in G from u to v, denoted as $(u, v) \in G$. Suppose that there are n security domains with $G_i = <V_i, A_i>$ associated with the the ith domain. To facilitate secure interoperation, mappings can

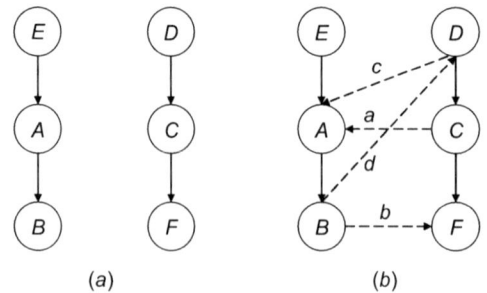

(a)   (b)

Fig. 3. (a) ACL model; (b) Interoperation example.

be represented as a set of permitted accesses F and a set of restricted accesses R over all the nodes of the n domains, that is, $\cup_{i=1}^{n} V_i$. Both F and R are the sets of entity pairs in which the two entities are from two different domains. For each element $(e_1, e_2) \in F$, e_1 *can access* e_2; for any entity pair $(e_1, e_2) \in R$, e_1 *cannot access* e_2. R is used to explicitly prevent the undesirable cross-domain accesses. It is possible that F and R contain the same entry indicating a conflict. In such a case, the elements in R take precedence over those in F; in effect, the entry in F should be removed. Secure interoperation can now be ensured if (1) F and R do not contain the same entity and (2) the principles of *autonomy* and *security* are not violated. The first condition can be verified easily by one traversal of F and R. The second condition in general is not easily detected and prevented. Fig. 3(b) shows an example of a possible interoperation between two domains as shown in Fig. 3(a). Here, note that *Bob* can access *Alice* indirectly through *Diana*, even though this access is illegal within the local domain. In cases like this, F may need to be modified to remove such security violations. The secure interoperation problem can be generalized for a multidomain environment as follows (Gong and Qian, 1996):

Given n security domains $G_i < V_i, A_i >$, $i = 1, \ldots, n$, a set of permitted access F and a set of restricted accesses R, find a multidomain system $G < V, A >$ such that $V = \cup_{i=1}^{n} V_i$, and $A \subseteq (\cup_{i=1}^{n} A_i \cup F) - R$ is a secure interoperation.

Given a multidomain system $G < V, A >$, determining whether A is a secure interoperation has shown to be in P (Gong and Qian, 1996). If A is not secure, the security violations introduced can be removed by removing items from F until the resulting interoperation is secure. It is easy to see that removing all entities in F is a trivial solution. To find a nontrivial solution, one natural optimality measure is to maximize *direct data sharing*, which involves removing the least number of items in F to satisfy the principles of *autonomy* and *security*. Another option is to specify an integer k and require that the number of entities left in F be not less than k. Given such a k, the problem of determining which items to remove from F to ensure A is secure and $|F| \geq k$ is *NP*-complete (Gong and Qian, 1996). For an *NP*-complete problem, one naturally seeks a good approximation algorithm. Unfortunately, even finding approximate solutions has been shown to be *NP*-complete (Gong and Qian, 1996).

Another optimality goal is to *maximize direct* and *indirect* information sharing by considering all the domains in the target multidomain environment. The aim is to find a secure interoperation solution with a *maximum number of legal accesses*, instead of aiming for maximizing the size of F, as in the case of *direct data sharing*. The key difference between the two is that in this one, entities from both ($\cup_{i=1}^{n} A_i$) and F can be removed. This problem has also been shown to be *NP*-complete (Gong and Qian, 1996). It is worth noting that the key factor for these complexity results for maximizing secure interoperation is because of the use of *restrictive accesses* (i.e., the set R).

In other words, if we allow both positive and negative access modes, the problem of finding a maximum secure interoperation becomes very complex. In some multidomain systems, especially early federated systems, secure interoperation is accomplished by having a master system interacting with other systems in local interoperation. In such a configuration, the global interoperation is secure *if and only if* each local interoperation is secure (Gong and Qian, 1996).

3.2   Mediator-based integration of multilevel secure systems

MLS model is widely used in a military-like organization (Dawson et al., 2000). In a MLS model, all subjects and objects are assigned security labels that form a lattice. The MLS model uses the following two rules to govern the accesses that can be allowed (Bell and La Padula, 1975).

- *Simple security property*: A subject with a given security level l_s (also called *clearance level*) can *read* an object with the security level l_o (also called *classification level*) *if and only if* $l_s \geqslant l_o$;
- **-Property*: A subject with a given security level l_s can *write* an object with the security level l_o *if and only if* $l_o \geqslant l_s$.

Dawson et al. (2000) propose a secure interoperation framework for integrating MLS systems. In essence they do not assume that each domain employs the MLS model, but they assume that a "wrapper" can translate the policies of each local domain into MLS policies. They introduce a mediator component that communicates directly with these wrappers. Although the global policy mentioned in the previous section combines all the local policies in a secure manner, the mediator "creates" a central policy and connects it with each local policy in a secure manner. Key issues in this mediator-based approach include determining how to relate the mediator with different local domains and how to effectively process the access requests.

Figure 4 shows an example mediator *MedInfo* connecting three local databases: *Clinic*, *Medline*, and *Hospital* (from Dawson et al., 2000). The solid arrows indicate each lattice and the dashed arrows indicate the interoperation links between the lattices. For example, there is a dashed arrow between *prv* and *pub* indicating that the *prv* security level in the *MedInfo* dominates the *pub* security level in the *Medline*. Dawson et al. (2000) do not discuss who should create or how to create interoperation links between different lattices. Moreover, they assume that the interoperation links in the system introduce no conflicts. Such assumptions may be too simple (Gong and Qian, 1996; Shafiq et al., 2005).

The proposed mediator-based approach only considers the "read" requests that are invoked by the subjects in the mediator and require that all the "write" requests be handled locally in the individual domain.

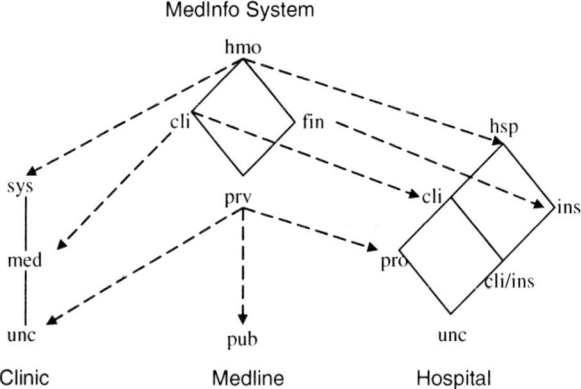

Fig. 4. An example of the MLS system.

Table 1
Example rules in the mediator

Labels	Application		Resource
prv	*research*	←	*M.publiction*[*pub*], *M.author*[*pub*], *M.keyword*[*pub*]
cri	*research*	←	*C.events*[*med*], *C.physicians*[*unc*]
cri	*research*	←	*H.providers*[*pro*], *H.events*[*cli*]

The "read" request is modeled as a query of one of the relations stored in the mediator. Whether such an access request is granted or not depends on the *clearance level* of the subject issuing the request and the *classification level* of the relation, which is determined by all the rules that contain the queried relation as the head (called the "related" rules of a relation). A rule is of the form: $event_1, \ldots, event_n \to relation$, where events are related to the local domains and the relation is in the mediator. The security level of the rule is defined as the least secure label that dominates the least upper bound (LUB) of all events. The access request is granted *if and only if* the security level of the subject dominates at least one of the security levels of the related rules of the queried relation. Table 1 shows some example rules in the system as shown in Fig. 4. Consider a subject with level *prv* that issues a query on relation *research*. Table 1 contains three rules that are related to *research*. The first rule has level *prv* and the other two rules have level *cli*. As the level of the subject (*prv*) dominates the level of the first related rule (*prv*), the access request is granted in this case.

3.3 *Role-based secure interoperation for tightly coupled environments*

Recently, secure interoperation approaches based on RBAC models are being considered very promising. In RBAC, users and permissions are associated through roles. Any user assigned to a role can use the permissions assigned to that role. We can change user-permission relationship by changing user-role assignments and role-permission assignments. This gives us better flexibility especially in large, distributed systems. A distinguished characteristic of RBAC is the role hierarchy. A role hierarchy defines inheritance semantics among roles. For example, a senior role can have the permissions of its junior roles without having to assign those permissions explicitly to the senior roles. SoD constraints are another important feature in the RBAC model.

Joshi et al. (2008) have established a clear distinction among the following three types of role hierarchies: *permission-inheritance*-only hierarchy (*I*-hierarchy, $\geqslant_i$), *activation-inheritance*-only hierarchy (*A*-hierarchy, $\geqslant_a$), and the combined *permission-inheritance and activation* hierarchy (*IA*-hierarchy, $\geqslant$). Semantically, $s \geqslant_i j$ (*s* is *I*-senior of *j*) means that permissions available through *j* are also available through *s*; $s \geqslant_a j$ (*s* is *A*-senior of *j*) means that any user who can activate *s* can also activate *j*; and $s \geqslant j$ (*s* is *IA*-senior of *j*) means that permissions available through *j* are available through *s* and users who can activate *s* can also activate *j*. It has been shown that such a fine-grained hierarchy has much clearer semantics and can allow specification of a wider range of security requirements, including specification of dynamic SoD constraints, and user-centric as well as permission-centric cardinality constraints on roles (Joshi et al., 2008).

Shafiq et al. (2005) proposed a secure interoperation framework in multidomain environments employing RBAC policies. They use the graphical model to represent elements in RBAC as well as the hybrid hierarchy, as illustrated in Fig. 5. The proposed framework addresses three types of security violations that may be introduced during interoperation:

- *Role assignment violation*: An interoperation policy causes a violation of role assignment constraint of domain *d* if it allows a user *u* of domain *d* to access a local role *r* even though *u* is not directly assigned

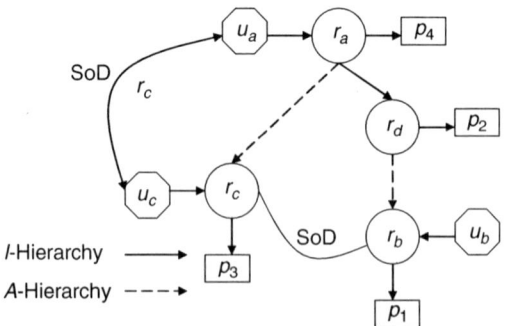

Fig. 5.   Graphical model of RBAC.

to r or any of the roles that are senior to r in the role hierarchy of domain d.

- *Role-specific SoD violation*: An interoperation policy causes a violation of role-specific SoD constraint of domain d if it allows a user to simultaneously access any two conflicting roles r_i and r_j of domain d in the same session or in concurrent sessions.
- *User-specific SoD violation*: Let U_r^c denote the conflicting set of users for role r belonging to domain d. An interoperation policy causes a violation of user-specific SoD constraint of domain d if it allows any two distinct users from the set U_r^c to activate role r in the same session or in concurrent sessions.

Note that all three types of conflicts are due to the violation of the principle of *security*. That is, a user u of domain d is not authorized for permission p of d according to d's local policy, but u is authorized for p under the interoperation. Shafiq et al.'s (2005) framework assumes that each domain employs RBAC model. Hence, the secure interoperation problem becomes finding a policy mapping that supports maximum *sharing* without introducing any of the three security violations. Shafiq et al. (2005) used two steps to solve the problem: (1) do the policy mapping (form a global policy) to facilitate as much interoperation as possible and (2) solve the conflicts introduced into the global policy using an *integer programming* (IP)-based approach. The overall process is depicted in Fig. 6. The first step is policy mapping. This may involve adding new roles and hierarchical relations. Introducing new roles and relations needs to be done systematically. To facilitate this, several possible relations between cross-domain roles need to be considered.

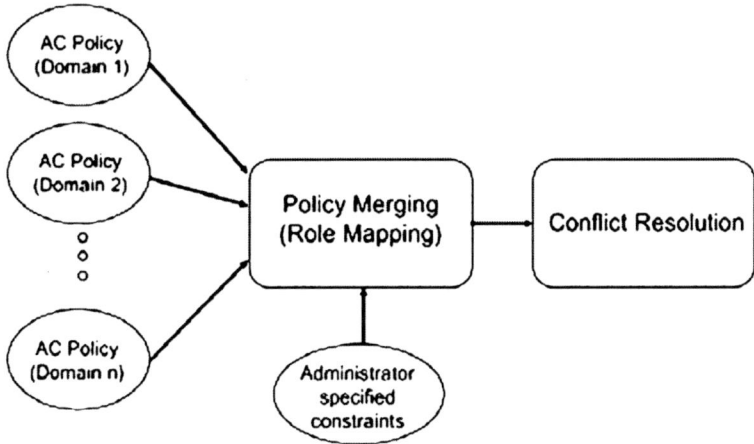

Fig. 6.   Policy integration framework of Shafiq et al.'s (2005) approach.

Four types of relations can be defined between two cross-domain roles r_A and r_B belonging to domains A and B, respectively.

- *Contain*: r_A contains r_B if the following holds:
  - ○ The permission set, $Pset(r_B)$, of role r_B is included in the permission set $Pset(r_A)$ of role r_A.
  - ○ All the permissions in the set $Pset(r_B)$ are shareable with domain A.
- *Equivalent*: r_A is equivalent to r_B if r_A contains r_B and r_B contains r_A.
- *Overlap*: r_A overlaps with r_B if $Pset(r_A)$ and $Pset(r_B)$ have some common shareable permissions and neither r_A contains r_B nor r_B contains r_A.
- Not related: r_A is not related to r_B, if roles r_A and r_B do not share any common permissions.

In the policy-mapping step, different local policies are added to the global policy one by one. When mapping two policies, the roles are integrated pair-wise—any pair of roles (r_1, r_2) that are from different domains are mapped based on how they are related. More specifically, if r_1 is equivalent to r_2, the hierarchical relations $r_1 \geqslant_i r_2$ and $r_2 \geqslant_i r_1$ are introduced. If r_1 and r_2 are not related, then nothing needs to be done. If r_1 contains r_2, then (i) a new role r' is created and $r_1 \geqslant_i r'$ is added, (ii) the shareable permissions of r_1 and r_2 are assigned to r', and (iii) $r' \geqslant_i r_2$ and $r_2 \geqslant_i r'$ are added. Figure 7 shows such role mappings.

Once the global policy is formed, the redundant roles that are not assigned to any users or permissions can be removed. This ensures that the global policy created is order-independent. The next step is to remove the three types of conflicts that may have been introduced into the global policy. The straightforward way to resolve the conflicts is to remove the hierarchical relations caused by the role mappings that cause the conflicts. However, an arbitrary selection of removable role mappings may

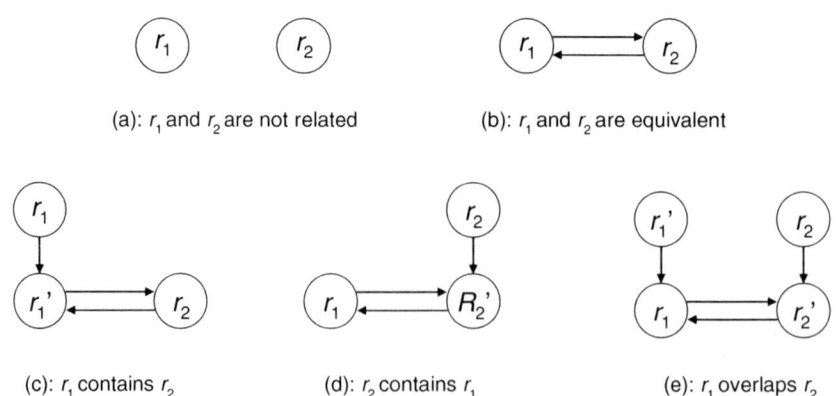

(a): r_1 and r_2 are not related   (b): r_1 and r_2 are equivalent

(c): r_1 contains r_2 (d): r_2 contains r_1 (e): r_1 overlaps r_2

Fig. 7.   Role mapping algorithm.

significantly reduce interoperation. The problem of conflict resolution can be formulated as an optimization problem with the objective of maximizing permitted accesses. Various optimality measures such as maximum *data sharing* and maximum *prioritized accesses* can be used. When conflicts occur, the IP approach, mentioned earlier, is used. In this approach, all the policy specifications are expressed as linear inequalities. The optimization criteria are expressed as the weights in the objective function, as follows:

$$\text{maximize } \mathbf{c}^T u_r$$

$$\text{s. t. } \mathbf{A}u_r \leq b$$

$$\forall u_{ir_j} \in u_r, \ u_{ir_j} = 0 \text{ or } 1$$

Here, $\mathbf{A}$ is the constraint matrix and $\mathbf{c}$ a vector defining the optimality criteria in terms of the weight of the decision variables corresponding to user-role authorizations. The IP-based approach can then be solved to obtain the optimal solution based on the specified optimization criteria, expressed by assigning weights in $\mathbf{c}$. For example, assume maximum data sharing is the optimization objective. It can be specified in the objective function as a sum of all decision variables representing interdomain user-to-role accesses, *i.e.*, all $\mathbf{c}_i$s corresponding to the cross-domain user-role variables are assigned a value of "1" and the remaining $\mathbf{c}_i$s are set to "0."

Note that in Shafiq et al.'s (2005) approach, a trade-off exists between maximum interoperability and ensuring autonomy of individual domains. In other words, we need to remove some legal accesses in the local policy to ensure maximum interoperability. Otherwise, some conflicts will remain. The underlying reason for such trade-off is still the role assignment violation. Consider the interoperation example in Fig. 8, there is a role assignment violation between r_1 and r_2 since r_2 can now access r_1 through the interoperation. To remove this conflict, we need to remove at least one edge in $\{a, b, c, d\}$. Note that edges a and c ensure the autonomy, whereas edges b and d ensures maximum interoperation. Therefore, ensuring both autonomy and maximum interoperation at the same time is not feasible in this example.

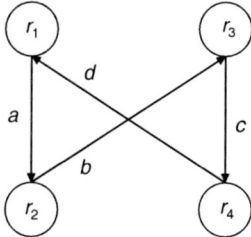

Fig. 8.   Tradeoff between maximum interoperation and autonomy.

3.4 Decentralized role-based secure interoperation

Piromruen and Joshi (2005) proposed a role-based *decentralized* approach for secure interoperation where no global policy exists for all the domains. In their approach, the policy mapping is dynamically driven by the access requirements between every pair of interacting domains. Their approach also assumes that each domain employs **RBAC** model with hybrid hierarchy, which is illustrated in Fig. 9.

As shown in Fig. 9, assume that domain d_1 interoperates with domain d_2. It first sends its access requests (a set of permissions) to d_2 (d_2 can also send its access requests to d_1 in the same way). Once the requirements have been received, d_2 attempts to fulfill the requests by identifying and creating a role set (say R_2) that collectively have the requested permissions. The external role set (say R_1) from d_1, which are the roles through which d_1 allows its users to access authorized permissions in d_2, are mapped to exported roles (R_2) from d_2 through *A*-hierarchy relations—this semantically means, the external entity has to activate the specified exported roles in the other domain. At this time, d_1 can establish activation conditions to restrict these mappings, for instance, to capture context-based cross-domain accesses.

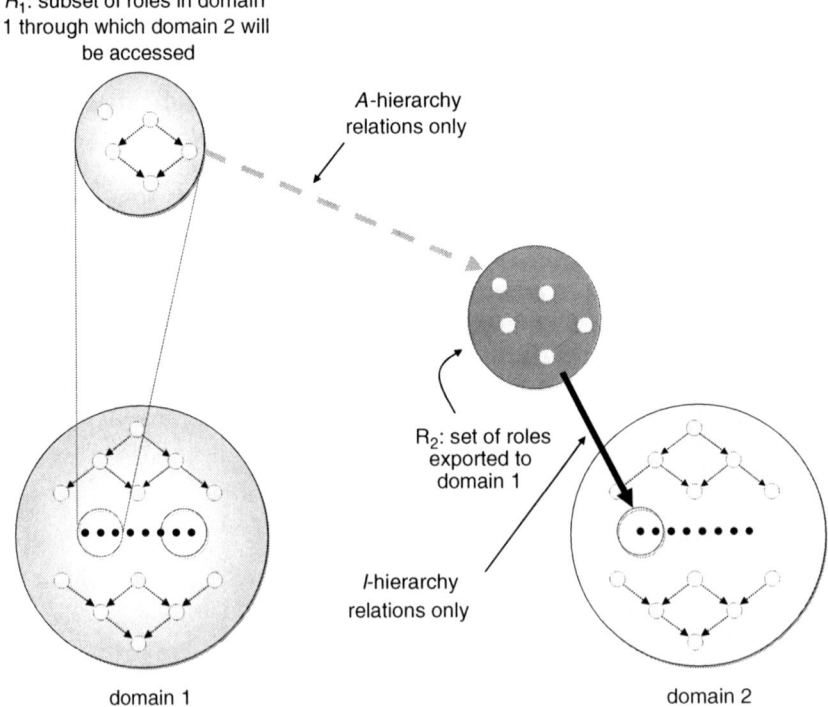

Fig. 9.   Framework of Piromruen & Joshi's (2005) approach.

The exported roles in R_2 are themselves made I-seniors of local roles of d_2 that provide the requested permissions to ensure that the external entities do not activate other local roles.

The use of the A and I hierarchy relations, as described above, prevents the transitivity of the activation semantics that is usually the underlying problem in interdomain accesses (Gong and Qian, 1996). Figure 10 shows how the A-hierarchy followed by the I-hierarchy can be used to prevent the transitivity of activation semantics problem. Here, assume that users of r_1 in d_1 need to access permissions of r_2 in d_2, and $r_3 \geqslant_i r_1$ and $r_2 \geqslant_a r_4$ according to each local policy. According to the policy-mapping approach shown in Fig. 9, r_2' is an exported role. There are four ways to connect r_1, r_2', and r_2 using the three hierarchical relations—note that IA-hierarchy includes both I-hierarchy and A-hierarchy. In Fig. 10(a), $r_1 \geqslant_a r_2' \geqslant_a r_2$. Now, users of r_1 can activate r_4 and acquire the permissions of r_4. The principle of *security* is violated in this case. In Fig. 10(b), $r_1 \geqslant_i r_2' \geqslant_a r_2$, users of r_1 cannot acquire permissions of r_2. Hence, the interoperation is not supported. In Fig. 10(c), $r_1 \geqslant_i r_2' \geqslant_i r_2$, users of r_3 can acquire permissions of r_2. Again, the principle of *security* is violated. In Fig. 10(c), $r_1 \geqslant_a r_2' \geqslant_i r_2$, this indicates that users of r_1 can acquire permissions of r_2 by activating r_2'. Moreover, no security breach occurs here, since users of r_3 cannot acquire permissions of r_2 and users of r_1 cannot acquire permissions of r_4.

The key step in this approach is called "role mapping." Role mapping involves finding a role set R_{RQ} that exactly contains a requested permission set P_{RQ}. Formally,

- $P_{au}(r) = \{p \in P:\ p\ is\ assigned\ to\ r_1,\ r \geqslant_i r_1\}$
- $P_{au}(R_1) = \bigcup_{r \in R_1} P_{au}(r)$
- *Given R_{RQ}, find P_{RQ} such that $P_{RQ} = P_{au}(R_{RQ})$*

In Fig. 9, on receiving the requested permission set P_{RQ1} from domain d_1, domain d_2 finds $R_{RQ2} \subseteq R_2$ (the role set in domain d_2) such that

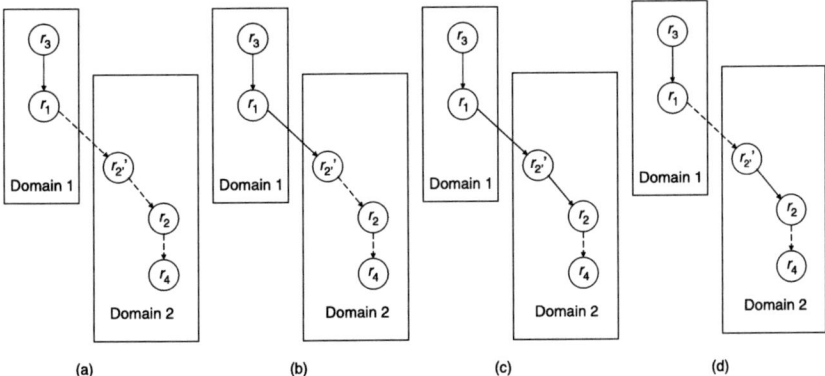

Fig. 10. Transitivity of activation problem.

$P_{au}(R_{RQ2}) = P_{RQ1}$ and exports R_{RQ2}' for d_1 to use. All roles in R_{RQ2}' is made *I*-senior of corresponding roles in R_{RQ2}. The situation where d_2 requests permissions from d_1 is handled similarly. Note that, given P_{RQ}, R_{RQ} does not always exist, and hence the local policy needs to be changed to find such an R_{RQ} in such a way that the authorization semantics for the local policy is not affected.

In the local policy shown in Fig. 11, if $P_{RQ} = \{p_a, p_b\}$ then $R_{RQ} = \{r\}$. However, if $P_{RQ} = \{p_a\}$, we cannot find R_{RQ} since $P_{au}(r)! = \{p_a\}$. The local policy needs to be changed accordingly. As shown in Fig. 11(a), role r can be split into r_a and r_b, with p_a assigned to r_a and p_b assigned to r_b; now, we have $R_{RQ} = \{r_a\}$. In Fig. 11(b), the new role r_a is added as *I*-junior of r p_a assign to it. Now, $R_{RQ} = \{r_a\}$. Although both of these two changes work, we note that splitting roles can cause other problems in the local policy. For example, if r is in the role hierarchy and there are several senior and junior roles of r, an issue would be how to connect r_a and r_b without changing original permission acquisition semantics. Piromruen and Joshi (2005) adopts the second approach (Fig. 11(b)) in their framework and propose a *FindRoleSet* algorithm to implement such a role-mapping process. The algorithm traverses the role hierarchy using *breadth first search* (BFS). For each role r, if all the permissions available to r (i.e., $P_{au}(r)$) are in the P_{RQ}, then r is selected; if $P_{au}(r)$ overlaps with P_{RQ}, the algorithm partitions roles as illustrated in Fig. 11(b) to reconstruct the role hierarchy and then the newly created *I*-junior role of r is selected; otherwise, r is not selected. The *FindRoleSet* algorithm is essentially a greedy algorithm and tries to partition as few roles as possible to satisfy P_{RQ}. Note that the algorithm is carefully designed to maintain the original authorization semantics in the role hierarchy. An alternative role-mapping algorithm is proposed by Du and Joshi (2006). They assume that one can always find a role set R_{RQ} that exactly matched the requested permission set P_{RQ} (maybe after role splitting), so they focus on finding the minimum R_{RQ}. They prove that such

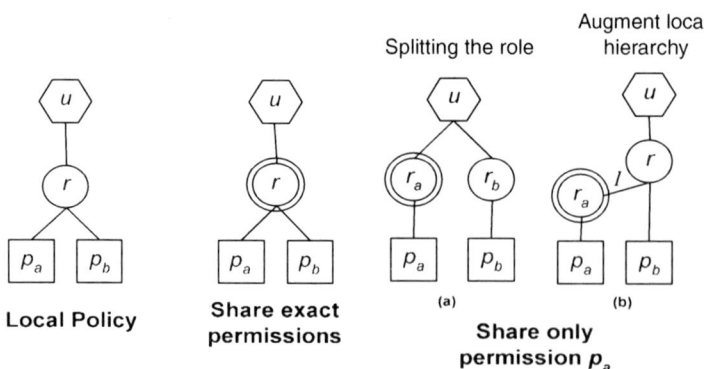

Fig. 11.   Role mapping example.

problem is NP-complete and propose a Greedy-Search algorithm to find a suboptimal solution (Du and Joshi, 2006).

3.5 A role-based request-driven secure interoperation framework

The decentralized role-based approach described earlier assumes that a domain can receive all the requested services from another domain. However, in a loosely coupled environment, such simple assumption may not be realistic. For example, how does the individual domain know which domain contains the desired service? And what if several domains need to collaborate to provide the full service required by a requesting domain? Zhang and Joshi (2007) proposed a request-driven secure interoperation framework in loosely coupled environments to address these issues.

Figure 12 illustrates the architecture proposed by Zhang and Joshi (2007). Here, d_{RQ} represents the service-requesting domain that initiates the service request, and d_S represents the service-providing domain that d_{RQ} requests the services from. In a loosely coupled environment, d_S itself may not be able to satisfy all the services requested by d_{RQ}. In such a case d_S may initiate collaboration with other assistant domains to provide services to d_{RQ}. In this framework, if d_S cannot provide all the services requested, it aggregates the services securely from assistant domains and make it available to d_{RQ}. d_{RQ} does not need to be aware of the existence of other assistant domains. The dashed arrow in Fig. 12 indicates that it is not necessary to include other assistant domains if d_S can provide all the services itself.

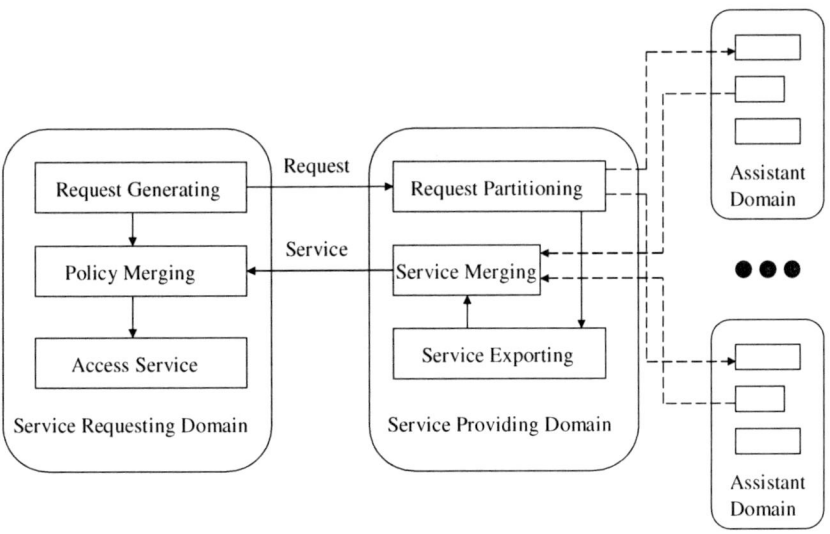

Fig. 12. The architecture of Zhang and Joshi's (2007) framework.

The service-requesting domain d_{RQ} uses three modules. The *request generating* module is responsible for generating the service request and sending it to the service-providing domain. The *policy merging* module is responsible for merging the initial service request in d_{RQ} and the service provided by d_S to form an integrated interoperation policy. The framework allows use of any existing RBAC-based policy-merging approaches in the literature. For example, Shafiq et al.'s (2005) approach can be used here to facilitate such policy mapping. Once the merged RBAC policy is built, d_{RQ} can simply access the services mediated through the *access service* module.

The service-providing domain d_S also uses three modules. The *request partitioning* module is responsible for checking whether d_S can provide all the services requested by d_{RQ}. If so, the *request partitioning* module simply forwards the service request to the *role mapping* module; if not, besides forwarding the part of the request that d_S can satisfy to the *role mapping* module, the *request partitioning* module also exports the part of requests that cannot be satisfied by d_S and forwards them to other assistant domains to see whether they can satisfy such requests. The *service exporting* module is responsible for finding the roles in d_S that can satisfy the service requests, exporting the service policy, and sending the service to the *service merging* module. The *service merging* module simply merges the services provided by the *service exporting* module and by other assistant domains (if necessary) and sends them back to the d_{RQ}.

Since the *policy merging* module exists in the d_{RQ}, and d_S provides services only based on the permission set P_{RQ} in RQ, d_{RQ} only needs to send P_{RQ} to the d_S as the service request. Note that in a loosely coupled environment, it is typical that each domain serves as both service-requesting domain in some scenario and service-providing domain in another scenario. Therefore, each domain will essentially have all the six modules as shown in Fig. 12. For convenience, we have shown only the necessary modules in each domain in Fig. 12.

Figure 13 shows the scenario where d_S needs to integrate some other assistant domains to provide d_{RQ}'s request. When d_S sends the request that

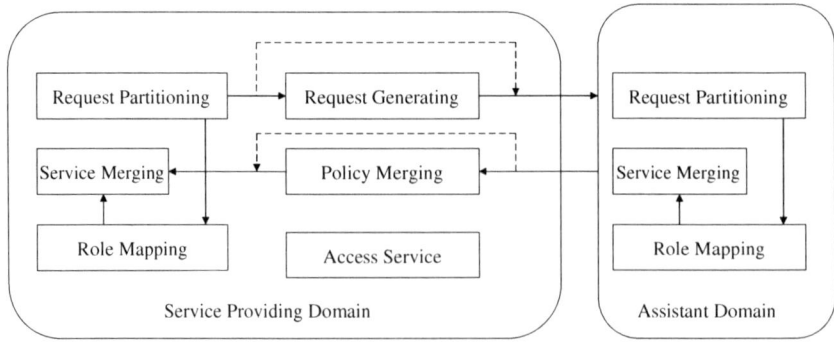

Fig. 13.   Collaboration scenario.

cannot be provided by itself to other assistant domains, d_S serves as a service-requesting domain. In such a case, d_S is essentially a "relay point" between d_{RQ} and other assistant domains. The working mechanisms of *request generation, policy merging,* and the *access service* modules of d_S are different from those modules in d_{RQ}, as shown by the dashed arrows in Fig. 13. The *request generation* module in d_S simply forwards the request it cannot satisfy, as returned by its *request partitioning* module, to the *request partitioning* module of other assistant domain(s). Similarly, the *policy merging* module in d_S simply forwards the services provided by other assistant domains to its *service merging* module. The *access service module* in d_S does nothing in this case.

Using this framework, d_{RQ} does not have to know which domains it should interoperate with. d_{RQ} can simply send the request to its neighborhood (say, d_S), and if d_S cannot provide the requested service, or can only provide part of the service it will automatically forward the service request to other domains, as shown in Fig. 13. Note that d_{RQ} is not aware of such kind of collaboration at all.

4 Integrating trust and access control for secure interoperation

In a loosely coupled environment, the secure interoperation needs to be achieved between transient partners both of which may provide and receive services from each other. As these partners may be formed in an *ad hoc* way, dynamically, it is important that they are able to trust each other. The level of trust that they can have on each other may define how much sharing each may be interested in. Although integration of the access policies is important, it is intricately interleaved with the process through which trust is established. If the desired level of trust is not established during negotiation, the level of sharing may need to be renegotiated; at the same time, the level of trust needed may govern the trust negotiation process. Hence, to address the overall secure interoperation problem in emerging systems that are primarily loosely coupled in nature, trust negotiation/management and access control policy integration issues should be addressed together. In this section, we overview efforts toward integrated approach to trust and access control issues that are applicable to distributed, loosely coupled multidomain environments.

4.1 *TrustBAC: integrating trust level with RBAC model*

Chakraborty and Ray (2006) proposed a TrustBAC model that integrates trust management with the RBAC model. Their model can be used in multidomain environments.

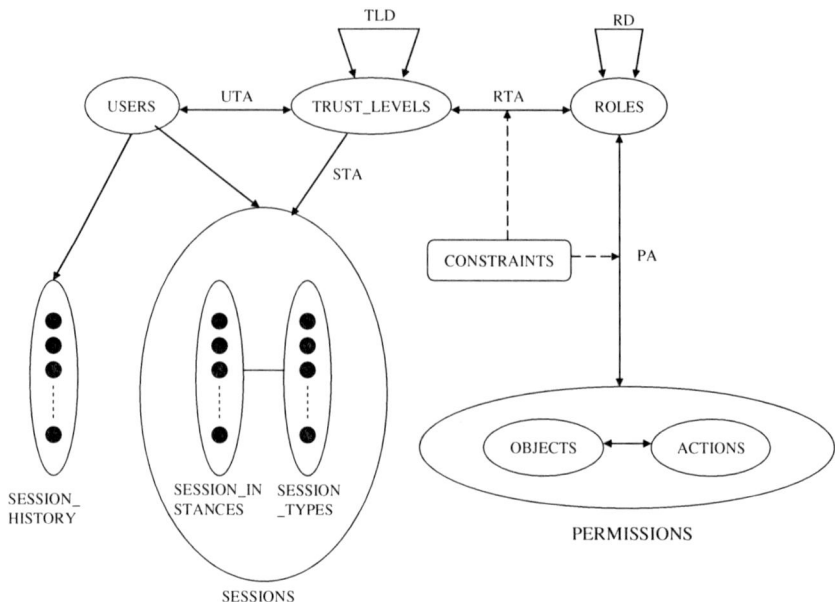

Fig. 14.   TrustBAC model.

Figure 14 shows the TrustBAC model including its elements and various relationships between those elements. The USERS, ROLES, PERMISSIONS, and CONSTRAINTS are the same as those in RBAC. A role domination (RD) relationship is used to represent the role hierarchy. Unlike the RBAC model, which associates users with roles, TrustBAC associates users to a trust level, and trust levels to different roles. Intuitively, the trust level is the measurement of how the system trusts the particular user, based on his/her history and disclosed credentials. TrustBAC uses *session type* and *session instance* to represent a session. The *session type* defines which properties/credentials a user needs to have to create a *session instance* of this *type*. The *session instance* serves as the context to compute the *trust level*, since the *trust level* between the system and a particular user could be different in different context. The session history of a user is an important factor when calculating the associated *trust level*.

The most important issue in TrustBAC is how to calculate the trust level given a user (*trustee*), a system (*truster*), and a context (session type, user history, etc.). Assume that B is the *trustee*, A is the *truster*, and c is the context. TrustBAC uses the following three components to model the trust level: *experience component* ($_AE_B{}^c$), *knowledge component* ($_AK_B{}^c$), and *recommendation component* ($_\psi R_B{}^c$). Each of these measure is a real number between $[-1, 1]$ or $\perp$ (not applicable). The computation of the experience component is done as follows:

$$_AE_B^c = \sum_{i=1}^{n} w_i I_i, \text{ where } I_j = \frac{\sum_{k=1}^{n_j} v_k^j}{\sum_{k=1}^{n_j} |v_k^j|}$$

Given time interval, it is first divided into n nonoverlapping time intervals. Let I_j denote the incidents in the jth time interval. In each time interval, e_k^j denotes the kth event in jth time interval and v_k^j is the trust value gained from e_k^j. Specifically, $v_k^j \in [-10, 0]$ if e_k^j contributes to a negative trust value, $v_k^j \in (0, +10]$ if e_k^j contributes to a positive trust value, and $v_k^j = 0$ if e_k^j has no effect on trust value. Therefore, I_j is essentially the normalized sum of all the trust values associated with each event in jth time interval, and the overall value of $_AE_B^c$ is the weighted sum of I_j of all time intervals.

The value of knowledge component is given by

$$_AK_B^c = w_d \cdot d + w_r \cdot r$$

Here d denotes the direct knowledge that A has about B, whereas r denotes the indirect knowledge that A has about B. A is allowed to assign different weights, w_d and w_r, for these two factors, such that $w_d + w_r = 1$. In practice, d could be calculated from the user session history and r is similar to the "*reputation*" of the user.

The recommendation component is given by

$$_\varphi R_B^c = \frac{\sum_{j=1}^{n} \left(v\left(A \xrightarrow{\text{rec}} j \right)_t^N \right) \cdot V_j}{\sum_{j=1}^{n} \left(v\left(A \xrightarrow{\text{rec}} j \right)_t^N \right)}$$

where ψ is a group of n recommenders, $v(A \xrightarrow{\text{rec}} j)_t^N$ the trust value of jth recommender, and V_j the jth recommender's recommendation value about the trustee B.

Given the fact that different *trusters* may give different trust values for the same trustee under the same context, TrustBAC uses trust vector to define the overall trust value of a *trustee*, given by

$$\left(A \xrightarrow{c} B \right)_t^N = \left[W_E \cdot {}_AE_B^c, W_K \cdot {}_AK_B^c, W_R \cdot {}_\varphi R_B^c \right] = \left[{}_A\hat{E}_B^c, {}_A\hat{K}_B^c, {}_\varphi\hat{R}_B^c \right]$$

The *trustee*'s trust level, is defined by

$$v\left(A \xrightarrow{c} B \right)_t^N = {}_A\hat{E}_B^c + {}_A\hat{K}_B^c + {}_\varphi\hat{R}_B^c$$

If this value is below 0, then the trustee is deemed as distrusted; and if this value is above 0, then the trustee is deemed as trusted. Moreover, the user will be assigned to different roles based on its trust value, and hence can acquire the corresponding permissions of the roles.

4.2   Traust: a trust negotiation-based authorization framework in multidomain environments

Lee et al. (2006) have proposed trust negotiation-based authorization framework for multidomain environments. Their focus is not on the specific trust computation model. Rather, they focus on building a framework that integrates the existing access control model, service exchange protocol, trust computation model, and applications.

The architecture of the Traust framework is shown in Fig. 15. The Traust server acts as a broker for the access rights to a set of resources in its domain. A Traust server contains a protocol interpreter to interact with the Trust Negotiation Agent (TN Agent). It also maintains a repository of access tokens used to grant access to the resources. The Traust client is a process designed to acquire access tokens for resources of interest to its owner. Traust client also contains a protocol interpreter to interact with the TN Agent. A Traust client can be accessed directly by a user or by a Traust-aware application. The TN Agent is responsible for understanding the protocol used for trust negotiation (e.g., the approaches by Blaze et al., 1998a,b) and carrying out trust negotiation sessions. In addition, a TN Agent manages its owner's attribute certificates and their corresponding release policies. Each Traust server maintains a repository of access tokens that can be used to access the services that it protects. The tokens could be either static or generated during run time. Finally, resources are the logical and physical objects that Traust servers broker the access rights to.

The service exchange/trust establishment protocol is shown in Fig. 16. The TN Agent of the Traust Client first requires the information from the corresponding TN Agent of the Traust Server to find out whether the server contains the services of interest. The server then sends the requested information to the client. Once the client finds out that the server can provide the service, it will initiate trust negotiation with the server. This trust negotiation process invoked by the client (labeled as A in Fig. 16) is to determine whether the client can trust the server to send its credentials. After this step, the client sends the specific resource request to the server and the server responds by specifying a set of tokens required to access the recourses. The trust negotiation process invoked by the server (labeled as C in Fig. 16) determines whether the client has disclosed enough credentials to access the corresponding service. Finally, if the negotiation succeeds, the server responds to the client with the requested service.

4.3   An integrated trust and access control framework

One of the main motivations to ensure secure interoperation in multidomain environments is to facilitate the service exchange. Therefore, the trust negotiation should be integrated with service exchange properly.

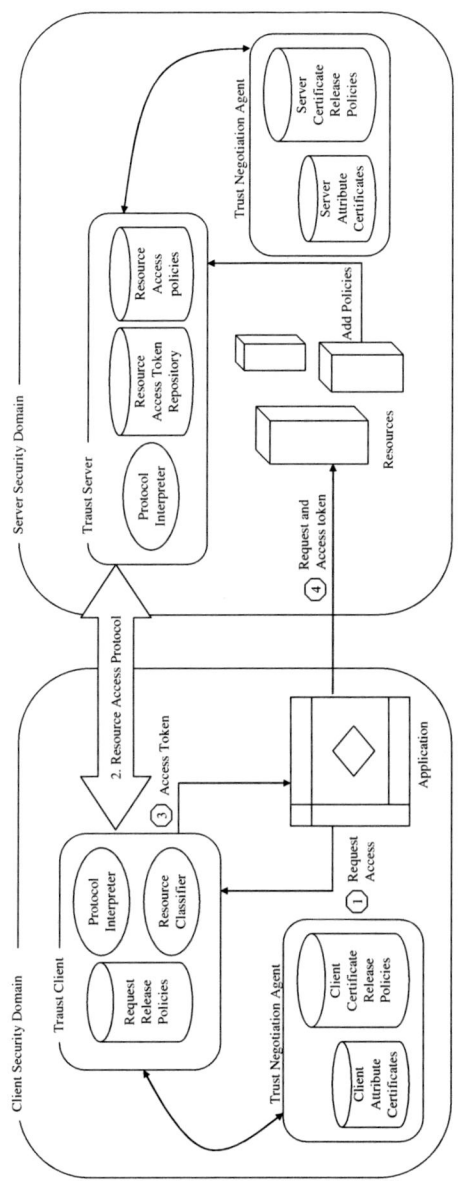

Fig. 15.   Traust system architecture.

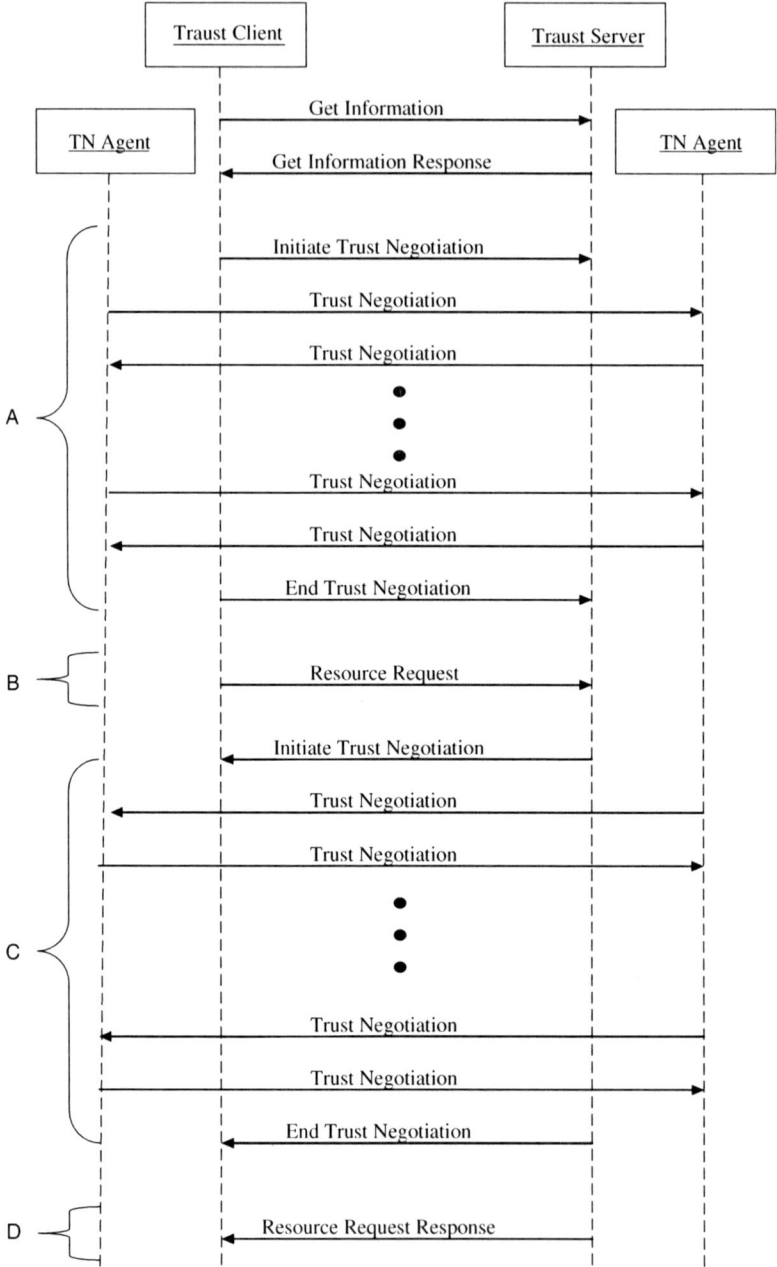

Fig. 16.　Traust negotiation protocol.

For example, if the service-providing domain does not trust the service-requesting domain, it may choose to deny the access request. Even if the service-providing domain permits the service-requesting domain to access some of its data, to what extent the data should be shared also depends on the trust level established between the two domains. Such trust negotiation framework has been proposed by Chandran et al. (2006). Figure 17 shows their trust-based secure interoperation framework. It is composed of two principle modules: the *requirements-based trust establishment* (TE) module and the *trust sustenance and evolution* (TSE) module.

TE contains two modules: *service/context negotiation* and *trust negotiation*. The service requested from one domain may not be fully provided by the other domain depending on the different context. Therefore, the service/context negotiation module is responsible for establishing an acceptable level of service/context provided to the external domain. For each kind of service, the service-providing domain associates a *trust token type* to it. The service-requesting domain needs to disclose the *trust token*s based on the trust token type to access the service. However, sometimes the service-requesting domain may not be able to provide all the required information in the trust token type. The *trust negotiation* module is responsible to establish a trust level that is acceptable for both of the interacting domains.

The TSE is responsible to maintain or change trust levels when domain characteristics change during the period of interoperation. There are four

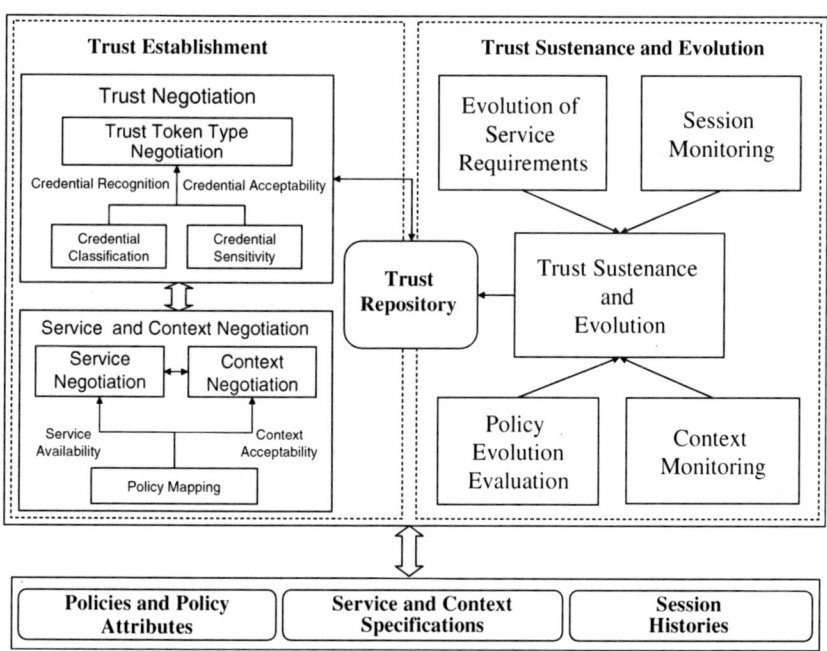

Fig. 17. The requirement-driven trust framework.

situations that the trust level needs to be reconsidered (either maintain or change the trust level): (1) there is a new service requirement or some services may no longer be required; (2) the service exchanging context changes; (3) the underlying policy changes, for example the trust-token type of the service changes; and (4) the anomalous and malicious behavior are detected.

The key part of the framework is the service and trust negotiation. During negotiation, various cost factors need to be considered to establish a trust level that is acceptable for both domains d_x and d_y, as shown in Table 2. Intuitively, the cost incurred to a domain during interoperation should be less than the benefits and incentives it gets. Therefore, given those cost factors, the convergence point of the service negotiation is defined as $c \leq b + i$ for both d_x and d_y.

Before negotiation, the interoperating domains also compute $\mathrm{tr}_{S,C}^{d_y \to d_x}$, which denotes the trust d_x has on d_y for services defined by S in context C. This is a value that is used to compute the payoff of a negotiation strategy, which is given by Table 2. From Table 1, we can see that the trust level that d_y has on d_x is the weighted sum of the recommended trust $\mathrm{rtr}_{S,C}^{d_y \to d_x}$ and direct trust $\mathrm{dtr}_{S,C}^{d_y \to d_x}$. The direct trust variables are *historical satisfaction level* (h) and *risk* (rk). Here, h indicates the cumulative level of satisfaction that a domain has had for another domain on their previous interactions and is computed based on session histories and older h values. Variable rk captures risks associated with the desired interoperation. An example is the risk of too many claimed trust tokens being invalid. Another risk is that of

Table 2
Trust level computation

$$\mathrm{tr}_{S,C}^{d_y \to d_x} =$$ $$(\alpha \times \mathrm{dtr}_{S,C}^{d_y \to d_x}) + (\beta \times \mathrm{rtr}_{S,C}^{d_y \to d_x})$$	• $\alpha, \beta, \gamma, \delta, \psi, \lambda,$ and ε are weights • α is typically greater than β, as direct trust is usually more influential than recommended trust • Very often α is a result of a time-decay function that represents the degradation in the trust for a domain, due to the lack of interaction
$$\mathrm{dtr}_{S,C}^{d_y \to d_x} =$$ $$(\gamma \times h_{S,C}^{d_y \to d_x}) - (\delta \times \mathrm{rk}_{S,C}^{d_y \to d_x})$$	• $h_{S,C}^{d_y \to d_x}$ is the historical satisfaction level that d_y has for d_x • $h_{S,C}^{d_y \to d_x}$ is bound by the previous risk levels as follows: $h_{S,C}^{d_y \to d_x} = \eta \times \mathrm{rk}_{S,C}^{d_y \to d_x}$, where $0 \leq \eta \leq 1$
$$\mathrm{rtr}_{S,C}^{d_y \to d_x} =$$ $$(\psi \times \mathrm{tr}_{R,C}^{d_y \to d_R}) + (\lambda \times r_{S,C}^{d_R \to d_x})$$	• $\mathrm{rk}_{S,C}^{d_y \to d_x}$ is the *risk* • $r_{S,C}^{d_R \to d_x}$ is the recommendation given by d_R for domain d_x

services promised but not provided. The historical satisfaction level is also affected by the result of the verification of trust tokens in the earlier sessions. That is, if a domain presents valid trust tokens, then in inter-operation, during actual cross-domain accesses, the historical satisfaction level will not be negatively affected.

They take a game-theoretic approach of defining payoffs for different strategies to determine the convergence point of the negotiation. On the basis of the choice of trust tokens for disclosure, corresponding domains have gains or losses. The payoff for each domain is the linear sum of the payoffs from services and trust token negotiations, respectively. The trust token negotiation pay off is the difference between the trust level established and the *protection level* required of the trust tokens disclosed, as given below

$$\phi'_{ij}\left(p_i^{d_x}, p_j^{d_y}\right) = \left(\left(\text{tr}_{S,C}^{d_x \to d_y} - \text{ProtLevel}(d_x.T_i)\right), \left(\text{tr}_{S,C}^{d_y \to d_x} - \text{ProtLevel}(d_y.T_j)\right)\right)$$

The service negotiation payoff is the difference between the benefits from usage of services and the losses incurred through service exchange and service provision.

$$\phi''_{ij}\left(p_i^{d_x}, p_j^{d_y}\right) = \left(b_{d_y}^{d_x} - c_{d_y}^{d_x} - i_{d_y}^{d_x}, \ b_{d_x}^{d_y} - c_{d_x}^{d_y} - i_{d_x}^{d_y}\right)$$

Thus, the overall negotiation payoff is given as

$$\phi_{ij}\left(p_i^{d_x}, p_j^{d_y}\right) = \phi'_{ij}\left(p_i^{d_x}, p_j^{d_y}\right) + \phi''_{ij}\left(p_i^{d_x}, p_j^{d_y}\right)$$

The negotiation is essentially modeled as a negotiation tree. The different strategies used by the domains are the disclosure of different trust tokens that satisfy the other domain's requirements but have different protection requirements. It is reasonable to assume that protection requirement of a trust token is directly related to trust level desired. For instance, a passport is a more trustworthy proof of age, but it also contains more sensitive details. Traversal of the tree represents negotiation exchanges between the domains. Each domain computes the payoffs at the leaf nodes and selects a set of *candidate payoffs*. Using a goal-driven approach (goal being any of the candidate payoffs), the domains negotiate the payoffs. Ideally, both domains select the same candidate payoffs, because in game-theory-based negotiation, strategies are selected that optimize payoff for both parties. The candidate payoff values are selected through empirical studies. Consequently, backtracking is also facilitated in the negotiation—if say d_y proposes a set of services and trust tokens that would lead to poor payoff for say d_x, then d_x will reject the proposal and d_y will have to go back and try another proposal.

5 Discussion and open research problems

We have overviewed several ongoing efforts related to the problem of secure interoperation in current and emerging multidomain application environments. The major contributions of Gong and Qian's (1996) work is the introduction of principles of *autonomy* and *security* to capture the key requirements of secure interoperation, and the analysis of various complexity issues related to secure interoperation. One key reason for these complexity issues is the need to support negative access rights. Dawson et al.'s (2000) work focuses on the secure interoperation among systems that employ MLS policies. The basic idea of their model is still specifying the cross-domain access rights manually through label matching. A key difficulty with MLS-based systems is the classification schemes that may be quite different in different domains, requiring possibly re-evaluation of the classification levels to facilitate the interoperation. There are several other problems including cascading problem, and the inference problems that are difficult to address. Shafiq et al.'s (2005) role-based approach provides a framework to integrate policies and generate optimal solutions based on required criteria. They also consider SoD constraints that currently make their approach most advanced. The use of role-based approach has been motivated by the fact that a diverse set of policies can be expressed by RBAC models and the notion of roles are typically similar in different domains, thus providing a semantic basis for integration. In their approach, some of the cross-domain access rights are created automatically according to each local policy, and some of the cross-domain access rights are specified manually by the administrators. The resulting global policy supports more fined-grained access control than the one done by the administrators only.

Piromruen and Joshi's (2005) decentralized approach addresses policy integration in loosely coupled environments. This mechanism is significantly different from the centralized approach where all local policies are statically merged into one global policy. However, their approach assumes simple RBAC policies with hybrid hierarchy and does not support domain policies with SoD and other constraints. Furthermore, they assume that the interacting domains fulfill each other's sharing requirements. Zhang and Joshi's (2007) work attempts to provide a more comprehensive decentralized secure interoperation framework to allow requirements of a domain to be fulfilled by aggregation of services from multiple domains, with one domain acting as a provider domain and aggregating the services from assistant domains transparently. Moreover, their proposed framework is generic and supports use of various role-mapping algorithms.

Integration of trust with access control, in particular policy integration, is important for holistically addressing the secure interoperation among entities unknown to each other. Chakraborty and Ray's (2006) TrustBAC integrates trust management with access control model by adding the "trust level" element in the traditional RBAC model. The users are made member of the trust level and each trust level is assigned to some roles. Here, the resources that a user can access depend on how much the system trusts the user. And the trust level associated with the user also depends on his/her access history. However, the main focus of the paper is how to compute the trust level based on user credentials and session histories, similar to the general trust management approaches in the literature. Lee et al.'s (2006) work related to Traust focuses on an integration framework and negotiation protocol for trust management and service exchange, and is policy neutral since any existing trust computation model can be used in their framework. The trust and access control integration framework by Chandran et al. (2006) is similar to Traust in that it also emphasizes the strong need of integrating the trust management and access control models into one framework. They propose a fine-grained trust level computation and negotiation protocol using game-theory-based approach that is integrated with the policy integration process. A key aspect of this work is that it motivates the fact that the trust negotiation and policy integration issues are interrelated and need to be interleaved to facilitate trust-based information sharing among different domains.

Open research problems: Although the various work discussed earlier indicate recent efforts toward access control and trust issues related to the multidomain secure interoperation environments, they are in preliminary stages of development and several research problems remain open and unsolved. In particular, we see the following three are the crucial problems that need to be addressed:

1. *Fine grained access control and practical trust models*: As the afore-mentioned discussion indicates, the solutions that have been proposed are very limited in terms of expressiveness of the access control and the trust models. Most of the access control models considered are specific to MLS or discretionary (Gong and Qian, 1996) policies or a simplified RBAC model. Emerging systems demand more fine-grained, context-based and content-based access control models. Integrating such policy models for emerging applications is a daunting challenge. Piromruen and Joshi's (2005) and Zhang and Parashar's (2003) approaches supported some basic temporal context-based access control policies. Efforts toward integrating trust and access models are very recent and in a very early stages. Work on trust models are still in early stages of development. Issues related to verification and validations of integrated policies have not been well-addressed.

2. *Semantic heterogeneity and evolution management*: Heterogeneity of protection requirements and the very dynamic nature of the individual domains make the issue of multidomain security very complex. Issues related to establishing proper semantic mapping among policy elements to achieve policy integration are yet to be addressed. Approaches discussed earlier typically assume that semantic mapping is already established. Emerging semantic web-related technologies provide possible approaches

to address such semantic heterogeneity issues. Even if the solutions are available to achieve perfect integration of policies, the issue of managing the evolving policies in the individual domains and it effects on the integrated policies presents another level of challenge.

3. *Usability and prototype development*: The complex problem of solving multidomain security problem will likely face severe usability challenge because of its complex nature. Although automation is a goal that will be difficult to achieve and humans will be required to facilitate secure interoperation at some level. The sensitive nature of the access policies themselves present a crucial challenge in the policy integration and trust negotiation processes. Prototype development and testing need to be extensively done to create acceptable practical, viable solutions.

6   Conclusions

In this chapter, we discussed the crucial issues related to the problem of secure interoperation in multidomain application environments. We first discussed the secure interoperation problem and motivated that proper access control and policy integration, as well as trust management mechanisms are needed to facilitate information sharing among multiple domains. We overviewed several existing work that deals with policy integration in multidomain environments and integrated access control and trust management approaches to provide viable secure interoperation solutions. With the growing trend in information sharing that has been facilitated by recent advances in IT, it is clear that the secure interoperation problem will be one of the most critical security issues in the coming years and effective and efficient solutions are becoming critically important, whereas the research work toward it is still in a nascent stage. We finally presented the key challenges that need to be addressed to develop viable solutions for the complex multidomain secure interoperation problem.

Acknowledgments

This work has been supported by the US National Science Foundation award IIS-0545912.

References

Aberer, K., Z. Despotovic (2001). Managing trust in a peer-2-peer information system, in: *Proceedings of the Tenth International Conference on Information and Knowledge Management* (CIKM01), November 5–10, ACM Press, New York, pp. 310–317.

Bell, D.E., L.J. La Padula (1975). Secure computer system: unified exposition and multics interpretation. Technical Report MTIS AD-A023588, MITRE Corporation.

Blaze, M., J. Feigenbaum, A.D. Keromytis (1998a). KeyNote: trust management for public-key infrastructures, in: *Security Protocols International Workshop*. Cambridge, England.

Blaze, M., J. Feigenbaum, M. Strauss (1998b). Compliance checking in the policymaker trust management system, in: *Financial Cryptography: Second International Conference*. Springer-Verlag, Anguilla, British West Indies.

Bonatti, P., S.D.C. Vimercati, P. Samarati (2002). An algebra for composing access control policies. *ACM Transactions on Information and System Security* 5(1).

Bonatti, P.A., M.L. Sapino, V.S. Subrahmanian (1996). Merging heterogeneous security orderings. in: *Proceedings European Symposium Research in Computer Security (ESORICS)*, pp. 183–197.

Chakraborty, S., I. Ray (2006). TrustBAC: integrating trust relationships into the RBAC model for access control in open systems, in: *Proceedings of the Eleventh ACM Symposium on Access Control Models and Technologies* (Lake Tahoe, CA, USA, June 7–9, 2006), SACMAT '06. ACM, New York, NY, pp. 49–58.

Chandran, S.M., K. Panyim, J.B.D. Joshi. (2006). A requirements-driven trust framework for secure interoperation in open environments, in: *The Fourth International Conference on Trust Management, (iTrust-06), May 16–19*, Pisa, Tuscany, Italy.

Chuang, M., S. Phoomvuthisarn, J.B.D. Joshi (2006). An integrated framework for trust-based access control for open systems. CollaborateCom, GA, USA.

Cornwall, L.A., J. Jensen, D.P. Kelsey, A. Frohner, D. Kouril, F. Bonnassieux, S. Nicoud, et al. (2005). Authentication and authorization mechanisms for multi-domain grid environments. *Journal of Grid Computing* 2(4), 301–311. Springer Science and Business Media B.V, ISSN:1570-7873.

Damiani, E., D. di Vimercati, S. Paraboschi, P. Samarati, F. Violante (2002). A reputation-based approach for choosing reliable resources in peer-to-peer networks, in: V. Atluri (ed.), *Proceedings of the 9th ACM Conference on Computer and Communications Security* (Washington, DC, USA, November 18–22, 2002), CCS '02. ACM, New York, NY, pp. 207–216.

Dawson, S., S. Qian, P. Samarati (2000). Providing security and interoperation of heterogeneous systems. *Distributed and Parallel Databases* 8, 119–145.

Du, S., J.B.D. Joshi (2006). *Supporting authorization query and inter-domain role mapping in presence of hybrid role hierarchy*. The 11th ACM Symposium on Access Control Models and Technologies, June 7–9, Lake Tahoe, CA, USA.

Ferraiolo, D., R. Sandhu, S. Gavrila, D. Kuhn, R. Chandramouli (2001). Proposed NIST standard for role-based access control. *ACM Transactions on Information and Systems Security* 4(3), 224–274.

Foster, I., C. Kesselman, S. Tuecke (2001). The anatomy of the grid: enabling scalable virtual organizations. *International Journal of High Performance Computing Applications* 15(August 3), 200–222.

Gong, L., X. Qian (1996). Computational issues in secure interoperation. *IEEE Transaction Software Engineering* 22(1), 43–52.

Jajodia, S., P. Samarati, M.L. Sapino, V.S. Subrahmanian (2001). Flexible support for multiple access control policies. *ACM Transaction on Database Systems* 26(2), 214–260.

Joshi, J.B.D., E. Bertino, A. Ghafoor, Y. Zhang (2008). Formal foundations for hybrid hierarchies in GTRBAC. *ACM Transactions on Information and System Secutity (TISSEC)* 10(4), 1–39.

Lee, A.J., M. Winslett, J. Basney, V. Welch (2006). Traust: a trust negotiation-based authorization service for open systems, in: *SACMAT '06: Proceedings of the Eleventh ACM Symposium on Access Control Models and Technologies*. ACM Press, New York, NY, USA.

Li, N., J.C. Mitchell, W.H. Winsborough (2002). Design of a role-based trust-management framework, in: *Proceedings of the 2002 IEEE Symposium on Security and Privacy* (May 12–15, 2002), SP. IEEE Computer Society, Washington, DC, 114pp.

Piromruen, S., J.B.D. Joshi (2005). An RBAC framework for time constrained secure interoperation in multi-domain environment. Tenth IEEE International Workshop on Object-oriented Real-time Dependable Systems (WORDS 2005), February 2–4, Sedona, Arizona, USA.

Ramakrishnan, L., H. Rehn, J. Alameda, R. Ananthakrishnan, M. Govindaraju, A. Slominski, K. Connelly, V. Welch, D. Gannon, R. Bramley, S. Hampton (2002). An authorization framework for a grid based component architecture, in: M. Parashar (ed.), *Proceedings of the Third international Workshop on Grid Computing*. Lecture Notes in Computer Science, Vol. 2536, Springer-Verlag, London, pp. 169–180.

Sandhu, R., E.J. Coyne, H.L. Feinstein, C.E. Youman (1996). Role-based access control models. *IEEE Computer* 29(2), 38–47. IEEE Press.

Shafiq, B., J.B.D. Joshi, E. Bertino, A. Ghafoor (2005). Secure interoperation in a multi-domain environment employing RBAC policies. *IEEE Transactions on Knowledge & Data Engineering* 17(11), 1557–1577.

Shehab, M., E. Bertino, A. Ghafoor (2005). SERAT: SEcure role mApping technique for decentralized secure interoperability, in: *Proceedings of the Tenth ACM Symposium on Access Control Models and Technologies* (Stockholm, Sweden, June 1–3, 2005), SACMAT '05. ACM, New York, NY, pp. 159–167.

Winsborough, W., K. Seamons, V. Jones (2000). Automated trust negotiation, in: *DARPA Information Survivability Conference and Exposition (DISCEX '2000)*, *January 25–27*, Hilton Head, South Carolina, USA.

Zhang, G., M. Parashar (2003). Dynamic context-aware access control for grid applications, in: *Proceedings of the Fourth international Workshop on Grid Computing* (November 17–17, 2003), GRID. IEEE Computer Society, Washington, DC, 101pp.

Zhang, Y., J.B.D. Joshi (2007). *A request-driven secure interoperation framework in loosely-coupled multi-domain environment employing RBAC policies*. TrustCol' 2007, White Plains, New York.

Rao & Upadhyaya, Eds., *Handbooks in Information Systems, Vol. 4*
Copyright © 2009 by Emerald Group Publishing Limited

Chapter 16

Privacy, Access Control, and Location in Mobile Applications

Yi Zheng, Michelle Watson, Stephanie Chow, Amanda Paul, Ryan Bishop, Ranny Huang and Patrick C.K. Hung

Faculty of Business and Information Technology, University of Ontario Institute of Technology (UOIT), 2000 Simcoe Street North, Oshawa, Ontario, Canada, L1H 7K4

Jordanne Christie

Innovation Centre, University of Ontario Institute of Technology (UOIT), Canada

Abstract

Privacy is one area of security referring to a state or condition of limited access to a person. In particular, information privacy relates to an individual's right to determine how, when, and to what extent information about the self will be released to another person or an organization. Privacy can often be guaranteed through security measures. The protection of information security and privacy against unauthorized access is a key issue in any information systems including mobile computing. Additionally, access control is the process of limiting access to the resources of a system only to authorized users, programs, processes, or other systems. Access control is synonymous with controlled access and limited access. Although access control technologies can be directly applied to protecting personal data, privacy issues such as purpose, obligation, recipient, retention, and location also have to be addressed. Privacy access control is usually not concerned with individual subjects. A subject releases his or her data to the custody of an organization while consenting to the set of purposes for which the data may be used. The traditional view of the access control model should be expanded to include an organization-wide privacy policy for managing and enforcing individual privacy preferences. On the contrary, misuse of information, such as the location of an individual, is a major contributing factor for privacy violations in mobile applications. To meet the security and privacy requirements of mobile applications, it is necessary to extend the existing access control model with location constraints. Location-related control requires accurate location information. This chapter will discuss a privacy access control model with location information for supporting mobile applications with an illustrative mobile healthcare application.

---

1 Introduction

Privacy is a state or condition of limited access to a person (Schoeman, 1986). In particular, information privacy relates to an individual's right to determine how, when, and to what extent information about the self will be released to another person or to an organization (Leino-Kilpi et al., 2001). In general, privacy policies describe an organization's data practices, what information is collected from individuals (subjects), what the information (objects) will be used for, whether the organization provides access to the information, who the recipients are of any result generated from the information, how long the information will be retained, and who will be informed in the event of a dispute. One can imagine that information privacy is usually concerned with the confidentiality of Personal Identifiable Information (PII) such as electronic medical records (EMR). Although access control technologies can be directly applied to protecting personal data, privacy issues such as purpose, obligation, recipient, and retention also have to be addressed. Threats to information privacy can come from insiders and from the outsiders in each organization (Fischer-Hubner, 2001). Privacy control is usually not concerned with individual subjects. A subject releases his or her data to the custody of an enterprise while consenting to the set of purposes for which the data may be used. The traditional view of the access control model should be expanded to include an enterprise-wide privacy policy for managing and enforcing individual privacy preferences (Powers et al., 2002).

Access control is the process of limiting access to the resources of a system only to authorized users, programs, processes, or other systems. Access control is synonymous with controlled access and limited access. In general, access control is defined as the mechanism by which users are permitted access to resources according to their identities, authentication, and associated privileges authorization (CSIS, 2003). Protecting information against unauthorized access is a key issue in any information systems including mobile computing. This chapter discusses the research issues of location constraints in a privacy access control model, such as which components in the privacy access control model are related to location and the effect of location in making access control decision. In general, the term "location" denotes the position of an object in physical space with respect to a specific frame of reference (e.g., the position of another point or thing) that varies across applications. There are two major approaches to describe a location. The first approach is to describe a location as an absolute location, meaning the exact location of an object. Absolute location is a spot in the global frame of reference, where a few nodes are already aware of their locations and act as beacons or anchors for the remaining nodes within a specific context. A good example would be the latitude and longitude of a place. For instance, Lake Maracaibo of Venezuela is at 10°39' N latitude and 71°36' W longitude (Savarese et al., 2001). This kind of location information can be directly retrieved by using some location-based services (LBS). Another approach is to describe a location as a relative location, where only relative positioning of nodes with respect to each other is known. A local frame of reference does not require any beacons that reside at a known location. A good example of relative location is if you were to give directions to somebody and you used terms such as "it is across the street from the market," "it is to the left of the gas station," and "it is very close to a certain city" (Ahmed et al., 2005). Besides, civil addresses are commonly used to describe a location. For outdoor locations, a civil address can refer to a specific building; for building-level indoor locations, a civil address can refer to a specific room; for room-level indoor locations, a civil address can refer to a specific part of a room (Wu and Schulzrinne, 2005). Civil addresses are written in formats that are easier for us to comprehend. Location attributes indicate if a place is private, public, protected, unclassified, or if this location is stationary or mobile with certain speed. In this chapter, we describe the location as civil addresses.

Furthermore, with the increase in the growth of wireless networks and mobile devices, we are moving toward an age of ubiquitous computing where location information will be an important component of access control. Denning and MacDoran (1996) and other researchers have advocated that location information can be used to provide additional security (Ray and Yu, 2005). The traditional access control models, such as role-based access control (RBAC), cannot provide such location-based access control (LBAC). These traditional models need to be augmented so that they can provide location-based access (Ray and Yu, 2005). In particular, mobile devices can be more intelligent in terms of user's locations and service needs, with the ability to adapt to the user's changing geographical area, offering LBS (Savvides et al., 2000). In ubiquitous computing, location is one of key contexts that determine which mobile devices are available (Schulzrinne et al., 2003). This chapter presents an extended framework of RBAC with privacy-based extensions and location constraints to tackle such a need. The remainder of this chapter is organized as follows: Section 2 addresses a literature review. Then, Section 3 discusses the privacy access control model with location constraints, and Section 4 concludes the chapter.

2 Literature review

Information security ensures the *confidentiality, integrity, authentication, availability,* and *non-repudiation* of information system (Adaikkalavan, 2006). *Confidentiality* is defined as keeping information private or secrect and preventing unauthorized users from reading sensitive information. *Integrity* prevents information from being modified by unauthorized users. *Authentication* verifies users' identity before accessing any system. *Availability* prevents Denial of Service (DoS) or any unauthorized withholding of information. *Non-repudiation* gives proof of the information's origin. In general, protecting confidential information is required by businesses and by law. This section discusses the background and recent related works of these research areas, which include security and privacy policy, the access control models, LBS, and location or context aware access controls in the research community.

2.1 Security and privacy policy

A *security policy* is a set of rules and practices that specify or regulate how a system or organization provides security services to protected resources. It is a consistent and unambiguous specification that states the required behavior of the system with respect to some specific security properties (Anderson, 1996). In general, a security policy starts with *risk analysis* and ends with a set of *security assertions* for integration into the security architecture of a subject such as a service locator. *Risk analysis* identifies security threats in a business process and forms a set of security assertions, which refer to rules and practices that regulate how sensitive or activity information is managed and protected. A *security assertion* is typically scrutinized in the context of a security policy (Hooda et al., 2004). A security policy is often formalized or semi-formalized in a security model that provides a basis for a formal analysis of security properties.

Privacy is one area of security; it is a state or condition of limited access to a person (Schoeman, 1984). In particular, information privacy relates to an individual's right to determine how, when, and to what extent information about the self will be released to another person or to an organization (Leino-Kilpi et al., 2001). In general, privacy policies describe an organization's data practices, what information is collected from individuals (subjects), what the information (objects) will be used for, whether the organization provides access to the information, who the recipients are of any result generated from the information, how long the information will be retained, and who will be informed in the event of a dispute. On the contrary, *privacy policies* are often expressed in natural language to specify or regulate how a system or an organization is to preserve privacy. To restrict unnecessary or illegitimate access to sensitive information, it is necessary to represent a privacy policy in a formal and technical way similar to an access control mechanism. Privacy rules are therefore used to present system-level specifications when enforcing natural language privacy. Powers et al. (2002) defined terminology to express privacy rules by specifying what requested data accesses are allowed or denied and under what conditions as follows:

```
ALLOW [Data User]
to perform [Operation] on [Data Type]
for [Purpose] provided [Condition].
Carry out [Obligation].
```

One can see that the format of privacy rules (Powers et al., 2002) is the extended concept from general access control rules as follows, which is discussed in Section 2.2:

```
ALLOW [Subject]
to perform [Operation] on [Object]
```

2.2   Access control model

Access control is used to monitor whether a user has proper permission to access a particular object (e.g., EMR) or to perform a particular operation assuming that the user is successfully authenticated. A typical access control model involves querying for membership in a particular user group, possession of a particular clearance, or looking for that user on a resource's approved access control list (Powers et al., 2002). Most access control models are described in terms of subjects, objects, and the operations on objects. A *subject* is a computer system entity that can initiate requests to perform an operation or series of operations on objects; it can be users, processes, or domains. An *object* is a system entity on which an operation can be performed. An *operation* is an active process invoked by a subject. *Permissions* are authorizations to perform some actions on the system. *Access rights* to an object (e.g., EMR) are mainly governed by a set of access control rules (Louwerse, 1998). In the following sections, we discuss three traditional types of access control models.

2.2.1   Mandatory access control

The *mandatory access control* (MAC) assigns objects and subjects to a system security level. The access rule is based on a predefined predicate, which compares the security levels between objects and subjects. When a system security policy controls access to an object and an individual user cannot alter the access, the control is called MAC (Bishop, 2003). Neither the subject nor the owner of the object can determine whether access is granted. An example of MAC is in military security, where an individual data owner does not decide who has *Top Secret* clearance, nor can the owner change the classification of an object from *Top Secret* to *Secret*. Usually, a labeling mechanism and a set of interfaces are used to determine access based on the MAC policy; for example, a user who is running a process at the Secret classification should not be allowed to read a file with the label Top Secret. This is known as the "no read up," not above the subject's clearance level. Conversely, a user who is running a process with a label of *Secret* should not be allowed to write to a file with a label of *Confidential*. This rule is called the "no write down."

2.2.2 Discretionary access control

The *discretionary access control* (DAC) is used to model the security of objects on the basis of a subject's access privileges. Generally, it is used to limit a user's access to a file. Only those users specified by the owner may have a combination of read, write, execute, and other permissions to the file. If an individual user can set an access control mechanism allowing or denying access to an object, the mechanism is called DAC (Bishop, 2003). The DAC policy tends to be flexible and is widely used in commercial and government sectors. DAC leaves a certain amount of access control to the discretion of the object's owner or anyone who is authorized to control the object's access, rather than through a system-wide policy. However, DAC has two main drawbacks. First, granting read access is transitive. Therefore, information can be copied from one object to another and there is no real assurance on the flow of information in a system. Secondly, no restrictions are applied to the usage of information when the user has received information. For example, when Alice grants Bob read access to a file, then Bob can copy the contents of Alice's file to an object that Bob controls. Bob may also grant any other user access to the copy of Alice's file without Alice's knowledge.

2.2.3 Role-based access control

The RBAC model is defined in terms of individual users and permissions being assigned to roles. In RBAC, instead of assigning access permissions to individual users (e.g., Alice and Bob), permissions are assigned to roles. Roles are job functions that have certain access rights on resources such as "Doctor," "Nurse," or "Patient." Access decisions are based on the roles that individual users embody in an organization or system. Users therefore share the same access rights under the same role. Each user can be assigned to one or more roles and each role can be assigned to one or more users. The use of resources is restricted to individuals authorized to assume the associated role. For example, within a hospital system, the role of a doctor can include operations to perform a diagnosis, prescribe medication, and order laboratory tests; the role of researcher can be limited to gathering anonymous clinical information for studies. The use of roles to control access is effective for developing and enforcing domain-specific security policies. It simplifies the administration and management of privileges, allowing old operations to be deleted as organizational functions change and evolve, while removing the necessity to update privileges for each user when roles are updated.

When a user is associated with a role, the user cannot be given additional privileges other than what is necessary to perform the job. Since many of the responsibilities overlap between job categories, maximum privileges for each job category could cause unauthorized access. This concept of *least privilege* requires identifying the user's job functions, determining the minimum set of privileges required to perform those functions, and restricting the user to a domain where his/her privileges apply and nothing more. In less precisely controlled systems, *least privilege* is often difficult or costly to achieve because it is difficult to tailor access based on various attributes or constraints. The RBAC model has been further refined and adopted by the American National Standards Institute (ANSI) and by the International Committee for Information Technology Standards (INCITS) such as ANSI INCITS 359-2004 (NIST, 2005). The National Institute of Standards and Technology (NIST) also stated that the RBAC model has a natural fit with many healthcare applications.

In summary, DAC controls the access from subjects to objects, whereas MAC controls the data flow between subjects and objects. Both models are used primarily in system-oriented resources such as databases and file systems. The RBAC model was found to be the most effective solution for providing security features in a multi-level access control (Joshi et al., 2001). It is considered a promising alternative to the traditional MAC and DAC models in healthcare (Osborn et al., 2000). There are few variations of the RBAC extension proposed to meet the security needs of different sectors. For example, the task-based access control (TBAC) is an example of an extended RBAC model based on a task-based approach. It is used primarily to secure workflow management for addressing the synchronization of authorization flow and workflow. Another example, the temporal role-based access control (TRBAC), is also extended from the RBAC by considering the temporal issues such as time constraints. TRBAC can be used for supporting periodic role enabling and disabling and temporal dependencies such as actions in a session.

2.3 Introduction to location-based services

Personal location information is very useful in many domains to individuals and services. It can provide additional security and privacy protection to sensitive information. Recent widespread deployment of LBS and location technologies such as Global Positioning System (GPS) and infrared sensors can provide a geographical location detection mechanism and the exact location information of a mobile user or requested object. The location can also describe the attributes of a place, such as place type and privacy status, that may correspond to the past, present, or future location of a person, event, or device (Wu and Schulzrinne, 2005). A real location can often be designated using a specific pairing of latitude, longitude, and altitude; a Cartesian coordinate grid (e.g., State Plane Coordinate System); a spherical coordinate system; or an ellipsoid-based system (e.g., World Geodetic System) (Savvides et al., 2000).

2.3.1 The definition of LBS

Mobile phones and the Internet have changed the communication and the lifestyle of people. An increasing number of personal digital assistants (PDAs) and smartphones allow people to access the Internet wherever they are and whenever they want. In healthcare, LBS can help find the nearest hospital or clinic based on the user's current position, time, and special type or aid ambulance and rescue teams to locate and track people who are in a medical emergency. LBS are information services accessible with mobile devices through the mobile network, utilizing the ability to make use of the location of the mobile device (Location Based Services, http://www.geo. unizh.ch/publications/cartouche/lbs_lecturenotes_steinigeretal2006.pdf); or defined by the international OpenGeospatial Consortium (Open Geospatial Consortium (OGC), http://www.opengeospatial.org/): LBS are wireless IP services that use geographic information to serve a mobile use or any application service that exploits the position of a mobile terminal. These definitions describe LBS as an intersection of multiple technologies, namely mobile devices, Internet, a communication network that transfers data and requests back and forth to the service provider, positioning component, service, and application provider that offers services to the users and processes all the requests from the user, data, and content provider that stores and maintains all the data and content like geospatial database. Particularly, the positioning component is responsible for determining a user's position such as the mobile communication network, the GPS, WLAN stations, active badges, or radio beacons.

2.3.2 Location determination

Positioning components use different ways to determine location information. In GPS, to determine a location, a transmission of the location is received. This method usually requires existing infrastructure, which causes additional costs but has limited accuracy (GMS localization, http:// en.wikipedia.org/wiki/GSM_localization). Outdoor location determination, like navigation systems in cars, relies on GPS technology. Another application of LBS is in cell phones. The provider of the radio network can determine the user's location and supply third party services accordingly. These technologies usually obtain the location by a mix of triangulation and distance measure from a set of fixed nodes (e.g., PDAs and smartphones) or mobile nodes with a known position and movement (e.g., GPS).

Based on known characteristics of signal propagation, several measurement technologies are being used to detect location, such as signal-strength-based methods, time-based methods, and directional methods. Signal-strength-based methods make use of signal attenuation with distance to determine proximity. In the work by Garg et al. (2002), the signal strength of the client was used, observed by the access point it connects to, to indicate the distance between the access point and the client. A client may gain access if the observed signal strength is above a certain threshold specified for that client; however, there are inherent problems in determining location only from the signal strength caused by the direction of antenna and the nature of the physical medium.

Directional methods use Angle of Arrival (AoA) or Direction of Arrival (DoA) for computing locations. Triangulation uses angle measurements together with at least one known distance to calculate the subject's location. In a relative positioning system, which only requires prior knowledge of relative positioning of nodes with respect to each other, the subject's location can be easily determined with only two reference points. Time-based methods measure distances by recording the time of flight (ToF) from the transmitter to the receiver. Trilateration uses the known locations of two or more reference points and measures the distance between the subject and each reference point. To accurately and uniquely determine the relative location of a node in two-dimensional space by using trilateration alone, generally at least three measurements to reference points with known locations are required. The location of an object lies at the intersection of three circles with radii equal to the distance between the object and the emitters. Similarly, multilateration estimates location by measuring the time difference of arrival (TDOA) of a signal from the emitter at three or more receiver sites. For instance, Global System for Mobile communication (GSM) localization is the use of multilateration to determine the location of GSM mobile phones, usually with the intent to locate the user.

Besides location detection, there has been earlier work done on detecting user mobility mode. Given the GSM signal strengths observed from fixed base stations, they are consistent in time, but variable in space, Timothy et al. (2006) propose a method to calculate the average Euclidean distance between consecutive GSM measurements. By capturing the similarity between GSM measurements, they infer changes in the set of nearby towers and signal strengths as indicative of motion mode such as standing still, walking, and running. In general, we are interested in the application of an extended notion of "context" (computing, user, and physical contexts) of the environment (Chiu et al., 2007) in the enforcement of privacy policies.

2.4 Location-related access control model

There are several existing access models based on location information and context-aware constraints or extensions. The role- and context-based access control (RCBAC) model proposed by Yao et al. (2005) extends traditional RBAC with context-related constraints. RCBAC dynamically grants and adapts permissions to users based on a set of security-relevant contextual information collected from the grid environments. Every constraint is evaluated dynamically against the current context of the access request. Michalakis (2002) presents pervasive access control (PAC) architecture for anonymous authentication. PAC uses a lightweight security solution to authenticate a user's location by avoiding heavy security at the end points and minimizing the number of trusted components. The Location ID (LID) authority authenticates the membership of a user in a location group by mapping between location groups and the client's LID and keeping track of the corresponding time-varying location code. Ray and Yu (2005) introduced another model for extending RBAC to incorporate LBAC. This model is applied to applications consisting of static and dynamic objects, where location of the subject and object must be considered before granting access. They show relationships between the different components of the core RBAC model and location and what constraints are needed to perform location-based access.

In addition, Covington et al. (2001) enhanced the RBAC by adding in some environment roles. Environment roles can describe any state of the system such as locations or time. Environment roles can be used to implement controllable properties such as granularity of returned information. They show that environment roles are constrained to similar issues as traditional subject roles in RBAC such as role activation, revocation, and hierarchies. Damiani et al. (2005) present GEO-RBAC, which extends the RBAC mode with spatial- and location-based information. GEO-RBAC relies on the Open Geospatial Consortium (OGC) spatial model to model spatial objects, user positions, and geographically bounded roles. Moreover, this model has the ability to deal with both real positions, obtained from a given mobile terminal such as PDAs or smartphones, and logical position, represented at different granularities. They introduced a role schema concept to specify the name of the role as well as the type of the role spatial boundary and the granularity of the logical position.

In the research area of location description and LBS, some works on end-user-related location information technology have been completed. Wu et al. (2004) focuses on the application layer, human-understandable location descriptions, and performing end-user-oriented, LBS. Recently, Ardagna et al. (2006) presented a location-based condition integrating an access control model (LBAC). Their approach to LBAC considers the specific techniques and algorithms to ascertain the location from the service requester, representing the underlying location technologies in terms of a set of standard interfaces.

Meanwhile, location information is also sensitive privacy data that needs to be protected. Ray (2006) incorporates the MAC model to the notion of location. They show how to control the disclosure of location information in the context of subjects and objects to prevent any illegal information flow. Their approach includes adding location and security level components into the MAC model. Hengartner and Steenkiste (2004) have designed an access control mechanism for controlling location information in their proposed model. Although there are many proposals on the RBAC model extensions, there is not yet a comprehensive model in handling privacy access requirements based on location information and conditions.

3 Privacy, access control, and location in mobile applications

This section presents the approach to tackle privacy access control issues in the context of mobile applications with location awareness. The basic concept of RBAC is that users are assigned to roles, permissions are assigned to roles, and users acquire permissions when they are members of roles. As we mentioned in Section 2, the features of RBAC have received broad attention both from the research community and from the industry. These features have been widely adopted and implemented in database management, security management, and network operating systems. For mobile applications, this section presents an RBAC model with privacy extensions and location extensions to control privacy information in location-sensitive activities. This section starts with the fundamental model, namely core RBAC model, and then moves to the location aware privacy access control model.

3.1 Core role-based access control model

The core RBAC model proposed by the NIST defines the fundamental aspects of this model. The core model introduces minimum collection of RBAC elements, elements sets, and relations to completely achieve a RBAC system (Ferraiolo et al., 2001). Referring to Fig. 1, it includes five basic entities, namely USERS, ROLES, OPS, OBJECTS, and SESSIONS, as well as the user-role assignment (UA) and permission-role assignment (PA) relations. The SESSIONS is a mapping of one user to possibly many roles.

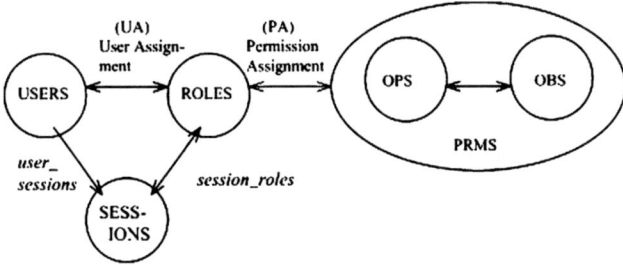

Fig. 1.   Core role-based access control model.

That is, a user establishes a session during the activation of the subset of roles assigned to the users (Ferraiolo et al., 2001). Each session associates with one user, and the user can associate with more than one session. The entities, relations, and functions in core RBAC in the context of a system can be described as follows (Ferraiolo et al., 2003):

Entities

- SUBJECTS is the set of subjects in the system. Generally, it can be in the form of a person, a process, or devices that cause information to flow among objects, or it can change the system states (National Computer Security Center (NCSC), 1988).
- USERS $\subseteq$ SUBJECTS is the set of persons in the system.
- ROLES is the set of roles that contain a collection of permissions to use resources appropriate to a person's job function, such as nurse, doctor, and administrator.
- OBJECTS is the set of information entities in the system, such as medical records and insurance files.
- OPS is the set of operations that can be executed in the system, such as read and write.
- SESSIONS is the set of sessions in the system.

Relations

- PRMS $= 2^{\{OPS \times OBJECTS\}}$ is the set of permissions that approve a particular operations to one or more objects in the system.
- UA $\subseteq$ USERS $\times$ ROLES is a many-to-many mapping between users and roles (UA relation).
- PA $\subseteq$ PRMS $\times$ ROLES is a many-to-many mapping between permissions and roles (PA relation).

Functions

- assigned_users: (r: ROLES) $\rightarrow 2^{USERS}$ is the mapping of role r onto a set of users. Formally, assigned_users(r) $\subseteq \{\forall_{i = 1,2, \ldots, n}\ u_i \in$ USERS $\mid (u_i, r) \in$ UA$\}$.
- assigned_permissions: (r: ROLES) $\rightarrow 2^{PRMS}$ is the mapping of role r onto a set of permissions. Formally, assigned_permissions(r) $\subseteq \{\forall_{i = 1,2, \ldots, n}\ p_i \in$ PRMS $\mid (p_i, r) \in$ PA$\}$.
- subject_user: (s: SUBJECTS) $\rightarrow$ USERS is the mapping of subject s onto the subject's associated user(s).
- subject_role: (s: SUBJECTS) $\rightarrow 2^{ROLES}$ is the mapping of subject s onto a set of roles. Formally, subject_role(s) $\subseteq \{\forall_{i = 1,2, \ldots, n}\ r_i \in$ ROLES $\mid$ (subject_user(s), $r_i) \in$ UA$\}$.
- user-sessions: (s: SUBJECTS) $\rightarrow 2^{SESSIONS}$ is the mapping of subject s onto a set of subject's associated session(s).
- session-roles: (se: SESSIONS) $\rightarrow 2^{ROLES}$ is the mapping of session se onto a set of this session associated role(s).

Role authorization property

- A subject *s* can never have an active role that is not authorized for its user:
  $\forall s \in SUBJECTS, u \in USERS, r \in ROLES,$
  $r \in subject\_roles(s) \wedge u \in subject\_user(s) \Rightarrow u \in assigned\_users(r)$

Basic access authorization property

- *basic_access:* $SUBJECTS \times OPS \times OBJECTS \rightarrow DECISIONS$
  basic_access(s, op, o)
  = *allow*, if subject *s* can access object *o* using operation *op*,
  = *deny*, otherwise.

A subject *s* is allowed to perform an operation *op* on object *o* only if there exists a role *r* that is included in the subject's active role set, and there exists a permission that is assigned to *r* such that the permission authorizes the performance of *op* on *o*: $s \in SUBJECTS, o \in OBJECTS, op \in OPS$, $basic\_access(s, op, o) = allow \Rightarrow \exists r: ROLES, p: PRMS, r \in subject\_roles(s)$ $\wedge p \in assigned\_permissions(r) \wedge (op, o) \in p$.

In core RBAC, a subject cannot be granted an active role that it has not been authorized to complete. The core RBAC model will allow access or deny decisions that are traditionally based on low-level operations such as read and write. For instance, a user *A* with role *R* is allowed to read data *D*. In this case, the user *A* is a subject, the data *D* is an object, and *read* is an operation. The core RBAC does not comply with privacy regulatory mandates, since privacy legislation is not only defined in terms of such low-level operations such as read and write but also presented with some other high-level entities such as a set of purposes or recipients before access is granted. It is also necessary to make clear the obligations and the retention period if access is granted. In such a scenario, it is evident that the core RBAC-based access authorization system is not adequate to satisfy privacy-related requirements.

3.2 Privacy access control model

Cheng and Hung (2005) proposed the privacy access control model by extending the core RBAC model with a set of privacy-related entities concerning the Health Insurance Portability and Accountability Act (HIPAA), namely *PURPOSES, RECIPIENTS, OBILIGATIONS, RETENTIONS, EVENTS, COMMUNICATION_CHANNELS, TIME-STAMP*, and *ACCESS_LOGS* as shown in Fig. 2. As Fig. 2 shows, the privacy access control model consists of a core RBAC model, privacy-based entities (*PURPOSES, RECIPIENTS, OBLIGATIONS*, and *RETENTIONS*), and other entities (*EVENTS, COMMUNICATION_ CHANNELS, TIMESTAMP*, and *ACCESS_LOGS*). This model processes

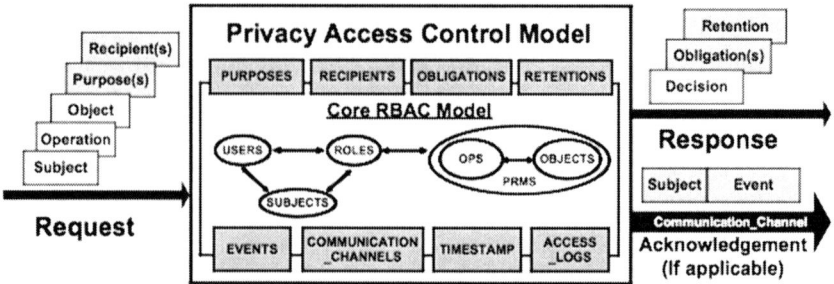

Fig. 2.   The extended privacy access control model (Cheng and Hung, 2005).

an input request *<Subject, Operation, Object, Purpose(s), Recipient(s)>* and generates a corresponding response *<Decision, Obligation(s), Retention>* and an optional acknowledgement *<Subject, Event>* through a communication channel. The extended entities and mappings are defined as follows:

- *PURPOSES* is the set of purposes that describe his/her purpose(s) of a request submission.
- *RECIPIENTS* $\subseteq$ *SUBJECTS* is the set of recipients of the result generated by the set of collected object(s) such as analysis reports.
- *OBLIGATIONS* is the set of obligations that may be taken after the decision of permission is made. In general, an obligation is opaque and is returned after the permission is granted. The obligations describe what promises a subject must make after gaining the permission.
- *RETENTIONS* is the set of retention policies that are to be enforced in the effected object(s). Each data custodian may have its own retention policy to enforce the usage of datasets (Cheng and Hung, 2005).
- *COMMUNICATION_CHANNELS* = $\{c_1, c_2, ..., c_n\}$ is a set of communication media in the system. It is used to specify how the acknowledgement is sent to a subject, for example, email, telephone, and so on.
- *TIMESTAMP* is a set of positive integer Z^+, representing the system time in partial order.
- *ACCESS_LOGS* = $\{e_1, e_2, ..., e_n\}$ is a set of n events to keep track of the access control log history of all events that occurred in the system. Initially, the system starts with an empty access log.
- *DECISION*: {ALLOW, DENY} is a decision for describing whether the access is granted or denied.
- *PRIVACY_RULES* $\subseteq$ *ROLES* × *OPS* × *OBJECTS* × *PURPOSES* × *RECIPIENTS* × *DECISIONS* × *OBLIGATIONS* × *RETENTIONS* is a set of privacy rules arranged in the system. For the *DECISIONS* = *allow*, the rules denote a positive authorization,

meaning it states who is allowed to perform which operation, on which object, based on what purposes, to which recipients, and under what obligations and retention. Otherwise, *DECISIONS = deny.*

- *EVENTS* $\subseteq$ SUBJECTS $\times$ OPS $\times$ OBJECTS $\times$ PURPOSES $\times$ RECIPIENTS $\times$ DECISIONS $\times$ OBLIGATIONS $\times$ RETENTIONS $\times$ TIMESTAMP is an event of an access request and the corresponding response.
- *EVENTS* $\subseteq$ *SUBJECTS* $\times$ *ACCESS_LOGS* $\times$ *TIMESTAMP* is an event of an acknowledgment.
- *EVENTS* $\subseteq$ *SUBJECTS* $\times$ *PRIVACY_RULES* $\times$ *PRIVACY_ RULES* $\times$ *TIMESTAMP* is an event of a change in privacy rules or restrictions.
- *EVENTS* $\subseteq$ *SUBJECTS* $\times$ *COMMUNICATION_CHANNELS* $\times$ *TIMESTAMP* is an event of a change in an acknowledgment communication channel.
- OWNER $\subseteq$ SUBJECTS $\times$ OBJECTS, is a one-to-many mapping between subjects and objects. It is a set of tuples (s, o), where s $\in$ SUBJECTS and o $\in$ OBJECTS.
- object_owner: OBJECTS $\rightarrow$ SUBJECTS is the mapping of an object *obj* to its owner *s*. Formally, object_owner(*obj*) = {*s* $\in$ SUBJECTS | (*s*, *obj*) $\in$ OWNER}.
- owner_object: SUBJECTS $\rightarrow 2^{\text{OBJECTS}}$ is the mapping of a subject *s* to all the objects {o_1, o_2, ..., o_n} that the subject owns. Formally, owner_object(*s*) $\subseteq$ {$\forall_{i=1,2,...,n}$ o_i $\subseteq$ OBJECTS | (*s*, o_i) $\in$ OWNER}.
- To restrict the one-to-many mapping between subjects and objects, this model adds the following rules: $\forall$ *obj* $\in$ OBJECTS, $\exists$ s_i, s_j $\in$ SUBJECTS, $s_i \neq s_j$, such that object_owner(*obj*) = s_i $\Rightarrow$ s_j $\oplus$ object_owner(*obj*) = $\varnothing$, s_i $\oplus$ object_owner(*obj*) = s_i, where $\oplus$ means logical exclusive-or.

The role authorization with all the privacy-based extension can be described as a function *access* as follows (Cheng and Hung, 2005):

- access: SUBJECTS $\times$ OPS $\times$ OBJECTS $\times$ PURPOSES $\times$ RECIPIENTS $\rightarrow$ DECISION $\times$ OBLIGATIONS $\times$ RETENTIONS, is the core part in determining whether an access is granted or denied with any obligations and retention policies according to the subject that invokes the access, operation of the access, the objects that the subject is requesting, the purposes for this request, the recipients of the result generated by the set of collected objects. Formally, access(*s*, op, {o_1, o_2, ..., o_i}, {pp_1, pp_2, ..., pp_j}, {rp_1, rp_2, ..., rp_k}) = (ALLOW, {obl_1, obl_2, ..., obl_m}, {rt_1, rt_2, ..., rt_i}) if subject *s* can access any object in {o_1, o_2, ..., o_i} using operation op, for any purpose in {pp_1, pp_2, ..., pp_j}, with any recipient in {rp_1, rp_2, ..., rp_k}, (DENY, $\varnothing$, $\varnothing$) otherwise. If the access is granted, a set of obligations {obl_1,

$obl_2, \ldots, obl_m$} and also a set of retention policies {$rt_1, rt_2, \ldots, rt_i$} for a corresponding set of objects {$o_1, o_2, \ldots, o_i$} are returned to subject s.

3.3 An illustrative mobile healthcare application

Health information is among the most personal and guarded data that can be collected and shared. The information that needs to be protected in the healthcare sector is often referred to as Protected Health Information (PHI). PHI includes individually identifiable health information and the provision of healthcare to an individual relating to past, present, and future physical and mental health conditions. PHI can influence an individual's access to credit, admission to educational institutions, and his or her ability to secure employment and obtain insurance, making it very important to ensure that proper measures are taken to ensure the accuracy, confidentiality, and integrity of the data.

Traditionally, PHI was paper-based and kept in the doctor's clinic. Doctors and nurses were the only users who retained access to patients' PHI. As a result, protecting privacy as required by law was relatively easy because the system was isolated. At the present time however, doctor-patient relationships are no longer limited to one-on-one communication but may include referral physicians, specialists, financial staff in insurance companies, and so on. In addition, the introduction of EMR gradually shifted the storage medium away from paper-based to electronic-based, leaving the PHI much more distributed among all involved parties. Furthermore, as the Internet is now viewed as more reliable, and we have become more familiarized with its capabilities, physicians, researchers, and patients are now using the Web to gather (e.g., view medical records), distribute (e.g., electronic billing), and exchange (e.g., email) health information. From the perspective of patients and doctors, accessing patients' health information over an electronic medium is becoming easier and more common throughout the world; however, this also leads to increases in threats and vulnerabilities. The threats to information privacy can come from insiders and outsiders within an organization (Fischer-Hubner, 2001).

To enhance the privacy protection of PHI, some legislative schemas and practice guidelines have been proposed by healthcare organizations such as the HIPAA and the European Union (E.U.) Data Protection Act. In general, access control is defined as the mechanism by which users are permitted to access resources (e.g., EMR) according to their identities, authentication, and associated authorization privileges (CSIS, 2003), or other policies. It uses control policies to evaluate requests to the resources and returns a permit or deny association. For instance, HIPAA defines policy rules to protect and enhance the rights of consumers, clients, and patients to control how their health information is used and disclosed according to an American national standard. HIPAA can be implemented into access control systems as access control policies to ensure the PHI privacy.

To realize mobile healthcare applications, the adoption of mobile technologies is applicable to an array of healthcare scenarios. Physicians and specialists have already begun using these devices for general medical reference, storing patient's PHI, and maintaining medical orders. Devices such as PDAs and smartphones can be used to meet the needs of highly mobile patients and medical personnel. Particular to the homecare area, there is an increasing demand for mobile computing technologies. Due to cost and efficiency issues, some chronically ill or disabled patients require medical care at home, after a stay in hospital. Today, many patients across Europe receive care in their familiar surroundings—around 200,000 times per year in Germany alone. During homecare services, nurses or physicians go to the patient's home regularly to retrieve and update the patient's medical data. This data can be loaded to the patient's mobile device (e.g. PDAs and smartphones) before the nurse sends any requests to access this information at the patient's home. Since healthcare service providers and patients have to work together in a highly cooperative and collaborative manner, mobile devices are well suited for such scenarios.

These advanced technologies benefit healthcare delivery; however, protecting PHI becomes more complicated in highly mobile and distributed circumstances. There are a number of security and privacy implications that must be explored. Although access control technologies can be directly applied to protecting PHI, it is not adequate to tackle all privacy-related issues in the environment of prevalent mobile healthcare services. We relate the illustrative example based on the following scenarios of healthcare services where location information is an important fact, which influences the control of access to PHI.

Scenario 1. *Homecare nurse A visits patient B's home regularly to collect information on B's health and progress. B received dialysis results facilitated by him/herself or another family member. These data collection processes have to be restricted at the patient's home in accordance with privacy reasons.*

Scenario 2. *An important meeting about patient B's surgery is held where all the doctors and surgeons are present. B's medical records and related personal information are distributed to their handheld devices (e.g., PDAs and smartphones) before the meeting starts. The final decision about B's coming surgery and the surgery memo are also available in the same way so that the participants do not miss any points. Any unauthorized parties are not allowed to access the sensitive information due to privacy policies.*

Scenario 3. *Sometimes more than one clinician staff (e.g., doctor, physician) comes to visit patient B, and not necessarily the same staff visits every time. Clinics offer mobile devices (e.g., PDAs and smartphones) to each visiting homecare nurse to help in navigating and locating B's home efficiently. Since B's home address is not public information, the nurse's location plays an important role in getting the patient's EMR only at the patient's home.*

In general, the illustrative example lies in the need to obtain location-based information in mobile healthcare service scenarios. As we can see, if malicious users can observe the presence of a person in a certain location and infer the activities being performed by the person, this attack may cause disastrous consequences. In short, a formal model containing location information is critical. We will base the following example on the process on home hemodialysis.

Hemodialysis is the process of filtering wastes and excess water from the blood when an individual is experiencing chronic kidney disease or kidney failure (Watson et al., 2006). The process will involve the use of a dialyzer (dialysis machine, which will cleanse the blood as it travels through the machine and is returned to the body). The dialyzer is capable of capturing volumes of data, multiple times per second. Other information systems such as tele-monitoring and patient communication systems are also used for hemodialysis. Patient data that is transferred to a central observer in real time includes heart rate, blood pressure, respiration, and oxygen saturation, and so on. Based on these sets of data, the physicians or doctors need to analyze the patient's physiology and give further instructions or prescriptions to the patient through a patient communication system.

Nowadays, patients are able to undergo hemodialysis in the comfort of their own home. Patients can attend training sessions where they will be taught everything they need to know about administering their own treatments. Dialysis conducted at their homes allows patients to dialyze themselves on their own schedule; have more options of control over decisions that are made; undergo treatment in familiar surroundings; and have the ability to continue working and living a relatively normal life, leaving the limited hospital space for those patients whose homes are not equipped for home dialysis treatments. This has lead to a vast adoption of home dialysis in the United States and Canada, as it is more comfortable, convenient, and less costly.

During each appointment with a nurse at home, patients will provide the homecare nurse with his or her journal logs (diary logs) consisting of input and output values from the dialyzer as well as the vital signs taken from the dialysis machine. If the nurse notices any inconsistencies or abnormal results, the nurse will immediately notify the nephrologist as well as the family physician. The nephrologist will use the information to make any necessary changes to the current prescriptions and send the data to the supplier who will deliver new or different supplies to the patient's home.

The nephrologist will also notify the patient of the changes that need to be made to his/her treatment plan. Any changes made to the patient's medical records would be updated in a database maintained by the patient at his or her home. In other cases, the nurse will update the patient's data to the central server when they return to the hospital, allowing the patient's physician to monitor the progress and prepare any new directions or care plans for the nurse's next visit to the patient's home. Mobile devices suit these homecare scenarios in terms of aiding to transfer patient's health information and make the collaboration and cooperation between different practitioners efficiently.

In all scenarios, the nurse plays a role in the security of the patient's information. It is the nurse's obligation to ensure that the medical records are protected from theft, loss, and unauthorized disclosure, copying, modifications, and disposal. In ensuring privacy, the nurse and other hospital personnel such as doctors, nephrologists, or medical suppliers are required to ensure that the personal health information is used in a secure manner and that the information is accurate, complete, and up-to-date. Proper access control mechanisms in terms of privacy rules from legislation could be applied to restrict and control access to patient's health information.

Figure 3 illustrates the major practitioners, their job functions, and the flow of patients' medical data in the hemodialysis process. The dialysis machine and database contain the patient's journal log, which cannot be accessed without an internal login. The patient's PDA can download his or her diary logs from the dialysis machine and any updates can be made through the patient's PDA to the database at home. The nurse's PDA is responsible for downloading the patient's information, viewing the diary logs, and updating the patient's EMR to the patient's PDA, at the patient's home. When in the

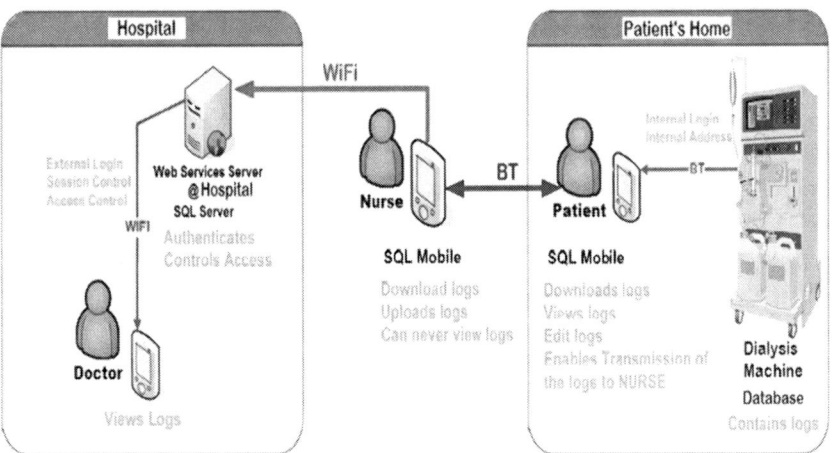

Fig. 3.   Hemodialysis scenario illustrations.

hospital, the nurse's PDA will communicate with the Web service server to upload the patient's data and download the EMR that has been modified by the physician, along with any instructions provided by the physician, before the nurse visits the patient again. The physician's PDA can view and document a patient's EMR for medical purposes. In each transmission of the patient's data between devices, corresponding security and privacy mechanisms need to be applied to secure the data. In the following sections, we look at some security and privacy mechanisms based on location information.

3.4   Location aware access control model

Location aware access control model adopts civil addresses to describe location information. For example, the civil address of the University of Ontario Institute of Technology is shown below as:

2000 Simcoe Street North
Oshawa, Ontario
Canada L1H 7K4

Location information may contain privacy and physical attributes. For example, in a hospital, some rooms are considered as "private," such as the operation rooms, whereas other rooms are "public," such as the clinics. These classifications indicate different privacy clearance for different locations. The "private" rooms have more strict limitations to enter than the "public" rooms. It is because "public" rooms can be accessed by the public in the hospital and the public rooms do not need to be authorized by administers in the hospital. Physical attributes are data from physical systems such as speed or signal strength. These kinds of information can affect a mobile subject's location detection. Here, we revise the general privacy policy rule based on the work by Powers et al. (2002) as follows:

```
ALLOW [Subject]
to perform [Operation] on [Object]
In authorized [Location]
only for legitimate [Purposes] to [Recipients]
Carry out [Obligations] and [Retentions].
DENY otherwise.
```

A subject only has access to an object if the access is authorized by the core RBAC. In addition, the subject needs to specify the purpose(s) of the access and recipient(s) of the result of the access operation in an authorized location. The purpose(s) and the recipient(s) must be legitimate according to the access of the object defined by the owner or an authority such as the government. Thus, obligations and a retention policy will be returned as a response message if the access is allowed. The subject must also comply with the obligations and the retention policy. The access request will be denied otherwise. For illustration, the privacy rule with location awareness in an illustrative healthcare example can be expressed as follows:

A *homecare nurse* is allowed to use his or her *PDA* to *download* and *read* the *medical record* of his or her hemodialysis patient from a *patient's PDA*, at the patient's *home* for *collection* purpose, that is,

```
ALLOW [homecare nurse's PDA]
to perform [download and read] on [his or her patient's
  medical record]
In authorized [patient's home]
only for legitimate [collection purpose] to [patient's
  doctor]
```

This chapter proposes to use *location beacons* to determine the location information of *subjects* and *objects* in the extended RBAC. This model assumes that some of these entities, *subjects* and *objects*, may be encapsulated by a beacon-enabled device such as Bluetooth beacons, wireless USB devices, infrared/radio frequency programmable badges, and a Dynamic Host Configuration Protocol (DHCP) extended with location information. For example, a subject is holding a PDA with Bluetooth beacon functionality or an object is stored in a PDA with BlueTooth beacon functionality. This works well as long as the coverage region of a location beacon corresponds roughly to the desired location accuracy (Schulzrinne et al., 2003). Thus, the concept of locations, beacons, and groups is expressed in the extended RBAC as follows:

- LOCATIONS is the set of civil addresses that are used to describe the location of subjects and objects.
- BEACONS $\subseteq \{\forall_{i\,=\,1,2,\,\ldots,\,n}$ device$(e_i) \mid e_i \in$ SUBJECTS $\cup$ OBJECTS$\}$, where *device* can be any devices with beacon functionalities.
- GROUPS $\subseteq$ BEACONS is the set of beacons.

In some cases, we can group beacons into different groups based on their locations. We choose the community with highest density of beacon nodes as the location reference group. The concept of location reference group and civil address of a subject or an object can be defined as follows:

- location_reference_group: LOCATIONS → GROUPS, where the relative location of a group of *beacons* are consistently referenced in a specific location within a certain period of time. Formally, location_reference_group(*location*) = $\{b_1, b_2, \ldots, b_m\}$.
- civil_address: (SUBJECTS $\cup$ OBJECTS) → LOCATIONS, the mapping of a subject or an object to its civil address.

One of the beacons with least mobility within the group could be the master. The master decides the network coordinate system. The rest of the nodes adjust their position and direction according to the master. A newcomer who wants to communicate with members of the reference group can first send a request to the master. Furthermore, we integrate the concept of hierarchy to the location reference groups shown as follows:

- *Mobility hierarchy*: This hierarchy is based on different mobility levels of each beacon. The root beacon's mobility level is the lowest, meaning almost stationary. Any other beacons below it have higher mobility levels and properties, such as direction and speed.
- *Location hierarchy*: This hierarchy depicts the relationships between beacons' location detection abilities, that is, the different ranges they detect. For instance, there are four beacons, namely A, B, C, and D. The detection range covered by A is larger than B and C. B's and C's are likely the same. D can detect the location between B and C. Thus A, B, C, and D form a location reference group in a hierarchical structure.

This section presents the location information of a subject and an object as constraints in the access control rules. Constraints are used to specify configurations of the model that the specific requirements need to be enforced in the system. Referring to the illustrative mobile healthcare example (Watson, 2006), the nature of hemodialysis suits the healthcare settings with mobile devices and highlights the privacy concerns. The hemodialysis process is an asynchronous cooperation between the visiting nurses over a long period of time, with many temporal ruptures. Data about the hemodialysis process was obtained from medical records that are kept at the simulator machine and health monitoring machines at the patients' homes and is updated by the nurses' mobile devices (e.g., PDAs) after every visit (Hamek et al., 2005). In this scenario, the nurse can only collect the medical records (i.e., object) while both the nurse (i.e., subject) and the patient (i.e., subject) are at the patients' homes (i.e., civil address). Both the nurse and the patient hold a PDA with Bluetooth beacon functionality, and the nurse can simply download the medical records from the patient's PDA to his/her PDA. For this reason, there is a constraint for this access control rule as follows:

$\forall\ s_1, s_2 \in$ SUBJECTS,
subject_user(s_1) $\not\subset \varnothing$, subject_user(s_2) $\not\subset \varnothing$,
$r_1 = $ "nurse" $\in$ subject_role(s_1) $\subseteq$ ROLES,
$r_2 = $ "homecarePatient" $\in$ subject_role(s_2) $\subseteq$ ROLES,
subject_user(s_1)$\in$ assigned_user(r_1) ,
subject_user(s_2)$\in$ assigned_user(r_2) ,
$op_1 = $ "download" $\in$ OPS,
$o_1 = $ "medicalRecords" $\in$ owner_object(s_2),
$pp_1 = $ "Collection of home hemodialysis patient's medical records" $\in$ PURPOSES,
$s_3 = $ "homecareDepartment" $\in$ RECIPIENTS
$\Rightarrow$
(access(s_1, op_1, $\{o_1\}$, $\{pp_1\},\{s_3\}$) = (ALLOW, $\{obl_1, obl_2, \ldots, obl_m\}$, $\{rt_1, rt_2, \ldots, rt_n\}$),
$\{obl_1, obl_2, \ldots, obl_m\} \subseteq$ OBLIGATIONS,
$\{rt_1, rt_2, \ldots, rt_n\} \subseteq$ RETENTIONS) AND (location_constraint (s_1, s_2, o_1,
    location_reference_group(civil_address(s_2))))

For all users in the system, if the users s_1 and s_2 have the role "nurse" and "homecarePatient," respectively, s_1 is allowed to read s_2's own medical record o_1 on the purpose of "collection of home hemodialysis patient's medical records." The homecare department will be the only recipient for the medical record o_1, and s_1 has to follow a set of obligations $\{obl_1, obl_2, \ldots, obl_m\}$ and retention policies $\{rt_1, rt_2, \ldots, rt_n\}$. Please note that $\{obl_1, obl_2, \ldots, obl_m\} \subseteq$ OBLIGATIONS and $\{rt_1, rt_2, \ldots, rt_n\} \subseteq$ RETENTIONS would need to be defined by the homecare services provider. Here, this chapter introduces a location constraint that requires o_1, s_1, and s_2 must be located at the civil address of s_2 (e.g., patient's home). The detection of location is determined by the reference group located at the civil address of s_2.

4 Conclusions

This chapter presents a location aware privacy access control model for supporting mobile applications. We adopt the location-related privacy rules into a hemodialysis scenario to prove our model. Extended from the Core RBAC model, the location aware privacy access control model is designed to meet the location requirements for supporting mobile healthcare applications, since the misuse of location information could cause a breach of privacy and security. For this reason, we will view location information as protected objects instead of being parameters of constraints in our proposed model and adopt our model to maintain the confidentiality of location information and control its disclosure.

5 Questions for discussion

1. There are some limitations in the design of our model. Firstly, as we adopt the core RBAC model and the privacy access control model, the access control decision is limited by the authorization of core RBAC model and the privacy access control model. In core RBAC, each access request involved requires one (role) subject to perform one operation on one object. This limits our ability to obtain permission for accessing a group of objects, but only a single object. What do you suggest to revise the model to tackle this limitation?
2. Beside the illustrative mobile healthcare, what other mobile applications can adopt the privacy access control with location awareness?

Acknowledgment

This work was supported by Privacy Commissioner of Canada (PCC) Contributions Program Grant, Natural Sciences and Engineering Research Council of Canada (NSERC) Discovery Grant, NSERC Collaborative

Research and Development Grant, Privacy Commissioner of Canada, and Bell University Laboratories (BUL), Canada.

References

Adaikkalavan, R. (2006). *Generalization and enforcement of role-based access control using a novel eventbased approach.* Doctor Thesis, University of Texas at Arlington. Available at http://hdl.handle.net/10106/231

Ahmed, A.A., H. Shi, Y. Shang (2005). SHARP: a new approach to relative localization in wireless sensor networks, in: *Proceedings of the 25th IEEE International Conference on Distributed Computing Systems Workshops, June 6–10,* IEEE Computer Society Press, pp. 892–898.

Anderson, R.J. (1996). A security policy model for clinical information systems, in: *Proceedings of the 1996 IEEE Symposium on Security and Privacy, SP, May,* IEEE Computer Society Press, Oakland, CA, USA, pp. 30–43.

Ardagna, C.A., M. Cremonini, E. Damiani (2006). Supporting location-based conditions in access control policies, in: *Proceedings of the 2006 ACM Symposium on Information, Computer and Communications Security (ASIACCS'06), March,* the Association for Computing Machinery (ACM), pp. 212–222.

Bishop, M. (2003). *Computer Security: Art and Science.* Addison Wesley Professional, USA, p. 1136.

Cheng, V.S.Y., P.C.K. Hung (2005). Health Insurance Portability and Accountability Act (HIPAA) compliant access control model for web services. *The International Journal of Health Information Systems and Informatics (IJHISI)* 1(1), 22–39.

Chiu, D.K.W., D. Hong, S.C. Cheung, E. Kafeza (2007). Adapting ubiquitous government services with context and views in a three-tier architecture, in: *Proceedings of the 40th Hawaii International Conference on System Sciences (HICSS40), January,* CDROM, IEEE Computer Society Press, Waikoloa, Big Island, Hawaii, USA.

Covington, M.J., W. Long, S. Srinivasan, A. Dey, M. Ahamad, G. Abowd (2001). Securing context-aware applications using environment roles, in: *Proceedings of 6th ACM Symposium on Access Control Models and Technologies (SACMAT '01), May,* Chantilly, Virginia, USA, pp. 10–20.

CSIS. (2003). *Security Glossary,* Information Systems Security Organization. Available at http://www.security-online.com/info/glossary.html

Damiani, M.L., E. Bertino, B. Catania, P. Perlasca (2005). GEO-RBAC: a spatially aware RBAC, in: *Proceedings of the ACM Symposium on Access Control Models and Technologies,* Stockholm, Sweden, pp. 29–37.

Denning, D.E., P. F. MacDoran (1996). Location-based authentication: grounding cyberspace for better security, in: *Computer Fraud and Security,* February, Vol. 1996, No. 2, Elsevier Science, USA, pp. 12–16.

Ferraiolo, D.F., D.R. Kuhn, R. Chandramouli (2003). *Role-based access control,* Computer Security Series. Artech House Publishers, USA.

Ferraiolo, D.F., R. Sandhu, S. Gavrila, D.R. Kuhn, R. Chandramouli (2001). Proposed NIST standard for role-based access control. *ACM Transactions on Information and System Security (TISSEC)* 4(3), 224–274.

Fischer-Hubner, S. (2001). *IT-Security and Privacy: Design and Use of Privacy-enhancing Security Mechanisms.* Springer, USA.

Garg, S., M. Kappes, M. Mani (2002). Wireless access server for quality of service and location based access control in 802.11 networks, in: *Proceedings of Seventh International Symposium on Computers and Communications, July,* Taormina, Italy, pp. 819–824.

Hamek, S., D. Anceaux, S. Pelayo, M.C. Beuscart-Zéphir, J. Rogalski (2005). Medical applications: cooperation in healthcare—theoretical and methodological issues: a study of two situations: hospital and home care, in: *Proceedings of the 2005 Annual Conference on European Association of Cognitive Ergonomics (EACE '05)*, Chania, Greece, pp. 233–240.

Hengartner, U., P. Steenkiste (2004). Implementing access control to people location information, in: *Proceedings of the Ninth ACM Symposium on Access Control Models and Technologies (SACMAT'04)*, June, Yorktown Heights, New York, USA, pp. 11–20.

Hooda, J., E. Dogdu, R. Sunderraman (2004). Health level-7 compliant clinical patient records system, in: *Proceedings of the 2004 ACM Symposium on Applied Computing*, March, Nicosia, Cyprus, pp. 259–263.

Joshi, J.B., W.G. Aref, A. Ghafoor, E.H. Spafford (2001). Security models for web-based applications. *Communications of the ACM* 44(February), 38–44.

Leino-Kilpi, H., M. Valimaki, T. Dassen, M. Gasull, C. Lemonidou, A. Scott, M. Arndt (1967). Privacy: a review of the literature. *International Journal of Nursing Studies* 38, 663–671.

Louwerse, K. (1998). The electronic patient record; the management of access—case study: Leiden University Hospital. *International Journal of Medical Informatics* 49(1), 39–44.

Michalakis, N. (2002). PAC: location aware access control for pervasive computing environments. Available at http://www.cs.nyu.edu/~nikos/personal/pubs/sow2002.pdf

National Computer Security Center (NCSC). (1988). *Glossary of computer security terms*, NCSC-TG-004, NCSC, October 21.

NIST. (2005). Role based access control standards roadmap, May. National Institute of Standard and Technology (NIST). Available at http://csrc.nist.gov/rbac/rbac-stds-roadmap.html

Osborn, S., R. Sandhu, Q. Munawer (2000). Configuring role-based access control to enforce mandatory and discretionary access control policies. *ACM Transactions on Information and Systems Security (TISSEC)* 3(2), 85–106.

Powers, C.S., P. Ashley, M. Schunter (2002). Privacy promises, access control, and privacy management—Enforcing privacy throughout an enterprise by extending access control, in: *Proceedings of the Third International Symposium on Electronic Commerce*, Washington, DC, USA, pp. 13–21.

Ray, I. (2006). Towards a location-based mandatory access control model. *Computer and Security* 25(1), 36–44. February.

Ray, I., L. Yu (2005). Short paper: towards a location-aware role-based access control model, in: *First International Conference on Security and Privacy for Emerging Areas in Communications Networks (SecureComm 2005)*, September 5–9, Athens, Greece, pp. 234–236.

Savarese, C., J. Rabaey, J. Beutel (2001). Locationing in distributed ad-hoc wireless sensor networks, in: *Proceedings of IEEE International Conference on Acoustics, Speech, and Signal Processing (ICASSP'01)*, May, Washington, DC, USA, pp. 2037–2040.

Savvides, A., F. Koushanfar, M. Potkonjak, M.B. Srivastava (2000). Location Discovery in Ad-Hoc Wireless Networks, UCLA EE and CS Departments, USA.

Schoeman, E.D. (1984). *Philosophical Dimensions of Privacy: An Anthology*. Cambridge University Press, New York.

Schoeman, F.D. (1986). Privacy: philosophical dimensions of the literature, in: F. D. Schoeman (ed.) *Philosophical Dimensions of Privacy: An Anthology*, April, Vol. 96, No. 3, Cambridge University Press, New York, NY, pp. 1–33.

Schulzrinne, H., X. Wu, S. Sidiroglou, S. Berger (2003). Ubiquitous computing in home networks. *IEEE Communications Magazine*, November, pp. 128–135.

Timothy, S., V. Alex, L. Anthony, M.Y. Chen (2006). Mobility detection using everyday GSM traces, in: *Proceedings of the 8th International Conference on Ubiquitous Computing (UbiComp)*, September, Springer, Berlin, pp. 212–224.

Watson, M. (2006). Mobile healthcare applications: a study of access control, in: *Proceedings of the Fourth Annual Conference on Privacy, Security and Trust (PST'2006)*, October 30–November 1, Toronto, Canada, pp. 525–528.

Watson, M., W. Stanyon, P.C.K. Hung, J. Andrade (2006). *A Study of Privacy Access Control in a Mobile Homecare Application*, December. University of Ontario Institute of Technology, Oshawa, Canada.

Wu, X., H. Schulzrinne (2005). Location-based Services in Internet Telephony, in: *Proceedings of Consumer Communications and Networking Conference (CCNC 2005), January 3–6*, Las Vegas, Nevada, USA, pp. 331–336.

Wu, X., R. Shacham, M.J. Mintz-Habib, K. Singh, H. Schulzrinne (2004). Location based communication services, in: *Proceedings of the 2004 ACM SIGMM Workshop on Effective Telepresence (ETP '04), October*, ACM, NY, USA, pp. 55–56.

Yao, H., H. Hu, B. Huang, R. Li (2005). Dynamic role and context-based access control for grid applications, in: *Proceedings of Sixth International Conference on Parallel and Distributed Computing (PDCAT'05), December*, Dalian, China, pp. 404–406.

Online resources

Center for Democracy and Technology. Personally identifiable information. Available at http://www.cdt.org/privacy/issues/pii/

Online Privacy Alliance. Effective enforcement of self regulation. Available at http://www.cdt.org/privacy/guide/protect/

Suggested readings

Fischer-Hubner, S. (2001). *IT-security and privacy. Lecture Notes in Computer Science*. Vol. 1958. Springer New York, Inc., New York.

Westin, A. (1967). *Privacy and Freedom*. Atheneum, New York, p. 487.

Rao & Upadhyaya, Eds., *Handbooks in Information Systems, Vol. 4*

Chapter 17

Employee Location Sensing: Implications for Security and Privacy

Laurel A. McNall

Department of Psychology, The College at Brockport, State University of New York,
350 New Campus Drive, Brockport, NY 14420, USA

Jeffrey M. Stanton

School of Information Studies, Syracuse University, 316 Hinds Hall, Syracuse,
NY 13244-4100, USA

Abstract

Although electronic monitoring of employees' work performance has occurred for years, new technology developments have facilitated the development of techniques that allow managers to track the location and movements of employees whose work takes them outside the confines of the company's facilities. Such location technologies frequently rely on the global positioning system (GPS) and other telecommunications technologies to provide a map of employees' movements that managers can use to help ensure both the performance of employees as well as the protection of the firm's mobile assets (e.g., vehicles). In this chapter, we review literature on employee monitoring, organizational security, and privacy to provide a framework for analyzing location sensing technologies. Then we provide preliminary data on a study that examines employee reactions to these technologies. Finally, we offer research based recommendations to organizations that plan to implement employee location sensing technologies.

---

1 Introduction

New technology developments have led to profound changes in the manner in which organizations supervise their employees. Electronic monitoring systems are defined as electronic technologies used to collect, store, analyze, and report the actions or performance of workers (Nebeker and Tatum, 1993). According to the American Management Association and The ePolicy Institute (2005), employers are increasingly using monitoring technology to manage productivity and protect resources. A 2003 study by Bentley's Center for Business Ethics found that 92% of employers conduct some form of workplace monitoring. A recent development in electronic monitoring is the deployment of location sensing technologies that allow managers to track the location and movements of employees beyond the confines of the company's facilities. Such location technologies frequently rely on the global positioning system (GPS), radio frequency identification devices (RFID), and other telecommunications technologies to provide constant, real time location tracking of employees' movements, even off-site.

In 2005, the American Management Association and The ePolicy Institute found 5% of organizations using GPS to monitor cell phones, 8% using GPS to track company vehicles, and 8% using GPS to monitor employee ID/Smartcards, with the latter mostly (53%) to control physical security and access to buildings (American Management Association and The ePolicy Institute, 2005). According to the U.S. Mobile Resource Management Systems Market Study, nearly 1.9 million GPS/wireless devices are used to monitor fleet vehicles, trailers, construction equipment, and mobile workers. Moreover, this same study found that the market for GPS-equipped cellular phones is rapidly expanding, with mobile resource management revenues expected to grow to over $2 billion in 2009. A variety of industry analysts have suggested that by 2010, roughly half of cell phone users will have location sensing technologies and services enabled within their handsets (Anthony et al., 2007).

GPS-tracking devices are being installed for a variety of different job roles, from behind the grills of police patrol cars to GPS-enabled delivery scanners for United Parcel Service employees to snowplow drivers with GPS-enabled cell phones (Forelle, 2007). Many employees expect their performance to be monitored and few are surprised by their supervisors' needs to oversee their work activities, but these location sensing technologies allow managers to have highly detailed records about employees' location beyond corporate walls, into their nonwork lives, with or without their knowledge (Alge et al., 2006). Thus, location technologies can greatly expand the range of monitoring organizations can perform. Lane points out that in a remarkably short time, an employer can develop a highly detailed profile of exactly how a worker spent his or her day using various methods of electronic monitoring (Lane, 2003). This is especially true with location sensing technologies given the capability to know where a worker spent his or her time outside regular business hours.

The use of electronic monitoring in the workplace is controversial. Critics contend that these devices are equivalent to "electronic whips" that turn workplaces into "electronic sweatshops" (Alder, 1998). Studies have found that electronic monitoring is related to elevated levels of stress, and ultimately contributes to employee health problems (Aiello, 1993; Nussbaum and duRivage, 1986; Rogers et al., 1990; Smith et al., 1992). In one study, 75 % of electronically monitored workers believed that the practice of electronic performance monitoring (EPM) lowered morale (McLaughlin, 1989). Perhaps the most serious criticism stems from concerns over invasion of privacy (U.S. Congress, 1987). This seems especially salient when nonwork activities are monitored, which often violates the expectation of privacy that most workers feel is their right (Ambrose et al., 1998). Some states have introduced legislation to limit the use of RFID devices due to privacy concerns as well as data security issues (Songini, 2008). However, from the organization's point of view, there are numerous advantages for using electronic monitoring devices, such as increasing productivity, improving quality and service, reducing fraud, combating theft of company resources, and reducing operating costs (Ambrose et al., 1998). Increasingly, organizations are turning to electronic monitoring as a way to protect intellectual property and prevent employee lawsuits (Lane, 2003) as well as protection from liability due to claims related to employees' on the job behavior.

With respect to location sensing technologies, many of these same concerns apply, while others are magnified. For instance, because location technologies are pervasive and less well bounded by the primary work location, privacy issues are paramount. Harmon (2003) notes that "location devices lift the curtain on a zone of privacy many Americans value, even if they rarely have anything serious to hide (p. 2)." In turn, this threatens worker autonomy in that "the devices ... promote the scrutiny of small decisions – where to have lunch, when to take a break, how fast to drive—rather than general accountability" (Harmon, 2003, p. 1).

Yet, companies using tracking devices in company-provided vehicles and cell phones often find increases in employee productivity (Canoni, 2004; Gruber, 2005b). For instance, Waxer (2006) discusses how one plumbing contractor installed GPS devices into his company's trucks to track vehicle location, speed, fuel consumption, mileage and the engine performance over the Internet. He found that he could cut response times by 10% and increase the number of clients from four to six per truck each day.

Proponents also contend that location sensing technologies offer safety benefits which outweigh privacy issues (Harmon, 2003; Sovocool, 2000). For instance, a GPS-enabled dispatch and routing system can provide 911 operators with which ambulance is closest to the call and provides the best route to get to that address (Forelle, 2007). Kightlinger (2004) also argues that GPS technology can include silent alarms for drivers to use in emergencies and monitoring equipment that shows whether drivers followed safety procedures or whether an emergency exit had been deployed.

RFID-based access cards can also have benefits for security and public safety (Balkovich et al., 2005). Gruber (2005a) noted that RFID-enabled identification cards enable organizations to study workplace patterns and improve efficiency, track workflow and theft, and restrict access to sensitive areas. In a case study within six organizations, Balkovich et al. (2005) found access cards were often integrated with other surveillance technologies (e.g., video cameras) and in addition to controlling access to areas within the workplace, were often used to investigate workplace incidences, misconduct allegations, and compliance with corporate policy.

1.1 Location sensing and organizational security

Location monitoring systems may contribute to organizational security in three inter-related ways: security of mobile assets, usage privileges related to mobile assets, and both perceived and actual personnel security. In this context, we construe organizational security quite broadly as referring to the protection of a variety of physical assets such as vehicles and tools as well as information assets such as databases. Likewise, we encompass location sensing as it occurs onsite, within the confines of the firms facilities, as well as off-site, although we note any distinctions between onsite and off-site monitoring when it is important to do so. Location sensing frequently provides benefits in maintaining security, albeit at the cost of greater complexity of organizational processes and systems as well as possible privacy concerns.

Mobile asset security: To an ever-increasing extent, organizations deploy a variety of assets into the field for the benefit of employees, partner organizations, and customers. These assets include vehicles, heavy machinery, tools, electronic devices, computers, original and replacement equipment for installation at customer sites, merchandise, and negotiable instruments such as gift cards. RFID, GPS, and various telecommunication technologies (e.g., cellular telephone) have been molded and integrated in a variety of ways to allow centralized or distributed monitoring of these assets (Werb and Lanzl, 1998). Conducting this location monitoring allows firms to reduce shrinkage (the loss of assets through theft and breakage) because items that "go astray" can be tracked to their last or current location depending on the type of sensing technology in use. Knowledge of this tracking capability among employees naturally reduces the amount of employee-initiated shrinkage through a deterrent effect, whereas recovery of misplaced assets or those stolen by non-employees may be facilitated through the tracking of missing items.

A secondary benefit of the capability for tracking the location of mobile assets is the avoidance of liability problems related to those assets. For example, by having computer-based records of vehicle routes, times, and locations, some metropolitan governments have been able to fend off lawsuits by demonstrating that the vehicle was not present at the accident scene at the time of the problem. A tertiary effect closely related is that employees can be held harmless if it can be shown that their tools, vehicles, and/or equipment were not present at the time when a problem occurred.

On the flip side, however, location tracking of mobile assets does make it easier to implicate an employee if he or she appears to have been "on the scene" when a problem occurred. Some employees (or their unions) may find this problematic because of the possibility that location sensing records might be tampered with or selectively mined or filtered as a way of targeting the activities of a particular employee.

Location sensing for personnel security: In the earlier discussion, we have examined the use of location sensing technology as applied to objects in the work environment, or, more broadly, assets owned or controlled by the firm. In addition to tagging and tracking objects, however, it is becoming increasingly common to track people in the work environment for security purposes. The use of RFID-enabled badges for employees is now commonplace in many work environments (Rieback et al., 2006). Many of the firms that use RFID badges do so as a way of controlling access to various locations within their facilities. When combined with a centralized database of employee roles and privileges, RFID badges make possible a fine-grained control of who goes where within the facility. Such systems can also maintain records on unsuccessful attempts to gain access to an area that an employee has not been given the rights to access. Although, older RFID badge systems used "near field" technology that required swiping a badge over a reader plate, newer implementations of "far field" RFID technology permit firms to extend the sensing beyond simply tracking door access. Using far field technology it is possible to learn quite precisely where within a facility an employee is located. Naturally this enhances the security applications of the badge because it can deliver a level of detail about an employee's movements that might detect, for example, when an employee came too close to a dangerous, restricted area on a factory floor.

Of further interest, some organizations have begun deploying RFID-enabled badges for personnel other than employees. For example, hospitals have recently begun a consideration of the risks and benefits of having RFID-enabled badges worn by patients (Aguilar et al., 2006; Cangialosi et al., 2007; Halamka, 2006). The benefits with respect to security are numerous and straightforward. Hospitals and other medical facilities have a well-established need to know where each admitted patient is within the facility at all times. Many dangerous or restricted locations exist within a typical hospital (e.g., nuclear medicine) and patients' access to these areas must be carefully controlled. Likewise, if a patient leaves the hospital facility unexpectedly, patient care teams need to become aware of this as quickly as possible. The same logic and reasoning generally applies when badge systems for non-employees are used for populations of guests/ visitors, temporary or contract staff members, and vendor staff members.

The costs and risks of using an RFID badge system on non-employee personnel are not as clear-cut. If a location system for non-employees is deployed as a "piggyback" on top of an existing system for tracking employees, the incremental cost of deployment may not be too significant. However, a brand new system that replaces existing guest/visitor or patient badges or wristbands may incur new costs that substantially exceed those used in simpler printed badge or barcode systems. Risks associated with the use of location sensing technologies on non-employees center on privacy concerns and the possibility of badge loss, misidentification, or unauthorized badge reuse. Although, employees represent a fairly stable population—a badge issued to an employee will probably be used for months or years—non-employees' presence in a facility is by definition ephemeral, making the management and control of badges and related infrastructure considerably more complex.

1.2   Usage privileges and location sensing

One promising new security application of personnel location sensing is in the granting and control of access to information systems. Most information systems access control systems center on "something you are" (i.e., your username) and "something you know" (i.e., your password). The use of personnel location sensing technologies expands these possibilities to "something you have" (e.g., an RFID-enabled tag) and/or "someplace you are." This latter option reflects the capability of a location sensing system to prevent access by one user to systems in more than one location. Additionally, such systems can be used to ensure that a user only accesses a system in a particular context (e.g., in a supervised computer cluster). Likewise, when a personnel tracking system is used in conjunction with tracking mobile assets (e.g., a laptop or personal digital assistant [PDA]), access control and privilege-granting systems can be used to ensure that the user possessing the device has permission to use the device and that the device provisions the user with only those privileges he or she is authorized to use at a particular location. To describe a concrete example, a nurse might use a PDA to access a patient's records in that patient's hospital room, but general access to all patient records would be prevented in that location.

2 A framework for analyzing employee location sensing technologies

Given the controversial nature of electronic monitoring, and in particular, employee location sensing technologies, a major challenge for organizations is balancing the expectations and preferences of employees with the security needs of the company. Stanton and Stam (2006) reported that monitoring systems to which employees strongly objected tended to be less effective, because employees expended time, effort, and creativity trying to "beat the system" (i.e., by finding ways to circumvent monitoring systems). Thus, before implementing such a system, it is important for planners to have a framework for analyzing location sensing technologies, so that the effects of a proposed system might be anticipated before implementation. To provide a framework for analyzing location sensing technologies, we review the organizational privacy literature (Bies, 1993; Stone and Stone, 1990) as it pertains to organizational monitoring (Alge et al., 2006; Ambrose et al., 1998).

2.1 Privacy

Privacy can be defined as the extent to which individuals believe they have control over their personal information and interaction with others (Stone and Stone, 1990). In other words, individuals have privacy when they are able to control information (Stone and Stone, 1990) and losing this sense of control can be viewed as an invasion of privacy (Alge, 2001). When it comes to location sensing technologies, Sovocool (2000) argued that many employees do not think organizations have a right to detailed information regarding how they traveled from point of pickup to point of delivery. This may be related to a loss of control that these employees have enjoyed in the past. Yet, courts have generally failed to affirm that employees have privacy rights protecting them from electronic monitoring or that electronic monitoring violates any privacy rights (Tabak and Smith, 2005). On a related note, Stanton and Stam (2006) confirmed that many managers hold beliefs consistent with those of the courts—i.e., that the firm has the right to monitor virtually any aspect of the job behavior. Having the right to do so, however, does not guarantee the wisdom of doing so, and thus it is important to understand employees' beliefs with respect to privacy.

According to Alge et al. (2006), privacy serves several basic human needs, including the need for control, belonging, and self-regard. In their identity-based model of organizational monitoring, employees' knowledge of monitoring triggers awareness of self, which in turn leads to a comparison of a standard. As employees engage in self-evaluation, they seek out information on how to evaluate their identity by looking at features of the monitoring system (Alge et al., 2006). Later, we review various features of electronic monitoring and discuss how these features have implications for privacy perceptions related to location sensing technologies.

Advanced notification: According to Bies (1993), offering advance notice for policies provides employees with a greater ability to control information about themselves, which in turn influences perceptions of invasion of privacy. For instance, Stone and Kotch (1989) found that attitudes toward drug testing are less negative when employees are provided with advance notice. In Ambrose and Alder's (2000) model of computer performance monitoring, they asserted that employees who receive advanced notification of monitoring will perceive the system as more ethical. Alge et al. (2006) argued that one dimension of monitoring richness is transparency—the degree to which monitoring systems are open and transparent to monitored employees. Transparency can affect privacy in both positive and negative ways. On the one hand, high transparency clarifies to employees what, when, and how they are being monitored, yet it can also undermine privacy by violating perceptions of information control by knowing that the organization is collecting all of this detailed personal information (Alge et al., 2006). However, silent or covert monitoring is often problematic because employees who find out about monitoring after implementation are more likely to see the monitoring as unfair (Hovorka-Mead et al., 2002). Indeed, Picard (1993) equated silent monitoring with spying and intruding on employee privacy. Thus, providing employees with adequate notice for the implementation of location technologies (thereby making the monitoring process more open and transparent) should reduce threats to privacy and possibly simultaneously enhance beliefs about fairness.

Purpose of monitoring: Stone and Stone (1990) argued that the extent to which individuals perceive a procedure as invasive depends on the purpose of the information collection. For instance, people are more likely to accept drug testing if there is a reasonable suspicion of drug use compared to random testing of employees (Stone and Bowden, 1989). Applying this notion to location sensing technologies, employees may find it less invasive to track locations of employees who are suspected of theft or breaking company policies compared to tracking any employee at any time.

Participation: Both Ambrose and Alder (2000) as well as Alge (2001) noted that participation in the design or implementation of electronic monitoring systems can enhance one's feelings of control. Indeed, Alge (2001) found that participants who were given the opportunity to voice concerns over monitoring had lower levels of invasion of privacy compared to those who did not have this same opportunity. Therefore, organizations which give employees the opportunity to provide input on the policies surrounding location sensing technologies may have lower perceptions of invasiveness.

Types of activities monitored: According to Stone and Stone (1990), the type of information being collected from individuals is likely to affect privacy perceptions. Ambrose et al. (1998) argued that electronic monitoring types vary in terms of the kinds of activities captured via monitoring, with computer monitoring (defined as computer hardware and software to record computer-driven activities) being generally confined to capturing work-related activities compared to surveillance (defined as visual equipment to observe employee behavior or track movements), which captures a much broader range of information (both work and nonwork-related activities). Ambrose et al. (1998) assert that monitoring personal, nonperformance-related activities may be considered unethical "because it ignores individuals' right to privacy" (p. 74). Indeed, McNall and Roch (2007) found that participants viewed surveillance devices as more invasive than computer monitoring devices, perhaps because they lead to a greater sense of uncontrollability due to the types of activities monitored.

Similarly, Bies (1993) claimed that the relevancy of information collected may play a key role in determining if it is viewed as an invasion of privacy. Tolchinsky et al. (1981) found that subjects reported greater levels of invasion of privacy when the data collected was based on personality information (irrelevant) as opposed to performance data (relevant). Moreover, Woodman et al.'s (1982) study of employees in five multinational companies revealed that employees regarded relevancy of personal information for organizational decision making as central to perceptions of invasion of privacy. Applying the notion of relevancy to electronic monitoring, Alge (2001) found that individuals who were exposed to electronic monitoring systems that monitored relevant activities reported lower levels of invasion of privacy compared to those exposed to systems capturing both relevant and irrelevant activities.

Stone and Stone (1990) noted that "concerns about organizational privacy should be exacerbated by attempts to collect information that seem unrelated or only tangentially related to a given purpose" (p. 364). Accordingly, organizations that use tracking devices to capture relevant, work-related activities may be perceived as less invasive.

Intensity/pervasiveness of monitoring: Smith et al. (1996) noted one major concern that individuals have with organizational information privacy practices is the amount of data being collected. Bies (1993) noted that the procedures used to collect information about workers' behavior may be considered psychologically intrusive to the individual, and therefore an invasion of privacy. For instance, Stone and Bowden (1989) conducted a study to see if the direct monitoring of providing a urine sample would impact whether an applicant accepted a job offer. Indeed, applicants were more likely to agree to a job offer if they were not monitored while giving a urine sample. Zweig and Webster examined monitoring technologies that enable geographically separated employees to determine if other colleagues are available for collaboration. They found that these awareness-monitoring systems can invade employees' psychological barriers. Participants reported a violation in interpersonal space, which drove perceptions of privacy and fairness (Zweig and Webster, 2002). According to Alge et al. (2006), high intensity and pervasiveness of monitoring can help managers provide accurate, detailed explanations for behavior but as more intimate details are collected, employees are more likely to experience privacy violations. Therefore, location sensing technologies that are higher in intensity and pervasiveness are more likely to be viewed as a greater threat to privacy.

Precision of monitoring: Location technologies may differ in the precision they offer for tracking movements. According to Griffin (2002), the accuracy of a position determined by GPS depends on the type of receiver, with handheld receivers having an approximately 10–20 m accuracy. It is possible that the precision of the monitoring device may influence perceptions of privacy. For instance, Zweig and Webster examined whether image clarity was related to privacy invasion. They found that a blurred image (i.e., a less precise image) to convey availability was related to lower perceptions of privacy invasion compared to a clear image (i.e., a more precise image) (Zweig and Webster, 2002).

Outcome of information disclosure: According to Bies (1993), the outcomes people receive may influence their perceptions of invasion of privacy. For example, employees react more negatively if the outcome of drug testing is termination rather than counseling (Stone and Kotch, 1989). Thus, employers who use location technologies to "catch" employees doing something wrong and use this information as the basis for termination may be perceived as more invasive. In fact, union officials are watching closely to make sure location-tracking devices are used to improve customer service rather than discipline drivers (Forelle, 2007), presumably so privacy rights are retained.

Target of monitoring: Many researchers have noted that monitoring systems can target individual employees or provide more general, unit-wide information where one particular employee is not identifiable (Alge et al., 2006; Ambrose and Alder, 2000). Stanton (2000) proposed that monitoring systems displaying aggregated performance records would be more satisfactory to workers. Likewise, Alge et al. (2006) argued that group based monitoring would be less threatening to a person's identity and privacy, thus leading employees to feel less vulnerable about a loss of personal information control. We would expect tracking devices that capture group-level data to be perceived as less invasive compared to those which capture individual-level data.

3 A preliminary study: employee reactions to locating sensing technologies

To examine some initial reactions to employee location sensing technologies, we asked participants to imagine themselves as an employee in a hypothetical organization. We provided participants with the following information:

> You work for Quality Logistics Inc. as a senior level associate. As a regular part of your job you must do quite a bit of local automobile travel, in some weeks as much as 100 miles per day with multiple stops. Because of this schedule, the company provides you with a company car. Company policy requires that this car must be used only for company purposes, not for personal driving/travel.

Next, participants read about a policy change instituted by management. Participants are told that the company car will be fitted with a locating device allowing the position of the car to be monitored and tracked. In addition, keys to the car and the various sales and marketing kits will be tagged with RFID tags to facilitate inventory tracking of these items.

In the notification condition, half of participants were told that management announced the policy change three months ago (advance notice), whereas the other half of participants read that management made this announcement yesterday (short notice). In the precision condition, half of the participants were told that the locating device on the company car could allow the position of the car to be monitored and tracked to a precision of roughly one city block (high precision) compared to a five-mile radius (low precision). Lastly, in the target of monitoring condition, participants were told that management is planning on aggregating the data for each department (group monitoring) or each individual (individual monitoring).

The following hypotheses will be tested:

Hypothesis 1a. Participants receiving advance notice will perceive monitoring as less invasive compared to short notice.

Hypothesis 1b. Participants receiving advance notice will be more satisfied with monitoring compared to short notice.

Hypothesis 1c. Participants receiving advance notice will have more positive reactions to monitoring compared to short notice.

Hypothesis 2a. Participants monitored by a low precision device will perceive monitoring as less invasive compared to a high precision device.

Hypothesis 2b. Participants monitored by a low precision device will be more satisfied with monitoring compared to a high precision device.

Hypothesis 2c. Participants monitored by a low precision device will have more positive reactions to monitoring compared to a high precision device.

Hypothesis 3a. Participants monitored as a group will perceive monitoring as less invasive compared to being monitored as an individual.

Hypothesis 3b. Participants monitored as a group will be more satisfied with monitoring compared to being monitored as an individual.

Hypothesis 3c. Participants monitored as a group will have more positive reactions to monitoring compared to being monitored as an individual.

3.1 Participants

Four thousand participants were drawn from a provider of Internet-based research volunteers. Of these 4000, 329 responses were obtained. After filtering out partial and duplicate responses, 225 usable cases remained, for an effective response rate of 5.6%. Participants included a range of ages from 18 to 82, with a mean age of 35.4 years and a standard deviation of 11.1 years. All participants had self-reported as being employed full time or part time at the time when they registered with the Internet research service. The sample consisted of even proportions of males and females (50.4% female).

3.2 Measures

All self-report scales were rated on a 5-point Likert-type scale ranging from 1 (*Strongly disagree*) to 5 (*Strongly agree*) (see Appendix for a full list of items used in the study).

Invasion of privacy: Invasion of privacy was measured using a nine-item scale derived from Alge (2001). Cronbach's alpha was .96. A sample item is "I feel like the manner in which I will be evaluated is an invasion of my privacy."

Satisfaction with monitoring: A three-item measure of satisfaction with monitoring from Alder (1999) was adapted for the current study. Cronbach's alpha was .83. A sample item is "I am satisfied with the way the company monitors my activities."

Reactions to monitoring: A six-item measure of general reactions to monitoring was created by the authors. Cronbach's alpha was .90. A sample item is "I think the use of this type of monitoring device is acceptable for this type of job."

4 Results

Given the early stage, exploratory nature of this research, we used a liberal significance criterion of $p < .10$. Thus all results should be considered

Table 1
Summary of four conditions

		Precision (low or high): the level of precision that the location sensing device captures
Target (individual or group): the extent to which the location sensing device targets individual employees or provides more general, unit-wide information	Low precision individual	High precision individual
	Low precision group	High precision group

Table 2
Descriptive statistics for dependent variables

		M	SD	1	2	3
1.	Invasion of privacy	3.64	1.09		−.77**	−.81**
2.	Satisfaction with monitoring	2.51	1.05		—	−.80**
3.	Reactions toward monitoring	2.82	.97			—

**p < .01.

preliminary and subject to further confirmation. We began our analysis by considering the manipulation checks for the three factors. The manipulation check for precision was statistically significant, F (1, 217) = 11.0, $p < .01$. Similarly, the manipulation check for target was statistically significant, F (1, 217) = 3.71, $p < .10$. However, the manipulation check for notice was not statistically significant. Thus, participants did not adequately distinguish between the scenario stimuli for advance notice and short notice. Given the problem with this manipulation, we dropped it from further analysis and were unable to test Hypotheses 1a–c. We conducted an analysis of variance (ANOVA) for each of our remaining hypotheses. See Table 1 for a summary of the four conditions. See Table 2 for the means, standard deviations, and intercorrelations of the dependent variables.

4.1 Invasion of privacy

We tested perceptions of privacy invasion and the results of the ANOVA revealed no significant interaction. There was not a significant main effect for precision, thus Hypothesis 2a was not supported. There was, however, a significant main effect for target, F (1, 221) = 4.31, $p < .05$. In accordance with Hypothesis 3a, participants perceived group monitoring as less invasive ($M = 3.44$, $SD = 1.18$) than individual monitoring ($M = 3.76$, $SD = 1.01$).

4.2   Satisfaction with monitoring

Next we tested satisfaction with the new monitoring system and once again, the results of the ANOVA indicated that there was no significant interaction. There was a significant main effect for precision, $F(1, 220) = 3.52$, $p < .10$. In support of Hypothesis 2b, satisfaction with "low precision" monitoring was higher ($M = 2.63$, $SD = 1.04$) than "high precision" monitoring ($M = 2.37$, $SD = 1.06$). There was also a significant main effect for target, $F(1, 220) = 4.00$, $p < .10$. In accord with Hypothesis 3b, satisfaction with aggregate location sensing monitoring was higher ($M = 2.70$, $SD = 1.13$) than individual location sensing monitoring ($M = 2.40$, $SD = 1.00$).

4.3   Reactions to monitoring

In testing reactions to monitoring, there was no significant interaction and no significant main effect for precision (thus, Hypothesis 2c was not supported). Yet, there was a significant main effect for target, $F(1, 220) = 5.93$, $p < .05$. In support of Hypothesis 3c, reactions were more positive for group monitoring ($M = 3.02$, $SD = 1.01$) than individual monitoring ($M = 2.70$, $SD = .93$).

5   Discussion

As location sensing technologies become more widely deployed, organizations need guidance on how to use these devices to optimize benefits but at the same time preserve employees' privacy rights. The benefits to organizations include better control over valuable assets such as vehicles, possible improvements to productivity for employees who work in the field, and avoidance of liability through accurate assessment of the locations and activities of personnel and assets. These benefits must be balanced against the essential rights of employees to a measure of autonomy in the professional sphere and basic human needs for occasional seclusion—two of the basic ingredients of privacy. As one writer noted, "we are moving into a world where your location is going to be known all times by some electronic device. It's inevitable. So we should be talking about its consequences before it's too late" (Harmon, 2003, p. 1). Safeguards are needed to ensure that location technologies minimize threats to privacy (Forelle, 2007).

Our preliminary study provides a useful first view for understanding how individuals react to employee location sensing technologies but results should be interpreted cautiously given our liberal significance criterion of $p < .10$. As predicted, when monitoring data was aggregated to the departmental level, individuals perceived fewer threats to privacy, more satisfaction with monitoring, and more favorable reactions toward monitoring in general. Moreover, participants were more satisfied with monitoring when it was less precise compared to more precise. Surprisingly, precision was not related to privacy perceptions or general reactions toward monitoring, although given the limits of out study strategy, these may be methodological artifacts and should be subjected to further analysis.

As with any study, several limitations exist that readers should consider when interpreting the results. The use of written scenarios about the introduction of a new location sensing technology system instead of actually experiencing the monitoring first-hand is likely to reduce psychological realism. Yet, according to Eddy et al. (1999), the results of scenario studies tend to *underestimate* the impact of procedural variables in real-world contexts. Future research should investigate the relationship between location sensing devices and various reaction measures using a realistic simulation or actual field settings. In addition, more research is needed to test other features offered in our framework of location sensing (e.g., purpose of location monitoring, personnel outcomes related to the use of location monitoring data) and assess the impact of these characteristics on a variety of employee reaction measures.

5.1 Recommendations for implementing employee location sensing technologies

Based on previous electronic monitoring research, along with the results from our initial study, we can offer several recommendations for organizations that are considering implementing employee location sensing technologies. Before the implementation of new monitoring policies, Alge et al. (2006) urged organizations to conduct readiness assessments to better understand employee preferences related to monitoring. In addition, soliciting opinions and giving employees some say or "voice" in the design of the monitoring system is likely to yield higher perceptions of fairness (Alge, 2001).

Organizations should also consider need or mandate for the various types of information collected by location sensing technology, and should request employee input on the perceived intensity and pervasiveness of each type of data the organization proposes to collect. Canoni (2004) as well as Stone and Stone (1990) suggested imposing procedural restrictions on monitoring, such as monitoring activities only during work hours, to combat the notion of "big brother is watching" that employees may take away from more pervasive procedures. One possible way to limit perceived intensity of monitoring is to give employees some level of control over monitoring, such as the ability to shut down tracking features during lunch time, personal breaks, and after hours, as a means to protect privacy. In fact, some union officials have only approved of tracking device when these types of concessions have been made (Gruber, 2005b). Previous research demonstrates the positive impact of having the ability to turn monitoring devices off. For instance, Stanton and Barnes-Farrell (1996) found that participants who were given the ability to delay or prevent electronic monitoring indicated higher feelings of personal control, even when they did not actually use the feature. In examining the effects of being monitored for availability purposes, Zweig and Webster (2002) found that control over when awareness information was made available to others was significantly related to lower perceptions of privacy invasion.

Once a decision has been to implement a monitoring program, care should be given in how to effectively communicate the policy to employees. Canoni suggested that the employer's policies should advise employees that location sensing technologies exist within company vehicles, cell phones, and access cards (in addition to other types of electronic monitoring that may be used). The policy should also be clear on what information will and will not be collected with these technologies (Gruber, 2005b). Employees should actively sign off on their understanding of these policies and should be periodically reminded of the presence and use of the monitoring technologies (Stanton and Stam, 2006). Over time, companies should periodically and systematically review policies to see if changes are necessary (Stone and Stone, 1990).

Finally, organizations should provide training to educate supervisors on the various capabilities of location sensing technologies as well as appropriate and inappropriate uses of the technology. Alge et al. (2006) noted that managers will need assistance at developing monitoring competencies and training should be one way to accomplish this.

The inevitable advancement of electronic technologies, both in terms of sophistication and reductions in costs, ensures that new developments in location sensing will continue to emerge. These trends, together with the growing sophistication of cellular communication networks throughout the world, suggest that organizational capabilities for tracking the location of people and material will continue to grow, and probably at an accelerating pace. By adapting best practices from earlier generations of monitoring technologies and engaging employees in the processes surrounding deployment of new location sensing technologies, organizations can ensure that they obtain the expected benefits from the enhanced capabilities that new location sensing systems will permit.

Acknowledgment

Portions of this research were supported by the StudyResponse Center for Online Research at Syracuse University.

Glossary

Electronic monitoring: Electronic technologies used to collect, store, analyze, and report the actions or performance of workers.

Global positioning system (GPS): An international location sensing standard based on precisely timed signals sent from a network of satellites.

Radio frequency identification devices (RFID): Any of a variety of electronic tags that permit short range (centimeters to tens of meters), nonline of sight sensing of tagged devices.

References

Aguilar, A., W. van der Putten, F. Kirrane (2006). Positive patient identification using RFID and wireless networks, in: *HISI 11th Annual Conference and Scientific Symposium*, Dublin, Ireland.

Aiello, J. (1993). Computer-based work monitoring: electronic surveillance and its effects. *Journal of Applied Social Psychology* 23, 499–507.

Alder, G.S. (1999). *Computer performance monitoring and fairness: The role of feedback*, Unpublished doctoral dissertation, University of Colorado, Boulder.

Alder, S. (1998). Ethical Issues in electronic performance monitoring: a consideration of deontological and teleological perspectives. *Journal of Business Ethics* 17, 729–743.

Alge, B. (2001). Effects of computer surveillance on perceptions of privacy and procedural justice. *Journal of Applied Psychology* 86, 797–804.

Alge, B.J., J. Greenberg, C.T. Brinsfield (2006). An identity-based model of organizational monitoring: integrating information privacy and organizational justice. *Research in Personnel and Human Resources Management* 25, 71–125.

Ambrose, M., S. Alder, T. Noel (1998). Electronic performance monitoring: a consideration of rights, in: M. Schminke (ed.), *Managerial Ethics: Moral Management of People and Process*. Lawrence Erlbaum Associates, Mahwah, NJ.

Ambrose, M.L., G.S. Alder (2000). Designing, implementing and utilizing computerized performance monitoring: enhancing organizational justice. *Research in Personnel and Human Resources Management* 18, 187–219.

American Management Association and The ePolicy Institute (2005). Workplace Monitoring and Surveillance. Available at http://www.amanet.org/press/amanews/ems05.htm

Anthony, D., D. Kotz, T. Henderson (2007). Privacy in location-aware computing environments. *Pervasive Computing* 6(4), 64–72.

Balkovich, E., T., Bikson, G. Bitko (2005). 9 to 5: Do You Know If Your Boss Knows Where You Are? Case Studies of Radio Frequency Identification Usage in the Workplace. Available at http://www.rand.org/pubs/technical_reports/2005/RAND_TR197.pdf

Bies, R.J. (1993). Privacy and procedural justice in organizations. *Social Justice Research* 6, 69–86.

Cangialosi, A., J.E. Monaly, S.C. Yang (2007). Leveraging RFID in hospitals: patient life cycle and mobility perspectives. *Communications Magazine, IEEE* 45(9), 18–23.

Canoni, J. (2004). Employers are using location awareness technology to keep track of their employees. Available at http://www.nixonpeabody.com/publications_detail3.asp?ID = 486

Eddy, E., D. Stone, E. Romero-Stone (1999). The effects of information management policies on reactions to human resource information systems: an integration of privacy and procedural justice perspectives. *Personnel Psychology* 52, 335–358.

Forelle, C. (2007). GPS units keep tabs on employee loafing. Available at http://www.careerjournal.com/hrcenter/articles/20040603-forelle.html

Griffin, D. (2002). How does global position system (GPS) work? Available at http://www.pocketgpsworld.com/howgpsworks.php

Gruber, J. (2005a). RFID and workplace privacy. Available at http://www.workrights.org/issue_electronic/RFIDWorkplacePrivacy.html

Gruber, J. (2005b) On your tracks: GPS tracking in the workplace. Available at http://www.workrights.org/issue_electronic/NWI_GPS_Report.pdf

Halamka, J. (2006). Early experiences with positive patient identification. *Journal of Healthcare Information Management* 20(1), 25–27.

Harmon, A. (2003). Lost? Hiding? Your Cellphone is Keeping Tabs. Available at http://query.nytimes.com/gst/fullpage.html?res = 9A02E0DD133FF932A15751C1A9659C8B63

Hovorka-Mead, A.D., W.H. Ross, T. Whipple, M.B. Renchin (2002). Watching the detectives: seasonal student employee reactions to electronic monitoring with and without advance notification. *Personnel Psychology* 55, 329–362.

Kightlinger, C. (2004). Schools Looking to the Skies to Track Buses. Available at http://www2.indystar.com/articles/8/135547-9318-P.html

Lane, F.S. (2003). *The Naked Employee*. AMACOM, New York.

McLaughlin, M. (1989). An attempt to tether the electronic workplace. *New England Business* October, pp. 13–16.

McNall, L.A., S.G. Roch (2007). Effects of electronic monitoring types on perceptions of procedural justice, interpersonal justice, and privacy. *Journal of Applied Social Psychology* 37, 658–682.

Nebeker, D.M., C.B. Tatum (1993). The effects of computer monitoring, standards and rewards on work performance, job satisfaction and stress. *Journal of Applied Social Psychology* 23, 508–536.

Nussbaum, K., V. duRivage (1986). Computer monitoring: mismanagement by remote control. *Business and Society Review* Winter, 16–20.

Picard, C. (1993). Working under an electronic thumb. *Training* 47–51.

Rieback, M.R., B. Crispo, A.S. Tanenbaum (2006). The evolution of RFID security. *IEEE Pervasive Computing* 5(1), 62–69.

Rogers, K.S., M.J. Smith, P.C. Sainfort (1990). Electronic performance monitoring, job design, and psychological stress, in: *Proceedings of the Human Factors Society 34th Annual Meeting*, Orlando, FL.

Smith, H.J., S.J. Milberg, S.J. Burke (1996). Information privacy: measuring individuals' concerns about organizational practices. *MIS Quarterly* 20, 167–196.

Smith, M., P. Carayon, K. Sanders, S.Y. Lim, D. LeGrande (1992). Employee stress and health complaints in jobs with and without electronic performance monitoring. *Applied Ergonomics* 23, 17–27.

Songini, M. (2008). Wisconsin law bars forced RFID implants. Available at http://www.computerworld.com/action/article.do?command = viewArticleBasicandarticleId = 1112. Retrieved on April 24.

Sovocool, D.R. (2000). GPS: Charting new terrain: legal issues related to GPS-based navigation and location systems. Available at http://www.thelen.com/index.cfm?section = articlesandfunction = ViewArticleandarticleID = 443

Stanton, J.M. (2000). Reactions to employee performance monitoring: framework, review, and research directions. *Human Performance* 13, 85–113.

Stanton, J.M., J.L. Barnes-Farrell (1996). Effects of electronic performance monitoring on personal control, task satisfaction, and task performance. *Journal of Applied Psychology* 81, 738–745.

Stanton, J.M., K.R. Stam (2006). *The Visible Employee*. Information Today, Medford, NJ.

Stone, D.L., C. Bowden (1989). Effects of job applicant drug testing practices on reactions to drug testing, in: F. Hoy (ed.), *Academy of Management Best Paper Proceeding*. Academy of Management, Atlanta, GA.

Stone, D.L., D. Kotch (1989). Individuals' attitudes toward organizational drug testing policies and practices. *Journal of Applied Psychology* 3, 518–521.

Stone, E.F., D.L. Stone (1990). Privacy in organizations: theoretical issues, research findings and protection mechanisms. *Research in Personnel and Human Resources Management* 8, 349–411.

Tabak, F., W.P. Smith (2005). Privacy and electronic monitoring in the workplace: a model of managerial cognition and relational trust development. *Employee Responsibilities and Rights Journal* 17, 173–189.

Tolchinsky, P., M. McCuddy, J. Adams, D. Ganster, R. Woodman, H. Fromkin (1981). Employee perceptions of invasion of privacy: a field simulation experiment. *Journal of Applied Psychology* 66, 308–313.

U.S. Congress (1987). *Office of Technology Assessment, the Electronic Supervisor: New Technology, New Tensions.* U.S. Government Printing Office, Washington, DC.

Waxer, C. (2006). Satellite plumbing. Available at http://money.cnn.com/magazines/fsb/fsb_archive/2006/02/01/8368208/index.htm

Werb, J., C. Lanzl (1998). Designing a positioning system for finding things and people indoors, spectrum. *IEEE* 35(9), 71–78.

Woodman, R.W., D.C. Ganster, J. Adams, M.C. McCuddy, P.D. Tochinsky, H. Fromkin (1982). A survey of employee perceptions of information privacy in organizations. *Academy of Management Journal* 25, 647–663.

Zweig, D., J. Webster (2002). Where is the line between benign and invasive? An examination of psychological barriers to the acceptance of awareness monitoring systems. *Journal of Organizational Behavior* 23, 605–633.

Suggested readings

Boreham, P., R. Parker, P. Thompson (2006). *New Technology @ Work.* Routledge, New York.

Hearn, J., T. Heiskanan (2003). *Information Society and the Workplace: Spaces, Boundaries and Agency.* Routledge, New York.

Taras, D.G., J.T. Bennett, A.M. Townsend (2004). *Information Technology and the World of Work.* Transaction Publishers, New Brunswick.

Weckert, J. (2004). *Electronic Monitoring in the Workplace: Controversies and Solutions.* Idea Group Publishing, Hershey, PA.

Online resources

http://www.workrights.org/issue_electronic/RFIDWorkplacePrivacy.html
http://www.workrights.org/issue_electronic/NWI_GPS_Report.pdf
http://www.rand.org/pubs/technical_reports/2005/RAND_TR197.pdf
http://www.amanet.org/press/amanews/ems05.htm

Appendix

All self-report scales were rated on a 5-point Likert-type scale ranging from 1 (*Strongly disagree*) to 5 (*Strongly agree*).

Satisfaction with Monitoring (Alder, 1999)
1. Given the opportunity, I would change the way the company monitors my activities.[a]
2. I am satisfied with the way the company monitors my activities.
3. I feel good about having the company monitor my activities.

General Reactions (developed by the authors)
1. If the job were appropriate, I would find this company an acceptable place to work.
2. If the job were appropriate, I would not want to work for this organization.[a]
3. I feel like this tracking device is appropriate for determining my location.
4. I feel that I would like this tracking device.
5. I think the use of this type of monitoring device is acceptable for this type of job.
6. My general attitude toward the use of this monitoring device is negative.[a]

Invasion of Privacy (Alge, 1999)

1. I feel that some of the monitoring that occurred was an invasion of my privacy.
2. Some of my time did not need to be monitored.
3. I feel like the manner in which I was evaluated was an invasion of my privacy.
4. I feel that the methods used to monitor my performance were invasive.
5. I am not at all happy about the fact that my activities were monitored.
6. I feel uncomfortable with the way in which some of my time was monitored.
7. The methods used to monitor my activities make me feel uneasy.
8. I feel that some of the information being electronically collected is none of anybody's business but my own.
9. To some extent, I feel like my privacy has been invaded.

[a]Reverse coded items.

Part VI
Economic Aspects of Security

Rao & Upadhyaya, Eds., *Handbooks in Information Systems, Vol. 4*
Copyright © 2009 by Emerald Group Publishing Limited

Chapter 18

Security Investment and Information Sharing for Defenders and Attackers of Information Assets and Networks

Kjell Hausken

Faculty of Social Sciences, University of Stavanger, N-4036 Stavanger, Norway

Abstract

Six main focus points for firms in cyber war are the efficient use of resources, information sharing, internal controls, technical improvements, behavioral/ organizational improvements, and cyber security insurance. This chapter overlays an economic framework on these points. Two firms invest in security and share information to protect their assets that are under attack by a strategic attacker. The attacker is subject to an income effect, which influences its resources, and substitutes its attack optimally across the two firms. The firms' and attacker's strategic decisions and profits depend on the income and substitution effects, and on the interdependence between firms, which can be positive or negative. Each firm invests maximally in security when the average attack level is 25% of the firm's required rate of return. Increasing interdependence between firms causes free riding in security investment, which means that each firm hopes to cash in on the other firm's security investment. A firm increasing its security investment usually benefits from the substitution effect, which shifts some of the attack over to other firms. The substitution effect is not conducive to information sharing. Information sharing and security investment for two firms are inverse U shaped in the aggregate attack. A social planner imposes unreasonably high levels for the variable it controls, and firms respond by free riding in the variable they control. A social planner moving first and controlling both information sharing and security investment is collectively beneficial and may deter the attack. Four kinds of marginal returns to security investment are discussed and how these depend on the asset vulnerabilities.

1 Introduction

The Internet revolution has intensified cyber warfare. The number of security breaches increases exponentially (www.cert.org). Firms invest increasingly in security technology. Attackers act strategically and are increasingly motivated by financial gain. Fundamentally, firms in cyber war compete with each other and external intruders over assets. Six main focus points are the efficient use of resources, information sharing, internal controls, technical improvements, behavioral/organizational improvements, and cyber security insurance. This chapter focuses on how firms choose the optimal investment, how they are influenced by the income, interdependence, and substitution effects, how they allocate resources to defend assets and interlinked components, how they choose to share information with and without the influence of a social planner, and how attackers allocate resources between attacking assets under the various scenarios.

The main shortcomings of today's literature are that the external threat is usually considered to be fixed and immutable in quantity and quality, directed in a fixed and immutable manner against each firm, and does not depend on the kind of interaction between the firms. The interaction with other firms and attackers are essential when determining security investment. Attackers are as sophisticated in their attack as defenders are in their defense. Both sides act strategically, maximize profits, and account for costs. This chapter depicts cyber war between firms as strategic players on the one hand and the external threat phrased as a strategic player on the other hand. The warring sides adapt to each other. The resources available to the players, and their strategic choices, depend on all strategic choices and the nature of cyber war. The firms and the attacker wage war over the firms' assets.

Accounting for the strategic nature of cyber warfare means accounting for three effects, which have usually not been considered within the information security literature. The first is the income effect. It reduces the attacker's ability or willingness to conduct cyber war, through eliminating parts of the attacker's resource, or weakening the attacker's ability to convert resources into an attack. The second is the interdependence effect. Two firms are in varying degrees intertwined, dependent, and influenced by each other. Hence, one firm's security investment may benefit or be detrimental to other firms, and the attack on one firm may impact other firms. The third is the substitution effect. It causes the attacker to consider the firms' strategies and substitute into the most optimal and least costly attack allocation across the firms.

Attackers can be perceived as hackers or perpetrators intending to break through the security of firms to get access to assets. Attackers differ, many are unknown, and their skills and objectives differ. See Kjaerland (2005) for a classification of computer security incidents and attacker objectives.

Porter's (1980) competitor analysis, adopted to information security by Gordon and Loeb (2001), is one way of accounting for the strategic nature of cyber warfare. They suggest identifying one's competitors, and thereafter determining the type of information about one's firm that competitors would find most beneficial. Gordon and Loeb (2003) developed a formal model of how two rivals invest in competitor analysis and information security. Competitor analysis enables a firm to capture a portion of the market's profits currently earned by the rival. Information security is a way of reducing the threat that the firm's information system will be breached by the firm's rival or by others. Firms apply competitor analysis when adjusting the size and kind of security investments to protect assets, and attackers apply competitor analysis when adjusting their attacks to appropriate assets.

Firms' security investments are also influenced by law. Not being law-abiding is costly. The economics of information security means adhering especially to the 2002 Sarbanes–Oxley Act (SOX). Bagby (2005) suggested that a confluence of SOX, privacy law, national and institutional security, and trade secrecy, reinforcingly place pressures for internal control progress on various functions within firms and across industries and professions. Control systems are the key security methods for information assets, which are pathways to other assets. An alternative viewpoint presented by Dhillon et al. (2004, p. 551) is "that organisations which focus exclusively on technical and formal control measures in their systems fall short of protecting their resources." They propose "that organizations should focus more on the pragmatic control measures" "related to good management practices and management communication."

From an economic point of view, one can argue that firms abide by formal control requirements directed by law if the benefits of such compliance exceed the costs. This is satisfied when the fines and sanctions for noncompliance are large. Firms abide by the informal, pragmatic, and other control requirements directed by culture, custom, good management practices, and other concerns if the benefits are larger than the costs. For example, firms' assets are reduced through loss of reputation and customers, which may follow from noncompliance. Firms do not invest in security when the required rate of return is lower than the average level of attack, or the threat is overwhelming. Then normal control requirements do not dictate investment, and pragmatic control measures may or may not exist. Formal and informal control measures, and attackers, can have the same impact. The reason is that firms' assets can be reduced when firms invest insufficiently in security, which may mean not complying with the control measures, or not successfully preventing attackers from appropriating their assets.

The security of an interlinked information system depends on the strategies for security investment and information sharing chosen by all actors. Illustrating the role of multiple actors is a key objective of this chapter. Examples of actors involved in information systems are those that generate and maintain it, those that are players in it, those that run it or attempt to administer or regulate it, those that are affected by it and attempt to affect it in return, those that attempt to use it to their advantage, those that attempt to reshape it, and those that attempt to shut it down.

Section 2 gives an overview of the field. Relevant literature is provided and systematized as a timeline in a table. A figure is provided as a framework for the chapter. The figure shows two firms protecting one asset each, and one attacker seeking to attack these two assets. The firms choose security investment and information sharing. The figure shows how the income, interdependence, and substitution effects operate within the framework. Section 3 develops mathematically a benchmark model with two firms and one attacker. Sections 4–6 present and discuss the income, interdependence, and substitution effects. It is shown how these influence security investment, information sharing, and profits for the firms and attacker. Section 7 analyzes information sharing. It is first shown how firms individually choose optimal information sharing and balance information sharing against security investment. Thereafter, a social planner is introduced which controls information sharing and security investment in a simultaneous game and a two period game. Section 8 considers returns to information security investment, and discusses four classes of return functions. Section 9 suggests future developments. Section 10 concludes the chapter.

2 An overview of the field

Anderson (2001) provided an early paper that influenced security people to think about information security from an economic perspective. The paper considers issues such as why software contains many bugs, why security mechanisms are difficult to manage, why government evaluation schemes lack in quality. An influential book on how to manage cyber security resources from an economic point of view, readable also for practitioners, was published by Gordon and Loeb (2006). In earlier work, Gordon and Loeb (2002) analyzed returns to security investment, referred to as the Gordon–Loeb model. Tanaka and Matsuura (2005) found empirical support for the work. Anderson and Moore (2006) considered the economics of information security, arguing that incentives are as important as technical design in achieving dependability. They discuss peer-to-peer systems, the optimal balance of effort by programmers and testers, why privacy gets eroded, the politics of digital rights management, bugs, spam, phishing, and law enforcement strategy. Hausken (2006b) considered the properties of alternative security breach functions. Cavusoglu et al. (2004b) developed a model for evaluating IT security investments accounting for the

IT security infrastructure. Cavusoglu et al. (2005) analyzed the value of intrusion detection systems in information technology security architecture.

The strategic behavior of attackers has earned increased analysis in recent years. Enders and Sandler (2003) and Hausken (2006a) considered the attackers' resource base phrased as an income effect. Enders and Sandler (2003), Lakdawalla and Zanjani (2002, p. 11), and Hausken (2006a) analyzed how attackers substitute attacks across targets, and Keohane and Zeckhauser (2003) considered substitutions across time. Kunreuther and Heal (2003) and Hausken (2006a) determined the impact of interdependence between firms.

Schenk and Schenk (2002) considered incentives for reporting security breaches, and Campbell et al. (2003) and Cavusoglu et al. (2004a) analyzed the cost and impact of security breaches. Security breaches and vulnerabilities are analyzed by Gordon and Loeb (2002, 2003), Gordon et al. (2006a), Hausken (2006b), Schenk and Schenk (2002), and Tanaka et al. (2005). Schechter and Smith (2003) considered the benefits of sharing information to prevent information security breaches. Choi et al. (2005) and Nizovtsev and Thursby (2005) considered incentives to disclose security flaws and provided the appropriate patches. Kannan and Telang (2005) considered the market for software vulnerabilities, and Arora et al. (2006) considered the impact of patching on software quality through selling first and fixing later. Png et al. (2006) considered how end-users interact with each other and with hackers assuming a continuum of user types. Users' effort in fixing depends on hackers' targeting and vice versa. Ghose (2007) considered information disclosure and regulatory compliance, Kannan et al. (2007) provided an empirical analysis of market reactions to information security breach announcements, Axelson (2007) analyzed security design with investor private information, and Garcia and Horowitz (2007) addressed game-theoretically the economic motivations for security investments and suggested a possible market failure with underinvestment.

Gal-Or and Ghose (2003) analyzed how market characteristics affected information sharing and security investment, which in turn affected demand and costs. Gal-Or and Ghose (2005) presented a two-stage model where firms choose security investment and information sharing in the first stage, and they compete by choosing prices as their strategies in the second stage. They focused on demand side effects, which highlight the strategic implication of competition in the product market. Gordon et al. (2003) focused on the cost side effects of how security breaches and information sharing affects the overall level of security. They show that free riding may cause under-investment in security. The free-rider dilemma is further analyzed by Anderson (2001), Varian (2002), and Hausken (2002).

The free-rider dilemma expresses a tension between individual and collective rationality where individual firms suffer low profit since they cannot jointly commit to strategies that would benefit them collectively.

Free riding is especially common for information sharing and has been analyzed by Hausken (2007) linked to social welfare (joint profit). Each firm prefers to receive information from other firms, but is reluctant to provide information, for example, about security breaches to other firms since it then suffers information leakage costs and possibly bad reputation. The implication is that each firm does not provide information, or only to a limited degree. This places both firms at a strategic disadvantage relative to the attacker. A social planner aimed at maximizing social welfare for all firms may be able to commit the two firms to share information with each other. If successful, this may prevent the free-rider dilemma, and the firms may become better equipped to protect their assets against the attacker.

Hausken (2008) considered information security and networks, Bodin et al. (2008) considered information security and risk management, and Anderson and Choobineh (2008) considered enterprise information security strategies, Hui et al. (2008) considered the economics of shareware, and Katos and Patel (2008) developed a partial equilibrium view on security and privacy. The timeline for the development of some key issues is shown in Table 1. Section 3 considers a benchmark model with two firms and one attacker. Sections 4–6 present the income, interdependence, and substitution effects. Section 7 analyzes information sharing. Section 8 considers returns to information security investment.

Figure 1 shows a framework we refer to as we develop this chapter. There are two firms i and j with assets r_i and r_j that they seek to defend. Firm i invests t_i in security and shares information s_i with firm i. The parameter γ scales the relative weight of t_i and s_j. Each firm enjoys contest success, and incurs investment expenditure and information leakage costs. ϕ_1, ϕ_2, and ϕ_3 are information leakage parameters. The attacker has resource R that is converted into cyber attacks $T_i + T_j$ against the two firms. c_i and c_j are unit costs of defense. C is the unit cost of attack. The attacker enjoys contest success, and incurs cyber attack expenditure. There is interdependence between firms expressed with α. The attacker is subject to an income effect, and substitutes optimally across the two attacks.

3   A benchmark model with two firms and one attacker

This section provides a reference point against which the subsequent sections are compared. Consider two firms with assets r_i and r_j. Two firms are sufficient to account for the kind of interaction we need between two strategic defenders. Each firm invests t_i at unit cost c_i in security to protect its asset. The attacker has a resource R that is transformed at unit cost C into the investment $T_i + T_j$ directed against the two assets. One attacker is sufficient to model the external threat as a strategic actor. Two firms and one attacker provide a benchmark general enough to predate the timeline in

Table 1
Timeline for the development of key issues

Year	Author	Contribution	Section
2001	Anderson (2001)	Information security from an economic perspective	3, 8
2002	Gordon and Loeb (2002)	Returns to security investment	8
	Schenk and Schenk (2002)	Incentives for reporting security breaches	7
	Lakdawalla and Zanjani (2002, p. 11)	Substitution effect for attacker	6
	Schenk and Schenk (2002)	Security breaches and vulnerabilities	3, 8
2003	Gordon et al. (2003)	Information sharing	7
	Gal-Or and Ghose (2003)	Information sharing	7
	Schechter and Smith (2003)	Information sharing	7
	Enders and Sandler (2003)	Income effect for attacker's resource	4
	Kunreuther and Heal (2003)	Interdependence between firms	5
	Enders and Sandler (2003)	Substitution effect for attacker	6
	Gordon and Loeb (2003)	Competitor analysis and information security	3, 8
	Campbell et al. (2003)	Cost and impact of security breaches	
	Keohane and Zeckhauser (2003)	Time substitution for attacker	6
2004	Cavusoglu et al. (2004a)	Cost and impact of security breaches	3, 8
	Cavusoglu et al. (2004b)	Security and infrastructure	3, 8
	Choi et al. (2005)	How vulnerabilities affect firms and consumers	3, 8
2005	Nizovtsev and Thursby (2005)	Incentives to disclose software vulnerabilities	7
	Cavusoglu et al. (2005)	Value of intrusion detection systems in information technology security architecture	3, 8
	Tanaka and Matsuura (2005)	Empirical support for Gordon and Loeb (2002)	8
	Kannan and Telang (2005)	Market for software vulnerabilities	3, 8
	Png et al. (2006)	End-users and hackers	3, 8
	Tanaka et al. (2005).	Security breaches and vulnerabilities	3, 8
	Gal-Or and Ghose (2005)	Information sharing	7
2006	Gordon and Loeb (2006)	Managing cyber security resources	3, 7, 8
	Anderson and Moore (2006)	Economics of information security	3, 8
	Hausken (2006a)	Income effect for attacker's resource	4
	Hausken (2006a)	Interdependence between firms	5
	Hausken (2006a)	Substitution effect for attacker	6
	Gordon et al. (2006a)	Security breaches and vulnerabilities	3, 8
	Arora et al. (2006)	Impact of patching on software quality	3, 8
	Hausken (2006b)	Returns to security investment	8

Table 1. (*Continued*)

Year	Author	Contribution	Section
2007	Hausken (2007)	Information sharing and social welfare	7
	Ghose (2007)	Information disclosure and regulatory compliance	7
	Kannan et al. (2007)	Market reactions to security breaches	3, 8
	Axelson (2007)	Security design and investor private information	3, 8
	Garcia and Horowitz (2007)	Security and market failure	3, 8
2008	Hausken (2008)	Information security and networks	3, 8
	Bodin et al. (2008)	Information security and risk management	3, 8
	Anderson and Choobineh (2008)	Enterprise information security strategies	3, 8
	Hui, Yoob, and Tam (2008)	Economics of shareware	3, 8
	Katos and Patel (2008)	Security and privacy	3, 8

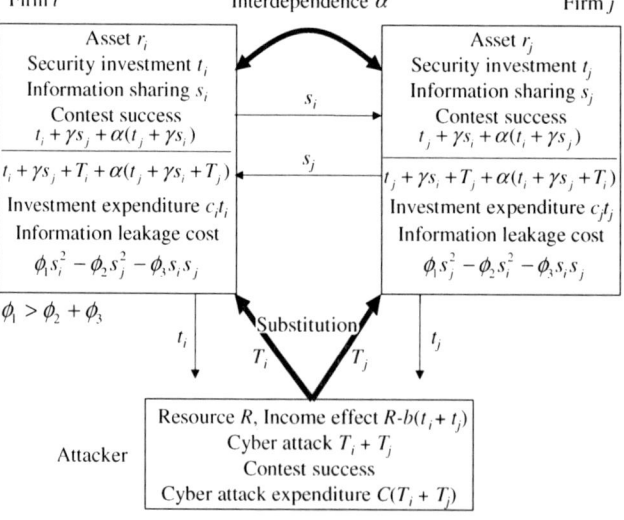

Fig. 1.   Framework for interaction between two firms.

Table 1. On the other hand, the treatment in this section intermingles with or is tangential to several of the topics in Table 1.

The defense consists in employing security experts, installing firewalls, applying encryption techniques, access control mechanisms, developing intrusion detection systems, etc. The attack consists in breaking through the defense to appropriate and get access to information or something else of value, which can be used to control fractions of the firms' assets. Each firm's profit is u_i, and the attacker's profit is U, expressed as

$$u_i = \frac{t_i}{t_i + T_i} r_i - c_i t_i, \quad U = \frac{T_i}{t_i + T_i} r_i + \frac{T_j}{t_j + T_j} r_j - C(T_i + T_j) \quad (1)$$

We refer to $t_i/(t_i + T_i)$ as the firm's contest success (Hausken, 2005), and $T_i/(t_i + T_i)$ as the attacker's contest success. In the symmetric case $r_i = r$ and $c_i = c$, the attacker attacks each asset equally much, $T_i = R/2C$. Solving the defender's first-order condition (second-order condition always satisfied) yields

$$t_i = \sqrt{\frac{R}{2C}} \left(\sqrt{\frac{r}{c}} - \sqrt{\frac{R}{2C}} \right), \quad u_i = c \left(\sqrt{\frac{r}{c}} - \sqrt{\frac{R}{2C}} \right)^2, \quad T_i = \frac{R}{2C},$$

$$U = \sqrt{\frac{2Rrc}{C}} - R \quad (2)$$

Eq. (2) shows that a firm invests in security technology when the required rate of return from security investment, r/c, exceeds the average attack level, $R/2C$. This means that each firm's asset value divided by its unit cost of investment is higher than the attacker's resource divided by the attackers unit cost of attack and divided by the number of firms. Not investing in security can occur against an overwhelming threat. For example, investing into security codes is not useful if attackers have developed means of breaking security codes. The attacker attacks if the product of a firm's asset value and unit cost is higher than the attacker's resource and unit cost divided by the number of firms.

Eq. (2) also shows (Hausken, 2006a) that a firm's security investment increases concavely in the required rate of return from security investment, and is inverse U shaped in the average attack level. The concavity accounts for diminishing marginal return on investment. Each firm invests maximally in security when the average attack level is 25% of the firm's required rate of return. The attacker poses an especially large threat when $R/2C = r/4c$, which yields $t_i = r/4c$ and $u_i = r/4$. The inverse U shape means that if the attacker's resource divided by its unit cost and divided by the number of firms is below 25%, then the attacker constitutes a limited threat and each firm can cut back on its security investment. This is realistic for small threats that require only modest effort. Sufficiently small threats can simply be ignored, not deserving security investment. Conversely, if the specified ratio is above 25%, then the attacker constitutes an overwhelming threat. Then a high expenditure to contain the threat is not cost effective, and each firm cuts somewhat back on its investment. If the threat by the attacker is especially overwhelming, each firm withdraws from security investment. This can occur if there is a technological breakthrough for how to break through security defenses, during times of economic hardship, when asset values are low, or for firms on the brink of bankruptcy.

These results can be compared with Gordon and Loeb's (2002) analysis, although they consider one firm in isolation. They consider one class of functions where the investment increases concavely in the vulnerability, and a second class that is inverse U shaped, and equals zero for a sufficiently high vulnerability. For computer viruses attacking Japanese firms, Tanaka and Matsuura (2005) and Tanaka et al. (2005) find support for the second class. Hausken's (2007) result is compatible with the second class if a firm is more vulnerable if the attacker's resource is higher, or the attacker's unit cost of attack is lower, or if fewer firms are under attack.

With this benchmark, we now proceed to analyze the income, interdependence, and substitution effects, and we thereafter focus more thoroughly on information sharing, and finally return to security investment and future developments.

4   The income effect

The attacker's resource is not necessarily fixed. It can sometimes be altered by the two firms, or external actors, or other factors. We refer to this as the income effect. The firms prefer the attacker's resource or income to be reduced in various ways. They thereby ensure that their assets are better preserved which benefit them, their shareholders, and their customers. In the timeline in Table 1, the income effect has been analyzed by Enders and Sandler (2003) related to terrorism, and by Hausken (2006a) related to information security.

Three main ways in which the attacker's resource or income to be reduced are as follows. The attacker's unit cost of attacking can be increased, the attacker's resource base can be decreased or eroded, and the attacker's resource, attack and scanning tools, and competence can be "frozen" or eliminated. This can be modeled such that the attacker has a lower resource $R - b(t_i + t_j)$, where b is an income reduction parameter that scales the sum of the security investments relative to the attacker's resource. In the symmetric case, the attacker attacks each asset with $T_i = (R - 2bt_i)/2C$. Naturally, a strong income effect, $R - 2bt_i < 0$, eliminates the external threat. This occurs when $R - 2bt_i < 0$. Hausken (2006a) shows that security investments decrease in the parameter b when the attacker's resource is low. Firms cash in on the income effect, and the attacker's income is eventually eliminated. When the resource is intermediate, the security investment is inverse U shaped as a function of *b*. Investing is expensive when the parameter is low, and the firms cash in when the parameter is large. When the attacker's resource is large, the security investment is zero when the parameter is low since the firms find investment against an overwhelming threat to be wasteful. Security investments increase when the parameter increases above a certain level.

For terrorism, Enders and Sandler (2003) refer to "freezing terrorist's assets" which "reduces their 'war chest' and their overall ability to conduct a campaign of terror." Various authorities can implement such freezing. Firms' security investments in antivirus, intrusion detection systems, firewalls, virtual private networks, and access control can have a similar impact, rendering parts of the attacker's resource as useless, obsolete, or removed from circulation. Many of today's cyber-security investments are less aggressive than for antiterrorism, particularly in terms of eliminating the attacker's resource, but this may change in the future. Firms and authorities increasingly confiscate hackers' computers, software, and hacking tools. Future efforts to combat cyber attacks may well turn out to be more aggressive than the current war on terror.

As an example, assume that the attacker has two tools labeled X and Y. Tool X runs through all combinations of 32-digit passwords and breaks into a system when the correct password is found. Tool Y has another function. Without security investment, the attacker can use both tools. If the firm abandons 32-digit passwords in favor of more sophisticated security, the reduced income situation for the attacker can be interpreted as follows. That tool X becomes useless can mean that the attacker's unit cost gets increased since he can now only use tool Y, that his resource gets reduced, and that parts of his resource (tool X) gets eliminated. For the latter interpretation, abandoning 32-digit passwords is not equivalent to confiscating tool X, but it might as well have been confiscated since it is now useless for the attacker.

Summing up, the attacker's resource or income can be reduced by increasing the attacker's unit cost of attack, eroding the attacker's resource base, and freezing or eliminating the attacker's tools and competence. A parameter is introduced which scales how effectively firms reduce the attacker's resource. The firms' security investment decreases in this parameter when the attacker's resource is low, is inverse U shaped when the resource is intermediate, and equals zero when the external threat is large. A strong income effect eliminates the external threat. In the next section, we proceed to analyze the interdependence effect.

5 The interdependence effect

Two firms may operate independently in different markets, share markets, be strong competitors, be interlinked through vertical integration upstream or downstream, outsourcing, or other arrangements. We refer to this as the interdependence effect, and express it with an interdependence parameter α. Examples are firms that frequently exchange products, services, information, personnel, and competence with each other, have developed elaborate contact surfaces against each other, and may have developed information flow systems that are somehow interlinked. In the timeline in Table 1, the interdependence effect has been analyzed by Kunreuther and Heal (2003) and Hausken (2006a). The objective of this section is to analyze the role of interdependence between firms, and the impact interdependence has on security investments by firms, the attack, and the profits of the firms and the attacker.

Assume that a firm's security is compromised by a hacker. If the firm is connected to other firms via a common network, its security can also be compromised through the network. If the firm's security is good, it is less likely to be hacked. But, if the security of other firms in the network is low, the likelihood of being hacked indirectly increases, especially if the linkages through the network are strong. Hence, a firm's security depends on the security investments by all the interconnected firms. Examples of interdependent systems are computer networks, the airline industry, computer networks, fire protection, theft protection, bankruptcy protection, and vaccinations (Kunreuther and Heal, 2003). Interdependence can be modeled by generalizing Eq. (1) to

$$
\begin{aligned}
u_i &= \frac{t_i + \alpha t_j}{t_i + T_i + \alpha(t_j + T_j)} r_i - c_i t_i, \\
U &= \frac{T_i + \alpha T_j}{t_i + T_i + \alpha(t_j + T_j)} r_i + \frac{T_j + \alpha T_i}{t_j + T_j + \alpha(t_i + T_i)} r_j - C(T_i + T_j)
\end{aligned}
\tag{3}
$$

where α is the interdependence parameter, $-1 \leq \alpha \leq 1$. Firm j's investment t_j gets channeled to degree α to firm i, and the attacker's investment T_j also gets channeled to degree α to firm i. When α is positive, this causes larger defense for each firm, but also larger attack against each firm. Firms may be so strongly interconnected that an attack on one is tantamount to an attack on the other. This occurs when $\alpha = 1 \cdot$ The interdependence may also be negative. This is likely in competitive and conflictful environments and means that a firm's security investment is detrimental to other firms. It occurs when one firm's increase in security investment redirects the attacker's attack to other firms and therefore reduces other firms' cyber war success. Assume that a firm succeeds through investment to attract another firm's Security Officer, which brings more defending experience to the firm. This causes increased cyber war success for the firm, and less cyber war success for the firm losing its security officer.

Solving the defender's first-order condition (second-order condition always satisfied) for the symmetric case yields

$$t_i = \sqrt{\frac{R}{2C}}\left(\sqrt{\frac{r}{c(1+\alpha)}} - \sqrt{\frac{R}{2C}}\right), \quad u_i = r - \frac{(2+\alpha)\sqrt{Rrc}}{\sqrt{2C(1+\alpha)}} + \frac{Rc}{2C},$$

$$T_i = \frac{R}{2C}, \quad U = \sqrt{\frac{2Rrc(1+\alpha)}{C}} - R \tag{4}$$

Eq. (4) shows that a firm's security investment decreases in α, with a positive second derivative. The firm's profit decreases in α, with a negative second derivative. The attacker attacks if $2rc(1+\alpha) > RC$, which means that higher interdependence increases the likelihood of attack. The attacker's profit increases in α, with a negative second derivative.

Eq. (4) further shows that a firm invests in security technology when the required rate of return from security investment, divided by $1+\alpha$, exceeds the average attack level, that is when $r/(c(1+\alpha)) > R/2C$. Comparing with Eq. (2), where $\alpha = 0$, a firm considerably exposed with high α through a network may find an interest in cutting back somewhat on its security investment, and instead encouraging other firms in the network to invest, or assessing how the network as a whole can be secured. This means that interdependence between firms introduces a free rider effect by which firms rely on other firms' investment to benefit themselves through the network. The firms' problem is that firms with weak security become convenient entry points for hackers seeking to compromise firms with good security within the network.

Summing up, the firms' security investment decreases as the interdependence between firms increases due to free riding. This means that each firm seeks to cash in on the other firm's security investment. The attacker benefits from this and hence more interdependence causes lower profits for the firms and higher profits for the attacker. Later in this chapter, we show how the interdependence effect plays an essential role to facilitate beneficial information sharing. But first we consider the substitution effect.

6   The substitution effect

If a firm becomes increasingly difficult to attack, a hacker may substitute to attack another firm. Hackers can be expected to tune in on firms with low security assessed comparatively with high asset value, and to substitute optimally across firms. Hence, a firm needs to be concerned not only about its own security, but also how its security compares with other firms. A firm's relative security determines how attractive it is as a target compared with other firms. We refer to this as the substitution effect. The substitution effect is particularly interesting related to how firms are different, and how attackers substitute back and forth between firms dependent on such differences. For equivalent firms, substitution is irrelevant since the attacker has no reason to treat them differently. In the timeline in Table 1, the substitution effect has been analyzed by Lakdawalla and Zanjani (2002, p. 11) and Enders and Sandler (2003) related to terrorism, by Keohane and Zeckhauser (2003) for attacker substitution across time, and by Hausken (2006a) related to information security.

Enders and Sandler (2003) exemplify for terrorism the substitution effect with "the installation of screening devices in US airports in January 1973" which "made skyjackings more difficult, thus encouraging terrorists to substitute into other kinds of hostage missions." Lakdawalla and Zanjani (2002, p. 11) used the term displacement that occurs when "protection by one target increases the terror investments directed at other targets." Three kinds of substitution are common. First, an attacker may adjust its attack optimally across firms dependent on the firms' characteristics. Second, when attacks and investments are multidimensional, an attacker may substitute across attack tools. If a firm has a good firewall, but invests modestly in security manpower, the attacker may exploit the inferior manpower situation. Third, attackers may substitute across time, keeping a low profile during times when security investment is rampant, awaiting times with more lax security. Substitutions of such kinds also apply for firms. Keohane and Zeckhauser (2003) find that the optimal control of terror stocks relies on both periodic cleanup and ongoing abatement. Economy of scale in reducing the cyber threat may make it optimal to do so only periodically.

Hausken (2006a) finds that an attacker does not attack the most valuable firm if a low unit cost of investment for that firm, which makes security investment cheap, ensures that it is too well protected. Furthermore, if one firm is x times more valuable than another firm, but has a unit cost of investment that is a fraction $1/x$ of the other firm's unit cost, the substitution effect causes, *ceteris paribus*, equally large attacks on the two firms. This occurs because the first firm's large security investment deters the attacker, which gains nothing by attacking the first firm more than the second. A firm increasing its security investment usually benefits from the substitution effect since it thereby shifts some of the attack over to other firms, and especially to valuable firms with comparatively low cyber security.

Summing up, an attacker substitutes its attack optimally across firms searching for high value combined with weak protection. By increasing its security, a firm may shift some of the attack over to other firms and hence the firm benefits from the substitution effect. We now proceed with information sharing between firms.

7 Information sharing

A firm compiles information about its security breaches, compiles a log history of events including successful and unsuccessful attacks, and develops exposure profiles for how its security handles the threats it has been and is subject to. In addition to security investment as a strategic variable, a firm can also choose to share information with other firms, as a strategic variable. To the extent information about security breaches, log histories, and exposure profiles become readily available across firms, the firms as a collective unit become better equipped to protect their assets, and it becomes more difficult for the attacker to attack the assets. In the timeline in Table 1, the main contributors to information sharing are Gordon et al. (2003), Gal-Or and Ghose (2003, 2005), Schechter and Smith (2003), and Hausken (2007). Authors have further focused on disclosures of various kinds.

For the income effect, information sharing, which is a strategic complement to security investment under some assumptions (Gal-Or and Ghose, 2003), may eliminate parts of the attacker's resource. This may occur if the reporting of security breaches allows for straightforward elimination as useless some of the attacker's attack tools. Similarly, Schechter and Smith (2003) showed that information sharing by firms can deter hackers.

The substitution effect is not conducive to information sharing since a firm that shares information with another firm risks information leakage, and additionally causes a benefit for the other firm. This makes the first firm a more vulnerable target, and the attacker substitutes its attack from the other firm toward the first firm. Aside from cases when confidentiality constrains, information sharing is usually collectively beneficial, and there is an obvious free rider dilemma.

When firms exist in isolation from each other, no firm has an incentive to share information, but would prefer to receive information. The classical free rider dilemma explains why information sharing does not occur, as also found by Gordon et al. (2003). The need to free ride becomes in principle even stronger for negative interdependence, since sharing information then gives a competitive advantage to the other firm that has direct negative impact on one's own defense.

Although security investment is directly costly for firms, information sharing is relatively costless to perform but carries costs through increased risk of information leakage. Information sharing can be modeled by generalizing Eq. (3) to

$$
u_i = \frac{t_i + \gamma s_j + \alpha(t_j + \gamma s_i)}{t_i + \gamma s_j + T_i + \alpha(t_j + \gamma s_i + T_j)} r_i - c_i t_i - (\phi_1 s_i^2 - \phi_2 s_j^2 - \phi_3 s_i s_j),
$$

$$
u_j = \frac{t_j + \gamma s_i + \alpha(t_i + \gamma s_j)}{t_j + \gamma s_i + T_j + \alpha(t_i + \gamma s_j + T_i)} r_j - c_j t_j - (\phi_1 s_j^2 - \phi_2 s_i^2 - \phi_3 s_i s_j),
$$

$$
U = \frac{T_i + \alpha T_j}{t_i + \gamma s_j + T_i + \alpha(t_j + \gamma s_i + T_j)} r_i
$$

$$
+ \frac{T_j + \alpha T_i}{t_j + \gamma s_i + T_j + \alpha(t_i + \gamma s_j + T_i)} r_j - C(T_i + T_j)
$$

(5)

Firm i shares (delivers) an amount s_i of information with firm j, and firm j shares s_j with firm i. Each firm succeeds better against the attacker when it receives information from the other firm. Hence, both s_j and t_i strengthen firm i's defense. This gives substitutability between own security investment and information received by the other firm, but allows for complementarity when the interdependence between firms is negative. The parameter γ scales how effective is information from the other firm relative to own security investment when regarding contesting the attacker's attack. With positive interdependence, $\alpha \gamma s_i$ strengthens firm j's competitive effort $t_j + \gamma s_i$ which gets channeled back to firm i moderated by α. With negative interdependence, γs_i strengthens firm j's competitive effort $t_j + \gamma s_i$, which has negative impact on firm i just as t_j has negative impact when $\alpha < 0$. Since information exchange is risky for both firms. Gal-Or and Ghose (2005, pp. 190–191) suggested leakage costs $g^i = \phi_1 s_i^2 - \phi_2 s_j^2 - \phi_3 s_i s_j$, where $\phi_1 \geq \phi_2 + \phi_3$. The parameter ϕ_1 is the unit cost of own leakage, ϕ_2 the unit benefit of the other firm j's leakage (which benefits firm i), and ϕ_3 the unit benefit of joint leakage.

In Eq. (5), the two firms have the free choice variables t_i, s_i, t_j, and s_j, and the attacker has the free choice variable T_i and T_i. Solving the six first-order conditions in the simultaneous symmetric game $r_i = r$, $c_i = c$, $t_i = t$, $s_i = s$, and $u_i = u$, implies

$$
t = \frac{Cr}{[C + c(1 + \alpha)]^2} - \frac{c\alpha\gamma^2}{2\phi_1 - \phi_3} \geq 0, \quad s = \frac{\alpha\gamma c}{2\phi_1 - \phi_3}, \quad T = \frac{cr(1 + \alpha)}{[C + c(1 + \alpha)]^2},
$$

$$
u = \frac{Cr(C + c\alpha)}{[C + c(1 + \alpha)]^2} + \frac{c^2\alpha\gamma^2[(2 - \alpha)\phi_1 + \alpha\phi_2 - (1 - \alpha)\phi_3]}{(2\phi_1 - \phi_3)^2},
$$

$$
w = 2u, \quad U = \frac{2c^2 r(1 + \alpha)^2}{[C + c(1 + \alpha)]^2}
$$

(6)

where w is social welfare (joint profit) for the two firms. Hence, information sharing increases in the interdependence, is zero with negative or no interdependence, and increases more in one's own than in the other firm's unit cost of security investment. That information sharing increases in the interdependence between firms is illustrated by the interdependent U.S. telecommunications industry, where information sharing is common. The high degree of competitiveness has been suggested as a tentative explanation of the need to share information, but competitiveness seems better characterized with negative interdependence, which reduces information sharing. A firm becomes vulnerable through information sharing that is not reciprocated, and may lose its competitive edge. Furthermore, a firm shifts some of its emphasis from security investment to information sharing as the interdependence, unit cost of security investment, effectiveness of information sharing, or unit benefit of joint leakage increase, or the unit cost of own leakage decreases. The firm with the highest unit cost of security investment is least inclined to free ride in information sharing.

Introducing a social planner that controls information sharing means replacing the two first-order conditions $\partial u_i/\partial s_i = 0$ and $\partial u_j/\partial s_j = 0$ with $\partial \hat{w}/\partial s_i = 0$ and $\partial \hat{w}/\partial s_j = 0$ where $\hat{w} = u_i + u_j$, and keeping the remaining four first-order conditions unchanged. Solving the simultaneous symmetric game yields

$$t = \frac{Cr}{(C + c(1 + \alpha))^2} - \frac{c(1 + \alpha)\gamma^2}{2(\phi_1 - \phi_2 - \phi_3)} \geq 0, \quad \hat{s} = \frac{(1 + \alpha)\gamma c}{2(\phi_1 - \phi_2 - \phi_3)},$$

$$T = \frac{cr(1 + \alpha)}{[C + c(1 + \alpha)]^2}, \quad u = \frac{C(C + c\alpha)}{(C + c(1 + \alpha))^2}r + \frac{c^2(1 - \alpha^2)\gamma^2}{4(\phi_1 - \phi_2 - \phi_3)}, \tag{7}$$

$$\hat{w} = 2u, \quad U = \frac{2c^2 r(1 + \alpha)^2}{[C + c(1 + \alpha)]^2}$$

Furthermore, the social welfare $\hat{w}$ where the social planner controls information, minus the social welfare w in the absence of a social planner is

$$\hat{w} - w = (1 - 2\alpha)\gamma^2 c^2/2\phi_1 \tag{8}$$

which is positive when $\alpha < 1/2$. This illustrates the importance of interdependence. Highly interdependent firms are collectively best off regulating their own information sharing without external interference in a simultaneous game. The reason is that positive interdependence makes information sharing directly beneficial since what gets delivered makes its way back to the firm through the interdependence. Conversely, firms with low interdependence are collectively best off adhering to the social planner's regulation of information sharing. In this case, the social planner prevents free riding.

Solving the corresponding two period symmetric game where the social planner determines s_i and s_j in the first period, whereas the firms and attacker determine t_i, t_j, T_i, and T_j in the second period, yields

$$t = \frac{Cr}{[C + c(1 + \alpha)]^2} - \frac{c\gamma^2}{2(\phi_1 - \phi_2 - \phi_3)} \geq 0, \quad \tilde{s} = \frac{\gamma c}{2(\phi_1 - \phi_2 - \phi_3)},$$

$$T = \frac{cr(1 + \alpha)}{[C + c(1 + \alpha)]^2}, \quad u = \frac{Cr(C + \alpha c)}{[C + c(1 + \alpha)]^2} + \frac{c^2\gamma^2}{4(\phi_1 - \phi_2 - \phi_3)}, \quad (9)$$

$$\tilde{w} = 2u, \quad U = \frac{2c^2 r(1 + \alpha)^2}{[C + c(1 + \alpha)]^2}$$

where $\tilde{s}$ is more than $1/\alpha$ times higher than the individually optimal information sharing in Eq. (6). This again illustrates how a social planner can facilitate information sharing in the absence of interdependence. The social welfare $\tilde{w}$ in the two-period game where the social planner determines s_i and s_j in the first period, minus the social welfare w in the absence of a social planner (in a simultaneous game) is

$$\tilde{w} - w = \frac{\gamma^2 c^2 [2\phi_1 - 2\alpha(\phi_1 - \phi_2 - \phi_3) - \phi_3]^2}{2(\phi_1 - \phi_2 - \phi_3)(2\phi_1 - \phi_3)^2} \quad (10)$$

which is always positive. Hence, regardless of interdependence, if the social planner moves first, the firms prefer it to do so. The two-period game is realistic when a credible social planner, such as a security based information sharing organization (SB/ISO), can commit firms in advance to information sharing. Commitment can occur through enforceable laws and procedures backed with sanctions and punishment for noncompliance. Such a social planner must usually have a long-term perspective, be well respected with a sustained reputation, so that its recommendations are taken seriously.

The 2002 SOX places strict requirements on firms. The future will likely show attempts to work incentives, inducements, and possibly requirements to share information, into laws and regulations. A possible further development is to require firms to invest in security. For example, certain security installations and procedures may be required. Firms may be required to invest a percentage of its profit into security, or to invest relatively to its size, type, or other characteristics. Security investment may alternatively be controlled by a budget imposed or dictated by someone else. For example, the budget may be determined by the CEO who may overrule the CISO, or determined by historic events, future goals, external conditions, shareholders, laws, regulations, etc. These examples imply that the social planner determines security investment. Letting the social planner control security investment means introducing $\partial w / \partial t_i = 0$ and $\partial w / \partial t_j = 0$, and keeping the remaining four first-order conditions from the individual optimization game unchanged. Solving the simultaneous game yields

$$t = \frac{Cr}{(C+c)^2} - \frac{c\alpha\gamma^2}{(1+\alpha)(2\phi_1 - \phi_3)} \geq 0, \quad \check{s} = \frac{\alpha\gamma c}{(1+\alpha)(2\phi_1 - \phi_3)},$$

$$T = \frac{cr}{[C+c]^2}, \quad u = \frac{C^2 r}{(C+c)^2} + \frac{c^2\alpha\gamma^2[(2+\alpha)\phi_1 + \alpha\phi_2 - \phi_3]}{(1+\alpha)^2(2\phi_1 - \phi_3)^2}, \qquad (11)$$

$$\check{w} = 2u, \quad U = \frac{2c^2 r}{[C+c]^2}$$

where $\check{s}$ is lower than the individually optimal information sharing in Eq. (6). Comparing t in Eqs. (11) and (6), the social planner dictates more security investment than when the firms optimize individually. This causes firms to free ride on information sharing, thus sharing less information with each other.

A more ambitious scenario is a social planner controlling both information sharing and security investment in a simultaneous game. This yields $\partial w/\partial s_i = 0$, $\partial w/\partial s_j = 0$, $\partial w/\partial t_i = 0$, and $\partial w/\partial t_j = 0$, whereas $\partial U/\partial T_i = 0$ and $\partial U/\partial T_j = 0$ for the attacker remain as before. This means that the firms have no free choice. Solving the simultaneous game yields

$$t = \frac{Cr}{(C+c)^2} - \frac{c\gamma^2}{2(\phi_1 - \phi_2 - \phi_3)} \geq 0, \quad \bar{s} = \frac{\gamma c}{2(\phi_1 - \phi_2 - \phi_3)} = \check{s},$$

$$T = \frac{cr}{[C+c]^2}, \quad u = \frac{C^2 r}{(C+c)^2} + \frac{c^2\gamma^2}{4(\phi_1 - \phi_2 - \phi_3)}, \qquad (12)$$

$$\bar{w} = 2u, \quad U = \frac{2c^2 r}{[C+c]^2}$$

where $\bar{s}$ happens to equal $\check{s}$ in Eq. (9). Hence, the social planner imposes more information sharing than the firms would individually choose, but less than a social planner that controls only information sharing. In the latter case, the social planner compensates for not controlling security investment, extracting unreasonably high information sharing, and the firms respond by free riding on security investment. This shows how a social planner with reduced power may exploit the subset of instruments it controls, and firms may respond suboptimally in their choice of the set of instruments they control.

The most ambitious scenario for a social planner is to control all instruments in a two-period game where the social planner moves first and the attacker moves second. Solving the two-period game yields

$$t = \frac{Cr}{4c^2} - \frac{c\gamma^2}{2(\phi_1 - \phi_2 - \phi_3)} \geq 0, \quad \widehat{s} = \frac{\gamma c}{2(\phi_1 - \phi_2 - \phi_3)} = \bar{s} = \tilde{s},$$

$$T = \frac{(2c - C)r}{4c^2} \geq 0, \quad u = \frac{Cr}{4c} + \frac{c^2\gamma^2}{4(\phi_1 - \phi_2 - \phi_3)}, \tag{13}$$

$$\widehat{w} = 2u, \quad U = \frac{(2c - C)^2 r}{2c^2}$$

where $\widehat{s}$ happens to equal $\bar{s}$ in Eq. (9) and $\tilde{s}$ in Eq. (12). Comparing Eqs. (13) and (12), when $c < C$, then a social planner controlling both information sharing and security investment is more beneficial for the firms in a two-period game than in a simultaneous game. Moving second, the attacker observes the high defense, and reduces the attack below that of the simultaneous game. Eq. (13) finally shows that when $c \leq C/2$, the attack ceases, causing zero profit to the agent. This control scenario, which deters the attacker, altogether is the collectively most beneficial one for the firms.

A firm seeks to establish the perception that its information activities are secure. Reputation building presupposes circulation of information. A firm may state that it applies the most advanced security technology without releasing further specifics. Attackers with malevolent objectives can thus not exploit the information, but customers, clients, cooperation partners, and competitors may find it problematic to trust a firm that withholds specifics. Alternatively, a firm may release all information about technology and procedures. Then all attackers know how well the firm is protected. The firm can thus be attacked more easily by attackers with malevolent objectives, but may benefit from other attackers than trusting the firm more thoroughly. The benefits may outweigh the costs. Gordon et al. (2006b) found that voluntary disclosure increased 100% in 2003–2004 compared with 2000–2001. In practice, firms often choose an intermediate route between the two extremes.

Three classes of information disclosure are voluntary disclosure of information security breaches, voluntary disclosure of information security vulnerabilities, and voluntary disclosure of proactive steps toward improving information security (Gordon et al., 2006b). The U.S. federal government has encouraged establishing SB/ISOs. Examples are Information Sharing And Analysis Centers (ISACs), CERT, INFRAGARD, etc. Also, SOX places strict requirements on firms to establish and maintain controls for financial reporting, and assessing annually the effectiveness of those controls.

Gal-Or and Ghose (2005, p. 193) find that "security technology investments and security information sharing act as 'strategic complements.'" In contrast, Gordon et al. (2003) assume a different cost function and "find that when firms share information, each firm has reduced incentives to invest in information security." Gal-Or and Ghose (2005) state that "the main reason for the different result is the existence of the demand enhancing effects of information security sharing and technology investments in our model."

Gal-Or and Ghose (2005) assume a fixed and immutable external threat, but account for how market characteristics, consumer demand, and sensitivity toward price and quantity depend on the strategic choices of the two firms. They find that "a lower level of firm loyalty leads to lower levels of security information sharing and security technology investment," and that "the extent of information sharing and amount of security technology investment by both firms increase when the degree of product substitutability increases." Furthermore, "security information sharing and security technology investment levels increase with firm size," which is "consistent with the well known result that a monopolist benefits more from cost-reducing innovations than a firm competing in a duopoly, given that it can extract a higher proportion of the surplus from the market." In an industry with one strong dominant firm and one weak inferior firm, this result will likely be different. The strong firm may not trust the weak firm and may refuse to share information with it. Also, attackers with low competence may attack weak firms as easier targets.

In Gal-Or and Ghose's (2005) two-stage game, two firms choose security investment and information sharing simultaneously in the first stage. The firms choose prices simultaneously in the second stage. The second stage is solved first, which gives prices dependent on all the four first stage decision variables. Inserting the prices into the first stage gives an optimization problem where both firms choose positive security investment and information sharing. This means that each firm chooses information sharing in the first stage taking into account how the price it chooses optimally in the second stage depends on information sharing by both firms. Hence, information sharing by the other firm has a direct impact on the information sharing chosen by the first firm. This direct impact reduces the incentive each firm has to free ride on the other firm's information sharing. Hence, Gal-Or and Ghose's (2005) two-stage game, and other two-stage games in the literature, partly eliminate the free rider dilemma.

Summing up, information sharing is an important strategic tool for firms in addition to security investment. The free rider dilemma is prominent since each firm prefers to receive information from other firms, but is reluctant to provide information. Interdependence between firms is conducive to information sharing since information provided benefits the security of other firms, which flows back as a benefit to one's own firm which provides better protection for both firms against the attacker. A social planner can sometimes curtail or prevent the free rider dilemma. But, a social planner tends to impose unreasonably high levels for the strategic variable it controls, since the firms free ride on the variable they control. A social planner controlling both information sharing and security investment in a two period game, where the social planner moves first, is the most collectively beneficial control scenario for firms, and may prevent the attack altogether if the unit cost of defense is low. We now turn to consider returns to security investment.

8 Returns to information security investment

Everyone agrees that firms need to take steps to defend their assets and information networks. But, such steps are costly and compete with other steps firms need to survive, such as maximizing high quality production and profit, and serving customers successfully. The challenging questions are how much to invest in security, and how much information to share about security breaches. There are benefits and costs. In the timeline in Table 1, an early contribution was made by Gordon and Loeb (2002), supported empirically by Tanaka and Matsuura (2005), followed up by Gordon and Loeb (2006), and Hausken (2006b). Furthermore, the treatment in this section intermingles with or is tangential to several of the topics in Table 1.

Gordon and Loeb (2002) assume that the probability of an information set being breached decreases at a decreasing rate as the firm increases security investment. They demonstrate for three classes of such functions that a risk-neutral firm would optimally invest no more than 37% of the expected loss from a security breach. For one of the classes, the optimal investment increases strictly in the initial vulnerability level, and for the other class, the optimal investment is inverse U shaped. They propose that protecting moderately, rather than extremely vulnerable information sets may be optimal. Preliminary empirical work of Tanaka and Matsuura (2005) applying empirics from Japan is consistent with the assumption of decreasing marginal returns to information security investment.

Hausken (2006b) presents four kinds of functions where the optimal investment is not confined to 37% of the expected loss. The first is the logistic function where marginal returns first increase and then decrease as security investment increases. The logistic function (S curve) is the common function to explain the impact of marketing effort. The optimal security investment is zero for low vulnerabilities, jumps abruptly to a positive level for intermediate vulnerabilities, and thereafter increases concavely in absolute terms. The second is an alternative class of decreasing marginal returns where the investment increases convexly in the vulnerability until an upper bound is reached. This means, contrary to Gordon and Loeb (2002), investing most heavily to protect the extremely vulnerable information sets. The third and fourth are increasing and constant marginal returns to security investment. Optimal investment is then zero for low vulnerabilities, and jumps to high investment for intermediate vulnerabilities.

Summing up, four kinds of marginal returns to security investment to protect a firm are decrease, first increase and then decrease, increase, and constancy. Gordon and Loeb (2002) suggests protecting moderately rather than extremely vulnerable information, whereas Hausken (2006b) develops more detailed recommendations dependent on the marginal return function.

9 Future developments

Future research on security investment and information sharing accounting for the income, substitution, and interdependence effect can introduce more complexity. Firms allocate resources into production versus security investment, share information, compete with each other on quality and price, compete with attackers, serve customers, and comply with laws and regulations. Firms have different size and market power, and attackers have different capabilities.

A distinction can be introduced between various kinds of security investment, in particular investments of offensive versus defensive nature. Gordon et al. (2003), Gal-Or and Ghose (2005), and Hausken (2007) assume information scaled along one dimension. Different kinds of information are then given different weights according to their relative importance. Future research may account for information being multi-faceted, of different kinds, and with different degrees of importance for different purposes. It can also be analyzed how attackers share information.

The time dimension should be introduced. The income of firms and external attackers fluctuates over time, interdependence between firms fluctuates over time according to market conditions, and attackers make substitutions through time. As profits change, firms make tradeoffs between R&D, maintenance, and security investment adapting to changing threats. At the same time attackers search for the most cost efficient attack scenario, may accumulate resources during times when security defenses are high, awaiting optimal times for attack.

Learning and acquiring information about how to invest and share information wisely need further research, accounting for information being inaccurately received and interpreted. Industry-pervasive vulnerabilities need to be understood more thoroughly as these can be exploited by firms and attackers to gain competitive advantage.

Further modeling possibilities are to account for risk, uncertainty, and incomplete information, which may be one sided or two sided. Firms are uncertain and have incomplete information about attackers' income resources, attack capabilities and preferences, and substitution preferences across firms and through time. Firms are also uncertain about other firms' production, security investments, investment efficiencies, information sharing, and customer demand. Attackers are better informed about their own capabilities and preferences, but are uncertain about firms' assets, production, security investment, investment efficiencies, information sharing, capacities and willingness to withstand cyber attack, and are uncertain about other attackers' capabilities and preferences.

10 Conclusion

This chapter has considered strategic interaction between firms and attackers. Firms compete with attackers, invest in security, and share information to maximize profit. Attackers choose the optimal attack scenario across firms to break through security defenses and maximize profit.

For two firms competing with one attacker, each firm invests in security technology when the required rate of return from security investment exceeds the average attack level. Each firm invests maximally in security when the average attack level is 25% of the firm's required rate of return. An income effect means that the attacker's resource gets reduced by the firms' security investments. The income effect eliminates or freezes parts of the attacker's resource, attack tools, and competence, or ability to convert resources into an attack. An income reduction parameter scales how much firms' security investments reduce the attacker's income. The security investment decreases in the income reduction parameter when the attacker's resource is low, is inverse U shaped when the resource is intermediate, and equals zero when the external threat is large. A strong income effect eliminates the external threat.

For two interdependent firms, security investment by one firm impacts the other firm, and an attack against one firm impacts the other firm indirectly. As the interdependence increases, each firm free rides by investing less, earns lower profit, whereas the attacker earns higher profit. The substitution effect allows an attacker to substitute across firms, across attack tools, and through time. Substitution across firms means endogenizing the attack distribution across firms. Each firm's security investment increases in its asset and unit cost of investment. The attack against each firm increases in the firm's asset and the firm's unit cost of investment. The attacker does not attack a valuable firm if a low unit cost of security investment implies that it is too well protected. A firm increasing its security investment usually benefits from the substitution effect since it thereby shifts some of the attack over to other firms.

Information sharing becomes increasingly important. The U.S. federal government encourages establishing SB/ISOs. For the income effect, information sharing may eliminate parts of the attackers' resources. The substitution effect is not conducive to information sharing since a firm sharing information with other firms risks information leakage, which benefits other firms. Providing information to other firms is costly because of the risk of leakage. For firms in isolation, firms have no incentives to share information, but prefer to receive information. The free rider dilemma is well documented. Interdependence between firms impacts information sharing positively. An example is the U.S. telecommunications industry.

Accounting for demand enhancing effects of information sharing and security investments, Gal-Or and Ghose (2005) find that security investments and security information sharing are strategic complements. In contrast, Gordon et al. (2003) find that when firms share information, each firm has reduced incentives to invest in information security. Hausken (2007) finds that information sharing and security investment for two firms are inverse U shaped in the aggregate attack, and interlinked through the interdependence and the firm's unit cost of security investment. When security investment is fixed, social welfare is inverse U shaped in information sharing. Individual optimization implies free riding, which can be curtailed by a social planner. A social planner controlling information sharing imposes unreasonably high information sharing. Conversely, a social planner controlling security investment imposes unreasonably high security investment. The reason is that firms free ride in the variable they control, and the social planner compensates too much with the variable it controls. The social planner shows restraint through imposing more moderate levels in two period games, but this requires a highly respected social planner with a good track record who credibly moves first. A social planner controlling both information sharing and security investment in a two period game, where the social planner moves first, is the most ambitious control scenario. It is also the most collectively beneficial control scenario when the firms' unit security investments are low. If these are sufficiently low, the attack is deterred altogether. To facilitate increased information sharing, firms are well advised to build up increased interdependence with other firms, but the risk is increased free riding in security investment.

Various marginal returns to security investment are considered to protect information sets. As investment increases, these can decrease, be logistic (first increase and then decrease), increase, and be constant. Gordon and Loeb (2002) analyze a broad subset of the first common class and show that a firm invests maximum 37% of the expected loss from a security breach. Protecting moderately rather than extremely vulnerable information sets is optimal. Hausken (2006b) analyzes all four classes. Optimal investment is not generally confined to 37%. For a subset of the first class, investment increases convexly in the vulnerability until a bound is reached. The extremely vulnerable information sets are protected most heavily. For the logistic function, investment is zero for low vulnerabilities, jumps moderately for intermediate vulnerabilities, and thereafter increases concavely in absolute terms. For the third and fourth classes, investment is zero for low vulnerabilities, and jumps to a high level for intermediate vulnerabilities.

11 Questions for discussion

Section 2

1. Perform a literature review to extend the timeline in Table 1.
2. Assess in which ways Fig. 1 can be generalized.
3. In which directions do you expect this field to develop in the future?
4. Which parts of Table 1 and Fig. 1 do you think firms should focus most on?
5. Imagine being a defender, how would you go about defending?
6. Imagine being an attacker, how would you go about attacking?

Section 3

1. Do you think two firms and one attacker adequately captures this phenomenon?
2. What does a firm's asset consist in?
3. What does a firm's security investment consist in?
4. Should a firm overinvest or underinvest, and if yes, when, why, how, and how much?
5. Which factors influence a firm's unit cost of defense?
6. What does an attacker's resource consist in?
7. Does the notion of contest success adequately capture the interaction between firms and attackers?
8. What kinds of attack can an attacker launch, and through which channels?
9. Which factors influence an attacker's unit cost of attack?
10. What kinds of firms do you think an attacker is motivated to attack?
11. Is an attacker motivated by economic gain, political factors, leisure, status, a desire to create destruction, or other factors?
12. Is a firm's loss equal to an attacker's gain, or does something get lost in the attack?
13. Which factors influence whether the conflict between firms and attackers is fierce or lenient?
14. Are the interests of firms and attackers 100% opposite as when sharing a pie, or do they have some common interest?
15. Describe exhaustively the asymmetries between firms and attackers.
16. Is the interaction between firms and attackers adequately described as a predator–prey situation? What happens to the prey if the predator goes extinct?
17. Is external regulation needed to govern the interaction between firms and attackers?
18. Should security investment be mandatory and absence thereof punishable?
19. Should attackers be prosecuted when detected, or provided with alternative incentives?
20. Can attackers be eliminated?

Section 4

1. Do you agree with the three ways in which the attackers' resource or income can be reduced?
2. In which other ways do you think the attackers' resource can be reduced?
3. Which characteristics of firms do you think influence the attackers' resource?
4. Which societal characteristics do you think influence the attackers' resource?
5. Is the income reduction parameter is appropriate?
6. Which factors influence the income reduction parameter?
7. Do you think attackers of information assets and networks have sponsors and interests aligned behind them?
8. Do you see advantages or disadvantages from allowing attacker resources to flourish, or attempting to eliminate attacker resources?
9. Is elimination of attacker resources periodically or permanently a goal?
10. Can elimination of attacker resources be counterproductive and cause a society with undesirable characteristics?

Section 5

1. What kinds of interdependence exist between firms?
2. How do you think interdependence varies across industries, and across private and public sector?
3. Do you think competitiveness, industry size, the size and number of firms, profits, and other factors influence interdependence between firms?
4. Describe exhaustively which factors influence interdependence between firms.
5. How do you think the emergence of the Internet impact interdependence between firms?
6. Is an interdependence parameter appropriate?
7. Describe exhaustively when interdependence between firms is positive or negative.
8. Do you think firms take interdependence between firms into account when choosing strategies for security investment?
9. Do you think attackers take interdependence between firms into account when designing attack strategies?
10. How do you think interdependence between firms impacts the firms' incentives to free ride on their security investments?
11. Should governments take interdependence between firms into account when designing procedures against attackers, and should interdependence somehow be regulated?

Section 6

1. What does it mean for an attacker to substitute its attack optimally across firms?
2. What kinds of substitutions can attackers make?
3. Which factors influence how an attacker substitutes its attack across firms?
4. Should a firm substitute into attacking a highly valuable firm regardless of its security defense and regardless of the attackers' unit cost of attack and regardless of other factors?
5. How should a firm handle an attacker that substitutes its attack across firms?
6. Should a firm invest into security without considering how other firms invest in security, and without considering how attackers substitute its attack across firms?
7. Should firms that are equivalent in some or many respects be concerned about the substitution effect?

Section 7

1. Do you see upper or lower limits to how much information about security breaches, events, exposure, and other characteristics a firm should compile?
2. Under what circumstances does a firm benefit or suffer from security breaches by other firms?
3. What kinds of information can, may, and should a firm exchange and not exchange?
4. How widely should information be shared, that is, to partners, competitors, firms in other industries, or public announcement also available for customers and attackers?
5. How specific should a firm's policy be with respect to information sharing?
6. Should a firm practice information sharing equivalently to or differently from its officially formulated information sharing policy?
7. Which implications related to reputation and profit flow from following versus deviating from an information sharing policy that can be specific versus vague?
8. Why should a firm exchange information with other firms and actors?
9. What is the linkage between information sharing and the free rider dilemma?
10. Should information sharing be routinized?
11. Should amount and kind of information sharing be somehow linked to a firm's security investment and other characteristics?

12. Should amount and kind of information sharing be somehow linked to how aggressively and in what manner attackers target one's firm or other firms?

13. In what different or similar senses are security investment and information sharing costly?

14. Are security investment and information sharing strategic complements or strategic substitutes?

15. Which factors may facilitate information sharing?

16. What barriers do you see against information sharing?

17. Should governments or others intervene with laws, advice, or funding to facilitate or prevent information sharing?

18. Should governments or others intervene with laws, advice, or funding to facilitate or prevent the design of Security Based Information Sharing Organizations? If yes, what mandate and power should such organizations have?

19. How is information sharing influenced by the income, interdependence, and substitution effects?

20. If a social planner controls information sharing, how does that influence firms' security investment, social welfare, and attacker profits?

21. If a social planner controls security investment, how does that influence firms' information sharing and social welfare, and attacker profits?

22. If a social planner controls both information sharing and security investment, how does that influence firms' social welfare and attacker profits?

23. Which factors influence whether a social planner can control its instrument (information sharing and security investment) simultaneously with or prior to the firms' and attacker's choice of strategy, and what are the implications for the firms' social welfare and attacker profits?

24. Envision all the different ways in which a social planner, firms, and attackers can move first, second, or simultaneously, and determine which ways are most realistic and under what circumstances and with what implications?

25. How does the 2002 Sarbanes–Oxley Act regulate information sharing and security investment, and for what kinds of firms?

Section 8

1. How important is security investment compared with other investments that firms make?

2. How can a firm determine returns to security investment?

3. How can a firm weigh benefits and costs against each other when determining security investment?

4. How should a firm assess the probability of an information set being breached?
5. Describe the four classes of functions characterizing returns to security investment, as discussed in this chapter?
6. Which of these classes do you find most descriptive, under which circumstances, and for which industries?
7. Envision other classes than these four, and assess their realism?
8. How much should a firm invest in security as a percentage of expected losses, as a percentage of the value of the asset it protects, dependent on the four classes of functions, or dependent on other factors?
9. Should moderately vulnerable information sets be more or less protected than highly vulnerable information sets, for which classes of functions, and under what circumstances?
10. Assess the appropriate security investment and information sharing as a function of how vulnerable and valuable an information set is.

Glossary

Asset: An object that has value for a firm.
Attacker: An agent attacking an asset or information set with the objective of acquiring or destroying it.
Cyber war: Competition or struggle between firms and attackers over assets.
Firm: An organization protecting an asset or information set.
Free riding: How a firm cuts back on its contribution in the hope that the other firm contributes. A firm that consumes more than its fair share, or shoulders less than a fair share of the production cost.
Income effect: How the attacker's resource or income is affected by the firms' strategies or other factors.
Information set: A piece of information that has value for a firm.
Information sharing: The amount of information about security breaches and other events and characteristics that a firm provides to another firm.
Interdependence effect: How interdependent firms are in their exchange of products, services, information, personnel, competence, common contact surfaces, linked information systems, etc.
Returns to security investment: How a firm benefits from incurring a cost of investing in security.
Security investment: The amount that a firm invests in security to protect its asset.
Social planner: A third party intervening to maximize the social welfare (joint profit) of two firms.
Substitution effect: How the attacker substitutes its attack optimally across firms.
Vulnerability: How exposed an asset or information set is for attack.

References

Anderson, E.E., J. Choobineh (2008). Enterprise information security strategies. *Computers & Security* 27(1–2), 22–29.
Anderson, R. (2001). Why information security is hard: an economic perspective, in: *Proceedings of 17th Annual Computer Security Applications Conference, December*, IEEE Computer Society, Washington, DC, p. 358. Available at http://portal.acm.org/citation.cfm?id = 872155, ISBN: 0-7695-1405-7.
Anderson, R., T. Moore (2006). The economics of information security. *Science* 314(5799), 610–613.
Arora, A., J. Caulkins, R. Telang (2006). Sell first, fix later: impact of patching on software quality. *Management Science* 52(3), 465–471.

Axelson, U. (2007). Security design with investor private information. *The Journal of Finance* 62(6), 2587–2632.

Bagby, J. (2005). *The confluence of public policy on information security controls.* Ms., Pennsylvania State University.

Bodin, D., L.A. Gordon, M. Loeb (2008). Information security and risk management. *Communications of the ACM* 51(4), 64–68.

Campbell, K., L. Gordon, M. Loeb, L. Zhou (2003). The economic cost of publicly announced information security breaches: empirical evidence from the stock market. *Journal of Computer Security* 11(3), 431–448.

Cavusoglu, H., B. Mishra, S. Raghunathan (2004a). The effect of Internet security breach announcements on market value: capital market reactions for breached firms and Internet security developers. *International Journal of Electronic Commerce* 9(1), 69–104.

Cavusoglu, H., B. Mishra, S. Raghunathan (2004b). A model for evaluating IT security investments. *Communications of the ACM* 47(7), 87–92.

Cavusoglu, H., B. Mishra, S. Raghunathan (2005). The value of intrusion detection systems in information technology security architecture. *Information Systems Research* 16(1), 28–46.

Choi, J., C. Fershtman, N. Gandal (2005). *The economics of Internet security.* December 6. Department of Economics, Michigan State University.

Dhillon, G., L. Silva, J. Backhouse (2004). Computer crime at CEFORMA: a case study. *International Journal of Information Management* 24, 551–561.

Enders, W., T. Sandler (2003). What do we know about the substitution effect in transnational terrorism? in: A. Silke, G. Ilardi (eds.), *Researching Terrorism: Trends, Achievements, Failures.* Frank Cass, Ilfords, UK. Available at http://www-rcf.usc.edu/~tsandler/substitution2ms.pdf

Gal-Or, E., A. Ghose (2003). The economic consequences of sharing security information, in: *Proceedings of the Second Workshop on Economics and Information Security*, May 29–30, University of Maryland.

Gal-Or, E., A. Ghose (2005). The economic incentives for sharing security information. *Information Systems Research* 16(2), 186–208.

Garcia, A., B. Horowitz (2007). The potential for underinvestment in Internet security: implications for regulatory policy. *Journal of Regulatory Economics* 31(1), 37–55.

Ghose, A. (2007). Information disclosure and regulatory compliance: economic issues and research directions, in: H.R. Rao, M. Gupta, S. Upadhyaya (eds.), *Managing Information Assurance in Financial Services.* Idea Group, Hershey, PA.

Gordon, L.A., M. Loeb (2001). Using information security as a response to competitor analysis systems. *Communications of the ACM* 44(9), 70–75.

Gordon, L.A., M. Loeb (2002). The economics of information security investment. *ACM Transactions on Information and System Security* 5(4), 438–457.

Gordon, L.A., M. Loeb (2003). Expenditures on competitor analysis and information security: a managerial accounting perspective, in: A. Bhimani (ed.), *Management Accounting in the New Economy.* Oxford University Press, Oxford, pp. 95–111.

Gordon, L.A., M. Loeb (2006). *Managing Cybersecurity Resources: A Cost-Benefit Analysis.* McGraw-Hill, New York.

Gordon, L.A., M. Loeb, W. Lucyshyn (2003). Sharing information on computer systems security: an economic analysis. *Journal of Accounting and Public Policy* 22(6), 461–485.

Gordon, L.A., M. Loeb, W. Lucyshyn, R. Richardson (2006a). 2006 CSI/FBI computer crime and security survey. Available at http://www.gocsi.com/

Gordon, L.A., M. Loeb, W. Lucyshyn, T. Sohail (2006b). The impact of the Sarbanes–Oxley Act on the corporate disclosures of information security activities. *Journal of Accounting and Public Policy* 25(5), 503–530.

Hausken, K. (2002). Probabilistic risk analysis and game theory. *Risk Analysis* 22(1), 17–27.

Hausken, K. (2005). Production and conflict models versus rent seeking models. *Public Choice* 123, 59–93.

Hausken, K. (2006a). Income, interdependence, and substitution effects affecting incentives for security investment. *Journal of Accounting and Public Policy* 25(6), 629–665.

Hausken, K. (2006b). Returns to information security investment: the effect of alternative information security breach functions on optimal investment and sensitivity to vulnerability. *Information Systems Frontiers* 8(5), 338–349.

Hausken, K. (2007). Information sharing among firms and cyber attacks. *Journal of Accounting and Public Policy* 26(6), 639–688.

Hausken, K. (2008). Strategic defense and attack for reliability systems. *Reliability Engineering & System Safety* 93(11), 1740–1750.

Hui, W., B. Yoob, K.Y. Tam (2008). Economics of shareware: how do uncertainty and piracy affect shareware quality and brand premium? *Decision Support Systems* 44(3), 580–594.

Kannan, K., J. Rees, S. Sridhar (2007). Market reactions to information security breach announcements: an empirical analysis. *International Journal of Electronic Commerce* 12(1), 69–91.

Kannan, K., R. Telang (2005). Market for software vulnerabilities? Think again. *Management Science* 51(5), 726–740.

Katos, V., A. Patel (2008). A partial equilibrium view on security and privacy. *Information Management & Computer Security* 16(1), 74–83.

Keohane, N., R.J. Zeckhauser (2003). The ecology of terror defense. *The Journal of Risk and Uncertainty* 26(2/3), 201–229.

Kjaerland, M. (2005). A classification of computer security incidents based on reported attack data. *Journal of Investigative Psychology and Offender Profiling* 2(2), 105–120.

Kunreuther, H., G. Heal (2003). Interdependent security. *The Journal of Risk and Uncertainty* 26(2/3), 231–249.

Lakdawalla, D., G. Zanjani (2002). *Insurance, self-protection, and the economics of terrorism*. Ms., RAND and NBER, Federal Reserve Bank of New York.

Nizovtsev, D., M. Thursby (2005). Economic Analysis of Incentives to Disclose Software Vulnerabilities, The Fourth Workshop on Economics of Information Systems, Boston, MA.

Png, I., C. Tang, Q. Wang (2006). Information Security: User Precautions and Hacker Targeting, Working Paper, National University of Singapore. Available at http://papers.ssrn.com/sol3/papers.cfm?abstract_id = 912161

Porter, M. (1980). *Competitive Strategy: Techniques for Analyzing Industries and their Competitors*. Free Press, New York, NY.

Schechter, S., M. Smith (2003). How much security is enough to stop a thief? in: *Proceedings of the Financial Cryptography Conference*, January, Guadeloupe.

Schenk, M., M. Schenk (2002). Defining the value of strategic security. *Secure Business Quarterly* 1(1), 1–6.

Tanaka, H., K. Matsuura (2005). Vulnerability and effects of information security investment: A firm level empirical analysis of Japan. Presented at Forum "Financial Information Systems and Cyber Security", College Park, Maryland, May 26, 2005.

Tanaka, H., K. Matsuura, O. Sudoh (2005). Vulnerability and information security investment: an empirical analysis of E-local government in Japan. *Journal of Accounting and Public Policy* 24, 37–59.

Varian, H. (2002). System reliability and free riding, in: *Proceedings of the First Workshop on Economics and Information Security*, May 16–17, University of California, Berkeley.

Rao & Upadhyaya, Eds., *Handbooks in Information Systems, Vol. 4*

Chapter 19

Economic Determinants of Piracy of Digital Goods: Using Market Forces to Shape a Secure Solution

Sudip Bhattacharjee, Ram Gopal, James R. Marsden and Ramesh Sankaranarayanan

Department of Operations & Information Management, School of Business, University of Connecticut, 2100 Hillside Road, U-1041, Storrs, CT 06269, USA

Abstract

The wide, enabling reach of the Internet has fostered a growth in illicit copying and use of such goods that can be easily transported through this channel. Chief among such digital goods are software and music, whose producers have faced significant revenue erosion created by a perfect storm of technological, legal, and economic issues in the past several years. Consequently, we have witnessed various technological measures, legal approaches, and economic incentives to thwart the menace of Internet-based piracy of digital goods. There have been several claims on which method works best to increase revenues, or at least slow its decline; however, there is a paucity of comparison studies on the effectiveness of such market forces. Here, we present a comparative analysis of how to reduce the threat of piracy and create a secure flow of digital goods and associated revenues using the Internet channel.

This chapter looks at two digital goods most affected by the scourge of online sharing and piracy—software and music. We start by showing that there are certain similarities between these goods, as well as uniqueness in each one, such that different approaches are necessary to have an appreciable effect to stop piracy and secure the supply of goods and revenues. We compare the technological measures that have been proposed to deter sharing and piracy of software and music and conclude that such technological impediments are short-term solutions that are quickly overcome by savvy users. Furthermore, cumbersome technological solutions may in fact hurt legitimate buyers in their enjoyment and use of the good, creating a less than favorable overall consumer experience.

We then turn our attention to several legal tactics adopted by the respective industries against pirates. Although there are preventive and deterrent aspects of a legal solution which work to the benefit of the industry, we show that software and music are impacted in different ways by such approaches. Furthermore, the legal approach is slow in a fast-evolving technical world and sometimes has the unintended consequence of snaring the unsuspecting potential customer in its attempt to catch the pirating thief.

Finally, we review several economic models and incentives designed to deter piracy and increase sales of these digital goods. We initiate the discussion by highlighting studies that model the consumer incentives that determine a buy/pirate decision. We show that for experience goods such as music, which has to be consumed to understand its true value, sharing and sampling may have a beneficial effect. However, it is a double-edged sword, as sharing may enhance the value of a high-quality good and increase its sales, while it may reveal the true quality of a lower quality good and hurt its sales. Furthermore, the cost of search and sampling is a significant component in users' ability to accurately sample and buy such products. Properly designing the search, sampling and buying experience of consumers, and providing them with a rich and satisfying environment that fosters positive network externality, are crucial to the continued revenue flow for the concerned industries. We conclude by suggesting a framework where a triangulated approach works best to secure the marketplace from piracy of digital goods and help in generating associated revenues through the Internet channel.

1 Introduction

In the Information Age, the raw materials for value creation lie in knowledge and information. Intellectual property rights, including copyrights, constitute a framework to protect such value creation and dissemination. In the past decade, these industries have created jobs at a faster rate than many leading sectors in the US economy, for example, and have continued to expand their worldwide sales and exports. More importantly, in the current atmosphere of faster information collection and dissemination through Internet-based technologies, the rate of growth of such intellectual property-based industries continues to be higher than the US economy as a whole.

The core "copyright" industries encompass those whose major operations include creation of copyrighted material. These include the music recording industry, the motion picture industry, the book, journal publishing industry, software industry, and others. The "total" copyright industries include the core industries and parts of other industries that create, distribute, or depend on copyrighted materials. In 2005, the core copyright industries added $819.06 billion to the US GDP (a 6.56% share), while the total copyright industries added $1.38 trillion (11.92% of US GDP) (Siwek 2004, 2006). In 1997–2002, core copyright industry had an

Table 1
Annual growth rate of foreign sales and exports of US copyright industries

Year	1991	1996	2000	2001	2002	2003	2004	2005
Growth rate	6.4%	13.3%	8.3%	3.4%	1.1%	10.7%	7.5%	4.3%

annual growth rate of 3.51%, while the overall US economy grew at a 2.40% rate. In 2005, the core copyright industries were responsible for 12.96% of the US GDP. Lastly, the growth rates of worldwide sales and exports of core copyright industries have been significant (Table 1). In 2004, exports from selected core copyright industries totaled $110.8 billion, which was higher than the US Commerce Department's export estimates of several other major industry sectors.

Emerging information technology breakthroughs, including peer-to-peer (P2P) file sharing networks, interconnection of web sites and easy creation of web logs (blogs for politics, science, products, etc.), scanning and online search of out-of-print books (e.g., Google Print Project), and other approaches have made it faster, easier, and cheaper to share content as well as information about the content in a manner not available earlier. Digitization of information has also made it possible to make such information sharing more focused and targeted to a specific audience. Although these technologies bring significant opportunities that may be exploited to further enhance the growth and profitability of these industries, several challenges have cropped up, including illegal file sharing and possible copyright violations, which have impeded the growth of existing copyright industries. There is an urgent need to study and recommend solutions to secure copyrighted and other information products, and the associated revenue, for the continued growth of this high-value industry. This is especially true for digital goods, which have been hit the hardest in the shifting landscape.

Digital goods encompass a wide variety of products, including software, digital music, video games, electronic books, digital movies, and others. Among these, the most prominent ones in the market that have faced the scourge of illegal online sharing and copying have been software and music products. Certain features of software and music, such as smaller file sizes, close ties to the computer platform, and positive network externalities, have contributed to these products being shared online and copied at a massive scale. In addition, for both software and music items (in their digital form), perfect copies can be made and shared with others. Hence, these products have the characteristics of a quasi-public good, in that once the good is provided to some consumers, it is very difficult to preclude other consumers from consuming it.

Audio piracy, the illegal act of copying sound and, mostly music, without explicit permission from and compensation to the copyright holder, has exploded with the growth of digitized audio. Incentives to indulge in such behavior are influenced by economic, technological, and ethical considerations. Key technological factors that have aided such behavior include the growing pervasiveness of the Internet, rapid adoption of broadband technology, writeable CD[1] and DVD technology, and the emergence of better compression technology.[2] This technological advancement has several interesting consequences:

(i) CDs can now be created that contain over 160 compressed digital music files that can play for over 14 h on a personal computer. With DVDs, it increases by several magnitudes.
(ii) A compressed music file (e.g., encoded in MP3) is much smaller than the original version and can be easily transmitted over the Internet.
(iii) Digital music can be downloaded from any point from the world-wide reach of the Internet into a portable music player. These players can store several hours of digital-quality music and are smaller than a personal CD player.

These recent technological changes have transformed, what was until recently a mostly domestic problem for individual countries, into an effective and effortless cross-border and transcontinental music piracy. Much of the audio piracy activity is through the illegal copying of compact discs and the downloading of audio files through the Internet. According to International Federation of the Phonographic Industry (IFPI), a music watchdog body, the piracy of digital audio has spread exponentially in the past three years. The number of infringing music files available on the Internet has increased 25-fold in just three years, with 3 million downloads of music a day. The global music piracy market was estimated to be 1.9 billion units in 1999 with an estimated value of $4.1 billion.[3]

Interestingly, there is economic rationale behind the actions of users who illegally copy and use such digital products. If piracy behavior is modeled as a utility maximizing behavior where individuals choose between illegal behavior that yields a positive consumer surplus, but carries the risk of punishment, and legal behavior that carries lower consumer surplus but no punishment, higher music purchasing cost would increase the payoff from piracy, *ceteris paribus*. Such an increase in the payoff would naturally increase the likelihood for piracy, leading to greater illegal behavior (Givon et al., 1995). In the domain of software piracy, such behavior has indeed been found, and increasing software prices are generally correlated with increased piracy behavior (Gopal and Sanders, 1997, 1998). Gopal and

---

[1] In this chapter, reference to CD includes all recording media of high sonic quality.

[2] MP3 (Mpeg 1 Audio Layer 3), a well-known audio compression technology, uses a compression algorithm based on a complicated psycho-acoustic model to create CD quality music at a fraction (about 10%) of the file size of the original song.

[3] IFPI's Music Piracy Report 2000. 1999 IFPI, http://www.ifpi.org

Sanders (2000) have reported on a significant price and income effect related to software piracy rates.

The response of the recording industry to combat the piracy phenomenon has primarily been two-pronged. The main emphasis has been to adopt legal measures against online sites that facilitate widespread audio piracy. Claiming that the impact of online music sharing on the music business has been devastating, Recording Industry Association of America (RIAA) has aggressively pursued stronger copyright enforcement and regulations (Harmon, 2003). RIAA's initial legal strategy was aimed at Napster, which RIAA succeeded in shutting down largely due to potential liability around Napster's centralized file search technology. The so-called Sons of Napster quickly emerged to fill the vacuum, attempting to escape legal wrath by deploying further de-centralized structures. In response, RIAA has since altered its legal strategy by seeking sanctions against individuals "who offer a significant number of songs for others to copy" (Bhattacharjee et al., 2006a; Logie, 2006). However, this has not been able to stem the tide of losses from illegal sharing and use.

Simultaneously, the recording companies have realized the economic potential of offering online music services and are working on developing technological solutions that enable the viable provision of such services while protecting the copyrights of the legitimate owners.

1.1   Software and digital music—distinct digital goods

Digital goods have high initial production costs and very low—approaching zero—reproduction costs. They also have characteristics of a *public good* in that sharing with others does not reduce a consumer's utility for the product. These traits facilitate their widespread and often illegal distribution worldwide.

Although software and music are both "information goods" in that the marginal cost of production is virtually zero, certain key characteristics differentiate the two: (i) quality of an original CD song is better than that of its electronically transferable compressed version; software, on the contrary, requires a lossless compression for proper functioning; (ii) music files are much smaller than a typical software application, hence they take much less time to transfer and consume; (iii) consumption of music requires little specific skills as compared to software, hence the increased consumer base adds significant dynamics to the issue; (iv) consumers closely relate a performer with a music product, unlike developers with a software product, which create issues of personalized valuations for that musical product that depend on the performer; and (v) the volume of available music is significantly larger than the existing volume of software products. This provides a far greater product sampling base, compared to software products, which introduces additional levels of dynamics in music sampling and its analysis.

Music is an experience good, a type of hedonic product whose valuation is based on the experience it provides to a consumer (Dhar and Wertenbroch, 2000). A music item must be experienced (heard) to be accurately valued by a consumer. Additionally, each music item, even from the same artist, is potentially unique. While physical piracy (through CDs) may be common in certain markets, our focus is on those markets where increasing broadband connections provide the means for legal online markets while at the same time enabling online sharing and piracy (mainly through P2P networks).

There are also differences in the nature of piracy between software and music. While several studies on software piracy have examined consumer decisions to purchase or pirate the product (Conner and Rumelt, 1991; Givon et al., 1995; Gopal and Sanders, 1997, 1998, 2000), several key factors distinguish music from software. Music files are typically much smaller (and thus easier to copy) than computer software. Another important difference to keep in mind is the quality of the shared good. The acoustic quality of original music (high-quality recording media) is better than that of a compressed digital music file, the format typical for music items shared or pirated online. Shared computer software, on the contrary, requires lossless compression for proper functioning (Bhattacharjee et al., 2003).

1.2   Why are existing models not sufficient?

Here, we briefly identify relevant existing literature on experience goods, sharing, piracy, and subscription models. We discuss how the unique characteristics of these digital products need a reevaluation of existing models. This necessitates a new understanding and approach toward these new products and markets, such that we can secure the products from illegal activity and assure a steady revenue stream for producers.

Experience goods and assumption of restrictions on sharing: Existing research on experience goods primarily focuses on models related to physical goods at a given location, that is, conditions where sharing or redistribution is not easy. Focusing on a monopolistic market of entertainment experience goods, Oi (1971) implicitly assumed that sharing or redistribution of the good across different locations was difficult. Shapiro (1983) focused on a personal experience good, but dealt with a scenario with impediments to the resale and redistribution of the product. Additional related studies include the works by Gale and Rosenthal (1994), Holbrook and Schindler (1989), Jedidi et al. (1998), Liebeskind and Rumelt (1989), and Riordan (1986). While the markets we study here involve experience goods, the possibility of broad sharing and redistribution (based on the product and environmental characteristics) makes these market dynamics quite different from those in earlier studies.

Economic models with subscription pricing: Models on economics of subscription pricing and shared goods have usually focused on products where private sharing occurs among only a small group of consumers. In analyzing the journal subscription market, Glazer and Hassin (1982) and Ordover and Willig (1978) assumed that individual customers or subscribers do not share journals. Coyte and Ryan (1991) extended the subscription model and examined a consumer's decision to purchase or renew a subscription of an *information* good, a book. Borrowing a library book has low cost, but such borrowing has a time limitation and sharing can only occur in a limited way. On the contrary, a downloaded software or digital music file from a subscription service potentially can be owned permanently and shared very widely.

Going forward in this chapter, we detail a three-legged approach to understand the incentives and motivations of users in pirating digital goods and provide solutions that can be used to combat the revenue losses and a steady business model for digital products.

2 Technological measures to deter piracy

The copyright owners of digital products—in most cases large corporations—have been pressing for protections that will inhibit consumers' ability to reproduce copyrighted content cheaply. Digital rights management (DRM) technologies are being developed, which can restrict the actions of users with respect to the digital goods they purchase, for example, restricting portability among different platforms, and availability of downloaded product after subscription period has ended. DRM can be viewed as a type of preventive control (Gopal and Sanders, 1997), as opposed to deterrent controls such as threat of lawsuits (Bhattacharjee et al., 2006a).

2.1 Can DRM be profitable for copyright owners?

DRM is primarily intended to protect unlawful consumption of copyright protected content, so that copyright owners can realize the full economic benefits of their intellectual property. Given this goal, researchers have examined whether DRM does indeed improve a firm's profitability. Conner and Rumelt (1991) find that increases in protection technologies could actually hurt a firm's profit if the product displays positive network externalities. A product that displays such externalities becomes more valuable to each user as the user base grows larger, whether the users consume the product legally or otherwise. To the extent that protection technologies inhibit the growth of the user base, it could hurt a firm's profit. Gopal and Sanders (1997) find that while preventive and deterrent controls can deter piracy, preventive controls such as DRM could also hurt a seller's profit. Sundararajan (2004) outlines one mechanism by which the seller's profit could be hurt: DRM technologies often degrade the quality of product for legitimate users. For instance, incorporating DRM requires encryption that can increase file size and download time; restricting a music file to one device only increases the inconvenience to a legitimate user who may wish to use different devices in different locations. DRM can therefore diminish consumer surplus, which can limit profits to the seller.

DRM and the law: DRM could place unlawful restrictions on "fair use" of copy protected content. While the legal system provides for "fair use" of copyrighted content, the actual implementation of DRM systems could result in customers being denied "fair use" (Erickson, 2003). "Fair use" criteria include purpose and character of use (e.g., educational use), effect of use on potential market, and so on, which are not rule based. These criteria require human judgment, and it is difficult for DRM technology to substitute for this.

DRM, privacy and security: DRM could sometimes result in the violation of users' privacy (Cohen, 2003). When a user consumes DRM-protected media, the DRM system often needs to collect and report information on the user's activities, for instance to implement a pay per use arrangement. Sometimes DRM could also incorporate Spyware—in 1999, RealNetworks' media player had spyware that searched users' computers for information on users' musical preferences and other software products installed in the computers. DRM could sometimes compromise the security of the host computer on which it is installed—in 2005, Sony BMG introduced new DRM software that was installed on user's computers without their informed consent. This software created serious security vulnerabilities for the host computer that could be exploited by hackers (McMillan, 2006).

2.2   Technological measures used in digital music

While individual firms may take steps to secure their digital goods, such constraints have two major drawbacks. First, such measures tend to impede the consumer's use of the digital good since they can restrict portability or require additional steps (e.g., security actions) that reduce consumer utility (Halderman, 2002). Second, the measures have proven less than "foolproof" and rather easily beaten (Felten, 2003). For example, Sony BMG's recent use of a rootkit with the XCP technology (Bergstein, 2005; Reuters, 2005) provides a prominent illustration of how an attempted technological security constraint can backfire:

> Part of Sony's anti-pirating strategy is that some of its music will play only with media software included on the CD. When a user inserts the CD, he or she is asked to consent to an "end user licensing agreement" for a Digital Rights Management application. If the user agrees, the rootkit automatically installs and hides (or "cloaks") a suite of DRM software. (Bradley, 2005)

Unfortunately, the rootkit application created a possible secret backdoor for hackers that led Sony to "hastily" post a patch. However, the tool to remove the XCP application itself created new vulnerabilities. California quickly filed suit under both unfair and deceptive trace acts and consumer protection acts, Texas filed suit for including "spyware" in its media player, and the Electronic Frontier Foundation filed suit seeking class action status over its copy protection software (Smith, 2005). This gave rise to the following perspective (posting by concord (198387), 11/10/05, #13996982 in slashdot.org bulletin board):

> Now for the first time it is actually safer to download and listen to pirated music then (sic) it is to purchase and use compact disks and dvds. Piracy will become a matter of self-preservation.

In addition, security professionals have consistently noted that all CD and DVD encryption techniques that have been tried by the entertainment industry have been broken by savvy consumers (Associated Press, 2003; Clarke, 2005; Craver et al., 2001; Patrizio, 1999; Schneier, 2000). Given wide dissemination of the encrypted music product among users (factors that make breaking encryption easier), it is not unusual to observe such copy protection technologies being defeated by smart users (Bergstein, 2005; Felten, 2005). In the field of software product key activation, hardware dongle and other methods have been used as technological impediments to deter copying and other illegal activity.

Interestingly, Apple CEO Steve Jobs recently pointed out that iTunes customers were on average buying only 20–23 songs per iPod–a device that stores thousands of songs! Explanations include DRM restrictions on copying and constraints on portability of legally purchased downloads across music devices, both apparently at the insistence of major music labels (please see http://www.apple.com/hotnews/thoughtsonmusic/). Online music sales sites (such as Emusic, Amie Street, and Audio Lunchbox) offering downloads with "no copy protections, and few restrictions on per-track purchases" are anathema to the major labels who refuse to have their music sold at these sites.

Hence, securing digital goods through the DRM route may provide temporary relief from piracy activity; yet, all DRM copy protection security will be defeated in time. And DRM, if not used carefully, may itself lead to security breaches. Therefore, DRM acts as one leg of the three-leg approach to securing such digital products.

3   Legal measures to deter piracy

Here, we discuss some results of legal approaches to combat and secure digital goods from illegal activity, which forms the second leg of the security framework.

3.1   The threat of lawsuits

The RIAA, the legal arm of the world's largest music companies,[4] has repeatedly expressed concern over music sharing activities. The industry repeatedly cited lagging CD sales as clearly due to piracy (refer, e.g., Jenkins, 2003; Wagstaff, 2002). Jay Berman, IFPI Chairman, argued:

> ...the industry's problems reflect no fall in popularity of recorded music: rather they reflect the fact that the commercial value of music is being widely devalued by mass copying and piracy. (BBC News Online, 2002a)

During the 2002 Grammy Awards, Michael Greene, CEO of the National Association of Recorded Arts and Sciences (NARAS) suggested, "The most insidious virus in our midst is the illegal downloading of music on the Net" (Hellwig, 2002). Claiming that the impact of online music piracy on its business has been "devastating" (Feuilherade, 2004), the music industry has called for greater copyright enforcement and stronger regulations. In the past, RIAA has issued threats aimed only at the "operators" of P2P networks (Harmon, 2003). In 2000, RIAA sued and successfully shut down Napster, one of the first P2P file-sharing networks that facilitated digital music sharing. One of the main arguments employed against Napster was its facilitation of file copying and sharing by enabling a central directory of file repositories. But the popularity of music sharing, instead of being dampened by the forced closure of Napster, was reinvigorated by the advent of several second-generation P2P networks, the so-called Sons of Napster. The new networks do not maintain a central directory of files like Napster did; hence, they have avoided legal repercussions from appearing to aid illegal file sharing.[5] Consequently, these networks act as decentralized peer groups, where individual file sharers act as both file and information repositories. Among these networks, KaZaA, launched in March 2001, became the most popular with over 60 million subscribers in the year 2003–2004 (KaZaA.com, 2004).

In response to this "epidemic of illegal file-sharing," on June 26, 2003, RIAA redirected legal threats toward individual subscribers of these networks who, in the past, enjoyed anonymity in P2P environments (RIAA, September, 2003). Before RIAA's recent legal efforts, individual file sharers were almost completely immune from legal liability when violating copyright law. These recent legal developments considerably altered that perceived notion (Graham, 2003; Lichtman, 2003).

---

[4]The four major music companies are Universal Music Group, Warner Music Group, Sony-BMG, and EMI.

[5]The very recent Supreme Court holding in the "Grokster" case suggests that P2P operators must take care. In an online article by Jay Currie in *Tech Central* (2005), the author suggests that P2P operators must "not induce copyright infringement" and must make sure "that there is a non-infringing use for the software" such as sharing photos or personally developed software.

Due to the impracticality of filing lawsuits against every individual file sharer, RIAA chose to focus on a relatively small group of individuals and maximize the publicity surrounding their legal action to discourage the overall participation in file-sharing networks. The RIAA first threatened and then pursued legal action against numerous individuals who were sharing large amounts of music files. The legal actions against individuals were widely publicized. The results so far are limited and mixed—two cases have been reported (http://digitalmusicnews.com, December 28, 2006) as dismissed on summary judgments against RIAA while one went to the industry based on a failure to comply with pre-trial discovery motions. Several defendants are reported to have settled out of court while the RIAA has dropped several actions (http://punknews.org, December 24, 2006). Recently, the industry has shifted legal attention in another direction to fight AllofMP3, a Russian-based site that claims to operate legally while paying appropriate royalties to ROMS, the Russian music licensing society (http://arstechnica.com, December 21, 2006). AllofMP3 (actually its parent company, Mediaservices, Inc.) was sued in Federal Court in New York for $1.65 trillion (http://webpronews.com, December 28, 2006). Likely reasons include the fact that the site offers inexpensive music ($0.15 a song and $2.47 an album, versus iTunes, which offers $0.99 a song and $9.99 an album), a very large catalog, and DRM-free content.

3.2 Impact of legal threats

One of our research studies centered on illegal music sharing and involved the analysis of how individuals actually responded to legal threats from the recording industry (Bhattacharjee et al., 2006a). We developed an automated process to track the sharing behavior of 2056 individuals before and after four RIAA-related events. Three of the events were RIAA's formal threat that they would be pursuing legal action, the announcement that initial suits had been filed, and the announcement that a second round of suits had been filed. The other event involved an appellate court ruling that RIAA could not subpoena certain sharer identifying information from ISP's (Table 2).

Table 2
Description of RIAA events

Event	Description	Date
1	Announcement of intention to pursue legal actions	June 26, 2003
2	Lawsuits filed against alleged music file sharers	September 8, 2003
3	Court ruling against revealing identities of sharers	December 19, 2003
4	John Doe lawsuits	January 21, 2004

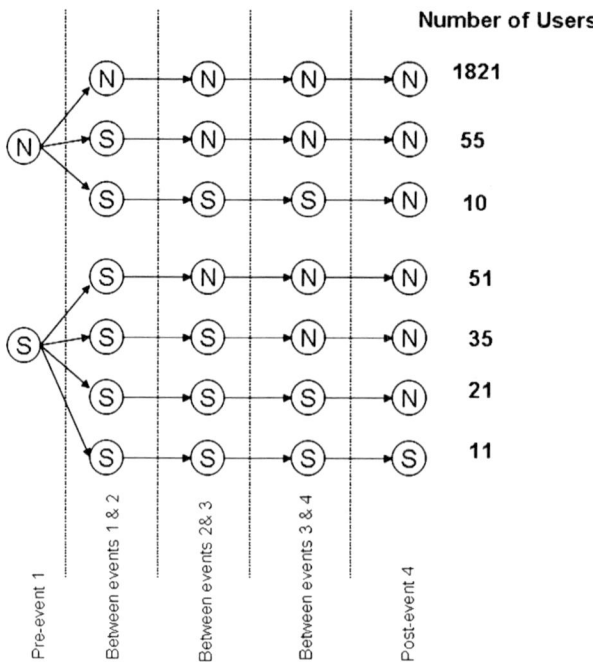

Fig. 1.   Learning effect on substantial and non-substantial sharers.

Our analysis indicated mixed success for RIAA's strategy (Fig. 1). On the positive side, before-and-after event comparisons suggested that over the course of the four events, the majority of substantial sharers decreased the number of files shared, typically by more than over 90%. During this period, a majority of non-substantial sharers dropped sharing activity, typically to a third of their original levels. Furthermore, a substantial number of sharers exhibited some risk mitigation behavior. Interestingly, a substantial number of sharers exhibited a learning effect, where the number of users sharing a substantial number of songs continued to decrease as the number of events increased (i.e., event 1—initial announcement of RIAA intention to go after sharers, event 2—actual lawsuits filed, etc.). As we see from Fig. 1, many of the substantial sharers (who were the target of RIAA) decreased the number of files shared after the first event, while several others continued decreasing their file sharing activity after the second and third event. After the fourth event (followed in this research), a majority of the substantial sharers had decreased their sharing behavior.

On the contrary, some findings pose concern for the recording industry. We found an upsurge in the frequency of usage after the event 3 from the sharers who continue to use the file-sharing network. These individuals continued to find value in accessing and using P2P networks. Next, although our analysis identified "RIAA intended" behavioral changes following RIAA's legal threats and legal actions, there remain fairly wide downloading options. That is, after the four events, we still found a fairly wide choice for anyone seeking to download music files. Another cause for concern is that even if the individual behavioral changes we observed are linked to an actual lessening of piracy, there is still the fact that the legal action did not come without a price to RIAA itself. Many critics of RIAA's actions against individual consumers suggested that their legal efforts may be perceived as heavy-handed and could backlash on the music industry itself (refer, e.g., Graham, 2003). In dealing with music piracy, the music industry's legal success in suing its own potential customers may not be as important as its potential future success in adjusting its business strategy.

While our results are consistent with the effect intended by RIAA, it is possible that the observed reduction in file sharing on KaZaA may have been at least partially linked to shift by sharers to other sharing networks. While we cannot rule this out, we do have information from another sharing network (WinMx). We found a similar general downward trend in the P2P file downloading opportunities, suggesting that there was no large-scale shift in usage from KaZaA (the largest sharing network during our observation period) to WinMX (the second largest sharing network during our observation period). Finally, we found no reported sharp increase in the usage of smaller networks in the popular press.

Taken as a whole, our results lead us to conclude that individuals have, to a very large extent, responded in the direction intended by RIAA through its lawsuits. In fact, the impact on US sharers may be stronger than our numerical results indicate because the few (11) who remained as stubborn sharers may well be foreign-based sharers. However, we also note that a significant number of sharers tended to move below the "threat levels" (800 or 1000 files shared) rather than exiting from sharing activity. RIAA could lower the "threat level" or number of files shared. But lawsuits cost real money. How many suits is it reasonable for RIAA to pursue? There have also been recent reports of consumers fighting back against the music industry's legal tactics for combating music piracy, with maneuvers that attack the heart of RIAA's legal tactics. At the present time, what we can say is that the previously "substantial sharers" are tending to still actively share (albeit fewer files) and downloading options still abound for those seeking to download. We continue to watch for the development by the recording industry of market mechanisms that might be more effective—will market options emerge that do not require costly legal actions and yet enhance industry net revenue while lowering the cost of music to consumers? We identify such market mechanisms in the next section.

4 Market mechanisms

Technological measures (e.g., DRM) and legal maneuvers are inherently linear approaches to a very complex issue—that of consumer utility and market choices. Recent work on market mechanisms to understand and model this emerging phenomenon of digital goods markets and associated piracy and security issues incorporate economic models of search, sampling, social groups, and superstar behavior, among other well-derived constructs. However, there are significant differences from classical economic models that warrant the development of new and modified approaches that incorporate several unique attributes of digital goods. Here, we discuss several models that show how market mechanisms may be included that help to incentivize consumers and users into increasing legitimate behavior and enhance security, thereby improving revenue assurance for firms selling such digital goods in the marketplace.

4.1 Digital music and sampling

Music is a hedonic product whose evaluation is based primarily on the experience it provides to a consumer rather than on specific product attributes (Dhar and Wertenbroch, 2000; Moe and Fader, 2001). Consequently, sampling of music is an important influencer for consumer purchase decisions. This has prompted record companies to employ radio airplay as a primary form of advertisement (Montgomery and Moe, 2000). From a historical perspective, individuals had the capability to record radio broadcasts on tape recorders since well before the 1960s. Quality, however, was not very good and record companies took little note. As technology improved, record companies began to take interest and strove to develop embedded signals that lessened the value of reproductions of commercial music cassettes. Technological improvements have continued to enhance consumers' capability to copy and share music products. But before today's P2P environment, copying required acts of "borrowing" and "returning" between trusted individuals—not always popular and certainly not prone to mass activities. Now, P2P networks have raised the possibility of sharing to entirely new levels, and the music industry has repeatedly raised the alarm, calling for enhanced enforcement of existing regulations (Clark, 2000; IFPI, 2002; Sarma, 2002) and the introduction of additional legislation (BBC News Online, 2002b; Freeman, 2003; IFPI, 2002).

But what do we really know about the impact of music file sharing on P2P? Is it possible that these exchanges actually serve as significant sampling mechanisms for individuals who, based on this "trial listening" information, subsequently purchase the higher quality production good? In fact, Peter Fader's expert report to the court in the Napster case suggests such positive impacts (Fader, 2000). However, there has been little analysis utilizing data collected from observing activities on P2P music sharing networks. It has been observed that while radio airplay, as measured by Broadcast Data Systems, measures the advertising effort for given music albums (Moe and Fader, 2001), airplay does not closely measure consumer interest in such albums (BusinessWeek Online, 2003). In fact, anecdotal evidence points to misjudgment of consumer interest and related promotional activities of new artists and albums by record companies (Love, 2000; Steinberg, 2002). Given the increasing interest in marketing hedonic products, Givon et al. (1995), Jedidi et al. (1998), Krider and Weinberg (1998), Radas and Shugan (1998), and Sawhney and Eliashberg (1996) observed "trial listening" information from P2P networks may be used to predict consumer interest and subsequent sales for music albums. Music is unique and different from, say, motion pictures as consumers need significantly less time to sample and repeatedly listen to the same music (over a period of time); hence, sampling is a natural prelude to subsequent purchase. It is also different from software as it takes much less skills to enjoy music, it is smaller in size and hence easier to share and sample, and the volume of available music is significantly larger than the volume of available software. Hence, sampling before purchase is an innate characteristic of music.

The music industry repeatedly cited lagging CD sales as clearly due to piracy. But there are various other explanatory factors for declining CD sales including cited decreases in new album releases by major labels, a generally sluggish economy, and pricing issues. Simon Goodley (2003) offered the following information on new releases:

> Figures posted on the Recording Industry Association of America's website reveal that the number of new US music releases has fallen by 31 percent to about 27,000 from 38,000 in 1999. Throughout the 1990's, the trend was for the number of new releases to rise.

Mike Shalett, President and Chief Executive of SoundScan, suggested the inevitable quality issue in his comments that, quite simply, he did not think "the music was as exciting in 2001" (Ordonez, 2002). Despite claims of piracy on P2P networks, a recent article suggested that the music industry may actually be trying to collect and utilize "trial listening" information from P2P networks to predict sales (BusinessWeek Online, 2003). Hence, it is clear that sampling is an integral component for consumers to discover and potentially purchase new music. However, sampling music is fundamentally different from traditional models of sampling, say for a brand of tuna, as explained in Section 4.2. This necessitated the development of new models to understand and capture the unique nature of sampling in such digital goods.

4.2   Models of sampling for digital products

Gopal et al. (2006) focused on the economic dynamics of online digital music sampling and information sharing and its implications for consumers and sellers of such goods. An economic model that incorporates the incentive structure for consumers and sellers was developed and tested.

The analysis provides several interesting insights. We show that decreasing sampling costs would not only lead more potential consumers to sample unknown music items but it would actually lead more consumers to buy the music items that they have sampled. This directly follows from the fact that lower sampling costs have a positive effect on the consumer surplus of samplers, which in turn has a positive effect on their purchasing intentions. This has major implications for the music industry, in that the industry can potentially reverse the effects of online audio piracy by providing more legal and efficient sampling techniques that consumers could use. This is contrary to the anecdotal belief that online availability of digital music leads only to a drain on profitability. This efficient sampling may be offered in the form of easily searchable indexes of music items, fast download access to music items in different secure formats, provisions of posting consumer reviews on items, creation of fan club sites within the search portal, and so on. Some of these components of faster and more efficient sampling are now being made available on online music portals—several years after research pointed to that direction—however, there is little evidence of an integrated offering of such strategies.

The effect of sampling on sales depends on the true intrinsic value of the music item, *ceteris paribus*. The impact of music availability online has a differential impact based on the realized value of the music to the consumers. For higher valued songs, online search and sampling capabilities have a beneficial impact on sales. Lower valued music items are pirated more than higher valued items, *ceteris paribus*, and consequently sales of those suffer. If a producer is aware of the true value of a song to consumers, he can set the price accordingly to maximize profits. For producers, the model shows that in the presence of online music sampling, uniform pricing for all music items is a sub-optimal strategy. The key challenge is to obtain priors on this realized value, so that differential pricing schemes can be effectively implemented based on music valuations. Techniques to obtain this critical information and derive appropriate pricing schemes are of critical importance. However, at this time, we see a preponderance of uniform pricing of music items, especially from online music vendors, which provides a sub-optimal quality signal to consumers and may be leading to poor price discrimination and demand satisfaction of consumers.

The empirical evaluation in the research described earlier provides strong support to the hypotheses that the existing superstar phenomenon in the music business is positively aided by high sampling costs and that this superstar status is threatened by the advent of efficient online music sampling services. Superstars come under increasing threat from two fronts: (a) a greater proportion of sampling of a superstar's music may lead to piracy—users who sample do so with increased intention to pirate and

(b) decreasing sampling costs lead to erosion of superstardom. However, there is a greater probability of discovering other high-quality music items by lesser known artists with the new technology, which will hurt a superstar's sales—and hence status. Hence online music sharing technologies tend to threaten some superstars and favor other lesser known artists, *ceteris paribus*, and it is understandable that some superstars would have reservations toward it. This has created a schism in the artistic community. There is anecdotal evidence that some superstars, such as the heavy metal group Metallica and rapper Dr. Dre, have opposed such sampling technology (Gomes and Mathews, 2001). Others, including Don Henley[6] and Alanis Morisette and other lesser known artists and groups, have supported it, including in US Judiciary subcommittee hearings. This poses a potentially disruptive question in music business circles—how does one change a well-known and existing business model, dependent on superstars for its revenue stream, to another one that would secure the revenue stream and assure business continuity? We detail some such business models below.

4.3 Search process and costs—why is digital music different?

Search costs have been widely studied in the literature (refer, e.g., Chircu and Kauffman, 2003; Gastwirth, 1976; Stigler, 1961; Telser, 1979). Nelson (1970) modeled a consumer who searches through different brands of canned tuna fish (a prototypic *experience* good) to find her favorite brand. Once the consumer finds the brand she likes, she no longer needs to search further for her next purchase since the same brand would be expected to have the same taste over time. While there has been increasing interest in the marketing of hedonic products (Krider and Weinberg, 1998; Radas and Shugan, 1998; Sawhney and Eliashberg, 1996), we suggest that that the search process for digital music is significantly different from a prototypical search process. Each piece of musical performance contains its own unique characteristics. For a consumer, searching and finding a music item by a particular artist that the consumer likes is no guarantee that the next music item by the same artist (read *brand*) would be similarly liked by the consumer (have the same "value"). This variability together with a large volume of music items available suggests that consumers are likely to perform additional searches for additional products, a process quite different from that modeled in earlier studies.

In sum, differences relating to ease of sharing, potential permanence of the product, characteristics that set music files apart from computer software, and a rather different search process lead us to the development of new models specifically for the evolving digital music market.

---

[6]Don Henley was a founding member of the legendary group Eagles, of *Hotel California* fame.

In Section 4.4, we detail some business models that incorporate the nature of search and sampling in digital goods.

4.4 Search- and sampling-based profitability models

Here, we examine the conditions under which online sharing networks might benefit retailers. Might it be the case that electronic music sharing/ piracy options actually foster increased searching by consumers seeking to experience the product before making the purchase decision? Is it possible that increased searching is linked to increased sales and thus increased benefits for retailers? In fact, there is anecdotal evidence pointing toward online sampling as increasing sales (Kot, 2002; Matthews, 2000). In addition, there is some indication that the music industry is realizing that these networks cannot be closed down by legal means alone. In short, the industry needs to develop new business models, pricing strategies, and licensing schema (Healey, 2003; Weber, 2002).

We present a model of consumer search for such a hedonic product where each item might produce a unique experience (Bhattacharjee et al., 2006b). Utilizing this consumer search process, we analyze a series of market models for a monopolistic retailer of such digital goods, which represent differing environments, pricing options, and licensing arrangements. Our models include the traditional brick-and-mortar retailer, an online retailer offering per unit pricing, an online retailer offering subscription pricing, and an online retailer offering both types of pricing options.

Our theoretical results suggest that under certain conditions, contrary to common perception, a retailer may actually do better in an environment with piracy, largely due to consumers' use of downloads as a means of pre-purchase sampling. We find that revenues from an online model offering both subscription and per unit pricing dominate other online models studied. However, pricing and retailer profits do not have closed form solutions under various licensing structures and piracy environments. Hence, we extend our investigation with computational analyses to study the interactions of these retailer controllable factors and environment variables–in the absence of publicly available empirical data—and gain insights into these and other emerging online market scenarios, some of which are not yet available to consumers. Key results from these experiments are the following:

  (i) online selling strategies for an existing traditional retailer can provide additional profits even under piracy environments;
  (ii) efficient search techniques are essential to attract consumers to legal online markets;
 (iii) maximum profit solutions do not occur in the absence of piracy; and
 (iv) licensing cost structures of online retailers with music publishers have a significant impact on pricing and profits.

5 Discussion and conclusion

To summarize, our broad-based research on illegal procurement of digital products and subsequent development of technological, legal, and economic measures to secure the products and associated revenue streams indicate that all these measures are a necessary component to fight the growing menace of illegal activity in this domain. Several times, popular opinion and media commentary runs counter to the fact, which points to the need for rigorous data- and model-based research in these affected areas. For example, our research has found that decreasing piracy does not necessarily imply increasing profits. Rather, maximum profit outcomes occur in the presence of piracy (Bhattacharjee et al., 2006b). Seeking regulatory means to stop piracy is likely to be a self-harming strategy. Part of access to unauthorized networks enabling music sharing may well be pre-purchase sampling, an activity aiding consumers to make better purchases. Our analysis also suggests that online music sale is a dominant strategy for retailers.

Our results also indicate that a *mixed* model, where a consumer can either subscribe or purchase music *ala carte*, is the dominant strategy for the retailer. Interestingly, this dominance continues to hold even when the search cost in the legal channel exceeds that in the illegal channel. Various companies, including Apple, Roxio, Musicmatch, Wal-Mart, Sony, and Microsoft, have or are planning online music services (Matthews and Wingfield, 2003). Our analysis suggests that some of them may be missing a dominant strategy—the *mixed* strategy. Likewise, license fee structure with music publishers is a significant factor affecting pricing and overall profits. We show that a lump sum or percent of revenue payment model dominates a per-download cost structure, suggesting a need for new licensing models for online music sales (for details, please refer Bhattacharjee et al., 2006b).

There is also a perception that well-known artists and their high-value albums are the biggest losers in the scourge of piracy of digital music. However, one of our empirically driven studies shows that although a music album's survival on the Billboard charts has decreased significantly in the years following the P2P technology explosion, superstars (and solo female artists) continue to survive long. This is potentially a result of search and sampling costs remaining high even with the advent of basic P2P services. In fact, an interesting result was that P2P sharing did not hurt the survival of top-ranked albums but has a negative impact on low-ranked albums. This result is extremely important for several genres of digital goods and points to an increased risk from rapid information sharing for all but the cream of the crop (Bhattacharjee et al., 2007).

The overall economic implications of this analysis are generally applicable to other similar digital goods. A subsequent critical issue for producers and distributors of such goods is to estimate market demand and set differentiated prices to maximize returns. Additional research needs to be conducted to derive enhanced pricing models for such goods that incorporate individual consumer valuations and other marketing models that utilize consumer attitudes toward such goods. The enormous level of monetary resources at stake demands further investigation into newer models that maximize the value of digitized intellectual property.

Online technologies are fundamentally altering the landscape of the digital goods industry. While consumers clearly stand to gain from these opportunities, the music industry can also reap significant benefits through effective strategies. Technology has forever changed the way consumers sample and procure these items, and the pot of gold awaits retailers who can understand the new landscape and adapt appropriately.

References

Associated Press. (2003). Norwegian hacker cracks iTunes code, November 27. Available at http://www.chinadaily.com.cn/en/doc/2003-11/28/content_285577.htm

BBC News Online. (2002a). Global music sales drop. April 16. Available at http://news.bbc.co.uk

BBC News Online. (2002b). Internet boss challenges piracy fears. April 25. Available at http://news.bbc.co.uk

Bergstein, B. (2005). Copy protection still a work in progress. *Associated Press*, November 18. Available at http://www.accessmylibrary.com/coms2/summary_0286-11641609_ITM

Bhattacharjee, S., R.D. Gopal, K. Lertwachara, J. Marsden (2006a). Impact of legal threats on individual behavior: an analysis of music industry actions and online music sharing. *Journal of Law and Economics* 49(1), 91–114.

Bhattacharjee, S., R.D. Gopal, K. Lertwachara, J.R. Marsden (2006b). Consumer search and retailer strategies in the presence of online music sharing. *Journal of Management Information Systems* 23(1), 129–159.

Bhattacharjee, S., R.D. Gopal, K. Lertwachara, J.R. Marsden, R. Telang (2007). The effect of digital sharing technologies on music markets: a survival analysis of albums on ranking charts. *Management Science* 53(9), 1359–1374.

Bhattacharjee, S., R.D. Gopal, G.L. Sanders (2003). Digital music and online sharing: software piracy 2.0? *Communications of the ACM* 46(7), 107–111.

Bradley, M. (2005). Sony aims at pirates - and hits users. *Christian Science Monitor* (November 9). Available at http://www.csmonitor.com/2005/1109/p14s01-stct.html

BusinessWeek Online. (2003). File trading as CD sales predictor? *BusinessWeek Online*, February 20.

Chircu, A.M., R.J. Kauffman (2003). Special section: competitive strategy, economics, and the internet. *Journal of Management Information Systems* 19(Winter), p. 3.

Clark, D. (2000). Steps by music industry to halt internet piracy may be futile. *The Wall Street Journal*, Tech Center, June.

Clarke, G. (2005). DVD Jon hacks media player file encryption. *The Register* (September 2). Available at http://www.theregister.co.uk/2005/09/02/dvd_jon_mediaplayer/

Cohen, J.E. (2003). DRM and privacy. *Communications of the ACM* 46(4), 46–49.

Conner, K.R., R.P. Rumelt (1991). Software piracy: an analysis of protection strategies. *Management Science* 37, 125–139.

Coyte, P.C., D.L. Ryan (1991). Subscribe, cancel, or renew: the economics of reading by subscription. *Canadian Journal of Economics* 24, 101–123.

Craver, S.A., M. Wu, B. Liu, A. Stubblefield, B. Swartzlander, D.W. Wallach, D. Dean, E.W. Felten (2001). Reading between the lines: lessons from the SDMI challenge. *Proceedings of 10th USENIX*

Security Symposium, August 13–17, Usenix Association, Washington, DC. Available at http://www.usenix.org

Dhar, R., K. Wertenbroch (2000). Consumer choice between hedonic and utilitarian goods. *Journal of Marketing Research* 37, 60–71.

Erickson, J.S. (2003). Fair use, DRM, and trusted computing. *Communications of the ACM* 46(4), 34–39.

Fader, P.S. (2000). Expert report of Peter S. Fader, Ph.D. in: *Record Companies and Music Publishers vs. Napster*, July 26, United States District Court, Northern District of California.

Felten, E.W. (2003). A skeptical view of DRM and fair use. *Communications of the ACM* 46(4), 56–61.

Felten, E.W. (2005). Inside RISKS: DRM and public policy. *Communications of the ACM* 48(7), p. 112.

Feuilherade, P. (2004). Online piracy devastates music. *BBC News Online*, March 4. Available at http://news.bbc.co.uk/go/pr/fr/-/2/hi/technology/3532891.stm

Freeman, K.L. (2003). A Mickey Mouse Ruling from the U.S. Supreme Court: Intellectual Property Challenges, Rejection of them, Dissents, The Legal Intelligencer. *American Lawyer Media*, January 30.

Gale, D., R.W. Rosenthal (1994). Price and quality cycles for experience goods. *The RAND Journal of Economics* 25, 590–607.

Gastwirth, J.L. (1976). On probabilistic models of consumers search for information. *Quarterly Journal of Economics* 90, 38–50.

Givon, M., V. Mahajan, E. Muller (1995). Software piracy: estimation of lost sales and the impact on software diffusion. *Journal of Marketing* 59, 29–37.

Glazer, A., R. Hassin (1982). On the economics of subscriptions. *European Economic Review* 19, 343–356.

Gomes, L., A.W. Mathews (2001). Napster suffers a rout in appeals court—Decision casts grave doubt on operating prospects for web music entity. *The Wall Street Journal* (February 13), p. A3.

Goodley, S. (2003). Disharmony over music pirates on the internet. *The Telegraph*, January 9. Available at http://www.telegraph.co.uk

Gopal, R.D., G.L. Sanders (1997). Preventive and deterrent controls for software piracy. *Journal of Management Information Systems* 13(44), 29–48.

Gopal, R.D., G.L. Sanders (1998). International software piracy: analysis of key issues and impacts. *Information Systems Research* 9(4), 380–397.

Gopal, R.D., G.L. Sanders (2000). Global software piracy: you can't get blood out of turnip. *Communications of the ACM* 43(9), 82–89.

Gopal, R.D., S. Bhattacharjee, G.L. Sanders (2006). Do artists benefit from online music sharing? *The Journal of Business* 79(3), 1503–1534.

Graham, J. (2003). RIAA lawsuits bring consternation, chaos. *USA Today Online*, September 10. Available at http://www.usatoday.com/tech/news/techpolicy/2003-09-10-riaa-suit-reax_x.htm

Halderman, J.A. (2002). Evaluating new copy-prevention techniques for audio CDs. *Proceedings of 2002 ACM Workshop on Digital Rights Management*, November 18, 2002, Association of Computing Machinery, Washington, DC.

Harmon, A. (2003). Suit settled for students downloading music online. *The New York Times*, May 2, p. A22.

Healey, J. (2003). Song sharing by iTunes users stirs piracy concerns; Apple's music-buying software can be used to access other people's collections on the Net. *Los Angeles Times*, May 14.

Hellwig, E. (2002). Memo to the record companies: downloading can't be stopped. *Business 2.0*, March 6.

Holbrook, M.B., R.M. Schindler (1989). Some exploratory findings on the development of musical tastes. *Journal of Consumer Research* 16, 119–124.

IFPI. (2002). Music Piracy Report. International Federation of the Phonographic Industry, June, London.

Jedidi, K., R.E. Krider, C.B. Weinberg (1998). Clustering at the movies. *Marketing Letters* 9(4), 393–405.

Jenkins, H.W., Jr. (2003). Business world: the music stops, again. *The Wall Street Journal*, January 15, p. A11.

KaZaA.com. (2004). About the Revolution! KaZaA.com. Available at http://www.KaZaA.com/revolution/revolution.htm. Accessed on June 10.

Kot, G. (2002). Wilco defies experts as 'FoxTrot' gallops. *Chicago Tribune*, May 2.

Krider, R.E., C.B. Weinberg (1998). Competitive dynamics and the introduction of new products: the motion picture timing game. *Journal of Marketing Research* 35, 1–15.

Lichtman, D.G. (2003). KaZaA and punishment. *The Wall Street Journal*, September 9.

Liebeskind, J., R.P. Rumelt (1989). Markets for experience goods with performance uncertainty. *The RAND Journal of Economics* 20, 601–621.

Logie, J. (2006). *Peers, Pirates and Persuasion: Rhetoric in the Peer-to-Peer Debates.* Available at http://www.parlorpress.com/pdf/PeersPiratesPersuasion-Logie.pdf. Parlor Press, West Lafayette, IN.

Love, C. (2000). Courtney Love does the math. Salon.com, Technology and Business. Available at http://dir.salon.com/tech/feature/2000/06/14/love/index.html. Accessed on June 14.

Matthews, A.W. (2000). Sampling free music over the internet often leads to a sale—poll adds to conflicting data as recording industry sorts out Web's impact. *The Wall Street Journal*, June 15, p. A3.

Matthews, A.W., N. Wingfield (2003). Apple's planned music service for Windows attracts rivals. *The Wall Street Journal Online*, May 9.

McMillan, R. (2006). Settlement ends sony rootkit case. *PC World*, May 23.

Moe, W.W., P.S. Fader (2001). Modeling hedonic portfolio products: a joint segmentation analysis of music compact disc sales. *Journal of Marketing Research* 38(August), 376–385.

Montgomery, A.L., W. W. Moe (2000). Should Record Companies Pay for Radio Airplay? Investigating the Relationship Between Album Sales and Radio Airplay, June, Working paper, Marketing Department, The Wharton School, University of Pennsylvania.

Nelson, P. (1970). Information and consumer behavior. *The Journal of Political Economy* 78, 311–329.

Oi, W.Y. (1971). A Disney Land dilemma: two-part tariffs for a Mickey Mouse monopoly. *Quarterly Journal of Economics* 85, 77–96.

Ordonez, J. (2002). Album sales fell 2.8% in '01 as top bands failed to strike a chord with listeners. *The Wall Street Journal*, January 4.

Ordover, J.A., R.D. Willig (1978). On the optimal provision of journals qua sometimes shared goods. *The American Economic Review* 68, 324–338.

Patrizio, A. (1999). Why the DVD hack was a cinch. *Wired News*, November 2. Available at http://www.wired.com/news/technology/0,1282,32263,00.html

Radas, S., S.M. Shugan (1998). Seasonal marketing and the timing of new product introductions. *Journal of Marketing Research* 35, 296–315.

Recording Industry Association of America (RIAA). (2003). Recording industry begins suing P2P file sharers who illegally offer copyrighted music online, September 8. Available at http://www.riaa.com/newsitem.php?news_month_filter = 9&news_year_filter = 2003&resultpage = 2&id = 85183A9C-28F4-19CE-BDE6-F48E206CE8A1

Reuters (2005). Sony tests technology to limit CD burning. *CNET News*, June 1. Available at http://news.cnet.co.uk/digitalmusic/0,39029666,39189658,00.htm

Riordan, M.H. (1986). Monopolistic competition with experience goods. *Quarterly Journal of Economics* 101, 265–280.

Sarma, N.A.K. (2002). The life and death of a copyright. *Business Line, The Hindu*, December 4.

Sawhney, M.S., J. Eliashberg (1996). A parsimonious model for forecasting gross box office revenues. *Marketing Science* 15(2), 113–131.

Schneier, B. (2000). *Secrets and Lies: Digital Security in a Networked World.* Wiley, New York.

Shapiro, C. (1983). Optimal pricing of experience goods. *The Bell Journal of Economics* 14, 497–507.

Siwek, S.E. (2004). Copyright Industries in the US Economy: The 2004 Report, produced by Economists Incorporated for the International Intellectual Property Alliance. Available at http://www.iipa.com/

Siwek, S.E. (2006). Copyright Industries in the US Economy: The 2006 Report, produced by Economists Incorporated for the International Intellectual Property Alliance. Available at http://www.iipa.com/

Smith, E. (2005). Sony BMG faces civil complaint over CD software. *The Wall Street Journal,* November 22.

Steinberg, B. (2002). A CD spins full circle at AOL—A hard-to-peg band named Wilco was out—Then back in. *The Wall Street Journal,* May 8, p. B9H.

Stigler, G.L. (1961). The economics of information. *Journal of Political Economy* 69, 213–225.

Sundararajan, A. (2004). Managing digital piracy: pricing and protection. *Information Systems Research* 15(3), 287–308.

Telser, L.G. (1979). A theory of monopoly of complementary goods. *Journal of Business* 52, 211–230.

Wagstaff, J. (2002). Music industry may be exaggerating losses from file-sharing, Net radio. *The Wall Street Journal,* May 15.

Weber, T.E. (2002). Record companies should attempt to compete for music's fan loyalty. *The Wall Street Journal Online,* April 15.

Rao & Upadhyaya, Eds., *Handbooks in Information Systems, Vol. 4*

Chapter 20

Advances in the Economics of Information Security

Vineet Kumar and Tridas Mukhopadhyay

Tepper School of Business, Carnegie Mellon University, Pittsburgh, PA 15213, USA

Byung Cho Kim

Pamplin College of Business, Virginia Tech., Blacksburg, VA 24061, USA

Abstract

A great deal of research based on economic theory has emerged recently on a cross section of problems of information security. In this chapter, we review, evaluate, classify, and synthesize the published and on-going research at the intersection of economic theory and information security. We specifically describe and examine the topics and concepts on which economic tools from game theory, industrial organization, and microeconomics can be applied. These include works examining the roles of various actors involved in information security decision making namely, security managers, CIOs, regulators, firms as well as hackers and insiders. Each actor differs in terms of goals, private information and available strategy sets. We consider areas of the literature that involve both multi-agent optimizations with shared goals as well as strategically opposed agents with different goals. We evaluate the role of incentives in shaping the behavior and strategies of decision makers in various contexts (e.g., firms protecting themselves from hackers or regulators deciding on optimal information-sharing policies). We also look at how economic principles can improve the design of security technology. Specific examples of economic analysis on the selected topics are provided to show how economic tools can be applied in the domain of information security.

1 Introduction

The information security industry has experienced a high growth rate in the past few years due to increasing Internet usage, broadband adoption as well as the increasing complexity of software systems and regulatory requirements. Anderson (2001) discusses various misaligned economic incentives in the context of information security and argues that socio-economic factors contribute more than technical risks to poor security. He observes that the economics of the software industry gives software vendors little incentive to create secure software. Many firms spend significant fractions of their IT budgets on security, and are interested in under-standing the economic factors that underlie the market. In this chapter, we selectively survey the extant literature on the economic aspects of Information Security that illustrates, generally, applicable concepts and modeling approaches. We consider perspectives that we believe will be helpful to researchers in computer science and related areas as well as to economists who are interested in examining research issues in the economics of information security. In doing so, our objective is also to classify much of the research in this field by developing a broad framework that applies to this research area. We focus on outcomes at the level of users, firms, and markets as well as public policy implications in several settings. From a theoretical standpoint, most papers in the literature use tools and concepts from microeconomics, game theory as well as regression-based econometric methods.

To characterize the major contributions made to the literature, in Fig. 1 we illustrate the information security event sequence[1] that captures most of the actions, decisions and key constructs from the discovery of a vulnerability to the effects of a breach and consequent damages.

The reasoning is that exploits and attacks leading to breaches of security have their origins in software or hardware vulnerabilities or in policy design, implementation or enforcement. When vulnerabilities are discov-ered by hackers, they could create exploits that can attack systems that suffer from the vulnerability. If the discovery is made by the firm or a benign user, then it could potentially be disclosed to the software producer and patched before it is exploited. The attack on systems may be asynchronous (e.g., a worm) or triggered by user action (like opening an e-mail with a malicious attachment). Countermeasures like firewalls can also block attacks from succeeding, but if they do not, the attacks can lead to breached systems and cause damages to users and firms. Finally, in case the user or firm has a cyber-insurance policy, the impact of the losses are diminished according to the terms of the policy.

In employing a microeconomic (or game-theoretic) framework, a first step is to identify the key constructs in the framework. In the context of information security, the following constructs and examples apply[2]:

Actors or Agents: Agents correspond to real-world decision makers like users, hackers, firms, or regulators. Each agent in microeconomic and

---

[1]The arrows merely depict a process through time, and are not meant to signify causation.
[2]See Gibbons (1992) for an accessible treatment of these concepts.

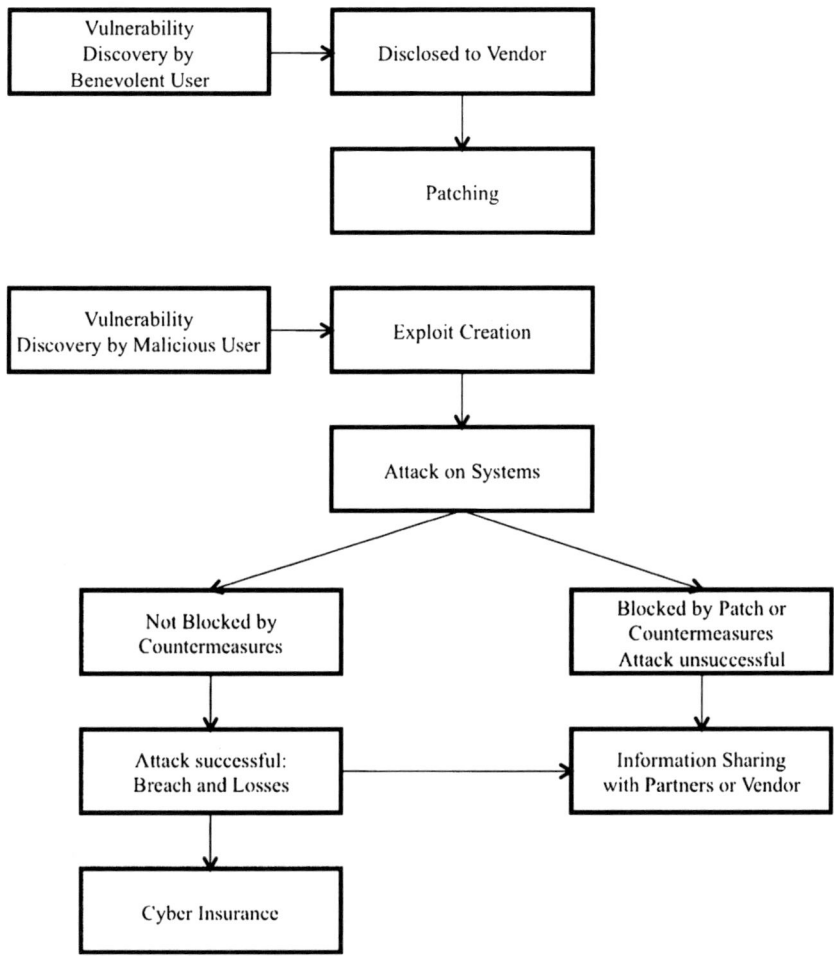

Fig. 1. Sequence of potential events.

game-theoretic models has a well-defined objective function that must be maximized. The actions chosen by the agent serve to optimize the specified objective. The objective of a firm deploying countermeasures is to minimize expected loss or risk exposure.

Strategies: A strategy for an agent characterizes the complete playbook, that is, the entire set of possible decisions that an agent may take at any given time as a function of information available to the agent. Strategies are not synonymous with actions since they represent each player's decision as a function of the decisions of all other players. An example in the security context is that a user's strategy on whether to install a patch can depend on whether other users have patched. A strategy profile is a set comprising of a strategy for each agent playing the game. Mixed strategies involve probabilistically assigning (pure) strategies.

Equilibrium: The literature uses several equilibrium concepts but all of them share the following underlying intuition; an equilibrium is a set of strategies so that no player can profitably deviate from his strategy if all other agents follow their equilibrium strategies. An example of an equilibrium strategy profile might be for all users to install patches or for no user to install patches.

In Table 1, we characterize some of the important research papers along the above dimensions, listing the actors making decisions and the decision factors that result in equilibrium choices.

2 Review of selected literature

The research papers in the literature have chosen some of the areas detailed in Fig. 1 to explore in depth. For tractability, authors often have to make the decision to leave out several of the factors we have detailed, although in several cases the results might not change qualitatively when additional factors are added. We place in sequential context papers that address the issues illustrated in Fig. 1.

2.1 Vulnerabilities

It is useful to define vulnerability in a technological system (hardware or software) as the presence of a flaw in design or in implementation that permits unauthorized usage or access to a resource (data, computer systems, etc.). During the process of creating or writing software, designers and programmers can and do make mistakes. These errors if not caught during the quality analysis and testing phase can develop into vulnerabilities or bugs that do not affect security. Carnegie Mellon University's CERT (Computer Emergency Response Team) publishes a publicly accessible vulnerability list (http://www.kb.cert.org/vuls/) that is submitted by researchers and users. The important questions answered by the literature concerning vulnerability discovery, announcements, information sharing, and patching are

(a) Should software producers be held liable for vulnerabilities caused by software errors? Will this solve the quality issue?
(b) If an ordinary user discovers a bug, should he report it to the producer? Or to an intermediary like CERT? Or auction it off to the highest bidder?
(c) When a software producer discovers a vulnerability, should he make a public disclosure? Wait until a patch is developed? Never report the vulnerability?

Table 1
Select studies in economics of information security

Study	Actors	Decisions studied
Arora et al. (2006)	Software vendor Consumers	Product release timing Quality choice
Arora et al. (2007)	Software vendor Consumers	Vulnerability disclosure Purchase choice
August and Tunca (2006)	Users, software vendor	Patch installation choice, effect of incentives for patching
Boehme (2005)	Firms, insurers	Correlation of platforms, availability of insurance
Campbell et al. (2003)	Firms, stock market	Change in valuation by investors due to breach
Cavusoglu et al. (2005)	Users, firm and hackers	IDS configuration using ROC characteristics
Chen et al. (2006)	Firm	Recovery and platform
Gal-Or and Ghose (2005)	Firms and ISAC	Level of security technology, information sharing
Gordon and Loeb (2002)	Firms	Investments in countermeasures
Huang et al. (2007)	Access providers	Filtering of malicious traffic, incentives for cooperation
Hausken (2006)	Firms	Investment decisions by interconnected firms, income and substitution effect
Hausken (2007)	Firms, social planner	Information sharing, security investments
Kannan and Telang (2005)	Consumers, benign identifiers, hackers and information intermediary	Disclosure, patching
Png et al. (2006)	Users, hackers	Hacker targeting, user precautions
Yurcik and Doss (2002)	Firms, insurers	Policy design, investment in countermeasures

(d) Should users be incentivized (or penalized) to ensure patches are installed? Is it better to make patches mandatory or provide subsidies?

(e) Should firms join a consortium to share information among members regarding vulnerabilities?

Kannan and Telang (2005) model whether markets in vulnerabilities can outperform intermediaries and whether it would help to regulate such a market rather than for its existence. The agents in the model are benign identifiers, users, an attacker, and an intermediary. The intermediary may be a profit maximizing monopolist or a CERT-type nonprofit. Users can choose to subscribe to the intermediary to receive information on discovered vulnerabilities. Both the benign identifiers and the attackers can exert effort to identify the vulnerability quicker. Additionally, they model two cases

   (a) the intermediary may leak the vulnerability information which then exposes nonsubscribers to attacks thus adding the value of being a subscriber and
   (b) a regulated market where the intermediary cannot leak information.

The authors find that in most cases CERT outperforms the unregulated market on the metric of social welfare. They find that if there is a significant likelihood that the vulnerability will be discovered without effort, then CERT always outperforms the regulated market. Additionally, if CERT incentivizes benign identifiers by paying them for reporting vulnerabilities, this can reduce user loss as well as increase social welfare though it may also induce perverse incentives for identifiers who choose not be benign. The presence of an unregulated monopolist can actually worsen user welfare as compared to no market being present. These findings point out that markets in vulnerability are not a panacea and must be treated with caution from a public policy standpoint.

Explicitly examining the role of the software producers, Choi et al. (2007) evaluate the decisions of firms along the following dimensions: investment in measures to improve quality, price of the software whether to announce a discovered vulnerability. The consumer's decision is whether to buy the software and whether to install a patch upon vulnerability discovery where the patching process is costly for the consumer. If the firm does not make a vulnerability announcement, then hackers may independently find the vulnerability and create an attack for it. The decision on whether to announce is nontrivial because some consumers may not patch, and under some parameter conditions, all consumers patching is not a Nash equilibrium. The intuition is driven by the following effect: if everyone else patches and patching is costly, the likelihood of attack is low enough that not patching is optimal. Firms choose not to announce vulnerabilities when the probability of a hacker discovering them is low, and may announce when it is socially optimal not to announce. The assumptions to keep the model tractable are (a) patching cannot be done without announcing the vulnerability—several software publishers provide service packs and updates that fix unknown vulnerabilities; (b) consumers who do not patch can be identified at the time the software is purchased (or that purchasing can be made mandatory); and (c) there is a single vulnerability and patch. The authors choose to abstract away from intermediaries like CERT as well as benign identifiers who may be incentivized to report vulnerabilities—this makes the focus of the chapter complementary to the aforementioned research that choose to model intermediaries or identifiers. Arora et al. (2006) develop a dynamic model to evaluate a software producer's incentive to release buggy software who knows that it can be patched by consumers with little cost and show that software products will be released with more errors than a comparable nonsoftware product. This finding has received support from several anecdotal instances in the news media regarding vulnerabilities in major platforms like Windows Vista and Mac OS X.

Arora et al. (2007) develop a theoretical framework to analyze the optimal timing of vulnerability disclosure and find that vulnerability disclosure policy affects the speed and quality of the software vendors patch. The results show that the software vendor does not have any incentive to release the patch at the socially optimal timing unless threatened with a disclosure policy, which also motivates the software vendor to fix bugs. August and Tunca (2006) study the economic incentives of individual software users under costly patching and negative security externalities. The externalities are present because the larger the number of users with unpatched systems, the easier is the spread of the attack. They find that a subsidy-based policy outperforms mandatory or tax-based policy and suggest that making patching easy and reliable will lead to better security. For open source software, they suggest that a usage-based fee might be appropriate to align users incentives with the social optimum. However, they do not model the vulnerability discovery or publishing process and also abstract away competitive effects between software publishers by focusing on a monopolist.

Gordon et al. (2003a) discuss how information sharing affects the overall level of information security by examining the cost-side of information sharing. They study the firm's trade-off between improving information security and under-investing in security by free riding. Gal-Or and Ghose (2005) develop a game-theoretic model to study the consequences of security information sharing in Information Sharing and Analysis Centers (ISACs). They find that security technologies and information sharing act as strategic complements and that information sharing is more valuable for firms when the substitutability between their products is higher. Hausken (2007) models the interplay of firms' choices: information sharing and security investment. He finds that both information sharing and security investment increase in the interdependence between firms.

Several well-known viruses and worms (e.g., SoBig.F) have exploited known vulnerabilities and caused damages to millions of computer systems. This begs the question of whether software can be improved if procedures were made to ensure that producers bear part of the costs of damages. This issue is commonly debated in the business press (see, e.g., Bank, 2005). In the case of physical products, liability is commonly enforced and defective products are recalled. Kim et al. (2007) study whether this might work in a software setting and we describe their model in detail in the case study section. In this model, information asymmetry between the seller and the buyer leads to incentives for the seller to pass off a low-quality good as a higher-quality one. As a result, bad products drive out good ones, which is even worse when the liability is imposed on the party who is able to evaluate the quality. Since software users are not well informed about security quality, it is easy to find markets dominated by software with poor security quality. Researchers suggest two approaches to improving security quality of software: software liability and cyber insurance. In classical economic theory, Spence (1977) examines the effectiveness of producer liability in terms of preventing product failure in the presence of information asymmetry. He finds that consumer's overestimation of the likelihood of product failure gives the seller incentive for liability and that the product liability can be a signal of quality.

2.2 Exploit creation and deployment

The presence of vulnerabilities by itself is obviously not enough for damages to occur. There must be attackers who create exploits that take advantage of vulnerabilities to either gain access to resources (breaching systems or data assets) or prevent legitimate users from accessing the resources (denial of service). The literature has been cognizant of the importance of attack modeling and examined some of the research questions of critical importance in this area

(a) What are the motivations of attack creators? Does it differ from the attack launchers? Do most of the attackers (creators and launchers) do this for fame and satisfaction, for political reasons, or for profit?
(b) When attackers must exert effort to find vulnerabilities, what is the optimal level of effort from the attackers' viewpoint? Can law enforcement deter such activity by prosecuting offenders?
(c) How do the attacker's objectives influence the decisions of users and firms in their countermeasure provision? Should systems reveal their monitoring or security strategies to deter attackers?

Cremonini and Nizovtsev (2006) examine the role of information where attackers have incomplete information on the type of targets. In the presence of multiple targets, hackers could choose to attack targets that are known to be high value as well as more insecure. However, there is an additional externality in the sense that when certain targets are well secured, hackers shift their attention to other targets (they term this a behavioral shift) and the paper points out the fact that investments in security by specific types of targets may have a larger than proportional change in the breach probability.

Huang et al. (2007) study the important issue of distributed denial of service (DDoS) attacks that use hosts distributed at multiple locations on the Internet to overwhelm a target by simultaneously sending requests to the target. They evaluate the effectiveness of cooperative filtering, which is a process where all the access providers along the path to the target evaluate whether a DDoS is taking place and filter out the traffic in that case.

They identify that the incentives for such cooperative behavior are lacking due to the subscription-based pricing, and suggest usage-based pricing as well as capacity provision networks (CPN) as alternatives that are more appropriate to deal with the problem of DDoS.

2.3 Countermeasures

It is clearly not practical to expect that vulnerabilities are always discovered by software producers or benign users, so end-users (consumers and firms) have to secure their systems with countermeasures to block attacks from succeeding. From an end-users' viewpoint the decision on countermeasure deployment must take into consideration economic considerations. The economic factors obviously involve monetary costs to purchase, install, and deploy the countermeasures, but may also incur additional costs due to business process adjustments and productivity effects. The key research questions involving countermeasures explored in the literature are

(a) What is the optimal amount to invest in each type of counter-measure? When is it critical to consider interaction effects between countermeasures?

(b) In targeted attacks, how does taking the attackers motives change the strategies for securing systems?

(c) When systems are interconnected but managed by different units or individuals, how can they be incentivized to take actions that maximize the social good?

Countermeasures are often designed with specific threats in mind (e.g., antivirus software that attempts to identify viruses by signature) or to only permit specified activities (e.g., a firewall that blocks traffic on all nonessential ports). A single vulnerability may be protected against in several ways: consider a buffer overflow in a software program deployed by an enterprise. To exploit this vulnerability via a network-based attack, an attacker must be able to communicate to the program via specific ports— the traffic passes through the enterprise firewall and host-based protection measures and may be blocked by any of them. However, there are several vulnerabilities in software and hardware that are available for exploitation by attackers. The intricate interaction between these factors contributes to the complexity of modeling security countermeasures at a very detailed level, so reasonable abstractions must be made to achieve tractable models.

Gordon and Loeb (2002) modeled security investments as reducing the probability of attack. Their model provided a starting point for rigorously thinking about marginal effectiveness of security countermeasures. They showed that there are conditions under which firms are better off not investing in countermeasures, depending on the loss caused by a breach, the lower probability of breach due to security investments and the cost of security investments. However, from a practical standpoint, several important factors like interconnected systems, the variety of loss, and countermeasure types needs to be explicitly modeled to better understand the subtleties of economic effects. Cavusoglu et al. (2005) evaluate the functioning of an Intrusion Detection System (IDS) using both decision- and game-theoretic approaches. The primary purpose of an IDS is to evaluate whether traffic is legitimate. Their chapter shows that it is critical to consider the objectives of hackers to optimally configure the system. It is important to note that they used game theory to help in designing and configuring the technology and operating policies, rather than evaluating current systems in place since most extant research has focused on the presence of exogenous technology and modeled its effects on strategies and decisions. Hausken (2006) examines firms' incentive to invest in security technology using an economic model, and finds that increasing interdependence between firms leads to firms' free riding by investing less in security.

Although the importance of factors like security awareness and training has been noted by practitioners, academic research has not rigorously explored the real-world effects of these factors alone or in conjunction with other security measures. A notable exception is a detailed empirical examination of security investments in Japanese enterprises carried out by Tanaka et al. (2006) who use and characterize investment using Annual Loss Expectancy (ALE).

In a related study, they employ a holistic model factoring in the effects of countermeasures, security policies and human cultivation issues like awareness, training, and security education. Controlling for firm and industry-specific factors, they found that policy and human cultivation factors are significant and can play a complementary role to counter-measures. This points out that there is a need for more research from a resource allocation viewpoint that balances investments in countermeasures with appropriate policies and training and education programs for users.

2.4   Recovery measures

Recovery and restoration measures are useful to bring systems back into operation after attacks that affect their availability. An example would be to recover a breached system after a worm attack. Such a measure might involve an IT expert installing patches, reconfiguring the system software, etc. When there are several systems to be restored, the restoration experts often have to prioritize the systems. Chen et al. (2006) model the expected recovery time when all the systems within a firm face a concerted attack and systems share a common platform. Kumar et al. (2007) (detailed in the case study section) also explicitly model the recovery process with two systems and characterize the optimal investment in recovery resources.

Another aspect of recovery is action by the law enforcement in the context of data theft. Although, there have been reports in the trade press on the effectiveness of such actions, researchers have not explicitly modeled the motivations of cyber-criminals as well as insiders. There is a rich literature on the economics of crime with seminal work by Becker (1968) that can serve as a reference when modeling criminal behavior.

2.5 Insurance and risk management

There are several examples of risks that are transferred and can be insured at the enterprise level, for example, theft insurance or fire insurance. Yurcik and Doss (2002) have pointed to the benefits of an insurance market for security risks, that insurance firms will price policies differentially which would result in firms installing security measures to receive lower premiums. Gordon et al. (2003b) identify two categories of risks policy holders may bear (a) direct (or first-party) risks caused by failure of business processes, etc.; (b) indirect (or third-party) risks caused by damages to interconnected firms (suppliers or clients) via a firm's network. Boehme (2005) adds the cause of damage to this classification, differentiating accidental failures from adversarial attacks. The additional problem in cyber-security is that attackers are not likely to be detected or even if identified, they are often not in the same jurisdiction as the victim. In addition to the earlier factors, the following are critical for an insurance market to develop successfully:

(a) accurate data on the probability of damages and the extent of damage,
(b) the applicability of such data in future cases,
(c) there must be advantages due to pooling risks,
(d) verifiability of occurrence and extent of damages, and
(e) countermeasures to diminish risks must be incentivized.

Insurance for cyber-security has failed to become prevalent because it is lacking to some extent on each of the earlier factors. It is well known that correlation in damages will reduce the positive effects of risk pooling. Examining the decisions of insurance firms, Boehme (2005) identifies various software and technological effects that lead to correlation in damages. The first is the presence of similar platforms (versions of Windows or Linux) within enterprises. Second, countermeasures are also often standardized (a hardware firewall may have a default configuration that many users do not change). In addition, there can be attack correlation in the sense that a worm outbreak may attack thousands of hosts virtually simultaneously. Firms can also have standardized policies or best security practices that may reduce expected loss but can have a negative effect in terms of correlation. Boehme (2005) finds that the insurance market may fail to provide coverage due to the negative effects of correlation. There are significant implications for software and hardware producers that standardized products with lower production costs may not always be a good idea from a security viewpoint. Apple Inc. has recently announced a randomized memory allocation scheme in the OS X 10.5 operating system that would reduce such correlation.

In Boehme and Kataria (2006), the authors present an extended classification of correlation at the firm-level (intra-firm correlation) and at the global level, as well as empirically estimating levels of correlation using data from honeypots situated at several world-wide locations. They find that for the development of the cyber-insurance market, high internal correlation, and low global correlation are favorable. The latter effect is because insurance firms can diversify their risk whereas the former effect makes insurance attractive to clients because they cannot self-insure. Chen et al. (2006) evaluate the effect of intra-firm correlation on recovery time and losses caused by unavailable systems. They model the recovery process by an $M/G/1$ queue and find that not just the variance but the expected availability loss increases with the degree of correlation between the systems. This demonstrates the importance of correlation to a risk-neutral decision maker.

3   Case studies

In this section, we explore three studies on different aspects of information security that we hope will serve as examples on how to develop economic models in this area. The first two models use a game-theoretic framework whereas the third uses an empirical econometric approach. These two approaches are often complementary in economics studies, with empirical research serving to test theories as well as provide real-world validation.

3.1   Study 1: an economic analysis of the software market with a risk-sharing contract

Low-security quality of software has been blamed for poor security of our computer networks as major viruses and worms have exploited the vulnerabilities of such software. Software liability has been intensely discussed among computer scientists and jurists for years as a possible solution for software security quality improvement. Kim et al. (2007) propose a risk-sharing mechanism as a way to impose software liability, and analyzes a software vendor's decision on the levels of the security quality and risk-sharing to indemnify the potential loss from the vulnerability exploitation, using an economic model of quality differentiation (Mussa and Rosen, 1978; Ronnen, 1991). The authors examine the feasibility and the effectiveness of the risk-sharing mechanism in the presence of information asymmetry.

There are two players in their model: a software vendor and customers. Let q be the security quality of the software product where $q \in [0, 1]$. Security quality measures vulnerability of the software to attacks at the product launch. Bug-free software can be considered to be of perfect security quality. V is the baseline utility if the software is bug-free. V can be interpreted as the value from the software that a customer enjoys if the software provides perfect security quality. The study focuses on the interplay between security quality and risk-sharing. $K(q)$ is the expected loss in the product lifespan when q-quality software is installed under nontargeted attacks that exploit the vulnerabilities of the software due to imperfect code. Under the proposed risk-sharing mechanism, the vendor takes some proportion of the risk, denoted by r where $r \in [0, 1]$. Thus, the expected utility of a customer who purchases the software with price p is

$$U = \theta[V - (1 - r)K(q)] - p$$

The authors assume that $K'(q) < 0$ and $K''(q) > 0$, so that the expected loss decreases as the security quality level increases at a diminishing rate. θ captures customer heterogeneity indicating how much utility a customer derives from the software. The same attack may cause more severe damage to some firms than others. If θ is high, the customer is more sensitive to security features of the product. θ is assumed to be uniformly distributed on $[0, 1]$. The software vendor's expected profit is

$$\pi = D(p, q, r)(p - rK(q)) - C(q)$$

where $D(p,q,r)$ is the demand for the product, p the price and $C(q)$ represents the initial cost for producing software with security quality level q. A cost function is assumed to be convex, that is, $C'(q) > 0$ and $C''(q) > 0$, so that the cost increases as the security quality level rises at a growing rate. $rK(q)$ is the expected loss, for which the vendor is responsible per unit of the product sold.

3.1.1 Perfect information: a benchmark case

The model is set up in a way that the software vendor first decides the security quality level q, and then the risk-sharing level r, followed by setting up the price p for the software. Finally, the customers decide whether to buy the software based on the baseline utility V, security quality q, risk-sharing level r, and the price p. Demand for the software derived from the expected utility of the customers is

$$D(p, q, r) = 1 - \frac{p}{V - (1 - r)K(q)}$$

The expected profit for the monopolist becomes

$$\pi = \left(1 - \frac{p}{V - (1-r)K(q)}\right)(p - rK(q)) - C(q)$$

The first-order condition for p is $\partial\pi/\partial p = 1 - (2p/(V - (1-r)K(q))) + (rK(q)/(V - (1-r)K(q))) = 0$ and the second-order condition for p is $\partial^2\pi/\partial p^2 = -(2/(V - (1-r)K(q))) < 0$. Thus, solving for the first-order condition for p yields the optimal price that maximizes the vendor's profit as $p^* = (V - (1-2r)K(q))/2$. Substituting p^* in the software vendor's expected profit function leads to $\pi = (V - K(q))^2/(4(V - (1-r)K(q))) - C(q)$. Since $(V - K(q))^2 > 0$ and $K(q) > 0$, zero risk-sharing maximizes the expected profit. The expected profit is maximized with respect to q when

$$\frac{\partial\pi}{\partial q} = -\frac{K'(q)(V - K(q))}{2(V - (1-r)K(q))} + \frac{(1-r)K'(q)(V - K(q))^2}{4(V - (1-r)K(q))^2} - C'(q) = 0.$$

Let M and P in the subscript represent the monopolist software vendor and the case of perfect information, respectively. $r^*_{M,P}$ denotes the optimal risk-sharing level and $q^*_{M,P}$ is the optimal security quality at equilibrium provided by the monopolist software vendor under perfect information. The optimal choice of the risk-sharing and the security quality levels are

$$r^*_{M,P} = 0 \text{ and } \frac{K'(q^*_{M,P})}{C'(q^*_{M,P})} = -4$$

A social planner is one whose priority is to maximize the benefit of the entire society, not like the vendor who pursues profit. The benefit of the entire society in the software market means the sum of all the customers' benefit and the software vendor's profit. The social benefit is maximized when the price is set at the marginal cost, which is $rK(q)$ in their model. Hence, the social benefit can be written as

$$S = \int_{\theta^*}^{1} \theta[V - (1-r)K(q)]d\theta - (1 - \theta^*)rK(q) - C(q)$$

where $\theta^* = rK(q)/(V - (1-r)K(q))$ which simplifies to $S = (V - K(q))^2/2(V - (1-r)K(q)) - C(q)$. Note that $r^* = \arg_r \max \pi(q,r) = 0$ since $(V - K(q))^2 > 0$ and $K(q) > 0$ and the outcome is socially optimal at q which satisfies $\partial S/\partial q = 0$. Let SP in the subscript denote the social planner in the monopoly market. The social benefit in the monopoly market under perfect information is maximized when

$$r^*_{SP,P} = 0 \text{ and } \frac{K'(q^*_{SP,P})}{C'(q^*_{SP,P})} = -2.$$

Neither the social planner nor the software vendor under monopoly wants to share any risk with the customers. This implies that sharing risk with customers may be less cost-efficient than increasing security quality to achieve their goals: maximizing profit or social benefit. The outcome is socially optimal when the social planner allocates all resources to improve security quality rather than to share risk. The social planner is left with no resource to share the loss when it serves the entire market by offering a price at marginal cost. Thus, it turns out that even the social planner does not want to share any risk. Comparison of security qualities provides evidence of under-provided security quality of software under monopoly, as has been observed in the market. The authors also examine the feasibility and the effectiveness of the risk-sharing mechanism under information asymmetry, where customers are misinformed about the possible outcome due to software vulnerabilities.

3.2 Study 2: optimally securing interconnected systems against confidentiality losses

In their study focusing on optimal security decision making Kumar et al. (2007) consider a model of an enterprise with two divisions where the information systems located at each division are connected by an enterprise network. The systems contain confidential data assets so that if they are breached the divisions face a loss. The firm faces attacks by contagious threat sources so that once a threat has breached one division's systems, it can become "trusted traffic" internal to the enterprise network which leaves the other division vulnerable to the attack. Hence, by protecting the systems of a division there is an externality effect where the other division faces lower expected losses as well. The firm is represented by a CIO who seeks to minimize the overall loss of the firm but does not know the characteristics of each division's information systems which is a problem of asymmetric information. The division managers know their system characteristics but since they are ordinarily motivated to minimize the costs of their division, they are likely to ignore the positive externality effect of deploying a higher security level.

Although the authors consider two dimensions of loss, namely availability and confidentiality, we focus our attention here on the latter. The model of the contagious threat source is motivated by Internet worms and viruses, but can apply to more general attack vectors. The major components of the model are as follows $j \in \{1, 2\}$:

1. Susceptibility α_j is the probability that an attack will breach an unsecured information system.
2. Vulnerability $p_j = v(\alpha_j, s_j)$ is the breach probability by external attack in the presence of protection measures of level.

3. L_j is the loss faced when division j is breached.
4. η is the probability of breach by internal attack, that is, by an attack through the enterprise network.
5. The cost of countermeasures is linear in the deployment, $C(s_j) = c \cdot s_j$.

For simplicity, the authors consider a single time period and normalize the cost of countermeasures by the expected number of attacks.

The mutually exclusive and exhaustive events and their associated probabilities are given in the chapter that details nine possible events. For example, in one of the events division 1 is breached via both direct and indirect attacks whereas division 2 is breached only via direct attack. The authors posit that losses due to direct and indirect attacks are not additive since the attacker merely receives access to the same data asset by another means. The overall loss faced by the firm is the weighted sum of the event probability and the loss corresponding to the event (Fig. 2).

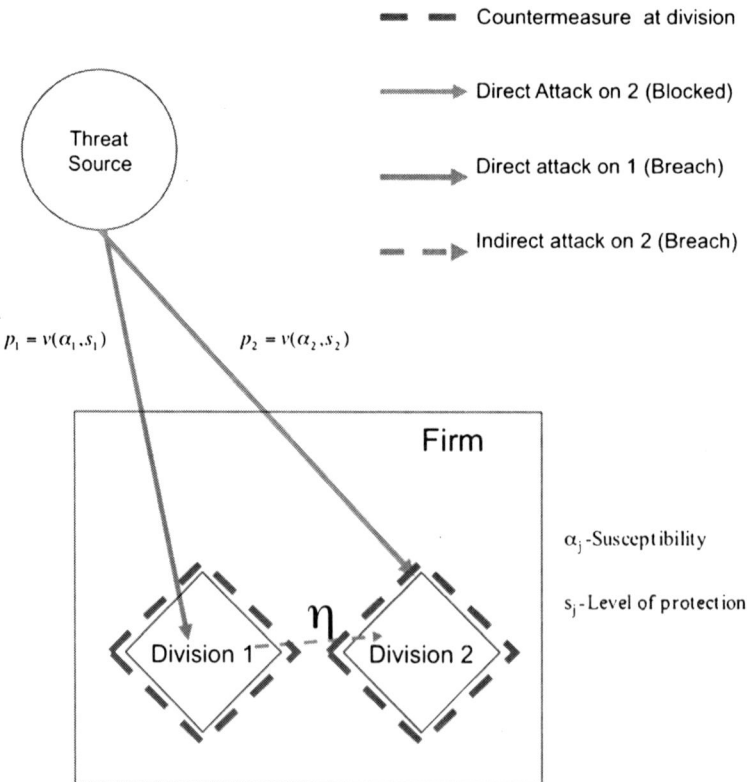

Fig. 2.   Model of contagious threat.

The firm's expected confidentiality loss is then

$$[v(\alpha_1, s_1) + \eta v(\alpha_2, s_2) - \eta v(\alpha_1, s_1) v(\alpha_2, s_2)]L_1$$
$$+ [\eta v(\alpha_1, s_1) + v(\alpha_2, s_2) - \eta v(\alpha_1, s_1) v(\alpha_2, s_2)]L_2 + c(s_1 + s_2)$$

The study evaluates the CIO's decision problem to minimize the expected loss, and compares it to the case where the division managers have decision rights to deploy protection levels for their divisions. The CIO's complete information optimization (first-best) is considered as a benchmark for comparison as well as an aid in designing optimal contracts to incentivize division managers to deploy first-best levels of protection measures. The first order condition (FOC) for the CIO with full information is evaluated for divisions $j \in \{1, 2\}, k = 3 - j$

$$F_j^{CIO}(s_j^{CIO}) = v_s(\alpha_j, s_j^{CIO})\left[(1 - \eta v(\alpha_k, s_k^{CIO}))L_j + \eta(1 - v(\alpha_k, s_k^{CIO}))L_k\right] + c = 0$$

A similar equation results for FOCs with respect to s_k. These combined FOCs result in a set of implicit equations that characterize the first-best solution. When the division managers are vested with decision rights, we need to set $L_k = 0$ when taking the FOCs for s_j and χ_j and vice versa. Doing this analysis results in the following implicit equations for s_j^{DIV}:

$$F_j^{DIV}(s_j^{DIV}) = v_s(\alpha_j, s_j^{DIV})(1 - \eta v(\alpha_k, s_k^{DIV}))L_j + c = 0$$

The authors make several inferences from F_j^{DIV} and F_j^{CIO} regarding the optimal level of protection measures chosen by the CIO and by the division managers.

The optimal level of protection is always higher when the CIO makes deployment decisions—again this effect due to externality is not surprising because division managers do not consider the positive effect of higher security deployments on other divisions. Observe that comparing the FOCs gives us $v_s(\alpha_j, s_j^{CIO}) > v_s(\alpha_j, s_j^{DIV})$, which simplifies to the earlier result.

When the losses are not significantly different, the protection level deployed by the CIO increases with internal vulnerability (η) whereas if protection is deployed by the division mangers, it decreases with η. The authors then apply the implicit function theorem to evaluate $\partial s_j / \partial \eta$ to be negative.

The protection levels at the two divisions are strategic complements.

Protection measures may increase or decrease in susceptibility levels—the degree of convexity and the shape of the function $v(\cdot, \cdot)$ determine the direction.

In general, subsidies will not work to align the incentives of the division managers with the CIO. However, a residual liability mechanism works in theory but imposes demanding informational requirements to implement in practice.

This study illustrates the tensions between asymmetric information and goal divergence, while providing the result that an incentive mechanism can be designed to achieve the optimal result from the point of view of the firm. The important parameters in the model were the susceptibilities and internal vulnerability (η) so it was instructive to do a comparative statics analysis to answer the following question, for instance, as η increases, does the divergence between the protection levels chosen by the CIO and by division mangers increase or decrease? The analysis in the chapter provides well-specified conditions such that the divergence always increases with η. Note that it is not necessary to assume functional forms if closed-form solutions are not required. For example, other researchers have modeled the vulnerability function as $v(\alpha, s) = \alpha e^{-s}$, and have proceeded to derive optimal investments as an explicit function of model parameters. This has the advantage that the protection levels are easily characterized once the parameters are known, and the intuition is easier to grasp. However, the assumption of a specific functional form is to be treated with care to ensure that it is indeed applicable and a reasonable approximation for the phenomenon under study.

3.3   Study 3: the economic costs of publicly announced security breaches

In this study, we consider one of the first empirical contributions to the literature. Campbell et al. (2003)—termed CBLZ (Campbell, Gordon, Loeb, and Zhou) henceforth—performed this study to quantitatively examine the negative effects on firms that had suffered security breaches. As argued in CBLZ, there are several reasons why breaches are materially important: the negative impacts include lost business, efforts to correct and restore systems and legal liability. However, there are valid arguments for the magnitude of such effects being minimal, the most notable is that any activity that was prevented would just occur later when systems become available. Another compelling argument is that firms have secured their critical assets and the breaches represent only the relatively unimportant systems and assets. In this context, the key contribution made by CBLZ is to distinguish between two classes of attacks: those that involve the violation of confidential data assets and those that do not (such denial of service attacks). The distinction is that once confidential information has been compromised it is extremely difficult to ensure that there are no unauthorized copies in circulation. Availability losses, however, are of a temporal nature and are usually recoverable and in most cases fully recoverable. However, the question remains as to how to develop a measure of how firm value is affected. There can be several drivers of such losses including business process continuity—any survey administered to the firm managers, besides being inherently subjective, might fail to capture the full effects.

The authors used an event study methodology with the event being a publicly announced security breach. The data was gathered for a 6-year period from major newspapers for terms that indicate a security breach (e.g., "computer attack" or "hacker"). Note that this restricts attention to major breaches at large corporations that are publicly traded. So, the information is almost surely available to any interested investor in the corporation. The breaches are classified as "confidential" or not as discussed earlier. The hypotheses tested by the authors are reproduced later:

H1o. There is no stock market reaction to public reports of corporate information security breaches.

H2A. There is no stock market reaction to public reports of corporate information security breaches involving unauthorized access to confidential information.

H2B. There is no stock market reaction to public reports of corporate information security breaches that do not involve unauthorized access to confidential information.

The study uses a seemingly unrelated regressions (SUR) approach since several firms experience breaches on the same dates and the ordinary least squares (OLS) assumption of uncorrelated error terms would not hold. For daily returns in the absence of attacks, they use a standard capital asset pricing model (CAPM) model over 120 days to estimate

$$R_{it} = \alpha_i + \beta_i R_{mt} + \varepsilon_{it}$$

where R_{it} denotes the return on day t for firm i (over the risk-free rate), R_{mt} the market return on day t and α_i and β_i parameters are firm-specific intercepts and slopes. The last term is the error. The authors use the data on 121 days before the breach announcement to get firm-specific paramter estimates $\hat{\alpha}_i$ and $\hat{\beta}_i$. The abnormal returns are then computed to be

$$AR_{it} = R_{it} - (\hat{\alpha}_i + \beta_i R_{mt})$$

They then take the sum of the abnormal returns over a 3-day window around the announcement date to get CAR_i, and determine the mean CAR for all announcements.

Using the alternative SUR methodology, the basic model is $R_{it} = \alpha_i + \beta_i R_{mt} + \gamma_i D + \varepsilon_{it}$, where the new variable $D = 1$ if the time period under consideration lies within the 3-day window. The authors test their hypotheses by evaluating whether the coefficients are nonzero and significant.

The authors find that the support for H1o is less robust and depends on the specification used, whereas for confidentiality breaches, the null hypothesis is rejected at a high significance level. This lends support to the assertion that the market treats breaches differently even when controlling for press coverage as this study does.

4 Discussion and future research directions

We have surveyed a wide range of research that has focused on the economic aspects of information security. Several areas, notably vulnerability detection, disclosure and patching as well as investments in countermeasures have been relatively well-explored. Looking to the future, we expect the following issues to gain prominence:

1. *Social networks*: There is increasing focus on social networks due to the popularity of networking sites like Facebook.com. However, in addition to these, cell phone networks are becoming increasingly capable and present new security challenges as these networks open up to applications and services. In this context, it would be critical to examine how security strategy can be optimized to recognize the structure of the underlying network.
2. *Evaluating security countermeasures as a portfolio*: Most studies in the literature have neglected the links between countermeasures. Several countermeasures share signatures and modules that would lead to the conclusion that the joint (or portfolio) effect is what firms and users should consider.
3. *Insider attacks*: According to the latest CSI/FBI survey, insider attacks and data theft are a growing problem and there need to be effective policies that balance the need for monitoring and access control with usability and productivity. How should insiders be monitored? How should access to data assets be allocated?
4. *Empirical studies on the effectiveness of countermeasures*: There is currently a growing body of research on empirically evaluating security investments, costs and losses but there needs to be more rigorous studies that go beyond descriptive statistics and evaluate and enumerate the constructs given by the large set of theoretical papers.

5 Conclusion

In this chapter, we have examined the process by which economic effects of information security are realized, studying consumers and firms as well as market-level issues. At the consumer level, there are several areas that have been studied extensively, for example, patching behavior. However, other areas like identity theft and protection are ripe for future exploration. At the firm-level, optimal investments in security counter-measures and aligning the incentives of decision makers and security portfolio decision making are actively researched but others including training and user-awareness analysis as well as empirical studies on "social engineering" need attention. At the market-level, competitive behavior between vendors has been shown to affect quality of software products and patch release behavior. The presence of intermediaries like CERT and information sharing consortia have been shown to be beneficial.

Overall, we have developed a characterization that places much of the literature at all the above levels in context, and we provide case studies from the literature to help the reader understand the issues in-depth as well as obtain a sense of the economic research methods as applied to information security. We hope this effort will stimulate researchers to undertake issues that have been overlooked or newly developing issues in this field.

6   Suggested readings and resources

1. *Secrets and lies*: Digital Security in a Networked World by Bruce Schneier (2004), published by Wiley. Schneier provides a nice overview of information security for those who want to begin an exploration of the technical computer science aspects.
2. Anderson (2001) provides a broad overview of the economic issues including incentives as well as adverse selection and moral hazard.
3. Gordon and Loeb (2002) is one of the first papers modeling information security from a microeconomic viewpoint.
4. Bibliography of Information Security Economics and Proceedings from the Workshops on the Economics of Information Security (2002–2008). Available at http://www.infosecon.net/workshop/bibliography.php.

References

Anderson, R. (2001). Why information security is hard—an economic perspective, in: *Proceedings of 17th Annual Computer Security Applications Conference*, December 10–14. Available at http://www.cl.cam.ac.uk/~rjal14/Papers/econ.pdf

Arora, A., J. Caulkins, R. Telang (2006). Sell first, fix later: impact of patching on software quality. *Management Science* 52(3), 465–471.

Arora, A., R. Telang, H. Xu (2007). Optimal policy for software vulnerability disclosure. *Management Science* 54(4), 642–656.

August, T., T. Tunca (2006). Network software security and user incentives. *Management Science* 52(11), 1703–1720.

Bank, D. (2005). Companies seek to hold software makers liable for flaws. *Wall Street Journal*, February 24, p. B1, ISSN: 00999660.

Becker, G. (1968). Crime and punishment: an economic approach. *Journal of Political Economy* 76(2), 169–217.

Boehme, R. (2005). *Cyber-insurance revisited.* 4th Workshop on the Economics of Information Security, Cambridge, MA.

Boehme, R., G. Kataria (2006). *Models and measures for correlation in cyber- insurance.* 5th Workshop on the Economics of Information Security, Cambridge, UK.

Campbell, K., L.A. Gordon, M.P. Loeb, L. Zhou (2003). The economic cost of publicly announced information security breaches: empirical evidence from the stock market. *Journal of Computer Security* 11(3), 431–448.

Cavusoglu, H., B. Mishra, S. Raghunathan (2005). The value of intrusion detection systems in information technology security architecture. *Information Systems Research* 16(1), 28–46.

Chen, P., G. Kataria, R. Krishnan (2006). *On Software Diversification, Correlated Failures and Risk Management,* April 8. Available at SSRN: http://ssrn.com/abstract = 906481

Choi, J.P., C. Fershtman, N. Gandal (2007). Network security: vulnerabilities and disclosure policy, in: *Proceedings of the Workshop on the Economics of Information Security (WEIS2007).* Carnegie Mellon University, Pittsburgh, PA.

Cremonini, M., D. Nizovtsev (2006). *Understanding and influencing attackers' decisions: implications for security investment strategies.* 5th Workshop on the Economics of Information Security, Cambridge, UK.

Gal-Or, E., A. Ghose (2005). The economic incentives for sharing security information. *Information Systems Research* 16(2), 186–208.

Gibbons, R. (1992). *Game Theory for Applied Economists.* Princeton University Press, Princeton, NJ, USA.

Gordon, L.A., M.P. Loeb (2002). The economics of information security investment. *ACM Transactions on Information and System Security* 5(4), 438–457.

Gordon, L.A., M.P. Loeb, W. Lucyshyn (2003a). Sharing information on computer systems security: an economic analysis. *Journal of Accounting and Public Policy* 22(6), 461–485.

Gordon, L.A., M.P. Loeb, T. Sohail (2003b). A framework for using insurance for cyber risk management. *Communications of the ACM* 46(3), 81–85.

Hausken, K. (2006). Income, interdependence, and substitution effects affecting incentives for security investment. *Journal of Accounting and Public Policy* 25(6), 629–665.

Hausken, K. (2007). Information sharing among firms and cyber attacks. *Journal of Accounting and Public Policy* 26(6), 639–688.

Huang, Y., X. Geng, A.B. Whinston (2007). Defeating DDoS attacks by fixing the incentive chain. *ACM Transactions on Internet Technology* 7(1), 1–19.

Kannan, K., R. Telang (2005). Market for software vulnerabilities? Think again. *Management Science* 51(5), 726–740.

Kim, B., P. Chen, T. Mukhopadhyay (2007). An Economic Analysis of the Software Market with a Risk-Sharing Contract, Working Paper, Social Science Research Network.

Kumar, V., R. Telang, T. Mukhopadhyay (2007). Optimally Securing Interconnected Information Systems and Assets, Working Paper, Social Science Research Network.

Mussa, M., S. Rosen (1978). Monopoly and product quality. *Journal of Economic Theory* 18, 301–317.

Png, I.P.L., C.Q. Tang, Q.H. Wang (2006). *Hackers, Users, Information Security: Welfare Analysis.* 5th Workshop on the Economics of Information Security (WEIS), Cambridge, UK.

Ronnen, U. (1991). Minimum quality standards, fixed costs, and competition. *RAND Journal of Economics* 22, 490–504.

Spence, M. (1977). Consumer misperceptions, product failure and producer liability. *Review of Economic Studies* 44(3), 561–572.

Tanaka, H., W. Liu, K. Matsuura (2006). *An Empirical Analysis of Security Investment in Countermeasures Based on an Enterprise Survey in Japan.* The 5th Workshop on the Economics of Information Security.

Yurcik, W., D. Doss (2002). *Cyberinsurance: A Market Solution to the Internet Security Market Failure.* Workshop on Economics and Information Security (WEIS), Berkeley, CA.

Part VII
Threat Modeling, Intrusion and Response

Rao & Upadhyaya, Eds., *Handbooks in Information Systems, Vol. 4*

Chapter 21

Threat Modeling and Dynamic Profiling of Networked Applications

Daniel Germanus, Andréas Johansson and Neeraj Suri

DEEDS Group, Department of Computer Science, Technische Universität Darmstadt,
Hochschulstr. 10, 64289 Darmstadt, Germany

Abstract

As networked computing objects become ubiquitous, consequently our reliance on their sustained functionality also increases. Unfortunately, the networked interactions also result in multifaceted threats arising at individual system level that may compromise the security of the entire networked system. To properly assess such threats, to devise countermeasures, and to enhance the design stage resilience of networked designs, a new methodology called threat modeling has emerged. This chapter introduces the basis of threat modeling and outlines its usage as applied to an actual networked application case study.

1 Introduction

The pervasiveness of networked applications concomitantly implies our growing reliance on their sustained functionality, also in the presence of any encountered perturbations be they operational (environment, connectivity, etc.) or deliberate (security breaches). As the components of an application may be spread over multiple systems and also utilizing rapidly evolving net-centric technologies, as a result multifaceted threats can arise at different levels both over design and deployment that might compromise the system's security. In this context, threat modeling (TM) pertains to a multitude of approaches aimed at the objective of threat discovery, threat prevention, and threat mitigation. TM can naturally be conducted at the application design time with access to source code. Obviously this has the benefit of early—and potentially less expensive—threat-discovery and remedial actions apart from a proper incorporation of "secure design and implementation" as a development basis. Alternatively, TM can also be performed *ex post*, *i.e., post application development* and often in the absence of source code, making vulnerability assessments of proprietary source applications possible.

In the following sections, the various TM processes are discussed in detail. We primarily focus on two alternate approaches for integrating TM into the development processes. A comprehensive case study of a real application, a related work section discussing a comparative metric regarding security as well as security testing, and a current work section concludes the chapter.

2   Threat modeling

The goals of TM are manifold such as (a) to discover potential weaknesses in software applications, (b) to model and uncover potential dependencies across operations required to successfully attack a software system, and (c) to categorize discovered threats to the system according to their criticality. In addition, a good threat model also supports other security-related efforts, such as mitigation planning, security testing, and development. During the entire TM process, five key developmental roles are involved

1. *Analysts* take on the main role during TM; they are responsible for collecting information, producing documents, scheduling meetings and so forth.
2. *System architects* impart their detailed knowledge of the software system's architecture and design. They participate during the whole development process to either answer questions or name other participants with detailed knowledge on a specific issue.
3. *Software engineers* answer questions concerning implementation work and offer technology-related knowledge.
4. *Security engineers* provide their experience with security-related technologies, implementations, and design decisions. Depending on the software development team size, this role might be taken over by software engineers.
5. *Software testers* are involved during mitigation planning and—if necessary—to eliminate/mitigate a discovered threat.

The aforementioned roles are engaged during the creation of a threat model, and its outcome is inserted into the next iteration of the software development process to rectify the discovered deficiencies. The outcome may also be of interest for quality assessment purposes.

The overall TM process often consists of three phases. Each phase consists of multiple steps (Fig. 1). In the inception phase, the system is analyzed to gain understanding of its composition, its interaction with

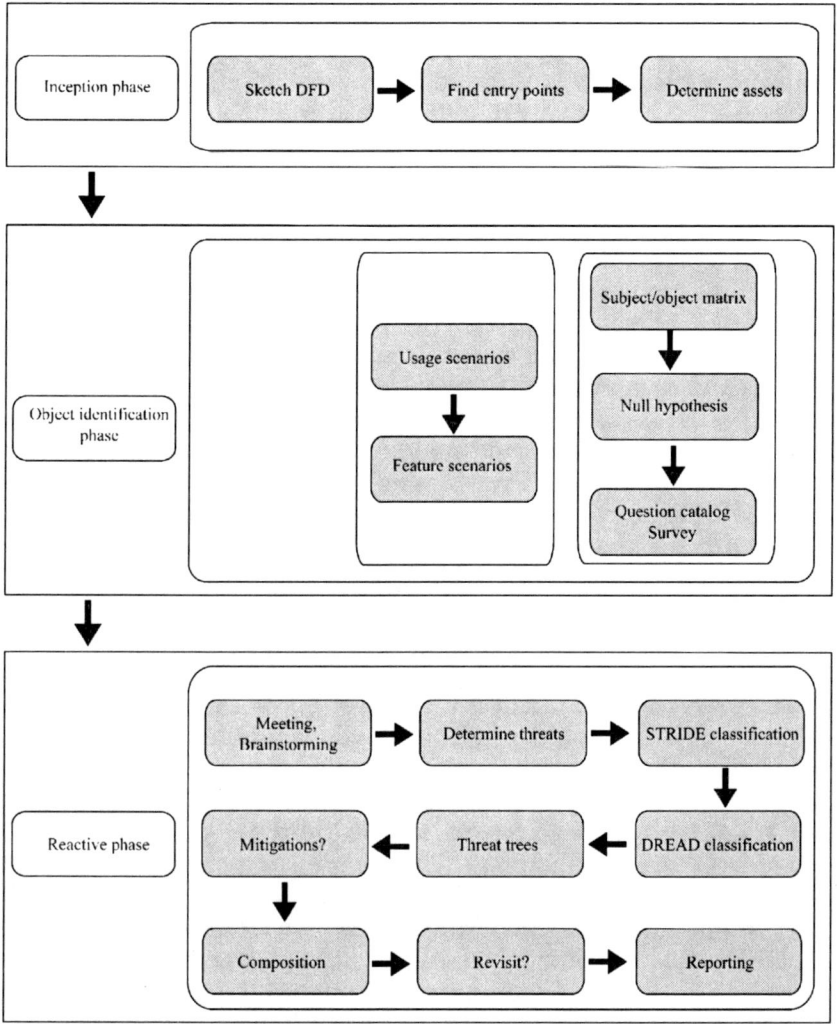

Fig. 1.   Threat modeling methodology.

external entities, and the assets in need of protection. The outcome is a data flow diagram (DFD) describing the system components and their interactions, a list of system entry points, and a list of the assets within the system. The assets are the targets for an attacker. The object identification phase uses this input to determine which actions can be performed in the system, and by whom. For such TM, two alternative approaches are described in this chapter namely, the classical approach and the subject/object (S/O) approach. The outcome of the second phase is a list of discovered vulnerabilities and external dependencies together with a set of questions about the system that needs answering. Finally, in the reactive phase, the threats to the system are identified and classified according to predefined criteria. This is done in a series of meetings where analysts, software and security engineers, and testers review the threats.

2.1   Phase 1

To model the potential threats to the system, we first need to understand the system, its composition and boundaries. This analysis is performed in three steps (1) sketching DFDs, (2) identifying the entry points, and (3) determining assets of the system. Large software systems are split into subsystems and each of them is threat modeled separately, the composition of several partial threat models is explained at the end of this section.

DFDs support analysts in understanding the connections across processes and resources in the system. Processes in TM are different from the process notion used for example in operating systems. A process describes a portion of application program logic and may expand to several subprocesses. Resources refer, for example, to devices or systems dedicated to storing data, network transmissions, or graphics processing. DFDs help in understanding how users (including potential attackers) may interact with the system and which processes and resources are involved in such interactions. Overall, the intent is a visual or graphical illustration of these interactions presented as a dependency graph. A typical threat model graph is drawn using three types of nodes with the requisite connecting edges. Rectangular nodes represent external dependencies, that is, entities beyond the control of the system architects, such as third party components whose source code is unavailable, or system libraries. A rectangular shape with open sides represents data stores. Processes have circular shape. Data flows are represented by edges connecting nodes. An example is illustrated in Fig. 2. DFDs can be built in a hierarchical fashion, where only the pertinent relations are displayed. As an example, process 1 on the left in Fig. 2 consists of several subprocesses (shown using double circles). On the right

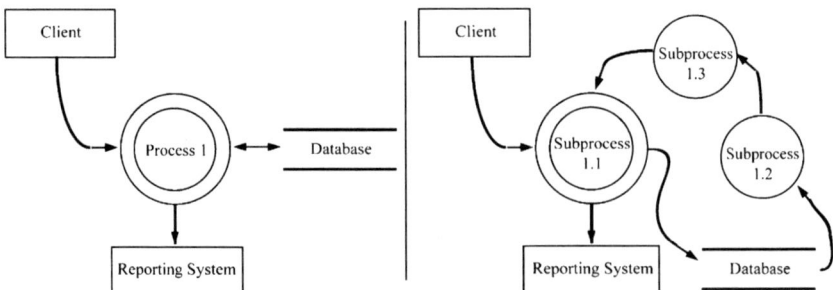

Fig. 2.   Dataflow diagram examples.

side, this process is expanded to include a subset of those subprocesses (process 1.1 contains further subprocesses). Not all diagrams need to offer the same level of detail; nonsecurity relevant components can remain hidden, aiding the analysts to focus on the relevant entities. It is often useful to first sketch an overall visualization for the entire system operations, and to selectively expand with more details if a specific component was identified as critical. Segregation of the overall DFD into smaller ones should be done pursuant to the software design. Three facets emerge, namely

External dependencies that have been discovered during DFD generation, such as third party components, are documented and used later in the process. Although they often cannot be modified, a well reviewed survey of dependencies and modifications to the software components dependent on them results in lessening the likelihood of a successful attack.

Entry points are used to interact with a software system, either in the desired way or during an attack. It is important to note that an attacker can only attack the system if it has access to an entry point to it. Common entry points are graphical user interfaces (GUIs), application programming interfaces (APIs), or network services awaiting connections.

Assets are the entities to be protected. Typically for a software system, assets include sensitive information or service availability. Even though service availability is an abstract asset, it can be made more tangible to make assessments and improvements possible: a company's web server represents an asset, which has a transitive relationship to the abstract assets service availability and the company's profit. Each asset is assigned a risk level representing the expected impact in case it is compromised.

2.2 Phase 2: overview

The information collected so far—DFDs, entry points, and assets—serve as input for the second phase. The crux of this phase is to determine the specific actions users of the software system are allowed to perform and the objects involved. There are two alternative approaches to this: the so-called "classical" approach and the "subject/object" (S/O) approach. The classical approach is either feature or scenario driven. The S/O approach examines the operations between different system entities in detail and produces an adaptable question catalog. We focus primarily on the S/O approach as it represents a development of the classical approach and takes a more defensive perspective, that is, a thorough identification of all possible operations among a system's entities minimizes the eventuality of ignoring facts.

Knowledge about possible operations and their implications provide a basis for threat assessments in the third phase.

2.3 Phase 2: classical approach

During the second phase, the application's operations are determined. Either by means of *use scenarios* or by *feature scenarios*. Use scenarios can be regarded as behavioral patterns of typical users. In a word processor application, this would be for instance typing, opening, saving, and printing documents. Feature scenarios can be derived from use cases of an application's specification. Information like which user class is allowed to perform a specific set of operations is relevant for the subsequent phase. A detailed discussion of the classical approach can be found in Swiderski (2004).

2.4 Phase 2: subject/object approach

The goal of the S/O approach is to identify both the subjects and objects in the system, and especially the allowed operations on them. Subjects are active entities that can carry out *operations* on other entities, the objects. The entities identified in DFDs are used as a basis. Processes and user classes are subjects. There are four object classes: processes, user classes, data stores, and flows. Note that each subject is also an object!

The subjects and objects are put into a matrix, where subjects are represented by rows and objects by columns. Table 1 lists the basic operations assigned to subject–object relations within the matrix. In this case, data stores are subject to fine granular operations resembling to access control lists. For instance, if the application to be threat modeled resides in a traditional UNIX environment, the operations may be simplified to *read, write, and execute.*

Table 1
Operations in subject/object matrix approach

Abbreviation	Object class	Operation
An	User, process	Authenticate
Az	User, process	Authorize
Noxs	User, data store, process	No access
L	Data store	Load
R	Data store	Read
E	Data store	Execute
W	Data store	Write
D	Data store	Delete
Own	Data store, process	Total control over the object
Send	Data flow	Send
Recv	Data flow	Receive

$$\left(\begin{array}{ccccccc} & \textit{Anonymous} & \textit{Client} & \textit{Login} & \textit{ChooseSeat} & \textit{GetBoardingPass} & \textit{DF}:\textit{CustomerDB} & \textit{DF}:\textit{AirplaneDB} \\ \textit{Anonymous} & & & \textit{An} & & & & \\ \textit{Client} & & & & \textit{Az} & \textit{Az} & & \\ \textit{Login} & & & & & & \textit{S/R} & \\ \textit{ChooseSeat} & & & & & & & \textit{S/R} \\ \textit{GetBoardingPass} & & & & & & \textit{S/R} & \textit{S/R} \end{array} \right)$$

Fig. 3.   Example for a subject/object matrix of an airline quick check-in terminal.

$$\left(\begin{array}{cccccc} & \textit{Users} & \textit{Login} & \textit{AirplaneUserOperations} & \textit{DF}:\textit{CustomerDB} & \textit{DF}:\textit{AirplaneDB} \\ \textit{Anonymous} & & \textit{An} & & & \\ \textit{Client} & & & \textit{Az} & & \\ \textit{Login} & & & & \textit{S/R} & \\ \textit{ChooseSeat} & & & & & \textit{S/R} \\ \textit{GetBoardingPass} & & & & \textit{S/R} & \textit{S/R} \end{array} \right)$$

Fig. 4.   Subject/object matrix after object contraction.

Figure 3 depicts an example for a S/O matrix of an airline's quick check-in terminal on a very coarse level. After having identified all matrix entries it may be that some objects (columns) have the same operations for the same subjects. Such objects can be grouped together as they contain redundant information. The same approach is used for subjects (rows). Column contractions are presented in Figs. 3 and 4. The objects representing the two processes *ChooseSeat* and *GetBoardingPass* have been contracted to a process called *AirplaneUserOperations*, because their only operation is authorization by a client subject. Also, the objects *Anonymous* and *Client* have been contracted to a single *Users* object. If necessary, subjects and objects can be expanded again to distinguish for instance different roles of subjects. For example, a subject *Users* could be split up into *Administrator*, *Clerk*, and *Guest* reflecting their different access levels. External dependencies, unresolved questions, and deployment constraints are noted on separate lists. Their entries are removed from the matrix.

Next, potential weaknesses in the system are exposed by inserting an omniscient subject: the *attacker*. The attacker is associated with all available operations on every object in the matrix. Besides, it is assumed that the attacker has miraculous knowledge of the whole system. These two assumptions, the existence of an attacker and its superior knowledge, help in determining the assets put at risk in the so-called *null hypothesis* discussion. A worst-case scenario is assumed and all operations found infeasible are successively removed. It is possible that new unresolved questions, external dependencies, or deployment constraints arise, and these are documented in the respective list for further discussions. The attacker's remaining operations are regarded as potential vulnerabilities to the software system. It is worth noting that in spite of the attacker's omniscience, the remaining attack scenarios could differ in required effort.

Subsequently, a *survey* is developed using a catalog of questions for each of the four object types. An excerpt of a catalog can be found in the appendix of this chapter. Experiences from projects in the past or recurring security flaws are included in the catalog as well. It can be compared to a set of building blocks and is adaptable to specific needs or technologies. The questions are answered by system architects, software and security engineers; more external dependencies, unresolved questions, deployment constraints, and possible vulnerabilities arise. The latter ones serve as input to phase 3.

2.5   Phase 3

In this phase, meetings are held involving all roles: analysts, system architects, software engineers, security engineers, and software testers. The actual amount of meetings depends on the size of the software, how many components originate from different software development teams, and possibly the number of different technologies used in the system. The purpose is to identify threats. *Threats* are directed against assets, put them at risk, and reflect an attacker's intentions. They are either discovered in a brainstorming fashion or derived from the lists of possible vulnerabilities and unresolved questions. Experiences from past projects, profound understanding of all technologies involved, and security bulletin awareness are important prerequisites.

To determine the expected impact of a successful attack, threats are classified according, for instance, to the *STRIDE* scheme (Howard and LeBlanc, 2003). A threat may be a member of multiple STRIDE classes. This method is used to prioritize mitigation planning: although spoofing is of interest in almost every sector, repudiation is of special interest in financial services. STRIDE is an acronym for the following terms:

- Spoofing—allows attackers to act as another user or component,
- Tampering—modification of data within the system as part of an attack or main incentive,
- Repudiation—ability to perform actions that cannot be traced back to a specific user,
- Information disclosure—attackers gain access to data in transit or in a data store,
- Denial of service—attackers interrupt a system's legitimate operation, and
- Elevation of privilege—attackers perform actions they are not authorized to perform.

Threat trees (Fig. 5) are trees, whose root node represents a threat and leaves represent entry points that can be used for an attack. An attack is

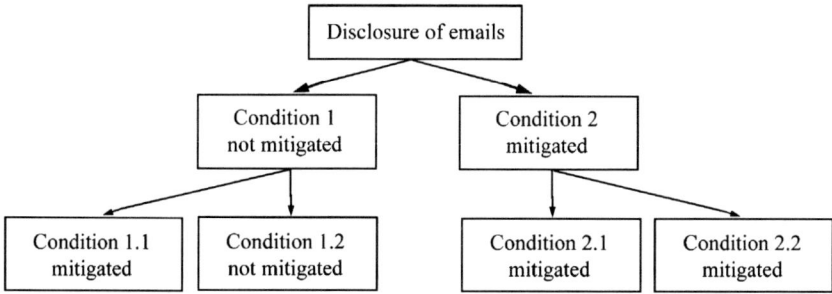

Fig. 5.   Threat tree example.

possible, if a path from any leaf to the root node can be traversed. In this case, a threat turns into an *attackable vulnerability* that can be exploited to gain access to one or more assets. Nodes on the same level in a threat tree are subject to a logical OR relationship, that is, it is sufficient to fulfill the conditions for one node on level n to proceed with its parent node on level $n-1$. Sometimes it is necessary to define a logical AND interconnection of nodes on the same level and to tag the nodes' emerging edges accordingly. Figure 5 depicts a threat tree whose nodes are subject to an OR relationship. The semantics of a threat tree is very similar to that of fault trees known from fault tree analysis (FTA; Vesely et al., 1981).

Each node in a threat tree, that is every partial condition of an attack, is associated with a risk according to the *DREAD* scheme (Howard and LeBlanc, 2003). *DREAD* is an acronym standing for the attributes of

- Damage potential—rates the affected assets and the expected impact,
- Reproducibility—rates the effort to bring the attack about,
- Exploitability—estimates the threat's value and an attackers' objectives,
- Affected users—estimates the fraction of installations, which are subject to the attack, and
- Discoverability—a measure for the likelihood of discovering the vulnerability.

The range of values (numerical or logical) assigned for each of the DREAD attributes should be chosen from a small set of values. For efficient modeling, in most cases it is sufficient to use a low/medium/high scale, as fine-granular ratings complicate the assessment and their expressiveness is questionable. The hierarchical visualization provided by threat trees, and the STRIDE and DREAD ratings are useful for mitigation planning. Multiple selection criteria can be used, for example, priority according to most easily reproducible vulnerabilities, conditions having occurrences in more than one threat tree, or strictly damage potential oriented.

2.6   Composition of partial threat models

When all relevant threat models exist, they may be composed of larger ones. During *composition* of threat models, their results are merged: dataflow diagrams, threat trees, scenarios, S/O matrices and surveys. Threat trees are linked such that a precondition of one subsystem is part of an attack path in another subsystem's threat tree. When merging surveys, analysts of all partial threat models must be present, as this task demands detailed discussions, especially for unresolved questions, external dependencies, and possible vulnerabilities. Deployment constraints are simply merged by concatenating both lists. Unresolved questions in one subsystem could be solved with knowledge gained from another subsystem's threat model. It may be the case that external dependencies become an internal part of the merged threat model and are not external anymore. Also, assumptions made for former external dependencies are likely to change, as they are covered by a partial threat model containing detailed information. In this case, the referring partial threat model needs to be revisited, as altered assumptions could reveal new threats. Finally, the lists of possible vulnerabilities are merged.

3   Process integration

TM can be performed at different stages of a software project's lifecycle, for example, when only a specification is available, when architecture or design decisions have been made, concurrent to implementation or integration, or during the deployment of third party software whose source code is not available. The early discovery of vulnerabilities using TM naturally gives rise to higher quality products. The design of a software component may be changed, if a threat is detected during the design phase: components are not implemented yet, changes involving classes or components other than the identified one are still possible, leading to a solid solution. However, patching implementations due to late threat discovery results in sporadic source code changes that possibly disregard far-ranging security requirements.

TM can be carried out as a standalone task or may be integrated into the development process. Later, we will present an overview of two such development processes containing TM stages. The first is called security development lifecycle (SDL) and originates from Microsoft (Howard and Lipner, 2006). The second (Bostroem et al., 2006) is an extended version of extreme programming (EP) (Beck, 2005), which is classified as an agile development process.

SDL is an integral part of the overall software development process. SDL's primary objective is to increase software security and reliability. Several security goals overlap with reliability goals such as availability

(Howard and Lipner, 2006). In addition, security techniques possibly affect reliability goals in a negative way, for example, intrusion detection systems might shut down services if abnormal usage has been detected repeatedly. In this case, security goals outrank reliability goals. Throughout this chapter, we focus on security aspects.

Contrary to SDL, EP is a complete software development process, defining subprocesses for collecting requirements, iteration planning, implementing, and testing. It is not document-centric, but encourages direct and frequent communication of all participants as well as short iterations.

3.1 SDL

The SDL is divided into 12 stages. Each will be explained briefly to give an overview of the actions performed in each stage:

During stage 1, it is ascertained if the software project needs to be covered by the SDL at all. With respect to today's omnipresent networking capabilities, "not to use SDL" decisions are to be expected only in very rare cases. Furthermore, the SDL team members are assigned and general objectives are defined.

Design decisions and best practices with respect to security are considered in stage 2. Moreover, an analysis of the attack surface—all operations and resources which are accessible through the software system—is performed. As far as possible, the attack surface is reduced by restricting or omitting features.

In stage 3, the so-called product risk assessment is carried out. A questionnaire consisting of the categories *setup, attack surface, mobile code, security features*, and *general questions* is answered.

The questionnaire serves as input for stage 4, which is the actual TM stage. It is performed according the previous section on TM.

The information gathered in TM helps driving stage 5, where documents and tools are developed responding to the discovered issues. The documents address developers, customers, and users. They offer detailed instructions on how to mitigate potential threats and vulnerabilities.

Stage 6 puts attention on proper configuration of the build environment and of those tools developed in the previous stage to enable all security-related features.

Policies for security testing are defined in stage 7, popular methods are fuzz testing (Sutton, 2006; Zimmer, 2006; see http://www.metasploit.com/, Metasploit LLC) and penetration testing (Lyon, 2008). Threat models are updated, if any relevant discoveries were made.

Legacy source code, originating from earlier projects and its interplay with the actual source code is handled in stage 8, called the security push. It consists of code reviews, revisiting and updating threat models, and rerunning stage 7 with respect to legacy code and its interfaces to the software project in the SDL.

A final security review takes place in stage 9, the central question during this stage being "Is the product ready to ship?". This involves reviewing all threat models and mitigations, evaluation of unmitigated threats, and discussing security relevant issues reported by developers. Furthermore, the application of all policies defined in stage 6 is audited. If any threat or uncertainty appears, the respective SDL stage required for mitigation needs to be revisited.

In stage 10, the organization necessary for security responses is defined. This involves processes for the customer support crew, security testers and developers, and for security patch releases.

Stages 11 and 12 define processes for the release of the software product and how to plan updates.

As previously mentioned, the SDL is not a complete software development process—its focus is on enhancing reliability and security aspects within the existing development processes. The process of integrating SDL into existing software development processes is described by Howard and Lipner (2006).

3.2   Secure extreme programming

Bostroem et al. (2006) propose to extend the EP paradigm (Beck, 2005) by seven security engineering activities:

1. Identification of security sensitive assets
2. Formulation of abuser stories
3. Abuser story risk assessment
4. Abuser story and user story negotiation
5. Definition of security-related user stories
6. Definition of security-related coding-standards
7. Abuser story countermeasure cross-checking

Clearly, activity 1 is identical to TM: high-level assets that need protection are identified. Activity 2 requires a security engineer to phrase the attacker's potential intentions of attacking the assets in so-called abuser stories. These are formulated in a high-level fashion, like "all communication between user terminals and backend systems need to be encrypted to anticipate man in the middle attacks and guarantee user data integrity." As is common practice in EP, each of the abuser stories is discussed with the customer and their importance is ranked. This discussion takes place during activity 3 and can be compared to TM's STRIDE- and DREAD-rating in collaboration with the customer. During activity 4, the next iteration is planned, that is, it is decided what will be implemented next. A single iteration in EP typically spans 5–10 days. Both, functionality (user stories) and mitigations to potential vulnerabilities (abuser stories) are under consideration for implementation; high-risk abuser stories should be considered first.

Activity 5 concerns the definition of security-related user stories. This is a necessary step as abuser stories themselves reflect only the requirements to achieve a secure system but do not comprise tangible instructions for software developers. Therefore, abuser stories need to be transformed into security-related user stories to offer developers more precise instructions. As an example abuser story, a security-related user story might read "the user's login credentials and the server's authentication cookie are hashed and sent to the authentication server whose returned token is used to obtain encryption services used for any user specific data flow between the terminal and the system's database services."

In case an abuser story requires changes of the software's deployment environment or of third party components, the formulation of a security-related user story might be impossible unless source code of all affected components is available. If no security-related user story can be derived, deployment constraints and unresolved questions are phrased to cover the abuser story.

The last activity, abuser story countermeasure cross-checking, helps keeping track of threats being mitigated. Each abuser story that has been selected in any iteration needs to be mapped either to a security-related user story or to deployment constraints/unresolved questions. No abuser story should be left without mapping.

4 Case study

A threat model of a real life application is presented by Germanus (2006); an excerpt of that thesis will be presented in this subsection. The author threat modeled ConferenceXP (CXP) (see Microsoft Research, CXP, http://research.microsoft.com/conferencexp/), a medium-sized networked application with publically available source code. The target of the study was the main application that is called CXP Client.

CXP aims at collaboration, wireless classrooms, and distance learning. It offers the Conference API and the CXP capability layer (Fig. 6) for creating new applications or extending existing ones with collaborative features.

CXP implements the real time transport protocol (RTP) (Schulzrinne et al., 2003) to realize network transport. RTP's scalability is suitable for large user groups having disparate bandwidth capacities. Simple access control mechanisms have been implemented to identify users and to delimit user groups in virtual rooms, the so-called Venues. The Conference API layer contains a DirectShow/Windows media component that provides a high-level interface for multimedia integration. The RTDocuments

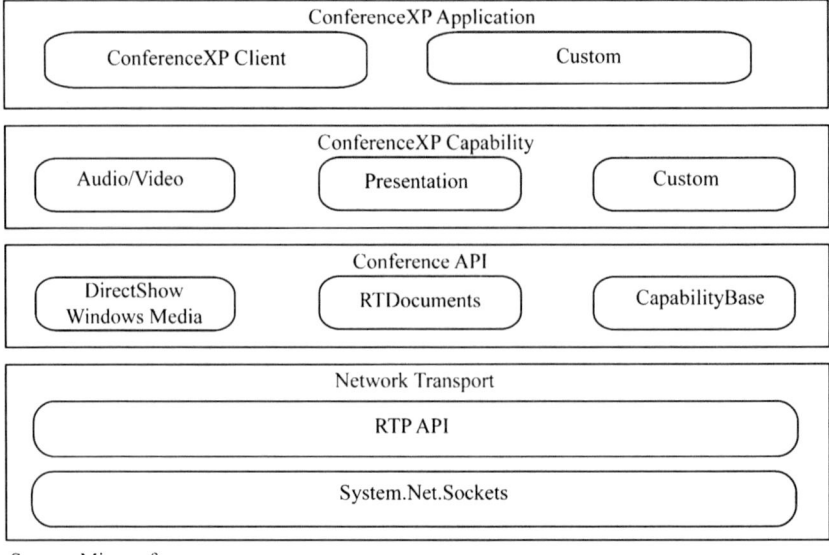

Fig. 6.   ConferenceXP architecture.

component, which is also part of the Conference API, embeds documents into a distributed networking context.

The client provides functionality of most CXP features, which are basically audio- and videoconferencing, instant messaging, and distributed viewing or editing of documents. As an example, Microsoft Powerpoint slides can be viewed and edited in a CXP session, providing identical onscreen experiences to all participants.

A CXP system consists of a client and a web service application called Venue Service. It is comparable to a directory service to define the virtual rooms that are called Venues and stores a user database. A reflector service can be installed additionally, if some or all participants' networks do not support multicast, that is, RTP messages encapsulated in UDP/IP packets cannot be sent to more than one destination at a time. Conferences may be recorded and replayed any time using the client and the archive service.

In the following, we will describe how the threat model for the CXP Client 3.2 was created. As each of the CXP applications shares many libraries—or more specific: .NET assemblies—and has a source code size beyond those of toy examples, methods were shadowed and logged to a database on each call. So, during the runtime of CXP Client, several scenarios of application usage were executed. Having this runtime logging information, all types were determined whose methods have been called. The full qualified type name points to the specific assembly. Assemblies represent in .NET's environment self-describing containers for common intermediate language (CIL) code. A .NET application consists of at least one assembly, namely the application's exe file. The two concepts encapsulation and separation of duties are supported by assembly oriented development. Accordingly, in the .NET context, we defined the assembly level as detail level in DFDs for the sake of clarity. The DFD's nodes represent all identified assemblies and if there exists a relation in terms of a cross assembly type use, an edge is incident to the corresponding assembly nodes. The dataflow diagram is depicted in Fig. 7.

As there was no team of involved developers at avail, the affected components had to be reviewed manually to get an idea of what functionality is encapsulated in which types and assemblies. With this knowledge in mind, participating roles, that is subjects, are identified and S/O matrices were created. An excerpt of the subsequent null hypothesis discussion is presented in Table 2.

A question catalogue has been created using a list of questions from Microsoft's latest TM method, known security issues of the .NET framework reported on MSDN (Microsoft Developer Network, see http://msdn.com), OWASP's (OWASP Organization, "Top ten most critical web application security vulnerabilities," see http://www.owasp.org.), "Writing Secure Code" (Howard and LeBlanc, 2003), "Programming .NET components" (Löwy, 2005), and "IT-Sicherheit" (Eckert, 2004). The complete list of questions can be found in Appendix A of Germanus (2006). We omit deployment constraints, unresolved questions, suggested enhancements,

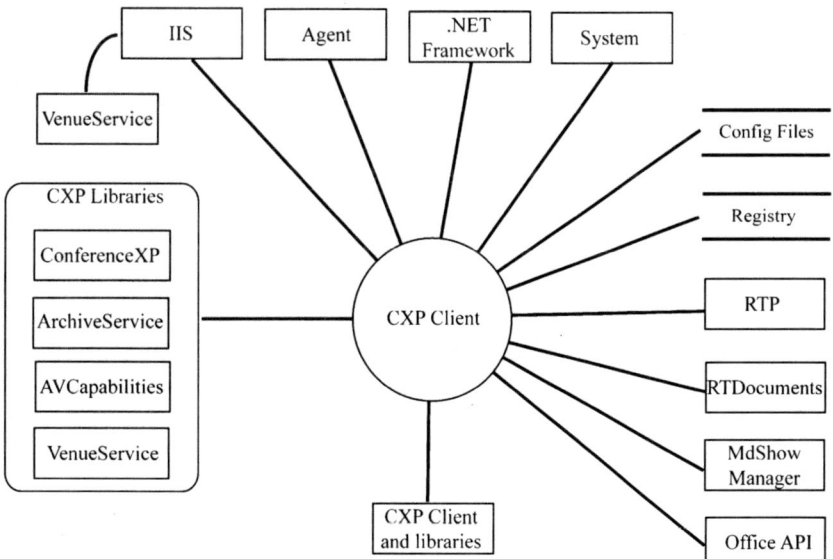

Fig. 7. Dataflow diagram of the ConferenceXP Client 3.2.

Table 2
Null hypothesis discussion results

Object	Discussion
CXP Client	There is no authentication mechanism in the CXP Client, access and execution of the client is delimited by file system ACLs, so an attacker needs appropriate rights, this is an external dependency of the file system.
User	Users authenticate implicitly by logging on to the operating system, so the attacker needs an account on the machine or domain. Proper and strict configuration is a deployment constraint and an external dependency, respectively.
IIS	Frequently reported security flaws concerning the IIS and ASP.NET engine denote that the remote site administrator should be outmost aware of securing the service. This is an external dependency. Trustworthy connections require the usage of SSL or TLS.
.NET framework & system	Security and proper configuration of the .NET framework and operating system are external dependencies.
Configuration files	Strictly set ACLs are important, this is a deployment constraint. Otherwise information disclosure about frequently used venue services is possible.
Registry	Only the installer writes values to the registry. The client has only read access to the registry and ACLs are set by the installer sufficiently. An attacker needs a user account with access rights to the CXP Client for reading the corresponding registry keys, but there is no hidden extra information, all the keys are visible from the client's configuration dialogs that can be executed as well.
RTP	RTP is a standardized protocol but the MS implementation and its specific extensions like forward error correction need to be assessed if a man-in-the-middle-attack or information disclosure is possible. If the attacker has network access, he is able to perform all operations regarding RTP, as the protocol does not encrypt or authenticate messages.
RTDocuments	This library is based on the LRN specification for exchanging educational content. An attacker could transmit a Powerpoint presentation with malicious content, hence it is an unresolved question, if the converter eliminates malicious content, scripts, etc. RTDocuments are not encrypted or authenticated, so messages could be spoofed and contents could be faked.

and external dependencies. The list of identified possible vulnerabilities is presented in Table 3.

With respect to possible vulnerability 7, Fig. 8 represents the corresponding threat tree for the threat of spoofing CXP Clients. A description, the assets put at risk, endangered security goals, detailed description, entry points, and known mitigations are presented in Table 4.

The root node represents the threat, namely a spoofing attack against the CXP Client. This kind of attack can only be carried out via network access, which is depicted on the second level of the threat tree. The third level, represented by three leaves, requires that actual messages are spoofed, that is, forging messages that pretend to be sent from someone else. Three different protocols are mentioned, by means of the threat tree semantic, either of them needs to be spoofed. Detailed knowledge of the protocols, and the handling of their state in the program logic, is needed. The next step is "obtaining network access" to inject the spoofed message. If the CXP Client accepts this spoofed message, the threat is realized and potentially causes an attackable vulnerability. Potential consequences are shown in

Table 3
Possible vulnerabilities of the ConferenceXP Client

	Possible vulnerability
1	Registry contains personally identifiable information, for example, the user's login and hostname.
2	Connections between IIS and VenueService are not authenticated or encrypted.
3	CXP Clients are not authenticated to the IIS or VenueService.
4	SOAP messages are not authorized or authenticated.
5	Channel between CXP Client and IIS is not trustworthy.
6	RTP network connections imply active conferences, participant IDs can be used to derive hostnames.
7	No RTP/RTCP authentication, packets might be spoofed or injected.

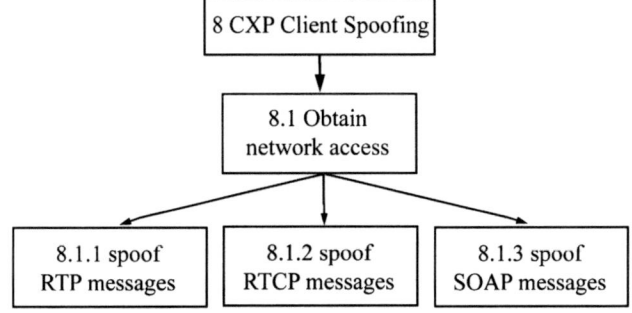

Fig. 8. Threat tree regarding ConferenceXP Client spoofing.

Table 4
Threat tree description

ID	8

Name	ConferenceXP Client Spoofing
Assets	Service availability, Venue contents, trustfulness of contents
Security goals	Information disclosure, privacy, denial of service, integrity, reputation
Description	8: Spoofing a CXP Client could result in information disclosure of the client's configuration, sending faked Venue contents, or disconnect the client from a Venue.
	8.1: The attacker needs appropriate access to network facilities directing Venue packets.
	8.1.1: Venues make use of the real time transport protocol called RTP. It handles single- and multicast connections, serving two to n participants with nearly constant bandwidth usage. The CXP RTP implementation does not authenticate or encrypt messages, so messages can be spoofed. An attacker can inject or replace RTP content and users participating in a Venue get the impression that this content was provided by a legal participant.
	8.1.2: RTP's control protocol does not support authentication either, hence spoofed messages can be injected.
	8.1.3: Spoofed SOAP messages can confuse the CXP Client, attackers could send corrupt or artificial messages.
Entry points	ConferenceXP Client
	Network
Known mitigation	8.1.1, 8.1.2: RTP and RTCP need authentication mechanisms or transmission in a protected VPN. SRTP or IPsec are recommended.
	8.1.3: HTTP/SOAP communication needs authentication. Usage of XMLsig is recommended.

Table 4 in the "Description" row. Also, mitigations are proposed and offer software engineers basic approaches to disable the possible vulnerability.

A key issue for creating any viable threat model is the comprehensive identification of the involved components. The case study presents an *ex post* threat model that was created without access to any detailed technical specifications such as use case diagrams, that is, participating subjects and objects were unknown in the beginning. Tools for static analysis, APIs for reflection in modern programming languages, or runtime profilers support analysts in the S/O identification process. Keeping the DFDs at a given level of detail is justified when the cost/time of effort for TM is limited; however, switching from the component level of detail to a type level would possibly have uncovered more threats. The coverage and comprehensiveness of the question catalogue tailored to the application's specifics is indispensable. The characteristics of the environment, the application itself, and all involved hard- and software technologies need to be considered to create a comprehensive catalog. The null hypothesis discussion and the preceding action of creating and condensing S/O matrices unveiled several possible vulnerabilities. One of these possible vulnerabilities was examined in detail and an attack on the conference service's communication control protocol was successfully conducted (Germanus, 2006). The main goal of TM, that is, discovering potential weaknesses in software applications, has been attained. Furthermore, the potential vulnerability discovery was helpful in security testing efforts.

5 Related work

In this section, we briefly discuss two[1] contemporary methods supporting the discovery of potential vulnerabilities in software, namely "Attack surface minimization" and "fuzz testing."

5.1 Attack surface minimization

"Attack surface minimization" (Manadhata and Wing, 2005; Manadhata et al., 2006) is based on the assumption that software systems should provide the smallest possible amount of externally accessible services, for example, API methods or resources, as an "attack surface" to enhance security. Application of this method does not yield an absolute measure, that is, at least two software projects of similar nature are considered during comparison; inherently different projects like text processors and music players are not comparable by means of this method. The attack surface consists of four entities, which need to be identified, namely

1. Entry points—methods that receive data from the environment,
2. Exit points—methods that send data to the environment,
3. Channels—communication media such as sockets and pipes, and
4. Untrusted data items—for example, databases or file systems, or more precisely, single elements like key/value pairs, database rows or tables, and files.

The actual computation result yields a three-dimensional vector $<M, C, D>$, where M is the weighted sum of entry and exit points, C represents the weighted channel sum, and D comprises all untrusted data items in the system multiplied by their weights. Clearly, all three components should be minimized. Each entity's privilege level, which is mapped to an integer

---

[1] A number of other techniques also exist though space constraints preclude our coverage of them and we limit ourselves to the representative approaches of attack surfaces and fuzzing.

value, forms the weight. The highest value is associated to root (or comparable) privileges and decreases with decreasing privileges.

The evaluation of the attack surface is not a trivial task. It is easy to identify untrusted data items, but different technologies offer different types of channels and entry/exit points. An example of an entry point in many programming languages is the main method that usually accepts parameters. More entry/exit points are those methods making up an API, because they provide interfaces to the environment. Consequently, the difference between an internal method (which cannot be called from the outside) and an API method (which receives data from or sends data to the environment) can be determined with call graph analyzers (see http://www.software-tomography. com/, Software-Tomography GmbH) as proposed by Manadhata and Wing (2005) and Manadhata et al. (2006). Low-level channels like TCP sockets exist in many programming languages, and are thus easily compared, but high-level channels like those coordinating distributed computing tasks differ significantly, for example, between Ruby (Matsumoto, 1995), .NET (see Microsoft Developer Network), and many other technologies. The authors (Manadhata and Wing, 2005; Manadhata et al., 2006) propose static analysis for the identification of entry and exit points and runtime monitoring to determine channels and untrusted data items.

A disadvantage of this approach is its static measure, although channels and untrusted data items are determined during runtime, no dynamic program execution is considered in entry/exit point analysis: attackability measures (Saydjari, 2006; Song et al., 2006) often incorporate different kinds of weights to express the likelihood of taking a certain attack path. These weights reflect for example access restrictions. The privilege level of a running process may be raised during runtime for operations that require more than the default privilege set. During this period of raised privilege utilization, a system might be susceptible to attacks. Therefore, it is interesting, how long a system remains under these conditions. Furthermore, which actions can be easily triggered from an adversary's point of view, that is, via an API call or using a GUI, to force the system on raising privileges? In addition, how often are these raises possible? One chance per day results in a poor attack attempt rate. These aspects cannot be discovered in static analysis.

5.2 *Fuzz testing*

Fuzz testing or "fuzzing" (Forrester and Miller, 2000; Miller et al., 1990) is a security testing method that provides irregular, that is "fuzzed," inputs to the software in the hope of exposing weaknesses in the software regarding handling external inputs. Several degrees of freedom exist regarding the locality of fuzz injection and how the injection values are generated. A major challenge in fuzz testing is to minimize the test case space while maximizing the code coverage. Another challenge is the definition of fuzz generating heuristics for inputs whose format is known. In the following, we distinguish between black box and white box fuzz testing approaches.

A detailed white box approach is described by Godefroid et al. (2007). To achieve a high degree of code coverage, the program is executed symbolically several times. Initially, a valid input is given to the program, for example, a valid document of a word processing program. After each symbolic execution, the input is altered and dependencies between input modification and branches taken by the program logic are determined and stored in a branch prediction database. Having this knowledge, different inputs are arranged in equivalence classes that provide a basis for test case generation. As an example, imagine a method body containing three if-statements, each checking a byte variable parameter for equality with a certain character. A naive approach yielding 100% code coverage is calling the method $3 * 2^8 = 768$ times, namely providing all possible bit configurations for each byte variable. Provided that none of the variables is modified within any of the if-blocks, only two calls are necessary to execute either none or all three if-blocks; all possible combinations yield $2^3 = 8$ calls. So, this white box approach minimizes in this example the amount of test cases with respect to conditional jumps by 96% compared to the naive brute force approach. However, a monitoring component is necessary to record test case results and deviations from the predicted branches to be taken. In the latter case, the respective test case needs adaption, as unintended jumps potentially lower the code coverage. A test case fails if the program encounters an access violation exception or if extreme memory consumption has been detected. SAGE is a system of multiple components and is introduced by Godefroid et al. (2007) to perform the duties mentioned earlier. It operates on machine-code level and does not rely on the presence of any source code. Unfortunately, SAGE is currently not publicly available.

Black box fuzzing, on the other hand, does not consider a program's code, it focuses on its interfaces and environment. Again, like in white box fuzzing, several methods exist to delimit the test case space. A method for black box fuzz testing networked applications is presented by Neves et al. (2006); it uses a framework which consists of three layers, namely a target protocol specification, an attack injector, and the target system monitor. The target protocol specification reflects the structure, semantics, valid value ranges, and also expected result values of the program's network protocol, which will be attacked during fuzz testing. In Neves et al. (2006), an example is given for the IMAP protocol and different IMAP server implementations. Beside standalone tests, the method can also be chosen for comparison of different applications using the same protocol and their coherence to the protocol's specification. The attack injector uses the target protocol specification to generate test cases that are actually injected into a running instance of the monitored target system. Test cases can be grouped into three classes: (1) syntax tests, (2) value tests, and (3) information disclosure tests. An example for each test class follows:

(1) Syntax tests distort the protocol's proper structure by adding, removing, or interchanging the fields within a single command or apply the same distorting actions on entities of command sequences.

(2) Value tests provoke abnormal program behavior by injecting invalid values. Valid ranges are known from the target protocol specification and boundary values, that is, values that are still valid, boundary exceeding values, that is, adding $+/-1$ to the boundary values, and "very invalid" values which are located far out from the valid range are chosen.

(3) Information disclosure tests aim for secret or private information stored within the program. Mostly, protocol commands are chosen which refer to interactions with data stores like file systems or databases. Commands that select or access data stores are modified to target data stores which are not subject to the current access rights or intended focus. In a UNIX system, such an attack might address the /etc/passwd or /etc/shadow files instead of an application specific data store like ∼/.application/data.

If the program can be transitioned into different states by network protocol messages, each transition message has to be recorded to apply each of the aforementioned test classes in every possible state.

The target system monitor handles program startups, synchronizes with the attack injector, and records the actual results after each injected test case has been processed, external tools provided by the operating system can be used to detect successful attacks in terms of extreme memory consumption or access violation exceptions.

Another black box fuzz testing method (Du and Mathur, 2000) focuses on the notion of program environment perturbation. The central assumption is that most security flaws result from inappropriate interactions with the environment. The authors differentiate between internal entities and states, and environment entities and states: internal entities refer to the process's data and memory space, internal states reflect variable values, object instances, etc. Environment entities and states refer to everything that is external to the application and anything that makes up a status in an environment entity is regarded as a state. The most important difference is the shared nature of the environment entity; a program cannot rely on its state. Imagine file system entities that are checked upon application startup but never again after this event. Although the check's result is valid only for a short time span, the check's result is provided to the application throughout its process lifetime. Disregarding potential changes made on the file system entity by an attacker or other users. Internal entities, on the other hand, are sealed off from the outside world, that is, other users cannot influence their state in unexpected ways. Developers tend to handle shared resources with care in concurrent programming to guarantee sane state to every executing thread. Nevertheless, few developers make the effort to secure environment interaction in a comparable way, for example, by using semaphores. Having this issue in mind, Du and Mathur (2000) developed an environment–application–interface fault model which will not be discussed in detail here; the bottom line of this model is a bipartition of faults into indirect and direct environment faults:

Indirect environment faults	Direct environment faults
User input	File system
Environment variable	Process
File system input	Network
Network input	
Process input	

The actual fuzz injection into the application takes place at the interaction level, for all eight-fault model categories. The actual fuzz is generated according to the fuzz column of Tables 5 and 6; we only present an excerpt for both fault classes: file system and network faults regarding direct and indirect environment faults.

Furthermore, Du and Mathur (2000) defined a test adequacy metric. It is a two-dimensional function, whose outcome vector needs to be maximized. One dimension describes the fault coverage, the other one the interaction

Table 5
Internal entities to be fuzzed

Internal entity	Semantic attribute	Fuzz
File system input	File name + directory name	Change length, use relative path, use absolute path, use special characters in the name such as "|", "&", or ">"
	File extension	Change to other file extension, for example, ".exe" in a Windows system, change length of the file extension
Network input	IP address	Change length of the address, use bad-formatted address
	Packet	Change size of the packet, use bad-formatted packet
	Host name	Change length of the host name, use bad-formatted host name
	DNS reply	Change length of the DNS reply, use bad-formatted DNS reply

Source: Du and Mathur (2000).

Table 6
Environment entities to be fuzzed

Environment entity	Semantic attribute	Fuzz
File system	File existence	Delete an existing file or make a nonexisting file exist
	File ownership	Change ownership to the owner of the process, other normal users, or root
	File permission	Flip the permission bits
	Symbolic link	If the file is a symbolic link, change the target it links to; if it is not a symbolic link, change it to a symbolic link
	File content invariance	Modify file
	File name invariance	Change file name
	Working directory	Start application in different directory
Network	Message authenticity	Change message origin to other network entity than the expected one
	Protocol	Purposely violate underlying protocol by omitting a protocol step, adding an extra step, or reordering steps
	Socket	Share the socket with another process
	Service availability	Deny services the application is demanding
	Entity trustability	Change the entity with which the application interacts to a untrusted one

Source: Du and Mathur (2000).

coverage. Both values are given as percentage: the fault coverage is the amount of tolerated faults divided by the total amount of faults being injected. Analogously, the interaction coverage is the amount of interaction points that were actually used for injections divided by the total amount of interaction points in the system. The authors' assumption is that the higher the fault coverage the more secure the software system is. Also, high interaction coverage stabilizes the previous assumption by demanding that preferably many "entries" of the system have been probed. In addition, such a metric helps to define a stopping criterion for fuzz testing.

6   Current work

The related work section presented an overview of the advantage of minimizing test case spaces. The presented fuzz testing approaches can be partitioned into high- and low-level methods. Although high-level approaches fuzz, for example, file system and network messages, low-level

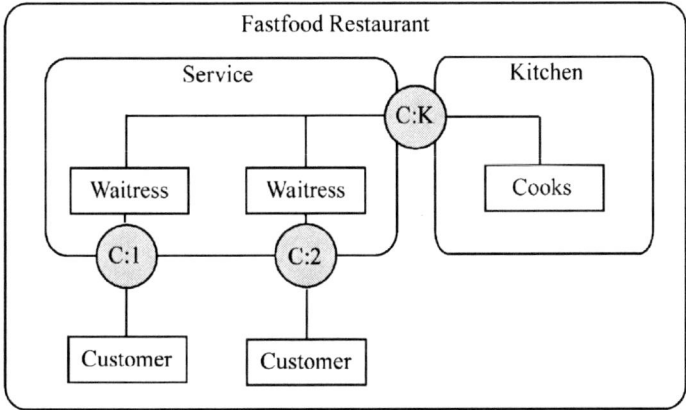

Fig. 9.   Example for software connectors.

approaches target shifting bit values, for example, in parameters, to maximize code coverage with a minimum of differing inputs.

We are currently evaluating the significance of metrics building up on the notion of Software connectors (Mehta et al., 2000), which embody the interactions among a software system's components. Connectors manifest themselves as shared variable accesses, table entries, buffers, instructions to a linker, procedure calls, networking protocols, pipes, SQL links between a database and an application, and so forth.

Figure 9 describes the notion of Software connectors, components, and class instances. To simplify matters, imagine that a fast food restaurant consists of two components: service and kitchen. The service component has several waitress instances waiting to service customers, which are external to the service component.

Customers are being serviced through connectors, called C:1 and C:2 in Fig. 9. These connectors are necessary for ordering, payment, and food delivery. Received orders are being passed via another connector to the kitchen component, where cook instances reside and wait for orders to return fresh fast food to the service component. There are more connectors than depicted: during peak times, many cooks are busy in the kitchen and they have to communicate among themselves to coordinate their duties. Likewise, there is a restaurant manager communicating with all the participating instances of the service component to carry on the business. Now imagine, there is not enough staff in at least one of the components, this could lead to an availability problem and customers start leaving the restaurant before being serviced, if the waiting queue increases excessively.

Hence, an attack against an application's Software connectors affects one or more of the following security goals: availability, confidentiality, and integrity.

Our method does not aim to reduce test case sets, but to highlight susceptible entities that interact with entities that are external to the monitored application. In the previous subsections, we discussed weights reflecting static analysis results, for example, the sum of entry and exit points, access restrictions, or probabilities. We will focus on two weights: frequency of use and estimated severity in case of a security vulnerability exploit.

Overall, we refer to execution frequencies or instantiations of type members and types respectively. Therefore, an application is run and profiled during runtime, as static analysis does not provide the desired insights. As runtime behavior differs based on how an application is used, a catalogue of feature-oriented actions is carried out while the runtime profile is created. Subsequently, we implemented a monitor prototype that addresses Microsoft.NET's common language runtime (CLR) to gain knowledge on object creation, garbage collection, method invocation, and the call graph of an application. The call frequency of a type's method is utilized as weight and also the type's intended use. The latter aspect reflects the estimated severity in case of a security vulnerability exploit: we categorized all types in the .NET framework taking the duties of a Software connector. Clearly, a method involving an unmanaged memory stream is associated to a higher risk than a method making a web request. As a result, we associate each method, type, and component, a value of its susceptibility in terms of the concepts described earlier. Entities with higher susceptibility values require detailed security audits. If the actual countermeasure is performed in an automated testing fashion or manually in a security review is left to the respective software development organization.

Our current work has evaluated the expressiveness of this method and the consideration of weighting factors.

7 Summary

Identifying an application's vulnerability to attack is the aim of TM. In this chapter, we have detailed two flavors of the TM process, namely (a) the feature/scenario-based approach and (b) the S/O matrix approach. These processes can be performed during design, development, or deployment stages, and can also be integrated into a software development organization. The section on process integration further exemplifies two development processes, which integrate the TM phases therein. To enumerate a step-by-step procedure for the TM processes, a medium-sized application— CXP—whose source code was available, has been threat modeled. The key results are presented in the "Case Study" section.

The section on related works presents contemporary approaches such as attack surface measurement and fuzz testing. Both methods tend to identify security weaknesses in software. The attack surface measurement approach is predominantly conducted as a static measurement. In contrast, fuzz testing entails a higher effort, as it monitors the application's behavior on fuzz injection during runtime. The section on "Current Work" concludes the chapter with its scope covering an approach for an attackability metric involving call frequencies and duties of concerned types.

Glossary

Abuser story: In contrast to a user story that specifies desired system functionality, an abuser story describes undesired system misuse which requires mitigation.

Asset: Abstract or concrete valuable entity that needs to be protected.

Attack surface: All operations and resources which are accessible through a software system.

Attackability: A measure for the likelihood of an attack to happen.

Black box fuzz testing: Behavioristic methods, which do not contemplate system internals.

Classical approach: Refers to the threat modeling method whose course of action may be performed in different ways, like the classical approach.

Code coverage: Measure for the percentage of source code that a method covers.

Data flow diagram (DFD): Visualizes connections and data flows between entities, be they classes, components, or subsystems.

Data store: Resources dedicated to persistently storing data.

DREAD: Acronym for the attributes Damage potential, Reproducibility, Exploitability, Affected users, and Discoverability. This method is used for ranking threats according to their expected criticality.

Entry point: A way used to interact with the software system, for example, APIs, user interface, and network service, either in the desired way or during an attack.

External dependency: These entities are beyond the influence of all threat modeling participants, although their thorough identification is required.

Extreme programming (EP): Agile software development process.

Feature scenario: Can be derived from use case descriptions; they describe the system's capabilities.

Fuzz testing or fuzzing: Testing method based on guessing or estimating input patterns to provoke unspecified system behavior.

Null hypothesis discussion: Informal method to cancel impossible scenarios.

Penetration testing: Testing method to assess a system's security goals.

Security development lifecycle (SDL): This software development process has been introduced by Microsoft. It aims at reducing maintenance and cost, and increasing reliability and security of software systems.

Security flaw: A synonym for vulnerability

Security goals: They describe the prevailing dimensions of system security, such as availability, authenticity, confidentiality, integrity, nonrepudiation, and privacy.

Security-related user story: Used in the secure extreme programming process to mitigate issues documented in abuser stories by provision of concrete implementation details.

Software connector: Entities within software systems whose primarily task is to connect portions of the system, for example, data access objects, instances of protocol implementations, etc.

Spoofing: This is an attack method which forges some or all of the data provided as input to a software system to provoke unspecified system behavior.

Static analysis: Source code evaluation technique; the code is not executed, no runtime behavior is considered.

STRIDE: Acronym for the terms Spoofing, Tampering, Repudiation, Information disclosure, Denial of service, and Elevation of privilege. This method is used for ranking threats according to their expected criticality.

Subject/Object (S/O) approach: Threat modeling approach focusing on subject and object identification within the system and their respective operations.

Subject/Object (S/O) matrix: This is a matrix representation of identified subjects and objects in the subject/object approach of threat modeling.

Survey: A structured document template that is helpful to achieve uniformity and traceability.

Threat: Faults in software systems turn to threats if exploitation endangers one or more assets.

Threat modeling: Threat modeling is an informal method to assess software system security during design, construction, or production stage.

Threat tree: Threat trees visualize the conditions to be met for a successful attack. The root node represents one or more assets; leafs are entry points.

Use scenario: They are derived from user behavior when interacting with the software system.

Vulnerability: Whenever a software system threat is exploitable, it turns to a known vulnerability, that is, an attacker is able to harm one or more assets.

Weakness: A synonym for threat.

White box fuzz testing: Explorative method, taking system internals into consideration.

References

Beck, K. (2005). *Extreme Programming Explained: Embrace Change.* Addison-Wesley Longman, Amsterdam, The Netherlands.

Bostroem, G., J. Waeyrynen, M. Boden, K. Beznosov, P. Kruchten (2006). Extending XP practices to support security requirements engineering, in: *Proceedings of the 2006 international workshop on Software engineering for secure systems,* Shanghai, China, pp. 11–18.

Du, W., A.P. Mathur (2000). Testing for software vulnerability using environment perturbation, in: *DSN '00: Proceedings of the 2000 International Conference on Dependable Systems and Networks,* New York, NY, USA, pp. 603–612.

Eckert, C. (2004). IT-Sicherheit. R. Oldenbourg Verlag.

Forrester, J.E., B.P. Miller (2000). An empirical study of the robustness of windows NT applications using random testing. in: *4th USENIX Windows Systems Symposium, August 2000,* Seattle, WA, USA.

Germanus, D. (2006). *Assessing software security using threat models.* Bachelor Thesis, DEEDS Group, Department of Computer Science, TU Darmstadt.

Godefroid, P., M.Y. Levin, D. Molnar (2007). Automated Whitebox Fuzz testing. Microsoft Research.

Howard, M., D. LeBlanc (2003). *Writing Secure Code.* Microsoft Press, Redmond, WA, USA.

Howard, M., S. Lipner (2006). *The Security Development Lifecycle.* Microsoft Press, Redmond, WA, USA.

Löwy, J. (2005). *Programming .NET Components.* 2nd ed. O'Reilly, Sebastopol, CA, USA.

Lyon, G. (2008). Network mapper (nmap). Available at http://insecure.org/nmap/

Matsumoto, Y. (1995). Ruby. Available at http://www.ruby-lang.org/

Manadhata, P., J. Wing (2005). An attack surface Metric. Technical Report CMU-CS-05-155, School of Computer Science, Carnegie Mellon University.

Manadhata, P., J. Wing, M. Flynn, M. McQueen (2006). Measuring the attack surfaces of two FTP daemons, in: *Proceedings of the 2nd ACM workshop on Quality of protection.* QoP '06, Alexandria, VA, USA, pp. 3–10.

Mehta, N.R., N. Medvidovic, S. Phadke (2000). Towards a taxonomy of software connectors, in: *Proceedings of the 2000 International Conference on Software Engineering,* Limerick, Ireland, pp. 178–187.

Miller, B.P., L. Fredriksen, B. So (1990). An empirical study of the reliability of UNIX utilities. *Communications of the ACM* 33(12), 32–44.

Neves, N., J. Antunes, M. Correia, P. Verissimo, R. Neves (2006). Using attack injection to discover new vulnerabilities, in: *Proceedings of Dependable Systems and Networks Conference,* 2006. DSN, Philadelphia, PA, USA, pp. 457–466.

Saydjari, O.S. (2006). Is risk a good security metric? in: *QoP '06: Proceedings of the 2nd ACM workshop on Quality of protection,* Alexandria, VA, USA.

Schulzrinne, H., S. Casner, R. Frederick, V. Jacobson (2003). RTP: a transport protocol for real-time applications. IETF Request for Comments: RFC 3550.

Song, X., M. Stinson, R. Lee, P. Albee (2006). An approach to analyzing the windows and linux security models, in: *5th IEEE/ACIS International Conference on Computer and Information Science.* ICIS-COMSAR '06, Honolulu, HI, USA.

Sutton, M. (2006). iDefense Filefuzz. Available at http://labs.idefense.com/software/fuzzing.php#more_filefuzz.

Swiderski, F. (2004). *Window Snyder. Threat Modeling*. Microsoft Press, Redmond, WA, USA.

Vesely, W.E., F.F. Goldberg, N.H. Roberts, D.F. Haasl (1981). Fault tree handbook. U.S. Nuclear Regulatory Commission.

Zimmer, D. (2006). iDefense ComRaider. Available at http://labs.idefense.com/software/fuzzing.php#more_comraider.

Online resources

Tool: Microsoft threat analysis & modeling. Available at http://www.microsoft.com/downloads/details.aspx?familyid = 59888078-9DAF-4E96-B7D1-944703479451

Weblog: Microsoft application threat modeling blog. Available at http://blogs.msdn.com/threatmodeling/

Weblog: Bruce Schneier's blog on threat modeling. Available at http://www.schneier.com/blog/archives/2007/10/threat_modeling.html

Website: OWASP's resources on "Threat risk modeling". Available at http://www.owasp.org/index.php/Threat_Risk_Modeling

Website: Threat modeling resources at cyberforge.com. Available at http://cyberforge.com/weblog/aniltj/archive/0001/01/01/550.aspx

Appendix

Table A.1
Sample question catalog for web service technology

	Description
1	Are SOAP contents validated?
2	Was the service designed to prohibit separation of privilege? Accessing other user accounts, viewing sensitive files, or using unauthorized functions is impossible?
3	Are account credentials and sessions properly protected?
4	Is the service hardened against cross-site-scripting attacks? Does it echo user input or URL parameters back to a web page? Is user input stored persistently to display it later on a web page?
5	Is the service hardened against buffer overflow attacks? Parameter bounds are checked?
6	Are web service interface commands passed directly to a data store or the operating system? Are there hooked black box modules enabling an attacker to inject malicious content that is executed?
7	Short error messages delimit retrieval of information about the service, its data flows, potential bottlenecks, etc. Is only an error code displayed that can be mapped on a detailed error message in the service host's event log?
8	If the service makes use of cryptographic methodologies, was the design and implementation reviewed by a crypto specialist team?
9	Are incoming connections limited? Does the service respond to control messages that do not correspond to requirements? This is important to prevent DoS attacks.
10	Is the service deployed with a strong configuration, that is, a maximum of limitations and restrictions, debugging options are deactivated?

Rao & Upadhyaya, Eds., *Handbooks in Information Systems, Vol. 4*

Chapter 22

Intrusion-Resilient Middleware Design and Validation

Paulo Verissimo, Miguel Correia, Nuno Neves and Paulo Sousa

Faculty of Sciences, University of Lisboa, LaSIGE, Bloco C6, Campo Grande, 1749-016 Lisboa, Portugal

Abstract

Intrusion tolerance (InTol) has become a reference paradigm for dealing with intrusions and accidental faults, achieving security and dependability in an automatic way, much along the lines of classical fault tolerance. This chapter is an introduction to the design and validation of intrusion-tolerant middleware and systems.

1 Introduction

Intrusion tolerance (InTol) is a new security and dependability paradigm that slowly emerged in the past two decades. While most security paradigms attempt to prevent intrusions from occurring, InTol assumes that systems are so complex that vulnerabilities are inevitable, therefore intrusions will happen and have to be tolerated. The approach is similar to classical fault tolerance (or dependability), in which systems are designed not only to prevent accidental faults from happening but also acknowledge that they will inevitably happen and that the system has to tolerate them automatically.

InTol has become a reference paradigm for dealing with faults and intrusions, achieving security and dependability in an automatic way, much along the lines of classical fault tolerance. The paradigm presents a significant added value in face of what are the current and future perceived threats to computer systems: it allows designers to address both faults and attacks in a seamless manner, through a common approach to security and dependability. InTol is bound not to replace but instead to amplify the reach of the classical paradigms in security, which have mostly consisted in trying to prevent security hazards from happening, or in deploying *ad-hoc* countermeasures when incidents are detected. In contrast, in InTol, it is assumed that systems remain to some extent faulty and vulnerable; attacks on components can happen and some will be successful, but automatic mechanisms ensure that the overall system nevertheless remains secure and operational.

The usual way to deploy InTol mechanisms in Internet-like or distributed systems is through middleware layers or Web services that are fault- and intrusion-tolerant, which can then be used by upper layer services and applications transparently, independently of how tolerance is achieved. The general idea is to implement the middleware offering the service through n replicas cooperating through distributed protocols. Replicas will be attacked and corrupted at the measure of the power of the attacker, but as long as there are sufficient replicas to perform the service correctly, the system continues to function, sometimes even without the user noticing anything.

Given the severity and the malicious intelligence behind the expected threats, there is a need for protocols to resist in general arbitrary faults as the top level of severity, in the line of what is called Byzantine fault/InTol. The necessary number of replicas varies with system configuration, the baseline being that if one expects a number f of faults or intrusions, then the middleware implementing the service should actually consist (typically) of at least $n = 3f + 1$ replicas.

However, these challenges are so intense that one must in practical cases resort to defences that attempt at shrinking the attackers' chances. Designers resort to representing the system along hybrid distributed systems models, which allow to include trusted-trustworthy components as enhancers of the baseline Byzantine algorithms, obtaining significantly better efficiency versus security ratios.

Furthermore, since faults erode systems inexorably, the next step towards high resilience is to offer strong enough resistance to attacks to prevent replica exhaustion. That is, to endow systems with the capability of preserving the needed resources (replicas) to perform correctly, throughout their mission. In other words, with the capability of achieving what is called exhaustion-safety. For our InTol middleware, this would mean to always preserve the number of replicas above the minimum threshold. This is a difficult task, since in the malicious-fault plane, threats can be exacerbated by factors such as attacker power and common-mode vulnerabilities. Techniques that make the life difficult to the attacker, for example, by exploiting diversity, rejuvenation, have been employed.

Last but not least, it is necessary to study and understand how malicious faults such as attacks are produced and what is their effect on existing vulnerabilities, to validate the fault assumptions underlying the above-mentioned intrusion-tolerant algorithms. This will allow algorithm and system designers to introduce more realistic assumptions. We are still far from a thorough understanding of the mechanisms behind the trilogy attack-vulnerability-intrusion.

1.1   Outline

Architecting intrusion-tolerant systems, to arrive at some notion of *intrusion-tolerant middleware* for application support, presents multiple challenges. InTol mechanisms can be selectively used at all layers starting with hardware, to build layers of progressively more trusted components and middleware subsystems, from baseline untrusted components (hosts and networks). This leads to an automation of the process of building resilience: for example, at lower layers, basic InTol mechanisms are used to construct a trustworthy communication subsystem. This subsystem can then be trusted by higher layer distributed software, to securely communicate amongst participants without bothering about network intrusion threats. Or alternatively, it can be used to build an even more trustworthy higher layer—by incrementally using InTol mechanisms—such as a replication management protocol resilient to both network and host intrusions. Section 2 introduces these middleware design principles.

Intrusion-tolerant middleware is usually based on the notion of replication, that is, in scattering a service in a set of server machines (Section 3). The section starts by presenting the main InTol paradigms in the literature and how they are used to ensure the integrity of a service, that is, the latter behaves as expected even if there are intrusions in some of its components (servers and clients). Then, how these paradigms can be extended to ensure also the confidentiality of information stored in a replicated service is also discussed. Finally, some system architectures are presented, showing how the paradigms can be used to build actual systems.

Intrusion-tolerant systems may have a long lifetime (e.g. online banking systems), and it should be guaranteed that no more than the maximum number of tolerated faults ever occurs, that is, InTol systems should be exhaustion-safe (Section 4). The section starts by presenting a model that allows assessing the exhaustion-safety of a system according to its fault and timing assumptions. Then, it is shown that to meet the exhaustion-safety predicate, InTol systems should be designed with diversity in mind and enhanced with proactive and reactive recovery mechanisms targeting, respectively, stealth/dormant faults and conspicuous attacks. It is also explained how recoveries can eliminate the effects of faults/attacks and how they can randomize certain parts of the system that vulnerabilities are somehow changed or removed, and the adversary cannot make use of knowledge learnt before the recovery.

An intrusion can only occur if the system contains vulnerabilities that can be exploited by an attack. Section 5 presents some of the techniques that can be utilized to locate security vulnerabilities and allow their subsequent elimination, both during the testing phases of the development cycle and when the system is in operation. The following techniques are examined: static vulnerability analyzers, fuzzing mechanisms and attack injection. Vulnerability removal is important because it causes an increase on the effort necessary to compromise a machine. This section also explains how these techniques can be applied to experimentally validate some aspects of the attack model and fault assumptions made during the design of the intrusion-tolerant system. Both aspects contribute to the deployment of cheaper intrusion-tolerant systems.

2 Intrusion-tolerant middleware design principles

In this section, we start by introducing the main concepts behind InTol. The reader may find a thorough treatment in the work by Verissimo et al. (2003). Then, we move on explaining how to architect and design intrusion-tolerant middleware.

2.1 Intrusion tolerance in a nutshell

What is InTol? As discussed earlier, the tolerance paradigm in security assumes that systems remain to a certain extent vulnerable, assumes that attacks on components or sub-systems can happen and some will be successful, ensures that the overall system nevertheless remains secure and operational, with a quantifiable probability. In other words:

- faults—malicious and other—occur;
- they generate errors, that is, component-level security compromises and
- error processing mechanisms make sure that security failure is prevented.

2.1.1 Attack-vulnerability-intrusion (AVI) composite fault model
The mechanisms of failure of a system or component, security-wise, range from internal faults (i.e. vulnerabilities) to external, interaction faults (i.e. attacks), whose combination produces faults (i.e. intrusions) that can directly lead to a security failure. Figure 1(a) represents the fundamental sequence of these three kinds of faults: attack → vulnerability → intrusion → failure. This well-defined relationship is called the *AVI composite fault model*.

Vulnerabilities are faults in a computing or communication system that can be exploited with malicious intention. They are the primordial faults existing inside the components, essentially requirements, specification, design or configuration faults (e.g. coding faults allowing program stack overflow, files with root setuid in UNIX, naive passwords and unprotected TCP/IP ports).

Attacks are malicious intentional faults attempted at a computing or communication system, with the intent of exploiting one or more of those

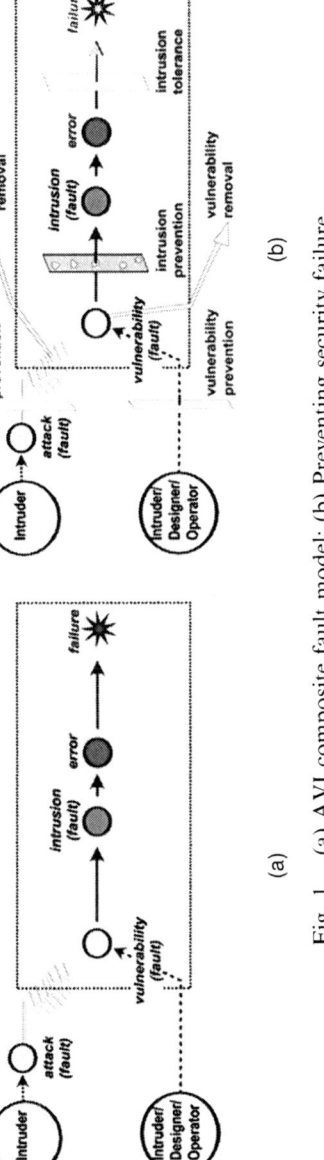

Fig. 1. (a) AVI composite fault model; (b) Preventing security failure.

vulnerabilities in the system (e.g. port scans, email viruses, malicious Java applets or ActiveX controls).

An *intrusion* is an intentionally malicious operational fault resulting from a successful attack on vulnerability. An intrusion has thus two underlying causes, as seen in the Fig. 1(a): vulnerability and attack.

2.1.2 Why the AVI model?

Firstly, the AVI model describes the mechanism of intrusion precisely: without matching attacks, a given vulnerability is harmless; without target vulnerabilities, an attack is irrelevant. Secondly, it provides constructive guidance to build in dependability against malicious faults, through the combined introduction of several techniques.

To begin with, we can prevent some attacks from occurring, reducing the level of threat, as shown in Fig. 1(b). *Attack prevention* can be performed, for example, by shadowing the password file in UNIX, making it unavailable to unauthorized readers, or filtering access to parts of the system (e.g. if a component is behind a firewall and cannot be accessed from the Internet, attack from there is prevented). We can also perform *attack removal*, which consists of taking measures to discontinue ongoing attacks.

However, it is impossible to prevent all attacks, and therefore, reducing the level of threat should be combined with reducing the degree of vulnerability, through *vulnerability prevention*, for example, by using best practices in the design and configuration of systems, or through *vulnerability removal* (i.e. debugging, patching, disabling modules, etc.), for example, it is not possible to prevent the attack(s) that activate(s) a given vulnerability.

The whole of the above-mentioned techniques prefigures what we call *intrusion prevention*, that is, the attempt to avoid the occurrence of intrusion faults. Figure 1(b) suggests, as we discussed earlier, that it is impossible or infeasible to guarantee perfect prevention. The reasons are obvious: it may be not possible to handle all attacks, possibly because not all are known or new ones may appear; it may not be possible to remove or prevent the introduction of new vulnerabilities.

For these intrusions still escaping the prevention process, forms of *InTol* are required, as shown in Fig. 1, to prevent system failure. As will be explained later, these can assume several forms: detection (e.g. of intruded account activity, of Trojan horse activity), recovery (e.g. interception and neutralization of intruder activity) and masking (e.g. voting between several components, including a minority of intruded ones).

2.1.3 Trust and trustworthiness

There is a well-defined relationship between the notions of 'trust' and 'trustworthiness'— in a sense, they relate strongly to the words 'dependence' and 'dependability' (Adelsbach et al., 2002). Whereas *trust* is the accepted dependence of a component or system, on a set of properties of another component or system, *trustworthiness* would be the measure in which the latter component or system meets that set of properties. Although this relation is often forgotten, leading designers concentrate on only one of them at a time, it is crucial to the design of intrusion-tolerant systems.

The relation can be metaphorically described as 'Thou Shalt Not Trust non-Trustworthy Systems' (Verissimo, 2006a). Let us understand this better. A trusted component has a set of properties that are relied upon by another component. If A trusts B, this means that a violation in those properties of B might compromise the correct operation of A. Observe that those properties of B trusted by A might not correspond quantitatively or qualitatively to B's actual properties. This happens when the relation is not taken into account by the designer. In consequence, trust should be placed *to the extent of* the component's trustworthiness. The trustworthiness of a component is thus, not surprisingly, defined by how well it secures a set of functional and non-functional properties, deriving from its architecture, construction and environment and evaluated as appropriate.

2.2   Models and assumptions

Surprising as it may seem, InTol is not just another instantiation of accidental fault tolerance. Architecting intrusion-tolerant systems, to arrive at some notion of *intrusion-tolerant middleware* for application support, presents multiple challenges, primarily because several of the paradigms and models used in accidental fault tolerance are not adequate for malicious faults: potential for maliciously caused common-mode faults makes probabilistic assumptions risky (number of 'independent' faulty components and fault types); error propagation is the rule rather than the exception (error detection delay and progressive intrusion); typical severity of malicious faults (Byzantine behaviour, attacks on timing and contamination of runtime support environment).

2.2.1   Failure assumptions

A crucial aspect of any fault-tolerant architecture is the fault model upon which the system architecture is conceived, and component interactions are defined. A system fault model is built on assumptions about the way system components fail. Classically, these assumptions fall into two kinds: *controlled failure* assumptions and *arbitrary failure* assumptions. These types of assumptions can be combined under *hybrid failure* assumptions and *architecturally hybrid failure* assumptions. The four kinds of assumptions are explained next.

Controlled failure assumptions specify constraints on component failures. For example, it may be assumed that components only fail by crashing or only have timing failures. This approach represents very well how common systems work under the presence of accidental faults, failing in a benign manner most of the time. However, it is difficult to model the behaviour of a hacker, and therefore, there is a problem of coverage that does not recommend this approach for malicious faults, unless a trustworthy solution can be found.

Arbitrary failure assumptions ideally specify no qualitative constraints on component failures. Practical systems do however specify quantitative bounds on the number of failed components. In this context, an arbitrary failure means the capability of generating a message at any time, with whatever syntax and semantics (form and meaning), and sending it to anywhere in the system. Arbitrary failure assumptions are costly to handle, in terms of performance and complexity, and thus are not compatible with the user requirements of the vast majority of today's online applications.

Hybrid failure assumptions combining both kinds of failures might be a way out of this dilemma (Meyer and Pradhan, 1987). Here, an undistinguished set of nodes are assumed to behave arbitrarily while others are assumed to fail only by crashing. These distributions are in essence postulating heterogeneous failure modes in sets of homogeneous components, a probabilistic foundation that makes sense in accidental fault scenarios, but which might be hard to sustain in the presence of malicious intelligence.

Architecturally hybrid failure assumptions introduce the necessary constraints (Verissimo et al., 2006): some parts of the system are justifiably assumed to exhibit fail-controlled behaviour, whilst the remainder of the system is still allowed an arbitrary behaviour. This is an interesting approach for modular and distributed system architectures, especially intrusion-tolerant ones, and therefore, we develop the principle a bit further in Section 2.2.2.

2.2.2 Intrusion tolerance under hybrid models

Consider a component or sub-system for which a given controlled failure assumption is made, the rest of the system being arbitrary on failure. How can we achieve coverage of such an assumption, given the unpredictability of attacks and the elusiveness of vulnerabilities?

A model featuring *architectural hybridization* is one where environment properties may vary from component to component. This includes failure assumptions, where the presence and severity of vulnerabilities, attacks and intrusions are in fact constrained by the architecture and the construction of those system components, and thus substantiated. For example, through intrusion prevention techniques combined with the recursive use of InTol mechanisms to build the component itself.

A modelling approach relevant to this discussion is the hybrid distributed systems model or Wormholes model (Verissimo, 2006b). Figure 2 shows a possible representation of a system under this model. Under such a model, a system is a hybrid of a 'normal' or payload part, which can exhibit weak properties such as asynchrony and arbitrary or Byzantine failure, and a 'privileged' or control part, a subsystem capable of providing a small set of services with stronger properties (e.g. timeliness, security and crash failure)

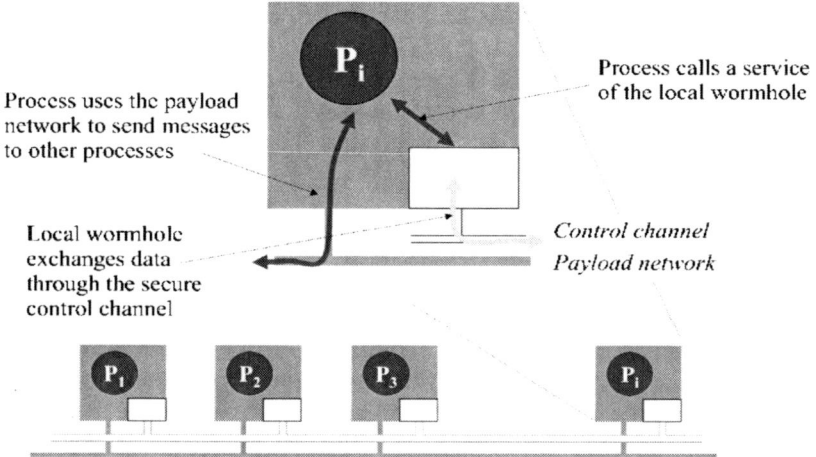

Process calls a service
of the local wormhole

Process uses the payload
network to send messages
to other processes

Local wormhole
exchanges data
through the secure
control channel

Control channel
Payload network

Fig. 2. Architecturally hybrid Wormholes system (payload displayed in dark and wormhole in white).

that are otherwise not available in the rest of the system. That latter part is also called a 'wormhole'. Wormholes can be either local or distributed, in which case they are interconnected through a control channel (the case depicted in Fig. 2). Practical wormholes should be kept small and simple to ensure their behaviour is verifiable.

Processes run in the payload, that part of the system that may experience arbitrary delays or failures (e.g. asynchronous Byzantine environment), and they communicate by sending messages through the payload network. However, during their execution, they can call the wormhole to perform (small) crucial steps. In contrast to the rest of the system, the wormhole always returns trustworthy results. Extremely resilient but performing secure protocols can be built with this powerful combination (Correia et al., 2002, 2005).

The approach yields implementations of fault- and intrusion-tolerant protocols that achieve the best of both worlds (Verissimo, 2003): (i) more efficient than protocol implementations that have to deal with truly arbitrary failure assumptions for all components and (ii) more robust than designs that make controlled failure assumptions without enforcing them.

Arbitrary failure assumptions are considered necessary. Note that the hybrid failure approach, no matter how resilient, relies on the coverage of the fail-controlled assumptions. Definitely, there will be a significant number of operations whose value and criticality is such that the risk of failure due to violation of these assumptions cannot be incurred. In consequence, an important area of research is still related to arbitrary-failure resilient building blocks, namely, communication protocols of the Byzantine class, which do not make assumptions on the existence of trusted or controlled-failure components. They reason in terms of admitting any

behaviour from the participants and allow the corruption of a parameteriz-
able number of participants, say f. The system works correctly as long as
there exist $n > 3f$ participants. These protocols do not make assumptions
about timeliness either and are in essence time-free. This has implications on
the operational aspects such as performance.

2.3   Architectural notions

One key aspect of *intrusion-tolerant middleware* is that it should lead to an
automation of the process of building resilience. In other words, each layer,
starting with hardware, should contribute to build a next layer of more
trusted functionality, progressively filtering the possible intrusions that may
occur in the baseline untrusted components.

Additionally, a good design practice is for the middleware to be modular
and tending to achieve incremental levels of trustworthiness. This is an
accepted design principle for building distributed fault tolerance into
systems. It facilitates the definition of different redundancy strategies for
different components and the placement of the relevant replicas.

For example, at lower layers, basic InTol mechanisms are used to construct a trustworthy communication subsystem. This subsystem can then be
trusted by higher layer distributed software, to securely communicate
amongst participants without bothering about network intrusion threats.
Or alternatively, it can be used to build an even more trustworthy higher
layer—by incrementally using InTol mechanisms—such as a replication
management protocol resilient to both network and host intrusions.

As such, there are several relevant levels at which trust can be built,
and the structure of an intrusion-tolerant host relies on a mix of a few
architectural options:

- The notion of *trusted*—versus untrusted—*hardware*. As a good
  practice, most hardware should be considered to be untrusted, but
  small parts of it may be considered to be trusted, if adequately
  trustworthy, for example, by being *tamperproof* by construction.
- The notion of *trusted support software*. Trusted to execute a few
  functions correctly albeit immersed in an environment subjected to
  malicious faults. The use of trusted hardware may help substantiate
  this assumption.
- The notion of *runtime environment*, extending operating system (OS)
  capabilities and hiding heterogeneity. A generic concept that is also
  useful in this context. Functions supplied by the above-mentioned trusted
  support software should be offered through the runtime application
  programming interface (API), vertically to all middleware layers.
- The notion of *trusted distributed component*. Implemented by each
  layer of the modular *middleware*: multipoint network abstraction,
  communication support services and activity support services. At each

level, the faulty behaviour of lower levels is partially or totally overcome. This depends on the different InTol strategies that can be followed at several levels of abstraction of the architecture. Versatile combinations of synchrony and failure assumptions are possible, from synchrony to asynchrony, from arbitrary to fail-silent.

A reference intrusion-tolerant architecture inspired by the Malicious- and Accidental-Fault Tolerance for Internet Applications (MAFTIA) project work (Verissimo et al., 2006) is depicted in at least three different dimensions in Fig. 3:

- First, there is the *hardware* dimension, which includes the host and networking devices that make up the physical distributed system.
- Second, within each node, there are the *local support* services provided by the OS and the runtime platform. These may vary from host to host in a heterogeneous system, and some services may even not be available on some hosts or may have to be accessed through the network using protocols providing an appropriate degree of trust. However, at a minimum, the local services include typical OS functionality such as the ability to run processes, send messages across the network and access local persistent storage (if it exists).
- Third, there is the *distributed software* provided by the specific systems: the layers of *middleware*, running on top of the runtime support mechanisms provided by each host, and any system's native *services* (Serv. x in Fig. 3).

Applications built to run on top of such an architecture use the abstractions provided by the middleware and the application services to operate securely across several hosts, and be accessed securely by users running on remote nodes, even in the presence of malicious faults.

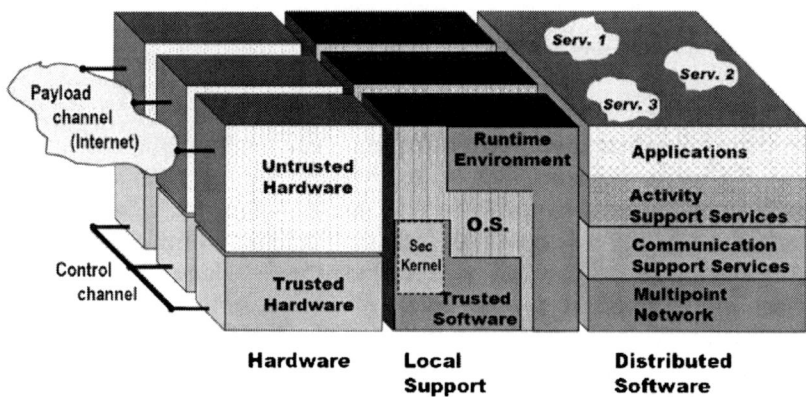

Fig. 3.   Dimensions of a reference intrusion-tolerant architecture.

As mentioned earlier, a middleware layer may host a trusted distributed component that overcomes the fault severity of lower layers and provides certain functions in a trustworthy way. These are in turn trusted by the layers above, in a recursive way. For example, a (distributed) transactional service trusts that a (distributed) atomic multicast component ensures the typical properties (agreement and total order), regardless of the fact that the underlying environment may suffer Byzantine malicious attacks.

The distribution dimension impacts on the protocol design but not on the services provided by each host. These are constructed on the functionality provided by the several middleware modules, represented in Fig. 3:

- The lowest layer is the *multipoint network* module, MN, created over the physical infrastructure. This component of the reference architecture should hide the particularities of the underlying network to which hosts are directly attached. It should provide a runtime compliant interface for any standard protocols to be used (e.g. internet protocol (IP); internet protocol security (IPSEC) and simple network management protocol (SNMP)). Typical properties are the provision of multipoint addressing, basic secure channels and management communications.
- The next reference layer, the *communication support services* module, CS, is where the designer should place: basic cryptographic primitives, Byzantine agreement, group communication with several reliability and ordering guarantees, clock synchronization and other core communication services. The CS module depends on the MN module to access the network.
- Finally, the *activity support services* module, AS, should host building blocks that assist execution of intrusion-tolerant applications such as replication management (e.g. state machine (SM) and voting), leader election, transactional management, authorization, key management and so forth. It depends on the services provided by the CS module.

2.4 Middleware design strategies

The goal of middleware is to support the construction of trusted applications, implemented by collections of components with varying degrees of trustworthiness. This is achieved by relying on distributed fault and InTol mechanisms supplied by that middleware.

Given the variety of possible intrusion-tolerant applications, several different strategies are pursued to achieve the above-mentioned goal. These strategies are applied at several levels of abstraction of the architecture, most importantly, in the implementation of the middleware and application services. In this section, we describe these strategies: fail-uncontrolled or arbitrary, fail-controlled with local trusted components (LTCs) and fail-controlled with distributed trusted components (DTCs).

The conventions used in Figs. 4–6 are as follows: grey means untrusted (the darker, the 'less trusted'), white means trusted, the presence of a clock symbol means a synchronous environment, a crossed out clock symbol means an asynchronous environment, a warped clock symbol means a partially synchronous environment, a key means a secure environment, dashed arrows means communication that can be interfered with and continuous arrows denote trusted paths of communication.

2.4.1 Arbitrary failure

The fail-uncontrolled or arbitrary failure strategy is based on the no-assumptions attitude discussed in Section 2.2. When a very large coverage is sought, we resort to making no assumptions about time, following an asynchronous model, and we make essentially no assumptions about the faulty behaviour of either the components or the environment. Of course, for the system as a whole to provide a useful service, it is necessary that at least some of the components are correct. This approach is essentially parametric: it will remain correct if a sufficient number of correct participants exist, for any hypothesized number of faulty participants f.

Figure 4 shows the principle in simple terms. The hosts and the communication environment are not trusted and are fully asynchronous. For a protocol to be able to provide correct service, it must cope with arbitrary failures of components and the environment. For example, component C_k is malicious, but this may be because the component itself or host C has been tampered with or because an intruder in the communication system simulates that behaviour.

Several protocols in the literature follow this strategy, to be resilient to arbitrary failure assumptions. They are Byzantine fault resilient and have probabilistic or deterministic structure, depending on whether they are subject to the Fischer–Lynch–Paterson (FLP) impossibility result (Fischer et al., 1985). They require a number of hosts $n > 3f$, for f faulty components. Different qualities of service exist, such as basic binary Byzantine agreement, reliable broadcast, atomic broadcast, multi-valued Byzantine agreement, quorums and state machine replication (SMR). These kind of protocols are detailed in Section 3.

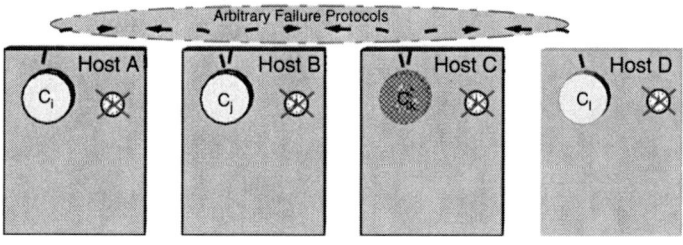

Fig. 4.   Arbitrary failure.

Some of these protocols have been featured in the literature under partially synchronous models (models where asynchrony is not absolute), but such a strategy has the problem of introducing vulnerabilities that can be attacked and as such is not recommended. When this is desired, time should be encapsulated in trusted components under a hybrid model. This problem is further discussed in Section 4.

2.4.2 *Fail-controlled with local trusted components*

Figure 5 exemplifies a fail-controlled strategy. As for the fail-uncontrolled strategy, it is assumed that hosts and communication environment are not trusted and asynchronous. However, hosts have a LTC, which supports functions they can trust for certain steps of their operation. This strategy can be substantiated by a hybrid, or wormholes model, with local wormholes, as discussed in Section 2.2. As such, we can construct protocols that cope with a hybrid of arbitrary and fail-silent behaviours, depending on whether a component is interacting with the other components or with the LTC.

In the example given earlier, component C_k may be arbitrarily malicious, either because the component itself or host C has been tampered with or because an intruder in the communication system simulates that behaviour. However, unlike the fail-uncontrolled strategy, the impact of this behaviour on the other components (i.e. error propagation) may be limited, if the protocol makes components perform certain checks and validations with the LTC (e.g. signature validation), which will prevent C_k from causing certain failures in the value domain (example.g. forging). Likewise, if host B is contaminated, component C_j may behave erroneously, but protocols can be designed in a way that prevents C_j from behaving in an arbitrary (e.g. Byzantine) way towards the other hosts.

2.4.3 *Fail-controlled with distributed trusted components*

The 'fail-controlled with DTCs' strategy amplifies the scope of trustworthiness of the local component support by making it distributed. As such, certain global actions can be trusted, despite a generally malicious

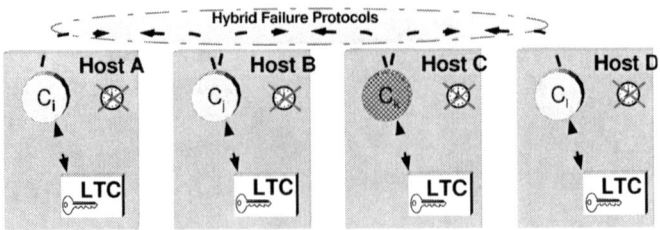

Fig. 5.   Fail-controlled with local trusted components.

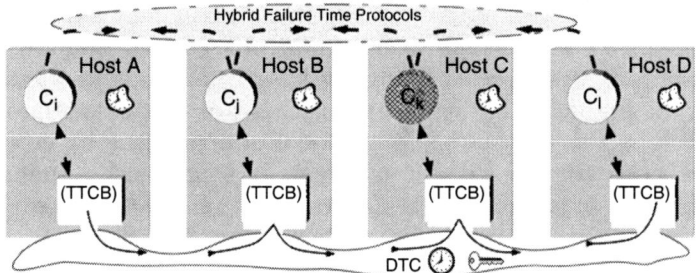

Fig. 6. Fail-controlled with distributed trusted components.

communication environment. This strategy can be substantiated by a wormholes model, with distributed wormholes, as discussed in Section 2.2.

A DTC has the advantage that trust can easily be built on global time-related and security-related properties (such as global time, distributed durations and block agreement). For example, timed behaviour can be supported globally in an intrusion-resilient way, as suggested by the warped clocks in Fig. 6: the system is assumed to be *partially synchronous*, that is, anywhere in the interval ranging from time-free to fully synchronous, depending on the environment.

Consider the example of Fig. 6, where again component C_k or host C may be arbitrarily malicious. Like the 'fail-controlled with LTCs' strategy, the impact of the faulty behaviour of these components may be limited by enforcing certain validations with the LTC. However, the fact that the LTCs are interconnected and can exchange information and perform agreement in a secure way—through the control channel—further limits the potential damage of malicious behaviour. For example, a very simple such service might be a generic low-level binary block consensus primitive: the DTC 'knows' directly what each of the payload components in different hosts 'say', unlike the solution with LTCs, where an LTC only 'knows' what a remote component 'says', through information coming through the local payload component. That service could be used, for example, to validate message authentication codes (MACs) used in higher level protocols (Correia et al., 2005).

Another advantage of a DTC is the ability to support timed behaviour in an intrusion-resilient way. Timed systems are fragile in that timing assumptions can be manipulated by intruders. The DTC may support trusted time-related services, namely, absolute time, duration measurement and timing failure detection, if constructed as a fully synchronous subsystem. The payload system can have any degree of synchronism, as suggested in Fig. 6 by the warped clock. The DTC does not make the latter 'more synchronous' but allows it to take advantage of its possible synchronism or to resist attacks against system timing.

Note that all strategies have one thing in common: they assume that both the hosts and the communication environment are not trusted and can thus be compromised. Stronger assumptions have been made previously in the literature, for example, that hosts are fortresses or trusted computing bases (TCBs). Whilst this may simplify protocol and middleware construction, there is a price to pay in that coverage is lesser and systems become more vulnerable: it is known that the construction of large, complex TCBs (i.e. a completely vulnerability-free system) is not feasible.

3 Tolerating intrusions

In Section 2, we presented the main InTol concepts and design principles. Here, we present the main paradigms for designing intrusion-tolerant systems: threshold cryptography, quorum systems, SMR and mechanisms for confidentiality. In the end of this section, we present example architectures.

This section summarizes the most common InTol paradigms, which are based on *error masking*. The idea in virtually all techniques considered is to *replicate* a *service* provided to a set of clients $C = \{c_1, c_2, \ldots\}$ in a set of n servers $U = \{s_1, \ldots, s_n\}$. The clients and servers (designated by the common word *processes*) run protocols that mask the failure of up to f servers and a possibly infinite number of clients. A process is said to be *correct* if it follows its protocol or algorithm specification during the runtime of the system and *faulty* otherwise. In InTol, we consider that a server may become faulty due to an intentional action of an attacker, and therefore, we have to substantiate in some way the assumption that no more than f servers are faulty. This substantiation is done by assuming that there is *diversity* among the servers, that is, that they are different and so they do not have the same vulnerabilities (Littlewood and Strigini, 2004; Obelheiro et al., 2006).

InTol aims to achieve the three classical security attributes: *availability* (readiness for providing the service), *integrity* (absence of unauthorized state modifications) and *confidentiality* (no unauthorized disclosure of information) (Avizienis et al., 2004). The first two techniques described in this section aim to enforce the availability and integrity of the service: quorum systems and SMR. Then in Section 3.4, we survey techniques that not only ensure availability and integrity but also confidentiality.

Distributed system models: Physical reality is always very complex, and therefore to reason about it in any science—for example, physics, chemistry or informatics—we need to simplify this reality using *models*. In distributed systems, there are several kinds of models. The *fault model* makes assumptions about the types of faults that can happen in the system and its environment. In InTol, the fault model assumed is usually the arbitrary fault model, in which components like the network, servers and clients are assumed to fail *arbitrarily*, that is, without restrictions on (physically possible) behaviour. *Arbitrary faults* are often called, somewhat loosely, *Byzantine faults*, after the seminal work by Lamport et al. (1982). An important distinguishing factor in InTol fault models is the *malicious* factor, to emphasize that the fault distribution is due to an attacker's action and not accidental facts of nature. To avoid a completely arbitrary behaviour, more complex to handle, several mechanisms are usually employed to exclude by construction some classes of faults. For instance, the communication is usually assumed to be authenticated, messages impossible to forge and often reliable, since these properties can be obtained using protocols such as IPSEC (Kent and Atkinson, 1998) or SSL/TLS (secure sockets layer/transport layer security) (Frier et al., 1996). In this section, we consider authenticated reliable communication. There are also *architecturally hybrid fault models* in which different fault assumptions are made about different components of the system architecture (see Sections 2.2 and 2.4).

The *time model* is a set of assumptions about the temporal behaviour of the system. Several works on InTol assume the *asynchronous model*, which makes no assumptions about processing and communication times. This model is used because systems that make assumptions about time can be vulnerable to certain attacks against time (e.g. delaying the communication beyond the assumptions). Other systems extend the asynchronous model with failure detectors (Chandra and Toueg, 1996), weak time assumptions (Dwork et al., 1988) or wormholes (Correia et al., 2004).

3.1 Threshold cryptography

Threshold cryptography is an expression that denominates a set of algorithms that seem as if they were designed specifically for InTol, although they appeared in a quite different context—information security. These algorithms are often important building blocks of intrusion-tolerant paradigms and systems, and therefore, we introduce them up-front. There is an extensive bibliography about the area. A nice survey can be found in the work by Gemmell (1997).

There are two basic forms of threshold cryptography. Consider n processes, each holding a secret *share*. The objective of *secret sharing*—first form—is to allow any k of the processes to combine their shares and reconstruct a secret s, ensuring at the same time that $k - 1$ (possibly malicious) processes cannot do the same and not even obtain any useful information about s. A function *sharing* algorithm—second form—allows k processes to compute a certain function, while preventing $k - 1$ (malicious) processes from doing the same. An especially useful form of function sharing are *threshold signature* functions, which allow k processes to do a digital signature while maintaining the private key secret, since it is not held by any of the processes, but collectively by all.

The relation between these forms of cryptography and InTol is immediate. If up to f servers can fail and k is set to $k = f+1$, then only a subset of correct processes can reconstruct a secret (with secret sharing) or compute a function/signature (with function sharing/threshold signature); on the contrary, a collusion of malicious servers can never do it (since $f = k - 1$).

A simple intuition about how threshold cryptography works can be given by one of the seminal secret sharing algorithms, due to Shamir (1979) (the other was proposed at the same time by Blakley, 1979). The algorithm is based on two properties of polynomials. Consider a polynomial of degree d: $p(x) = a_0 + a_1x + a_2x^2 + \ldots + a_dx^d$. Given up to d points of the curve defined by $p(x)$, it is impossible to discover the polynomial, but given $d+1$ points, it is possible to do it using Lagrange interpolation. Therefore, if we define a polynomial $p(x)$ of degree $k-1$ with $p(0) = s$ and give one point of the polynomial to each process, k processes can reconstruct the secret but not $k-1$. This is the basic idea behind Shamir's algorithm. However, the complete algorithm is more complex.

Shamir's algorithm has a few limitations. One is that a process cannot verify if its share is 'good', that is, if it serves to reconstruct the secret, and therefore, *verifiable secret sharing* algorithms were designed. Another limitation is that if a process provides a corrupt share, the secret that is reconstructed is not the real secret. To deal with this problem, *robust secret sharing* algorithms were designed.

To the best of our knowledge, threshold cryptography was rarely used to build intrusion-tolerant systems. An interesting exception is the use of a threshold signature scheme in the Mastercard/VISA SET system, in which the private key was shared by several independent organizations (Frankel and Yung, 1998).

3.2   Quorum systems

Recall that the objective in this section is to design intrusion-tolerant systems by replicating a service in a set of servers U, accessed by a set of clients C. A *quorum system* Q is a set of subsets of servers—called quorums—such that $\forall Q_1, Q_2 \in Q$, $Q_1 \cap Q_2 \neq \emptyset$ (Gifford, 1979; Malkhi and Reiter, 1997). This definition may not seem particularly enlightening, but it gives the most important idea about quorums: they provide a way to reason about subsets of servers.

Quorum systems for InTol are usually dubbed *Byzantine quorum systems* (BQS), after the initial works by Malkhi and Reiter (1997) and Malkhi et al. (1997). In this section, we start by discussing how to implement *data storage services* using BQS. These services are characterized as a set of *shared memory registers* or variables (each can store one value of a certain domain V). Afterwards, we briefly discuss the implementation of other shared memory *objects* using BQS. Shared memory registers or objects are implemented by the servers in U and accessed (written/read) by the clients.[1] In this section, the BQS are used to ensure the *integrity* and *availability* of the shared memory registers/objects.

3.2.1 Registers

Lamport (1986) presented a classification of shared memory registers that is still much used to characterize registers implemented with BQS. A first aspect of that classification is the number of readers (i.e. clients that are allowed to read the register) and writers (clients that are allowed to write the register). Here, we consider only the most generic case, that is, *multi-writer/multi-reader registers*.

A second aspect of that classification is the *consistency semantics* that states what happens to the register when accessed concurrently by several clients. An operation (read/write) o_1 *happens before* and operation o_2 if o_1 finishes before the beginning of o_2. Two operations o_1 and o_2 are *concurrent* if neither o_1 happens before o_2 nor o_2 happens before o_1. The three Lamport's consistency semantics can be defined in the following way for a certain register x (Lamport, 1986; Martin et al., 2002): *Safe*—a read operation that is not concurrent with any write operation returns the last value written in x; a read concurrent with one or more writes returns any value; *Regular*—the same as the safe semantics except that a read concurrent with one or more writes returns either the last value written in x or the value being written by one of the concurrent writes; *Atomic*—the same as the regular semantics except that reads and writes return values as if they were executed in some order.[2] Each semantics in the list above is stronger than the previous one, since it guarantees the same properties plus some others. In general, it is harder to implement registers with stronger than weaker semantics.

In the context of InTol, it is still important to differentiate two kinds of registers: those that tolerate Byzantine faults in the clients (or Byzantine clients for short) and those that do not. Furthermore, registers that do tolerate Byzantine clients can put some restrictions on the kinds of attacks those clients can do.

Register with f-dissemination BQS: Let us now illustrate the implementation of a register x with BQS using simple algorithms based on those in the works by Malkhi and Reiter (1997, 1998). Each server $u \in U$ stores the value of the register x_u and a timestamp $t_{x,u}$. All clients and servers know the content of a certain set W_x that contains the identifiers of the clients

---

[1] In this chapter, we consider that communication is done through a network and model this communication using *message passing*. *Shared memory* is an alternative communication model that appeared in the context of parallel systems. In distributed systems, shared memory registers/objects have to be implemented using message passing protocols, which is what we do in this section.

[2] Notice that this is not simple to enforce since the register is implemented by a set of servers, not by a single one.

allowed to write in x (e.g. it can be stored in another register or be coded in the register's name). For simplicity of presentation, the clients are assumed to communicate with the servers using a *quorum remote procedure call* (Q-RPC). A call to Q-RPC(m) sends a request m to a subset of the servers and collects replies from a quorum of servers. This can be implemented in several ways, for instance, first sending m to a quorum of servers, then sending m to more servers until a full quorum replies (since malicious servers may not reply). Neither the clients nor the servers communicate between themselves, which is a property common in algorithms with BQS and that favours scalability (Malkhi and Reiter, 2000).

There are several classes of BQS. We implement the register x using one of the simplest, *f-dissemination* quorum systems, which is specific for *self-verifiable data*, that is, data that a malicious server cannot modify unnoticed (e.g. the values stored are signed by the client using its private key, and the corresponding public key is known by all processes). The BQS used to implement x has to satisfy the following two properties:

- *Consistency.* $\forall Q_1, Q_2 \in Q, |Q_1 \cap Q_2| \geqslant f + 1$
- *Availability.* $\forall Q \in Q, |Q| \leqslant n - f$

The first is the condition required for the register to satisfy the desired consistency semantics: that the intersection of any two quorums has at least one correct server. The second is the condition for the register to be always available. The properties allow the quorums to be defined in several different ways. A possible instantiation is to consider $f = \lfloor (n-1)/3 \rfloor$ and the quorums to be any subset of the servers in U of size $\lceil (n+f+1)/2 \rceil$. The simplest case is to consider $n = 3f + 1$ and quorums to be any subset of servers of size $2f + 1$. This simplified form is in fact an alternative way of defining quorum systems, simpler to understand, used in less theoretical works like that of Martin and Alvisi (2004) and Martin et al. (2002).

Let us now implement a register x with *regular semantics*, considering initially that clients are always correct. The register is implemented using essentially two algorithms: one for writing a value v in x, and another to read the value in x.

The *client-side write algorithm* is the following: (1) do a Q-RPC to request a set of timestamps $\{t_{x,u}\}_{u \in Q_1}$ from a quorum Q_1, (2) choose the highest timestamp t from $\{t_{x,u}\}_{u \in Q_1}$ and (3) do a Q-RPC to send the signed pair $\langle v, t+1 \rangle$ to any quorum Q_2.

The *client-side read algorithm* is (1) do a Q-RPC to obtain a set of correctly signed pairs value/timestamp $\{\langle v_u, t_u \rangle_{wu}\}_{u \in Q_1}$ from a quorum Q_1 and (2) return the value with the highest timestamp written by a writer in W_x.

The server-side algorithms are not shown since they are trivially deduced from the client-side ones. It is also simple to understand that the register works as expected. In the write operation, even if the quorum Q_1 contains f Byzantine servers, there are still other $n - 2f$ correct servers in that quorum (availability property). In the read operation, if the client receives a value 'invented' by a set of Byzantine servers, it discards it because those servers will not be able to impersonate a writer in W_x. Also, a client will always get the most recent timestamp since all quorums intersect in $f+1$ servers (consistency property), at most f of which can be Byzantine. In case there are concurrent writes and a read, the value read is clearly the previous one or one of the values being written, and therefore, the semantics is regular.

Let us now consider the problem of Byzantine clients. With the above-mentioned algorithms, a malicious writer can leave the register in an inconsistent state by writing a pair with the same timestamp but different values in all servers (poisonous write). The solution is to use an *echo protocol* (Reiter, 1994) to ensure that all servers that accept the write accept the same pair $\langle v,t \rangle$. The modified client-side write algorithm is the following: (1) the writer sends the pair to the servers and obtains signed echoes from a quorum and (2) the writer sends the pair and the signatures to the same quorum. As all quorums intersect, it is impossible to the malicious writer to write two different values with the same timestamp in two different quorums.

Other registers and BQS: The requirement for self-verifiable (or signed) data of *f-dissemination* quorum systems is a restriction that may be inconvenient in many cases (e.g. distributing public keys is often difficult in large-scale systems). Therefore, Malkhi and Reiter defined a second class of quorum systems that does not have this restriction—*f-masking* quorum systems. This generalization, however, requires a modification to the consistency property since now the intersection of any two quorums must include a majority of correct servers, that is, at least $2f+1$ servers: $\forall Q_1, Q_2 \in Q, |Q_1 \cap Q_2| \geqslant 2f+1$. The availability property remains the same.

Martin, Alvisi and Dahlin studied the problem of implementing registers with BQS using a minimum of servers (Martin et al., 2002). They managed to implement atomic registers (the strongest semantics) with *f-masking* quorum systems and $3f+1$ servers. They also managed to implement regular registers with *f-dissemination* and *f-masking* quorum systems and only $2f+1$ servers.

The problem of Byzantine clients has also received some attention on the literature. The poisonous write mentioned earlier is only one of the possible attacks a malicious writer can attempt. Recently, (Liskov and Rodrigues, 2006) studied the problem of tolerating other attacks such as exhausting the timestamp space or not completing an algorithm.

3.2.2 Beyond registers

BQS can be used to implement shared memory objects other than registers. For instance, Malkhi and Reiter presented a mutual exclusion object (Malkhi and Reiter, 1998) and a (randomized) consensus object (Malkhi and Reiter, 2000).

The interesting question, however, is that what is the power of BQS to implement intrusion-tolerant services? Do they allow the implementation of registers plus some other objects/services or any intrusion-tolerant service?

The answer to this question depends on the system model considered. Most works on BQS (including all those cited earlier) consider that the system is strictly *asynchronous*, with no other time assumptions, failure detectors or other oracles. In fact, the asynchrony of systems based on BQS has always been pointed out as one of its positive aspects. Considering that model, is it possible to implement any service? The answer is no. Although BQS allow the implementation of read and write operations, with different semantics, it was recently shown that they do not allow the deterministic implementation of *update* operations, that is, operations that modify the state of the shared memory object (or service) taking into account the present state of the service (Bessani et al., 2007). For instance, $x = 1$ is a write operation, while $x = x + 1$ is an update operation (in C/Java syntax). The implementation of update operations requires timing assumptions (or randomization instead of determinism) (Bessani et al., 2007).

Guerraoui and Vukolic (2007) have been studying the performance of BQS without this restriction of a strictly asynchronous time model. Removing this restriction, BQS allow the implementation of SMR, which allows the implementation of any intrusion-tolerant deterministic service, as discussed in Section 3.3.

3.3   State machine replication

SMR is a generic solution for the implementation of fault-tolerant deterministic services (Schneider, 1990), including intrusion-tolerant services (Castro and Liskov, 2002; Reiter, 1995).

The basic idea is very simple. Consider a service, modelled as a SM S, that we want to make intrusion-tolerant. The state of S is defined by a set of *state variables* and is modified by a set of *commands*. Commands are atomic in the sense that there can be no interference between their executions. Clients send *requests* for the service to execute commands. SMR consists in replicating S in n servers and forces these servers to emulate the (non-replicated) service in such a way that the service still behaves as expected (i.e. satisfies availability and integrity) even if up to f servers are faulty. This emulation is done by enforcing the following four properties:

- *Initial state*: All correct servers start in the same state.
- *Agreement*: All correct servers execute the same commands.
- *Total order*: All correct servers execute the commands in the same order.
- *Determinism*: The same command executed in the same initial state in two different correct servers generates the same final state.

The first property is usually simple to enforce. The second and third are enforced by an (intrusion-tolerant) *atomic multicast protocol* (or total order multicast), which delivers the same requests in the same order to all (correct) servers. The fourth property is always problematic due to the need of diversity among the servers, and therefore, specific techniques such as software wrappers have to be used to enforce it (Castro et al., 2003).

SMR algorithms can be classified in two types: *primary-based* and *decentralized*. The former operate in a fashion similar to the classical Lamport's Paxos algorithm (Lamport, 1998), and therefore, they are often called *Byzantine Paxos* (Castro and Liskov, 2002; Martin and Alvisi, 2006; Ramasamy and Cachin, 2006; Reiter, 1995; Zielinski, 2004). There is a primary server that orders the requests; when the primary is suspected of being faulty, a new primary is chosen. In decentralized algorithms, the order of the messages is defined in a decentralized way, with the assistance of a consensus algorithm of some kind (Cachin et al., 2002; Correia et al., 2004). We give an example of each later.

3.3.1 BFT

A good example of a *primary-based SMR algorithm* is BFT, the algorithm that showed that Byzantine fault tolerance can be fast, to paraphrase the name of one of the papers about it (Castro and Liskov, 2002). The algorithm uses several techniques for efficiency, but probably the most useful is to use MACs based on a shared secret key, instead of asymmetric cryptography-based signatures. In BFT, messages multicast to all servers take an *authenticator*, that, a vector with one MAC calculated with the secret key shared between the sender and each of the recipients. This authenticator allows the recipient to verify if the message is authentic (i.e. is really from the sender) and has not been modified. Servers always discard messages with an invalid authenticator.

The algorithm is complex and can only be summarized in here. For simplicity, we consider $n = 3f + 1$ (in the general case, $f = \lfloor (n-1)/3 \rfloor$). The system evolves in *views*, which are numbered sequentially. In each view, one server is the *primary* and the others are the *backups*. There are two cases: *normal operation* and *view change*. Let us start with the normal operation, which is represented in Fig. 7.

When a client wants to make a request to the service, it multicasts a message with the command, a timestamp and an authenticator to all the servers (message m in Fig. 7). A client accepts the reply from the service when it receives $f + 1$ copies of the same reply from $f + 1$ different servers because this guarantees that at least one of the servers is correct (at most f can be faulty).

When the primary receives a request from the client it runs three phases. First, it gives an order number to the message and sends this number with a cryptographic hash of the request to all backups (*pre-prepare phase*). If the backups receive the request from the client and accept the order number

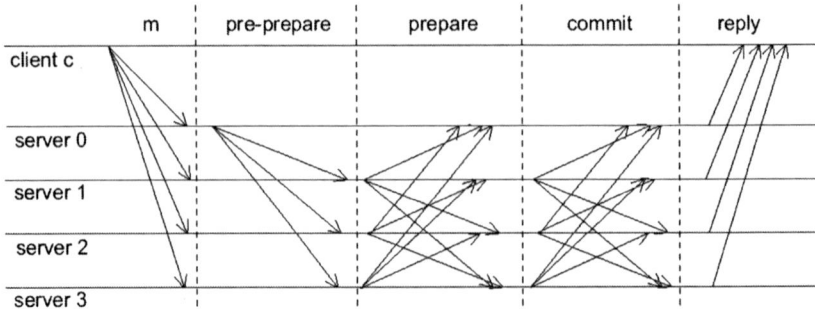

Fig. 7.   Normal operation of BFT (Castro and Liskov, 2002).

(e.g. if it was not given to another request yet and it corresponds to the present view), they send a prepare message (*prepare phase*). Finally, all servers that receive $2f$ prepare messages from other backups multicast a commit message (*commit phase*). When a server receives $2f + 1$ commit messages for a request, the request is accepted for execution. When all requests with lower order numbers are executed, this request is also executed and the result is sent in a reply message to the client.

Proving the correctness of this algorithm is complex and cannot be done here, but let us give an intuition that it works as expected. First, a Byzantine primary cannot 'invent' its own requests, since the backups only process requests that they receive from the client. Second, a Byzantine primary cannot give the same order number to two different messages (violating the agreement property) because (1) a correct backup sends a prepare message only for the first request it receives for a certain order number i, (2) a correct backup sends a commit message only if it receives prepare messages from $2f$ backups and (3) there cannot be two different sets of $2f$ backup that send prepare messages for the same i and different requests because $2f + 2f + 1 > 3f + 1$. To conclude, the algorithm gives order numbers to requests; correct servers only execute committed requests; it is not possible to create false requests or give the same number to two different requests.

However, there is still a problem. A Byzantine server can simply decide not to send pre-prepare messages to some requests or to skip some order numbers. To deal with this problem, when a backup receives a request from a client, it starts a timer, which is stopped when the request is executed. If the timer expires, the backup informs the other backups that it suspects of the primary. When enough backups suspect of the current primary, a new view is installed.

There are several publications that improve BFT in different ways: terminating faster in 'nice' conditions (Martin and Alvisi, 2006; Zielinski, 2004), ensuring progress when the primary changes frequently (Ramasamy and Cachin, 2006), extending it for wide area networks (WANs) (Amir et al., 2006, 2007).

3.3.2 SMR with 2f + 1 servers

BFT requires $3f + 1$ servers. This number comes from the minimum number of processes needed to solve intrusion-tolerant atomic multicast or consensus, which is equivalent in several system models. Example system models include extensions to the asynchronous model with weak synchrony properties (like BFT), with failure detectors or with randomization (Correia et al., 2006).

Although this is a common number of servers in InTol, it is important to reduce it as much as possible, since each server is a machine, with its own OS, application software and all the management costs involved. In this section, we briefly present only SMR algorithm in the literature that uses less than $3f + 1$ replicas, in fact, only $2f + 1$ replicas (Correia et al., 2004). This algorithm is also an example of a *decentralized SMR algorithm*.

The algorithm was designed under a hybrid distributed system model, where the asynchronous and Byzantine payload part was extended with a component of the *wormholes* class (see Section 2). The wormhole is *not* used to implement the SMR algorithm but only to provide a simple *ordering service* (just like failure detectors provide a detection service). In this environment, it was possible to achieve an algorithm that reduces the number of replicas to $2f + 1$. The system with wormhole-enabled servers is presented in Fig. 8.

The SMR algorithm works in the following way. A client sends a request protected with an authenticator (vector of MACs) to one of the servers. If after some time it does not get $f + 1$ equal replies from different servers, it retransmits the request to other servers. When a server receives the request from the client, it sends the request to all other servers and gives a cryptographic hash of the request to the wormhole. When the other servers

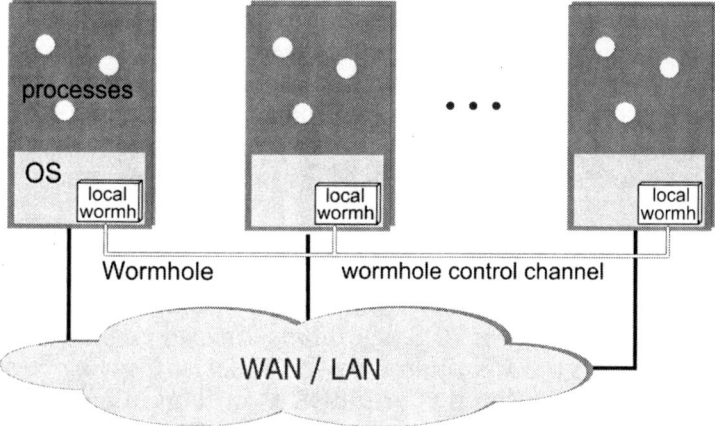

Fig. 8. Computers with a *wormhole* (Correia et al., 2004).

receive the request, they also give their hashes to the wormhole. When the wormhole collects $f + 1$ hashes from different servers, it gives the request an order number and gives that number to all servers. When all requests with lower numbers are executed, this request is also executed and a reply is returned to the client.

Let us give an intuition that the algorithm works as expected. The wormhole is a tiny tamperproof component, and therefore, it always behaves correctly, giving sequential numbers to the requests. A malicious server cannot fool the wormhole into giving order numbers to 'invented' requests because the wormhole only gives these numbers when it receives hashes of the request from $f + 1$ servers, one of which is correct by assumption, and correct servers only give the wormhole hashes of requests with valid authenticators.

3.3.3 SMR versus BQS

How does SMR relate to BQS? As discussed in Section 3.3.2, BQS are a way to reason about quorums of servers, whereas SMR is a specific form of service replication. SMR is based on a set of servers (U), and therefore, we can use BQS to reason about quorums of those servers, but SMR is in fact a more specific technique. A SMR system can be said to be based on BQS if we remove the restriction 'quorums $\Rightarrow$ asynchrony', discussed in Section 3.2. The problem is that intrusion-tolerant atomic multicast is equivalent to consensus that cannot be solved deterministically in an asynchronous system in which processes (servers in this case) can fail (Fischer et al., 1985). Therefore, SMR cannot be implemented deterministically in asynchronous systems, although it can be implemented using randomized protocols (Correia et al., 2006) (quite efficiently, as shown by project RITAS (Moniz et al., 2006)).

It is also important to emphasize that SMR is a generic technique that can be used to make any deterministic service intrusion-tolerant. If it was to be used to implement a data storage, then it would provide *atomic* registers, that is, the strongest of Lamport's semantics. In relation to the implementation of registers with 'light' BQS algorithms (like those presented earlier) versus SMR, some believe that the former are more efficient than the latter, but a recent work shows that this depends on several parameters (Dantas et al., 2007).

A few recent works tried to bring together the best of both worlds, that is, to use 'light' asynchronous BQS algorithms whenever possible and rely on 'heavy' atomic multicast only when needed. The above-mentioned work by Bessani et al. (2007) uses BQS algorithms for read and write operations and a Byzantine Paxos algorithm only for updates. Cowling et al. (2006) presented a SMR algorithm that uses BQS algorithms in normal operation but switches to Byzantine Paxos when it detects concurrency among write requests.

3.4 Enforcing confidentiality

SMR and the quorum protocols presented earlier have the objective of enforcing the *availability* and *integrity* of a service. This section is about ensuring the *confidentiality* of data stored. Recall that the challenge is that not only the clients but also up to f servers can be faulty/malicious and disclose any data stored in them (and modify that information and deny access to it).

3.4.1 Fragmentation-redundancy-scattering

Although we started with the problem of ensuring availability and integrity of a service, the seminal work that first discussed InTol was actually about a storage service that aimed to ensure the confidentiality of the data stored (Fraga and Powell, 1985). This work introduced a technique later called *fragmentation-redundancy-scattering* (FRS) (Deswarte et al., 1991). FRS had the important merit of introducing many of the ideas that reappeared more than a decade later when InTol started gaining momentum.

The basic idea is simple to understand. The service is a file storage, distributed among n servers. Each file F before being stored is fragmented into m fragments, which are scattered among the n servers. Each fragment is encrypted (for confidentiality) and stored in more than one server to guarantee the availability of the file even if there are faulty servers (redundancy). However, no server has enough fragments to reconstruct the file, also to tolerate faulty servers. Detection of corrupted fragments can be done with the assistance of MACs added to each fragment or by reading several fragments from different servers and voting. The location of the fragments of a file is stored in a specific server, which can also be made intrusion-tolerant using replication.

3.4.2 Asynchronous verifiable information dispersal with confidentiality (cAVID)

A few years after the appearance of FRS, in a different context, Rabin (1989) published a solution to fragment a file—an *information dispersal algorithm*—that optimizes the space used. The idea is to use a *(k,n)-erasure code* to divide the file into n fragments in such a way that it can be reconstructed with k fragments but not with $k - 1$. Rabin's scheme was purely mathematical. Krawczyk (1993) evolved the scheme to store information in a distributed service, and much later, Goodson et al. (2004) used a similar scheme to implement an intrusion-tolerant file storage with efficient space usage.

These works dealt with the problem of efficient storage but not of confidentiality. That further step was done more recently in the works by Cachin and Tessaro (2005, 2006). The basic mechanism, which provides only integrity and availability, is called *asynchronous verifiable information dispersal* (AVID). When a client wants to store/write a file F in the service, it starts by coding F as a vector $[F_1, \ldots, F_N]$ using a *(k,n)-erasure code*, with $k = f + 1$ for $n = 3f + 1$. Then, it obtains the *fingerprints* of the file (Krawczyk, 1993), that is, a vector with the hash of each of the file fragments $D = [D_1, \ldots, D_N]$. Finally, it uses a variation of Bracha's reliable multicast protocol (Bracha, 1984) to store each fragment F_i in server s_i and the fingerprints in all servers. Each fragment is sent only to its destination server, and therefore, the servers may have to reconstruct some of the fragments in case the client is malicious and does not send all fragments. When a client wants to read a file, it simply requests any k fragments and reconstructs the file, using the fingerprints to check if the fragments recovered were modified.

The confidentiality of the file is guaranteed using a variation of AVID, called cAVID. An obvious requirement for confidentiality is that only allowed clients can read the file, and therefore, cAVID stores a list L of clients with read access together with the file F. To guarantee the confidentiality of the file, the client starts by generating a random secret key K and then uses it to encrypt the file, which is stored using AVID. The main problem is how to give K to the clients that are allowed to read F. The solution is to use a *(n,k)-threshold encryption scheme*. Each server has a private key SK_i and all clients have the corresponding public key PK. When the client wants to store the file F, besides storing the encrypted file with AVID, it also stores the key K encrypted with PK and L. When a client c_1 wants to read a file, it sends that request to the servers; if $c_1 \in L$, then the correct servers send c_1 a decrypted share of K and the client uses $k = f + 1$ of those shares to reconstruct the key and decrypt F. On the contrary, no f malicious servers can disclose the content of F because they cannot reconstruct K.

Two final notes on InTol confidentiality schemes are as follows. First, confidentiality is an attribute of data, and therefore, these schemes make sense for data storage services. Therefore, the protocols presented can be considered to be quorum protocols. More specifically, cAVID implements a single-writer/multi-reader register. A second note is that *secret sharing* is an obvious candidate to implement confidential storage systems. However, only one system based on this kind of scheme was found in the literature, probably because current secret sharing algorithms are too slow for practical purposes (Lakshmanan et al., 2003).

3.5   Architectures

The earlier sections introduced the main paradigms for designing intrusion-tolerant systems: threshold cryptography, quorum systems, SMR and mechanisms for confidentiality. In Section 2, we also proposed a reference architecture for intrusion-tolerant middleware. The issue now is how to use these building blocks to build real systems. A few classical paradigms complement the former, such as encryption and access control, intrusion detection, firewalls and virtual private networks (VPNs). In this section, we briefly present actual architectures of intrusion-tolerant systems.

The basic architecture used up to now is composed by n servers accessed by clients through a network. Gupta et al. (2003) presented three additional architectures that, however, do not ensure the correctness of the system during all runtime. The first of these architectures is called centralized routing/centralized management. The basic idea is to protect the system using a small set of trusted components. The communication between clients and servers passes though a firewall that does some basic filtering/ protection and a gateway that routes each request to a server. Each request is executed by a single server. If there are intrusions in some of the servers, a component in the servers called configuration management daemon has to detect it and inform a special server, the configuration manager, which restarts the faulty server. In practice, it is not possible to ensure that this detection will be made before a malicious server replies to some requests, and therefore, this architecture does not mask all intrusions, on the contrary to SMR or registers based on BQS. The other two architectures presented in the work by Gupta et al. (2003), multicast routing/centralized management and multicast routing/decentralized management, are variations of the same ideas. A similar architecture that deals with dynamic content in the servers was present in the work by Saidane et al. (2003).

An interesting architecture for SMR was presented by Yin et al., (2003). The architecture is based on the observation that SMR involves two operations—*agreement* on the order of the commands and *execution* of the commands—and that while the first requires $3f + 1$ servers in asynchronous systems (plus failure detectors, weak synchrony assumptions or randomization), the latter requires only $2f + 1$. Furthermore, in a real system, the execution part, that is, the service software (say, database management systems (DBMSs), Web servers), is the bulk of the system, while, in comparison, agreement is probably a lighter operation, and therefore, it can also be done in more cheap machines. Therefore, in this architecture, the clients send the requests to $3f + 1$ *agreement servers*, which order them and send them to $2f + 1$ *execution servers*, which execute them. The architecture can also include between the two kinds of servers an intrusion-tolerant privacy firewall (with $(f + 1)^2$ servers) that guarantees that malicious execution servers do not disclose confidential data.

MAFTIA's precursor architectural work (Verissimo et al., 2006) has inspired several intrusion-tolerant architectures and in fact follows in general terms the reference intrusion-tolerant architecture presented in Section 2.3. It has been used to design several intrusion-tolerant services such as the SMR service with only $2f + 1$ servers (Section 3.3.2) and the Worm-IT group communication system (Correia et al., 2007). Trusted support software, some of which taking advantage from a few trusted hardware modules, is wrapped in the runtime environment, extending OS capabilities and hiding heterogeneity amongst host OSs. A modular and layered intrusion-tolerant middleware offers the top interface of the MAFTIA architecture to applications, implementing the notion of trusted distributed components. Some native application services run on top of the middleware and exist as default in any MAFTIA system: authorization, intrusion detection and trusted third party services. Applications built to run on top of MAFTIA are supposed to use the abstractions provided by the middleware and the application services to operate securely across several hosts, and be accessed securely by users running on remote nodes, even in the presence of malicious faults.

Critical utility infrastructural resilience (CRUTIAL) is an architecture following the same reference model, proposed for the protection of Critical Information Infrastructures (CII) in general and power infrastructures in particular (Verissimo et al., 2008). An infrastructure is modelled as a WAN-of-LANs (Fig. 9). The facilities of the CII are modelled as LANs that are interconnected by a WAN, which is not trusted. The LANs and the WAN are logical entities. For instance, a LAN can be a set of LAN segments, a control network or even boil down to a single computer. The architecture is hierarchical, and therefore, a LAN can also be 'zoomed in' and observed as a WAN-of-LANs. LANs can range from trusted to untrusted. An important objective in CRUTIAL is to control/filter the information flow between LANs, and therefore, the communication to/from a LAN is protected by a component called a CRUTIAL Information Switch (CIS)

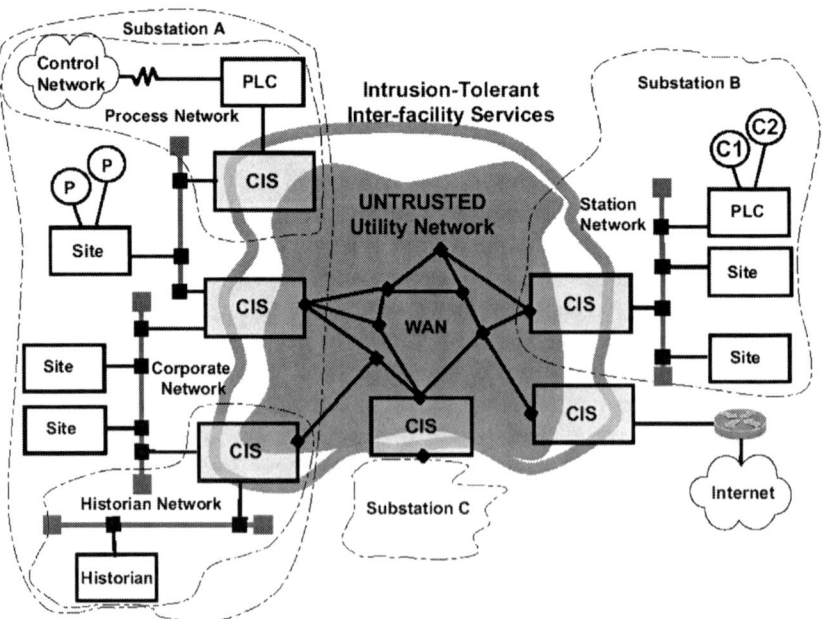

Fig. 9.   CRUTIAL WAN-of-LANs architecture for critical information infrastructures.

(Sousa et al., 2007b). The CIS has to be highly secure due to the criticality of CIIs, and therefore, it is made intrusion-tolerant using replication, building on the hybrid/wormhole architecture presented earlier.

An interesting architecture in the literature is designing protection and adaptation into a survivability architecture (DPASA), an architecture designed, implemented and evaluated in the DARPA OASIS Dem/Val program. The objective was to implement an intrusion-tolerant version of the Joint Battlespace Infosphere (JBI), a publish-subscribe-query application for military purposes (Pal et al., 2007; Stevens et al., 2004). A simplified presentation of the architecture is in Fig. 10. Each square represents typically more than one machine (e.g. two or three).

The core of the system is composed by four quadrants (quad 1 to 4). The quadrants replicate the same functions, and therefore, they are equivalent to the servers in the simple architecture we considered earlier for SMR and BQS. The machines from each of the quads run their own OS

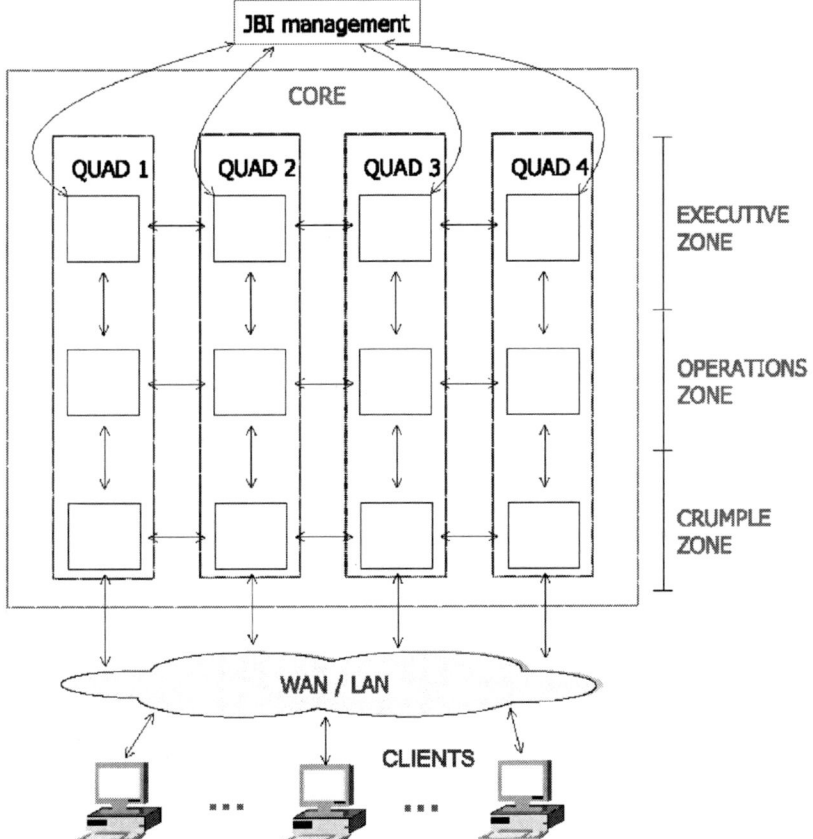

Fig. 10.   DPASA/JBI architecture (Pal et al., 2007).

(SELinux, Solaris, Windows XP and Windows 2000). The network adapters of all computers have an embedded firewall that do packet filtering and create VPNs with the machines they are supposed to communicate. The core is also divided into three zones. The crumple zone is the one that holds the first impact from an attack and has the middleware endpoints. The operations zone is where the publish-subscribe-query service itself is executed. The executive zone is used for system management and control, including intrusion detection and correlation. Replication among quads is based on SMR and BQS algorithms.

4 Resisting attacks

Intrusion-tolerant systems may have a long lifetime (e.g. banking systems and Web transaction servers), and the continued production of attacks may lead to the exhaustion of the necessary replicas. In consequence, a sometimes forgotten requirement of practical systems is that it should be guaranteed that no more than the maximum number of tolerated faults ever occurs. In other words, intrusion-tolerant systems should be *exhaustion-safe*.

One effective way of achieving this goal and keeping systems working perpetually is to enhance intrusion-tolerant systems with recovery mechanisms that re-establish the required level of redundancy by repairing failed components. These mechanisms may be either reactive or proactive, as will be seen.

However, an interesting observation is that the exhaustion-safety predicate is not just a mere artefact of an implementation, for example, of there being enough replicas to sustain the assumed level of threat, or of the recovery mechanisms being, say, fast enough. In fact, recent research has shown that the former property may never be attained unless the right distributed systems model is used.

In this section, we characterize the problem and discuss such a model. Then, we explain how proactive and reactive recovery can be implemented under such a (hybrid) model. We explain why reactive recovery should be used as a complementary approach to proactive recovery. Two concrete instantiations for two different intrusion-tolerant application scenarios serve to illustrate the concept and guide the reader: secret sharing and SMR. Finally, we discuss different ways of introducing diversity in intrusion-tolerant systems.

4.1 Exhaustion-safety

In Section 3, we explained the concepts of fault model and time model. The architect of an intrusion-tolerant system is responsible, on the one hand, for choosing the fault and time models under which the system will be designed and later operate and, on the other hand, for ensuring that those models correspond to what happens in the real world, that is, that the assumptions underlying the models have a good coverage in the environment where the system will execute (Powell, 1992). Part of those assumptions consists in an abstraction of the actual resources the protocol needs to work correctly. For example, when we assume that network messages are delivered within a known bound, we are in fact assuming that the network will have certain characteristics such as bandwidth and latency; when we assume that a service continues to operate despite faults, we are in fact assuming that there is enough redundancy, such as replicas, to compensate for the effect of those faults.

The violation of these resource assumptions may affect the safety or liveness of the protocols and hence of the system. In this section, we explain how system models may be augmented with the notion of the evolution of environmental resources along the timeline of system execution and its consequent impact on system assumptions. We are precisely concerned with the event of 'violation of any of the resource assumptions', which we call *resource exhaustion*, and on the conditions for its avoidance. We start by giving a name to failures caused by resource exhaustion.

Definition 1. *An exhaustion-failure is a failure that results from accidental or provoked resource exhaustion.*

Our goal is to prevent exhaustion-failures from happening. Therefore, we define exhaustion-safety in the following manner.

Definition 2. *Exhaustion-safety is the ability of a system to ensure that exhaustion-failures do not happen.*

Consequently, an exhaustion-safe system is defined in the following way.

Definition 3. *A system is said to be exhaustion-safe if it satisfies the exhaustion-safety property.*

We argue that an intrusion-tolerant system, to be resilient, has to satisfy the exhaustion-safety property. In other words, a resilient intrusion-tolerant system must be exhaustion-safe.

4.1.1 The model

To formally reason about how exhaustion-safety may be affected by different combinations of timing and fault assumptions, we conceived a model in which exhaustion-safety can be formally defined. This model takes into account the relevant system resources and their evolution with time. For this reason, we called it Resource Exhaustion model (REX, for short).

Our model considers systems (e.g. intrusion-tolerant systems) that have a certain mission. Thus, the execution of this type of systems is composed of various processing steps needed for fulfilling the system mission (e.g. protocol executions). We define three events regarding the system execution: *start*, *termination* and *exhaustion*. Only the start event is mandatory to happen: we cannot talk of a system execution if the system does not start executing. The termination and exhaustion events may or may not happen. More importantly, the causal relation between them is crucial to assess system exhaustion-safety.

We now formally define *REX*.

Definition 4. *Let A be a system. An A execution is defined by a triple*:

$$\mathcal{A} = <A_{t_{start}}, A_{t_{end}}, A_{t_{exhaust}}>,$$

where

- $A_{t_{start}} \in \mathcal{R}_0^+$ represents the real time start instant.
- $A_{t_{end}} \in [A_{t_{start}}, +\infty]$ represents the real time termination instant.
- $A_{t_{exhaust}} \in [A_{t_{start}}, +\infty]$ represents the real time instant when resource exhaustion occurs. If $A_{t_{exhaust}} \leq A_{t_{end}}$, system correctness may be corrupted through exhaustion-failures.

Therefore, under REX, a system is defined by a set of triples $\mathcal{A}$, one for each of its executions. Next, we formally define what is an exhaustion-safe system under REX.

Definition 5. *A system A is exhaustion-safe if and only if $A_{t_{end}} < A_{t_{exhaust}}, \forall \mathcal{A}$.*

Definition 5 states that a system is exhaustion-safe if and only if resource exhaustion does not occur during any execution. This does not mean that the system fails immediately after resource exhaustion. In fact, a system may even present a correct behaviour between the exhaustion and the termination events. Thus, a non exhaustion-safe system may execute correctly during its entirely lifetime. However, after resource exhaustion, there is *no guarantee* that an exhaustion-failure will not happen. Figure 11 illustrates the differences between an execution of an exhaustion-safe and a non-exhaustion-safe system. An exhaustion-safe system is always assuredly immune to exhaustion-failures. A non exhaustion-safe system has at least

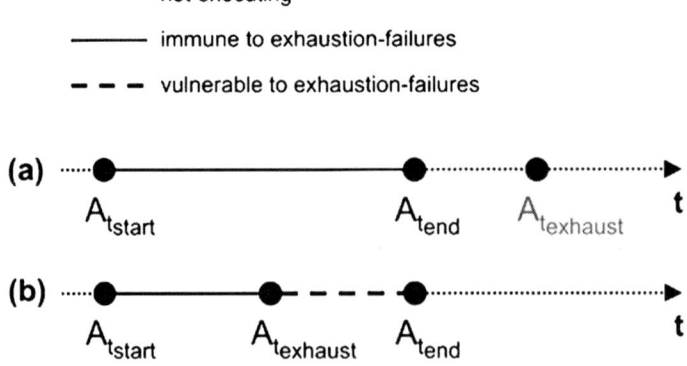

Fig. 11.   (a) Exhaustion-safe system; (b) Non-exhaustion-safe system.

one execution with a period or periods of vulnerability to exhaustion-failures where resources are exhausted and where correctness may be compromised.

4.1.2 Nodes as resources

As explained in Section 3, InTol is typically obtained by replicating a service in a set of nodes. Therefore, in an intrusion-tolerant system, nodes are important resources, so important that one typically makes the assumption that a maximum number f of nodes can fail during its execution, and the system is designed to resist up to f node failures. This type of systems can be analyzed under the REX model, nodes being the resource considered, and the exhaustion condition being $n_{fail} > f$, where n_{fail} represents the number of nodes that, during an execution, are failed at any time. In other words, this condition states that the system is exhausted when more than f nodes are failed simultaneously.

Notice that in a system in which failed nodes do not recover, this condition is equivalent to state that exhaustion-safety is guaranteed as long as no more than f node failures occur during the system execution. Thus, according to Definition 5, a system whose failed nodes do not recover is *node-exhaustion-safe* if and only if every execution terminates before the time needed for $f + 1$ node failures to be produced. To build a node-exhaustion-safe intrusion-tolerant system, one would like to forecast the maximum number of failures bound to occur during any execution, call it N_{fail}, so that the system is designed to handle $f = N_{fail}$ failures.

In the works by Sousa et al. (2005a, 2006b), a set of propositions are presented about the possibility/impossibility of exhaustion-safety for categories of algorithms and system fault and time models. The most important result is the *impossibility of building a node-exhaustion-safe intrusion-tolerant system under the asynchronous model and especially in the presence of a malicious adversary*. The intuition is the following: under the asynchronous model, it is not possible to upper-bound a system execution time, and thus it is not possible to guarantee that all executions will terminate before $f + 1$ node failures being produced and provoked.

4.1.3 Proactive recovery

To circumvent this impossibility result, one can add some mechanisms capable of increasing the time necessary to produce $f + 1$ node failures, such that it becomes unbounded and node exhaustion is avoided. One possible way of achieving this is by making use of proactive recovery (Ostrovsky and Yung, 1991), which can be seen as a form of dynamic redundancy (Siewiorek and Swarz, 1992). The aim of this mechanism is conceptually simple—components are periodically rejuvenated to remove the effects of malicious attacks/faults. If rejuvenations are performed sufficiently often, then an adversary is unable to corrupt enough resources to break the system. Proactive recovery has been suggested in several contexts.

For instance, it can be used to refresh cryptographic keys to prevent the disclosure of too many secrets (Cachin et al., 2002; Garay et al., 2000; Herzberg et al., 1995; Herzberg et al., 1997; Marsh and Schneider, 2004; Zhou et al., 2002; Zhou et al., 2005). It may also be utilized to restore the system code from a secure source to eliminate potential transformations carried out by an adversary (Castro and Liskov, 2002; Ostrovsky and Yung, 1991). Moreover, it may encompass the substitution of software components to remove vulnerabilities existent in previous versions (e.g. software bugs that could crash the system or errors exploitable by outside attackers). Vulnerability removal can also be done through address obfuscation (Bhatkar et al., 2003; Bhatkar et al., 2005; Forrest et al., 1997; PaX, 2001; Pucella and Schneider, 2006; Xu et al., 2003), which could be used to periodically randomize the memory location of code and data objects.

However, the effectiveness of proactive recovery is affected under asynchronous settings: in short, in an asynchronous system, a replica can delay its recovery (e.g. by making its local clock slower) for a sufficient amount of time to allow more than f replicas to be attacked. This may happen because (i) the replica's clock, although correct, is just very (asynchronously) slow and (ii) the replica has been compromised and actively sabotages recovery. A set of practical problems of existing systems that use asynchronous proactive recovery are presented in the work by Sousa et al. (2007a). Section 4.2 describes an effective way of using proactive recovery to overcome these problems.

4.2 Proactive resilience

The main difficulty with proactive recovery is not the concept but the system context in which it is used. The mechanism is useful to periodically rejuvenate components and remove the effects of malicious attacks/failures, as long as it has timeliness guarantees: it must act faster than the estimated speed at which faults develop. In fact, the rest of the system may even be completely asynchronous—only the proactive recovery mechanism needs synchronous execution. Now, this is impossible to realize under an asynchronous system model, so how do we solve this problem?

This type of requirement is correctly addressed under an architecturally hybrid distributed system model, or wormhole model, as presented in Section 2. One particular instantiation to proactive recovery is the Proactive Resilience Model (PRM) (Sousa et al., 2006b). Under PRM, the hybrid architecture of a system enhanced with proactive recovery has the following characteristics:

- It is composed of the payload (or normal) subsystem and the proactive recovery (wormhole) subsystem.
- The former is recovered by the latter.
- Each part is designed and built under a different time and fault model.

The payload subsystem executes the 'normal' applications. Thus, the payload synchrony and the fault model entirely depend on the applications executing in this part of the system. For instance, the payload may operate under an asynchronous and Byzantine environment.

The proactive recovery subsystem executes the proactive recovery protocols that rejuvenate the applications running in the payload part. With regard to the latter, the recovery subsystem wormhole has just the additional strength in synchrony and fault semantics that allow it to fulfil its job, implemented by specific proactive recovery protocols that are application dependent. In the following sections, we exemplify such a proactive recovery wormhole (PRW) and illustrate its use through a couple of application scenarios.

4.2.1 Proactive recovery wormhole

The architecture of a system with a PRW is suggested in Fig. 12: it has a local module in some hosts, called the *local PRW*. Depending on the particular instantiation, these modules may or may not be interconnected by a *control network*. This set up of local PRWs optionally interconnected by the control network is collectively called *the* PRW. This abstract secure and real-time distributed component executes the proactive recovery procedures on behalf of applications running in the payload part of the hosts concerned. This setting can be used in any usual distributed system architecture (e.g. on the Internet).

Conceptually, a local PRW should be considered to be a module inside a host and separated from the OS. In practice, this conceptual separation between the local PRW and the OS can be achieved in several ways: (1) the local PRW can be implemented in a separate, tamperproof hardware module (e.g. PC board), and therefore, the separation is physical and (2) the local PRW can be implemented on the native hardware, with a virtual separation and shielding implemented in software, between the former and the OS processes.

The local PRWs are assumed to be fail-silent (they fail by crashing). Every local PRW preserves, by construction, the following property:

P1. There exists a known upper bound T_{max}^{local} on the processing delays.

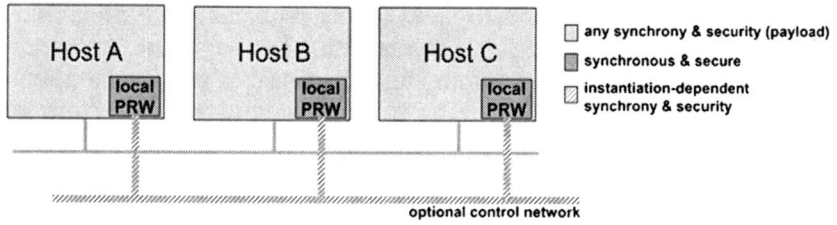

Fig. 12.   The architecture of a system with a PRW.

As mentioned, a **PRW** instantiation may or may not have a control network. For instance, if a proactive recovery procedure only requires local information, then the control network is expendable. Even when the control network is required, its characteristics will depend on the specific requirements of the proactive recovery procedure.

The PRW offers a single service, defined as follows:

Definition 6. *Given any function F, with a calculated worst case execution time of T_{Xmax}, an execution interval T_D, and a time interval (period) T_D, satisfying $T_{Xmax} < T_D < T_P$, then F is triggered by the PRW **periodic timely execution service** at real time instants t_i (the i-th triggering occurs at instant t_i), with $T_D < t_i - t_{i-1} \leq T_P$, and F terminates within T_D from $t_i, \forall i$.*

In short, the **PRW** has the ability to periodically execute well-defined functions in known bounded time. Moreover, the PRW allows the definition of a set of fail-safe measures to be triggered in certain situations. For instance, these fail-safe measures may shut down the system if the *periodic timely execution* service fails to satisfy its specification.

A triple $< D, <F, T_P, T_D>, S>$ defines a PRW instantiation, such that:

- *D* represents the set of *data* that is proactively recovered in all nodes.
- $<F, T_P, T_D>$ represents the *function F* that is periodically triggered with period T_P and timely executed within T_D of each triggering, through the *periodic timely execution* service, in all nodes. *F* makes operations over the data defined in *D*.
- *S* represents the set of (optional) *self-checking* mechanisms, which have the goal of guaranteeing a fail-safe behaviour of all the nodes.

4.2.2 *Building exhaustion-safe intrusion-tolerant systems*

To build an exhaustion-safe *f* intrusion-tolerant system, one has to guarantee that no more than *f* (accidental or malicious) faults occur during system execution. If the system maximum execution time is known, then one may choose a sufficiently high *f*—by endowing the system with sufficient nodes—so that exhaustion never occurs. However, if the system has an unbounded execution time, we have a problem—it is not possible to estimate how many nodes will be needed to avoid exhaustion. One possible approach to solve this problem is to use the **PRM**—enhance the system with a PRW that nodes are periodically and timely rejuvenated. Notice that this approach may even be applied in systems with a known bound on execution time when there is a need for minimizing the number of used nodes.

We propose a design methodology to build exhaustion-safe *f* intrusion-tolerant systems, under the **PRM**. The methodology has three steps.

1. Define the data *D* to rejuvenate, the rejuvenation procedure *F* and calculate *F*'s worst case execution time (T_{Xmax}). Then, define the execution interval T_D (greater than T_{Xmax}) and the periodicity T_P

(greater than T_D). Finally, define the actions S to be performed if F is not executed with the required periodicity and execution time.

2. Build a PRW instantiation $<D, <F, T_P, T_D>, S>$.
   - Notice that T_P and T_D may be increased if necessary. This will only impact the required fault tolerance degree, as explained in step 3.

3. Define the degree f_{safe} of fault tolerance, such that the minimum time necessary $(T_{exhaust_{min}})$ for $f_{safe} + 1$ faults to be produced satisfies the condition $T_{exhaust_{min}} > T_P + T_D$.

Given that at most f_{safe} faults are produced during any two consecutive rejuvenations, it is guaranteed that no more than f_{safe} faults will ever be produced at the same time during the entire execution of the system.

4.3 Reactive recovery

As described in the earlier sections, proactive recovery is crucial if one wants to build intrusion-tolerant system components that are simultaneously exhaustion-safe. Reactive recovery can be seen as a complementary approach to proactive recovery, in the sense that it may trigger recoveries sooner when malicious behaviour is detected. For instance, one can configure an intrusion detector that it triggers a recovery when an intrusion is detected. These early recoveries may have benefits not only in terms of performance but also in terms of system safety. Proactive recovery guarantees exhaustion-safety as long as recoveries are faster than fault production, that is, if recoveries take less time than a lower bound on the time needed to produce $f + 1$ node failures. This lower bound is calculated at deployment time and should be conservative to achieve a very high coverage. However, during system execution, malicious adversaries may prove to be more fierce than expected and may have the ability to compromise $f + 1$ nodes within the interval between two consecutive recoveries. Proactive recovery alone is not sufficient to maintain exhaustion-safety in this scenario (because design time assumptions were violated), but reactive recovery has the ability to defend the system against such fierce attacks if it is possible to detect the malicious behaviour of some nodes before $f + 1$ being compromised.

4.4 Diversity management

The different nodes of a distributed intrusion-tolerant system need to be different—or diverse—to have a different set of vulnerabilities. Otherwise, an attack that is effective against one node is effective against all of them, and a coordinated attack could compromise all the nodes at almost the same time. Many different diversity techniques have been proposed in the past targeting accidental and malicious faults. For instance, design diversity

(Randell, 1975) and N-version programming (Chen and Avizienis, 1978) consider only accidental faults. On the contrary, the work by Joseph and Avizienis (1988) is an early discussion on using diversity to improve security, and more recently Littlewood and Strigini (2004) presented an important study on diversity in the security domain. Obelheiro et al. (2006) identified several possible axes of diversity, that is, several components of a system that may admit different instances: application software, administrative domain, physical location, OS and hardware.

Recoveries should also introduce diversity. This can be done by randomizing certain parts of the system that vulnerabilities are somehow changed or removed, and the adversary cannot make use of knowledge learnt before the recovery. Such randomization can be achieved, for instance, through address obfuscation. By using this approach, it is possible to randomize the memory location of code and data objects in each recovery. Several techniques have been developed to achieve address obfuscation (Bhatkar et al., 2003; Bhatkar et al., 2005; Forrest et al., 1997; PaX, 2001; Xu et al., 2003).

Randomization can also be applied to OS functions (Chew and Song, 2002) and instruction sets (Barrantes et al., 2003; Kc et al., 2003). The former allows to mitigate buffer overflows through different types of randomization: system call mappings, global library entry points and stack placement, whereas the latter disrupts binary code injection attacks by randomizing their effect.

4.5 Application scenarios

This section describes two examples of application scenarios where proactive resilience can be applied. Section 4.5.1 describes the design of a distributed f intrusion-tolerant *secret sharing system*, which makes use of a specific instantiation of the PRW—the proactive secret sharing wormhole (PSSW)—targeting the secret sharing scenario. Section 4.5.2 describes a resilient f intrusion-tolerant *SMR architecture*, which guarantees that no more than f faults ever occur while ensuring availability. The architecture makes use of another instantiation of the PRW—the state machine PRW (SMW)—to periodically remove the effects of faults from the replicas.

4.5.1 Proactive secret-sharing wormhole

As explained in Section 3.1, secret sharing schemes protect the confidentiality and integrity of secrets by distributing them over different locations. In many applications, a secret s may be required to be held in a secret-sharing manner by n share-holders for a long time. If at most k share-holders are corrupted throughout the entire lifetime of the secret, any $(k + 1, n)$-threshold scheme can be used. In certain environments, however, gradual break-ins into a subset of locations over a long period of time may be feasible for the adversary. If more than k share-holders are corrupted, s may be stolen. An obvious defence is to periodically refresh s, but this is not possible when s corresponds to inherently long-lived information (e.g. cryptographic root and other long-term keys, legal documents).

Thus, what is actually required to protect the secrecy of the information is to be able to periodically renew the shares without changing the secret. Proactive secret sharing (PSS) was introduced by Herzberg et al. (1995) in this context. In PSS, the lifetime of a secret is divided into multiple periods and shares are renewed periodically. In this way, corrupted shares will not accumulate over the entire lifetime of the secret since they are checked and corrected at the end of the period during which they have occurred. A $(k+1,n)$ proactive threshold scheme guarantees that the secret is not disclosed and can be recovered as long as at most k share-holders are corrupted during each period, while every share-holder may be corrupted multiple times in several periods.

The PSSW (Sousa et al., 2006a) is an instantiation of the PRW presented in Section 4.2.1. The PSSW targets distributed systems that are based on secret sharing, and the goal of the PSSW is to periodically rejuvenate the secret share of each system node. A PSSW allows to timely trigger periodic share rejuvenations *with bounded execution time.*

The PSSW is defined by $<D_{PSSW}, F_{PSSW}, S_{PSSW}>$, such that:

- $D_{PSSW} =$ share, where share is the secret share to be periodically refreshed.
- $F_{PSSW} =$ <refresh, T_P, T_D>, where the refresh() function is based on the share renewal scheme of (Herzberg et al., 1995).
- $S_{PSSW} = \{shutdown$ *if share is not periodically and timely refreshed, as specified by* T_P *and* $T_D\}$.

Applying the methodology presented in Section 4.2.1, to build an exhaustion-safe intrusion-tolerant secret sharing system:

1. $D = \{share\}$, $F = refresh()$, $T_D = c_d T_{exec_{max}}$, $T_P = c_p T_{exec_{max}}$, and c_d and c_p are constants with $c_p > c_d > 1$, and $S = S_{PSSW}$.
2. Build the PSSW with the parameters defined in step 1.
3. k is chosen that $(c_p + c_d)T_{exec_{max}} <$ *'time needed to compromise* $k+1$ *shares'.*

Notice that in the secret sharing scenario, the degree of fault tolerance (f_{safe}) is represented by k.

4.5.2 The state machine proactive recovery wormhole

In this section, we describe a possible instantiation of a PRW for SMR (see Section 3.3)—the SMW (Sousa et al., 2005b). The goal of the SMW is to periodically rejuvenate replicas such that no more than f SM replicas are ever compromised.

Let the SMW be defined by the triple $<D_{SMW}, F_{SMW}, S_{SMW}>$, such that:

- $D_{SMW} = \{$OS code, SM code, SM state$\}$, where OS/SM code is the code of the OS/SM and SM state is the state of the SM. These are the three types of data to be periodically refreshed.
- $F_{SMW} = <$refresh, T_p, $T_d>$, where the concrete values of T_p and T_d depend on several factors that will be discussed later in the section, and the refresh function is presented as Algorithm 1. Each non-crashed local SMW P_i, $i \in \{1 \cdots n\}$ executes Algorithm 1 at some point of each time period defined by T_p. The precise execution start instant depends on the recovery strategy. More details can be found in the work by Sousa et al. (2005b).
- $S_{SMW} = \{$switch to a fail-safe state and alert an administrator, if the state is not periodically and timely rejuvenated, as specified by T_p and $T_d\}$.

A refresh function is presented as Algorithm 1. Regarding this algorithm, we assume that the state of both OS and local SM is stored in volatile random-access memory (RAM). Moreover, the state of the local SM is periodically saved to stable storage. Also, we assume that the local SM is automatically started after every boot of the OS and that the previous state is loaded from the stable storage.

In Algorithm 1, line 1 shut downs the OS and consequently stops the execution of the local SM. Notice that the algorithm continues to execute even after the OS being shutdown. This happens because the SMW does not depend on the OS, which can be achieved in practice by implementing each local SMW in a PC board. Line 2 checks if the OS code is corrupted. To accomplish this task, a digest of the OS code can be initially stored on some read-only memory, and then assessing if it is correct is only a matter of comparing the digest of the current code with the stored one. In line 3, the OS code can be restored from a read-only medium such as a read-only memory (ROM) or a write-protected hard disk (WPHD), where the write protection can be turned on and off by setting a jumper switch (e.g. Fujitsu MAS3184NP). In lines 5 and 6, the SM code can be checked and restored using similar methods to the ones we used to check and restore the OS code. Alternatively, both the OS and the SM code can be installed on a read-only medium, thus avoiding the execution of lines 2–5. Line 8 boots the OS from a clean code and thus brings it to a correct state. The local SM is also automatically started.

Algorithm 1. refresh() for each local SMW $P_i i \in \{1 \cdots n\}$
   1: *shut down OS*()
   2: **if** OS code is corrupted **then** { restore operating system code}
   3:   *restore OS code* ()
   4: **end if**

5: **if** SM code is corrupted **then** {restore state machine code}
6:    *restore SM code()*
7: **end if**
8: *boot OS()* {at this point, the OS and the SM can be safely booted because their code is correct}
9: wait until state recovery is finished

Given that the state of the local SM may have been compromised before the rejuvenation, it may be necessary to transfer a clean state from remote replicas. In line 9, we wait until a potential state recovery is finished. State recovery mechanisms are described in the work by Sousa et al. (2005b). This same work discusses how to deploy a recovery strategy that guarantees that (i) no more than f replicas are ever corrupted and (ii) the execution of the replicated SM is never interrupted, that is, the replicated SM is always available.

4.6   Proactive resilience in numbers

One may ask whether using a more complex (hybrid) model really leads to a more resilient system, in comparison with previous approaches to proactive recovery, namely, under the asynchronous model, as reviewed earlier.

An entire set of experiments was made in the work by Sousa et al. (2006c), using the Möbius (Deavours et al., 2002) modelling and simulation tool to assess the advantages of using proactive resilience.

In this section, we highlight the main results, focusing on the compared effects of *conspicuous* and *stealth* time attacks, on systems using proactive resilience versus asynchronous proactive recovery. Conspicuous time attacks are attacks that explicitly try to slow down the pace of recovery (e.g. a denial-of-service (DoS) attack aimed to increase cental processing unit (CPU) usage and thus increase recovery execution time). Stealth time attacks are attacks that implicitly try to slow down the pace of recovery (e.g. an attack aimed to slow down local clocks and thus increase recoveries interval). Notice that, in theory, stealth time attacks may not even be perceived by the essentially time-free logic of an asynchronous system, leaving it defenceless.

Figure 13 illustrates exhaustion time (measured by the percentage of time in which the system is exhausted) as a function of the combined strength of a conspicuous time adversary and a penetration adversary, for asynchronous recovery (Fig. 13(a)) and proactive resilience (Fig. 13(b)). The time adversary periodically slows down the recovery of a different replica, whereas the penetration adversary periodically (period = *mift*) corrupts a different replica.

With asynchronous recovery, the percentage of exhausted time depends on how small the conspicuous time attack period is (Fig. 13(a)), whereas proactive resilience renders the system immune to conspicuous timing

P. Verissimo et al.

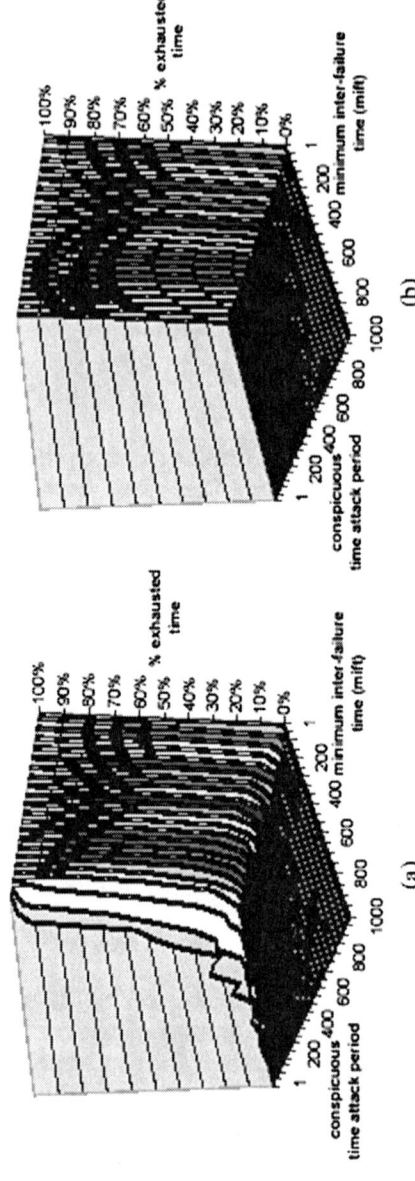

Fig. 13. Percentage exhausted time with conspicuous time attacks. (a) Asynch recovery and (b) Proactive resilience.

attacks (Fig. 13(b)), and the exhaustion time is only affected by the speed of the penetration adversary. Note that, in the latter case, recoveries are triggered and executed by a shielded recovery wormhole that is, by construction, immune to timing attacks launched on the payload system.

Figure 14 illustrates, again for asynchronous recovery (Fig. 14(a)) and proactive resilience (Fig. 14(b)), a second experiment: the impact of a stealth time adversary that periodically (the period is fixed) slows down the internal clock of a different node. The graphs depict increasing amounts of speed-down (time attack factor). As in the earlier scenario, the system exhausts much faster when the time attack factor increases (Fig. 14(a)), whereas proactive resilience also renders the system immune to this second type of attacks (Fig. 14(b)).

The stealth timing attack threat: Stealth timing attacks (on, e.g., clocks, timers or interrupt routines) have not deserved so far a great deal of attention. However, note that these attacks are very efficient, since with little power versus conspicuous direct attacks (e.g. of the DoS type) they achieve a more dire effect, as shown in Fig. 14(a): for attack factors of 200 and more, the system becomes almost permanently exhausted; for an attack factor of 1000, the system is exhausted 80% of the time.

Unlike the conspicuous time attack, in which the delay imposed is proportional to the power exerted, in the stealth attack the amount of delay inserted is virtually independent of the initial power used to gain control of the backdoors to the timing devices.

Some detection is possible in the case of conspicuous timing attacks: the delays injected by the conspicuous adversary may be detected programmatically if the system is partially synchronous and if the internal timebase is not compromised. Moreover, typically, these delays affect a large part or the entire system (e.g. DoS) and may get the attention of monitoring devices.

The stealth attacker can more easily evade detection than the conspicuous one. For example, attacks on the internal timebase hit the time references of the system and thus programmatic detections are not reliable, because they use these same time references. Moreover, the attack will not necessarily affect the entire system. For instance, the adversary may tamper with the kernel function that returns the current value of the local clock, and make it return different values to different applications, all the rest working perfectly. Or, alternatively, the attack may be applied to kernel scheduler/dispatcher code, selectively lengthening the execution of functions used by some processes.

Therefore, a stealth time adversary may be very difficult to defend against in classical asynchronous or even partially synchronous systems. The neutralization of this kind of attacks is one of the main achievements of proactive resilience.

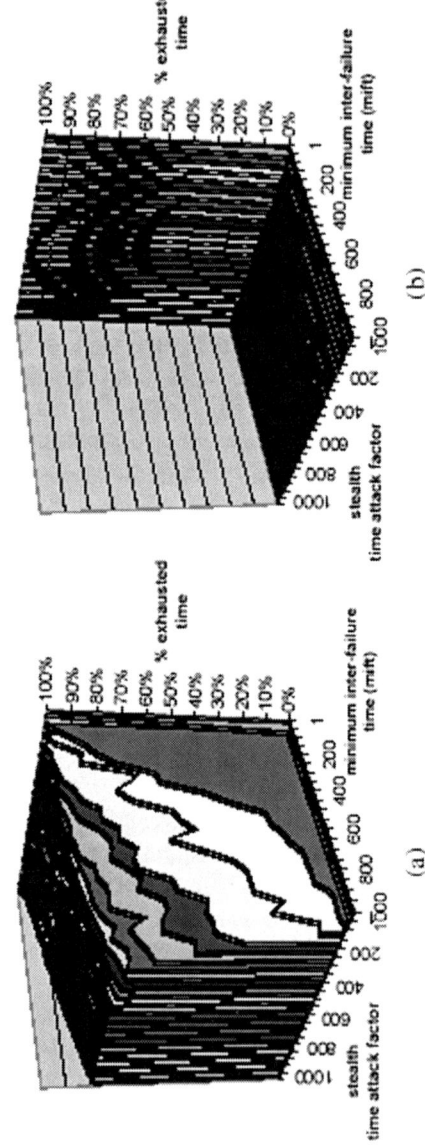

Fig. 14.   Percentage exhausted time with stealth time attacks. (a) Asynch recovery and (b) Proactive resilience.

5   Testing attacks and vulnerabilities

Intrusion-tolerant system designers need to have representative and realistic information about the threats and vulnerabilities their systems will experience once they are put in operation. Otherwise, the implementation of the systems will be flawed because it is based on wrong assumptions (or assumptions with small coverage), and as consequence, they will not perform as expected. It is therefore important to understand how intruders attack a system and how they proceed after a compromise, to develop dependable and secure systems that are able to cope with various threats.

5.1   *Trusting your assumptions*

Validating assumptions is often considered not a task of the algorithm or system designer, who considers his/her task finished when, for example, a successful proof is made that a protocol or algorithm is correct given a set of environmental assumptions. However, let us look at the big picture. Assume one wishes to design an algorithm offering a set of properties A, on a runtime support environment offering a set of properties H. The designer depends on the environment's properties H to implement the algorithm securing properties A. In other words, the designer *assumes* or *trusts* that the environment *has* properties H. What if it does not?

We have just discussed the trust side, now let us observe the trustworthiness side. H holds with a probability Pr_e, the environmental assumption coverage (Powell, 1992):

$$Pr_e = Pr(H|f), \ f \text{ any fault}$$

Pr_e measures the trustworthiness of the environment (to secure properties H). Given H, A has a certain probability of being fulfilled, the coverage Pr_o or operational assumption coverage. It measures the confidence on the algorithm securing properties A (given H as environment), or its trustworthiness:

$$Pr_o = Pr(A|H)$$

Pr_o can be 1 if the algorithm is deterministic and correct. This is the point of many designers. However, it is easy to understand that:

$$Pr_a = Pr_o \times Pr_e = Pr(A|H) \times Pr(H|f) = Pr(A|f), \ f \text{ any fault}$$

As such, in the end of the day, a very elegant and correct algorithm may very well do a poor job, if running over unrealistic or inadequate assumptions.

Particularly important for intrusion-tolerant systems are fault assumptions, and among other things, one would like to know what kind of faults will occur, at what rate they are produced, and if they happen simultaneously or are spread through time. Additionally, designers would like to have a good estimate on the level of vulnerability their systems have after development. This type of information is of utmost importance to keep security risk within certain limits. For instance, given a threat level, one would need to deploy enough replicas with a given degree of vulnerability, to maintain the risk below the desired magnitude.

5.2   Attacker profile

Since attackers conceal their activities and keep the operational tactics in close secrecy, it is usually very difficult to obtain information about their intents and behaviours. Additionally, attackers can come from anywhere in the world, have different backgrounds and motivations and, as humans, they constantly adapt to evolutions in the surrounding social and technological environment. For many years, their malicious activities were largely ignored by the security agencies, which meant that no serious effort was made to systematically collect and divulge data about them. Therefore, even with the important progresses made recently, it is quite challenging to build a profile that reasonably characterizes the attackers.

One of the early attempts to quantitatively describe intrusion actions used computer engineering students to act as hackers (Jonsson and Olovsson, 1997; Olovsson et al., 1993, 1995). The experiment was conducted over a 4-week period, during which attacks had to be carried out against the department workstations to fulfil the requirements of a course. Two interesting results came out from this research. The knowledge level of an attacker can be divided into three stages: low-skilled attackers, which are in the *learning phase*, are mostly unable to perform intrusions and they still need to educate themselves (e.g. take computer-related courses) to perform attacks in meaningful ways; attackers in the *standard attack phase* search the Internet and exchange information with other hackers, to obtain available expertise on vulnerabilities and exploits and in the *innovative attack phase*, attackers are able to invent new methods and try to exploit unknown vulnerabilities. During the standard attack phase, it was observed that *time to breach* was exponentially distributed, capturing the idea that activities in this phase are mainly done in a trial-and-error fashion. In another experiment, the attack threat in Internet Relay Chat (IRC) environments was assessed (Meyer and Cukier, 2006). Here, a combination of artificial (i.e. bots that simulated conversations) and regular users were employed during several weeks. From the recorded data, it was noticed that the attack level a user withstands is influenced by the gender of the name he or she uses—for example, users with female names are more likely to receive malicious private messages than users with ambiguous or male names. This implies that in IRC channels, most attacks are made by humans selecting targets, rather than automated scripts. More recently, a few other studies were made on the attackers' behaviour, which were based on information collected in honeypots.

5.2.1   *Honeypots*

Honeypots are computational systems that have been used in the security context with a few objectives (Honeynet Project, 2001; Pouget et al., 2003; Spitzner, 2002). They have been employed as decoys, to get the attention of the attackers away from the real systems and to waste their time and efforts. As a consequence, vital resources are kept unharmed until other protective measures can be put in place. Another major application of honeypots has been to study intrusions. In this case, honeypots can contain a number of vulnerabilities and can be successfully attacked, but they maintain detailed information about the various malicious actions. The analysis of this data allows, for example, a better understanding of the procedures that are followed after a machine compromise and the capture of hacker tools. Moreover, trends that emerge from the data can contribute to answer questions such as: Where do the attackers come from? What are their goals? Do they always behave in the same way? Are they alone or operating in groups?

The concept of honeypot appeared some time ago, in the context of monitoring and tracking activities done at the Lawrence Berkeley Laboratory (Stoll, 1988, 1990). During a reasonable period of time, intruder's actions were analyzed to determine which weakness were being exploited, what were the targets of the attacks and eventually to locate the person responsible for the break-in. Cheswick and Bellovin also describe how to implement and deploy a dedicated honeypot and give a discussion about ethical concerns associated with their use (Bellovin, 1992; Cheswick, 1992). At the end of the 1990s and beginning of the new millennium, there was an explosion on the number of projects developing systems (hardware architectures and software) whose only purpose was to act as honeypots (refer the work by Honeypots.net, 2007 for a list of available solutions). These systems can be implemented on a single machine, or they can be built as a network of several components, which are sometimes called honeynets (for a comparison, refer the work by Pouget and Dacier, 2003). As an example, a sophisticated honeypot can contain various target machines, a firewall to control network traffic, an intrusion detection system and a logging computer.

A honeypot facilitates the execution of two main tasks: it captures and stores as much data as possible and it prevents honeypot resources from being utilized to attack other external systems. The main challenge is to perform these actions without being detected by the intruders, and at the same time to give them as much flexibility as possible to do whatever they want within the honeypot. Normally, if less restrictions are placed on the attacker behaviour, more interesting information can be captured. However, it becomes much more difficult to contain the attacker.

Related to this idea, honeypots have been classified based on the level of the interaction that they allow (Spitzner, 2002). *Low-interaction* honeypots only emulate a few services, but they do not have any real OS where an intruder can operate on. Improved and more complete implementations of fake services are offered by the *mid-interaction* honeypots. A real OS, where attackers can upload and install tools, is only provided by the *high-interaction* honeypots.

Data collection in honeypots has lead to the unveiling of many intruder practices. These results have been reported in publications describing, for example, various kinds of attack methods, honeypot forensics techniques and trends (refer Honeynet Project, 2007 for papers on this topic). Some of the results related to the creation of an attacker profile are summarized next. Most of the studies demonstrate that any machine connected to the Internet can suffer several port scans per hour, on a limited set of ports, which correspond to some of the most used services (Panjwani et al., 2005; Pouget et al., 2004a,b). In a majority of cases, these probes seem to select targets in a random way, without being influenced by the OS of the machine. Most scan sources do not return to the same target for more than 1 day (this could be caused by the use of temporary addresses). Port scans *per se*, however, do not provide a good indication that an actual attack will follow, at least from the same source (Panjwani et al., 2005). A better indicator is provided by a port scan plus a vulnerability scan. This could in part be explained by the observation that attackers use in their activities two sets of machines, one to perform the scans with automatic scripts and another to do the actual manual break in (Alata et al., 2006; Pouget et al., 2004b). An initial statistical modelling of the attack process showed that the time intervals between scans/attacks do not follow a Poisson distribution (which is the traditional assumption for failure production in hardware reliability analysis) (Kaâniche et al., 2006). A state diagram describing the attacker behaviour after a machine compromise has also been proposed (Ramsbrock et al., 2007).

5.3 Vulnerability assessment

This section describes several techniques that contribute to estimate how vulnerable a system is. Some of these techniques can be applied in more than one stage of system development, but others are more specialized. They also have distinct requirements in terms of access to the system—for instance, some need to look into the source code to find flaws, whereas others only have to be able to provide malicious data to the system under test.

5.3.1 Manual, static and dynamic code analysis

The main objective of code analysis is to locate deficiencies in programs and reduce the risks for security. It is usually much less expensive to correct these problems if they are found earlier in the software development life cycle, that is, during the code production phases or while testing.

Manual analysis is one of the oldest methods for the detection of programming flaws. To carry out the analysis, the auditor needs to have a good knowledge about the specifications and architecture of the software and about the various coding errors that result in vulnerabilities. To increase efficiency and facilitate the life of the auditor, the program should be prepared for the review by including for instance relevant comments and a description of the functionality of each procedure. Manual code analysis however is a tiring activity because procedures have to be scrutinized carefully, and therefore, it can take a long time.

Static vulnerability analyzers automate some of the tasks of the auditor, as they look for potential flaws in the source code of the applications (Chess and McGraw, 2004). Analyzers process the code line by line and then produce a report telling where vulnerabilities might exist. Next, the programmer only needs to examine the parts of the code for which there were warnings. Depending on the method utilized in the analysis, more or less flaws are found. One of the most straightforward methods only takes into account the lexical rules of the programming language and looks for dangerous patterns that are usually associated with vulnerabilities (Bishop and Dilger, 1996; Haugh and Bishop, 2003; Viega et al., 2000). The main problem with this solution is that it produces a large number of false warnings, wasting effort of the person trying to correct the (non-existing) error. Therefore, throughout the years, several other techniques have been proposed and implemented, which utilize abstract syntax trees, model checking, theorem provers and integer range analysis (Beyer et al., 2005; Chess, 2002; Foster et al., 2002; Orlovich and Rugina, 2006; Wagner et al., 2000). The addition of annotations to the code has also been proposed as a way to improve the accuracy of the tools (Larochelle and Evans, 2001). Currently, a few commercial static analysis products are available and are being applied to all sorts of vulnerabilities, including buffer overflows, format strings and integer overloads.

Dynamic analyzers examine the program behaviour while it is running. Some of these tools require an understanding of the application's functionalities and the development of specific tests. Others are more generic, and they simply monitor the application's execution looking for erroneous actions. For example, some tools change the runtime environment of programs with the objective of thwarting the exploitation of vulnerabilities. The idea here is that removing all bugs from a program is infeasible, which means that it is preferable to contain the damages caused by their exploitation. StackGuard (Cowan et al., 1998) is a simple compiler extension that provides means to detect invalid changes in the stack return address and to prevent those changes from occurring. Stack Shield (Vendicator, 2001) also protects frame and function pointers from being changed. Other tools, such as PointGuard (Cowan et al.,

2003), add special code to the original program to prevent attackers from producing predictable pointer values. These solutions, however, are intrusive because besides requiring access to the source code, they also modify it.

5.3.2 Vulnerability scanners

Vulnerability scanners are tools whose purpose is the discovery of security weaknesses in computer systems already in production (or about to be put in operation). Consequently, they have to be employed with a certain care because people already working on the system should not be disturbed by the tests. Vulnerabilities can be of many types and flavours, and they can appear in any system component, from hardware to software. Some of the flaws can only be exploited within the system (e.g. a problem in the OS change directory command), requiring local access by the scanner to be able to find them. Others, however, can be exploited remotely by sending malicious packets to the system. Since vulnerabilities of this second class are much simpler to attack, many times they are critical to the overall security and are the main concern of the intrusion-tolerant systems designers.

Vulnerability scanners that look for remote exposure points are available with different levels of automation, accuracy of the checks and reporting capabilities. In their most basic form, which are called *port scanners*, they simply provide information about what ports are open and the OS version executing on the remote machine (an example of a well-known port scanner is Nmap (Fyodor, 2007)). Although this information is helpful, since it provides an indication of what services are running remotely, there are still too many details missing to determine if a vulnerability really exists. For example, just consider that an FTP service can be implemented by various programs, which go through many releases. Each of these releases has particular problems that one would like to identify to select the best solution to protect the system.

The analysis performed by a vulnerability scanner usually progresses in three steps. First, the scanner interacts with the target, by transmitting several well-crafted malicious messages, to obtain information about its execution environment. Besides discovering the type of OS, it is necessary to figure out what are the specific versions of the programs implementing each service that is running. Second, this information is correlated with the data stored in an internal database, to determine if vulnerabilities have previously been found for these services. A scanner to be effective needs to have a detailed and complete database of the most relevant (ideally all) vulnerabilities, which has to be periodically updated as new attacks appear. In the third step, the scanner needs to report its findings. The report can be simply a list of vulnerabilities, or it can give a more friendly diagnose, where vulnerabilities are ordered by their criticality level, and solutions are suggested for each problem.

Throughout the years, several scanners have been built and made available to users. One of the first examples was the Internet Security Scanner (ISS), created by Christopher Klaus in 1992 and distributed through the Usenet newsgroups (Klaus, 1993). ISS could be used to remotely to probe UNIX systems for a group of vulnerabilities. Another tool from approximately the same time was COPS (Farmer and Spafford, 1990), whose objective was to scan and locate vulnerabilities in the local machine. A few years later, another tool called SATAN (Security Administrator Tool for Analyzing Networks) was deployed (Farmer and Venema, 1995). SATAN could perform more checks and had a Web-based interface to display results. Currently, there are many other examples of these tools, some of which have been described in the literature and others are commercial products. Most of them are more sophisticated than the earlier examples, for instance, in the way they report the results. Some examples are Nessus (Tenable Network Security, 2007), SAINT (Saint Corp, 2007), QualysGuard (Qualys Inc, 2007), McAfee Foundstone Enterprise (McAfee, 2007) and PatchLink Scanner (Lumension Security, 2007).

5.3.3 *Discovering previously unknown vulnerabilities*

Fuzzers are testing tools that look for previously unknown vulnerabilities in software applications. They automatically generate invalid data and give it to a target component for processing (Oehlert, 2005). Then, the behaviour of the component is observed while the data is consumed, to determine how well that specific input is dealt with. If a failure is seen, this indicates the presence of some flaw that can potentially be exploited by some adversary. Fuzz was one of the first projects to explore these ideas, and it was designed to test UNIX commands (and was later applied to other OSs) (Miller et al., 1990). It generates large sequences of random characters that are used as command-line arguments of programs. Many programs failed to process the illegal arguments and crashed. In the recent years, fuzzers have evolved into more intelligent and less random tools, capable of testing different kinds of software components (refer, e.g., Biege, 2005; Greene, 2005; Mendonça and Neves, 2008; PROTOS—Security Testing of Protocol Implementations, 1999; Sutton, 2006).

Robustness testing probes various APIs of an OS to see how effective the latter is at handling erroneous input conditions. In a majority of cases, the testing engines of these tools have an almost complete knowledge of the many functions that compose the target interface, including the data types of the parameters and the expected return values. Consequently, they can produce relatively smart tests and can detect small deviations from the acceptable execution of a function. Most robustness tools have targeted the internal interfaces such as the kernel API to user-level processes. For instance, the Ballista tool was used to assess several OSs that implement the POSIX standard (Koopman and DeVale, 2000). Similarly, Shelton et al.

(2000) have made a comparative study of six variants of Windows. Other example studies with these tools include real-time microkernels (Arlat et al., 2002) and middleware support systems such as CORBA (Marsden et al., 2002; Pan et al., 2001). More recently, this technique has been applied at the OS device driver interface (Albinet et al., 2004; Durães and Madeira, 2002; Mendonça and Neves, 2007). Since robustness testing has mainly been used with the internal interfaces, which cannot be directly exploited by an external adversary, the discovered problems many times do not put security at risk. Nevertheless, their use in the past has shown that they can be very useful to find out problems in the implementation of the interfaces.

Attack injection is a method for vulnerability discovery that automatically generates a large number of malicious interactions (or attacks), which are then transmitted to the target system while monitoring its behaviour (Neves et al., 2006). The first tool to implement these ideas was attack injection on software components (AJECT), and it was specialized to look for flaws in network servers. The tool was composed of two main modules, an injector running in a remote machine and a monitor located in the server's system. A specification of the communication protocol employed by the server (e.g. internet message access protocol (IMAP) and domain name system (DNS)) was used to generate a broad spectrum of valid interactions, which were then maliciously modified accordingly to some predefined algorithms. The resulting attacks were then sent to the target by the injector. The monitor module closely watched the injection process and traced the server's execution and some basic resource usage (e.g. number of allocated memory pages and the time spent by the CPU). A vulnerability would be detected upon the observation of a *unusual* server behaviour such as the reception of segmentation violation (SIGSEGV) signal.

6   Conclusion

This chapter presented a comprehensive overview of the design and validation of intrusion-tolerant—or resilient—middleware and systems. It started by presenting the main design principles. Then, it presented the main InTol paradigms and how they can be used to ensure the integrity and confidentiality of a service. The next part of the chapter dealt with the problem of ensuring resilience, that is, of ensuring perpetual InTol, even if attackers periodically compromise components/hosts. The chapter finished with the problem of understanding how attacks are made and how vulnerabilities can be found.

InTol is still mostly an area of research, but we believe that soon it will serve to design commercial systems and be one of the foundations for a more secure information society.

Acknowledgments

We warmly thank our partners in several related projects over the past few years for many discussions on the topics of this chapter. We also thank our colleagues and students at the Navigators group for their collaboration and feedback on this work. This work was mainly supported by the EC, through project IST-FP6-STREP 027513 (CRUTIAL) and NoE IST-4-026764-NOE (ReSIST), by the FCT through the Large-Scale Informatic Systems Laboratory (LaSIGE) and the CMU-Portugal partnership.

Glossary

Attack: A malicious intentional fault attempted at a computing or communication system, with the intent of exploiting one or more vulnerabilities in the system.

Availability: The readiness of a system or component for providing its service.

BQS: See *Byzantine quorum system*.

Byzantine fault: A malicious fault, that is, an attack or an intrusion.

Byzantine quorum system: A set of quorums in which some of the processes/servers can be faulty/Byzantine.

Confidentiality: The absence of unauthorized disclosure of information.

Dependability: The measure in which reliance can justifiably be placed on the service delivered by a system.

Error: A fault when activated leads to an error, an erroneous state of the system which can lead to failure.

Failure: A deviation from the service the system is supposed to provide.

Failure assumptions: See *fault model*.

Fault: The hypothesized cause of a failure (see *vulnerability, attack* and *intrusion*).

Fault model: Set of failure assumptions about the system.

Integrity: The absence of unauthorized state modifications of a system or component.

InTol: See *intrusion tolerance*.

Intrusion: An intentionally malicious operational fault resulting from a successful attack on a vulnerability.

Intrusion Tolerance: The tolerance paradigm in security assumes that systems remain to a certain extent vulnerable; assumes that attacks on components or sub-systems can happen and some will be successful and ensures that the overall system nevertheless remains secure and operational, with a quantifiable probability.

Proactive recovery wormhole: A wormhole used to support proactive recovery, that is, the periodical rejuvenation of the replicas of a system.

PRW: See *proactive recovery wormhole*.

Quorum: A set of processes or servers.

SMR: See *state machine replication*.

State machine replication: A generic solution for the implementation of fault- and intrusion-tolerant deterministic services.

Trust: The accepted dependence of a component or system on a set of properties of another component or system.

Trustworthiness: See *dependability*.

Vulnerability: A fault in a computing or communication system that can be exploited with malicious intention.

Wormhole: A modelling approach under which a system is a hybrid of a 'normal' part that can exhibit weak properties (e.g. asynchrony and Byzantine failure), and a 'privileged' part capable of providing a small set of services with stronger properties (e.g. timeliness and security) that are otherwise not available in the rest of the system. The latter part is called a 'wormhole'.

References

Adelsbach, A., D. Alessandri, C. Cachin, S. Creese, Y. Deswarte, K. Kursawe, J.C. Laprie, et al. (2002). Conceptual Model and Architecture of MAFTIA. Project MAFTIA deliverable D21, January. Technical Report DI/FCUL TR-03-1, Department of Informatics, University of Lisbon, Portugal.

Alata, E., V. Nicomette, M. Kaâniche, M. Dacier, M. Herrb (2006). Lessons learned from the deployment of a high-interaction honeypot, in: *Proceedings of the 6th European Dependable Computing Conference*, October.

Albinet, A., J. Arlat, J.-C. Fabre (2004). Characterization of the impact of faulty drivers on the robustness of the Linux kernel, in: *Proceedings of the International Conference on Dependable Systems and Networks*, June, pp. 867–876.

Amir, Y., B. Coan, J. Kirsch, J. Lane (2007). Customizable fault tolerance for wide-area replication, in: *Proceedings of the 26th IEEE Symposium on Reliable Distributed Systems*, October, pp. 66–80.

Amir, Y., C. Danilov, D. Dolev, J. Kirsch, J. Lane, C. Nita-Rotaru, J. Olsen, D. Zage (2006). Scaling Byzantine fault-tolerant replication to wide area networks, in: *Proceedings of the 2006 International Conference on Dependable Systems and Networks*, June, pp. 105–114.

Arlat, J., J.-C. Fabre, M. Rodríguez, F. Salles (2002). Dependability of COTS microkernel-based systems. *IEEE Transactions on Computers* 51(2), 138–163.

Avizienis, A., J.-C. Laprie, B. Randell, C. Landwehr (2004). Basic concepts and taxonomy of dependable and secure computing. *IEEE Transactions on Dependable and Secure Computing* 1(1), 11–33.

Barrantes, E.G., D.H. Ackley, T.S. Palmer, D. Stefanovic, D.D. Zovi (2003). Randomized instruction set emulation to disrupt binary code injection attacks, in: *Proceedings of the 10th ACM Conference on Computer and Communications Security*, pp. 281–289.

Bellovin, S. (1992). There be dragons, in: *Proceedings of the Third Usenix UNIX Security Symposium*, September, pp. 1–16.

Bessani, A.N., M. Correia, J.S. Fraga, L.C. Lung (2007). Decoupled quorum-based Byzantine-resilient coordination in open distributed systems, in: *Proceedings of the 6th IEEE International Symposium on Network Computing and Applications*, July, pp. 231–238.

Beyer, D., T. Henzinger, R. Jhala, R. Majumdar (2005). Checking memory safety with BLAST, in: *Proceedings of the 8th International Conference on Fundamental Approaches to Software Engineering*, LNCS, Vol. 3442, Springer-Verlag, Germany, pp. 2–18.

Bhatkar, S., D.C. DuVarney, R. Sekar (2003). Address obfuscation: an efficient approach to combat a broad range of memory error exploits, in: *Proceedings of the 12th USENIX Security Symposium*, August, pp. 105–120.

Bhatkar, S., R. Sekar, D.C. DuVarney (2005). Efficient techniques for comprehensive protection from memory error exploits, in: *Proceedings of the 14th USENIX Security Symposium*, August, pp. 271–286.

Biege, T. (2005). Radius fuzzer, September. Available at http://www.suse.de/~thomas/

Bishop, M., M. Dilger (1996). Checking for race conditions in file accesses. *Computing Systems* 9(2), 131–152.

Blakley, G.R. (1979). Safeguarding cryptographic keys, in: *Proceedings of the National Computer Conference*, American Federation of Information, Processing Societies (AFIPS), New York, USA, Vol. 48, pp. 313–317.

Bracha, G. (1984). An asynchronous $\lfloor (n-1)/3 \rfloor$-resilient consensus protocol, in: *Proceedings of the 3rd ACM Symposium on Principles of Distributed Computing*, August, pp. 154–162.

Cachin, C., S. Tessaro (2005). Asynchronous verifiable information dispersal, in: *Proceedings of the 24th IEEE Symposium on Reliable Distributed Systems*, October.

Cachin, C., S. Tessaro (2006). Optimal resilience for erasure-coded Byzantine distributed storage, in: *Proceedings of the International Conference on Dependable Systems and Networks*, June, pp. 115–124.

Cachin, C., K. Kursawe, A. Lysyanskaya, R. Strobl (2002). Asynchronous verifiable secret sharing and proactive cryptosystems, in: *CCS '02: Proceedings of the 9th ACM Conference on Computer and Communications Security*, pp. 88–97.

Castro, M., B. Liskov (2002). Practical Byzantine fault tolerance and proactive recovery. *ACM Transactions on Computer Systems* 20(4), 398–461.

Castro, M., R. Rodrigues, B. Liskov (2003). BASE: using abstraction to improve fault tolerance. *ACM Transactions Computer Systems* 21(3), 236–269.

Chandra, T., S. Toueg (1996). Unreliable failure detectors for reliable distributed systems. *Journal of the ACM* 43(2), 225–267.

Chen, L., A. Avizienis (1978). N-version programming: a fault-tolerance approach to reliability of software operation, in: *Fault-Tolerant Computing 1995, Highlights from Twenty-Five Years*, FTCS, Pasadena, California, USA, pp. 113–119.

Chess, B. (2002). Improving computer security using extended static checking, in: *Proceedings of the Symposium on Security and Privacy*, May, pp. 160–173.

Chess, B., G. McGraw (2004). Static analysis for security. *IEEE Security and Privacy* (November/December), 32–35.

Cheswick, B. (1992). An evening with Berferd in which a cracker is lured, endured, and studied, in: *Proceedings of the Winter USENIX Conference*, January, pp. 163–174.

Chew, M., D. Song (2002). Mitigating buffer overflows by operating system randomization, December. Technical Report CMU-CS-02-197, Department of Computer Science, Carnegie Mellon University.

Correia, M., L.C. Lung, N.F. Neves, P. Verissimo (2002). Efficient Byzantine-resilient reliable multicast on a hybrid failure model, in: *Proceedings of the 21st IEEE Symposium on Reliable Distributed Systems*, October, pp. 2–11.

Correia, M., N.F. Neves, L.C. Lung, P. Verissimo (2005). Low complexity Byzantine-resilient consensus. *Distributed Computing* 17(3), 237–249.

Correia, M., N.F. Neves, L.C. Lung, P. Verissimo (2007). Worm-IT—a wormhole-based intrusion-tolerant group communication system. *Journal of Systems and Software* 80(2), 178–197.

Correia, M., N.F. Neves, P. Verissimo (2004). How to tolerate half less one Byzantine nodes in practical distributed systems, in: *Proceedings of the 23rd IEEE Symposium on Reliable Distributed Systems*. IEEE Computer Society, pp. 174–183.

Correia, M., N.F. Neves, P. Verissimo (2006). From consensus to atomic broadcast: time-free Byzantine-resistant protocols without signatures. *Computer Journal* 41(1), 82–96.

Cowan, C., S. Beattie, J. Johansen, P. Wagle (2003). Pointguard: protecting pointers from buffer overflow vulnerabilities, in: *Proceedings of the 12th USENIX Security Symposium*, August.

Cowan, C., C. Pu, D. Maier, J. Walpole, P. Bakke, S. Beattie, A. Grier, P. Wagle, Q. Zhang, H. Hinton (1998). StackGuard: automatic adaptive detection and prevention of buffer-overflow attacks, in: *Proceedings of the 7th USENIX Security Conference*, January, pp. 63–78.

Cowling, J., D. Myers, B. Liskov, R. Rodrigues, L. Shrira (2006). HQ-replication: a hybrid quorum protocol for Byzantine fault tolerance, in: *Proceedings of 7th Symposium on Operating Systems Design and Implementations*, November, pp. 177–190.

Dantas, W.S., A.N. Bessani, J. Fraga, M. Correia (2007). Evaluating Byzantine quorum systems, in: *Proceedings of the 26th IEEE Symposium on Reliable Distributed Systems*, October, pp. 253–262.

Deavours, D.D., G. Clark, T. Courtney, D. Daly, S. Derisavi, J.M. Doyle, W.H. Sanders, P.G. Webster (2002). The Möbius framework and its implementation. *IEEE Transactions on Software Engineering* 28(10), 956–969.

Deswarte, Y., L. Blain, J.C. Fabre (1991). Intrusion tolerance in distributed computing systems, in: *Proceedings of the 1991 IEEE Symposium on Research in Security and Privacy*, May, pp. 110–121.

Durães, J., H. Madeira (2002). Characterization of operating systems behavior in the presence of faulty drivers through software fault emulation, in: *Proceedings of the Pacific Rim International Symposium on Dependable Computing*, December, pp. 201–209.

Dwork, C., N. Lynch, L. Stockmeyer (1988). Consensus in the presence of partial synchrony. *Journal of the ACM* 35(2), 288–323.

Farmer, D., E.H. Spafford (1990). The COPS security checker system, in: *Proceedings of the Summer USENIX Conference*, June, pp. 165–170.

Farmer, D., W. Venema (1995). SATAN—security administrator tool for analyzing networks. Available at http://www.porcupine.org/satan/

Fischer, M.J., N.A. Lynch, M.S. Paterson (1985). Impossibility of distributed consensus with one faulty process. *Journal of the ACM* 32(2), 374–382.

Forrest, S., A. Somayaji, D.H. Ackley (1997). Building diverse computer systems, in: *Proceedings of the 6th Workshop on Hot Topics in Operating Systems*, May, pp. 67–72.

Foster, J., T. Terauchi, A. Aiken (2002). Flow-sensitive type qualifiers, in: *Proceedings of the Conference on Programming Language Design and Implementation*, June, pp. 1–12.

Fraga, J.S., D. Powell (1985). A fault- and intrusion-tolerant file system, in: *Proceedings of the 3rd International Conference on Computer Security*, August, pp. 203–218.

Frankel, Y., M. Yung (1998). Risk management using threshold RSA cryptosystems. USENIX; login, May.

Frier, A., P. Karlton, P. Kocher (1996). The SSL 3.0 protocol, November. Netscape Communications Corp.

Fyodor (2007). Nmap Security Scanner. Available at http://insecure.org/nmap/

Garay, J.A., R. Gennaro, C. Jutla, T. Rabin (2000). Secure distributed storage and retrieval. *Theoretical Computer Science* 243(1–2), 363–389.

Gemmell, P.S. (1997). An introduction to threshold cryptography. *Cryptobytes* 2(3), 7–12.

Gifford, D.K. (1979). Weighted voting for replicated data, in: *Proceedings of the 17th ACM Symposium on Operating Systems Principles*, pp. 150–162.

Goodson, G., J. Wylie, G. Ganger, M. Reiter (2004). Efficient Byzantine-tolerant erasure-coded storage, in: *Proceedings of the IEEE International Conference on Dependable Systems and Networks*, June.

Greene, A. (2005). SPIKEfile, July. Available at http://labs.idefense.com/labs-software.php?show = 14

Guerraoui, R., M. Vukolic (2007). Refined quorum systems, in: *Proceedings of the 1st Workshop on Recent Advances in Intrusion-Tolerant Systems*, pp. 8–12.

Gupta, V., V. Lam, H. Ramasamy, W. Sanders, S. Singh (2003). Dependability and performance evaluation of intrusion-tolerant server architectures, in: *Proceedings of the First Latin-American Symposium on Dependable Computing*, pp. 81–101.

Haugh, E., M. Bishop (2003). Testing C programs for buffer overflow vulnerabilities, in: *Proceedings of the Symposium on Networked and Distributed System Security*, February.

Herzberg, A., M. Jakobsson, S. Jarecki, H. Krawczyk, M. Yung (1997). Proactive public key and signature systems, in: *Proceedings of the 4th ACM Conference on Computer and Communications Security*. ACM Press, pp. 100–110.

Herzberg, A., S. Jarecki, H. Krawczyk, M. Yung (1995). Proactive secret sharing or: how to cope with perpetual leakage, in: *Proceedings of the 15th Annual International Cryptology Conference on Advances in Cryptology*. Springer-Verlag, pp. 339–352.

Honeynet Project. (2001). *Know Your Enemy: Revealing the Security Tools, Tactics, and Motives of the Blackhat Community*, August. Addison-Wesley Professional.

Honeynet Project. (2007). White papers. Available at http://www.honeynet.org/papers

Honeypots.net. (2007). Intrusion detection, honeypots and incident handling resources. Available at http://www.honeypots.net/

Jonsson, E., T. Olovsson (1997). A quantitative model of the security intrusion process based on attacker behavior. *IEEE Transactions on Software Engineering* 23(4), 235–245.

Joseph, M.K., A. Avizienis (1988). A fault tolerance approach to computer viruses, in: *Proceedings of the IEEE Symposium on Security and Privacy*. IEEE Computer Society, pp. 52–58.

Kaâniche, M., E. Alata, V. Nicomette, Y. Deswarte, M. Dacier (2006). Empirical analysis and statistical modeling of attack processes based on honeypots, in: *Proceedings of the Workshop on Empirical Evaluation of Dependability and Security*, June.

Kc, G.S., A.D. Keromytis, V. Prevelakis (2003). Countering code-injection attacks with instruction-set randomization, in: *CCS '03: Proceedings of the 10th ACM Conference on Computer and Communications Security*, pp. 272–280.

Kent, S., R. Atkinson (1998). Security architecture for the internet protocol. in: *IETF Request for Comments: RFC 2093*, November, The Internet Society, Washington, USA.

Klaus, C. (1993). Internet Security Scanner. Available at http://www.cert.org/advisories/CA-1993-14.html

Koopman, P., J. DeVale (2000). The exception handling effectiveness of POSIX operating systems. *IEEE Transactions on Software Engineering* 26(9), 837–848.

Krawczyk, H. (1993). Distributed fingerprints and secure information dispersal, in: *Proceedings of the 12th ACM Symposium on Principles of Distributed Computing*, pp. 207–218.

Lakshmanan, S., M. Ahamad, H. Venkateswaran (2003). Responsive security for stored data. *IEEE Transactions on Parallel and Distributed Systems* 14(9), 818–828.

Lamport, L. (1986). On interprocess communication (part II: algorithms). *Distributed Computing* 1, 86–101.

Lamport, L. (1998). The part-time parliament. *ACM Transactions on Computer Systems* 16(2), 133–169.

Lamport, L., R. Shostak, M. Pease (1982). The Byzantine generals problem. *ACM Transactions on Programming Languages and Systems* 4(3), 382–401.

Larochelle, D., D. Evans (2001). Statically detecting likely buffer overflow vulnerabilities, in: *Proceedings of the 10th Usenix Security Symposium*, August, pp. 177–189.

Liskov, B., R. Rodrigues (2006). Tolerating Byzantine faulty clients in a quorum system, in: *Proceedings of the 26th International Conference on Distributed Computing Systems*, June.

Littlewood, B., L. Strigini (2004). Redundancy and diversity in security, in: P. Samarati, P. Rian, D. Gollmann, R. Molva (eds.), *Computer Security—ESORICS 2004, 9th European Symposium on Research Computer Security, LNCS*, Vol. 3193, Springer, pp. 423–438.

Lumension Security. (2007). PatchLink Scan. Available at http://www.lumension.com/vulnerability-management.jsp

Malkhi, D., M. Reiter (1997). Byzantine quorum systems, in: *Proceedings of the 29th ACM Symposium in Theory of Computing*. ACM Press, pp. 569–578.

Malkhi, D., M. Reiter (1998). Secure and scalable replication in Phalanx, in: *Proceedings of the 17th IEEE Symposium on Reliable Distributed Systems*, October.

Malkhi, D., M. Reiter (2000). An architecture for survivable coordination in large distributed systems. *IEEE Transactions on Knowledge and Data Engineering* 12(2), 187–202.

Malkhi, D., M. Reiter, A. Wool (1997). The load and availability of Byzantine quorum systems, in: *Proceedings of the 16th ACM Symposium on Principles of Distributed Computing*, August, pp. 249–257.

Marsden, E., J.-C. Fabre, J. Arlat (2002). Dependability of CORBA systems: service characterization by fault injection, in: *Proceedings of the 21st International Symposium on Reliable Distributed Systems*, June, pp. 276–285.

Marsh, M.A., F.B. Schneider (2004). CODEX: a robust and secure secret distribution system. *IEEE Transactions on Dependable and Secure Computing* 1(1), 34–47.

Martin, J.P., L. Alvisi (2004). A framework for dynamic Byzantine storage, in: *Proceedings of the IEEE International Conference on Dependable Systems and Networks*, June, pp. 325–334.

Martin, J.P., L. Alvisi (2006). Fast Byzantine consensus. *IEEE Transactions on Dependable and Secure Computing* 3(3), 202–215.

Martin, J.P., L. Alvisi, M. Dahlin (2002). Minimal Byzantine storage, in: *Proceedings of the 16th International Conference on Distributed Computing, LNCS*, Vol. 2508, October, Springer-Verlag, pp. 311–325.

McAfee, Inc. (2007). McAfee Foundstone Enterprise. Available at http://www.mcafee.com/us/enterprise/products/risk_management/foundstone_enterprise.html

Mendonça, M., N. Neves (2007). Robustness testing of the windows DDK, in: *Proceedings of the International Conference on Dependable Systems and Networks*, June, pp. 554–564.

Mendonça, M., N. Neves (2008). Fuzzing wi-fi drivers to locate security vulnerabilities, in: *Proceedings of the European Dependable Computing Conference*, May.

Meyer, R., M. Cukier (2006). Assessing the attack threat due to IRC channels, in: *Proceedings of the International Conference on Dependable Systems and Networks*, June, pp. 467–472.

Meyer, F., D. Pradhan (1987). Consensus with dual failure modes, in: *Proceedings of the 17th IEEE International Symposium on Fault-Tolerant Computing*, July, pp. 214–222.

Miller, B., L. Fredriksen, B. So (1990). An empirical study of the reliability of UNIX utilities. *Communications of the ACM* 33(12), 32–44.

Moniz, H., N.F. Neves, M. Correia, P. Verissimo (2006). Randomized intrusion-tolerant asynchronous services, in: *Proceedings of the International Conference on Dependable Systems and Networks*, June, pp. 568–577.

Neves, N., J. Antunes, M. Correia, P. Verissimo, R. Neves (2006). Using attack injection to discover new vulnerabilities, in: *Proceedings of the International Conference on Dependable Systems and Networks*, June.

Obelheiro, R.R., A.N. Bessani, L.C. Lung, M. Correia (2006). How practical are intrusion-tolerant distributed systems? DI-FCUL TR 06–15, September, Department of Informatics, University of Lisbon.

Oehlert, P. (2005). Violating assumptions with fuzzing. *IEEE Security and Privacy* (March/April), 58–62.

Olovsson, T., E. Jonsson, S. Brocklehurst, B. Littlewood (1993). Data collection for security fault forecasting: pilot experiment, September. Technical Report 167, Department of Computer Engineering, Chalmers University of Technology.

Olovsson, T., E. Jonsson, S. Brocklehurst, B. Littlewood (1995). Towards operational measures of computer security: experimentation and modelling, in: B. Randell, J.-C. Laprie, H. Kopetz, B. Littlewood (eds.), *Predictably Dependable Computing Systems*. Springer-Verlag, Germany, pp. 555–572.

Orlovich, M., R. Rugina (2006). Memory leak analysis by contradiction, in: *Proceedings of the 13th International Static Analysis Symposium*, pp. 405–424.

Ostrovsky, R., M. Yung (1991). How to withstand mobile virus attacks (extended abstract), in: *Proceedings of the 10th Annual ACM Symposium on Principles of Distributed Computing*. ACM Press, pp. 51–59.

Pal, P., F. Webber, R. Schantz (2007). The DPASA survivable JBI–a high-water mark in intrusion-tolerant systems, in: *Proceedings of the 1st Workshop on Recent Advances on Intrusion-Tolerant Systems*, pp. 33–37.

Pan, J., P.J. Koopman, D.P. Siewiorek, Y. Huang, R. Gruber, M.L. Jiang (2001). Robustness testing and hardening of CORBA ORB implementations, in: *Proceedings of the International Conference on Dependable Systems and Networks*, June, pp. 141–150.

Panjwani, S., S. Tan, K. Jarrin, M. Cukier (2005). An experimental evaluation to determine if port scans are precursors to an attack, in: *Proceedings of the International Conference on Dependable Systems and Networks*, June, pp. 602–611.

PaX (2001). Available at http://pax.grsecurity.net/

Pouget, F., M. Dacier (2003). White paper: honeypot, honeynet: A comparative survey, September. Technical Report RR-03-082, Institut Eurecom.

Pouget, F., M. Dacier, H. Debar (2003). White paper: honeypot, honeynet, honeytoken: Terminological issues, September. Technical Report RR-03-081, Institut Eurecom.

Pouget, F., M. Dacier, H. Debar (2004a). Honeypots, a practical mean to validate malicious fault assumptions, in: *Proceedings of the 10th Pacific Rim International Symposium on Dependable Computing*, March.

Pouget, F., M. Dacier, V. Pham (2004b). Understanding threats: a prerequisite to enhance survivability of computing systems, in: *Proceedings of the International Infrastructure Survivability Workshop*, December.

Powell, D. (1992). Failure mode assumptions and assumption coverage, in: *Proceedings of the 22nd IEEE International Symposium of Fault-Tolerant Computing*, July, pp. 386–395.

Pucella, R., F.B. Schneider (2006). Independence from obfuscation: a semantic framework for diversity, in: *Proceedings of the 19th IEEE Workshop on Computer Security Foundations*, pp. 230–241.

Qualys Inc. (2007). QualysGuard Enterprise. Available at http://www.qualys.com

Rabin, M.O. (1989). Efficient dispersal of information for security, load balancing, and fault tolerance. *Journal of the ACM* 36(2), 335–348.

Ramasamy, H., C. Cachin (2006) Parsimonious asynchronous Byzantine-fault-tolerant atomic broadcast, in: *Proceedings of the 9th International Conference on Principles of Distributed Systems,* December, *Lecture Notes in Computer Science,* Vol. 3974, Springer-Verlag, pp. 88–102.

Ramsbrock, D., R. Berthier, M. Cukier (2007). Profiling attacker behavior following SSH compromises, in: *Proceedings of the International Conference on Dependable Systems and Networks,* June, pp. 119–124.

Randell, B. (1975). System structure for software fault tolerance, in: *Proceedings of the International Conference on Reliable Software,* pp. 437–449.

Reiter, M. (1994). Secure agreement protocols: reliable and atomic group multicast in Rampart, in: *Proceedings of the 2nd ACM Conference on Computer and Communications Security,* November, pp. 68–80.

Reiter, M. (1995). The Rampart toolkit for building high-integrity services, in: *Theory and Practice in Distributed Systems, LNCS,* Vol. 938, Springer, pp. 99–110.

PROTOS—Security Testing of Protocol Implementations (1999). Available at http://www.ee.oulu.fi/research/ouspg/protos/. Computer Engineering Laboratory, University of Oulu.

Saidane, A., Y. Deswarte, V. Nicomette (2003). An intrusion tolerant architecture for dynamic content internet servers, in: *Proceedings of the 1st ACM Workshop on Survivable and Self-Regenerative Systems,* October.

Saint Corp. (2007). SAINT Network Vulnerability Assessment Scanner. Available at http://www.saintcorporation.com

Schneider, F.B. (1990). Implementing fault-tolerant services using the state machine approach: a tutorial. *ACM Computing Surveys* 22(4), 299–319.

Shamir, A. (1979). How to share a secret. *Communications of the ACM* 22(11), 612–613.

Shelton, C., P. Koopman, K.D. Vale (2000). Robustness testing of the Microsoft Win32 API, in: *Proceedings of the International Conference on Dependable Systems and Networks,* June, pp. 261–270.

Siewiorek, D.P., R.S. Swarz (1992). *Reliable Computer Systems: Design and Evaluation.* 2nd Edition. Digital Press.

Sousa, P., N.F. Neves, P. Verissimo (2005a). How resilient are distributed *f* fault/intrusion-tolerant systems?, in: *Proceedings of the International Conference on Dependable Systems and Networks (DSN'05),* June, pp. 98–107.

Sousa, P., N.F. Neves, P. Verissimo (2005b). Resilient state machine replication, in: *Proceedings of the 11th Pacific Rim International Symposium on Dependable Computing (PRDC),* December, pp. 305–309.

Sousa, P., N.F. Neves, P. Verissimo (2006a). Proactive resilience through architectural hybridization, in: *Proceedings of the 2006 ACM Symposium on Applied Computing (SAC),* April, pp. 686–690.

Sousa, P., N.F. Neves, A. Lopes, P. Verissimo (2006b). On the resilience of intrusion-tolerant distributed systems. DI/FCUL TR 06–14, September, Department of Informatics, University of Lisbon.

Sousa, P., N.F. Neves, P. Verissimo, W.H. Sanders (2006c). Proactive resilience revisited: the delicate balance between resisting intrusions and remaining available, in: *Proceedings of the 25th IEEE Symposium on Reliable Distributed Systems (SRDS),* October, pp. 71–80.

Sousa, P., N.F. Neves, P. Verissimo (2007a). Hidden problems of asynchronous proactive recovery, in: *Third Workshop on Hot Topics in System Dependability (HotDep'07),* June.

Sousa, P., A.N. Bessani, M. Correia, N.F. Neves, P. Verissimo (2007b). Resilient intrusion tolerance through proactive and reactive recovery, in: *Proceedings of the 13th IEEE Pacific Rim International Symposium on Dependable Computing,* December.

Spitzner, L. (2002). *Honeypots: Tracking Hackers,* September. Addison-Wesley Professional.

Stevens, F., T. Courtney, S. Singh, A. Agbaria, J.F. Meyer, W.H. Sanders, P. Pal (2004). Model-based validation of an intrusion-tolerant information system, in: *Proceedings of the 23rd IEEE Symposium on Reliable Distributed Systems,* October, pp. 184–194.

Stoll, C. (1988). Stalking the wily hacker. *Communications of the ACM* 31(5), 484–497.

Stoll, C. (1990). *The Cuckoo's Egg: Tracking a Spy Through the Maze of Computer Espionage*. Pocket Books.

Sutton, M. (2006). FileFuzz, November. Available at http://labs.idefense.com/software/fuzzing.php

Tenable Network Security. (2007). Nessus Vulnerability Scanner. Available at http://www.nessus.org

Vendicator. (2001). Stack Shield: a stack smashing technique protection tool for Linux, January. Available at http://www.angelfire.com/sk/stackshield/.

Verissimo, P. (2003). Uncertainty and predictability: can they be reconciled?, in: *Future Directions in Distributed Computing, LNCS*, Vol. 2584, Springer, pp. 108–113.

Verissimo, P. (2006a). Thou shalt not trust non-trustworthy systems, in: *Keynote at the Workshop on Assurance in Distributed Systems and Networks, with the 26th IEEE International Conference on Distributed Computing Systems, July*, IEEE Computer Society, Lisbon, Portugal.

Verissimo, P. (2006b). Travelling through wormholes: a new look at distributed systems models. *SIGACT News* 37(1), 66–81.

Verissimo, P., N.F. Neves, M. Correia (2003). Intrusion-tolerant architectures: concepts and design, in: R. Lemos, C. Gacek, A. Romanovsky (eds.), *Architecting Dependable Systems, LNCS*, Vol. 2677, Springer, pp. 3–36.

Verissimo, P., N.F. Neves, C. Cachin, J. Poritz, D. Powell, Y. Deswarte, R. Stroud, I. Welch (2006). Intrusion-tolerant middleware: the road to automatic security. *IEEE Security and Privacy* 4(4), 54–62.

Verissimo, P., N.F. Neves, M. Correia (2008). The CRUTIAL reference critical information infrastructure architecture: a blueprint. *International Journal of System of Systems Engineering* 1(1/2), 78–95.

Viega, J., J.T. Bloch, Y. Kohno, G. McGraw (2000). ITS4: a static vulnerability scanner for C and C++ code, in: *Proceedings of the 16th Annual Computer Security Applications Conference*, December.

Wagner, D., J. Foster, E. Brewer, A. Aiken (2000). A first step towards automated detection of buffer overrun vulnerabilities, in: *Proceedings of the Network and Distributed System Security Symposium*, February, pp. 3–17.

Xu, J., Z. Kalbarczyk, R.K. Iyer (2003). Transparent runtime randomization for security, in: *Proceedings of the 22nd International Symposium on Reliable Distributed Systems (SRDS)*, October, pp. 260–269.

Yin, J., J. Martin, A. Venkataramani, L. Alvisi, M. Dahlin (2003). Separating agreement from execution for Byzantine fault tolerant services, in: *Proceedings of the 19th ACM Symposium on Operating Systems Principles*, October, pp. 253–267.

Zhou, L., F. Schneider, R. van Renesse (2002). COCA: a secure distributed on-line certification authority. *ACM Transactions on Computer Systems* 20(4), 329–368.

Zhou, L., F.B. Schneider, R. van Renesse (2005). APSS: proactive secret sharing in asynchronous systems. *ACM Transactions on Information and System Security* 8(3), 259–286.

Zielinski, P. (2004). Paxos at war, June. Technical Report UCAM-CL-TR-593, Computer Laboratory, University of Cambridge, Cambridge, UK.

Appendices

A1   Suggested readings

The following journals regularly present contributions in the area of resilience and InTol:

- *IEEE Transactions on Dependable and Secure Computing*
- *IEEE Security & Privacy*
- *ACM Transactions on Computer Systems*

A2   Online resources

We divided online resources into two categories: software packages and research projects.

A2.1   Software packages

There are not many software packages publicly available that can be used to build intrusion-tolerant distributed systems. We point out the following ones:

BFT: The aim of the BFT (Practical Byzantine Fault Tolerance) project was to develop algorithms and implementation techniques able to build practical Byzantine-fault-tolerant systems. BFT was implemented in C/C++ and it is available at the website http://www.pmg.csail.mit.edu/bft/

CODEX: CODEX (Cornell Data Exchange) is a distributed intrusion-tolerant service for storage and dissemination of secrets. At the same time, it comprises a set of general utility packages that provide useful primitives to build intrusion-tolerant systems. CODEX was implemented in C++ and it is available at the website http://www.umiacs.umd.edu/~mmarsh/CODEX/

JITT: The aim of the JITT (Java Intrusion Tolerance Tools) project was to develop a set of tools and libraries for InTol using the Java programming language. The objective was to provide a set of fully functional, clear-designed, building blocks to be used by the research community in Byzantine fault- and intrusion-tolerant systems. JITT was implemented in Java and it is available at the website http://www.navigators.di.fc.ul.pt/software/jitt/

RT-PSS: RT-PSS (Real-Time Proactive bSecret Sharing) is a library that provides an implementation of the Shamir's secret sharing scheme and Herzberg's PSS algorithm. It can be used to build intrusion-tolerant systems that make use of PSS. RT-PSS was implemented in C and it is available at the website http://sourceforge.net/projects/rt-pss/

TTCB: The TTCB (Trusted Timely Computing Base) is a distributed embedded component that provides a set of time and security-related services to client applications. It can be used as a fundamental building block for the development of intrusion-tolerant and real-time applications. TTCB was implemented in C/C++ and it is available at the website http://www.navigators.di.fc.ul.pt/software/ttcb/

A2.2   Research projects

Here we point out a list of research projects and networks of excellence (ongoing and already finished) that study/studied topics related with resilience and InTol.

CRUTIAL: CRitical UTility InfrastructurAL resilience (http://crutial.cesiricerca.it/)

ESFORS: European Security Forum for Web Services, Software and Systems (http://www.esfors.org/)

MAFTIA: Malicious- and Accidental-Fault Tolerance for Internet Applications (http://www.maftia.org)

OASIS: Organically Assured and Survivable Information Systems (http://www.tolerantsystems.org/oasis.html)

ReSIST: Resilience for Survivability in IST (http://www.resist-noe.org/)

SecureIST: ICT Security & Dependability Taskforce (http://www.ist-securist.org/)

TCIP: Trustworthy Cyber Infrastructure for the Power Grid (http://www.tcip.iti.uiuc.edu/)

Rao & Upadhyaya, Eds., *Handbooks in Information Systems, Vol. 4*
Copyright © 2009 by Emerald Group Publishing Limited

Chapter 23

Incentive-Based Methods for Inferring Attacker Intent and Strategies and Measuring Attack Resilience

Wanyu Zang and Meng Yu
Department of Computer Science, Western Illinois University, Macomb, IL, USA

Peng Liu
College of Information Sciences and Technology, Pennsylvania State University, University Park, PA, USA

Abstract

Although the ability to model and infer Attacker Intent, Objectives and Strategies (AIOS), and measure attack resilience of a defense system may dramatically advance the literature of risk assessment, harm prediction, and predictive or proactive cyber defense, existing AIOS inference techniques are *ad hoc* and system or application specific. In this chapter, we present a general incentive-based game theoretic approach to model AIOS and system resilience. On the one hand, we found that the concept of incentives can unify a large variety of attacker intents; the concept of utilities can integrate incentives and costs in such a way that attacker objectives can be practically modeled. On the other hand, we developed a game- theoretic formalization which can capture the inherent inter-dependency between AIOS and defender objectives and strategies in such a way that AIOS and intrusion resilience can be automatically inferred. Finally, we use a specific case study to show how AIOS can be inferred, and how attack resilience can be measured in real world attack–defense scenarios.

1 Introduction

The ability to model and infer Attacker Intent, Objectives and Strategies (AIOS) may dramatically advance the state-of-the-art of computer security. For example, for many "very difficult to prevent" attacks such as Internet Distributed Denial-of-Service (DDoS), given the specification of a system protected by a set of specific security mechanisms, this ability could tell us which kind of strategies are more likely to be taken by the attacker than the others, even before such an attack happens.

Such AIOS inferences may lead to more precise harm prediction and attack resilience (AR) measurement. AR quantifies the tolerance capability of the defense system against the attacks. It is an important metric for evaluating the performance of a defense system. Though a variety of defense methods are proposed to counter cyber attacks, AIOS modeling and inference are not well studied in the literature. Without knowing what the intents of the attacker are, or why a specific attack strategy is picked, the defense systems' cost-effectiveness cannot be fully understood. A comprehensive understanding of AIOS is the foundation of the attack resilience measurements.

Reversely, measuring attack resilience of the defense system can enhance peoples' understanding of AIOS. No matter what strategies are taken by the attacker, his/her final goal is to decrease the attack resilience of the system under a given risk or cost with specific intents and objectives. When measuring the attack resilience, we need to distinguish the attack strategies from the attack effects. Since the same attack effect may be caused by different attack strategies and the same attack actions may lead to different attack effects in different scenarios or states. Attack strategies and attack effectiveness are two basic elements of AIOS models. The measurement based on either attack strategies or attack effectiveness, but not both, may fail to yield comprehensive security evaluation results. Measuring resilience can help us distinguish attack strategies from attacker intents and objectives.

In fact, inferring AIOS and measuring resilience are just two sides of the same coin. They are highly interdependent on each other. By inferring AIOS, we can obtain realistic resilience quantification values. By measuring resilience, we can better understand the difference between attack actions and attacker intent and objectives.

However, with a focus on attack characteristics (Landwehr et al., 1994) and attack effects (Browne et al., 2001; Zou et al., 2002), most existing AIOS inference and resilience measurement techniques are *ad hoc* and system or application specific (Gordon and Loeb, 2001; Syverson, 1997). As a result, although a variety of attack taxonomies and attribute databases have been developed, people's ability to model and infer AIOS, to do proactive intrusion response and attack resilience evaluation is still very limited. Some general purpose attack analysis techniques, such as the attack graph analysis (Wing, 2006), and the statistics-based resilience-measuring approaches, consider either attack strategies or attack effectiveness. Therefore, they are not suitable for inferring AIOS and measuring resilience. For example, the attack graph analysis may be too pessimistic since they ignore the attackers' risks of been captured and punished. The statistics-based resilience-measuring approaches may not be able to capture all the better attack strategies. The statistics-based AIOS inference approaches may suffer from the same limitation.

In this chapter, we propose a generic game-theoretic AIOS/AR model to infer the attack intents, objectives, and strategies, and measure the system's attack resilience. First, we present a systematic incentive-based method to model AIOS and a game-theoretic approach in inferring AIOS. On the one hand, we use the concept of incentives to unify a large variety of attacker intents, and the concept of utilities to integrate incentives and costs in such a way that attacker objectives can be practically modeled. On the other hand, we develop a game-theoretic AIOS formalization that can capture the inherent interdependency between AIOS and defender objectives and strategies in such a way that AIOS can be automatically inferred.

Second, we present an incentive-based model to measure the attacker's intent and strategies, and the defense system's resilience. Through a case study, we explain how to measure the Internet's resilience against DDoS attacks, a serious threat to the Internet through the experiments. Although DDoS attacks with clear signatures can be effectively countered, DDoS attacks without clear signatures (e.g., brute-force DDoS attacks) are very difficult to counter cost-effectively, since the defense system is not clear which packets are DDoS packets and which are not. Although, several rate-limiting methods are proposed to counter such DDoS attacks, each may drop good packets and their cost-effectiveness are not clearly understood. In this chapter, we apply the generic AIOS formalization to do a game-theoretic analysis of the Internet's resilience against unclear signatures DDoS attacks when rate-limiting defense is deployed. Our analysis may substantially improve people's understanding about how resilient the Internet is against DDoS attacks. Further, our analysis can be used to improve the resilience of the defense system.

The rest of the chapter is organized as follows. In Section 2, we discuss the related work and in Section 3, we explain why we select game-theoretic framework. In Section 4, we present a game-theoretic formalization of this framework. Section 5 shows to infer AIOS, and measure resilience. In Sections 6 and 7, we use a specific case study to show how attack strategies can be inferred, and how system's resilience can be measured in real-world attack–defense scenarios. In Section 8, we mention several future research issues.

2 Related work

The use of game-theory in modeling attackers and defenders has been addressed in several other researches. In Syverson (1997), he talks about "good" nodes fighting "evil" nodes in a network and suggests using stochastic games for reasoning and analysis. In Lye and Wing (2002), they precisely formalize this idea using a general-sum stochastic game model and give a concrete example in detail where the attacker is attacking a simple enterprise network that provides some Internet services such as web and file transfer protocol (FTP). A set of specific states, regarding this example, are identified, state-transition probabilities are assumed, and the Nash equilibrium or best-response strategies for the players are computed. In Kodialam and Lakshman (2003), Kodialam uses a zero-sum game to model the detection of network intrusion. Aforementioned work assumes that the player knows other players completely. But in the real-world attacks, the system may not be able to distinguish the malicious user from legitimate users accurately. The zero-sum game with incomplete information can deal with such incomplete situation, however, the game among the user, attacker, and defense system is not a simple zero-sum game, in which whatever is gained by one player, is therefore lost by the other actor.

In Browne (2000), he describes how static games can be used to analyze attacks involving complicated and heterogeneous military networks. In his example, a defense team has to defend a network of three hosts against an attacking team's worms. The defense team can choose either to run a worm detector or not. Depending on the combined attack and defense actions, each outcome has different costs. Burke (1999) studies the use of repeated games with incomplete information to model attackers and defenders in information warfare. In Hespanha and Bohacek (2001), they discuss zero-sum routing games where an adversary (or attacker) tries to intersect data packets in a computer network. The designer of the network has to find routing policies that avoid links that are under the attacker's surveillance. Xu and Lee (2003) use game-theoretical framework to analyze the performance of their proposed DDoS defense system, and guide the system's design and performance tuning accordingly. Sallhammar et al. (2005) use stochastic game theory as a mathematical tool for computing the expected behavior of attackers. Zhuang and Bier (2008) proposed an optimal allocation of defensive investments to reduce the probability of damage from an attack through game-theoretic method. Liu et al. (2006a,b) uses Bayesian game to detect intrusion in wireless *ad hoc* networks.

Our work is different from the aforementioned game-theoretic attacker modeling that works in several aspects. First, these works focus on specific attack–defense scenarios, whereas our work focuses on general AIOS modeling and resilience measurement. Second, these works focus on specific types of game models, for example, static games, repeated games, or stochastic games, whrease our work focuses on the fundamental characteristics of AIOS/AR, and game model is one possible formalization of our AIOS framework. In addition, our AIOS/AR framework shows the inherent relationship between AIOS/AR and the different types of game models, and identifies the conditions under which a specific type of game models will be feasible and desirable. Third, our work systematically identifies the properties of a good AIOS/AR formalization. These properties not only can be used to evaluate the merits and limitations of game-theoretic AIOS/AR models, but also can motivate new AIOS/AR models that can improve the earlier game-theory models or even go beyond standard game-theoretic models.

The most similar work is our previous work in Liu et al. (2005) and Liu and Zang (2003), in which we focused on the analysis of the attacker, including AIOS. In this chapter, we consider both attacker and defense system. How to measure the resilience of the defense system against the attacker and how to improve the resilience are addressed in the chapter.

It should be noticed that AIOS modeling and inference are very different from intrusion detection (Lunt, 1993; McHugh, 2001; Mukherjee et al., 1994). Intrusion detection is based on the characteristics of attacks, whereas AIOS modeling is based on the characteristics of attackers. The attacker's objective and intent determine which attack strategy will be taken in the future. Intrusion detection focuses on the attacks that have already happened, whereas AIOS inference focuses on the attacks that may happen in the future. In the AIOS inference, the defense system uses current status to infer what the attacker will do in the next step, and picks an optimal strategy to optimize its resilience. So does the attacker, whereas the intrusion detection uses the current status to detect intrusions.

3 Why a game-theoretic framework?

In this section, we argue why a game-theoretic model is best to present AIOS and resilience measurement. Our model is quite abstract. To make our presentation more tangible, we first present the following example, which will be used throughout the chapter to illustrate our concepts.

Example 1. In recent years, Internet Distributed Denial-of-Service (DDoS) attacks have increased in frequency, severity, and sophistication and become a major security threat. When a DDoS attack is launched, a large number of hosts (called *zombies*) "controlled" by the attacker flood a high volume of packets toward the target (called the *victim*) to downgrade its service performance significantly or make it unable to deliver any service.

In this example, we would model the intent and objectives and infer the strategies of the attackers that enforce *brute-force* DDoS attacks. (Although some DDoS attacks with clear signatures, such as synchronize (SYN) flooding, can be effectively countered, most DDoS attacks without clear signatures, such as brute-force DDoS attacks, are very difficult to defend against since it is not clear which packets are DDoS packets and which are not.) An example scenario is shown in Fig. 1 where many zombies (i.e., a subset of source hosts $\{S_0, \ldots, S_{64}\}$) are flooding a couple of web sites (i.e., the *victims*) using normal HTTP requests. Here, $R_{x,y}$ denotes a router; the bandwidth of each type of links is marked; and the web sites may stay on different subnets.

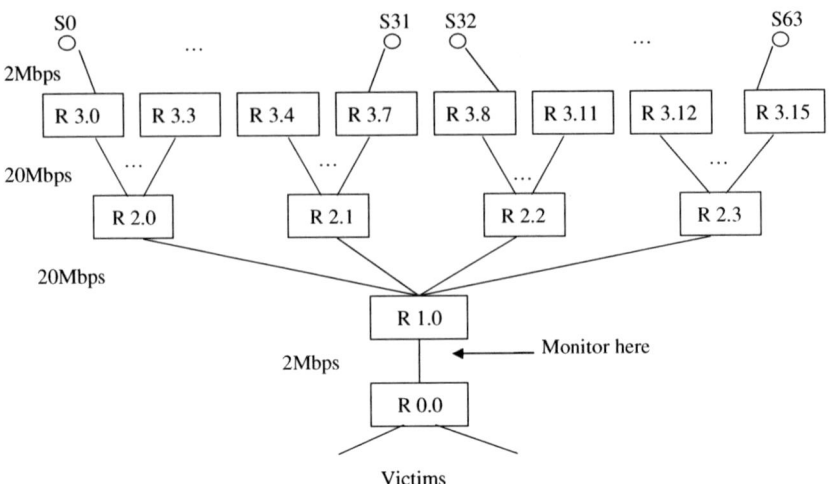

Fig. 1.   Network topology.

Although, our modeling and inference framework can handle almost every DDoS defense mechanism, to make this example more tangible, we select *pushback* (Ioannidis and Bellovin, 2002), a popular technique, as the security mechanism. Pushback uses *aggregates*, that is, a collection of packets from one or more flows that have some properties in common, to identify and *rate-limit* the packets that are most likely to cause congestion or DDoS. Pushback is a coordinated defense mechanism, which typically involves multiple routers. To illustrate, consider Fig. 1 again, when router R1.0 detects a congestion caused by a set of aggregates, R1.0 will not only rate-limit these aggregates, but also request adjacent upstream routers (e.g., R2.1) to rate-limit the corresponding aggregates via some pushback messages.

The effectiveness of pushback can be largely captured by four bandwidth parameters associated with the incoming link to the victims (i.e., the link that connects R1.0 and R0.0): (a) B_N, the total bandwidth of this link; (b) B_{ao}, the (amount of) bandwidth occupied by the DDoS packets; (c) B_{lo}, the bandwidth occupied by the legitimate packets; and (d) B_{lw}, the bandwidth that the legitimate users would occupy if there are no attacks. For example, pushback is effective if after being enforced B_{ao} can become smaller and B_{lo} can become larger.

The attacker-system relation has several unique characteristics (or properties), which are important in illustrating the principles of our framework. These properties are as follows:

 - *Intentional attack property*: Attacks are typically not random. They are planned by the attacker based on some intent and objectives.
 - *Dual property*: (a) Given two attack (defense) strategies, determining which one is a better attack (defense) strategy is dependent on the

defense (attack) strategies the system (attacker) is going to take. In other words, the capacity of either an attack or a defense posture should be measured in a relative way. (b) Each type of information useful for the attacker (system) to choose a good attack (defense) strategy will also be useful for the system (attacker) to choose a good defense (attack) strategy.

- *Uncertainty property*: The attacker usually has incomplete information or knowledge about the system, and vice versa. For example, in Example 1 the attacker usually has uncertainty about how pushback is configured when he or she enforces a DDoS attack.

We believe a game-theoretic formalization can be very valuable for AIOS modeling and attack resilience measurement because

(1) Such a formalization captures every key property of the attacker-system relation such as the Intentional attack property and the Strategy interdependency property. *Strategic interdependence* (Mas-Colell et al., 1995), normally handled by the noncooperative game theory, is the fundamental property of the attacker-system relation.

(2) Such a formalization captures every key element of our incentive-based AIOS modeling and interdependent-based measuring framework such as incentives, utilities, costs, risks, constraints, strategies, security mechanisms, security metrics, defense postures, vulnerabilities, attacks, threats, knowledge, and uncertainty.

(3) Game-theoretic models have been successfully used to predict rational behaviors in many applications such as auctions and their *rationality* notion (that each player plays an expected-utility maximizing best-response to every other player) is consistent with the goals of many, if not most, attackers and systems.

(4) Game-theoretic models have been successfully used to model the attacker-system behaviors in many applications.

(5) Nash equilibria of attacker-system games can lead to good AIOS inferences and resilient measurement since Nash equilibria indicate the "best" rational behaviors of a player, and when the system always takes a Nash equilibrium defense strategy, only a Nash equilibrium attack strategy can maximize the attacker's and system's utilities.

4 A game-theoretic formalization

Our general game-theoretic AIOS/AR formalization is shown in Fig. 2, where

- Instead of neglecting the attacker and viewing attacks as part of the system's environment, we model the attacker as a "peer" of the system, namely the *attacking system*.
- The *environment* only includes the set of good accesses by a legitimate user.

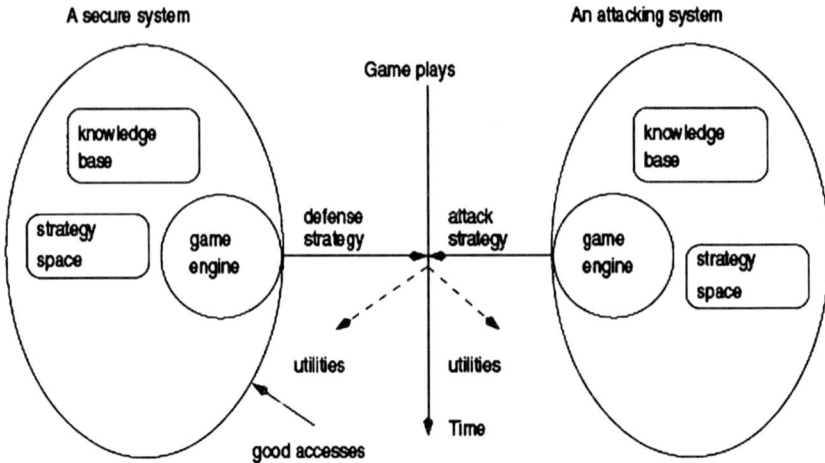

Fig. 2.   A game-theoretic formalization.

- We further split the system into two parts: the *service part* includes all and only the components that provide computing services to users; and the *protection part* includes the set of security mechanisms. For example, in Example 1 the service part mainly includes the hardware and software components (within the routers) that route packets; the pushback components belong to the protection part.
- Instead of passively monitoring, detecting, and reacting to attacks, the relation between the system and the attacker is modeled as a *game* (or battle) across the time dimension where the system may actively take defense actions.
- The game is a 6-tuple.
  - The two *players*, namely the (secure) system and the attacking system. Note that the "real" player for the system is the set of security mechanisms.
  - The *game type* (e.g., a Bayesian game or a stochastic game) and the set of type-specific parameters of the game.
  - The two strategy spaces of the two players, defined in the same say as in Section 3. The attacker's strategy space is denoted as $S^a = \{s_1^a, \ldots, s_m^a\}$ where s_i^a is an attack strategy. The system's strategy space is denoted as $S^d = \{s_1^d, \ldots, s_m^d\}$ where s_i^d is a defense strategy. Note that the constraints associated with the attacker and the cost of each attack imply the boundary of S^a. A more detailed formalization of attack strategies is described in Section 5.
  - A set of game *plays*. A play is a function $pl_i: S^a \times S^d \to O$, where O is the set of outcomes which indicate the effects of an attack. Each play involves one battle due to an attack. Each play may have several phases. We assume each player uses a *game engine* to determine

which strategy should be taken in a specific play. For example, in Example 1 a game play between the DDoS attacker and the network may involve attack strategy A1 and defense strategy D2.

- The two *utility* (or *payoff*) functions that calculate the utilities earned by the two players out of each play. The attacker's utility function is u^a: $S^a \times S^d \rightarrow R$, where R is the set of utility measurements. Given a play (s_i^a, s_i^d), the attack cost is an attribute of s_i^a, denoted $cost(s_i^a)$. The attacker's incentives are determined by $degradation(V_{t_1}^s, V_{t_2}^s)$ where t_1 is the time when the play starts; t_2 the time when the play ends; and security vector $V_{t_2}^s$ is dependent on the outcome of the play, namely $pl_i(s_i^a, s_i^d)$. And $u^a(s_i^a, s_i^d)$ is a distance between $cost(s_i^a)$ and the attacker's incentives. By contrast, the system's utility function is u^d: $S^a \times S^d \rightarrow R$. Given a play (s_i^a, s_i^d) the system's cost is $cost(s_i^d)$.

- A *knowledge base* maintained by each player. The attacker's (system's) knowledge base maintains the attacker's (system's) knowledge about the system's (attacker's) strategy space (including the system's (attacker's) cost and constraints), the system's (attacker's) value system, the system's metric and security vectors. Note that the attacker's (system's) knowledge may not always be true; it in fact captures the attacker's (system's) *beliefs*.

- Note that for simplicity, only the game-relevant components are shown in Fig. 2. Note also that the game model can be extended to cover multiple attackers who are either cooperating with other attackers (i.e., cooperative) or not (i.e., noncooperative). This extension is out of the scope of this chapter.

5   Game-theoretic AIOS inference and AR measurment

In this section, we further address how to apply the game-theoretic formalization to infer AIOS and measure AR.

5.1   Game-theoretic AIOS inference

As we mentioned in earlier sections, the ability to infer attacker intent, objectives and strategies (in information warfare) may dramatically advance the literature of risk assessment, harm prediction, and proactive cyber defense. In the earlier section, we show how to model AIOS via a game-theoretic formalization. In this section, we address how to exploit such formalizations to infer AIOS. In particular, we tackle two types of AIOS inference problems, which are illustrated later.

Type A—Infer attack strategies: Given a specific model of attack intent and objectives, infer which attack strategies are more likely to be taken by the attacker. The previous presentation implies the following pipeline in inferring attack strategies:

(1) Make assumptions about the system and the (types of) attacks that concern the system. Note that practical attack strategies inferences may only be able to be computed within some domain or scope (due to the complexity).

(2) Model the AIOS (conceptually). Specify the attacker's utility function and strategy space. Estimate the attacker's knowledge base.

(3) Specify the system's metric vector and security vector. Specify the system's utility function and strategy space. Build the system's knowledge base.

(4) Determine the game type of the game-theoretic attack strategy inference model that will be developed, then develop the model accordingly.

(5) Compute the set of Nash equilibrium strategies of the attack strategy inference game model developed in Step 4. Nash equilibria indicate the "best" rational behaviors of a player, and when the system always takes a Nash equilibrium defense strategy, only a Nash equilibrium attack strategy can maximize the attacker's utilities. One problem that we need to handle is the computation cost. If the cost is too much, we need to do (inference) precision-performance tradeoffs properly using some approximate algorithms. For example, both the attacker and the defense system may have infinite or very large strategy spaces. Consider all of them and compute the corresponding utilities are not practical. Therefore, we can reduce the strategy space by selecting the typical strategies.

(6) Validate the inferences generated in Step 5. The relevant tasks include but are not limited to *accuracy analysis* (i.e., how accurate the inferences are) and *sensitivity analysis* (i.e., how sensitive the inferences are to some specific model parameters). The relevant validation techniques include but are not limited to (a) investigating the degree to which the inferences match the real-world intrusions; (b) extracting a set of high-level properties or features from the set of inferences and asking security experts to evaluate if the set of properties match their experiences, beliefs, or intuitions.

(7) If the validation results are not satisfactory, go back to Step 1 to rebuild or improve the inference model.

Type B—Infer attacker intent and objectives: Based on the attack actions observed, infer the intent and objectives of the attacker in enforcing the corresponding attack. To a large degree, the pipeline for inferring attacker intent and objectives is the reverse of that for inferring attack strategies. In particular, the pipeline has two phases: the *learning* phase and the *detection* phase, which are as follows:

- *In the learning phase*: (1) Make assumptions of the attacker intent and objectives based on the observed attack actions. (2) Identify and classify the assumed attacker intent and objectives into a set of representative attacker intent and objectives models, for example, the intent and objective of an attacker is comprising one specific destination, or network bandwidth. (3) Model the attack strategies for each of the representative models. For example, the possible attack strategies can be packet flooding, SYN intrusion, and so on. (4) As a result, a (separate) set of attack strategy inferences will be generated for each of the representative models.
- In the detection phase, once an attack strategy is observed, match the observed attack strategy against the inferred attack strategies generated in the learning phase. Once an inferred attack strategy is matched, the corresponding attacker intent and objective model(s) will be the inference(s) of the real attacker's intent and objectives. (Note that sometimes an observed attack strategy may "match" more than one attacker intent and objective models.) Nevertheless, when none of the inferred attack strategies can be matched, go back to the learning phase and do more learning.

5.2 Game-theoretic AR measurement

Resilience measuring should start after the AIOS inference since attack strategies, intent, and objectives will be used to evaluate the resilience of the system. Given the model of attack intent and objectives, and attack strategies, the earlier presentation implies the following pipeline in resilience measurement:

(1) Use the attack strategies, attacker intent and objects obtained in AIOS inference (Section 5.1). Also use the system's utility function and strategy space defined in AIOS inference. Build the system's and attacker's knowledge base, and then estimate the attacker's and system's belief.
(2) Determine the game type of the game-theoretic resilience measurement model that will be developed, then develop the model accordingly.
(3) Compute the set of Nash equilibrium strategies of the resilience measurement game model developed in Step 2. Nash equilibria indicate the "best" rational behaviors of a player, and when the

system takes a Nash equilibrium defense strategy, the system can maximize its utilities (resilience).

(4) Validate the inferences generated in Step 3. The relevant tasks include but are not limited to accuracy analysis (i.e., how accurate the measurements are) and sensitivity analysis (i.e., how sensitive the measurements are to some specific model parameters). We can use the same relevant validation techniques listed in Section 5.1 to valid the resilience measurements.

(5) If the validation results are not satisfactory, go back to Step 1 to rebuild or improve the measurement model. For example, we can ask security experts to evaluate the resilience if the set of properties of the resilience match their experiences, or intuitions. If it does not match the experiences or intuitions, the payoff function, utilities, or knowledge base will be rebuilt.

In summary, both inference and resilience problems need a game-theoretic inference model. As we shown in Section 6, given a specific attack–defense scenario, once we have a good understanding of the attack, the defense, the attacker, and the system, most steps of the three pipelines are fairly easy to follow, but the steps of determining the game type of the AIOS inference and resilience measurement model are not naive and require substantial research. Therefore, in the following, before we show how the pipelines can be implemented in a real-world attack–defense scenario in Section 6, we would first show how to choose the right game type for a real-world AIOS inference and resilience measurement task.

5.3 Bayesian game-theoretic models

In this section, we present a concrete Bayesian game-theoretic model, which can be used to infer AIOS and measure resilience of the system. This model will be used shortly to do the case study in Section 6.

A Bayesian game-theoretic model is composed of two parts: a Bayesian *game model* that characterizes the attacker-system relation and a set of AIOS *inferences* and *resilience measurements* generated by the game model. In particular, the game model is a specific 2-player finitely repeated Bayesian game between the system and a subject, where (a) there can be multiple *types* of subjects. And the *type space* is denoted $T^{sub} = \{good, bad\}$. A subject's type is privately known by the subject. (b) A^{sys} is the *action space* of the system and A^{sub} the action space of the subject. One or more actions can build a *strategy*. (c) The game has a finite number of plays (or stages) and each play includes a pair of simultaneous actions (a^{sys}, a^{sub}). And each play will have an outcome denoted $o(a^{sys}, a^{sub})$. (d) The system is uncertain about the type of the subject. This uncertainty is measured by the system's *type belief*, denoted p_{sys}^{type}. For example, $p_{sys}^{type}(bad)$, a proba-bility denotes the system's belief about the statement that the subject is an attacker. (e) For each outcome o, the system's utility function is $u_{sys}(o) = p_{sys}^{type}(good)u_{sys}^{good}(o) + p_{sys}^{type}(bad)u_{sys}^{bad}(o)$. If the subject is a legitimate user, his or her utilities are determined by $u_{sub}(o; good)$, otherwise, his or her utilities are determined by $u_{sub}(o; bad)$. However, the set of AIOS inferences are determined by the Nash equilibria of the game model based on the rationality notion of an expected-utility maximizer. Note that mixed strategy Nash equilibria exist for every Bayesian game, although sometimes no pure strategy Nash equilibrium exists. Also a game may have multiple Nash equilibria. In particular, for each Nash equilibrium of the game, denoted $(a_{sys}^*, a_{bad}^*, a_{good}^*)$, the game model will output a_{bad}^* as the attack strategy inferences (i.e., a_{bad}^* indicates the kind of strategies that are more likely to be taken by the attacker); output $u_{sub}(o; bad)$ (i.e., the utility function) and $u_{sub}(a_{sys}^*, a_{bad}^*; bad)$ as the attacker intent and objectives inferences, where $u_{sub}(a_{sys}^*, a_{bad}^*; bad)$ can be mapped to the amount of security vector degradation caused by the attack. $u_{sys}(o)$ quantifies the security goals of the system, and $u_{sys}(a_{sys}^*, a_{bad}^*)$ measures the overall resilience of the system since if the system is *rational*, the system will at least earn $u_{sys}(a_{sys}^*, a_{bad}^*)$. We can use $u_{sys}^{good}(o)$ and $u_{sys}^{bad}(o)$ to quantify the various aspects of the system's resilience. Beside, a_{sys}^* is the best defense strategy for the system.

6   Case study: inferring the attack strategies and measuring attack resilience against DDoS attackers

In this case study, we want to infer the strategies of the attackers that enforce brute-force DDoS attacks, and measure the system's attack resilience against the DDoS attacks as well. Regarding the network topology, the attack model, the system model, and the defense mechanism, we make exactly the same assumptions as in Example 1. In particular, we assume pushback is deployed by the system. Based on the aggregates and the corresponding traffic volume, pushback classifies both the traffic and the users into three categories: good, poor, and bad. The bad traffic is sent by a bad user (attacker) and is responsible for the congestion. The poor and good traffics are legitimate traffics, and sent by the poor and good users (both legitimate), respectively. However, the poor traffic has the same aggregate properties as the bad traffic, but the good traffic has not, though the good traffic may share some paths with the bad traffic. To illustrate, in Fig. 1 assume the attacker compromises S_0 and sends "bad" packets to a victim denoted d_0. Simultaneously, S_{31} sends legitimate packets to d_0. If router *R1.0* uses destination address to identify the congestion aggregate, the poor packets sent from S_{31} to d_0 may be viewed as "bad" packets since they have the same destination address as the bad traffic, and dropped by the defense system. In summary, if the aggregates are destination-address-based in Fig. 1, then all packets sent to the same destination will belong to the same aggregate. Accordingly, when the attacker floods DDoS packets to a set of victims, all the legitimate packets sent to the victims are poor traffic and would be rate-limited together with the bad traffic. Nevertheless, the legitimate packets sent to other hosts are good traffic, such as the traffic between hosts in $\{S_0, \ldots, S_{64}\}$.

6.1 The game-theoretic AIOS/AR model

Now, we are ready to present the specific Bayesian game-theoretic AIOS/AR model for DDoS attack/defense, which is specified as follows. Without losing generality, we assume that in each DDoS attack, there is one attacker and multiple legitimate users. (Nevertheless, it should be noticed that our AIOS/AR model can be easily extended to handle collusive attackers.) For concision, we only mention the differences from the generic Bayesian game model proposed in Section 5.3.

$$\text{DDoSGM} = \{A_{\text{att}}, A_{\text{leg}}^1, \ldots, A_{\text{leg}}^i, A_{\text{sys}}, \ T_{\text{att}},$$
$$T_{\text{leg}}^1, \ldots, T_{\text{leg}}^i, T_{\text{sys}}, \ p_{\text{att}}, \ p_{\text{leg}}^1, \ldots, p_{\text{leg}}^i,$$
$$p_{\text{sys}}, \ u_{\text{att}}, \ u_{\text{leg}}^1, \ldots, u_{\text{leg}}^i, u_{\text{sys}}\}, \quad \text{where}$$

(1) The players are the attacker, the system, and several legitimate users. It should be noticed that we cannot model this game as a 2-player game and we must extend the 2-player Bayesian game model proposed in Section 5.3, since zombies and legitimate hosts are sending packets to the victim(s) simultaneously and neither zombies nor legitimate hosts can "control" the actions taken by the other side. Also note that our game model can be easily extended to model collusive DDoS attacks among multiple attackers.

(2) The attacker's action space is $A_{\text{att}} = \{A_1, \ldots, A_m\}$, where A_i is a DDoS attack launched by the attacker. No matter which kind of DDoS attacks A_i belongs to, there are typically some common properties among the attacking packets involved in A_i. For example, they may have the same destination address, or they may use the same protocol. In the case study, for the attacker's strategies, we mainly concern the *<number of zombies, ratio, traffic pattern, attacking traffic aggregates>*. We set the number of zombies as 12 (FewBad) or 32 (ManyBad). If the total rate of attacking traffic is stable, then each zombie has lower sending rates under ManyBad. We got three typical traffic values from http://ita.ee.lbl.gov/html/traces.html. They are rate1 = 67.1 kbps (the rates to a web site at the rush hour), rate2 = 290 kbps (the average rates from an Intranet to Internet), and rate3 = 532 kbps (the rates from an Intranet to Internet at the rush hour). In this chapter, we use three rates to set up three typical scenarios. We set the total poor rate as rate1, rate2, and rate3 since the poor traffic is sent to the same destination as the

bad traffic. The ratio is given by the total rate of the attacking traffic, divided by the total rate of the poor traffic. We set the ratio as 30, 35, 40, 45, and 50 (in rate3, the ratio is 30, 35, and 40). For example, when the poor rates is 67.1 kbps, the total attacking traffic rate is 2013 kbps, 2348.5 kbps, 2684 kbps, 3019 kbps, and 3355 kbps, respectively, which is larger than the bandwidth of the target link. There are four kinds of traffic patterns for attackers, Constant bits rate (CBR), Exponential (EXP), and ICMP and Mixed (half CBR and half ICMP). According to the different aggregate properties, the attacking traffic can be divided into several aggregates. For example, when the aggregate property is destination address prefix and zombies send packets to one victim, then the attacking traffic belongs to one aggregate. If zombies send packets to three destination prefix address, attacking traffic has three aggregates.

(3) The action space for legitimate user k is $A_{leg}^k = \{T_1, \ldots, T_m; \ 1 \leq k \leq i\}$, where T_i is a specific network application (or service). Regarding the legitimate users' strategies, the good traffic is always sent to different destinations from the victims and its aggregate differs from the attack aggregate. We set number of poor users as 2 (FewPoor) or 4 (ManyPoor) and number of good users as 5 (FewPoor) or 10 (ManyPoor). For simplicity, we just set the sending rate from each good user is same as that of the poor user. So when the poor rate goes up, even the legitimate rate goes up. Legitimate traffic only use CBR pattern. Notice, the bad traffic is sent by a bad user (attacker) and is responsible for the congestion. The poor traffic is sent by the legitimate users. However, the poor traffic has the same aggregate properties as the bad traffic, for example, having the same destination or source addresses.

(4) The system's action space A_{sys} is determined by the pushback postures of each router in the system. The system is composed of every router that is part of the pushback defense, denoted $\{R_1, \ldots, R_n\}$. In particular, the pushback behavior of a router can be described as *<aggregate property, congestion checking time, cycle time, target drop rate, free time, rate limit time, maximum session>*. The default values of the parameters are *<destination address prefix, 2s, 5s, 0.05, 20s, 30s, 3>*, which are explained as follows.

In pushback, agents identify the malicious traffic based on the aggregate property. The aggregate property usually includes the destination address prefix, source address prefix, the protocol layer, the flow id, or their combinations. *Congestion checking time* is the interval time that the router checks congestion. When serious congestion is detected, the Local Aggregate-based Congestion Control (ACC) will identify the aggregate(s) responsible for the congestion. *Cycle time* is the interval time that the agent reviews the limit imposed on the aggregates and sends refresh to the adjacent upstream routers to update the rate limit. The *target drop rate* is the upper bound of drop rate of the output queue. To achieve the given target drop rate, the rate limiter should let the rates sending to the output queue be less than $B/(1-\text{tdr})$, where B is the bandwidth of the output link and tdr is the target drop rate. *Free time* of the limited session is the earliest time to release a limited aggregate after it goes below the limit imposed on it. *Rate limit time* determines the period that the rate limiter controls for each identified aggregate. After the period, the agent will check whether the aggregate is still needed to be rate-limited. *Maximum session* determines the maximum sessions (aggregate) the rate limiter can control.

(5) The attacker's type space is $T_{\text{att}} = \{\text{bad,good}\}$. Legitimate user i's type space is also $T^i_{\text{leg}} = \{\text{bad, good}\}$. The system's type space is $T_{\text{sys}} = \text{sys}$.

(6) Regarding the system's type belief, since when a packet arrives at a router, the router cannot tell whether the sender of the packet is a zombie or not, the system's belief (or uncertainty) about every other player's type is the same, that is, $p^{\text{good}}_{\text{sys}} = \theta$, and $p^{\text{bad}}_{\text{sys}} = 1 - \theta$. In our simulation, for simplicity we assume there are one attacker and one legitimate user. Accordingly, $\theta = 0.5$. In the real world, the value of θ can be estimated based on some specific statistics of the DDoS attacks that have happened toward the system.

(7) Regarding the attacker and legitimate users' type belief, since both the attacker and the legitimate users know the system's type, $p^{\text{type}}_{\text{att}}(\text{sys}) = p^{\text{type}}_{\text{leg}}(\text{sys}) = 1$. Since the attacker knows who are zombies and who are legitimate nodes, the attacker's uncertainty about a legitimate user's type is $p^{\text{type}}_{\text{bad}}(\text{good}) = 1$. However, a legitimate user typically has uncertainty about the type of a node that is not involved in his application, since he is not sure whether the node is a zombie or not. So a legitimate user's uncertainty about the attacker's type and another legitimate user's type are the same, namely $p^{\text{type}}_{\text{leg}}(\text{bad}) = \beta$ and $p^{\text{type}}_{\text{leg}}(\text{good}) = 1 - \beta$.

(8) For each outcome o of a game play, the attacker's utility is $u_{\text{att}}(o) = \alpha u^{\text{sys}}_{\text{att}}(o) + (1 - \alpha)\sum^i_{k=1} u^{\text{legk}}_{\text{att}}(o)$, where $u^{\text{sys}}_{\text{att}}(o)$ measures the attack's impact on the network, whereas $u^{\text{legk}}_{\text{att}}(o)$ measures the attack's impact on legitimate user k. In particular, $u_{att}(o) = \alpha B_{ao}/B_N + (1 - \alpha)(1 - B_{lo}/B_{lw})$, where B_{ao} is the bandwidth occupied by the attacker; B_N the bandwidth capacity; B_{lo} the bandwidth occupied by the legitimate user (note that we assume there is only one legitimate user); B_{lw} the bandwidth that the legitimate user wants to occupy. For simplicity, B_{ao}, B_N, B^i_{lo}, and B^i_{lw} are all measured based on the incoming link to the edge router of the victim(s), as shown in Fig. 1. Note that B_{ao}/B_N indicates the absolute impact of the attack on the (whole)

network, whereas $1 - B_{lo}^k = B_{lw}^k$ indicates the relative availability impact of the attack on legitimate user k. α is the weight that balances these two aspects. Usually the attacker is mainly concerned with the attack's impact on legitimate users, so in this study we let $\alpha = 0.2$.

(9) The legitimate user's utility is $u_{leg}(o) = u_{leg}^{sys}(o) + p_{leg}^{type}(bad)u_{leg}^{bad}(o)$. Since the system controls both the legitimate and the bad traffic, and the attacker does not control the legitimate traffic directly, we simply let $u_{leg}^{bad}(o) = 0$. Therefore, $u_{leg}(o) = B_{lo}/B_{lw}$

(10) The system's utility function is $u_{sys}(o) = (1 - \theta)u_{sys}^{leg}(o) + \theta u_{sys}^{bad}(o)$. Since $u_{sys}^{leg}(o) = B_{lo}/B_{lw}$, and $u_{sys}^{bad}(o) = (-B_{ao}/B_N)$, the system's utility function is $u_{sys}(o) = (1 - \theta)B_{lo}/B_{lw} + \theta(-B_{ao}/B_N)$, and it is defined in the standard way.

Although in this case study several specific parameter values are set, the earlier DDoS attack strategy inference and resilience measurement model is a general model and can handle a variety of other DDoS attack scenarios beyond the case study. For example, our model can handle the scenario where the zombies adjust their strategies (e.g., attacking rate, traffic pattern) according to the response of the defense system. Moreover, although in our model the system's action space is pushback-specific, our model can be extended to support other DDoS defense mechanisms such as traceback.

We summarize the aforementioned notations in Table 1.

Table 1
Notations used in the chapter

Notations	Descriptions
A_{att}	Attacker's action space
A_{leg}^k	Action space of legitimate user k
A_{sys}	System's action space
T_{att}	Attacker's type space
T_{leg}^i	Legitimate user i's type space
T_{sys}	System's type space
p_{sys}^{good}	System's belief for a legitimate user
p_{sys}^{bad}	System's belief for an attacker
$p_{leg}^{type}(sys)$	Legitimate users' belief for the system
$p_{att}^{type}(sys)$	Attacker's belief for the system
$p_{att}^{type}(good)$	Attacker's belief for a legitimate user
$p_{leg}^{type}(bad)$	Legitimate user's belief for an attacker
$p_{leg}^{type}(good)$	Legitimate user's belief for a legitimate user
u_{att}	Attacker's utility
u_{leg}	Legitimate user's utility
u_{sys}	System's utility

7   Simulations

According to the pipelines in Section 5, after the game modeling, we also need to compute the set of Nash equilibrium strategies to infer the attack strategies, and measure the system resilience. In this section, we apply the game model to a real-world attack–defense scenario to calculate the Nash equilibrium strategies through extensive experiments. In our experiment, we assume there is one attacker attacks the system with multiple zombies. The different attack strategies (attack traffic and number of zombies), legitimate strategies, and defense strategies are simulated, and the corresponding utilities of the attacker, legitimate users, and the defense system are calculated in our experiment. Based on the sets of utilities $<u_{att}, u_{leg}, u_{sys}>$, we can identify the Nash equilibrium strategies where each player has the optimal utility in according to other players' actions, and the utility of the player will be reduced if he changes his action.

To obtain concrete attack strategy inferences of the real-world DDoS attackers, and accurate attack resilience of the populate defense systems, we have done extensive simulations on the game plays specified above using ns-2 (see http://www.isi.edu/nsnam/ns/, NS2, "The network simulator"). The network topology of our experiments is shown in Fig. 1, which is the same as the topology used in pushback evaluation (Ioannidis and Bellovin, 2002). There are 64 source hosts and 4 levels of routers. The link bandwidths are shown in the figure. Each router uses an ns-2 pushback module to enforce the pushback mechanism. It should be noticed that although there can be multiple victims staying on different subnets; we assume that all the victims share the same incoming link, namely R1.0-R0.0.

Figures 3 and 4 show how the system and attacker strategies affect the attacking capacities of attacker and system resilience, respectively. Axis X is for the attacker's strategies. Attacker has 40 (24) strategies in rate1 and rate2 (rate3). In the first 20 (12) strategies, the number of zombies is FewBad, followed by 20 (12) strategies with the number as ManyBad. For each 5 (3) strategies in each 20 (12) strategies, attacking traffic patterns are ordered as CBR, Exponential, ICMP and Mixed. In each 5 (3) strategies, the data is ordered according to the ratio, which is 30, 35, 40, 45, and 50 (30, 35, and 40). Axis Y is for system's strategies, which are ordered as congestion checking time (4 s), cycle time (10 s), drop rate (0.03), drop rate (0.07), free time (10), free time (30), default configuration, rate limit time (15), rate limit time (50), and maximum session (5). The aggregate property is of the defense system is DestPort (destination address prefix plus the port number).

7.1   The defense capacity vs. DDoS attack capacity

Figure 3 shows the attacker's attack effectiveness (capability) under different attack and defense strategies. Figure 4 shows the attack resilient

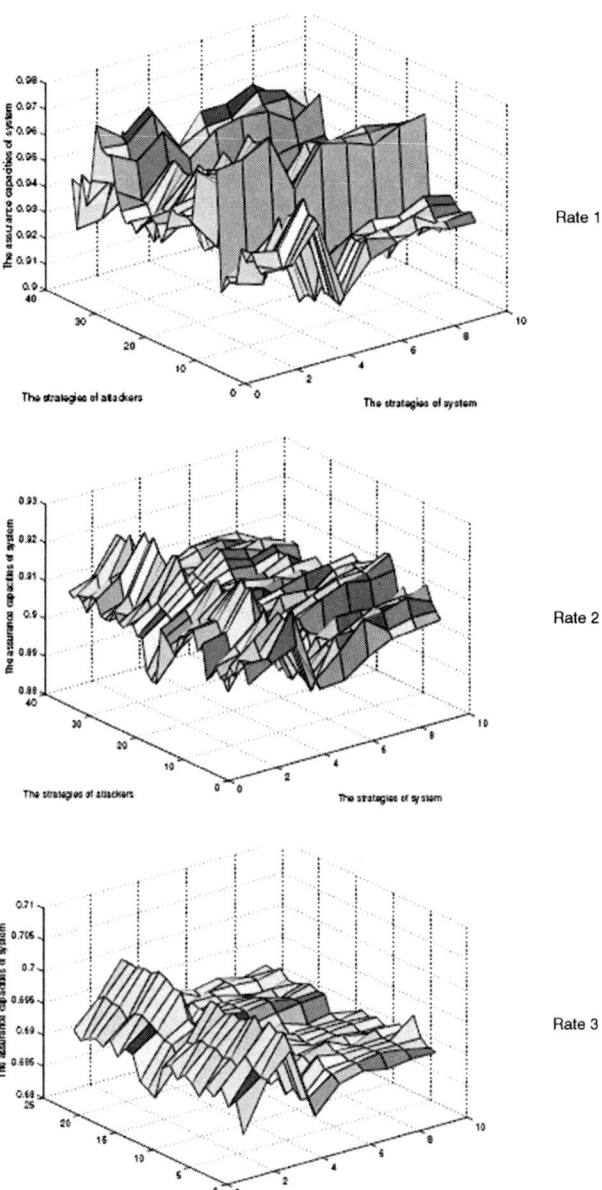

Fig. 3.   The resilience capacity of the defense system.

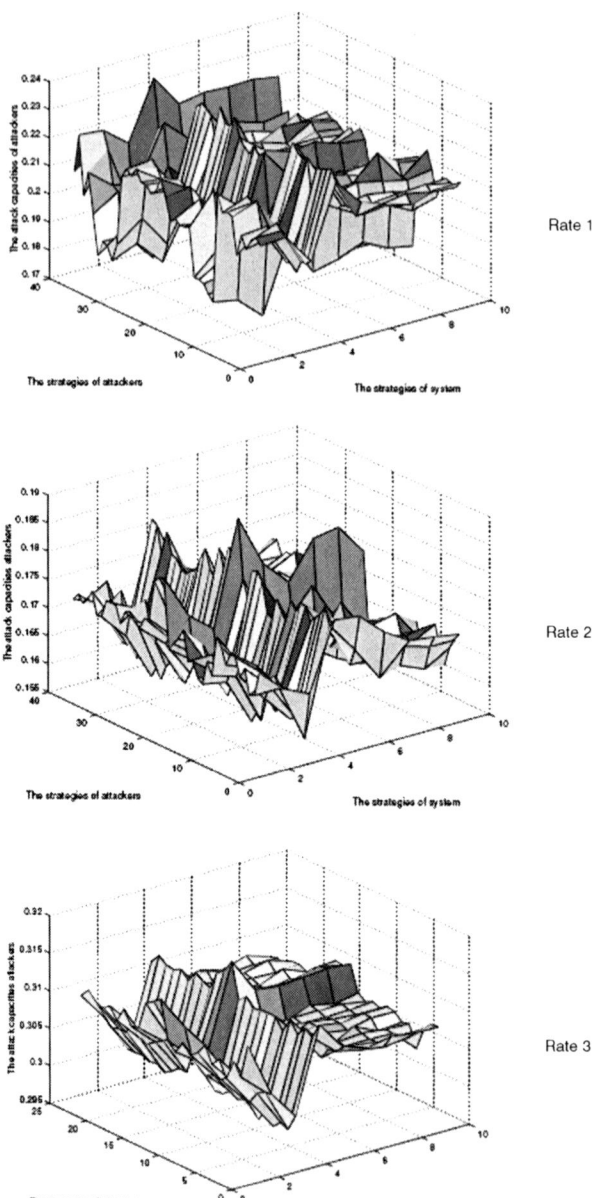

Fig. 4.   The attacking capacity of the attacker.

capacity of the defense system under different attack and defense strategies. We consider two parameters for attacker in our observations. The influence of attacker strategies is as follows.

Number of zombies: When the number of zombie is ManyBad, the system earns lower resilient capacity and the attacker earns higher attacking capability. When the aggregate property is Sour, the number of zombie affects the system and attacker's results greatly.

Ratio: The ratio affects the attacker's attack capacity only when the poor rate is 67.1 kbps, the traffic pattern includes ICMP (ICMP or Mixed) and the number of zombie is Many. In this situation, attacker gets higher attacking capacity when the ratio goes up. In other strategies, the ratio does not affect the attacker's attacking capacity much.

The influence of system's strategies is as follows: (1) The cycle time, drop rate, rate limit time and aggregate property affect payoffs; other system strategies do not affect the results much. (2) The system always gets high-resilient capacity when the drop rate is 0.03 and gets low resilient capacity when the drop rate is 0.07. The system sometimes also gets high-resilient capacity under cycle time (10 s) and rate limit time (50 s) strategies.

More analysis and simulation results can be found in our earlier work (Liu et al., 2005; Liu and Zang, 2003).

7.2 Converging to Nash equilibria

If the attacker and defense system are rational, they should take a Nash equilibrium (optimal) strategy. Even if they did not choose a Nash equilibrium strategy at the first step, they would change their choice and converge to the optimal strategies. In this section, we give a simple example in Fig. 5 to explain why and how they converge to a Nash equilibrium strategy.

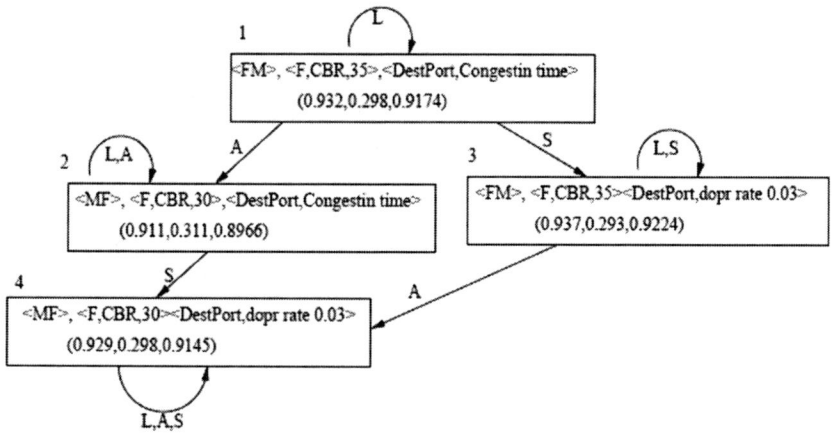

Fig. 5. Converging to Nash equilibrium strategy.

We assume that the legitimate user, attacker, and system start from state 1. The strategies and payoffs are list in the sequence of legitimate user, attacker, and defense system in box 1, where <FM> means Few-PoorManyGood, hF,CBR,35i means FewBad, CBR traffic, and ratio = 35.

The attacker does not satisfy with his attack capacity and the defense system does not satisfy its resilient capacity at state 1. The attacker found if he changes the strategy to <M, CBR, 30>, he could earn the highest attack capacity. Since the transition is good for the attacker, the state transits to 2. Consequently, the state will change to state 3 since the defense system can earn highest resilient capacity at target drop rate 0.03. At state 2, the attacker satisfies with his attack capacity and he does not want to change the strategy unilaterally. The system found it can earn his highest resilient capacity at <target-drop-rate 0.03> if it changes its strategy unilaterally. So the state finally transits to 4. Similarly, at state 3, the attacker wants to change his strategy to <F, CBR, 30> to maximize his attack capacity and the state finally transits to 4 too.

At state 4, everyone found if he changes the strategy unilaterally, his payoffs go down. Therefore no one wants to change his strategy. The strategy is at state 4 a Nash equilibrium strategy. In the example, ultimately no matter what the start state is the legitimate users, attacker, and defense system insist on a Nash equilibrium strategy to maximize their interests. If there is more than one Nash equilibrium point, which one will be converged into dependents on which they start with.

7.3   Improve attack resilience of the defense system

One benefit of our work is that the distribution of Nash equilibria and the payoff results could be used to optimize the system's defense posture for more resilience. For example, for the pushback defense system against DDoS attacks, our findings suggest the following ways to improve the resilience:

(1) *Target drop rate selection:* The lower the target drop rate is, the fewer packets will be sent to the output queue when a router is doing pushback, and more packets will be dropped by the defense system. But it is hard to say if a lower drop rate is always better than a higher drop rate, since lower drop rates may cause more legitimate packets to be dropped by the system, especially when the legitimate traffic volume is high. To find the best drop rate, we give the simulation results of the assurance capacity of the system and the attacking capacity under different drop rate {0, 0.005, 0.01, 0.02, 0.03, 0.04, 0.05, 0.06, 0.07, 0.08} and traffic rate (rate 1, rate2, and rate 3) in Fig. 6. We found when the percentage of poor traffic in the whole bandwidth is low, such as 15%, a lower drop rate is always better for the system even when the legitimate traffic rate is high. When the

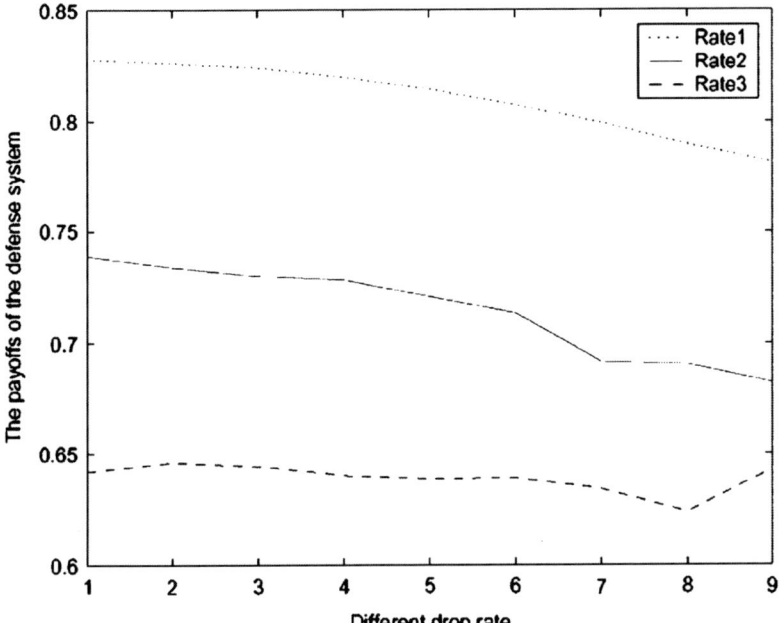

Fig. 6. The payoffs of the defense system under different drop rate and traffic rate.

percentage of poor traffic goes up to 25%, the system gets the best payoffs at the highest target drop rate. Hence, the target drop rate is dependent upon the percentage of poor traffic.

To improve the resilience of the system, when the percentage of poor traffic is low, the system should use a low drop rate, and vice versa. In practice, to find out the suitable target drop rate, the system needs to analyze the legitimate traffic when there are no attacks to get a profile of the legitimate traffic.

(2) *Configuration of the number of rate-limited sessions.* When the number of rate-limited sessions is less than the number of the attacking aggregates, there will be some malicious traffic not rate-limited and the system will be jeopardized by these attack traffic. Hence, we need to make the number of rate-limited sessions larger than the number of aggregates of the attacking traffic. Some people may believe that having too many rate-limited sessions are not good, since the legitimate traffic may be considered as malicious traffic and get rate-limited. However, since the volume of malicious traffic is much larger than the normal traffic, our experiment results show that a larger number of rate-limited sessions do not affect the system's resilience seriously. In the real world, it is usually hard to predict accurately the number of attacking aggregates; therefore, we suggest

the system just set a large number of rate-limited sessions for better resilience.

7.4   Experiments with a larger network topology

So far, our simulations are based on the original pushback topology composed of 64 hosts and 22 routers. To see whether the characteristics of the simulated DDoS attack/defense game (e.g., characteristics of the payoffs and Nash equilibria) and the corresponding conclusions we have drawn can still hold in a large-scale DDoS attack/defense game, we have done some experiments with a larger network topology. In particular, we use Brite (Medina et al., 2001), a popular topology generator, to create a network with 101 routers and more than 1000 hosts. We randomly select 200 hosts as zombies. To compare the experiment results with those generated with the pushback topology, we let the attacking bit rate (of each zombie) be the same as before, and we also let the legitimate bit rate be the same as before.

We found that with the Brite topology, the legitimate user's and system's payoffs are slightly smaller than those with the pushback topology, but the attacker's payoffs are slightly larger than those with the pushback topology. We believe the reason is mainly due to the fact that the pushback mechanism works in slightly different ways under different topologies. Nevertheless, the absolute values of payoffs are not very important for this comparison, and we are mainly concerned with the impact of the game parameters on the players' payoffs and the distributions of the Nash equilibria.

Through a comparison study, we found that compared with the DDoS attack/defense game with the pushback topology, the impact of the game parameters on the players' payoffs is of almost the same set of properties, and the distributions of the Nash equilibria, as shown in Table 2, are very similar. For example, with the Brite topology, (a) the legitimate user always gets the highest payoffs when the target drop rate is 0.03 and gets the lowest payoffs when the target drop rate is 0.07 and (b) most Nash equilibria occur when the target drop rate is 0.03 or when the max-number-of-sessions is 5. These encouraging results, though still preliminary, show that the set of

Table 2
The distribution of Nash equilibrium under different topologies

Topology	cont4	cyct10	dr0.03	dr0.07	ft10	ft30	default	sess5	rt15	rt50
Pushback	0	0	0.45	0	0	0.14	0	0.36	0	0.05
Britetopo	0.02	0	0.38	0	0	0	0.08	0.39	0.06	0.06

attack strategy characteristics (inferences) we have identified (computed) about DDoS attackers should hold in a large network and can be fairly consistent with the IOS of real-world DDoS attackers against the Internet.

8   Conclusion and future work

In this chapter, we present a general incentive-based method to model AIOS and a game-theoretic approach to infer AIOS and measure attack resilience. On the one hand, we found that the concept of incentives can unify a large variety of attacker intents; the concept of utilities can integrate incentives and costs in such a way that attacker objectives can be practically modeled. On the other hand, we developed a game-theoretic AIOS/AR formalization that can capture the inherent interdependency between AIOS and defender objectives and strategies in such a way that AIOS can be automatically inferred, and the system's attack resilience can be auto-matically measured. Finally, we use a specific case study on DDoS attack and defense to show how attack strategies can be inferred, and how attack resilience can be measured in real-world attack–defense scenarios.

Our game model can be extended to cover multiple attackers who are either cooperating with other attackers (i.e., cooperative) or not (i.e., noncooperative). In either case, we can consider an attacker as a player in the game and each one has the same strategies and utility function as the others. For the noncooperative attack, each attacker plays the game independently, and the goal of the attacker is to maximize his own utility. For the cooperative attack, the attackers play the game collaboratively, and the goal of the attackers is to maximize the sum of the utilities of all attackers instead of maximizing one attacker's utility.

Acknowledgments

This work was supported by DARPA and AFRL, AFMC, USAF, under award number F20602-02-1-0216, and by Department of Energy Early Career PI Award.

References

Browne, H., W.A. Arbaugh, J. McHugh, W.L. Fithen (2001). A trend analysis of exploitations. in: *Proceedings of IEEE Symposium on Security and Privacy*, IEEE Computer Society, Washington, DC, USA, pp. 214–229.

Browne, R. (2000). C4i defensive infrastructure for survivability against multi-mode attacks. in: *Proceedings 21st Century Military Communication-Architectures and Technologies for Information Superiority*, IEEE, Los Angeles, CA, USA.

Burke, D. (1999). Towards a game theory model of information warfare. Technical Report, Air force Institute of Technology. Master's thesis.

Gordon, L.A., M.P. Loeb (2001). Using information security as a response to competitor analysis systems. *Communications of the ACM* 9, p. 44.

Hespanha, J.P., S. Bohacek (2001). Preliminary results in routing games. in: *Proceedings of American Control Conference*, IEEE, Arlington, VA, USA.

Ioannidis, J., S.M. Bellovin (2002). Implementing pushback: Router-based defense against ddos attacks. in: *Proceedings of Annual Network and Distributed System Security Symposium*, The Internet Society, San Diego, California, USA.

Kodialam, M., T.V. Lakshman (2003). Detecting network intrusions via sampling: A game theoretic approach. in: *Proceedings of IEEE INFOCOM*, IEEE, San Francisco, USA.

Landwehr, C.E., A.R. Bull, J.P. McDermott, W.S. Choi (1994). A taxonomy of computer program security flaws. *ACM Computing Surveys* 26, p. 3.

Liu, P., W. Zang (2003). Incentive-based modeling and inference of attacker intent, objectives and strategies, in: *Proceedings 10th ACM Conference on Computer and Communications Security* (CCS '03), Washington, DC, October 28–31, pp. 179–189.

Liu, P., W. Zang, M. Yu (2005). Incentive-based modeling and inference of attacker intent, objectives and strategies. *ACM Transactions on Information and Systems Security* 8(1), 78–118.

Liu, Y., C. Comaniciu, H. Man (2006a). A Bayesian game approach for intrusion detection in wireless ad hoc networks. in: *Proceedings of GameNets*, Pisa, Italy (Workshop on Game Theory for Networks).

Liu, Y., C. Comaniciu, H. Man (2006b). Modelling misbehaviour in ad hoc networks: a game theoretic approach for intrusion detection. *IJSN* 1(3/4), 243–254.

Lunt, T.F. (1993). A survey of intrusion detection techniques. *Computers & Security* 4(12 June), 405–418.

Lye, K., J.M Wing (2002). Game strategies in network security, in: *Proceedings of IEEE Computer Security Foundations Workshop*, IEEE, Copenhagen, Denmark.

Mas-Colell, A., M.D. Whinston, J.R. Green (1995). *Microeconomic Theory*. Oxford University Press, New York, USA.

McHugh, J. (2001). Intrusion and intrusion detection. *International Journal of Information Security* 1, 14–35.

Medina, A., A. Lakhina, I. Matta, J. Byers (2001). BRITE: An approach to universal topology generation, in: *Proceedings of International Workshop on Modeling, Analysis and Simulation of Computer and Telecommunications Systems*, IEEE, Cincinnati, Ohio, USA.

Mukherjee, B., L.T. Heberlein, K.N. Levitt (1994). Network intrusion detection. *IEEE Network* 26–41.

Sallhammar, K., S.J. Knapskog, B.E. Helvik (2005). *Using stochastic game theory to compute the expected behavior of attackers.* Symposium on Applications and the Internet Workshops (SAINT 2005 Workshops), pp. 102–105.

Syverson, P.F. (1997). A different look at secure distributed computation. in: *Proceedings of IEEE Computer Security Foundations Workshop*, IEEE, Rockport, Massachusetts, USA.

Wing, J.M. (2006). Attack graph generation and analysis, in: *ASIACCS '06: Proceedings of ACM Symposium on Information, computer and communications security*. ACM Press, New York, USA.

Xu, J., W. Lee (2003). Sustaining availability of web services under distributed denial of service attacks. *IEEE Transactions on Computers* 52(4 February), 195–208.

Zhuang, J., V.M. Bier (2008). Katrina vs. 9/11–How should we optimally protect against both? in: H. Richardson, P. Gordon, J. Moore II, (eds.), *Natural Disaster Analysis after Hurricane Katrina: Risk Assessment, Economic Impacts and Social Implications*. Edward Elgar Publishing, Aldershot, England.

Zou, C., W. Gong, D. Towsley (2002). Code red worm propagation modeling and analysis. in: *Proceedings of ACM Conference on Computer and Communications Security*, ACM, Washington, DC, USA.

Online resources

http://staff.washington.edu/dittrich/misc/ddos/
http://www.gametheory.net
http://www.icir.org/pushback/
http://www.isi.edu/nsnam/ns/

Suggested readings

Game Theory: Analysis of Conflict by Roger B. Myerson, Publisher: Harvard University Press, ISBN-10: 0674341163, ISBN-13: 978-0674341166.

Game Theory for Applied Economists by Robert Gibbons, Publisher: Princeton University Press, ISBN-10: 0691003955, ISBN-13: 978-0691003955.